T0319645

LONDON RECORD SOCIETY
PUBLICATIONS

VOLUME XXV
FOR THE YEAR 1988

Dedicated to the memory of
Reginald Ralph Darlington
who encouraged both the initial undertaking
and its subsequent continuation

WESTMINSTER ABBEY
CHARTERS
1066–*c*. 1214

EDITED BY
EMMA MASON

ASSISTED BY
THE LATE
JENNIFER BRAY

CONTINUING THE WORK
OF THE LATE
DESMOND J. MURPHY

LONDON RECORD SOCIETY
1988

The preparation of this edition has been assisted by grants from the Leverhulme Trust and the Nuffield Foundation. Its publication has been made possible by generous grants from the Marc Fitch Fund, the British Academy, and the Publications Fund of Birkbeck College.

Phototypeset by
Wyvern Typesetting Ltd, Bristol
Printed in Great Britain by
The Bath Press

CONTENTS

SHORT TITLES
AND ABBREVIATIONS

MANUSCRIPT ABBREVIATIONS

BL	British Library, Department of Manuscripts
C	BL MS Cotton Claudius A VIII
CAY	College of Arms, London, Young MS 72
CC	BL Cotton Charter
F	BL MS Cotton Faustina A III
LN	Westminster Abbey, Liber Niger Quaternus (Muniment Book 1)
PRO	Public Record Office
T	BL MS Cotton Titus A VIII
WAD	Westminster Abbey Domesday (Muniment Book 11)
WAM	Westminster Abbey Muniment
WA Mun. Bk.	Westminster Abbey Muniment Book

SHORT TITLES

AASS	*Acta Sanctorum*, ed. J. Bollandus, G. Henschenius *et al.* (Antwerp, Brussels, Tongerloo, and Paris, 1643–)
Acta H II & R I	*Acta of Henry II and Richard I*, ed. J. C. Holt and R. Mortimer (List and Index Society Special Series 21, 1986)
Acts of Malcolm IV	*The Acts of Malcolm IV, King of Scots 1153–1165, together with Scottish royal acts prior to 1153 . . .*, ed. G. W. S. Barrow, Regesta Regum Scottorum I (1960)
Ann. Mon.	*Annales Monastici*, ed. H. R. Luard (5 vols., R.S., 1864–9)
ASC	*The Anglo Saxon Chronicle*, transl. and ed. Dorothy Whitelock, with D. C. Douglas and Susie I. Tucker (1961)
Barlow, *Edward the Confessor*	Frank Barlow, *Edward the Confessor* (1970)
Beauchamp Cartulary	*The Beauchamp Cartulary: charters 1100–1268*, ed. Emma Mason, PRS, new series 43, (1980)
Beaven, *Aldermen*	A. B. Beaven, *The Aldermen of the City of London*, 2 vols. (1908–13)

BEC LXVIII	L. Delisle, 'Notes sur les chartes originales de Henri II', *Bibliothèque de l'Ecole des Chartes* LXVIII (1907), 272–314
BEC LXIX	L. Delisle, 'Recueil de 109 chartes originales de Henri II, roi d'Angleterre et duc de Normandie', rassemblées, et photographiées par le Rév. H. Salter, *Bibliothèque de l'Ecole des Chartes* LXIX (1908), 541–81; 738–40
Bentley	S. Bentley, *Abstract of a Cartulary of . . . . . St Peter, Westminster* (1836, privately)
Bigelow	M. M. Bigelow, *Placita Anglo-Normannica* (London, 1879)
BIHR	*Bulletin of the Institute of Historical Research*
Bishop & Chaplais	*Facsimiles of English Royal Writs to A.D. 1100 presented to Vivian Hunter Galbraith*, ed. T. A. M. Bishop and P. Chaplais (1957)
Brett, *English Church*	M. Brett, *The English Church under Henry I* (1975)
Brooke & Keir	C. N. L. Brooke and Gillian Keir, *London 800–1216: the shaping of a City* (1975)
Browning & Kirk	A. G. Browning and R. E. G. Kirk, 'The Early History of Battersea', *Surrey Archaeological Collections* 10 (1891), 205–54
Cal. Chart. R.	*Calendar of Charter Rolls*
Cal. Letters Innocent III	*The Letters of Pope Innocent III (1198–1216), concerning England and Wales: a calendar, with an appendix of texts*, ed. C. R. Cheney and Mary Cheney (1967)
Cal. Pat. R.	*Calendar of Patent Rolls*
Cart. Aldgate	*Cartulary of Holy Trinity Aldgate*, ed. G. A. J. Hodgett, LRS 7 (1971)
Cart. Clerkenwell	*Cartulary of St Mary, Clerkenwell*, ed. W. O. Hassall (Camden Soc. third series LXXI, 1949)
Cart. Darley	*The Cartulary of Darley Abbey*, ed. R. R. Darlington, 2 vols. (1945)
Cart. St Bartholomew's	*Cartulary of St Bartholomew's Hospital*, ed. Nellie J. M. Kerling (1973)
Cat. Seals BM	A. B. Tonnochy, *Catalogue of British Seal-Dies in the British Museum* (1952)
Chaplais, 'Original Charters'	Pierre Chaplais, 'The Original Charters of Herbert and Gervase, abbots of Westminster (1121–1157)', *Med. Misc. DMS*, 89–110
Chaplais, 'Seals of Henry I'	P. Chaplais, 'The Seals and Original Charters of Henry I', *Essays in Medieval Diplomacy and Administration* (1981),

	260–75, reprinted from *EHR* 75 (1960), 260–75
Charters of the Honour of Mowbray	*Charters of the Honour of Mowbray 1107–1191*, ed. D. E. Greenway (British Academy Records of Social and Economic History, new series I, 1972)
Chron. Mon. de Abingdon	*Chronicon Monasterii de Abingdon*, ed. J. Stevenson (2 vols., RS 1858)
Councils & Synods	*Councils and Synods with other documents relating to the English Church*, I, 871–1204, ed. D. Whitelock, M. Brett and C. N. L. Brooke, 2 parts (1981); II, 1205–1313, ed. F. M. Powicke and C. R. Cheney, 2 parts (1964)
C & Y Soc.	Canterbury and York Society
Davis	G. R. C. Davis, *Medieval Cartularies of Great Britain: a short catalogue* (1958)
DB	*Domesday Book sive Liber Censualis*, ed. A. Farley (2 vols., Record Comm. 1783)
De Gestis Pontificum	William of Malmesbury, *De Gestis Pontificum Anglorum*, ed. N. E. S. Hamilton (RS 1870)
Diceto	Ralph de Diceto, *Opera Historica*, ed. W. Stubbs (2 vols., RS 1876)
DKR	Deputy Keeper's Reports
E. C. St Paul	*Early Charters of the Cathedral Church of St Paul, London*, ed. Marion Gibbs (Camden Soc. third series LVIII, 1939)
EHR	*English Historical Review*
EEA II	*English Episcopul Acta II: Canterbury 1162–1190* ed. C. R. Cheney and Bridgett E. A. Jones (1986)
EEA III	*English Episcopal Acta III: Canterbury 1193–1205*, ed. C. R. Cheney and E. John (1986)
EEA IV	*English Episcopal Acta IV: Lincoln 1186–1206*, ed. D. Smith (1986)
EETS	Early English Text Society
Eyton, *Itinerary*	R. W. Eyton, *Court, Household and Itinerary of King Henry II* (London, 1878)
Farrer, *H & KF*	W. Farrer, *Honours and Knights' Fees*, 3 vols. (1923–25)
Farrer, *Itinerary*	W. Farrer, *An Outline Itinerary of King Henry the First* (1920), reprinted from *EHR* 34 (1919)
Fasti I	John Le Neve, *Fasti Ecclesiae Anglicanae 1066–1300*, I: *St Paul's, London*, compiled by Diana E. Greenway (1968)
Fasti II	John Le Neve, *Fasti Ecclesiae Anglicanae*

	1066–1300 II: *Monastic Cathedrals* (Northern and Southern Provinces), compiled by Diana E. Greenway (1971)
Fasti III	John Le Neve, *Fasti Ecclesiae Anglicanae 1066–1300* III: *Lincoln*, compiled by Diana E. Greenway (1977)
Fines Essex	*Feet of Fines for Essex*, ed. R. E. G. Kirk, I (A.D. 1182–A.D.1272), (Colchester, 1899–1910)
Fines H II & Ric I	*Feet of Fines . . . of the reign of Henry II and of the first seven years of the reign of Richard I*, PRS XVII (1894)
Fines London & Mddx	*A Calendar to the Feet of Fines for London and Middlesex, I, Richard I to Richard III*, ed. W. J. Hardy and W. Page (London, 1892)
Fines Surrey	*Pedes Finium, or Fines relating to the County of Surrey*, ed. F. B. Lewis (Surrey Archaeological Soc., Extra Volume I, Guildford, 1894)
Fines 9 Ric. I	*Feet of Fines of the Ninth Year of King Richard I, A.D. 1197 to A.D. 1198*, PRS XXIII (1898)
Fines 10 Ric. I	*Feet of Fines of the tenth year of King Richard I . . . also a roll of the King's Court . . .*, PRS XXIV (1900)
Flete	John Flete, *The History of Westminster Abbey*, ed. J. Armitage Robinson (NDWA no. 2, 1909)
Florence of Worcester	*Florentii Wigorniensis monachi Chronicon ex Chronicis*, ed. B. Thorpe (2 vols., English Historical Society, London, 1848–9)
Foedera	T. Rymer, *Foedera, Conventiones, Litterae et Acta Publica*, ed. A. Clarke and F. Holbrooke (7 vols., London, 1816–69)
Formulare	T. Madox, *Formulare Anglicanum* (London, 1702)
Gams	P. B. Gams, *Series Episcoporum ecclesiae catholicae* (Leipzig, 1931)
Garnett, 'Coronation and Propaganda'	G. Garnett, 'Coronation and Propaganda: Some implications of the Norman claim to the throne of England in 1066', *TRHS* 5th ser., 36 (1986), 91–116
G.E.C.	*The Complete Peerage of England, Scotland, Ireland, Great Britain, and the United Kingdom*, ed. G. E. C[ockayne], new edn. V. Gibbs, G. H. White *et al.* (13 vols., 1910–59)

Geoffrey de Mandeville	J. H. Round, *Geoffrey de Mandeville. A study of the anarchy* (1892)
Gervase of Canterbury	*The Historical Works of Gervase of Canterbury*, ed. W. Stubbs (2 vols., RS 1879–80)
Gesta Abbatum	Thomas of Walsingham, *Gesta Abbatum Monasterii Sancti Albani*, ed. H. T. Riley (RS I, 1867)
Gesta Henrici	Roger of Howden, *Gesta Henrici II et Ricardi I*, ed. W. Stubbs (2 vols., RS 1867)
Gesta Stephani	*Gesta Stephani*, ed. and transl. K. R. Potter, introd. R. H. C. Davis (1976)
Gilbert Crispin	J. Armitage Robinson, *Gilbert Crispin, abbot of Westminster* (NDWA no. 3, 1911)
Harmer	F. E. Harmer, *Anglo-Saxon Writs* (1952)
Hart	C. Hart, *The Early Charters of Essex, The Norman Period* (Dept. of English Local History, Leicester, Occasional Papers, 1957)
Harvey, 'Fee Farms'	Barbara Harvey, 'Abbot Gervase de Blois and the Fee Farms of Westminster Abbey', *BIHR* 40 (1967), 127–41
Harvey, *WA*	Barbara Harvey, *Westminster Abbey and its Estates in the Middle Ages* (1977)
HBC	*Handbook of British Chronology*, third edition, ed. E. B. Fryde, D. E. Greenway, S. Porter and I. Roy (1986)
Heads	D. Knowles, C. N. L. Brooke and Vera C. M. London, *The Heads of Religious Houses: England and Wales 940–1216* (1972)
Hist. Novorum	*Eadmeri Historia Novorum in Anglia*, ed. M. Rule (RS 1884)
Historia Novella	William of Malmesbury, *Historia Novella*, transl. and introd. K. R. Potter (1955)
H Med Exch.	P. Spufford, with Wendy Wilkinson and S. Tolley, *Handbook of Medieval Exchange* (1986)
Hollister, 'Mandevilles'	C. Warren Hollister, 'The Misfortunes of the Mandevilles', *History* 58 (1973), 18–28
Honeybourne, 'Sanctuary Boundaries'	M. B. Honeybourne, 'The sanctuary boundaries and environs of Westminster Abbey and the college of St Martin-le-Grand', *JBAA* new series 38 (1932), 316–32
Howden, *Chronica*	Roger of Howden, *Chronica*, ed. W. Stubbs (4 vols., RS 1868–71)
Jaffé *RPR*	*Regesta Pontificum Romanorum . . . ad annum . . . 1198*, ed. P. Jaffé, 2nd edn. (2 vols., Leipzig, 1885–88)

JBAA	*Journal of the British Archaeological Association*
John of Worcester	*The Chronicle of John of Worcester*, 1118–1140, ed. J. H. R. Weaver (1908)
Keene & Harding	D. Keene and Vanessa Harding, *A Survey of Documentary Sources for Property Holding in London before the Great Fire* (LRS 22, 1985)
Kemble	J. M. Kemble, *Codex Diplomaticus Aevi Saxonici* (6 vols., London, 1839–48)
Knowles & Hadcock	D. Knowles and R. N. Hadcock, *Medieval Religious Houses, England and Wales* (1971)
L & C Foliot	*The Letters and Charters of Gilbert Foliot*, ed. A. Morey and C. N. L. Brooke (1967)
Landon, *Itinerary*	L. Landon, *Itinerary of King Richard I*, PRS, new series 13 (1935)
Lathbury, *Denham*	R. H. Lathbury, *The History of Denham, Bucks* (Uxbridge, 1904)
Letters of John of Salisbury	*The Letters of John of Salisbury, 1153–1180*, 2 vols., ed. W. J. Millor, H. E. Butler and C. N. L. Brooke (1955, 1979)
Letters of Osbert de Clare	*The Letters of Osbert de Clare*, ed. E. W. Williamson (1929)
Liber Niger Scaccarii	*Liber Niger Scaccarii*, ed. T. Hearne, 2nd ed. (2 vols., London, 1774)
LRS	London Record Society
Madox, *Hist. Exchequer*	T. Madox, *History of the Exchequer* (London, 1711)
Mansi	J. D. Mansi (ed.) *Sacrorum Conciliorum nova et amplissima Collectio* (53 vols., Florence, Venice, Paris, 1759–1927; reprinted Graz, Austria, 1960)
Mason, 'The Mauduits and their Chamberlainship'	Emma Mason, 'The Mauduits and their Chamberlainship of the Exchequer', *BIHR* 49 (1976), 1–23
Mason, 'Rutland Churches'	Emma Mason, 'Westminster Abbey's Rutland Churches', *Rutland Record* 5 (1985), 163–6
Med. Misc. DMS	*A Medieval Miscellany for Doris Mary Stenton*, ed. Patricia M. Barnes and C. F. Slade, PRS, new series 36 (1962, reprinted 1977)
Monasticon	W. Dugdale, *Monasticon Anglicanum*, revised H. Caley, H. Ellis and B. Bandinel (6 vols. in 8, London, 1817–30)
Moore, *Hist. St Bartholomew's*	N. Moore, *History of St Bartholomew's Hospital*, I (1918)

Morris, 'Sheriffs of Henry I'	W. A. Morris, 'The Sheriffs and the Administrative System of Henry I', *EHR* 37 (1922), 161–72
NDWA	Notes and Documents relating to Westminster Abbey (publication series)
Neufeldt	Ernst Neufeldt, *Zur Sprache des Urkundenbuche von Westminster (Cotton Faustina A III)*, Inaugural-Dissertation, Doctorate, University of Rostock (Berlin, 1907)
NPS *Facsimiles*	New Palaeographical Society: *Facsimiles of Ancient Manuscripts etc.*, ed. E. M. Thompson, G. F. Warner, F. G. Kenyon and J. R. Gilson, First Series, II (1904)
Orderic	*The Ecclesiastical History of Orderic Vitalis*, ed. and transl. Marjorie Chibnall (6 vols., 1969–80)
Oxley, 'Medieval Church Dedications'	J. E. Oxley, 'The Medieval Church Dedications of the City of London', *Transactions of the London and Middlesex Archaeological Society* 29 (1978), 117–25
Pearce, *Monks of Westminster*	E. H. Pearce, *The Monks of Westminster* (NDWA no. 5, 1916)
PL	*Patrologiae cursus completus, series Latina*, ed. J. P. Migne (221 vols., Paris, 1844–64)
Plac. Abbrev.	*Placitorum in domo capitulari Westmonasteriensi asservatorum Abbreviatio. Temporibus regum Ric. I, Johann., Henr. III, Edw. I, Edw. II* (Record Comm., London, 1811)
PN Mddx	J. E. B. Gower, A. Mawer and F. M. Stenton, with S. J. Madge, *The Place-Names of Middlesex apart from the City of London* (English Place-Name Society XVIII, 1942)
Poole, *Exchequer*	R. L. Poole, *The Exchequer in the Twelfth Century* (1912, new impression 1973)
PR	*Pipe Roll* (Great Roll of the Pipe, edited and published by the Pipe Roll Society. All references will be in the form *PR*, followed by the regnal year)
PR 31 Henry I	*The Great Roll of the Pipe for the thirty first year of the reign of Henry I (Michaelmas 1130)* ed. J. Hunter (Record Comm., London, 1833)
PRS	Pipe Roll Society
PUE	*Papsturkunden in England*, 3 vols., ed. W. Holtzmann (Abhandlungen der Gesellschaft der Wissenschaften in Göttingen,

	phil.-hist. Klasse, Berlin, Göttingen: I = neue Folge XXV, 1930–31; II = 3. Folge XIV–XV, 1935–6; III = 3. Folge XXXIII, 1952)
RBE	*The Red Book of the Exchequer*, ed. H. Hall (3 vols., RS 1896)
Recueil des actes de H II	*Recueil des actes de Henri II, roi d'Angleterre et duc de Normandie, concernant les provinces françaises et les affaires de France*, ed. L. Delisle & E. Bèrger (Academie des Inscriptions et Belles-Lettres: Chartes et diplômes relatifs à l'histoire de France, 4 vols., Paris, 1909–47)
Regesta	*Regesta Regum Anglo-Normannorum, 1066–1154*, 4 vols. ed. H. W. C. Davis, C. Johnson, H. A. Cronne and R. H. C. Davis (1913, 1956, 1968, 1969)
Reynolds, 'Rulers of London'	Susan Reynolds, 'The Rulers of London in the Twelfth Century', *History* 57 (1972), 337–57
Ric. of Devizes	Richard of Devizes, *Chronicle*, ed. J. T. Appleby (1963)
Richardson, 'William of Ely'	H. G. Richardson, 'William of Ely, the King's treasurer', *TRHS* fourth series, 15 (1932), 45–90
Richardson & Sayles	H. G. Richardson and G. O. Sayles, *The Governance of Medieval England* (1963)
Robinson & James	J. Armitage Robinson and M. R. James, *The Manuscripts of Westminster Abbey* (NDWA no. 1, 1909)
Rob. de Torigny	The Chronicle of Robert of Torigny, *Chronicles of the reigns of Stephen, Henry II and Richard I*, ed. Richard Howlett, IV (RS, 1889)
Rolls KC 1194–95	*Rolls of the King's Court . . . 1194–95*, ed. F. W. Maitland, PRS 14 (1891)
Rosser, 'Medieval Westminster'	A. G. Rosser, 'Medieval Westminster: the vill and the urban community 1200–1540', unpublished Ph.D. thesis, London University, 1984
Rot. Chart.	*Rotuli Chartarum in Turri Londoniensi asservati 1199–1216*, ed. T. Duffus Hardy (Record Comm., London, 1837)
Rot. Curiae Regis	*Rotuli Curiae Regis. Rolls and Records of the Court held before the King's Justiciars or justices, 1. From the sixth year of King Richard I to the accession of King John*, ed. F. Palgrave (Record Comm., London, 1835)

Rot. Litt. Claus.	*Rotuli Litterarum Clausarum in Turri Londiniensi asservati (1204–27)*, ed. T. Duffus Hardy (2 vols., Record Comm., London, 1833–44)
Rot. Litt. Pat.	*Rotuli Litterarum Patentium in Turri Londiniensi asservati*, ed. T. Duffus Hardy; I, pt. i (1201–1216), (Record Comm., London, 1835)
Rot. de Oblat. et Fin.	*Rotuli de Oblatis et Finibus in Turri Londiniensi asservati, tempore regis Johannis*, ed. T. Duffus Hardy (Record Comm., London, 1835)
RS	Rolls Series
Rutton, 'Eye next Westminster'	W. L. Rutton, 'The Manor of *Eia*, or Eye next Westminster', *Archaeologia* 62 (1910), 31–58
Saltman, *Theobald*	A. Saltman, *Theobald, archbishop of Canterbury* (1956, reprinted 1969)
Sanders	I. J. Sanders, *English Baronies: a study of their origin and descent 1086–1327* (1960)
Sawyer, *Anglo-Saxon Charters*	P. H. Sawyer, *Anglo-Saxon Charters: an annotated list and bibliography* (1968)
Scholtz, 'Canonization'	B. W. Scholtz, 'The Canonization of Edward the Confessor', *Speculum* 36 (1961), 38–60
Scholz, 'Sulcard of Westminster'	B. W. Scholz, 'Sulcard of Westminster; Prologus de Construccione Westmonasterii', *Traditio* 20 (1964), 59–91
Scholz, 'Two forged charters from Westminster'	B. W. Scholz, 'Two forged charters from the Abbey of Westminster and their relationship with St Denis', *EHR* 76 (1961), 466–78
Sheriffs	*List of Sheriffs for England and Wales . . . to A.D. 1831*, PRO Lists and Indexes IX (London, 1898; reprinted New York, 1963)
Symeon of Durham	*Symeonis Monachi Opera Omnia*, ed. T. Arnold (2 vols., RS 1882–85)
SR	T. A. M. Bishop, *Scriptores Regis: facsimiles to identify and illustrate the hands of royal scribes in original charters of Henry I, Stephen and Henry II* (1961)
Taxatio Nicholai IV	*Taxatio Ecclesiastica Angliae et Walliae auctoritate Papae Nicholai IV, circa 1291*, ed. S. Ayscough and J. Caley (Record Comm., London, 1802)
Taylor, *Our Lady of Batersey*	J. G. Taylor, *Our Lady of Batersey* (1925)
TRHS	*Transactions of the Royal Historical Society*

Van Caenegem	R. C. Van Caenegem, *Royal Writs in England from the Conquest to Glanvill*, Selden Soc., LXXVII (1959)
VCH	*Victoria County History*
Vita A Edwardi Regis	*Vita A Edwardi Regis qui apud Westmonasterium requiescit*, ed. and transl. Frank Barlow (1962)
West, *Justiciarship*	F. West, *The Justiciarship in England 1066–1232* (1966)
Wethered, *Lands of Hurley*	F. T. Wethered, *Lands and Tythes of Hurley Priory* (1909)
Wethered, *St Mary's, Hurley*	F. T. Wethered, *St Mary's Hurley, in the Middle Ages* (London, 1898)
Widmore	Richard Widmore, *A History of the Church of St Peter, Westminster, commonly called Westminster Abbey* (London, 1751)
Wilkins, *Concilia*	Wilkins, D., *Concilia Magnae Britanniae et Hiberniae* (4 vols., London, 1737)

EDITORIAL ABBREVIATIONS

cal.	calendared
pd.	printed
( )^c	cancelled
( )^I	inserted

ABBOTS OF WESTMINSTER
c. 1049–1222

EDWIN	*c.* 1049 –	1068
GEOFFREY	*c.* 1072 –	*c.* 1076
VITALIS	1076 –	1085 (?)
GILBERT CRISPIN	(?)1085 –	1117/18
HERBERT	1121 –	*c.* 1136
GERVASE	1138 –	*c.* 1157
LAURENCE	*c.* 1158 –	1173
WALTER	1175 –	1190
WILLIAM POSTARD	1191 –	1200
RALPH ARUNDEL	1200 –	1214
WILLIAM D'HUMEZ	1214 –	1222

INTRODUCTION

Westminster Abbey from its foundation to 1214

Saeberht, king of the East Saxons, and his wife founded a church dedicated to St Peter, on Thorney Island, in the Thames, to the west of London.[1] This couple were allegedly buried there, early in the seventh century but no further royal burials occurred on the site over the next 400 years or more.[2] Early in the eighth century, Offa of Essex restored this church.[3] Subsequently, Offa the Great of Mercia is said to have granted land to St Peter's, Westminster.[4] King Edgar, *c.* 959, sold the site to Archbishop Dunstan, who founded a monastery.[5] Edgar gave several manors to this foundation, and Ethelred Unraed gave or confirmed others.[6] Benefactions were received from further donors in the early eleventh century, by which time the house was moderately prosperous.[7] In 1040, King Harold I Harefoot was buried at Westminster, but his body is said to have been disinterred by his successor and half-brother, Harthacnut.[8] Since Harold was also regarded as a usurper by Harthacnut's uterine brother and successor, Edward, this royal burial presumably did not establish a precedent for him, when resolving to be buried at Westminster himself.[9] It is said in his biography, the *Vita A Edwardi Regis qui apud Westmonasterium requiescit*, that he was apprised of his belated accession to his realm by a vision of St Peter, whom he continued to hold in the highest regard.[10] The Westminster

1. Scholz, 'Sulcard of Westminster', 82–3; Harvey, *WA*, 20; Flete, 36.
2. Harvey, *WA*, 372, and notes 1–2. Saeberht became king *ante* 604, and d. 616 × 617 (*HBC*, 9).
3. Scholz, 'Sulcard of Westminster', 85–6; Harvey, *WA*, 21. Offa, who acceded 694 × 709, abdicated and went to Rome 708 × 709 (*HBC*, 10).
4. Sawyer, *Anglo-Saxon Charters*, no. 124. This text, in its present form, is of doubtful authenticity, but may represent a genuine grant (Harmer, 501). Offa perhaps supported the church with the intention of asserting Mercian supremacy in the neighbourhood of London (Brooke & Keir, 295).
5. Scholz, 'Sulcard of Westminster', 86–7; Harvey, *WA*, 22–3.
6. Harvey, *WA*, 341–2, 346, 352–4, 358–9; Sawyer, *Anglo-Saxon Charters*, nos. 670, 774 (spurious), 894 (spurious), 903.
7. Sawyer, *Anglo-Saxon Charters*, nos. 1487, 1522; Harvey, *WA*, 23–4.
8. *ASC* E, *sub an.* 1039, records Harold's burial at Westminster. C and D, *sub an.* 1040, record that Harthacnut ordered the body to be dug up and thrown 'into the fen'. Following a further removal into the Thames, it was recovered and buried by the Danes in their cemetery in London (Florence of Worcester, I, 194).
9. Scholz, 'Sulcard of Westminster', 91; *Vita A Edwardi Regis*, 44, 81.
10. *Vita A Edwardi Regis*, 9, 44. This earliest biography, ascribed to an anonymous monk of St Bertin's, at St Omer in Flanders (*ibid.*, xli–lix), is that usually referred to in the present volume. Further *Lives* of King Edward were subsequently written by Osbert de Clare, prior of Westminster, and by the Cistercian abbot Ailred of Rievaulx, a kinsman of Abbot Laurence (ibid., xiii–xiv). On King Edward's devotion to St Peter, see also J. H. Round, *Calendar of Documents preserved in France illustrative of the*

1

monk Sulcard, writing at the command of Abbot Vitalis (1076–*c.* 1085), maintained that Edward intended to make a pilgrimage to Rome, but abandoned this project in case the realm was endangered by his absence. Instead, he would honour St Peter by restoring the church which was dedicated to him at Westminster.[11]

This pre-existing dedication to St Peter may well have attracted Edward to Westminster, but perhaps equally important was its location near the reviving commercial centre of London, which commanded major routeways within England and also cross-Channel routes. A royal mausoleum would provide a better focus for national unity on this site than it would if built in Winchester, the old capital of Wessex.

Edward's endowment of St Peter's comprised almost twice the amount of land which the abbey already possessed.[12] He perhaps intended that Westminster should become the English counterpart of the abbey of St Denis, outside Paris.[13] Edward perhaps believed that the endowment of a comparable cult church[14] would help ensure the stability of the English monarchy, after the traumas of the previous decades.

During his last years, the church of St Peter at Westminster was rebuilt on a grand scale, as his mausoleum.[15] Earlier in the eleventh century, several large churches had been built throughout the western empire, designed intentionally to reflect the weight of the emperor's rule. Edward's grandiose plans for the rebuilding of Westminster may in part have consciously imitated these imperial projects.[16] Architectural influences probably drew heavily, too, on recent Norman buildings, especially Jumièges, no doubt due to the influence of its former abbot, Robert Champart, bishop of London from 1044, and archbishop of Canterbury 1051–2.[17] The rebuilt St Peter's was consecrated on 28 December 1065 and Edward died on the night of 4–5 January 1066.[18]

Both Harold II Godwinson and William I were crowned in the abbey,[19] establishing its traditional role as the coronation church, but the Norman dynasty established in 1066 made no attempt to associate its fortunes with St Peter's. In 1075, Queen Edith, widow of Edward, was buried in the abbey beside her husband. Queen Matilda, the Anglo-Scottish first wife

---

History of Great Britain and Ireland, I, A.D. 918–1206 (London, 1899), no. 1374; Barlow, *Edward the Confessor*, 36 and n.1.

11. Scholz, 'Sulcard of Westminster', 90–91. On Sulcard's monastic career and commission to write, see ibid., 59–60, 80, 91.

12. Harvey, *WA*, 27.

13. Brooke & Keir, 296–8. Two related grants of King Edward for the abbey of St Denis date from the 1050s (Sawyer, *Anglo-Saxon Charters*, nos. 1028, 1105).

14. On the supportive role of St Denis towards the contemporary French monarchy, cf. Gabrielle M. Spiegel, 'The cult of St Denis and Capetian Kingship', *Jnl. of Medieval History*, I (1975), 43–60.

15. *Vita A Edwardi Regis*, 44–6; J. Armitage Robinson, 'The Church of Edward the Confessor at Westminster', *Archaeologia* 62 (1910), 81–100.

16. R. H. D. Gem, 'The Romanesque Rebuilding of Westminster Abbey', *Proceedings of the Battle Conference on Anglo-Norman Studies III. (1980)*, ed. R. Allen Brown (1981), 52–3.

17. Ibid., 46, 50, 53–4; *HBC*, 214, 220.

18. *Vita A Edwardi Regis*, 73, 80; *ASC* C, D, *sub an.* 1065; E, *sub an.* 1066.

19. *ASC* D, E, *sub an.* 1066.

of Henry I, died at Westminster in 1118, when she was buried next to them,[20] but no further royal burials followed before that of Henry III. William I and his sons intermittently celebrated the feast of Christmas, or that of Pentecost, at Westminster.[21] A monetary offering was traditionally made to the abbey on such occasions (**58**).

Successive Anglo-Norman kings did not regard Westminster Abbey as having any special claim on their generosity. The royal charters, leaving forgeries aside, reveal their grantors as responding to requests for confirmations (e.g. **4, 27**), or for the rendering of justice (e.g. **22, 56**). King Stephen's charters display a certain generosity (**114, 118**), only natural in that his bastard son Gervase was abbot from 1138, but even this king chose to establish a new royal mausoleum at Faversham, rather than to regard the abbey as such. Henry II and his sons, like their Norman predecessors, looked elsewhere when establishing their mausolea,[22] and their attitude generally was one of response, rather than of active benefaction.

The composition of this volume
The present volume comprises only those charters, whether surviving in their original form or as transcripts, which were granted to the abbey, or were issued by the abbot, prior or monks, between the accession of William I and the deposition of Abbot Ralph Arundel in January 1214. The genuine charters granted to the abbey before the autumn of 1066 are excluded from this volume, but there is detailed discussion of them in other works.[23] Spurious charters of King Edward, and others, which contain clear signs of post-Conquest amendment, reflect the interests of the abbey in the period covered by this volume, and are briefly tabulated on pp. 321–2. The reader is there referred to their detailed discussion elsewhere.

There follows a calendar of royal, papal and episcopal documents issued for the abbey in the period October 1066 to January 1214. The decision not to print these in full was reached both on the pragmatic grounds of keeping the size and cost of this volume within manageable proportions, and also in order to avoid an overlap with the work of other editors. Papal documents are readily accessible, chiefly in the volumes of *Papsturkunden in England*. Episcopal charters are in some cases printed in monographs devoted to a single cleric, and the remainder are either already published in existing volumes of the *English Episcopal Acta*, or are intended for forthcoming volumes in that series. Royal charters are either already published, usually in the volumes of the *Regesta Regum Anglo-Normannorum*, or are in process of being edited for inclusion in its

---

20. *ASC* D, E, *sub an.* 1075; *ASC* E *sub an.* 1118; Harvey, *WA*, 373 and n.6; Barlow, *Edward the Confessor*, 270.
21. Martin Biddle, 'Seasonal Festivals and Residence; Winchester, Westminster and Gloucester in the Tenth to Twelfth Centuries', *Anglo-Norman Studies VIII*, ed. R. Allen Brown (1986), 51–72.
22. Knowles & Hadcock, 65; Elizabeth M. Hallam, 'Henry II, Richard I and the order of Grandmont', *Jnl. of Medieval History*, 1 (1975), 165–86; Emma Mason, 'St Wulfstan's Staff: a legend and its uses', *Medium AEvum*, 53 (1984), 157, 170–1.
23. Harmer; Sawyer, *Anglo-Saxon Charters*.

further volumes.[24] Yet by bringing together in calendar form the large number of charters pertaining to Westminster which have previously appeared in a wide variety of publications, the impact upon the abbey of the authorities of church and state can be more readily determined, while the content of their charters provides valuable background to those of the monks and the rank-and-file donors. The texts of these donors' charters, with those of the abbots and convent, are printed in full.

Some of the abbots' charters have previously been printed, as have a very small proportion of the donors' charters, but these have appeared in widely scattered publications. Their full texts are therefore included here, in their appropriate places among the unpublished charters in both groups.

Many twelfth-century documents which are now in the Abbey's possession are excluded from the present selection, on the grounds that they do not reflect Westminster's interests in the period 1066–1214. Charters concerning the foundation or endowment of the cells of Great Malvern, (**243**), Hurley, (**462**) and Kilburn (**249–50**) are included, since these documents take the form either of grants to the abbey or by the abbot and convent. Also included are a few charters concerning Westminster's relations with these cells (**280, 285**), and a rare document relating to that of St Bartholomew's, Sudbury (**72, 130**). Documents relating to further acquisitions by these houses are excluded entirely, as are other collections, such as the early charters of St Martin le Grand, or Poughley Priory, which came to the abbey only at the end of the middle ages. While the Luffield priory charters at the abbey have previously been published,[25] the opportunity remains for other scholars to produce self-contained editions of the charters of some of the houses whose estates supported the last great building phase of the medieval abbey church.[26]

The Manuscripts

In general, there have survived at the Abbey the originals, or in some cases the purported originals, of the most important royal grants of lands or privileges, while the texts of administrative writs are largely known from copies. Papal bulls usually survive only as copies, since the originals were lost at the Reformation (but see **179, 191**). More than half of the episcopal charters also survive only as transcripts, but the major proportion of the abbots' charters, and of those of the donors, survive in their original form. There are also a few original muniments, and purported originals, in the British Library, notably among the Harleian (e.g. **446–8**) and Cotton Charters (e.g. **1, 57**).

24. The charters of William I are being re-edited by David Bates, and those of Henry II and Richard I by J. C. Holt and R. Mortimer.

25. Luffield Priory Charters, ed. G. R. Elvey, I, Buckinghamshire Rec. Soc. 15 (1968); II, Northamptonshire Rec. Soc. 22 (1975). For the late acquisitions, see Harvey, *WA*, 31, 198–202, 337–8, 355.

26. Among the early charters excluded from the present volume are documents relating to Great Malvern, Worcestershire, and a group from Yorkshire, for some of which see *Yorkshire Deeds*, VII, ed. C. T. Clay, Yorks. Archaeological Soc. 83 (1932), nos. 8–9, 18, 132, 137–9, 450, 468.

The Abbey Muniments contained in this volume are generally in good condition, considering both their great age, and also their repeated consultation, as evidenced by endorsements of successive dates. A considerable number of originals even preserve their seals, the legends of which can sometimes contribute to the identification of donors (e.g. **387**). In a small number of cases, time has taken its toll, and the relevant description slip in the Abbey's boxed catalogue contains a terse note, such as 'damaged by damp'; 'damaged by damp and beetles', and, in a memorable instance, 'found in a rat's nest'.

Certain of the abbey's cartularies are invaluable, in filling the lacunae of damaged charters.[27] In the compilation of the present volume, two cartularies have proved invaluable. Muniment Book 11, usually known as the Westminster Domesday, and therefore cited in this volume as WAD, is a large volume dating from the early years of Edward II's reign.[28] It records in full many of the muniments, including most of those of the donors who appear in this edition, and normally gives full attestations. Separate sections of this manuscript are reserved for those charters relating to the income of particular obedientiaries. Probably at the time this cartulary was planned, many of the muniments were endorsed with the name of the relevant obedientiary, and numbered in red ink, but a check of such endorsements against folio headings and entries in WAD revealed that charters were not always entered systematically. A detailed index of this volume may be consulted at the abbey.

British Library MS Cotton Faustina A III, hereafter cited as F, is a handsome volume, slightly earlier than WAD, which includes copies of many of the muniments, but chiefly those of notables, such as kings, popes and bishops.[29] Although its texts are often clearer than those in WAD, attestations are frequently omitted.

Further Westminster cartularies which have proved useful in compiling the present volume[30] are British Library MS Cotton Titus A VIII, hereafter cited as T, a cartulary of privileges dating from the earlier fourteenth century; British Library MS Cotton Claudius A VIII, cited hereafter as C, compiled *c.* 1450, and largely comprising extracts, notably from John Flete's *History of Westminster*; Westminster Abbey Muniment Book I, known as the Liber Niger Quaternus, cited hereafter as LN, a fifteenth-century compilation; Westminster Abbey Muniment Books 3 and 12; and London College of Arms MS Young 72, hereafter cited as CAY.[31] These latter volumes usually contribute little beyond further late copies, abstracts or simply memoranda of texts known from their originals, or from WAD or F. On occasion, though, their corroborative detail can be helpful. The text of the fugitives' oath (**349**) is taken from LN, while the best surviving text of one charter of William I is transcribed in a

27. On the Westminster cartularies, see Robinson & James, 93–102; Davis, 116–17; Keene & Harding, no. 248.
28. Robinson & James, 93–4; Davis, 116.
29. Robinson & James, 98–100; Davis, 116.
30. Certain late medieval manuscripts record only transactions beyond the chronological range of this volume (Davis, 117).
31. Robinson & James, 94–8, 100–102; Davis, 116–17; Keene & Harding, nos. 247–8.

manuscript of the seventeenth century (**83**).

When original charters have been lost, their texts are often preserved in WAD, and sometimes additionally, or alternatively, in F. Occasionally, further copies are to be found in one or more of the later cartularies. On occasion, muniments have been mutilated as a result of a later medieval economy drive in the scriptorium. Some early-thirteenth-century documents were trimmed and stitched together at a later date, so that the backs could be used for an account roll. As an afterthought, a scribe queried on one, in a memorandum, whether the deed had been registered, i.e. copied into WAD or F. It had not (**347**). In many cases where texts survive only as late copies, it is likely that the originals were re-cycled at a later date.

Further muniments were lost in comparatively modern times. There are instances where an eighteenth-century editor, such as Thomas Madox, printed a text 'from the autograph in the Westminster archives', (e.g. **35**) but no such original is now to be found. Other originals disappeared even more recently. Indeed, until the red Martlet stamp was imprinted on each individual charter at the Abbey, a practice introduced *c.* 1900, a privileged researcher might abstract documents to work on at home, and then 'forget' to return them. The Dean and Chapter have, on occasion, been obliged to buy back documents which had earlier gone astray.

At the Dissolution, all but two of the illuminated manuscripts were seized from the abbey. The survivors each contained a text of the Coronation service.[32] Attendant upheavals caused the dispersal of certain of the cartularies (F, C and T) and charters (e.g. **36**, **45**) which eventually found their way into the collections of antiquarians, notably that of Sir Robert Cotton, and hence, ultimately, into the British Library.

At the Public Record Office, there are to be found some copies, or variants, of Westminster charters, normally in the form of enrolments in royal records. The Abbey possesses some early final concords, of which several (e.g. **310**, **314**, **316**), although not the very earliest (**287**, **296**), can be collated with the corresponding feet of fines now in Chancery Lane. Cartularies of other religious houses (e.g. Reading, Godstow), which are now in the British Library or the Public Record Office, occasionally preserve a text of a charter granted by an abbot of Westminster. The records of other major religious foundations in London, notably St Paul's cathedral[33] and the Augustinian priories of Holy Trinity Aldgate[34] and St Bartholomew, Smithfield,[35] while providing an occasional variant text (e.g. **367**, **377**), have been more useful as sources of background information.

Selection and dating of the texts
The transcripts made by Desmond Murphy were very largely confined to those royal, papal, abbatial and episcopal charters which were issued

32. The Liber Regalis and the Litlyngton Missal also contain the burial service, with illustrations of royal burials.
33. *E.C. St Paul.*
34. *Cart. Aldgate.*
35. *Cart. St Bartholomew's.*

1066–1214, but this collection was incomplete, since it was virtually confined to those which had been published in standard works such as the *Regesta Regum Anglo-Normannorum*, *Monasticon Anglicanum* and *Papsturkunden in England*. I added further texts in all existing categories, and discovered originals of others which were previously represented by transcripts from cartularies. This enlarged collection was further augmented by the addition of many contemporary grants by other donors.

Selection and dating were greatly facilitated by use both of the abbey's card-index of people and places in the muniments, and of the separate boxed catalogue of descriptions of the charters. In many cases, each Muniment has two distinct description-slips: one in copperplate longhand, and a more modern, typed one. While the latter is the more legible, it does not usually give all the attestations, unlike the handwritten slip. The vast majority of the early muniments are undated and have been assigned dates by the compiler of the earlier description slips. However, these notional dates, including the very popular 'early Henry III', are often too late, when compared with the attestations on the hand-written slip.

Donors' charters are normally undated, and the donor does not usually name the abbot of the day. Approximate dates can often be determined by the attestations of figures whose term of office, or whose date of death, is known, e.g. London's first mayor, Henry Fitz Ailwin, or the royal treasurer, William of Ely.

In the task of dating the charters, much use has been made of the work of Susan Reynolds, who identified the more prominent citizens of London in this period.[36] Another valuable work is Gervase Rosser's unpublished thesis on the development of the vill of Westminster,[37] in which he identifies the major property owners, and lists the reeves of the vill and the early seneschals of the abbots.

While the leading witnesses can be used to date the vast majority of donors' charters, there is one joker in the pack, Odo the goldsmith.[38] In fact there were two men of this name, probably grandfather and grandson, whose many attestations range over several decades, extending from the abbacy of Ralph Arundel (e.g. **327–8**) well into the reign of Henry III. Dating of donors' charters by attestations can be corroborated to some extent by the hand, terminology and content. In one or two cases (e.g. **439**), a charter known to be slightly later in date has been deliberately included, to round off a series of related documents. Inevitably, as with any edition of charters of this period, some borderline cases remain.

Royal, papal and episcopal charters which fall within the chronological span present problems only in rare cases. Occasionally, when a text survives only as a cartulary entry, it happens that the scribe, in reproduc-

36. Reynolds, 'The Rulers of London', 337–57. Miss Reynolds's Index of Londoners to c. 1216 is held by the Social and Economic Study of Medieval London, care of the Museum of London.

37. Rosser, 'Medieval Westminster'. The published version of Dr Rosser's thesis, *Medieval Westminster 1200–1540*, is forthcoming.

38. Richardson, 'William of Ely', 88n; R. Kent Lancaster, 'Artists, suppliers and clerks: the human factors in the art patronage of King Henry III', *Jnl. of the Warburg and Courtauld Institutes* 35 (1972), 97–8.

ing only the initial letter of the benefactor's name, has misunderstood it (e.g. **52**). This failing is more often found in attestations (e.g. **40**). Another problem in dating some royal charters is that the regnal style employed by William Rufus is identical with that of his father. While their respective charters can usually be identified on internal evidence, there are a few cases where the grant might have been issued by either, and the question is difficult to resolve.

Editorial method

The charters are presented here in the order of royal, papal, and episcopal, all in calendar form, followed by full texts of the abbots, prior and convent, and finally donors. The arrangement within each category is chronological, so far as the evidence permits, and the donors' charters are additionally grouped according to district and property.

The text of each charter is printed from the original, where it exists, and any gaps in a damaged document are supplied from the cartulary copies. The scribe's spelling, however unorthodox, is reproduced exactly; grammatical errors are amended and annotated; omissions are indicated in square brackets. Where texts are known only from copies, WAD is given, for the sake of its fuller attestations, in preference to F, although significant variations are noted. Punctuation is modernized and spelling of c/t, i/j and u/v is standardized throughout. Details of endorsements and of seals are given. Charters are numbered in one sequence. An asterisk following a number indicates that a text is less than genuine in its present form. Persons and places are indexed.

Comment on the texts has been kept as concise as possible. Variant transcripts are noted, but except in special circumstances, those dating from later than the reign of Edward III are excluded. Printed or calendared versions of texts are noted, and the reader is referred wherever possible to authorities on specific aspects of the abbey's charters, notably Barbara Harvey and Pierre Chaplais. Commentators on the abbey's muniments are heirs to a long tradition, which extends back through Armitage Robinson, dean of Westminster 1902–11[39] and M. R. James,[40] through the eighteenth-century antiquarian Richard Widmore[41] to the fifteenth-century monk John Flete.[42] The twelfth-century prior, Osbert de Clare, and the eleventh-century monk Sulcard should be considered as creators of Westminster manuscripts rather than as commentators upon them.

The political background and the forgeries

The monks of Westminster had good reason to be on the defensive in the later eleventh and twelfth centuries. The lavish patronage of Edward the Confessor was followed by the destabilizing of their endowment as a result of the Norman Conquest. William I ordered the exchange of

---

39. Flete; *Gilbert Crispin*; J. Armitage Robinson, *The Abbot's House at Westminster* (NDWA no. 4, 1911). On the dean himself, see also Edward Carpenter, *A House of Kings: the History of Westminster Abbey* (1966), 343–4.
40. Robinson & James.
41. Widmore.
42. Flete.

certain estates with Westminster, to facilitate the creation of Windsor Forest (**9**), and withheld from Westminster bequests which were due to take effect on the death of Queen Edith.[43] Following the death of the last English abbot, Edwin, probably within two years of the Conquest, there was evidently a vacancy of some years before the succession of Geoffrey, who was deposed during his fourth year in office.[44] During the twelfth century, the financial and territorial interests of the abbey were damaged during several vacancies,[45] notably that which ended with the election of Abbot Herbert, *c.* January 1121 (**73, 75**), while at his death in 1136 the finances of the house were probably again in a poor state.[46] Lands were confiscated at the time of Gervase's deposition, 1157 × 58,[47]; a two-year vacancy followed the death of Abbot Laurence,[48] and William Postard's election in 1191 was secured only after the fall of the justiciar, William Longchamps, who had been enforcing the candidacy of his brother.[49]

While successive kings and their agents were the chief predators on the abbey's financial and territorial rights, there were also other culprits. For instance, the London church of St Mary Newchurch was lost to Colchester abbey;[50] during the troubles of Stephen's reign, lands were attacked or appropriated by rapacious barons: in the West Midlands, by Earl Robert of Gloucester and his followers,[51] and by others further east (**195**). In the reign of Henry II, his minister Richard of Ilchester took a rapacious interest in the abbey's properties (**457**), while during the troubles in King John's reign, there were incursions into the very precincts (**151**). It is not surprising that the monks embarked upon a vigorous policy of self-help, namely to reinforce their title to their lands by judiciously augmenting their archives.

The creation of forged charters at Westminster can perhaps be traced back to the eleventh century, when a charter was drawn up which purported to have been issued by Offa the Great.[52] Propaganda designed to improve the status of the abbey was generated by the monk Sulcard, in the later eleventh century,[53] but the greatest flowering of imaginative literature in the guise of forged charters may be ascribed to the activities of Prior Osbert de Clare, in the 1120s and 1130s, and to those who worked under his direction.[54]

The career of Osbert was somewhat stormy. Successive abbots and indeed his fellow monks may have experienced difficulties in working with him, but his overriding motivation was zeal for the wellbeing of the

43. Harvey, *WA*, 27.
44. *Heads*, 76.
45. *Ibid.*, 77.
46. *Letters of Osbert de Clare*, pp. 5–6; ep. 2, p. 56; Harvey, 'Fee Farms', 128. On the situation during Herbert's abbacy, see *PR 31 Henry I*, 150.
47. *Curia Regis Rolls*, I, 464–5.
48. *Heads*, 77.
49. Diceto, II, 100–101; Ric. of Devizes, 39, 54–5.
50. *Gilbert Crispin*, 158–66.
51. Flete, 92.
52. There are two texts of this grant at the Abbey. WAM II is probably 12C, while WAM III is 11C or 12C: Sawyer, *Anglo-Saxon Charters*, no. 124.
53. Scholz, 'Sulcard of Westminster', 59–91.
54. Chaplais, 'Original Charters', 91–5, 97–8.

abbey, linked with a devotion to its patron, King Edward.[55] This zeal manifested itself in an indefatigable output of forged charters, designed to defend and strengthen the abbey's territorial and franchisal interests, and, tangentially, to promote the canonization of King Edward. To this end he composed a prose Life of the King, for production at the papal *curia*.[56]

Financial and managerial difficulties which grew during the abbacy of Herbert, 1121–36, evidently prompted the production of a forged bull of Pope Innocent II, designed to ensure that the new, young Abbot Gervase must henceforth act in concert with his chapter (**161**).[57] Other major products of Osbert and his subordinates included the texts, as they now survive, of Edward the Confessor's First, Second and Third Charters, and diplomas of Ethelred Unraed and Edgar. These and other 'pre-Conquest' forgeries are briefly tabulated, and references are given to those authorities who discuss them most fully.

The handiwork of Prior Osbert and his associates can also be detected in a considerable number of post-Conquest muniments, chiefly charters and writs of William I (e.g. **1**, **14–15**), of Henry I to a lesser extent (e.g. **57**, **70**), and perhaps in some spurious charters of King Stephen (**110–11**, **119**). Great energy and resourcefulness were displayed by Prior Osbert, and those who worked under, and followed after him. Their major productions have been examined in detail by Pierre Chaplais.[58] The output of less spectacular documents also presents a tantalizing challenge. The forgers were not complacent about their successes in this latter category, but strove to better their first efforts, notably in their steady output of spurious royal writs (e.g. **70**, **106**). Where the text of the genuine, original writ survives, it is sometimes possible to trace through several stages the accretion of alleged privileges which were later thought appropriate to the property in question (e.g. **62–4**). Sometimes a genuine writ has had inserted into it a clause, or clauses, awarding legal and fiscal exemption. Often, place of issue and attestations have been added, either to a genuine grant (e.g. **11–12**) or to one which, in an intermediate phase, had already been embellished with clauses of exemption. Genuine writs of William I sometimes lacked attestations, but Osbert and his team, working in the 1120s and 1130s, when attested writs were the norm, clearly decided to up-date their muniments by adding attestations to those which lacked them. The witnesses usually chosen are prominent men of the late eleventh century, but sometimes their mutual attestation of any one document is impossible, given the respective dates at which they acquired their offices and titles, or, conversely the dates of their deaths (e.g. **11**, **25**). The numbers of such charters are asterisked in the same way as documents which are more seriously suspect.

---

55. *Letters of Osbert de Clare*, 1–20.
56. Barlow, *Edward the Confessor*, 274. Spurious bulls were also incorporated into the texts of long, forged charters of King Edward, briefly tabulated in the present volume, relating to the circumstances surrounding his re-foundation and endowment of the abbey.
57. Harvey, 'Fee Farms', 128–9.
58. Chaplais, 'Original Charters', 91–5, 97–8.

The purpose of adding a place of issue to some of the eleventh-century charters was to build up evidence to suggest that in the latter part of William I's reign, the king, keeping Christmas in state at Westminster, traditionally made a gift to the abbey—perhaps a manor or two (e.g. **11, 28, 34**).

The majority of forged royal documents are those purporting to date from the reign of William I, when there was a need to demonstrate that certain lands were held in the reign of Edward the Confessor (e.g. **17, 20**) or, at latest, by the time of the Domesday Survey, (e.g. **13**) which would strengthen Westminster's title to them. The forgeries purporting to have been granted by Henry I were made largely to ascribe franchisal rights to genuine Westminster properties (**62–4, 74**). Forged documents ascribed to his successors are comparatively rare, apart from some imaginative documents purporting to have been issued by King Stephen (**119–21**), and a series of Charters of Liberties, allegedly issued by successive kings at their coronations or early in their reigns. This latter series exemplifies the virtue of economy of effort to be derived from recycling. Apart from adjustments to the attestations and dating clause, virtually the same improbable grant was ascribed to successive kings (**57, 110, 123**). The language of these charters is that of a monastic scriptorium rather than the royal chancery, but it might be argued that newly-crowned kings were willing to seal documents produced in the house where their coronation took place. However, the lavish concessions embodied in these grants are unlikely to have appealed to any King, however euphoric his mood at the outset of his reign. These, and a few later suspect charters suggest that Osbert de Clare's immediate subordinates left their own well-trained successors. Some Westminster forgeries known from the thirteenth century (e.g. **121, 271**) were designed to circumvent new legal impediments to the enjoyment of title, seignorial control or franchisal rights.[59]

Royal charters
The generous endowment of Edward the Confessor was quickly threatened by the circumstances of the Norman Conquest and settlement. It was essential that the abbey's lands and franchisal rights should be secured, and that the king's help should be enlisted for this purpose. Abbot Edwin (*c.* 1049–68) allegedly obtained the support of William I in several matters (e.g. **2, 3**). No surviving royal charter is addressed to the first Norman abbot, Geoffrey (*c.* 1072–*c.* 1076), which perhaps suggests his failure in the basic responsibility of obtaining royal support for the house. However, if, as is discreetly hinted, there were scandalous grounds for his removal, it is possible that his name was 'edited out' of the texts of such writs as were addressed to him as abbot.[60] When early writs of William I survive only as cartulary copies, it may be asked whether Geoffrey was indeed the recipient (e.g. **6–10**).

Geoffrey's successors, Abbot Vitalis (1076–85?) and Gilbert Crispin (?1085–1117/18), diligently enlisted royal protection of the abbey's interests (e.g. **19, 41**).

59. Harvey, 'Fee Farms', 132.
60. On Abbot Geoffrey, see Flete, 84, 141; Widmore, 18–19.

11

Despite the inflation by the staff of the scriptorium of the numbers of charters and writs ascribed to William I, and, to a lesser extent, to Henry I, the numbers of their genuine documents considerably exceed those of other kings, although most of their grants simply represent a response to Westminster's petitions, rather than any spontaneous benevolence towards the abbey.

During abbatial vacancies, the more remote of the Westminster properties no doubt offered a tempting prey to the unscrupulous. The first priority of Abbot Herbert, on obtaining office after a vacancy, was to petition Henry I for the recovery of lost rights and possessions (**75–82**). The flow of documents in Henry's name continued until his final departure from England in 1133 (**95–6**). The abbey possesses one charter issued by his first wife, Queen Matilda (**97**), and another by their daughter, the Empress (**98**). There are comparatively few genuine charters of King Stephen. These include several grants of exemption from legal and financial obligations (**105, 112–13, 116, 118**). The limited number of Stephen's genuine grants is remarkable in that he was the father of Abbot Gervase (1138–c. 1157).

Following the burial at Westminster of Queen Matilda in 1118, her brother Earl David granted land in Tottenham to finance the commemoration of her obit (**99**). Later, as King of Scots, he issued further charters concerning this property (**100–101**), and confirmations were also obtained from his son, Earl Henry (**102**), and grandsons Malcolm IV (**103**) and William (**104**).

The charters of Henry II and his sons do not display any particular interest in the abbey, notwithstanding the newly-sanctioned cult of Edward the Confessor.[61] Their tone overall is rather that of a perfunctory response to urgent petitions for support (e.g. **125, 127**). Given the length of Henry II's reign, the number of charters issued in his name on behalf of Westminster, even including his highly suspect charter of liberties (**123**), is not lavish, while those issued in the names of Richard and John total seven and five respectively. With the virtually continuous survival of the Pipe Rolls from this period, there is clear evidence that the abbot did not enjoy any special relationship with the crown, and that such royal support as the monks obtained might be purchased at considerable cost.[62]

Several charters issued in the later twelfth century suggested that the abbey was expected to present to some of its more lucrative livings royal clerks who were destined for high office (**286, 463**).[63] Moreover, the royal favour could be exercised to the detriment of the abbey's interests, as when its church of Bloxham was donated by Henry II to the nunnery of Godstow, where his mistress Rosamund Clifford was buried (**225**).

---

61. Barlow, *Edward the Confessor*, 278–85.
62. *PR 11 Henry II*, 33; *PR 4 John*, 19; *PR 5 John*, 11; *Rot. de Oblat. et Fin.*, 222, 325, 337; *PR 9 John*, 52.
63. Consultation did not necessarily occur. Henry II granted the church of Ashwell to Walter Map, during the vacancy which followed the death of Abbot Laurence (*Curia Regis Rolls* VI, 93).

Papal documents

Letters ascribed to popes down to Paschal II (**152–4**) are spurious, while those of Innocent II and his successors are normally genuine. One exception is a letter ascribed to Innocent II, rebuking Abbot Gervase (**161**). Barbara Harvey has demonstrated that this should be regarded as the handiwork of Prior Osbert de Clare.[64]

Numbers of letters increase from the pontificates of Eugenius III and Adrian IV, and markedly from the time of Alexander III. That of Pope Innocent II to Henry de Blois, concerning the restoration of the abbey's property (**159**) reflects the occasional vulnerability of its holdings. Letters of Innocent II (**158**) and Alexander III (**167–8**) pronounce on successive efforts to achieve the canonization of King Edward. The pope was also petitioned for privileges in such matters as liturgical dress (**173–4**). Papal rulings were also requested concerning the exclusion of the jurisdiction of the bishop of London (**172, 179**), or the confirmation of the abbey's lands and churches (**171, 177**).

Papal legates were usually dispatched to resolve some major problem which had arisen within the *ecclesia anglicana*. Consultations and legatine synods sometimes took place in London or even at Westminster itself,[65] when the legate was thus conveniently at hand to be petitioned in the interests of the abbey. In 1138, the legate Alberic of Ostia 'ordained' Abbot Gervase.[66] More often, the legate would be petitioned for an indulgence for those worshippers who attended the abbey on certain major feast days. These indulgences demonstrate how the monks encouraged first one, then another saint's cult, in the hope of attracting the devotions, and the offerings, of the populace. St Peter's cult was favoured in the earlier of these grants, sometimes in tandem with St Paul (**187–9**).[67]

The cult of St Edward was encouraged around the time of his canonization (**190**), but was never popular. By the early thirteenth century, the cult of the abbey's Holy Relics (**193**) was considered more promising.

Naturally there is no mention in these documents of any *quid pro quo*. The only hint of this appears in the register of Hugh of Wells, bishop of Lincoln, in an entry made just after the close of the period covered by this volume, where the nephew of Nicholas, bishop of Tusculum, is recorded as being presented to the church of Launton by the abbot and monks.[68]

64. Harvey, 'Fee Farms', 128–9.
65. *Councils and Ecclesiastical Documents relating to Great Britain and Ireland*, ed. S. W. Haddon and W. Stubbs (2 vols., Oxford, 1869), II, 317; *Councils and Synods*, II (i), 21, 36–8.
66. John of Worcester, 53.
67. In the twelfth century, St Paul's cathedral itself was fostering the cult of St Eorcenweald, an early bishop of London: Brooke & Keir, 272, 356; *A History of St Paul's Cathedral*, ed. W. R. Matthews and W. M. Atkins (1957), 5–6.
68. *Rotuli Hugonis de Welles episcopi Lincolniensis, A.D. MCCIX – MCCXXXV*, ed. W. P. W. Phillimore and F. N. Davis (Canterbury and York Soc., 3 vols., 1907–9), I, 70. This entry, of uncertain date, occurs in membrane 10, which covers the bishop's episcopate down to 1219 (I, iv). Although Nicholas is described simply as bishop of Tusculum, Westminster's obligation to him probably dates from his time as legate, for which see *Councils and Synods*, II (i), 36–8. The abbot who made the presentation would thus be William d'Humez.

The reader may conjecture whether this was in return for the indulgence recently granted to the abbey by Nicholas, in his capacity as papal legate (**193**), or for his role in the deposition of Abbot Ralph Arundel, whom the monks considered was overriding their interest in the management of their properties.[69]

With the increase in canon law jurisdiction in England in the later twelfth century came the regular employment of papal judges-delegate. Their rare verdicts concerning Westminster's interests in this period relate to the abbey's claim to certain churches (**194, 225**).

Episcopal charters

Most of these documents were issued by successive bishops of London. One was granted by Richard de Belmeis I (1108–27) (**203**) and another by his nephew, Richard II (1152–62) (**204**), but the majority were issued by Bishop Gilbert Foliot (1163–87) and by his successor, Richard Fitz Nigel (1189–98). These largely concern the abbey's claims to churches in the diocese, and in this respect, the bishop might be a valuable ally, since Westminster's claims to its parish churches were not always successful (**90, 93**). Charters of archdeacons of the diocese, concerning institutions to some of these churches' are printed in full among the Donors' charters (e.g. **368–9**). However, the monks claimed exemption from visitation by the bishop. Sulcard of Westminster related that St Peter himself had consecrated the earliest church on Thorney Island, thus forestalling the intention of Bishop Mellitus to perform this office.[70] A somewhat suspect Westminster account maintained that Bishop Gilbert 'the Universal' (1127–34) celebrated mass in the church, and took the offerings of the altar, thus challenging the abbey's claim to immunity, and prompting the monks to seek papal confirmation of their supposed rights.[71] Westminster's claim to be directly under papal jurisdiction to the exclusion of the bishop of London was confirmed in several bulls issued during the twelfth century (e.g. **155, 172**).

The bishops of Lincoln are also frequently represented, owing to Westminster's possession of several churches in that diocese (**222–27**). The abbey's lands and churches in other dioceses occasioned the infrequent issue of charters from the bishops of Chichester (**228**), Winchester (**231–2**) and Worcester (**233**), among others, while the acquisition of episcopal property in Westminster prompted the issue of one charter by a bishop of Exeter (**230**).

Charters of archbishops feature to a lesser extent. One royal charter refers to a territorial dispute between Westminster and Anselm of Aosta, at that time still abbot of Bec (**26**). Archbishop Theobald, towards the end of his primacy, issued several confirmations for the abbey (**197–9**). While there is no direct mention of Thomas Becket, the monks agreed to the presentation of his nephew John to one of their churches (**365**).

69. Harvey, *WA*, 83–4; Flete, 100.
70. Scholz, 'Sulcard of Westminster', 65, 83–85. See also Flete, 40–43.
71. Brett, *English Church*, 55; Beryl Smalley, 'Gilbert the Universal', *Recherches de Théologie Ancienne et Mediévale*, VII (1935), 245–7.

Archbishop Richard is represented by two confirmations, to successive members of one family, of land which was acquired by Westminster towards the end of this period (**201–2**).

There are, in the Donors' section, charters of three former senior royal clerks, who were appointed to Continental sees. Their charters for the abbey concern English properties in which they had earlier had an interest (**365, 401, 463**). The texts of these charters are printed in full, since they would not otherwise be readily accessible to readers in England.

Transactions with other religious houses

This collection includes surprisingly few charters concerning other religious houses in the London area. There is no charter issued on behalf of any house within the City of London. The Cluniac priory of Bermondsey claimed against Westminster the city church of St Magnus the Martyr (**287**) and there were dealings with the nunnery of Kilburn, a cell of Westminster (**280**); with St James's hospital (**392**); with the nunnery of Clerkenwell (**292**); and the canons of St Martin le Grand (**257**). One charter was issued by the Master of the Templars (**354**).

Further afield, the great Benedictine house of St Albans intermittently challenged Westminster over lands and other rights in Hertfordshire (**281–2**), disputes which were allegedly exacerbated by the activities of Abbot Laurence of Westminster. Prior Alquin of St Albans, on being deposed from office, following allegations concerning the existence of an illicit seal, fled to Westminster, where Laurence admitted him. In due course Alquin's exemplary conduct led to his election as Prior there, and he was eventually exonerated of charges detrimental to St Albans.[72]

The little Benedictine nunnery of Shouldham issued one charter after negotiations involving its patron, Geoffrey Fitz Peter (**476–7**). When papal judges-delegate awarded Bloxham church, previously held by Westminster, to the Benedictine nunnery of Godstow (**225**), its abbess issued a charter reserving a pension to the abbey (**481**). A memorandum survives of an exchange of land made with Merton priory (**268**). There is also one confirmation issued for the Cluniac priory of Lewes (**260**), and abbots of Bec occur in two charters (**26, 361**).

Confraternity agreements with other houses rarely survive from this period. Abbot Vitalis made one such with Durham cathedral priory (**235**), while in the later twelfth century another was made with the canons of St Victor, Paris, probably as a result of previous contacts between Abbot Laurence and that house (**400**). It may be conjectured that agreements with other religious houses were recorded in the martyrology, which is now lost.

Charters of the abbots of Westminster

No charter has survived in the name of Abbot Edwin (*c.* 1049–68), or in that of his successor, Geoffrey (*c.* 1072–*c.* 1076). Abbot Vitalis (*c.* 1076–85) has left only two charters (**234–5**). Seven charters survive from the

---

72. *Gesta Abbatum*, 107–10, 112, 133–4.

long abbacy of Gilbert Crispin (1085–1117/18) (**236–42**).[73] Herbert (1121– c. 1136) has left nine (**243–50**). Such limited numbers in proportion to the length of their abbacies preclude any realistic analysis of their policies.

Abbot Gervase (1138–c. 1157), in contrast, has left some twenty-four charters (**251–74**). His later reputation at Westminster, as recorded by John Flete in the fifteenth century, is that of an unsatisfactory abbot who had mismanaged the abbey's estates. In recent decades, the reputation of Gervase has been somewhat rehabilitated. H. G. Richardson and G. O. Sayles noted the extent to which his reputation suffered at the hands of his pro-Angevin successor, Laurence. They suspected, probably rightly, that the real reason for the dismissal of Gervase was his kinship to King Stephen.[74]

Barbara Harvey has re-examined the traditional allegations against Gervase, with particular reference to Flete's accusation that he granted several fee-farms on terms which were detrimental to the interests of the abbey. She demonstrated that several of the grants in question were actually made by other abbots. In particular, both the text and the hand of the Deerhurst grant reveal that, in its present form, it is a thirteenth-century product (**271**).[75] Of the remaining grants, the majority were made on reasonable terms, from Westminster's viewpoint, given the prevailing economic and political conditions. Of the charters in the present edition, many state that Gervase was acting in conjunction with his monks. Others are attested by Prior Osbert (**254**) or Prior Elias (**261**). There are three grants which were more favourable to their recipients than to the abbey (**258, 261–2**). On the evidence of these, later generations of monks, struggling to manage their portion of the Westminster estates without abbatial interference, came to regard Gervase as a symbol of abbatial autocracy. The most notorious of the grants was that of the manor of Chelsea to Gervase's mother Damette, 'the Little Lady' (**262**).[76] Richardson and Sayles suggested that it was the installation of King Stephen's mistress on a manor so close to the royal palace at Westminster which provoked much of the criticism of Gervase.[77]

Once England was firmly under Angevin rule, it is highly likely that Henry II instigated the deposition of Gervase, not wishing the coronation church to remain under the control of an abbot of the house of Blois.[78] At the outset of the new reign, Henry confirmed Gervase in the abbatial lands (**122**), but on the occasion of his deposition, probably in the latter part of 1157 (cf. **341**) took the opportunity to seize lands belonging to Westminster.[79]

---

73. It is possible that one lost charter of Abbot Gilbert concerned his grant of the manor of Powick to the priory of Great Malvern: *Monasticon*, III, 447–8; W. Thomas, *Antiquitates Prioratus Majoris Malverne* (London, 1725), iv.
74. Richardson & Sayles, 413–21. Gervase's kinship to King Stephen was probably a major consideration when the pope rejected him as a candidate for the see of Lincoln in 1148 (*L & C Foliot*, nos. 75, 80).
75. Harvey, 'Fee Farms', 131–3.
76. Ibid., 127–41.
77. Richardson & Sayles, 415–6.
78. Ibid., 421.
79. *Curia Regis Rolls*, I, 464–5.

Gervase was probably appointed at an early age,[80] but his numerous charters provide evidence of considerable exertions on behalf of the abbey. He granted a regular income for the repair of books (**251**), and made grants to supplement the monks' clothing allowance (**255, 258**) and to provide lights and other necessities for the high altar (**252–3**). He also utilized recent technological innovations in his administration of the abbey's lands. The mill which he constructed on the River Wandle in Surrey (**268**) was perhaps one of the earliest fulling mills in the region.[81] His assertion of Westminster's jurisdiction over Great Malvern was strongly endorsed by Archbishop Theobald and Gilbert Foliot, early in Henry II's reign, when support of Gervase might be considered courageous.[82]

Abbot Laurence (*c.* 1158–1173), left twelve charters (**275–86**), a small output considering his ambitions and his intellectual capacity.[83] His most notable achievement, reflected in two bulls of Pope Alexander III (**167–8**) is that he successfully steered the canonization process of Edward the Confessor through the papal curia.[84]

Charters of the prior and monks

Many of the abbatial charters in this volume were issued in the name of the abbot and convent, or in that of 'the abbot and monks'. A formal division of the Westminster estates, between those administered by the abbot, and those managed by the convent, dates only from the early thirteenth century, but there are earlier documents which illustrate the administration or acquisition of property by the prior and convent, or even simply by 'the monks'. Probably the earliest is a text recording 'the monks' farm', but this is not necessarily a document drawn up during an abbatial vacancy (**339**).[85] From the mid twelfth century there survive several documents which were issued collectively by the monks, concerning properties in the City of London (**340, 343–3**).

Prior Robert of Moulsham and the convent jointly issued several charters around the end of the twelfth century (**345–8**). Robert, like Osbert de Clare and Abbot Laurence before him, masterminded a project designed to further the interests of the abbey, and, perhaps, his own, simultaneously. Whereas the hopes of Osbert and Laurence rested largely on the projected canonization of King Edward, Robert of Moulsham, as precentor, actively fostered the cult of the Blessed Virgin, which was manifested at Westminster by devotion to the Lady Altar.

80. Richardson & Sayles, 413.
81. Emma Mason, 'Westminster Abbey's fulling-mills at Wandsworth', *Bulletin of the Wandle Group*, no. 13 (1984), 4. The known early fulling mills in England are mainly later in date: E. M. Carus Wilson, 'An Industrial Revolution of the Thirteenth Century', *Economic History Review* 11 (1941), 39–60; R. Lennard, 'Early English Fulling Mills: Additional Examples', *Econ. Hist. Rev.* second ser., 3 (1951), 342–3.
82. *Letters of John of Salisbury*, I, no. 45.
83. A further charter of Abbot Laurence, now lost, is cited by Abbot Walter in his grant to Robert of Wick of the vill of Upton Snodsbury (**305**). On Abbot Laurence, see Flete, 91–4; Richardson & Sayles, 420–21.
84. Flete, 92–4; Barlow, *Edward the Confessor*, 277–83.
85. On the division of possessions between abbot and monks in this period, see Harvey, *WA*, 85–6.

Numbers of the Donors' charters date from Robert's time as precentor, when he was also proctor of this altar, and administered the rent income which provided for its illumination (e.g. **411**, **429**). He continued as proctor after he became prior (**346–7**).

One rather different charter issued by Robert and the convent conceded the request of Abbot Ralph Arundel that four (additional) feasts in the year should be celebrated in copes, and with processions. As was usual on major festivals, these solemnities were to be followed by wine and pittances, no doubt to encourage hearty chanting beforehand (cf. **283**, **285**). The abbot, in return, gave back the monks' manor of Benfleet, which he had been holding at farm (**345**). There are no charters issued by other obedientiaries from this period, but two bulls of Pope Alexander III were issued respectively for Roger the infirmarer (**169**) and Walter the sacrist (**170**) confirming at their request and that of Abbot Laurence, certain churches of which they administered the income.

Donors and witnesses
In the aftermath of the Norman Conquest, it soon became clear that the abbey must look to benefactors other than the monarchy for the reinforcement of its endowment. The charters of the donors reflect the success which was achieved in this area. A small number of charters date from the late eleventh century, notably grants by Geoffrey de Mandeville I (**436**, **462**), whose descendants and territorial successors, down to the justiciar Geoffrey Fitz Peter, intermittently made further grants (**350**, **464**, **470**, **476**). There is a gradual build-up in the numbers of donors' charters surviving from the earlier twelfth century. A more marked increase can be discerned in the numbers of charters from the 1160s and 1170s, then a rapid acceleration from *c.* 1190, largely as a result of the acquisition of properties to support the Lady Altar.

From the middle years of Henry II's reign, Westminster effectively replaced Winchester as the centre of government. Consequently, royal officers, and especially the personnel of the Exchequer, began to acquire houses in the vill of Westminster.[86] Charters were increasingly granted to the Abbey by Exchequer personnel (e.g. **414**, **439**) and such men are also found among the witnesses (e.g. **449**).

Richard of Ilchester, both before and after his elevation to the see of Winchester, was involved directly and indirectly with Westminster. On occasion he appears as its benefactor (**231**) but he was on occasion recalled also as a predator (**457**). His kinsmen also appear in this collection, including Herbert le Poore, his reputed son (**457**); members of the Barentin family, of whom the younger generation were Richard's nephews (**134–5**, **139**), and the ubiquitous Adam 'nephew of the bishop' (**412–14**, **437**).[87] William of Ely, royal treasurer and near kinsman of his predecessor in office, Richard Fitz Nigel, bishop of London,[88] occurs as a donor (**439**), and also as a leading witness to the abbey's charters (**409**,

86. Rosser, 'Medieval Westminster', 18–21, 23, 26; *Beauchamp Cartulary*, nos. 183–203.
87. See also *Beauchamp Cartulary*, nos. 183–6, 191–2, 199–200; Richardson, 'William of Ely', 86n.
88. Richardson, 'William of Ely', 45–90; *Fasti* I, 35.

434, 446). Other leading officers who occur include Jocelin Fitz Hugh, marshal of the Exchequer (**409, 434**);[89] and the young Alexander of Swerford, who was employed as a clerk of Abbot Ralph Arundel (**327**) before joining the Exchequer staff (**414**), where he acquired a great reputation, and is now remembered as the compiler of the Red Book of the Exchequer.[90] His benefactions to the abbey were partly made in association with Edith de Barra, the mother of his children (**413–14**).

Joint donations by husband and wife, or by less formally-linked couples, occur several times in this collection. Robert Mauduit, an Exchequer chamberlain who accumulated considerable property in Westminster,[91] obtained from Abbot William Postard a licence to maintain a private chapel in his town house (**312**). Isabel Basset, Robert's wife, bought up properties in Westminster to bestow on the Lady Altar (**422, 450**) and in due course, the couple obtained from Abbot Ralph Arundel an agreement that all benefactors of this Altar should have their names inscribed in the martyrology (**329**).[92] Another benefactress was Rose *la custerere*, alias Rose de Bleis, the widow of William Turpin of the King's Chamber, acting with Ralph Mauduit (**386–7, 435**).[93]

The majority of donors and witnesses were inhabitants of London or of Westminster. Their surnames reflect the wide variety of trades and professions then practised in these places. The clergy of several of the city churches are named (**365, 368–9, 380–1**), while one charter was attested by nine goldsmiths (**381**). Similarly, the deeds concerning Westminster document the personnel of the Exchequer, down through the hierarchy to the smelters (**414, 446, 448**) and reckoners (**446**). The names also appear of a number of the lay personnel of the abbey—both its hereditary officers such as the seneschal (**411**) and the summoner (**402–3**), and lesser figures, including a bevy of sergeants, who often attest *en bloc* (**430, 443–4**) and some painters (**443–4, 447–8**). Gerin the engineer (*ingeniator*) attests a charter of Abbot Gervase (**255**), and it has been suggested that the reeve, Roger Enganet, a frequent witness to the later charters in this volume, was perhaps also named from the office of engineer.[94] Whether

---

89. *Beauchamp Cartulary*, xv, xxxij, xlj, nos. 199–200, 204, 226, 312–14; Richardson, 'William of Ely', 85n–86n.

90. *RBE*, I, xxxv–xlix; F. M. Powicke, *King Henry III and the Lord Edward* (1966), 90–1, 94, 97n–98, 315; *Fasti* I, 22, 43, 89.

91. *Beauchamp Cartulary*, nos. 183–200.

92. In 1221 × 22, Robert Mauduit granted rents to the abbey, in return for the solemn celebration of his obit: WAM 3456, printed in Mason, 'The Mauduits and their Chamberlainship', 22–3. On the donors of this period, see also Emma Mason, 'The Donors of Westminster Abbey Charters: *c.* 1066–1240', *Medieval Prosopography*, 8:2 (1987), 23–39.

93. Mason, 'The Mauduits and their Chamberlainship', 9, 23. In 1176–7, Ralph Mauduit was responsible for the collection of escheats in the New Forest. The sum due from him was entered on the Pipe Roll of the following year: *PR 34 Henry II*, 17.

94. Rosser, 'Medieval Westminster', 362. Roger Enganet was perhaps the son of Ailnoth the engineer (*ingeniator*), who, although a skilled engineer, was latterly employed as keeper of the King's houses at Westminster (C. T. Clay, 'The Keepership of the Old Palace of Westminster', *EHR* 59 (1944), 6–7; J. H. Round, 'The staff of a castle in the twelfth century', *EHR* 35 (1920), 93–4).

the activities of these men were confined to construction work within the immediate precincts, or extended to the harnessing of water power from the Wandle (**268**) and the Winterbourne (**486**) is uncertain.

Immigrants from overseas are found with surnames such as Burgundian (**278**), Lombard (**307**, **353**) or Fleming (**378**). High-flyers among the clerks of Henry II might find that successive promotions led them to cross the Channel first in one direction, then in the other (**365**, **463**). Church dedications are a further source of evidence on immigration patterns in this period, since settlers brought with them their native religious cults. Westminster, after a long struggle, acquired a half-share in the London church of St Magnus (**287**) dedicated to a martyred earl of Orkney.[95] The charters also contain briefer references to other churches whose dedications reflect non-native cults, such as St Denis (**259**), or St Clement Danes (**394–7**).

Properties in London and Westminster
Among the charters in the present collection, many relate to small residential plots of land in London and Westminster. In the absence of any sustained royal support after 1066, the abbey had to look elsewhere for the augmentation of its endowment. The growing population of London and Westminster might be enlisted to this end, particularly if attracted by the offer of the abbey's spiritual services. Barbara Harvey has demonstrated that it was never difficult for people of modest means to obtain burial within the abbey precincts, or an agreement that the anniversary of their deaths would be commemorated by the monks in perpetuity. Certain charters also grant the spiritual benefits of confraternity (**359**). In return for such concessions, the abbot and monks were able to consolidate their urban properties in certain parts of London and the growing suburb of Westminster, presumably those which would generate a good rent income.

In the vill of Westminster, there was evidently an early concentration on Charing, and on Tothill Street, in particular, with some concentration too on those areas which are now known as Ebury and St James's. Of the two latter, Ebury comprises only a part, but a substantial one, of the manor of Eye, granted by Geoffrey de Mandeville I, late in the eleventh century (**436**). Although part of this manor later became detached,[96] the term Ebury is used in the headings and notes in the present volume, for the convenience of non-specialist readers. The area now known as St James's takes its name from a leper house of that dedication (**288**). Another district of the vill which is mentioned several times in this volume is Endiff (e.g. **437–8**). This place-name, now lost, represents an area slightly down-river from the palace of Westminster.[97] The gradual urbanization of the whole vill, from the late twelfth century almost to the Reformation, has been admirably documented by Gervase Rosser, to whose work the reader is referred for a detailed account.[98] Since most

95. *Orkneyinga Saga*, transl. H. Palsson and P. Edwards (1981), 93–7, 103–8.
96. Rutton, 'Eye next Westminster', 31–58; *PN Mddx*, 167–8.
97. *PN Mddx*, 168; Rosser, 'Medieval Westminster', 21, 23.
98. Rosser, 'Medieval Westminster', *passim*.

charters are careful to give the boundaries of the tenements which accrued to the abbey, the names are known, in most cases, of the donors' neighbours, and it is possible to document the sequence in which particular groups of tenements were acquired (**416–18**). The major phase of consolidation can be dated to the 1190s onwards, when rents in Westminster were accumulated for the Lady Altar. In the case of many of the charters, both those concerning Westminster and others relating to the City of London, the measurements of each boundary of the tenement are given. Normally measurement is made in the ells of the reigning king (e.g. **367**), although there is an occasional instance where those of his predecessor appear to be cited (**419**), perhaps in order to correlate with an earlier title deed. The foot is sometimes used, too, in measuring these plots (**354, 356**).

In London, the abbey had interests from the mid-eleventh century, at latest, if the evidence of the spurious charters of King Edward, and of King William I (**25, 33, 36, 39–40**) can be accepted. One charter of Abbot Vitalis (**234**) reflects Westminster's interests in the City. These interests were enlarged during the reign of Henry I (**68, 77–9**), including an extension of the abbot's wharf (**97**). The systematic administration of property in various parts of London, already documented in the charters of Abbot Gervase (**255–9**), is amplified in those of Laurence (**275–8**) and in those of his immediate successor, Abbot Walter (**287–95**). During the abbacy of William Postard, the correlation of the charters of priors and donors reveals the accumulation of further tenements. On occasion, rents in the City were acquired for the Lady Altar, from the 1190s (**356**), but others were wanted for a variety of purposes (**350**).

Perhaps the overall majority of tenements were residential, in Ludgate, for instance (**358**), but there was a marked interest in areas with commercial potential, such as Cheapside (**355**) or the Fishmarket (**356–7**), while shops (**356–7**) and selds (**295**) were acquired on occasion, as were plots fronting the Thames (**353**). The occasional specific mention of stone buildings (**370**) suggests that others were of less durable materials.[99]

From the 1180s onwards, clauses of warranty are almost invariably found. In charters relating to London properties it seems to have become usual, *c.* 1200, to include a clause prohibiting the owner from dislodging the lessee on any pretext (**366–7**).

While rents, in both London and Westminster, were normally due on the standard English quarter-days, occasional charters specify payments in instalments other than quarterly, and consequently due on different dates (**340**). While most payments were reckoned in proportions of the mark (13*s.* 4*d.*), a few were stated in besants,[100] or in shillings and pence sterling. When a grant was made for a consideration (gersum), this was virtually always a monetary one.

---

99. According to City tradition, during the mayoralty of Henry Fitz Ailwin, regulations were made encouraging the use of stone in building walls, to lessen the spread of fires: *London Assize of Nuisance 1301–1431: a calendar*, ed. Helena M. Chew and W. Kellaway, (LRS 10, 1973), ix; T. Baker, *Medieval London* (1970), 202.

100. On the exchange-rate of the besant in shillings and pence sterling, in 1162 and 1213, see Spufford, *HME*, 295.

Grants concerning properties within the boundaries of the City of London were usually attested by the mayor and aldermen, and sometimes state explicitly that they were ratified in the Husting Court (**361**). Notable Londoners rarely attest deeds concerning property outside the walls, such as the district beyond Ludgate and the parishes of St Clement Danes and St Martin in the Fields. The location of extra-mural properties presents some difficulties, but these can often be resolved by reference to the attestations. The donors' charters afford good evidence of the development of the suburb of London, and its gradual expansion in the direction of Westminster.

Lands further afield

There is a relatively small number of donors' charters relating to lands further afield. These latter properties vary in size from a small plot bought to facilitate the making of a conduit (**486**) to large tracts of land (**475**). Most such charters relate to properties in the region which would now be termed the London commuter belt. The extension of control over churches (**459, 463, 469–70**) and tithes (**456, 478**) is a marked feature of this group. Properties in more remote counties were often held at farm, hence charters concerning any individual estate were normally issued only at infrequent intervals. Many of the more remote properties of the Abbey scarcely occur in the charters contained in the present volume.[101]

The Abbey Sanctuary

From an early date, the abbey claimed the right to offer sanctuary to fugitives from the law.[102] There survive, as copies in WAD and in F, texts of several writs concerning this right (**238–40, 248, 272–4, 279**). In most cases, the sheriff of the fugitive's home shire is notified of the man's flight and advised of the abbey's right, and later writs contain additional clauses. Presumably these writs represent only a small proportion of those which were issued, and were perhaps copied into the cartularies as examples of the formulae employed at various times. Related to these writs is the Fugitives' Oath (**349**), which survives only in two late transcripts. Its terms were designed to ensure the orderly conduct of these refugees from the law.

Acknowledgements

My thanks are offered to Phyllis Murphy who, on the untimely death of her husband, invited me to continue his work. The texts of Westminster Abbey Muniments, and of entries in the abbey's various Muniment Books, are published by courtesy of the Dean and Chapter of Westminster. Crown-copyright material in the Public Record Office is reproduced by permission of the Controller of Her Majesty's Stationery Office. I am also grateful to the British Library, and to St Bartholomew's Hospital, for permission to publish texts in their possession.

The staff of Westminster Abbey Library and Muniment Room have

101. On the administrative problems arising from the subinfeudated properties, see Harvey, *WA*, 70–85.
102. Honeybourne, 'Sanctuary Boundaries', 316–32.

given much invaluable advice and practical help. Regrettably, neither Nicholas MacMichael, Keeper of the Muniments, nor Howard Nixon, Librarian, lived to see the completion of this volume. I am also indebted to Enid Nixon, Acting Librarian, Christine Reynolds, and Richard Mortimer, Acting Keeper of the Muniments. My thanks are also offered to the staff of the British Library Students' Room, and to those of the College of Arms, the Public Record Office, the Archives Department of St Bartholomew's Hospital, and the Department of Manuscripts of the Guildhall Library.

Barbara Harvey commented on a considerable proportion of the calendar entries and the texts, besides advising on many specific points of detail. The remaining calendar entries were variously commented upon by Diana Greenway, Jane Sayers and David Bates, according to their respective areas of interest. Any remaining defects in text or calendar are my own responsibility.

Those who have generously advised on specific points include Janet Bately, Brenda Bolton, Christopher Brooke, Kenneth Cameron, Pierre Chaplais, Janet Cowan, the late R. R. Darlington, John Dodgson, Alison Finlay, Annabel Gregory, Bill Kellaway, Patrick McGurk, Shayne Mitchell, Philip Riebold, Jane Roberts, Gervase Rosser, Ian Short and David Smith. Eleanor Thomas typed the Introduction and some revised textual material.

Jennifer Bray died at a tragically early age, just as this volume was about to go to press. Her enthusiasm and commitment to the project went far beyond what would reasonably be expected of a research assistant. She typed the text and calendar onto a word-processor; exhaustively checked successive print-outs; did some preliminary work on the index and pursued many bibliographical references. Her assistance was generously financed, first by the Leverhulme Trust, which awarded me a Research Fellowship in 1983, and extended it in 1984, and secondly by a grant awarded in 1985 by the Nuffield Foundation. Contributions to the cost of publication were generously made by the Marc Fitch Fund, the British Academy, and the Publications Fund of Birkbeck College.

In the interval between the completion of this edition and its publication, the British Academy made me a most generous Personal Award, which financed the further assistance of Jennifer Bray in a detailed analysis of the Westminster Charters for the period 1066–1214. It is hoped that the results of this will be published in a series of articles on topics including the abbey's generation of propaganda; relations with both the crown and the papacy; dealings with the ecclesiastical hierarchy in England, and with other religious houses; the management of Westminster's parish churches; the prosopographical study of the men and women named in the charters; the policy of property management in London, Westminster and elsewhere, and the concomitant recourse to a variety of local courts; methods of record-keeping, fugitives to the sanctuary, and the fostering of various religious cults.

WESTMINSTER ABBEY CHARTERS
1066–*c.* 1214

CALENDARS OF ROYAL, PAPAL, AND EPISCOPAL CHARTERS

1.* 'First Charter' of W I, making offerings to the altars of the abbey; confirming its possessions (enumerated), and granting specified privileges. 1067.

CC VI,3 (12C forgery, with seal; MS damaged and lacunae filled from F). WAD, ff. 49–50v (incomplete); F, ff. 37v–44v; T, ff. 13v–16v (attestations omitted after that of the king); C, f. 30r–v (extracts); Rot. Ancient Charters, *olim* CC, PRO, C52/57, no. 2; Charter Roll 9 Ed. III, PRO, C53/122, mm.17–16.
Pd: *Cal. Chart. R.* IV, 330–6, from the confirmation of Ed. III; Flete, 54, 82 (extracts), from WAD; W. de Gray Birch, 'On the Great Seals of William the Conqueror, *Trans. Royal Soc. of Literature*, 2nd ser., 10 (1874), 161–70, from CC VI, 3.
Cal: *DKR* XXIX, App., 34–6; *Regesta* I, no. 11; Hart, no. 81; Bishop and Chaplais, xxi, no. viii, where it is erroneously stated that the seal is still attached. Browning & Kirk, 221–4 (transl. excerpts).
Note: Identified as a forgery by Birch (above), 170–1; Chaplais, 'Original Charters', 92; Bishop and Chaplais, xxi; C. N. L. Brooke, 'Approaches to Medieval Forgery', in *Medieval Church and Society: Collected Essays* (1971), 106 ff. On the churches confirmed in this charter, see Oxley, 'Medieval Church Dedications', 118.

2.* Writ of W I, notifying Rémy, bp. of Lincoln, William Fitz Osbern, and his barons and officers of Herts., that he has confirmed to St Peter, Abbot Edwin and the monks of Westminster their manor of Aldenham as they held it TRE. [Dec. 1066 × June 1068]

WAD, f. 186; F, f. 58v; T, f. 20 (attestations omitted). The variant texts omit *Dei gratia*, but complete the concluding phrase *torturam suam*.
Pd: *Regesta* I, no. IX. from WAD.

Cal: *Regesta* I, no. 53.

Date: Abbot Edwin d. 12 June 1068 (Flete, 83; *Heads*, 76). Bp. Rémy was nominated to Dorchester soon after the Conquest, ? 1067, and consecrated before April 1070. His see was transferred to Lincoln before 21 April 1073, and prob. in 1072 (*Fasti* III, 1). The bp.'s title on the original writ was presumably altered, at Westminster, before the copies were made.

Note: Textually, this appears to be a complete fabrication. On Aldenham, cf. Harvey, *WA*, 345.

3.* Writ of W I, informing Rémy, bp. of Lincoln, William Fitz Osbert and his officers of Oxon., that the church of St Peter of Westminster, Abbot Edwin and the monks are to have their manor of Islip, the birthplace of his kinsman King Edward, as that king granted it at the dedication of the abbey church. [1066 × 1068]

WAM XXV; F, f. 54; WAD, f. 270; CAY, f. lxxviii *verso* (memorandum).

Pd: *Regesta* I, no. X, from WAD; J. O. Halliwell, 'Historical Notices of Islip, Oxfordshire', *JBAA* 5 (1850), 42, from F.

Cal: *Regesta* I, no. 52, describing the muniment as a 12C copy; Bentley, 40, no. 284 (Item 3), from CAY.

Date: Abbacy of Abbot Edwin (*Heads*, 76).

Note: A forgery, perhaps composed when petitioning King John for this manor. There survive copies of two writs of King Edward, dating from 1065 × 1066, by which he granted Islip to Westminster. Both are of doubtful authenticity (Sawyer, *Anglo-Saxon Charters*, nos. 1147, 1148), although the substance of the abbey's claim was prob. true. Westminster did not hold this manor between 1066 and 1203 (Barbara Harvey, 'Islip', *VCH Oxon.*, VI, 208–9).

4. English writ of W I, informing Abp. Ealdred, Wulfstan, bp. of Worcester, Earl William Fitz Osbern and his thegns of Gloucs., Worcs., and Oxon., that he confirms to St Peter of Westminster the lands in Pershore and Deerhurst which were granted by King Edward. [1066 × Sept. 1069]

WAD, f. 278v; F, f. 113v; CAY, f. lxix (memorandum in Latin).

Pd: *Monasticon* I, 301, no. XL; Neufeldt, no. 34: from F.

Cal: *Regesta* I, no. 32; Bentley, 31, no. 254 (item 2), from CAY.

Date: Ealdred d. 11 Sept. 1069 (*ASC*, 149).

Note: Cf. Harvey, *WA*, 344, 363.

5. English writ of W I, informing Leofwine, bp. of Lichfield, Earl Edwin [of Mercia] and the thegns in Staffs., that the land of Perton pertains to St Peter of Westminster as fully as King Edward gave it. Abbot Æthelwig [of Evesham] and Thurkill the sheriff are to protect the land for the abbey. [1066 × 1071 (? 1066 × 1068)]

WAD, f. 648; F, f. 113v.

Pd: *Monasticon* I, 301, no. XXXIX; Neufeldt, no. 33: from F.

Cal: *Regesta* I, no. 25.
Date: Bp. Leofwine was deposed at the legatine council of Winchester at Easter 1070, and formally resigned his see to the king at Easter 1071 (*The Letters of Lanfranc archbishop of Canterbury*, ed. and transl. Helen Clover and Margaret Gibson (1979), 34–8 and notes). Earl Edwin d. in 1071, after some months passed as a fugitive rebel (*ASC*, 154; Orderic II, 258). It is unlikely that he would be addressed in such a writ following his brief rebellion in 1068 (Orderic II, 214–18).
Note: Cf. Harvey, *WA*, 357.

6. English writ of W I, informing Abp. Stigand, Count Eustace and his thegns in Surr., that he has granted land in Battersea and Pyrford to St Peter of Westminster, to hold as fully as Harold [II] held them at his death. [1066 × 10 April 1070]

F, f. 112v.
Pd: *Monasticon* I, 301, No.XXXV; Neufeldt, no. 29; Browning & Kirk, 'Early History', 225, from F.
Cal: *Regesta* I, no. 45.
Date: Abp. Stigand was deposed *c.* 11 April 1070 (*Fasti* II, 3).
Note: Cf. Harvey, *WA*, 357–9. On the boundaries of the Westminster estate in Battersea, see Taylor, *Our Lady of Batersey*, 9–20; Browning & Kirk, 'Early History', 225–35. The nuns of Barking held Battersea before the destruction of their house in 870. Harold Godwinson's subsequent possession of land there reflects the strategic importance of this site, which commanded an important ford on the Thames (Robin Fleming, 'Monastic Lands and England's defence in the Viking Age', *EHR* 100 (1985), 256, 262). On the style of Harold II, see Garnett, 'Coronation and Propaganda', 98–101.

7. English writ of W I, ordering Bundi the staller, Swawold the sheriff and his thegns in Oxon. that the abbey is to have its half hide in Marston. Anything alienated is to be returned within seven nights of the receipt of this writ. [1066 × *c.* 1068]

WAD, f. 273; F, f. 112v; CAY, f. lxxviii *verso* (memorandum in Latin).
Pd: *Monasticon* I, 301, no. XXXIV; Neufeldt, no. 28: from F.
Cal: *Regesta* I, no. 18; Bentley, 41, no. 284 (item 17), from CAY.
Date: English language and addressees; cf. the spurious 3.
Note: The abbey was granted this land by Edward the Confessor, but never gained possession of it: cf. Harvey, *WA*, 356n; Sawyer, *Anglo-Saxon Charters*, no. 1147.

8. English writ of W I, ordering Edmund the sheriff [of Herts.], Alfwine Gottune and Leofwine Scune that St Peter of Westminster is to have full possession of the land at Watton and Datchworth, and enquiry is to be made into the king's rights there. [1066 × *c.* 1070]

WAD, f. 227; F, ff. 112v–113.
Pd: *Monasticon* I, 301, no. XXXVI; Neufeldt, no. 30: from F.

Cal: *Regesta* I, no. 16.
Date: English language and addressees.
Note: Cf. Harvey, *WA*, 346.

9. English writ of W I, ordering William bp. of London, Sweyn the sheriff and the thegns of Essex, that the abbey is to have the two estates of Feering and Ockendon in exchange for Windsor, to hold with sake and soke, as he first granted them. Whosoever holds the lands, Sweyn is to convey them to the abbey, and all alienated goods or possessions are to be restored within eleven nights from the time this writ is read. [1066 × 1075]

WAD, f. 243; F, f. 113.
Pd: *Monasticon* I, 301, no. XXXVII; Neufeldt, no. 31: from F.
Cal: *Regesta* I, no. 87; Hart, no. 73.
Date: William, bp. of London, attended the Council of London in April
  or May 1075 (*Councils and Synods*, ii, 607), but d. later that year
  (*Fasti* I, 1). Sweyn the sheriff was in office before the Domesday
  Survey (*Sheriffs*, 43).
Note: Cf. Harvey, *WA*, 338, 341, 343; Garnett, 'Coronation and Propa-
  ganda', 99–100.

10. Writ of W I, notifying William bp. of London, S[weyn] the sheriff, and the men of Essex, that he has conceded and given to St Peter of Westminster the land of Ockendon and Feering with everything pertaining to it TRE, as Earl Harold Godwinson held it at that time. [1066 × 1075]

WAD, f. 243; F, f. 59v; T, f. 20.
Pd: *Regesta* I, no. XI, from WAD.
Cal: *Regesta* I, no. 86; Hart, no. 74.
Date: See **9**.
Note: Cf. Harvey, *WA*, 341, 343.

11.* Writ of W I, ordering William, bp. of London, Geoffrey de Mandeville, and the sheriff and officers of Mddx., that St Peter and the monks of Westminster are to have the land called Chalkhill (in Kingsbury), which he confirmed to augment their diet, to hold as Thurstan the housecarl held of King Edward, the king's kinsman, and as Thurstan gave it, and King Edward confirmed it, to the abbey. Westminster 25 Dec. [1066 × 1075]

WAD, f. 114v (only in this text is the attestation of Count Robert
  repeated); F, f. 58r–v; T, ff. 19v–20.
Pd: *Regesta* I, no. XII, from WAD.
Cal: *Regesta* I, no. 89; cf. ibid. II, 392.
Date: Prob. an authentic base, but with attestations added later. That of
  William of St Calais, bp. of Durham 1080–96, is incompatible with
  the address to William, bp. of London (cf. **9**). Franchisal clauses
  prob. also added.

Note: It is doubtful whether the abbey ever held this land in demesne (Harvey, *WA*, 349 and n.6).

12.* Writ of W I, ordering William, bp. of London, Geoffrey the sheriff, and his officers in Essex, that St Peter and the monks of Westminster are to have the manor of Kelvedon Hatch as Alric granted it, and King Edward confirmed it, with sake and soke, and other rights. Windsor [1066 × 1075]

F, f. 60.
Pd: Harmer, 494 ('not authentic').
Cal: Hart, no. 82.
Date: William, bp. of London, d. 1075 (see **9**). The first attestation, that of William of St Calais, bp. of Durham, is spurious, since he was elected only in Nov. 1080 (*Fasti* II, 85). The manor was given to the abbey when Alric the chamberlain (Harmer, 302, 554), who held it TRE, returned from a naval battle against W I, and the abbey occupied the manor in 1086 but was not seised of it (*DB* II, 14b). The authenticity of the Anglo-Saxon writ of Edward the Confessor confirming an earlier grant by Alric of the manor to the abbey has been queried, but Kelvedon Hatch was allegedly demesne manor from *c.* 1066 (Harvey, *WA*, 343), and therefore it is likely that the witness list was added at Westminster to a genuine writ, before the copy was made.

13.* Writ of W I, informing Bp. Walkelin of Winchester, Wulfwold, abbot of Chertsey, William Fitz Osbern, dapifer, Godfrey, son of Count Eustace, and the barons and officers of Surr., that he has confirmed to St Peter of Westminster, Abbot Edwin and the brethren the 'little manor' of Claygate, with appurtenant rights in Long Ditton and its woods, and legal and fiscal exemptions, as Earl Tostig and Countess Leofrune granted, and King Edward confirmed it. [1070 × 1071]

WAD, f. 465v.
Pd: Flete, 141.
Cal: *Regesta* I, no. 237.
Note: *Post descriptionem Anglie* follows the attestation of William, count of Mortain, who succeeded his father only in 1090 (Sanders, 14). These concluding phrases are a later addition, even if the text is based on a genuine grant, with the abbot's name miscopied. Abbot Edwin d. 1068, (*Heads*, 76) and William Fitz Osbern in 1071 (Sanders, 35). Bp. Walkelin was nominated 23 May, and consecrated 30 May 1070 (*Fasti* II, 85). The abbey held Claygate in 1086 (*DB* I, f. 32) but was not recorded as having any rights in Long Ditton (*DB* I, f. 35). Cf. Harmer, 305–6, 513; Harvey, *WA*, 358. Concerning the identity of Earl Tostig and Countess Leofrune, see Harmer, 303–4, 575–6; Barlow, *Edward the Confessor*, 30.

14.* 'Second Charter' of W I, confirming the privileges granted to the abbey by Edward the Confessor, as agreed at the Council of Westminster, with exemption from the jurisdiction of bps. or lay officers. Westminster, 22 May 1075.

WAM XXVII(b); WAD, f. 51 (second half of text, giving date as *vj Kal. Maij*); F, ff. 49–51; T, ff. 17v–18v (attestations omitted); BL Additional Roll 15895, no. 8 (extract).
Cal: *Regesta* I, no. 34; Bishop & Chaplais, xxxi, no. ix: date follows WAD.
Date: *Anno dominice incarnationis millesimo lxx^{mo} quinto, etiam adepti imperii . . . regis Willelmi anno iiii^{to} die predicti festi Pentecostes xi^{mo} kal. Junii.* The dates given are inconsistent: neither in 1075 (mlxxv) nor in 1070 (4 William I) did Pentecost fall on 22 May (11 kal. June). A synod was held in London in 1075, prob. in April or May–June (*Councils and Synods*, ii, 607) but the king did not attend, and is not known to have been at Westminster until Christmas (*Regesta* I, xxii). The attestations are impossible for either year, since Lanfranc was nominated to Canterbury only on 15 Aug. 1070 (*Fasti* II, 3), while William Fitz Osbern d. in 1071 (Sanders, 98). Forgery is also indicated by the language.

15.* 'Third Charter' of W I, confirming the property and privileges of St Peter of Westminster as granted by Edward the Confessor and his predecessors, and confirmed by successive popes. Westminster, 29 Dec. 1077.

WAD, ff. 51–52v; F, ff. 44v–49; T, ff. 16v–17v (attestations omitted after that of the king); BL Additional Roll 15895, no. 8 (extracts).
Cal: *Regesta* I, no. 90.
Note: The dating clauses and attestations contain inconsistencies, as do the language and purport of the charter (*Regesta* I, no. 90n.).

16. Writ of W I, notifying Sweyn the sheriff and his officers in Essex that he has granted to St Peter of Westminster and the brethren the manor of Feering, with its sokemen, and three appurtenant houses in Colchester, as Earl Harold Godwinson held it at the death of Edward the Confessor, and as he, William, held it. This grant is made on the advice of his barons, in exchange for Windsor. [Aug. 1070 × 1082]

WAD, f. 243; F, f. 59r–v; T, f. 20 (no witnesses). Both F and T omit *de Estsexa*.
Pd: *Regesta* I, no. XVII, from WAD. The third attestation is *recte Gosfrido Const'*.
Cal: *Regesta* I, no. 163.
Date: Cf. **9**.
Note: Cf. *DB* II, 14b; Harvey, *WA*, 338, 341; Garnett, 'Coronation and Propaganda', 99–100.

17.* Writ of W I, informing Walkelin, bp. of Winchester, and O. the sheriff and his officers in Surr., that St Peter of Westminster and the monks are to have the manors of Battersea, Wandsworth and Pyrford, with appurtenances and customs, as Earl Harold Godwinson held them TRE. [Aug. 1070 × 1082]

WAD, f. 161; F, ff. 55v–56; LN, ff. xlvj *verso*–xlvij; CAY, f. xlix.
Pd: *Regesta* I, no. XVIII, from WAD; Browning & Kirk, 225, transl. from F.
Cal: *Regesta* I, no. 162; Bentley, 23, no. 177, from CAY.
Date: Attestations of Bp. Odo, disgraced in 1082 (Orderic IV, 40–4), and of Abp. Lanfranc, nominated and consecrated Aug. 1070 (*Fasti* II, 3).
Note: Cf. *DB* I, f. 32. The sentence: *Et nolo . . . monasterii* is reminiscent of the forgers' language. This document, and its more elaborate version (**18**) were prob. designed to strengthen the abbey's title after lands in Battersea had been wrongfully seized (**82**). See also Garnett, 'Coronation and Propaganda', 99–100; Harvey, *WA*, 357–9, on these lands.

18.* Notification by W I to his officers in Surr. that he has granted St Peter of Westminster and the brethren, to augment their diet, the manors of Battersea, Wandsworth and Pyrford, with all appurtenances and privileges, as Earl Harold Godwinson held them TRE. [Aug. 1070 × 1082]

WAD, f. 161; F, f. 55v; T, f. 19v; LN, f. xlvj *verso*; CAY, f. xlix.
Pd: *Regesta* I, no. XIX, from WAD; Browning & Kirk, 224–5, transl. from F.
Cal: *Regesta* I, no. 164; Bentley, 23, no. 176, from CAY.
Note: Amplification of **17**, using extensively the inflated language of the forgers. Cf. Harvey, *WA*, 357–9. See also Garnett, 'Coronation and Propaganda', 99–100.

19. Writ of W I, notifying Abp. Lanfranc and Odo, bp. of Bayeux, that he has granted to Abbot Vitalis and the abbey hunting rights in Battersea wood (Surr.); the tithe of two hundred houses near the church; land in Chollington (Sussex); one house there and two in London; with Wick-by-Pershore and the tithes of all that the king holds in Droitwich (Worcs.). [1076 × 1082]

WAD, f. 161; F, f. 56r–v; BL Lansdowne 863, f. 100v.
Pd: *Regesta* I, XX (from WAD); Browning and Kirk, 225, transl. from F.
Cal: *Regesta* I, no. 166.
Date: Abbot Vitalis's term of office, limited by the downfall of Odo of Bayeux (Orderic IV, 40–44).
Note: Cf. *DB* I, f. 174b; *VCH Worcs.* I, 300, 302; Harvey, *WA*, 357–8, 359n.5; 363–4; and on Droitwich, 71n., 101, 113n., 125.

20.* Writ of W I, informing Abp. Lanfranc, Odo, bp. of Bayeux, and his officers in Kent that he has confirmed to St Peter of Westminster, Abbot

Vitalis and the monks the manor of Lessness, with its church, as King Edward conceded it. [1076 × 1082]

WAM XXII(1), pretended original; WAD, f. 647; F, f. 57r–v.

Pd: *Formulare*, no. LXII, from the pretended original; *Monasticon* I, 302, no. XLVI, from *Formulare*.

Cal: *Regesta* I, no. 54.

Date: Abbot Vitalis's term of office (*Heads*, 76), limited by the disgrace of Bp. Odo.

Note: The attestations are spurious (*Regesta* I, no. 54), and the hand is that of the scribe who wrote other Westminster forgeries (Bishop and Chaplais, xxii, n.1). In 1086, Robert Latimer held Lessness of Odo of Bayeux (*DB* I, f. 6v). In the reign of W II, Abbot Gilbert made an agreement with Robert Bloett concerning the abbey's manor there (**81**). See also Harmer, 299–301, on related documents concerning this estate.

21.* Writ of W I, informing Bp. Walkelin of Winchester and his barons and officers in Surr. that he has confirmed to St Peter, Abbot Vitalis and the monks of Westminster the three hides which Geoffrey, son of Count Eustace [of Boulogne] gave on behalf of his wife Beatrice, with the consent of Geoffrey de Mandeville: one hide in Balham, and the others in Walton near Morden, with quittance of murdrum, geld, and Danegeld. [1076 × April 1084]

WAD, f. 173.

Pd: *Regesta* I, no. XXV; *Gilbert Crispin*, 129, no. 3.

Cal: *Regesta* I, no. 202.

Date: Abbot Vitalis's term of office, limited by the attestation of Abbot Wulfwold of Chertsey (*Heads*, 38).

Note: The abbot's right in Balham is not recorded in 1086 (*DB* I, f. 36). Forgery indicated in the later clauses. The donor of this land is better known as Godfrey of Bouillon, Advocate of the Holy Sepulchre (*Gesta Francorum*, ed. Rosalind Hill (1962), 92 and n.2; see also *Gilbert Crispin*, 129).

22. Writ of W I, informing those wherever Vitalis, abbot of Westminster, holds land, that he is to have all his demesne in Worcs., insofar as he can demonstrate that Bp. Wulfstan, the abbot of Evesham and Rainbald the chancellor established Westminster's title to it. Similarly, he is to have his demesne throughout England, insofar as he can prove in the shire and hundred courts that Westminster had it of the grant of King Edward, and of the present king. The French and English of the fee are to come to terms with the abbot. [1076 × 1085 (? 1076 × 1077)]

WAD, ff. 52v–53; F, ff. 61v–62.

Pd: *Regesta* I, no. XXVIII; Flete, 84 (extract): from WAD.

Cal: *Regesta* I, no. 213.

Date: Abbot Vitalis's term of office (*Heads*, 76). The abbot of Evesham is almost certainly AEthelwig (cf. R. R. Darlington, 'Aethelwig, abbot of Evesham', *EHR* 48 (1933), 1 ff., 177 ff.) who d. in 1077

(*Heads*, 47), but the wording of the writ does not establish that he was still alive when it was issued. Similarly, Regenbald the chancellor is believed to have lost his office by 1069. See also Harvey, *WA*, 360–4.

23. Writ of W I, informing Sweyn, sheriff of Essex, that he has confirmed to St Peter of Westminster the land and marsh of Tilbury which Geoffrey de Mandeville granted for the soul of his wife [Alice]. [1068 × 1085]

WAD, f. 647, giving sheriff as S; F, f. 61.
Pd: *Gilbert Crispin*, 127, no. 1, from WAD.
Cal: *Regesta* I, no. 209.
Date: Sweyn's term of office ended before 1086 (*Regesta* I, no. 209n.) and Alice was d. by 1085 × 1086 (**462**; dated *c.* 1085 × 1086: Chaplais, 'Original Charters', 105). Alice was buried in the abbey cloisters (**436**).
Note: This grant was not fulfilled. In 1086 the abbey held no land in Tilbury, although Geoffrey held land in the hundred of Barstaple (*DB* II, 59b), land which probably lay in East Tilbury (*VCH Essex* I, 374). Sweyn, however, had wrongfully taken thirty acres of Geoffrey's land to add to his manor of West Tilbury (*DB* II, 59b; *VCH Essex* I, 374, 508).

24.* Writ of W I, informing Walkelin, bp. of Winchester, Hugh [de Aurea Valle], bp. of London, Ralph Baynard, Rannulf and Geoffrey [de Mandeville], the sheriffs, and their French and English barons of Surr. and Essex [and Mddx.], that he has confirmed to St Peter, Abbot Vitalis and the monks of Westminster those four hides in Tooting (Surr.) which Swein gave, and which his nephew, Ailnoth of London, now holds of St Peter and the monks. He also confirms the land in London, and the mill of Stratford (Essex) with its appurtenant land, of which Ailnoth made the abbey the heir. [1076 × 1085]

WAD, f. 496v; F, f. 56v; T, f. 19v (address includes the men of Mddx.).
Pd: *Gilbert Crispin*, 128, no. 2, from WAD.
Cal: *Regesta* I, no. 181.
Date: Abbot Vitalis's term of office (*Heads*, 76).
Note: A genuine writ (cf. *DB*, f. 32; Harmer, 311–13: see also Harvey, *WA*, 359), but with attestations added (*Gilbert Crispin*, 128).

25.* Writ of W I, informing the sheriffs and officers of London that he has reaffirmed to St Peter of Westminster and Abbot Vitalis the grant by Alwold of St Botolph's gate of his *curia*, with houses and a wharf lying at the head of London Bridge, as King Edward confirmed them. He orders that these are to be held peaceably, with all customary rights, as King Edward granted. [1076 × 1085]

WAD, f. 98; F, ff. 63v–64; T, f. 20v (attestations omitted).
Pd: *Regesta* I, no. XXXI, from WAD (reading *omnibus* for *domibus*).
Cal: *Regesta* I, no. 217 ('spurious').
Date: Abbot Vitalis's term of office (*Heads*, 76). The attestation of

Henry de Beaumont, earl of Warwick, is incompatible with this, since he was created earl *c.* 1088 (Sanders, 93). William of St Calais attests as bp. of Durham, implying that the earlier limit should be set at Nov. 1080 (*Fasti* II, 29).

Note: The substance of the writ appears unexceptionable, and it may be that a genuine confirmation was inflated by the addition of the concluding clauses: *Et volo . . . faciat*, and of the attestations, before the copies were made (cf. Harmer, 306–8, and no. 75).

26. Writ of W I, informing Peter de Valognes [sheriff of Essex], Rannulf [sheriff of Surr.] and all his sheriffs, that the land of St Peter of Westminster is to be as undisturbed as it was TRE, and at the king's coming to England; and that Abbot Vitalis is to have justice against Anselm [of Aosta, abbot of Bec]. [1076 × 1085]

WAD, f. 53.
Pd: *Regesta* I, no. XXIX.
Cal: *Regesta* I, no. 214.
Date: Abbot Vitalis's term of office (*Heads*, 76). Both sheriffs were in office in 1086 (*Sheriffs*, 43, 135).
Note: The land claimed by Abbot Anselm was evidently that in Tooting, which adjoined Bec's estate of Tooting Bec (cf. *Monasticon* VI, 1053; Harvey, *WA*, 359).

27. Writ of W I, informing Ilbert of Hertford and his men that he concedes to St Peter of Westminster the land of Wormley which Leofsin of London gave. He orders that the abbey should hold it as formerly, as King Edward conceded it, and as he himself afterwards granted. [1066 × 1086]

WAD, f. 647v; F, ff. 59v–60.
Pd: *Regesta* I, no. XLIII, from WAD.
Cal: *Regesta* I, no. 250.
Date: Ilbert was in office before 1086 but not at the time of the survey (*Sheriffs*, 64).
Note: In the Domesday Survey, Westminster is not recorded as holding this land either in 1086 or TRE. The land was confirmed to the abbey by Edward the Confessor as the gift of Leofsin, surnamed Dodesone (*Monasticon* I, 299, no. XVIII; Harmer, no. 90). He was a master-mason (Harmer, 566), presumably a kinsman of Alwin Dodesone, who held land in Wormley TRW, in succession to Wlward, a man of Esegar the staller, one of the landholders there TRE (*DB* I, f. 142). The transfer did not take effect. Presumably the W I writ was sought fairly early in his reign to remedy this, but it proved equally ineffective.

28.* Writ of W I, informing all in Worcs. and Gloucs. that he has confirmed to St Peter of Westminster and the brethren, towards their diet, the manors of Pershore (Worcs.) and Deerhurst (Gloucs.), with all appurtenances, as King Edward gave them. Westminster 25 Dec. [1066 × 1086]

WAD, f. 278v; F, f. 61r–v.
Cal: *Regesta* I, no. 234.
Date: Witnesses prob. added later.
Note: Although the language of these copies is inflated, they are based on a genuine writ (cf. Harmer, 330, and no. 99; *DB* I, ff. 166, 174b–175; Harvey, *WA*, 344, 363, 366); C. S. Taylor, 'Deerhurst, Pershore and Westminster', *Trans. Bristol and Gloucestershire Archaeological Society* 25 (1902), 230–50.

29. Writ of W I, informing his sheriffs throughout England that St Peter of Westminster is to have all those lands, with their customary rights, which Edward granted them. [1066 × 1087]

WAD, f. 53; F, f. 63.
Pd: *Regesta* I, no. II, from WAD.
Cal: *Regesta* I, no. 17.
Date: Prob. early in the reign.

30.* Writ of W I, generally addressed, confirming St Peter of Westminster and the monks in the possession of all the lands which King Edward gave them, with those immunities which he gave them. [1070 × 1087]

F, f. 64v.
Date: Attestations of Abp. Lanfranc and of Walkelin, bp. of Winchester (*Fasti* II, 3, 85). That of Edward the sheriff might indicate a date towards the end of the reign (*Sheriffs*, 54, 107).
Note: The inflated language indicates that the forgers were dissatisfied with the concise terms of **29**.

31. Writ of W I, informing Rémy, bp. of Lincoln, Hugh the sheriff and the other barons of Lincs., that St Peter of Westminster and Abbot Vitalis are to have the manor of Doddington and its appurtenant soke of Thorpe, which were granted by Ailric son of Meriet. *Wiht* [? Isle of Wight] [1076 × 1085]

WAD, ff. 500v–501; F, f. 62.
Pd: *Monasticon* I, 301, no. XLI, from F.
Cal: *Regesta* I, no. 212.
Date: Abbot Vitalis's term of office (*Heads*, 76).
Note: The Domesday Survey records the abbot as holding part of Ailric's former estate (*DB* I, f. 346), but, among the *clamores* for the Kesteven district of Lincs., the abbot claimed the land and soke of Ailric son of Meriet against a certain Baldwin, asserting his right to all the component parts, since the chief manor had been granted to St Peter (of Westminster). The whole shire court bore witness to the abbot's title (*DB* I, f. 377). The king's writ perhaps confirms this verdict. See also Harvey, *WA*, 348.

32. Writ of W I, informing Osmund, bp. of Salisbury, and Edward of

Salisbury, sheriff of Wilts., that he has confirmed to the church of St Peter of Westminster the land which Robert Fitz Wimarc granted. Cricklade [1078 × 1086]

WAD, f. 648v (giving sheriff's initial as O.); F, f. 62v.
Pd: *Regesta* I, no. LXX, from WAD.
Cal: *Regesta* I, no. 417.
Date: Absence of witnesses suggests temp. W I. Osmund became bp. of Salisbury in 1078 (Gams, 196), and d. 3 Dec. 1099 (Symeon of Durham, II, 230). Edward of Salisbury was sheriff of Wilts. before and at the time of the Survey (*Sheriffs*, 152). In 1086, the abbot of Westminster held in chief the church in Cricklade, with many (*plures*) burgesses and the third penny of the vill: total value £9 (*DB* I, f. 67r).

33.* 'Fourth Charter' of W I, notifying Hugh de Aurea Valle, bp. of London, Geoffrey de Mandeville, and others, including the citizens of London, that he confirms the property and privileges of the abbey in London, and grants protection to the merchants residing on the lands of St Peter. Westminster 2 Jan. 1081.

CC Aug.II, pt.54 (pretended original); WAD, ff. 96–97v; F, ff. 51–53v; T, ff. 18v–19; (attestations omitted, apart from that of the king).
Cal: *Regesta* I, no. 144.
Note: Attestations and language indicate forgery (*Regesta* I, no. 144). It appears to be a gross inflation of **36**, while **39** prob. represents the first stage of fabrication.

34.* Writ of W I, ordering Walkelin, bp. of Winchester, Hugh de Port, and his sheriffs and officers of Hants., that St Peter and the monks are to have the manor of Eversley, with the meadow of Streatfield, as King Edward gave it, towards his burial. Westminster 25 Dec. [1081]

WAM XXIII(2), (pretended original); WAD, ff. 647v–648; F, ff. 56v–57.
Cal: *Regesta* I, no. 143.
Date: Prob. based on a genuine grant. The manor was held by Westminster in 1086, although four thegns held it TRE (*DB* I, f. 43b). Attestations added. Count Robert attested a charter of Philip I on 6 Jan. 1082 (*Recueil des Actes de Philippe Ier Roi de France (1059–1108)*, ed. M. Prou, Chartes et Diplomes relatifs à l'Histoire de France (Paris, 1908), 270–1), therefore, it is unlikely that he had attended the Christmas court at Westminster. The phraseology and script indicate that this writ is a product of Osbert de Clare's forgery team (cf. Chaplais, 'Original Charters', 95).
Note: On the manor, see Harvey, *WA*, 345.

35.* Writ of W I, ordering William, bp. of London, Geoffrey de Mandeville, and the sheriff and officers of Essex that the church of St Peter of Westminster, Abbot Vitalis and the monks are to have the manor of Wennington with its church, and the appurtenant soke of Aveley, as

Eadser and Ealvida granted, and King Edward conceded. [Nov. 1080 × June 1085]

F, ff. 60v–61; T, f. 20r–v (attestations omitted).

Pd: *Formulare*, no. LXI, from the 'original' charter, then among the abbey muniments, but now missing; Harmer, 493, from F.

Date: Abbot Vitalis's term of office (*Heads*, 76), limited by the attestations of William of St Calais, bp. of Durham, elected 9 Nov. 1080, and consecrated at Gloucester 27 Dec., or 3 Jan. 1081 (*Fasti* II, 29; Symeon of Durham I, 119), and Robert, count of Meulan, who acquired his title in 1081 (G.E.C. VII, 523–6). But William, bp. of London, d.1075 (*Fasti* I, 1), and if a scribe wrote W[*illelmo*] for M[*auricio*], Bp. Maurice was elected only on 25 Dec. 1085 (*Fasti* I, 1), six months after Vitalis is said to have d.

Note: The place-name was defective in the abbey muniment: [. . .]*tun*', *Winiton*' (F); *Winton*' (T). The phrase *omnimoda* [*libertate*] was also defective but complete in F and T. The authenticity of this writ, and of a writ of Edward the Confessor confirming the grant of Wennington to Westminster by Aetsere Swearte and Aelfgyth his wife (Harmer, no. 73), is questioned by Harmer (301), but Wennington was held by the abbey in 1086 (*DB* II, 15) and it is possible that a genuine writ was addressed to Bp. William, 1066 × 1075, but that this was subsequently amended by the insertion of Vitalis's name and the addition of witnesses. See also Harvey, *WA*, 344.

36.* Notification by W I to Geoffrey de Mandeville, the sheriff of London, William the chamberlain and all the citizens and officers, that he has granted to St Peter, Abbot Vitalis and the monks the lands in London which Edward the Confessor gave, towards his burial, and those which he himself gave. He extends his protection over all merchants on the abbey's property. Westminster Pentecost [1081 × 1085]

CC XVI 30 (pretended original): last three lines damaged, missing text and attestations supplied from copies; WAD, f. 97v; F, f. 63r–v; T, f. 20v (attestations omitted).

Pd: *Gilbert Crispin*, 129–30, no. 4, from WAD.

Cal: *Regesta* I, no. 216, 'either a forgery or grossly interpolated'.

Date: Before the d. of Abbot Vitalis, 19 June, prob. 1085 (*Heads*, 76), and after the election to Durham of William of St Calais, who attests.

Note: Language is that of the Westminster forgeries.

37. Writ of W I, ordering Rémy, bp. of Lincoln, Peter de Valognes, and the sheriff and officer of Herts., that St Peter and the monks of Westminster are to have the manor of Ayot St Lawrence, as King Edward confirmed it. Windsor [Nov. 1080 × 1086]

WAD, f. 226v; F, ff. 58v–59.

Pd: *Regesta* I, no. XXXVIII, from WAD.

Cal: *Regesta* I, no. 235.

Date: W I's confirmation is recorded in *DB* (I, f. 135). Attestations prob. added later. William, bp. of Durham, was nominated to his see in Nov. 1080 and consecrated 27 Dec. or 3 Jan. following (*Fasti* II, 29). See also Harvey, *WA*, 72, 74.

38.* Writ of W I, notifying his sheriffs and officers in Mddx. that he has confirmed to St Peter of Westminster and the brethren, to augment its diet, the manor of Staines with all appurtenances and privileges as King Edward gave it, and additional exemptions of his own. Westminster 25 Dec. [1081 × 1086]

WAD, f. 133r–v; F, ff. 54–55; LN, f. xij *verso*; CAY, f. xiii *verso*.
Pd: *Regesta* I, no. XXXVII, from WAD.
Cal: *Regesta* I, no. 233; Bentley, 6, no. 47, from CAY.
Date: Witnesses prob. added later.
Note: Although the language of the copies is inflated they were probably based on a genuine writ (cf. Harmer, nos. 97–8; *DB* I, f. 128a–b). The value of the manor differs TRE from when it was subsequently received (or reacquired) by the abbot, although the manor was held by the abbey before the survey (Harvey, *WA*, 354).

39.* Writ of W I, informing his officers and burgesses of London that he has confirmed to St Peter of Westminster all the lands in London which King Edward gave. Westminster [1080 × 1087]

WAD, ff. 97v–98; F, ff. 64v–65.
Pd: *Regesta* I, no. XXX, from WAD.
Cal: *Regesta* I, no. 215.
Note: The inflated language indicates forgery. See also **33** and **36**.

40.* Writ of W I, informing Maurice, bp. of London, Geoffrey de Mandeville and his officers in London that he has conceded to St Peter of Westminster and Abbot Gilbert the grant which Alward of London made of St Mary Newchurch, which he confirms with its land and houses, sake and soke and other customary rights. Westminster [1085 × 1087]

WAD, f. 505r–v; F, f. 64.
Pd: *Gilbert Crispin*, 131, no. 5, from WAD; *Monasticon* I, 302, no. XLV, from F.
Cal: *Regesta* I, no. 278, as a writ of W I.
Date: Attestation of William of St Calais (*Fasti* II, 29).
Note: This is prob. based on the writ of W I to which W II refers (**54**), but interpolated with franchisal liberties, and attestations added later. They include a group often utilized by the forgery team (*Regesta*). That of the earl of Warwick is given as *R* (WAD); *Hugone* (F), but the first earl, 1088–1119, was Henry.

41. Writ of W I, informing his officers in Essex that he has confirmed to St Peter and Abbot Gilbert the manor of Moulsham with the land of Broomfield (*Brom'*), which Wlmar held of the abbey, with all customary rights as King Edward conceded. [1085 × 1087]

F, f. 60r–v.

Pd: Harmer, 507.
Cal: Hart, no. 99.
Date: Abbot Gilbert's term of office (*Heads*, 77).
Note: Cf. Harmer, no. 84; *DB* II, 15; Harvey, *WA*, 343.

42. English writ of W I, informing his 'true friends' in all shires in which St Peter has lands, that Abbot Gilbert is to enjoy sake and soke, and other judicial privileges. [1085 × 1087]

WAD, f. 53; F, f. 113r–v.
Pd: *Monasticon* I, 301, no. XXXVIII; Neufeldt, no. 32: from F.
Cal: *Regesta* I, no. 279, 'spurious'.
Date: The king's last years, following the appointment of Abbot Gilbert (*Heads*, 77).
Note: The English grammar is bad, although this might be due to the copyist's errors. It is unlikely that the Chancery would issue writs in English at this late date. An English writ survives in Abbot Gilbert's name (**238**), and it might be that an abbey scribe drew up the present document for the king to ratify.

43.* Land-book (*Telligraphus*) of W I, confirming the abbey's lands in numerous shires. [1085 × 1087]

WAM XXVI, pretended original, a twelfth-century work; WAD, ff. 46v–49; F, ff. 120–128v.
Cal: *Regesta* I, no. 251 ('an obvious forgery'); Hart, nos. 80, 96 ('spurious'; both entries relate to this charter).
Date: Mention of Abbot Gilbert Crispin, succeeded *c.* 1085 (*Heads*, 77), and of Geoffrey de Mandeville [I]'s second wife (Chaplais, 'Original Charters', 105), suggest that this complete forgery claimed to date from the last years of the reign.
Note: 'Telligraphus' is the title in the rubric of WAD text. The language clearly indicates forgery. Cf. also Hart, 6–7 (extended n. to no. 80), and 12 (n. to no. 96).

44. Writ of W I, informing Rannulf the sheriff and his officers in Surr. that he has granted to St Peter of Westminster and Abbot Gilbert eight hides of the manor of Pyrford, which are in his demesne, within Windsor Forest, quit of scot and geld. [1086 × 8 Sept. 1087]

WAM XXIV(3), original; WAD, f. 174v; F, f. 56v; LN, f. xvij *recto*; CAY, f. xlix.
Pd: *Formulare*, no. CCCXCVI; *Foedera* I, 4; *Monasticon* I, 307, no. XLVIII; Bishop & Chaplais, 26 and plate XXIV; *Gilbert Crispin*, 29n.: from WAM.
Cal: *Regesta* I, no. 236; Bentley, 23, no. 178, from CAY.
Date: *Post descriptionem totius Anglie* follows attestations. Rannulf was in office at the time of the Domesday Survey (*Sheriffs*, 135).
Note: Cf. Harvey, *WA*, 359.

45. Writ of W I, informing Hugh de Port that he has granted the tithe of

Rutland to St Peter of Westminster and ordering him to deliver seisin. [1086 × 1087]

CC XVI(2) (original); WAD, f. 594; F, f. 62v.
Pd: *Monasticon* I, 302, no. XLIV; *Formulare*, no. CCCCXCII: from F; Bishop & Chaplais, no. 27, and plate XXV (a) and (b), from CC.
Cal: *Regesta* I, no. 382.
Date: There is no mention in the Domesday Survey that the abbey held the tithe in 1086. The seal is that of W I.

46.* Writ of W I, informing Rémy, bp. of Lincoln, Hugh de Port and his officers in Notts., that he has confirmed to St Peter of Westminster and the monks the churches of Uppingham and Wardley in Rutland, with the church of Belton (Lincs.), with lands, tithes and appurtenant chapels, and all rights pertaining to those churches TRE. [1086 × 1087]

WAD, f. 242v; F, f. 62r–v.
Pd: *Monasticon* I, 301, no. XLII, from F; *Regesta* I, XLIV, from WAD.
Cal: *Regesta* I, no. 275.
Note: The Domesday Survey did not record these churches as being held by Westminster. The language is inflated: *Et volo* . . ., and this combination of witnesses is suspect. Prob. this document was composed at Westminster in order to identify the churches, and to amplify the terse wording of the genuine royal writs (**55–6**) concerning them. On the subsequent history of these churches and their dependencies, see Mason, 'Rutland Churches', 163–6; Harvey, *WA*, 404.

47.* Notification of W II, generally addressed, that he has confirmed the grant which Abbot Gilbert and the convent made to Hugh de Coleham and his heirs, of being dapifer of the abbey, and proctor under the abbot. Westminster [1085 × July 1100]

PRO, Carte Antique Rolls, C52/21.
Pd: *Foedera* I, pt.i, 2; *Gilbert Crispin*, 30 (extracts).
Cal: *Regesta* I, no. 437.
Date: Limited by the d. of W II (in Hants.), and the appointment of Abbot Gilbert (*Heads*, 77), hence prob. a writ of W II. Hugh was prominent among the abbot's men, although given no title, in a record of a transaction *ante* Jan. 1098 (**488**).
Note: The abbey would have no further need to keep its own record of this grant after Hugh's descendant surrendered the office to Abbot William in 1198 (**310**). The authenticity of this document has been questioned (*Regesta* I) because of the attestation of an otherwise unknown Robert de Beaumont. It is possible that the witnesses were a later addition, although the suspect may simply have been an obscure kinsman of Robert, count of Meulan, who also attests.

48. Writ of W II, ordering Peter de Valognes and the sheriff and officers of Essex to restore to the church of St Peter of Westminster the land of Broomfield (*Brom'*), where Wlmar was tenant, and which was wrongfully taken by Thurold, dapifer of [Odo] the bp. of Bayeux. He confirms the abbey's possessions of Moulsham, to which Broomfield pertains, as it was granted by King Edward, and confirmed by W I. Windsor [Sept. 1087 × *ante* March 1093]

F, f. 60v.
Pd: Harmer, 507.
Cal: Hart, no. 100.
Date: Attested by Robert Bloet without a title. He was nominated bp. of Lincoln prob. March 1093 and consecrated shortly before 22 Feb. 1094 (*Fasti* III, 1). Peter de Valognes was still sheriff of Essex when the Domesday Survey was compiled (*Sheriffs*, 43).
Note: Cf. Harvey, *WA*, 343.

49. Writ of W II, informing Maurice, bp. of London, Geoffrey de Mandeville and the sheriff and barons of London that he has confirmed to St Peter of Westminster [St. Mary] Newchurch as Alward the clerk gave it, and as W I confirmed by writ. Winchester [1091 × *ante* 2 Feb. 1093]

F, f. 76 (*Henricus rex*).
Pd: *Gilbert Crispin*, 137, no. 10.
Cal: *Regesta* I, no. 306.
Date: Attested by Geoffrey, bp. of Coutances, who d. 2 Feb. 1093 (Gams, 542; J.-F. Lemarignier, *Etude sur les Privilèges d'Exemption et de Jurisdiction ecclésiastiques des Abbayes normandes depuis les Origines jusqu'en 1140*, Archives de la France monastique 44 (Paris, 1937), 167), and by William of St Calais, bp. of Durham, who rebelled in the spring of 1088 (F. Barlow, *William Rufus* (1983), 70, 74, and n.97). He was restored to favour in 1091, and d. 2 Jan. 1096 (*Fasti* II, 29).
Note: St Mary Newchurch is also known as St Mary Woolchurch (Keene & Harding, 229–30). See also W. A. Carter, 'St Mary of Westcheap, London, called Newchurch', *JBAA*, n.s. 25 (1913), 83–110. Compare the wording of **54**.

50. Writ of W II, informing Peter de Valognes, sheriff of Essex, and his officers, that he has conceded to Abbot Gilbert the manor of Feering, with customary rights which Abbot Vitalis had, and his other predecessors TRE. [Sept. 1092 × *ante* 6 March 1093]

WAD, f. 243; F, f. 59v.
Pd: *Gilbert Crispin*, 140, no. 17, from WAD.
Cal: *Regesta* I, no. 436; Hart, no. 106.
Date: Attested by Abbot [Anselm] of Bec, who arrived in England Sept. 1092, when he met the king briefly. They next met at the Christmas court at Westminster, and subsequently at Gloucester, on 6 March 1093, when the king appointed him to Canterbury (*The Life of St Anselm archbishop of Canterbury*, ed. and transl. R. W. Southern (1962), 63–5 and notes; R. W. Southern, 'St Anselm and Gilbert Crispin, abbot of Westminster', in *Medieval and Renaissance Studies*, ed. R. W. Hunt and R. Klibansky, III (1954), 87–115).

Note: Feering had been granted by W I in exchange for Windsor (**9**; Harvey, *WA*, 341; cf. **10**).

51. Writ of W II, informing Hugh de Beauchamp and the men of Bucks. that, on his order, and before named judges, Abbot Gilbert proved his title to the land of Burnham and Cippenham, granted by W I, and he is to hold it peaceably. [1091 × Dec. 1095]

WAD, f. 499; F, f. 55r–v.
Pd: *Gilbert Crispin*, 136, no. 9, from WAD.
Cal: *Regesta* I, no. 370.
Date: One of the judges was Robert Dispenser, who d. 1095 × 1100 (*Beauchamp Cartulary*, xx), and prob. *ante* 1098, since his restitution to the abbey, seemingly made on his deathbed (**488**), was witnessed by Bp. Walkelin of Winchester, who d. 3 Jan. 1098 (*Fasti* II, 85). The (unnamed) bp. of Winchester was a judge in the present suit, but the see was vacant Jan. 1098–Aug. 1100 (ibid.). The (unnamed) bp. of Durham was also a judge, whereas this see was vacant Jan. 1096–May 1099 (ibid., 29), following the d. of William of St Calais, who had been in disgrace 1088–1091 (ibid.).
Note: Cf. Harvey, *WA*, 338.

52. Writ of W II, informing his barons and men of Mddx. that he has conceded to St Peter of Westminster and Abbot Gilbert the manor of Ebury (Eye), as granted by Geoffrey de Mandeville and his (second) wife Lecelina, with sake and soke, and other customary rights. London [1087 × *ante* 3 Jan. 1098]

WAD, f. 100; F. ff. 57v–58; LN, f. v *verso*; CAY, f. v *verso* (rubric attributes to W I).
Pd: *Regesta* I, no. LXV, from WAD; *Gilbert Crispin*, 140, no. 16, from WAD and LN.
Cal: *Regesta* I, no. 402; Bentley, 4, no. 16, from CAY, as a charter of W I.
Date: Attested by Bp. Walkelin of Winchester, who d. 3 Jan. 1098 (*Fasti* II, 85). H I's confirmation states that this earlier one was made by W II (**59**). Geoffrey de Mandeville still held Ebury in 1086 (*DB* I, f. 129b).
Note: Cf. Harvey, *WA*, 350–1. The abbot's house, 'La Neyte', and its adjacent lands were subsequently regarded as distinct from Ebury, the name used from the 13C for the manor as a whole (ibid., 350n.4). See also Rutton, 'Eye next Westminster', 31–58.

53. Writ of W II, ordering Hugh of Buckland and the sheriff of Mddx. that St Peter of Westminster is to hold the land of Yeoveney, which is pasture pertaining to the manor of Staines, and which Abbot Vitalis recovered in a lawsuit against Walter Fitz Oter. Abbot Gilbert is not to be impleaded of the land, except in the presence of those bps. and barons who gave judgement in the plea. The land is to be held as fully as King Edward gave it. [1087 × 1100]

F, f. 55; T, f. 19r–v; LN, f. xxv *recto*; CAY, f. xxvii *verso* (extracts).
Pd: *Gilbert Crispin*, 138, no. 12, from F with LN.
Cal: *Regesta* I, no. 455; Bentley, 11, no. 104, from CAY.
Note: Harvey, *WA*, 354–5; Harmer, nos. 97–8; *DB* I, f. 128a–b.

54. Writ of W II, informing the men of London that he has conceded to St Peter of Westminster St Mary Newchurch as Alward of London gave it, and ordering that the abbey is to hold it as fully and peaceably as W I commanded by his writ. [1087 × 1098]

WAD, f. 505; F, f. 64r–v.
Pd: *Gilbert Crispin*, 137, no. 11, from WAD.
Cal: *Regesta* I, no. 454.
Date: Attested by Count Alan (of Brittany, lord of Richmond). Alan 'the Red', d. 4 Aug. 1093 (R. W. Southern, *Saint Anselm and his Biographer* (1966), 187n.2, where the evidence emanating from Bury St Edmunds, Count Alan's burial place, is preferred to that of other sources. Southern does not, however, consider the York evidence for 1089: *The Chronicle of St Mary's, York*, ed. H. E. Craster and M. E. Thornton, Surtees Soc. 148 (1934), 113). The count's younger brother, Alan 'the Black', was d. by 1093 (C. T. Clay, *Early Yorkshire Charters* IV, 87).
Note: St John's Abbey, Colchester, later claimed that, at the death of W II, the church pertained to the fee of Eudo dapifer (*Cartularium Monasterii Sancti Johannis Baptiste de Colecestria*, ed. Stuart A. Moore (Roxburghe Club, 2 vols., London, 1897), I, 50). The present writ, like **49**, appears genuine. They were perhaps successively requested following Eudo's appropriation and retention of the church. A further writ ordering restitution of the church was issued by Henry I (**90**) but Abbot Herbert did not succeed in recovering it (**244**). The Colchester claim was supported by blatant forgeries (*Gilbert Crispin*, 158–66. See also Oxley, 'Medieval Church Dedications', 118).

55. Notification of W II, generally addressed, that he has granted to St Peter of Westminster and Abbot Gilbert the churches in Rutland with their appurtenant lands, as Albert the Lorrainer held them of the king. [1087 × 1096]

WAD, f. 594; F, f. 62v.
Pd: *Monasticon* I, 301, no. XLIII, from F.
Cal: *Regesta* I, no. 381.
Date: Hugh de Port, who attests, d. 1096 (G.E.C. XI, 317). Alberic (*sic*) still held three churches in Rutland in 1086 (*DB* I, f. 294).

56. Writ of W II, ordering W. the sheriff to act justly towards the abbot concerning the churches in Rutland, which Osbern the clerk holds of him, and their customary rights. [Sept. 1087 × *ante* 29 May 1099]

WAD, f. 594; F, f. 65 (*Hosbertus*).

Pd: *Gilbert Crispin*, 139, no. 14, from WAD; *Formulare*, no. LXIII, from F.

Cal: *Regesta* I, no. 420.

Date: Rannulf Flambard, who attests without a title, was nominated to Durham, received the temporalities, 29 May 1099, and was consecrated 5 June (*Fasti* II, 29).

Note: The reading *Hosbertus* in F may be a corruption of *Albertus*, and therefore indicate that this clerk is identical with the earlier holder of these churches (**55**).

57.* Charter of H I, taking the abbey into his protection; acknowledging it as the coronation church, and confirming its liberties and privileges. [Westminster, 5 Aug. 1100]

CC VII.8, pretended original, no trace of seal; F., ff. 65–67; WAD, ff. 53v–54; T, f. 21r–v (attestations omitted); PRO Rot. Ancient Charters CC no. 3 (in part: text ends at *frydhsocne*); C, f. 30v (extracts only).

Pd: *Regesta* II, no. I, from CC VII.8, collated with F; *Flete*, 54–5 (excerpts only), from CC VII.8 with WAD.

Cal: *Regesta* II, no. 489; Farrer, *Itinerary*, no. 2.

Note: 'Not authentic' (*SR*, no. 348). The *dei gratia* style would suggest a date of 1172/3 or later (ibid., 19). The attestations are those of the principal witnesses to H I's coronation charter (F. Liebermann, *Die Gesetze der Angelsachsen* (Halle A.S., 1903), I, 521–3; F. Liebermann, 'The Text of Henry I's Coronation Charter', *TRHS* new ser. 8 (1894), 45; C. Bemont, *Chartes des Libertés anglaises* (Paris, 1892), 3–6; W. Stubbs, *Select Charters*, 9th edn. (Oxford, 1913), 117–19; *English Historical Documents II, 1042–1189*, ed. D. C. Douglas and G. W. Greenaway, 2nd edn. (1981), no. 19 (in translation). See also Scholz, 'Two Forged Charters from Westminster', 473.

58. Mandate of H I informing Eudo dapifer and Herbert the chamberlain that on all feasts when he wears his crown in the churches of Westminster, Winchester and Gloucester, these are to have an allowance, and their cantors an ounce of gold, as Maurice bp. of London testified that they had in the time of the king's predecessors. Westminster [1100 × 1107]

WAD, f. 339; F, f. 78v; T, f. 24r–v (omitting place of issue).

Pd: *Gilbert Crispin*, 141, no. 18, from WAD and F; J. H. Round, *The King's Sergeants* (1911), 322 (salutation and attestation omitted), from *Gilbert Crispin*.

Cal: *Regesta* II, no. 490; Farrer, *Itinerary*, no. 3.

Date: Prob. issued at the king's coronation on 5 Aug. 1100 (*ASC, sub an.* and note 11). Attested by William Giffard as bp.-elect of Winchester. He was nominated on 3/4 Aug. 1100, and consecrated 11 Aug. 1107 (*Fasti* II, 85).

Note: On the location of earlier crown-wearings, see Biddle, 'Seasonal Festivals and Residence', 51–72. Westminster became a venue for crown-wearings only in 1062 and remained so down to 1109. In addition to the three venues named in this writ, there were others, notably Windsor and York, but Westminster was chosen frequently at Christmas, and often at Pentecost (never at Easter).

59. Notification by H I to Hugh of Buckland, William the chamberlain, William de Mandeville and the men of Mddx., that he has conceded to God and St Peter, and Abbot Gilbert the grant of the manor of Ebury which Geoffrey de Mandeville and his wife made for their souls. The abbot is to hold it as W II conceded by his writ (**52**). London [Nov. 1100 × July 1106]

F, ff. 73v–74; LN, f. vj; CAY, f.v *verso*-vj.
Pd: *Gilbert Crispin*, 142, no. 20, from F and LN.
Cal: *Regesta* II, no. 769; Farrer, *Itinerary*, no. 66; Bentley, 4, no. 17, from CAY.
Date: Attested by Queen Matilda (married 11 Nov. 1100: *ASC*, 177; Orderic V, 298), and by W. the chancellor (extended to *Willelmo* in LN and CAY). William Giffard remained chancellor to *c.* April 1101 (*Regesta* II, ix); Waldric became chancellor late in 1102, until late 1106 (ibid.). Hugh of Buckland was sheriff of Mddx. in 1103 (Morris, 'Sheriffs of Henry I', 163 n.5) and possibly already by July 1101 (*Regesta* II, no. 532). The king was in Normandy from Aug. 1106 to late Mar. 1107 (*Regesta* II, xxix).
Note: Cf. Harvey, *WA*, 350–1.

60. Writ of H I, informing William Giffard, bp. of Winchester, and the barons of Surr. that he has confirmed to St Peter, Abbot Gilbert and the monks four hides at Tooting, as these were held in the time of W I and H's (other) antecessors. The abbot is not answerable for any claim to this land except in the king's presence. Winchester [Aug. 1100 × 1107]

WAD, f. 505; F, f. 67v (where the additional attestation of Richard de Reviers appears before that of Nigel d'Oilly).
Pd: *Gilbert Crispin*, 142–3, no. 21, from both MSS.
Cal: *Regesta* II, no. 1173.
Date: Richard I de Reviers d. 1107 (Sanders, 137). William Giffard was nominated to Winchester 3/4 Aug. 1100, and consecrated 11 Aug. 1107 (*Fasti* II, 85). Like other episcopal nominees in the early years of H I's reign, he was probably styled *episcopus* from the date of his nomination (*Beauchamp Cartulary*, no. 159n).
Note: The unnamed royal predecessor was Harold II Godwinson, in whose reign Tooting was given by Alnod of London. He had bought the land from Waltheof, who acquired it from Sweyn (*DB* I, f. 32; cf. Harmer, 357, no. 92, where Sweyn, a kinsman of Edward the Confessor, is named as the donor; cf. also *VCH Surrey* IV, 98; Harvey, *WA*, 359).

61. Writ of H I, informing Robert Bloet, bp. of Lincoln, Ranulf Fitz

Ranulf, and the barons of Lincs., that, in his presence and with his consent, Hugh de *Evremou* restored to Abbot Gilbert the manor of Doddington, which he received from the abbot in presence of W II, in exchange for the manor of Duxford. But King Henry restored Duxford to Count Eustace, and gave Hugh a grant in exchange, therefore Hugh restored his manor to the abbey. Westminster, Pentecost [1102 × 1107 (? 1102 × 1103)]

WAD, f. 501; F, f. 74r–v.
Pd: *Gilbert Crispin*, 145, no. 26, from both MSS.
Cal: *Regesta* II, no. 818; Farrer, *Itinerary*, no. 90.
Date: Attested by William Warelwast, without any title. He was consecrated bp. of Exeter in 1107, but prob. used the style bp.-elect from 1103, following the d. of Bp. Osbern, whom he allegedly attempted to have removed from office on account of blindness (*De Gestis Pontificum*, 202n). Before William's consecration, the king kept Pentecost at Westminster only in 1102, 1104 and 1107 (*Regesta* II, xxix, no. 818n).
Note: Hugh's companion notification to the bp. is **475**. See also Harvey, *WA*, 339, 348.

62.* Writ of H I, informing the sheriffs of those shires where the almonry holds lands that he has quitclaimed Paddington (Mddx.), Fanton (Essex) and Claygate (Surr.), and whatever it held TRE in the wood of Ditton (Surr.) and elsewhere, from pleas, scots, aids, plaints, and all other customary exactions, for the souls of his father and brother, Queen Matilda and himself, and their children. London *post* 2 Feb. [*c.* 1103 × 1104]

WAM XXIX(2); WAD, f. 458.
Pd: *SR*, no. 521, plate X(a) (facsimile); *Gilbert Crispin*, 144, no. 24: from WAM XXIX(2).
Cal: *Regesta* II, no. 667; Farrer, *Itinerary*, no. 63.
Date: Early in the reign, but after the birth of the future Empress Matilda, Aug. 1101 × Aug. 1102, and perhaps also after that of William Aetheling, Aug. 1102 × Aug. 1103 (Gervase of Canterbury I, 91–2). The hand is that of Scribe ii, the narrowest limits of whose Chancery career are 1095–1103 (*SR*, facing plate X(a); Bishop & Chaplais, xix). See also Chaplais, 'Seals of Henry I', 272.
Note: Cf. Harvey, *WA*, 341, 353, 358. There is no evidence in DB that the abbey held any property in Ditton. Moreover, a pre-Conquest assignment of land to the almonry would be improbable. The contents of this writ suggest either that the king's clerks did not scrutinize Westminster's claims or that a royal scribe was persuaded to produce a forgery for the abbey.

63.* Writ of H I, informing the sheriffs in whose shires the almonry holds lands that he has quitclaimed Paddington (Mddx.), Fanton (Essex) and Claygate (Surr.), and whatever it held TRE in the wood of Ditton (Surr.) and elsewhere, from pleas, scots, aids, all plaints and murder-fine, and all other customary exactions, for the souls of his father and brother, at the request of Queen Matilda. London [1101 × *ante* 1 May 1118]

WAD, f. 458; F, f. 75v.
Cal: *Regesta* II, no. 668 (conflated with **64**); Farrer, *Itinerary*, no. 65; *Gilbert Crispin*, 144.
Date: Before the death of Queen Matilda on 1 May 1118 (*ASC*, sub an.). The queen was married on 11 Nov. 1100 (*ASC*, sub an.).
Note: Possibly a fabrication, designed to include the murder-fine, based on **62**. See also Harvey, *WA*, 341, 353, 358.

64.* Writ of H I, informing the sheriffs of those shires where the almonry holds lands that he has quitclaimed Paddington (Mddx.), Fanton (Essex), Claygate (Surr.), and whatever it held TRE and TRW in the vill or the wood of Ditton (Surr.), from pleas, plaints, shire and hundred courts, murder-fine, scots, aids, wardpenny and all incidents and customary exactions, as the charters of King Edward and W I bear witness. London [*for* 1100 × 1110]

WAM XXX; WAD, f. 458; F, f. 75v; T, f. 23v (attestations omitted).
Pd: *SR*, no. 522, plate VII(c) (facsimile); *Gilbert Crispin*, 143–4, no. 23: from WAD XXX.
Cal: *Regesta* II, no. 668, conflated with **63**; Farrer, *Itinerary*, no. 64.
Date: Intended for the early years of the reign. See also notes to **62**.
Note: Not authentic (*SR*, 8–9). An elaboration of **63**, itself a suspect document.

65. Writ of H I, ordering Gilbert the sheriff of Surrey that those lands of the abbey and of Abbot Gilbert which are in the king's demesne, within Windsor Park and forest, namely eight hides of the manor of Pyrford which W I granted, are to be quit henceforth from all geld and scot, specifically from the new geld, and other gelds as W I and W II conceded by their writs. Bisley [*c.* 1104 × 1107]

F, f. 67r–v.
Pd: *Gilbert Crispin*, 141, no. 19.
Cal: *Regesta* II, no. 851; Farrer, *Itinerary*, no. 191.
Date: Roger Bigod, who attests, d. 1107 (Sanders, 12, 47). Roger was still sheriff of Surr. *c.* 1104. Gilbert is known to have been in office *c.* 1110–1125 (*Sheriffs*, 135). Royal exactions are mentioned *sub an.* 1104 by chroniclers (e.g. *ASC*, 179; Florence of Worcester II, 53).
Note: Cf. Harvey, *WA*, 359. For W I's writ, see **44**; the writ of W II appears to be lost.

66. Writ of H I, informing Urse d'Abetot and his barons of Worcs. that he has conceded to the abbey the land of Comberton which Robert Dispenser gave (**488**). Windsor [Aug. 1100 × 1108]

WAD, f. 292v; F, f. 74; CAY, f. lxix *verso* (memorandum).
Pd: *Gilbert Crispin*, 147, no. 28, from WAD collated with F.
Cal: *Regesta* II, no. 903; Farrer, *Itinerary*, no. 94; Bentley, 33, no. 254 (item 43), from CAY.

Date: Urse d'Abetot d. in 1108 ('Winchcombe Annals', ed. R. R. Darlington, *Med. Misc. DMS*, 122.) His brother Robert Dispenser d. before the end of 1097 (**488**).

67. Writ of H I, informing his barons and officers of Essex that the abbey is to have its land of Feering and Ockendon freely, with all customary rights, as W I granted and conceded (**9–10**). Havering [Aug. 1100 × 1114]

WAD, f. 243; F, f. 74.
Pd: *Gilbert Crispin*, 143, no. 22, from both MSS.
Cal: *Regesta* II, no. 1179; Farrer, *Itinerary*, no. 312.
Date: Attestation of William de Curcy (Sanders, 143). No attestation of royal charters can certainly be ascribed to his son, W II (Farrer, *H & KF* I, 104).
Note: Cf. Harvey, *WA*, 341, 343.

68. Writ of H I, informing Hugh of Buckland, the sheriffs, loyal men and officers of London, that he has conceded to the abbey the lands in London which the three daughters of Deormann gave for their souls and their burial, and for confraternity, with the advice and consent of their brother Ordgar, to hold with sake and soke, and lawful rights. [*ante* 26 Sept. 1107 × *c.* 1114]

WAD, f. 492v; F, f. 77v.
Pd: *Gilbert Crispin*, 147–8, no. 29, from WAD.
Cal: *Regesta* II, no. 1123.
Date: Term of office of Ranulf the chancellor, who attests (*Regesta* II, ix; T. F. Tout, *Chapters in the Administrative History of Medieval England* (1933), VI, 2), further limited by that of Hugh of Buckland as sheriff of London and Mddx., *c.* 1103 × 1109, who had been succeeded by William of Eynsford by *c.* 1114 (*Sheriffs*, 199).
Note: The king's overlordship of the lands suggests that the women's father was Deorman the moneyer (prob. son of Algar the moneyer), who is named on coins of King Edward and W I. Deorman was succ. as moneyer in London by several of his descendants in turn: Pamela Nightingale, 'Some London Moneyers and Reflections on the Organization of English Mints in the Eleventh and Twelfth Centuries', *Numismatic Chronicle*, 142 (1982), 34–50; James Campbell, 'Some Agents and Agencies of the Late Anglo-Saxon State', *Domesday Studies*, ed. J. C. Holt (1987), 209–10. In 1086 Derman (*sic*) of London held in chief half a hide in Islington (Iseldone) as successor to Algar (*DB* I, 130v. See also Brooke & Keir, 219, 344; Bishop & Chaplais, no. 16 and plate XV).

69. Writ of H I, ordering his justices, sheriffs, and officers throughout England and in the seaports that the whole supplies of the monks, and whatever pertains to their victuals and clothing, which their men can swear to be their demesne property, are to be quit of toll, passage-dues, and all customary exactions. Tower of London [Spring 1107 × *ante* April 1116]

WAD, f. 54; F, f. 130r–v.
Pd: *Gilbert Crispin*, 150, no. 34, from WAD.
Cal: *Regesta* II, no. 1175; Farrer, *Itinerary*, no. 307.
Date: Issued by Otwel Fitz Count, drowned 25 Nov. 1120 (Orderic VI, 304). The king was in Normandy from early April 1116 until 25 Nov. 1120 (*Regesta* II, xxx). Attested by Rannulf the chancellor (*Regesta* II, ix).

70.* Writ of H I, instructing [Richard de Belmeis I] bp. of London, the archdeacon, and the chapter of St Paul's, that the abbot and church of St Peter of Westminster and their priests are to have those churches which his father gave them, namely: the wooden chapel of St Margaret, Eastcheap, with the parish, lands and houses pertaining to it; half the stone chapel of St Magnus the Martyr with the whole parish; the church of St Laurence [Candlewick Street] with all appurtenances, and the church of St James on the riverbank (? St James, Garlickhithe), as they held them in King William's time and his own, and in the episcopates of Hugh [de Aurea Valle] and Maurice. London [24 May 1108 × *ante* mid-April 1116]

WAD, f. 98.
Pd: *Gilbert Crispin*, 148, no. 30.
Cal: *Regesta* II, no. 1177.
Date: The attestation of Queen Matilda indicates a date before the king's departure from England in 1116 (*Regesta* II, xxx). Internal evidence indicates that the bp. addressed is intended as Richard de Belmeis I, elected and temps. 24 May, consecrated 26 July 1108 (*Fasti* I, 1).
Note: The bp.'s name is represented by the initial *G*, indicating that a forger was working from a text of **93**, purportedly dating from Dec. 1127 × *ante* Aug. 1133. Moreover, there can have been no chapel dedicated to St Magnus the Martyr in the reign of W I. The date of his d. is uncertain. It is said to have taken place in 1091, but prob. occurred 16 April 1117 (*Orkneyinga Saga*, transl. and introd. H. Palsson and P. Edwards (1981), 95–96n.). Alternative years of 1104 and 1109 have been given (*AASS, April* II, 438–41), although there are internal inconsistencies in both of these. Even on Orkney itself, his translation, and the observance of his cult date only from some twenty-one years after his death (*Orkneyinga Saga*, 104). Whereas a related forged charter of H I confirmed the whole church of St Magnus (**93**), the present text confirms only half, as does the spurious First Charter of W I (**1**). On 23 April 1182, Westminster Abbey and Bermondsey Priory agreed to hold half each (**287**). See also Oxley, 'Medieval Church Dedications', 117–25.

71. Writ of H I, ordering Richard de Monte to cause the abbot to have

10*s.* annually from the royal alms, as contained in his rolls. Cannock [? 1110 × 1116]

F, f. 79.
Pd: *Gilbert Crispin*, 149, no. 32; Poole, *Exchequer*, 37n.
Cal: *Regesta* II, no. 1053; Farrer, *Itinerary*, no. 330.
Date: Richard de Monte was sheriff of Oxon. 1110 × 1116 (*Sheriffs*, 107).

72. Writ of H I, notifying Herbert Losinga, bp. of Norwich, Haimo the dapifer, the burgesses of Sudbury and his officers in Suffolk that he has conceded to the abbey St Bartholomew's church, Sudbury, which his moneyer Wulfric gave when he became a monk at Westminster, to hold with all liberties which they had at any time, and as it was adjudged in his court, in presence of his barons. Westminster [May 1114 × *ante* 3 April 1116]

F, f. 79r–v; T, f. 24v (first attestation only).
Pd: *Monasticon* III, 459, no. I; *Gilbert Crispin*, 34n. (extracts): from F.
Cal: *Regesta* II, no. 1178; Farrer, *Itinerary*, no. 348.
Date: Herbert Losinga (d. 1119) was consecrated in 1091; moved his see to Norwich in 1094 or 1095, and was consistently styled bp. of Norwich from *c.* 1103 (*Fasti* II, 55; Barbara Dodwell, 'The Foundation of Norwich Cathedral', *TRHS* fifth ser. 7 (1957), 6–7). The king was in Normandy from 3 or 4 April 1116 until 25 Nov. 1120 (*Regesta* II, xxx). The first witness, Ralph d'Escures, abp. of Canterbury, was postulated 26 April 1114 and enthroned 16 May 1114 (*Fasti* II, 3). The council held at Westminster in Sept. 1115 was a likely setting for this grant (*Gilbert Crispin*, 34).
Note: Wulfric struck coins of W II (Types iv and v) and H I (Types iii and v) at Sudbury (G. C. Brooke, *A Catalogue of English Coins in the British Museum, I The Norman Kings* (1916), clxxxiii–clxxxiv).

73. Writ of H I, instructing all sheriffs and collectors in whose administrative districts the abbey holds lands that all the land and men of the abbey are to be acquitted of all gelds, pleas, Danegelds, murder-fines and everything else exacted while the abbey was in the king's hand. Anything taken from them is to be restored. Brampton [*c.* New Year 1121]

F, ff. 130v–131.
Pd: *Regesta* II, no. CXXV.
Cal: *Regesta* II, 152, no. 1239.
Date: Prob. issued immediately after Abbot Herbert's election, *c.* Jan. 1121 (*Hist. Novorum*, 291). The king spent Christmas 1120 at Brampton (Henry of Huntingdon, *Hist. Anglorum*, 243), but was in London by 6 January 1121 (*Regesta* II, xxx).
Note: The problem of wrongful exactions was a major and recurring one. At Michaelmas 1130, it was recorded that Abbot [Herbert] owed 1,000 marks to secure restoration of goods which had been

unjustly dispersed. Thanks to successive royal pardons, the total liability was reduced to 150 marks (£100): *PR 31 Henry I*, 150.

74.* Writ of H I, ordering all sheriffs and collectors in whatever administrative districts there are lands of Westminster Abbey, that the whole land and men of the abbey are to be quit of all pleas, gelds, Danegelds, murder-fines, sheriffs' aids and all other exactions, since he quitclaimed these for the soul of his wife, Queen Matilda, and as King Edward acquitted them by his charters. Brampton [*post* 1 May 1118 × *c.* 4 Jan. 1121]

WAD, f. 54v; F, ff. 75v–76.
Pd: *Regesta* II, 337–8, no. CXXVI, from F.
Cal: *Regesta* II, no. 1240.
Date: After the d. of Queen Matilda (*ASC* 'E', 186). The king was at Brampton at Christmas 1120 (*Regesta* II, xxx).
Note: Prob. a fabrication based on **73**.

75. Writ of H I, ordering his barons, sheriffs and officers that Abbot Herbert is to be given seisin of all lands which were alienated from the abbey, or granted without the assent of the chapter. If anyone brings a claim concerning these lands, the abbot may do justice to him in his own court. Windsor [1121 × 1122 (? *c.* 30 Jan. 1121)]

F, f. 75v.
Pd: *Regesta* II, no. CXXX.
Cal: *Regesta* II, no. 1252; Farrer, *Itinerary*, no. 412.
Date: As for **77**.

76. Writ of H I, notifying those in whose shires St Peter of Westminster holds lands, that he has granted to St Peter and Abbot Herbert, for his soul and for those of King Edward, his predecessors and successors, certain liberties, as King Edward confirmed by charter. Windsor [Jan. 1121 × May 1122]

WAD, f. 54; F, ff. 77v–78 (omitting attestations of Robert bp. of Lincoln and John bp. of Bayeux); F, f. 129r–v; T, f. 24 (attestations omitted).
Pd: *Gilbert Crispin*, 163–4 (no MS cited).
Cal: *Regesta* II, no. 1248; Farrer, *Itinerary*, no. 109 (witnesses correct, but erroneously stating that the charter concerns London).
Date: As for **77**.
Note: The opening clause of the attestations is defective and should read: *R. archiepiscopo Cant'*, *G. archiepiscopo Rothom'*, as in **77**.

77. Notification by H I to the bp., sheriffs, barons and officers of London, that, for the stability of the realm, and for the souls of named members of the royal family, he has confirmed to St Peter of Westminster all lands given by King Edward and others in London, to hold with the privileges confirmed in King Edward's charter. Merchants, both native and alien, dwelling on the abbey's land, are to be exempt from customary dues and exactions, rendering lawful payment to the abbot, as King Edward and W I confirmed by charter. Windsor [Jan. 1121 × May 1122]

WAM XXXI, Fourth Great Seal in white wax; WAD, f. 98r–v; F, ff. 76v–77 (only the first seven attestations); T, ff. 23v–24 (attestations omitted).

Pd: *NPS Facsimiles*, plate 20a (facsimile and transcript); *Formulare*, no. CCCCXCVI: from original; *Monasticon* I, 308, no. LII, from *Formulare*.

Cal: *Regesta* II, no. 1249; *SR*, no. 523; Farrer, *Itinerary*, no. 410, wrongly listed as a general charter.

Date: The principal witness, Ralph d'Escures, abp. of Canterbury, d. 19 Oct. 1122 (*Fasti* II, 3). Evidently issued after the d. of William Aetheling, 25 Nov. 1120 (Orderic VI, 294–8). The king was at Windsor 29–30 Jan. 1121, and 14–15 May 1122 (*Regesta* II, xxx). The preamble indicates the earlier visit (cf. *Geoffrey de Mandeville*, 429).

Note: In the hand of Scribe vii, active *ante* 1120 × *c.* 1130 (*SR*, 30). Seal is genuine (Chaplais, 'Seals of Henry I', 265, 273). The authenticity of the hand and seal indicate that this is indeed a genuine charter, and not, as first appears, an inflation of **78**, designed to incorporate the mercantile privileges.

78. Notification of H I, addressed both generally and specifically to his officers and burgesses in London, that he has conceded to St Peter and Abbot Herbert those lands in London which King Edward gave, and those which the abbey formerly held there, whosoever gave them, with the laws and customs granted by King Edward and confirmed by privilege of his charter. Any further donations of lands or churches within London are to be held with similar exemptions. Windsor [1121 × *ante* 20 Oct. 1122]

WAD, f. 98.

Pd: *Formulare*, no. LXV, from the original charter, endorsed *Libertates Lundoniae*, then at Westminster Abbey; *Monasticon* I, 307, no. LI, from *Formulare*; Flete, 88 (*Henricus . . . dedisset*) from WAD.

Cal: *Regesta* II, no. 1247.

Date: The first witness, Ralph d'Escures, abp. of Canterbury, d. 19 or 20 Oct. 1122 (*Fasti* II, 3). Also attested by Robert 'the king's son'. He was created earl of Gloucester in June–Sept. 1122 (*HBC*, 463). See also *Regesta* II, no. 1347. Herbert became abbot *c.* Jan. 1121 (*Hist. Novorum*, 291). The charter was possibly issued on the occasion of his appointment.

79. Writ of H I, ordering William the chamberlain and Aubrey de Vere, and their successors as chamberlains and sheriffs of London, to pay the sacrist of St Peter of Westminster $\frac{1}{2}d.$ daily, from the farm of London, to maintain the light burning before the tomb of Queen Matilda, from Michaelmas last past, in perpetuity. Westminster [*post* 25 Nov. 1120 × *ante* 10 Jan. 1123 (? 7 Jan. 1121)]

WAD, f. 339v.

Pd: *Gilbert Crispin*, 156, no. 39.

Cal: *Regesta* II, no. 1377; Farrer, *Itinerary*, no. 470.
Date: Attested by Robert Bloet, bp. of Lincoln, d. 10 Jan. 1123 (*Fasti*
  III, 1), and by Rannulf the chancellor, d. *c.* New Year 1123 (*Regesta*
  II, ix), after the king's return to England following a four-year
  absence (ibid., xxx), during which the Queen d. The king was at
  Westminster on 7 Jan. 1121 (ibid.). Aubrey de Vere was sheriff of
  London 1120–1122 (*Sheriffs*, 199).

80. Writ of H I, ordering the sheriffs of those shires where St Peter and
the abbot of Westminster hold lands, and their officers, that Abbot
Herbert is to hold his lands, men and property quit of pleas and suits,
shire and hundred courts, as the abbey held them TRE, and as confirmed
by a charter of King Edward. Any plea concerning murder or larceny
committed on his land shall be pleaded there, as the aforesaid charter
bears witness and commands. Windsor [1121 × 1122 (? *c.* 30 Jan. 1121)]

WAD, f. 54; F, ff. 78r–v, 129v–130 and 130 (i.e. three transcripts).
Pd: *Regesta* II, no. CXXIX, from F, f. 78r–v, collated with WAD.
Cal: *Regesta* II, no. 1251.
Date: Rannulf the chancellor, who attests, d. Jan. 1123 (John of Worces-
  ter, 17; Henry of Huntingdon, 244). Abbot Herbert was appointed
  c. Jan. 1121 (*Hist. Novorum*, 291).

81. Writ of H I, ordering Robert Bloet, bp. of Lincoln, to abide by his
agree- ment with Abbot Herbert and the monks concerning their manor
of Lessness (Kent), which he holds of them, as firmly as he observed the
agreement with Abbot Gilbert and the convent in the time of W II, so that
the king hears no further complaint. Woodstock [Jan. 1121 × *ante* 10 Jan
1123]

F, f. 67v.
Pd: *Gilbert Crispin*, 157, no. 42.
Cal: *Regesta* II, no. 1383; Farrer, *Itinerary*, no. 473.
Date: Robert Bloet d. at Woodstock 10 Jan. 1123 (*ASC*, 188; *De Gestis*
  Pontificum, 313; John of Worcester, 17; Henry of Huntingdon, 244).
  Abbot Herbert was appointed in Jan. 1121 (*Hist. Novorum*, 291).

82. Writ of H I, ordering Gilbert the sheriff of Surr. that Abbot Herbert
is to be seized of the land of Battersea as Rannulf the chancellor was
formerly, and especially that land of which Gilbert unjustly gave seisin to
Hugh Fitz Hedric. Waltham [*c.* Jan. × *ante* 11 June 1123]

WAD, f. 161r–v.
Pd: *Regesta* II, no. CLXXI.
Cal: *Regesta* II, no. 1416.
Date: Gilbert ceased to be sheriff *c.* 1125 (*Sheriffs*, 135; cf. Morris,
  'Sheriffs of Henry I', 70). Henry was in Normandy from 11 June 1123
  to 11 Sept. 1126 (*Regesta* II, xxx). Rannulf the chancellor d. January
  1123 (John of Worcester, 17; Henry of Huntingdon, 244). Herbert
  became abbot *c.* Jan. 1121 (*Hist. Novorum*, 291) but the writ was
  prob. issued after Rannulf's d. See also note to **83.**

Note: Cf. Harvey, *WA*, 357–8.

83.* Writ of H I, informing Roger bp. of Salisbury, Geoffrey de Clinton, and his sheriffs and officers in Oxon., Surr. and Mddx., that he has restored to Abbot Herbert and the convent those lands which the chancellor held of them, namely Battersea (Surr.), Islip (Oxon.), Pyrford (Surr.) and Shepperton (Mddx.), as they held them TRW. Woodstock [Jan. 1121 × *ante* 2 Aug. 1133 (? × 1123)]

WAD, f. 54v; F, f. 67v, repeated f. 130v; BL Harleian MS 6148, f. 139v
   (transcribed *c.* 1607–1621 from the sealed original, which was owned
   by Oliver St John, Lord Grandison. His interests in Battersea
   developed over many years, and he bought the manor in 1627:
   Taylor, *Our Lady of Batersey*, 67).
Pd: *Regesta* II, no. CCCIII, from WAD.
Cal: *Regesta* II, no. 1881.
Date: Before the king's final departure from England (*Regesta* II, xxxi),
   and after Herbert's accession *c.* Jan. 1121 (*Hist. Novorum*, 291). A
   likely date would be shortly after the d. of the chancellor Rannulf, in
   Jan. 1123 (John of Worcester, 17).
Note: The writ is attested by Nigel d'Oilly, who is believed to have d.
   c. 1115 (Sanders, 54), and in *Regesta* II it is calendared as spurious
   for this reason. On Islip, see the note to the spurious restoration
   attributed to William I (**3**) ; Harvey, *WA*, 356. On the other lands,
   see Harvey, *WA*, 354, 357–9. The chancellor in question has been
   identified as Rannulf Flambard (ibid., 354, 359n.2), although H. W.
   C. Davis argued that he was never chancellor (*Regesta* I, xviii). In the
   reign of W II, the chancellors were successively Robert Bloet and
   William Giffard (ibid.), who remained in office after the accession of
   H I. He was followed by Roger, later bp. of Salisbury, Waldric,
   another Rannulf, and finally by Geoffrey *rufus* (*Regesta* II, ix–x).
   Robert Bloett held other land of the abbey (**81**), but of all these
   chancellors, only the second Rannulf did not acquire a bishopric,
   and would therefore most naturally be styled chancellor in
   retrospect: cf. **82**.

84. Writ of H I, ordering Richard [de Belmeis I], bp. of London, to render justice to the abbot of Westminster, concerning the men who, armed and by night, broke into his church at Wennington (Essex). [24 May 1108 × Jan. 1127]

F, f. 74 (no attestations).
Pd: *Gilbert Crispin*, 149, no. 31; A. L. Poole, *The Exchequer in the
   Twelfth Century* (London, 1973 impression), 39–40, n. 4; Bigelow,
   127; Madox, *Hist. Exchequer*, 141n.(a); T. Stapleton, *Magni Rotuli
   Scaccarii Normanniae* I (London, 1840), xx. n.(v).; Van Caenegem,
   418, no. 13.
Cal: *Regesta* II, no. 1538.
Date: Richard de Belmeis I's term of office (*Fasti* I, 1).

85. Writ of H I, ordering his sheriffs and officers throughout England that the entire supplies and goods of the abbot, which his men can swear are his own, are to be quit of toll, passage dues and all customary exactions, as they were in the time of his predecessors. Marlborough [Aug. 1100 × *ante* 1129]

F, f. 76r–v.
Pd: *Gilbert Crispin*, 149, no. 33.
Cal: *Regesta* II, no. 867.
Date: Before the king's final departure from England. A similar, but not identical, charter for Abingdon Abbey has the same attestation and place of issue, but is addressed to Hugh of Buckland in his capacity as sheriff of Berks. (*Chron. Mon. de Abingdon*, II, 79). If the Westminster writ was issued on the same occasion, its limits are those of Buckland's term of office in Berks, before 1129 (*Sheriffs*, 6).

86. Writ of H I, instructing Robert de Bertherol and all the barons of the honor formerly held by Otwel Fitz Count, that he has granted to St Peter and the monks of Westminster the church of Sawbridgeworth (Herts.), to hold with its appurtenant lands, tithes and rights. [*post* 25 Nov. 1120 × *ante* 2 Aug. 1127]

F, f. 75.
Pd: *Gilbert Crispin*, 156, no. 40.
Cal: *Regesta* II, no. 1884; Farrer, *Itinerary*, no. 472.
Date: Otwel Fitz Count d. in the White Ship disaster (Orderic VI, 304). Richard de Belmeis I, bp. of London, d. 16 Jan. 1127, caused seisin of this church to be delivered to the convent (**203**).
Note: Cf. Harvey, *WA*, 388, 409.

87. Writ of H I, generally addressed, ordering that the entire supplies and goods which the convent's officers at Sawbridgeworth (Herts.) can swear to be their demesne possessions are to be kept quit of toll, passage-dues and all customary exactions. [*post* 25 Nov. 1120 × *ante* 2 Aug. 1133]

F, f. 75.
Pd: *Gilbert Crispin*, 156–7, no. 41.
Cal: *Regesta* II, no. 1885.
Date: No earlier than **86**, and possibly issued on the same occasion. It is prob. later than H I's writ granting general exemption from toll (**85**), since this property was not held in the time of the abbot's predecessors (**86**).

88. Writ of H I, informing the bp. of London, and the justices, sheriffs and barons of Mddx., that he has conceded to Richard de Balta and his heirs the land of the fee of the abbot of Westminster in Hampstead, rendering to the abbot and convent £2 annually, as they granted him by charter. Westminster [*post* 25 Nov. 1120 × *ante* Aug. 1133 (? Jan. × *ante* 25 Aug. 1127)]

WAD, f. 120v.
Pd: *Regesta* II, no. CCLXIX.

Cal: *Regesta* II, no. 1758.

Date: Before the king's final departure from England, 2 Aug. 1133 (*Regesta* II, xxxi). The attestation of Eustace Fitz John indicates a date of 1116 or later (Sanders, 103n.1), so that the writ dates from after the king's return to England, 25 Nov. 1120 (*Regesta* II, xxx). The attestation of Hugh Bigod also suggests this (Sanders, 47). The absence of the bp.'s name (assuming that this is not an omission of the cartulary scribe) may indicate that the writ was issued during the vacancy in the see (*Fasti* I, 1). In 1127, the king was at Westminster 13–16 May, and crossed to Normandy on 26 Aug. (*Regesta* II, xxx).

Note: Cf. Harvey, *WA*, 352.

89. Writ of H I, notifying the sheriff and officers of London that all merchants residing in the soke of St Peter and of the abbot of Westminster may come and go peaceably, without harassment. No-one except the abbot and his monks has authority there, as Kings Edward and W I conceded by their charters. Windsor [c.Jan. 1121 × Aug. 1133]

WAD, f. 98v; F, f. 76v.

Pd: *Regesta* II, no. CXXVIII (from WAD).

Cal: *Regesta* II, no. 1250; Farrer, *Itinerary*, no. 411 (a reference to contents of F, ff. 75–8).

Date: Farrer suggests *c.* 30 Jan. 1121; followed by *Regesta* II, giving outside limits of *c.* 1110 × 1133, presumably on the grounds that the writ is attested by Geoffrey de Clinton. The king was at Windsor in Jan. 1121 (Farrer, *Itinerary*, 91; *Regesta* II, xxx) and it is likely that this writ is one of the group of privileges obtained by Abbot Herbert at the time of his appointment.

90. Writ of H I, ordering the sheriff and barons of London that Abbot Herbert and the monks of Westminster are to have the church of St Mary (Newchurch) which Goslan gave, with its appurtenant lands. No one may administer it without the permission of the abbot. Windsor [Jan. 1121 × *ante* 2 Aug. 1133]

WAD, f. 505v; F, f. 79.

Pd: *Gilbert Crispin*, 159, from WAD.

Cal: *Regesta* II, no. 1880.

Date: Before the king's final departure from England (*Regesta* II, xxxi) and after Herbert's appointment (*Hist. Novorum*, 291).

Note: The church is identified in the rubric to the entry in WAD. Control over this church was already lost in the reign of W II (**49, 54**), and the present writ, whether or not a fabrication, was intended to assist in its recovery. Despite subsequent confirmations by King Stephen (**109**) and Pope Adrian (IV) (**166**), it was not recovered. The donor is named as Alward in the three eleventh-century royal writs concerning this church (**40, 49, 54**), and also in the spurious First Charter of W I (**1**).

91. Writ of H I, ordering Aubrey de Vere, sheriff of Essex, to convene the shire court concerning the dispute between the abp. of Canterbury and the abbot of Westminster concerning the land of Alestan [in West Ham]; to cause a verdict to be delivered on who has the better title, and to put him lawfully in seisin. Westminster [1129, *ante* Nov.]

F, f. 76.
Pd: *Regesta* II, no. CCIV; Van Caenegem, 419, no. 14.
Cal: *Regesta* II, no. 1539.
Date: Attested by Nigel d'Aubigny, who d. in Normandy in Nov. 1129 (*Charters of the Honour of Mowbray*, xviii and n. 2). Aubrey de Vere is recorded in office in 1130, and succeeded his predecessor after 1128 (*Sheriffs*, 43).
Note: Alestan held a manor of eight hides, thirty acres in West Ham TRE, and this was given by W I to Rannulf Peverel and Robert Gernon (*DB* II, ff. 64, 72b).

92. Writ of H I, ordering Hugh Mascherell to restore to St Peter at Westminster the tithe of Roding (Essex) which his brother gave, and also any arrears. Windsor [*c.* 1120 × *ante* 2 Aug. 1133]

WAD, f. 648v.
Cal: *Regesta* II, CCCII, breaking text at *concessit*, but continuing *T. G. de Clinton apud Windr'*; Van Caenegem, 433, no. 44.
Pd: *Regesta* II, no. 1878.
Date: Limited by the king's final departure from England. The earlier limit is indicated by the attestation of Geoffrey de Clinton (C. Warren Hollister, 'The Origins of the English Treasury', *EHR* 93 (1978), 262, 266).
Note: Hugh Mascherell attests both the genuine (*c.* 1085 × 1086) and the forged charter of Geoffrey de Mandeville I granting Hurley to Westminster, the latter in association with Walter Mascherel, evidently his social inferior, whose relationship is unspecified (Chaplais, 'Original Charters', 108). Hugh with his brother Roger attests Geoffrey I's grant of Ebury (**436**). Armitage Robinson suggested that Hugh of the present writ was of a younger generation than Geoffrey's contemporary (*Gilbert Crispin*, 134). The attestation of Geoffrey de Clinton may support this contention, but all references may yet be to the same man. Presumably Roger granted the tithe of Roding, but Hugh, as his feudal superior, declined to ratify the grant.

93.* Writ of H I, ordering Gilbert the Universal, bp. of London, the archdeacon and the chapter of St Paul's, that the abbot and church of St Peter of Westminster and their priest are to hold peaceably the church of St Magnus the Martyr in London, and its parish, as in the time of W I and W II, and earlier in his own reign; and during the episcopates of Hugh [de Aurea Valle], Maurice and Richard de Belmeis I. He prohibits anyone from impleading them. Woodstock [Dec. 1127 × *ante* Aug. 1133]

WAD, f. 98v; F, f. 77r–v.
Pd: *Regesta* II, no. CCCIV (from WAD).

Cal: *Regesta* II, no. 1883.

Date: Before the king's final departure from England. Gilbert was elected bp. *c*. Dec. 1127, and consecrated 22 Jan. 1128 (*Fasti* I, 1).

Note: St Magnus's cult is unlikely to have spread to London until after the end of Henry's reign (**70**), and the writ is presumably a fabrication. Both the spurious First Charter of W I (**1**) and another spurious charter of H I (**70**) confirm to the abbey only half of this church, the portion awarded in a lawsuit of 1182 between Abbot Walter and the prior of Bermondsey (**287**).

94. Writ of H I, instructing Richard Basset and Aubrey de Vere that the abbot is to have his stalls in the new work as in the old, and as the king has ordered, so that he hears no complaint arising from default of right. [? *c.* 1129 × 1133]

F, ff. 78v–79.

Pd: *Gilbert Crispin*, 157, no. 43.

Cal: *Regesta* II, no. 1988.

Date: Prob. before the king's final departure from England. From 1129 onwards, Richard Basset and Aubrey de Vere were associated as sheriffs in various counties (*Sheriffs*, 12, 43, 75, 86, 92, 135), including Surr. (ibid., 135). They were not sheriffs of London in that year, nor is it likely that they would be, from *c.* 1130, when H I granted the city the right to elect its sheriffs (*PR 31 Henry I*, 148).

Note: If Basset and De Vere were addressed as sheriffs of Mddx., the 'new work' would seem to be in Westminster and Armitage Robinson suggested that it was a building being constructed outside the abbey precincts on the king's orders (*Gilbert Crispin*, 157). The abbot's stalls were prob. those for the fair in Westminster, or, if this did not yet exist, for a market there.

95. Writ of H I, ordering William II, constable of Chester, that the abbot and convent are to have their land of Perton (Staffs.), as the earl's father granted in alms for his wife's soul, quit of scutage and secular services, as William's father granted it, and as they held it afterwards, and in the time of Hugh, earl of Chester. No-one is to exact escheats, and anything unjustly taken must be restored. Woodstock [*c.* 1130 × *ante* 2 Aug. 1133]

WAM XXXII.

Pd: *SR*, plate XVIII(a) (facsimile); Bigelow, 127; Madox, *Hist. Exchequer*, 435.

Cal: *Regesta* II, no. 1882; *SR*, no. 524.

Date: Limited by the king's final departure from England (*Regesta* II, xxxi). The attestation of Richard Basset is unlikely to date from *ante* 1127 (*Regesta* II, no. 1838n). The hand is that of Scribe xv, active *c.* 1133 (*SR*, note facing plate XVIII(a); see also Chaplais, 'Seals of Henry I', 275). William succeeded his father in the constableship of Chester and the barony of Halton in, or shortly before, 1130 (G. Barraclough, 'Some charters of the earls of Chester', *Med. Misc. DMS*, 25).

Note: Westminster had lost possession of this land *post* 1086, and eventually recovered it only after the accession of Richard I, when it was immediately farmed by Abbot Walter and the convent to Hugh de Nonant, bp. of Coventry (**304**; see also Harvey, *WA*, 79, 82, 357n).

96. Writ of H I, informing his barons of Sussex and Mddx. that, by judgement of his barons of the Exchequer, Abbot Herbert proved his title to Parham (Sussex) and *Mapleford* against Herbert Fitz Herbert, and may hold this land in demesne. Woodstock [*c.* 1130 × *ante* Aug. 1133]

WAD, f. 571v; F, f. 74v; T, f. 23v (attestations omitted); PRO, KB 26/54, m. 18d.

Pd: *Curia Regis Rolls* VI, 176–7, from KB enrolment; *Plac. Abbrev.*, 84b (attestations omitted): citing original; *Gilbert Crispin*, 46, from WAD.

Cal: *Regesta* II, no. 1879; Farrer, *Itinerary*, no. 666.

Date: Before the king's final departure from England in Aug. 1133 (*Regesta* II, xxxi). An allowance was made to Herbert the chamberlain in 1129–1130 (*PR 30 Henry I*, 104), but Herbert Fitz Herbert succeeded his father in that year (ibid., 378).

Note: Cf. Harvey, *WA*, 359. *Mapleford* is presumably a holding in Mddx.

97. Writ of Queen Matilda, informing Richard [de Belmeis I], bp. of London, and the sheriff and barons of London, that she has conceded to Abbot Gilbert the tenement on the abbot's wharf which Hugh of Buckland held of her in London, with sake and soke and customary rights, for the souls of King Henry and herself, and their children. [*c.* Dec. 1113 × 1 May 1118]

WAD, f. 492v.

Pd: *Gilbert Crispin*, 155, no. 38.

Cal: *Regesta* II, no. 1180; Farrer, *Itinerary*, 80, no. 376.

Date: Abbot Gilbert d. 6 Dec., either 1117 or 1118 (*Heads*, 77). Queen Matilda d. 1 May 1118 (*ASC* 'E', 185). Attested by the queen's brother David, as earl of Huntingdon, a title acquired *c.* Christmas 1113 (*ASC* 'H', 183). Hugh of Buckland was still living in May 1114 (*Chron. Mon. de Abingdon* II, 147). He is said to have d. *c.* 1115 (*Regesta* II, xx).

98. Notification by the Empress Matilda, 'Lady of the English', generally addressed, that she has conceded to William of Darnford the manor of Deerhurst (Gloucs.) as Abbot Gervase and the chapter granted and confirmed to him by charter. [April 1141 × 1147]

WAD, f. 317.

Pd: *Regesta* III, no. 259.

Date: The empress finally left England *ante* 4 March 1148 (*Regesta* III, xliv). The first attestation is prob. that of Robert, earl of Gloucester, who d. 31 Oct. 1147, according to the annals of his foundation, Margam (*Ann. Mon.* I, 14). The Tewkesbury Annals and the Waverley Annals agree that he d. 1147 (*ibid.* I, 47; II, 232). The empress adopted the style 'Lady of the English' after 7 or 8 April 1141 (*Regesta* III, xxix, following *Historia Novella*, 52–4). If Abbot Gervase was involved in the transaction, the probable year of issue would be 1141, in the course of which the empress visited Devizes in March, and again *post* 14 Sept. (*Regesta* III, xliv).

Note: Cf. Harvey, *WA*, 344–5. Gervase's grant survives only in a spurious form (**271**). The empress's writ was acquired by Westminster when Abbot Walter de Wenlok recovered this manor (Flete, 116; Barbara Harvey, *Documents Illustrating the Rule of Walter de Wenlok, abbot of Westminster, 1283–1307*, Camden Soc. fourth series 2 (1965), 239n).

99. Grant by David earl of Huntingdon to the chapter of £1. 10*s.* worth of land which Aldwin, the queen's chamberlain, holds in Tottenham (Mddx.), to provide lights, love-feasts and pittances on the anniversary of his sister, Queen Matilda, and the anniversary of his parents [Malcolm III, king of Scots, and Queen Margaret]. Westminster [May 1118 × *ante* 23 April 1124]

WAD, ff. 157v–158.
Pd: *Acts of Malcolm IV*, no. 6.
Date: David became king of Scotland shortly after the d. of his brother, King Alexander, on 23 April 1124 (*Acts of Malcolm IV*, 124 and n. 1; cf. Symeon of Durham II, 275, where the date given is a misreading of the MS, which has *vij. Kal. Maj.*). Queen Matilda d. 1 May 1118 (*ASC*, 186). David's itinerary was within England for almost the whole of this period, down to the middle of 1123, at least (*Acts of Malcolm IV*, 113).
Note: Aldwin, chamberlain of Queen Matilda, attested charters of hers (*Regesta* II, nos. 675, 971), and had some jurisdiction in Waltham (ibid., nos. 1090, 1108–9), near to Tottenham.

100. Notification by David I, king of Scotland, to his dapifers, barons and officers, that he has granted and conceded to the abbey the land which Aldwin the chamberlain held in Tottenham (Mddx.), and which Adam his son held after him. He makes this grant to sustain an anniversary for the soul of his sister, Queen Matilda, and for those of his parents, ancestors and successors. Adam and his heirs may hold this land of the abbey, but if they default on the rent, the convent may treat the land as demesne. London June [1141]

WAD, f. 157.
Pd: *Acts of Malcolm IV*, no. 13.
Date: King David is unlikely to have been in London on any later occasion than his visit of June 1141 (*Acts of Malcolm IV*, no. 13n.; cf. *Regesta* III, nos. 328, 377, 393, 429, 629, 899, which confirm David's

presence in southern England in June–July 1141; cf. also Symeon of Durham II, 309).

Note: The inclusion of the phrase *fidelibus suis Francis et Anglis*, implies that a Westminster scribe, rather than a clerk of David's household, drew up this charter. Prob. too, an English scribe, or else the WAD copyist was responsible for David's incorrect title, since the style 'King of Scots' was usual (cf. *Acts of Malcolm IV*, 69).

101. Writ of David I, king of Scots, instructing Eustace Fitz John that he has granted and conceded to the abbey the land which Adam son of Aldwin the chamberlain holds in Tottenham (Mddx.), for the soul of his sister, Queen Matilda, and of his ancestors and successors. Eustace and his officers are forbidden to intrude into that land, and he must restore anything he took from it after he was seized of Tottenham. London [*c*. June 1141]

WAD, f. 157.
Pd: *Acts of Malcolm IV*, no. 14.
Date: Cf. notes to **100**.
Note: Eustace Fitz John received from David's son Henry, in 1139 × 1141, a grant of Tottenham with its appurtenances, except for the land previously granted to Robert Foliot (*Acts of Malcolm IV*, no. 12).

102. Writ of Earl Henry, son of King David of Scotland, informing his dapifers and officers in England, especially those in Tottenham (Mddx.), that he has conceded to the abbey and convent the land in Tottenham which his father conceded for the soul of Queen Matilda, to support her anniversary annually. Aldred and his wife, who hold that land, are to occupy it in peace, answering only to the convent. Henry's officers are to make no further demands on them. [5 Feb. 1136 × *ante* 12 June 1152 (? Feb. 1136 × early 1139)]

WAD, f. 157v.
Pd: *Acts of Malcolm IV*, no. 36.
Date: Earl Henry d. 12 June 1152 (*Acts of Malcolm IV*, 124; cf. Symeon of Durham II, 327; *Chronica de Mailrose*, ed. J. Stevenson, Bannatyne Club (Edinburgh, 1835), 52, 74). He received the honor of Huntingdon in place of his father on 5 Feb. 1136, and finally lost it in the latter part of 1141 (*Acts of Malcolm IV*, 102). Since Henry names Aldred (Aldwin) as the tenant in Tottenham, this writ appears to be earlier than the related mandates of King David, issued in June 1141 (**100–101**), and prob. also than Henry's grant of the land to Eustace Fitz John, 1139 × 1141 (*Acts of Malcolm IV*, no. 12). But it is possible that the copyist's error over the tenant's name represents a misreading of *Adam*, in which case Henry's restoration postdates David's.
Note: The style of the earl's father indicates the work of an English scribe or copyist (cf. **100**).

103. Charter of Malcolm IV, king of Scots, conceding and confirming to

Abbot Laurence and the convent the land which Aldwin the chamberlain, and afterwards Adam his son, held in Tottenham (Mddx.), as King David his grandfather granted and confirmed by charter, to provide an annual anniversary for the souls of Queen Matilda, King David and Earl Henry and his wife, and all Malcolm's ancestors and successors. If Adam and his heirs default on their rent, the convent may treat the land as demesne. [*c.* 1158 × *ante* 24 Jan. 1162 (? Spring or Autumn 1159)]

WAD, f. 157r–v.
Pd: *Acts of Malcolm IV*, no. 154.
Date: Attested by William bp. of Moray, who d. 24 Jan. 1162 (*Acts of Malcolm IV*, 125), and by Walter (de Bidun), Malcolm's chancellor, who was not in office after 1162 (ibid., 125), while Abbot Laurence was elected *c.* 1158 (*Heads*, 77). While most of the witnesses were members of the Scottish court, Robert earl of Leicester also attests, and the writ was therefore prob. issued in England. In 1159, Malcolm joined H II on the Toulouse expedition, and was on the Continent between 16 June and *c.* mid Oct. He had travelled south through England in late May × early June, and prob. returned through England in late Oct. × early Nov. (*Acts of Malcolm IV*, 114–5).
Note: The phrase *fidelibus suis Francis et Anglis* occurs in the address (cf. no. **100**).

104. Notification by William I 'the Lion', king of Scots, that he has confirmed to the abbey and convent, for the soul of Queen Matilda, his grandfather's sister, the land of Tottenham (Mddx.) which was held by Aldwin the chamberlain, and afterwards by his son Adam. [1165 × 1173 (? 14–15 June 1170)]

WAD, f. 157v.
Pd: *The Acts of William I, King of Scots 1165–1214*, ed. G. W. S. Barrow, with W. W. Scott (1971), no. 52.
Date: Outer limits assigned (ibid.). William was at Westminster 14–15 June 1170, for the coronation of the Young King (ibid., 96).
Note: The phrase *Francis et Anglis* occurs in the address (cf. ibid., 76–7, and no. **100**), reinforcing the probability that an English scribe worked on the document.

105. Writ of King Stephen, informing the bps., sheriffs, and officers in whose shires the almoner of Westminster holds lands, or tithes, that he has quitclaimed the lands and tithes of the abbey from pleas, and certain other actions and specified financial obligations, in the land of Paddington (Mddx.), Fanton (Essex) and Claygate (Surr.), and whatever the almoner held TRE in the wood of Ditton (Surr.), namely the third oak and common pasture, as he held it in the time of King Henry, and as King Edward's charter testifies, lest the archdeacon, sheriff or other officer should intrude on the monk-custodian. The grant is made for the souls of himself, his wife and their children; for the repose and redemption of his father; for the wellbeing of his mother, and for the soul of his uncle, King Henry. London [Dec. 1135 × 1137]

WAM XXXIX; WAD, f. 458r–v.
Pd: *Regesta* III, no. 936; *SR*, plate VII(a), facsimile.
Cal: *SR*, no. 531: scribe vii.
Date: The king's mother d. in 1137 (D. C. Douglas, *William the Conqueror* (1964), 395).
Note: It is remarkable that an archdeacon should have intruded in the matters listed here. At this period, the archdeacons of London, Mddx. and Essex were all members of the entrenched Belmeis dynasty (*Fasti* I, 9, 12–13, 15), and perhaps presumed to extend their own jurisdiction during the crisis in that of the bishopric of London, 1134–41 (ibid., 1–2). For King Edward's grants, see Sawyer, *Anglo-Saxon Charters*, nos. 1040, 1043, 1137.

106.* Writ of King Stephen ordering the sheriffs in whose shires the [minister of the] alms holds lands that the lands of [this minister] in Paddington (Mddx.), Fanton (Essex) and Claygate (Surr.) are to be quit of pleas, shire and hundred courts, and specified financial obligations. The abbey is to have whatever it held in the vill or wood of Ditton (Surr.), TRE or TRW, as the charters of those kings bear witness, namely the third oak and acre, and the third of all other things, as King Henry conceded by charter, lest anyone trespasses on the monk-custodian. [1135 × 1154]

WAM XXXVII; WAD, f. 458.
Pd: *Regesta* III, no. 937; *SR*, plate VII(b), facsimile.
Cal: *SR*, no. 529.
Note: T. A. M. Bishop allows that this text may represent an instance of a genuine charter having been written by the beneficiary's scribe, but suggests that if so, **64** is modelled on it (*SR*, 8, 8*n*.). The present writ supplements **62–3** by stating that these privileges were confirmed in a charter of W I, as does the spurious **64**, but there is no such grant among his genuine charters, and the writs of H I and Stephen which mention it are prob. forged.

107. Writ of King Stephen ordering the abbot and convent and their officers that Gilbert of Hendon is to have his land of Hendon (Mddx.) which he holds in fee-farm, as peaceably as Abbots Gilbert and Herbert and the chapter granted it to him by charter. Westminster [*post* 22 Dec. 1135 × *c*. 1137]

WAD, f. 124.
Pd: *Regesta* III, no. 926.
Date: Attested by Robert Fitz Richard, who is said to have d. in 1137 (*Geoffrey de Mandeville*, 13), and by Hugh Bigod. By 1141 at latest, he went over to the empress, who recognized him as earl of Norfolk in that year (*Regesta* III, nos. 275, 634). Although this text is only a cartulary copy, it may be significant that the abbot is not named. The writ was prob. issued soon after the d. of Herbert, 3 Sept.

1136 × 1138 (*Heads*, 77; cf. Flete, 142), when Gilbert would need to seek a renewal of his grant in fee.

Note: Cf. Harvey, *WA*, 352.

108. Writ of King Stephen informing the bp. of London, and the justices, sheriffs and barons of Mddx. that he has conceded to Richard de Balta and his heirs the land of the abbot's fee in Hampstead, rendering £2 annually to the abbot and convent, as they granted by charter. Westminster [22 Dec. 1135 × c. 1137]

WAD, f. 120v.
Pd: *Regesta* III, no. 925.
Date: Attested by R[obert] Fitz Richard, who is said to have d. in 1137 (*Geoffrey de Mandeville*, 13). The King was first at Westminster 22–26 Dec. 1135 (*Regesta* III, xxxix). Although this text is only a cartulary copy, it may be significant that the bp. of London is not named. Anselm, abbot of Bury, was elected 1136 and enthroned in 1137, but his election was quashed by the pope in 1138 and the see remained vacant until July 1141 (*Fasti* I, 1–2). The attestation of the bp. of Salisbury indicates a date *ante* June 1139 (*Gesta Stephani*, 72–8; *Historia Novella*, 26–8).
Note: Cf. Harvey, *WA*, 352.

109. Writ of King Stephen, ordering his justice, sheriff, barons and officers of London that they are to guard and maintain the lands and tenements of his son, Abbot Gervase, as they would the royal demesne, and to enable him to have his rents and dues, and especially St Mary Newchurch, which Gislan gave him, with its appurtenant lands. Westminster [17 Dec. 1138 × 1154]

WAD, f. 57.
Pd: *Regesta* III, no. 930; *Gilbert Crispin*, 159.
Date: Prob. issued following the consecration of Gervase by the legate Alberic, 17 Dec. 1138 (John of Worcester, 53). The omission of the bp. of London from the addressees suggests that it was issued during the vacancy in the see, 1138–41 (*Fasti* I, 1–2).

110.* Confirmation by King Stephen, generally addressed, of the abbey's lands, liberties and privileges. Westminster, 13 Dec. 1138.

WAM XXXIII; WAD, ff. 55–56v; F, ff. 68r–71v; T, ff. 21v–22 (ending at *regis confirmata sunt*); C, ff. 30v–31 (extracts only); BL MS Lansdowne 992, f. 147 (brief note).
Pd: *Regesta* III, no. 928, 'a forgery'; Flete, 55–6 (extracts only).
Cal: *SR*, no. 525.
Date: Attestation of Abp. Theobald inconsistent with date given in charter, since he was elected only on 24 Dec. (*Fasti* II, 4).

Note: Cf. Chaplais, 'Original Charters', 97.

111.* Confirmation by King Stephen, generally addressed, of the abbey's lands and customary privileges. [8 Jan. × *ante* 24 June, 1139]

PRO, E40/15911 (pretended original); WAD, f. 80r–v.
Pd: *Regesta* III, no. 929, 'spurious'.
Date: Attestations of Roger of Salisbury and his nephews (*Gesta Stephani*, 72–8; *Historia Novella*, 26–7), and of Abp. Theobald (*Fasti* II, 4).
Note: The text, clearly indicative of forgery, is almost identical to the alleged confirmation of H I (**57**).

112. Writ of King Stephen addressed to Andrew Buccuinte and the citizens of London, ordering that the men in the soke of St Peter are to be quit of the Hustings and Folkmoot as fully as their charter attests. If anyone makes any claim against them, let justice be done. Clare [Dec. 1135 × 1139]

WAD, f. 98v.
Pd: *Regesta* III, no. 927.
Date: Andrew Buccuinte's term of office as justiciar of London (*Regesta* III, no. 927*n*; Brooke & Keir, 327).

113. Writ of King Stephen, informing the justice, sheriff, barons and officers of Essex that he quitclaims to the church of St Peter of Westminster and the monks the sheriff's aid called justice-aid, at the rate of 1*s.* annually on each hide in Essex. London [late 1138 (× *ante* May 1152)]

WAD, f. 647.
Pd: *Regesta* III, no. 931.
Date: Attested by Robert de Vere, whose d. occ. before that of the queen, May 1152 (*Regesta* III, xxx; cf. *ASC*, 202, *n.* 7). Also attested by Richard de Lucy, out of England until late 1138 (*Regesta* III, no. 931, n.; Orderic VI, 526). Since Gervase is not named, the writ prob. dates from before his consecration, 17 Dec. 1138 (*Heads*, 77).

114. Writ of King Stephen informing the bp. of London, and the justice, sheriff, barons and officers of Essex, that he has granted to the church of St Peter of Westminster and to the abbot and monks, in perpetual alms, forty acres of assarts in Kelvedon for the soul of King Henry his uncle, and for those of himself, his wife Queen Matilda, their son Eustace and his other children. London [Dec. 1135 (× 1154)]

WAD, f. 269v.
Pd: *Regesta* III, no. 932.
Date: Since the bp. of London is not named, the writ may date from the interregnum in the see, 1138–41, or perhaps that during the first months of the reign (*Fasti* I, 1–2). The wording implies a date close to Stephen's coronation, and the abbot's name is not given, suggesting

that the writ was issued in the vacancy between Herbert and Gervase (cf. *Heads*, 77).

Note: Cf. Harvey, *WA*, 342. Eustace was prob. named because he was the king's heir, but the wording may be designed not only to include children of the marriage as yet unborn, but specifically to encompass Stephen's other offspring, notably Gervase, whose subsequent appointment to Westminster was perhaps already planned.

115. Writ of King Stephen ordering Gerbod de Scalt that the monks are to be allowed to hold their manor of Doddington (Lincs.) peaceably. Gerbod must not seize anything, nor exact forfeiture, nor intrude into any part of it, since he, Stephen, will warrant that manor to no-one but the church and monks of Westminster. Westminster [Dec. 1135 × 1154 (? Sept. 1136 × 1138)]

WAD, f. 649v.

Pd: *Regesta* III, no. 933.

Date: Since the abbot is not mentioned, the writ may date from the vacancy between the death of Herbert and the election of Gervase (*Heads*, 77). The only witness, William Martell, attests Stephen's charters throughout the reign.

Note: Cf. Harvey, *WA*, 348–9.

116. Writ of King Stephen ordering William Martell to bring justice to bear, without delay, upon the abbot of Chertsey (Surr.) and other tenants of the abbot of Westminster who deprived him of his rights, and did not render from their tenements the Danegeld due to the king. Meanwhile, the abbot of Westminster is to have respite on the balance due on the hidage exacted from his land. Martell is to name a day for agreement to be made between the abbots of Westminster and Chertsey. London [Dec. 1138 × 1143 (*or* 1149 × 1154)]

WAD, f. 650v.

Pd: *Regesta* III, no. 934.

Date: Attestation of Henry of Essex without a title. He witnesses from the early years of the reign, and succeeded Robert de Vere as constable 1151 × *ante* May 1152 (*Regesta* III, xx). The abbot of Westminster is prob. Gervase, consecrated 17 Dec. 1138 (*Heads*, 77). The abbot of Chertsey is prob. William of St Helen, appointed by Stephen but removed by the pope at the instance of Bp. Henry of Winchester (*Chron. Mon. de Abingdon* II, 291–2), prob. during his legateship, 1 March 1139 × 24 Sept. 1143 (*Fasti* II, 85). William's successor, Hugh, nephew of King Stephen, succeeded to Chertsey in 1149 (*Regesta* III, no. 169, dated by *Chertsey Abbey Cartularies* (Surrey Record Soc., 1958), II, x); see also Rob. de Torigny, 218–19; *St Benet Holme 1020–1210*, ed. J. R. West, Norfolk Record Soc. 3 (1932), II, 194–5.

117. Writ of King Stephen informing his justices, barons, sheriffs and officers of Sussex and Mddx. that, since Abbot Herbert proved his title to the land of Parham (Suss.) and *Mapelefort* (Mddx.) against Herbert Fitz Herbert, in the presence of King Henry's barons at the Exchequer, by their verdict, the abbot may hold it in demesne if he wishes, and may do as he pleases with it. The king orders that the (present) abbot is to hold that land peaceably as the said abbot proved his title, and as King Henry's charter bears witness (**96**). London [*post* 24 June 1139 × 1154]

WAM XXXVIII.

Pd: *Regesta* III, no. 935.

Cal: *SR*, no. 530: scriptor xx.

Date: The narrowest limits of scriptor xx's chancery career are 1139–Dec. 1141 (*SR*, facing plate XXI(a) and XXI(b)). Attached to the charter is a fragment of Stephen's second seal, adopted after 24 June 1139, and used for the rest of the reign (*Regesta* III, xv, following *Geoffrey de Mandeville*, 50–1).

Note: Cf. Harvey, *WA*, 359–60. The writ was presumably issued for (the unnamed) Abbot Gervase.

118. Notification by King Stephen, generally addressed, that he has conceded to the church of St Peter and to the monks there quittance of geld and customary exactions on six and a half hides in the manor of Westminster, since his court and palace, and the infirmary of St Giles, are established there. The grant is made for the souls of his wife Queen Matilda and himself and his children; and for the souls of King Henry and his other predecessors as kings of England. St Albans [*c.* 1150 × *ante* 3 May 1152]

WAM XXXV, with fragment of Stephen's second seal; WAD, f. 80v; LN, f. j; CAY, f. j.

Pd: *Regesta* III, no. 938; Chaplais, 'Original Charters', 109–10; *NPS Facsimiles*, plate 20*b* (plate and transcript).

Cal: *SR*, no. 527, scriptor xxii; Bentley, 1, no. 2, from CAY.

Date: Issued before the d. of the queen, 3 May 1152. Attested by R. abbot of St Albans, either Ralph (1146–51) or Robert (1151–66) (*Heads*, 67), and by Daniel, abbot of St Benet of Hulme, in office *c.* 1141–46 (deposed), and *c.* 1150–53 (*Heads*, 68).

Note: It is interesting both that the grant is made for the king's children (presumably including Gervase and others born out of wedlock), and also that the king styles his predecessors as kings 'of England' (see also **119–20**), rather than kings 'of the English'.

119.* Notification by King Stephen, generally addressed, that he has quitclaimed gelds, Danegelds, and specified financial exactions and other obligations on six and a half hides in the manor of Westminster, since the royal court and palace, and also the infirmary of St Giles, are established there, for the souls of himself, Queen Matilda and his children, and the souls of King Henry and his other predecessors as kings of England, with an anathema on transgressors. St Albans [early 1150 × *ante* 3 May 1152]

WAM XXXIV, with fragment of second seal; WAD, ff. 80v–81; LN, f. j *verso*; CAY, f. j *recto–verso*.

Pd: *Regesta* III, no. 939; Chaplais 'Original Charters', 109–10 (both texts presented to indicate extent of borrowing from **118**; *Formulare*, no. D; *Monasticon* I, 308, no. LIII.

Cal: *SR*, no. 526; Bentley, 1, no. 3, from CAY.

Date: Intended as for **118**.

Note: A forgery based on **118**, and virtually contemporary (Chaplais, 'Original Charters', 97). Scribe discussed by Bishop & Chaplais, xxii; Chaplais, 'Original Charters', 97n.3. In comparison with **118**, Abp. Theobald is now styled 'primate and legate', but neither this, nor the additional attestations of Robert de Chesney, bp. of Lincoln, Richard de Lucy and Osbert Martell has any conclusive effect on the dating.

120.* Notification by King Stephen, generally addressed, that he has conceded to the abbey and convent for their manor of Battersea (Surr.) quittance of gelds, Danegelds and certain other exactions on twenty-eight hides; with quittance of geld on forty-four hides which were formerly required to contribute, for the souls of himself, his wife Queen Matilda and his (*sic*) children, and for those of his uncle King Henry and his other predecessors as king of England, with an anathema on transgressors. St Albans [early 1150 × *ante* 3 May 1152]

WAM XXXVI, with a seal resembling Stephen's second seal; WAD, f. 161v.

Pd: *Regesta* III, no. 940, with italics indicating derivations from **119**.

Cal: *SR*, no. 528.

Date: Intended as for **118**.

Note: Scribe not identified (*SR*) and the handwriting prob. 13C (Chaplais, cited *Regesta* III, no. 528n.).

121.* Notification of King Stephen, generally addressed, concerning his grant to the church of St Peter of Westminster and the monks of exemptions for their manor of Battersea (Surr.) as applicable to twenty-eight hides; his quittance of geld on forty-four hides there (all as in **120**), and on six and a half hides in the manor of Westminster (as in **119**), and quittance of all secular service on a virgate in Hanwell (Mddx.). St Albans [early 1150 × *ante* 3 May 1152]

WAD, f. 56v; PRO Pat. Roll 3 Ric. II, pt. i, m. 7; Pat. Roll 1 Ed. IV, m. 21; Confirmation Roll 2 Hen. VII, pt. 2, no. 12; Conf. Roll 2 Hen. VIII, pt. 6, no. 1.

Pd: *Regesta* III, no. 941, with distinctive typefaces to indicate derivations from **119** and **120**; *Cal. Pat. R. 1461–7* (Ed. IV's confirmation of Ric. II's confirmation).

Cal: *Cal. Pat. R. 1377–81*, 407.

Date: Intended as for **118**. Derivations from **120** suggest the composition is 13C.

122. Writ of H II, ordering that Abbot Gervase is to have all his lands, tenants and liberties as any of his predecessors held them TRE, and as

King Edward and H I granted by their charters to the abbey, with pleas, including murder and theft. The sheriff may not intrude without the consent of the abbot and monks. Dover [Dec. 1154 × 1157 (? 2 × 10 Jan. 1156)]

WAM XLIV(5); WAD, f. 58; F, f. 131r–v.

Pd: *NPS Facsimiles*, plate 98(a), facsimile; Chaplais, 'Original Charters', plate VIII(b), partial facsimile: from original; L. Delisle, 'Notes sur les chartes originales de Henri II', *B.E.C.* LXVIII (1907), 279, no. 17, extracts only, from *NPS Facsimiles*.

Cal: *S.R.*, no. 536, scribe not identified; *Acta H II and R I*, 160–1, no. H 292.

Date: Gervase was still in office *c.* 1 June 1157 (**165–6**; cf. *Letters of John of Salisbury* I, no. 45), but removed by H II (Symeon of Durham II, 330), prob. *c.* 1157 (Flete, 143). The attestations suggest that this document was among those issued at Dover, 2 × 10 Jan. 1156 (cf. Eyton, *Itinerary*, 15–6; *Monasticon* (1823) IV, 538–9, no. IX).

Note: 'Apparently genuine' (Chaplais, 'Original Charters', 96, and n. 6).

123.* Charter of liberties of H II, granted for his own soul; for those of his parents; and those of H I and King Edward, taking the abbey, the coronation church, under his protection; confirming its exemption from episcopal or other temporal authority; its right of free election, and all lands granted by his predecessors, magnates or citizens of London, and extensive exemptions. Dover [19 Dec. 1154 × *ante* 14 Aug. 1158 (? 2 × 10 Jan. 1156)]

WAM XLIII, with seal, attached on parchment tag, on which is written 'Prima Carta Duplicata'; BL Cotton Charter VI 5, also an 'original', damaged, therefore uncertain whether it was ever sealed; WAD, ff. 57v–58; F, ff. 72–73v; T, f. 23r–v (attestations omitted).

Cal: *B.E.C.* LXIX, 555, no. 32 (WAM XLIII); *B.E.C.* LXVIII, 276, no. 6 (Cotton Charter); *S.R.*, no. 535: scribe not identified; *Acta H II and R I*, 161–2, no. H 294; 161, no. H 293 (Cotton Charter VI 5).

Date: Attestation of Warin Fitz Gerold as chamberlain. He was succeeded by his brother Henry before the king left England 14 Aug. 1158 (Eyton, *Itinerary*, 39–40). The witnesses all attest charters issued by Henry at Dover, 2 × 10 Jan. 1156 (ibid., 15–16).

Note: A forgery, closely modelled on the spurious charters of liberties of H I (**57**) and Stephen (**111**): cf. Chaplais, 'Original Charters', 96 n. 6. The *Dei gratia* formula was introduced into the royal style only in 1172/3 (*S.R.*, 19, 35).

124. Writ of H II, ordering the abbot and monks to allow Gilbert of Hendon to hold his manor of Hendon (Mddx.) in fee farm as well and as peaceably as Abbots Gilbert and Herbert and the chapter granted it to his father, and to Gilbert himself, and as Gilbert or his father held it in the reign of H I, as H I's charter bears witness. Northampton [Dec. 1154 × *ante* 14 Aug. 1158 (? × summer 1157)]

WAD, f. 124.

Date: Attested by Thomas Becket as chancellor, *ante* his election to Canterbury, 23 May 1162 (*Fasti* II, 4). Prior to that date, the king was continuously out of England from 14 Aug. 1158 (Eyton, *Itinerary*, 40–58), and since Abbot Gervase issued a charter to Gilbert Fitz Gunter, in response to this mandate (**263**), Henry's writ cannot have been issued much later than June 1157.

Note: King Stephen's writ ordering the abbey to observe Gilbert's tenancy (**107**) makes no mention of any charter of H I. Abbot Gilbert granted Hendon in farm to Gunter (**241**), and Abbot Herbert confirmed it to Gunter and his unnamed heir (**245**). See also Harvey, *WA*, 352.

125. Writ of H II, ordering the sheriff of Surrey that, if the abbot has been disseised unjustly and without judgement of any part of his land of Claygate (Surr.), then the sheriff is to reseise him justly and without delay, as he was seised at the d. of H I. Winchester [1155 × c. Aug. 1158]

WAM XLII(3); WAD, f. 471.
Pd: *S.R.*, plate XXV(b), facsimile; *B.E.C.* LXIX, 563, no. 66: from original.
Cal: *S.R.*, no. 534: scribe xxvi; *Acta H II and R I*, 160, no. H 291.
Date: Scribe xxvi was employed from 1155, but prob. down to the early 1160s, at latest, and he worked only in England (*S.R.*, 30, and note facing plate XXV(b)). The king was abroad from 14 Aug. 1158 to early Jan. 1163 (Eyton, *Itinerary*, 40–58). The contents of the writ also indicate a date soon after the king's accession (cf. Van Caenegem, 64, 66, 278).
Note: Cf. Harvey, *WA*, 358.

126.* Writ of H II, informing the justices, sheriffs, ministers and bailiffs in whatever shires or jurisdictions the almonry holds lands, that he has quitclaimed to the almonry all pleas, legal actions, suit of shire and hundred courts, geld, Danegeld, scots, sheriffs' aids, murder fines, and customary exactions in Paddington (Mddx.), Fanton (Essex) and Claygate (Surr.), and whatever it held in the wood and vill of Ditton (Surr.) TRE and in the reigns of W I and H I, as their charters bear witness, with sake and soke, etc. Westminster [Dec. 1154 × *ante* Michaelmas 1158]

WAD, f. 458v.
Date: Issued by Warin Fitz Gerold, who was succeeded as chamberlain by his brother Henry *ante* Michaelmas 1158 (*PR 4 Henry II*, 123–4; cf. *PR 3 Henry II*, 80–1, 107).
Note: The tone and content suggest that this writ, like others on the subject ascribed to H I and Stephen (**62–4, 106**), is spurious. See also Harvey, *WA*, 341, 353, 358.

127. Writ of right of H II, ordering Geoffrey de Jarpunville to restore to the monks without delay their tithes of Bushey (Herts.), as they held them in the reign of H I, otherwise the bp. of Lincoln will do so. Woodstock [Dec. 1154 × *c.* 1165]

WAD, f. 648v.

Date: *Dei gratia* absent from the royal style. John of Oxford attests without a title, which suggests a date before his appointment as dean of Salisbury in 1165 (*L & C Foliot*, 537; *Letters of John of Salisbury* II, xxxii–xxxiii, 112, 170; E. Turk, *Nugae Curialium* (Geneva, 1977), 48). He became bp. of Norwich late in 1175 (*Fasti* II, 56).

Note: The bp. of Lincoln, Dec. 1148–Dec. 1166, was Robert de Chesney (*Fasti* III, 2).

128. Writ *praecipe* of H II, ordering John of Bushey (Herts.), clerk, to render to the abbot, justly and without delay, the tithe pertaining to his parish of Aldenham (Herts.), as the abbey held it in the reign of H I, or else the bp. of London will see to it. There must be no delay, because of the king's sea-crossing or the appeal which he (the abbot) made to the king. Portchester [Dec. 1154 × mid March 1166]

WAD, f. 203v.

Date: Attested by Joscelin de Bailliol, who does not attest after 1166 (Eyton, *Itinerary*, 91, 94, 97; cf. p. 312). The king crossed to France 16–23 March 1166 (ibid., 92).

Note: Cf. Harvey, *WA*, 345, 403.

129.* Writ of H II, ordering Hilary, bp. of Chichester, the justices, sheriffs and officers of Sussex, that the abbey and monks are to hold their vill of Parham, with the church and its other appurtenances, quit of shire and hundred courts, geld, Danegeld, sheriffs' aids and other exactions, as a royal demesne chapel. It is not to be disseised of anything with which it was seised on 15 Aug. next after his crossing to Normandy. Southampton [Dec. 1154 × Mar. 1166]

WAM 4075; WAD, f. 572; F, ff. 74v–75; PRO, KB 26/54, m. 18d. The copies supply the place of issue.

Pd: *S.R.*, plate VI(b), facsimile; *B.E.C.* LXIX, 560, no. 54, extracts only: from original; *Curia Regis Rolls* VI, 177.

Cal: *S.R.*, no. 553, 'supposed original'; imitates hand of **132** (ibid., 8 and plate VI); *Acta H II and R I*, 160, no. H 290.

Date: Hilary bp. of Chichester d. 1169 ('Winchester Annals', 'Waverley Annals', *Ann. Mon.*, ci, 239). The king crossed to Normandy mid-March 1166, and returned to England 3 March 1170 (Eyton, *Itinerary*, 92, 135).

Note: Cf. Harvey, *WA*, 359–60.

130. Writ of H II, informing William de Turba, bp. of Norwich, and the barons of Suffolk, that he confirms to the monks of St Bartholomew's, Sudbury, two parts of the tithe of *Torp*, which Ivo gave from his demesne when he became a monk there, to hold as King Henry confirmed by his charter. Winchester [Dec. 1154 × early May 1172 (? 29 Sept. 1155)]

F, f. 79v; T, f. 24v, giving first attestation only.

Pd: *Monasticon* III, 459, no. II, from F.

Cal: Eyton, *Itinerary*, 12.

Date: William de Turba d. Jan. 1174 (*Fasti* II, 56), although the absence of *Dei gratia* in the royal style indicates a date before the end of 1173 (cf. *S.R.*, 19). The king crossed to Normandy in May 1172, and returned to England 8 July 1174 (Eyton, *Itinerary*, 167, 179). Possibly issued at the Council of Winchester, 29 Sept. 1155 (ibid., 12).

Note: The one surviving charter of H I for Sudbury does not mention this tithe (**72**). No prior is known, and there were perhaps two inmates at any one time (Knowles & Hadcock, 77).

131. Writ of H II, ordering his sheriffs and officers throughout England, in whatever bailiwicks the abbey has lands and men, that the abbey is to have its liberty, as conceded in his own charter, and in those of his predecessors. No-one is to exact more from them. Rouen [Dec. 1154 × *ante* Feb. 1173 (? June 1157 × 1158)]

WAD, f. 58; F, f. 87v (royal style given *Henricus rex Anglorum etc.*).

Pd: *Regesta* II, no. CCCXXVII, from F.

Cal: *Regesta* II, no. 1987.

Date: *Dei gratia* absent from the royal style. The absence of the abbot's name, and the tenor of the writ, suggest that it was issued during an abbatial vacancy, prob. that following the removal of Gervase (*Heads*, 77). Use of *bailliva, teste, cancellario*.

Note: Perhaps in consequence of the issue of this writ, murder fines levied on the abbot's lands in Essex, Herts. and Northants. during the early years of the reign were pardoned *per brevem regis* (*PR 2–4 Hen. II*, 135; *PR 7 Hen. II*, 66, 69; *PR 8 Hen. II*, 8).

132. Writ of H II, ordering his justices, sheriffs and officers throughout England that the monks are to have all lands, tithes and rents pertaining to the almonry, as they did in the time of H I. Westminster [Dec. 1154 × *ante* 1 July 1175 (× *ante* Feb. 1173)]

WAM XLI; WAD, f. 471.

Pd: *S.R.*, plate VI(a): facsimile of original.

Cal: *S.R.*, no. 533: scribe not identified, but 'an authentic writ of Chancery origin' (ibid., note facing plate VI(a)); *Acta H II and R I*, 162, no. H 295; *B.E.C.* LXIX, 563, no. 67.

Date: Attested by Reginald, earl of Cornwall, who d. 1 July 1175 (Diceto, I, 401). *Dei gratia* absent from the royal style.

133. Writ of H II, ordering the abbot [Laurence] to render right, without delay, to Hugh Fitz Warner over three hides of land which were his in Teddington and Sunbury, otherwise the sheriff of Mddx. will do so. Westminster [*c*. 1158]

WAD, ff. 155v–156.

Date: Eyton, *Itinerary*, 38, and 25–58 passim; cf. **452**.

Note: Hugh surrendered this writ to the abbey following his subsequent lawsuit against Abbot Laurence (**452**). On Sunbury and Teddington, see Harvey, *WA*, 354. It was later believed that Abbot Gervase had granted a lease of three hides in these vills to Hugh Fitz Warner (Flete, 89, but see Harvey, 'Fee Farms', 129, n. 6).

134. Notification by H II, generally addressed, that William Fitz Durand declared in the king's presence his conversion to the monastic life, and requested that all his land should be confirmed to his kinswoman Margaret, wife of the king's sergeant, Alexander de Barentin. This comprised 8*s.* worth of land in Warnborough and Odiham (Hants.), which Durand 'the dwarf' (*nanus*) bought from Suffac in presence of H I and his justices, with certain herbage, and enclosures in H II's wood in Odiham. Henry therefore confirmed these lands to Alexander and Margaret, as Durand held them in the reign of H I. Woodstock [May × July 1175 (? 1–8 July 1175)]

WAM 661 (with Great Seal).
Pd: *Formulare*, no. DVIII, 295–6; *Foedera* I, i, ff. 45–6.
Cal: Eyton, *Itinerary*, 192; *Acta H II and R I*, 28, no. H 6.
Date: Outside limits given by the king's itinerary and the attestation of Herbert as archdeacon of Northampton (*Fasti* III, 30–1; cf. *Fasti* II, 14). Prob. issued during the Council of Woodstock (Eyton, *Itinerary*, 192).
Note: On the administrative activities of Alexander (de) Barentin c. 1173–1190, see *PR 20 Hen. II*, 133; *PR 21 Hen. II*, 187; *PR 22 Hen. II*, 12; *PR 24 Hen. II*, 112–13; *PR 25 Hen. II*, 125; *PR 30 Hen. II*, 151; *PR 31 Hen. II*, 239–40; *PR 32 Hen. II*, 180–1; *PR 33 Hen. II*, 207; *PR 34 Hen. II*, 204, 206; *PR 1 Ric. I*, 234.

135. Confirmation by H II, to his *pincerna*, Alexander de Barentin, of properties he has received from named donors, including a seld in Dowgate, London, which Richard [of Ilchester] archdeacon of Poitiers bought from Robert de Pont de l'Arche. Westminster [1175 × 1177 (? *c.* 18 May 1176)]

WAM 660 (with Great Seal).
Pd: *Formulare*, 47–8, no. LXXXVI, from WAM; *Recueil des actes de H II*, DLXXXIX (from *Formulare*).
Cal: Eyton, *Itinerary*, 202–3; *Acta H II and R I*, 27–8, no. H 5.
Date: The attestation of Gilbert Malet suggests a date no later than April 1177 (*HBC*, 75), while that of Herbert le Poer as archdeacon of Canterbury is no earlier than 1175 × 1176 (*Fasti* II, 14). Possibly issued during the Council or Synod of Westminster.

136. Notification of H II, generally addressed, that he has conceded and confirmed to William of Darnford and his heirs the manor of Deerhurst (Gloucs.) with all appurtenances, to be held of the abbot and convent at an annual rent of £30, as specified in the charter of the former Abbot Gervase, and in the charter of the convent. The king concedes all liberties and free customs which King Edward granted, and confirms any which may be granted by future kings. Oxford [May 1172 × *ante* Dec. 1184]

WAM 32669; WAD, f. 317.

Date: Attested by Count Geoffrey: prob. this is the king's son, usually styled 'count' rather than 'duke' of Brittany. He left England for the last time *c*. Dec. 1184 (*Gesta Henrici*, 320). *Dei gratia* absent from the royal style.

Note: Abbot Gervase's charter (**271**) had been confirmed by the empress, prob. in 1141 (**98**). The convent's charter apparently dates from shortly after Gervase's dismissal, *c*. 1157 × 1158 (**341**). Abbot Walter de Wenlock (1283–1307) purchased Deerhurst from the William of Darnford of his own day (Flete, 116), hence the presence of this charter among the Muniments. Cf. also Harvey, *WA*, 344–5.

137. Writ of H II, ordering the justices, sheriffs and bailiffs of Gloucs. and Worcs. that the abbot and monks and their possessions are under his protection, and everything belonging to them must be treated as though it is royal demesne. All tenants of the abbey are to be compelled to render the service they owe, without delay. Droxford [May 1172 × *ante* 10 July 1188 (? April 1173 × *ante* 8 July 1175)]

WAD, f. 58; F, ff. 131v–132.

Date: Before the king's final departure from England (Eyton, *Itinerary*, 288). *Dei gratia* in the royal style. The contents of the writ, and the omission of the abbot's name, suggest that it was issued in the interregnum between the d. of Abbot Laurence, 10 or 11 April 1173, and the election of Abbot Walter, *post* 8 July 1175 (*Heads*, 77). In that period, Henry was in England April–July 1173, and 8 July–8 Aug. 1174 (Eyton, 173, 179–83), and returned for a longer visit 8 or 9 May 1175 (ibid., 190).

138.* Confirmation by H II, in reverence for St Edward, and for his soul; and those of his predecessors and successors, of the manor of Denham (Bucks.), which Martin de Capella held, to hold in demesne. Westminster [*c*. 1181 × July 1188 (prob. *c*. 1181 × March 1182)]

WAD, f. 178v; LN, f. xxxiij *verso*; CAY, f. xxxvj *recto–verso*.
Cal: Bentley, 14, no. 137, from CAY.

Date: The first attestation to the WAD text is that of Abp. Richard, who d. 16 Feb. 1184 (*Fasti* II, 5), so that the limit would be the king's departure from England 10–11 March 1182 (Eyton, *Itinerary*, 247), since he returned only on 10 June 1184 (ibid., 256). The LN text gives the archbp. as B[aldwin], which would extend the limit to the king's final departure on 10 July 1188 (Eyton, *Itinerary*, 288). Since Hugh Bardulf attests as dapifer, an opening limit of 1181 is indicated (ibid., 239).

Note: Textually, this is plainly a product of the Westminster scriptorium, rather than of the royal chancery, and prob. spurious. Abbot Walter's confirmation of Denham to Martin de Capella in fee-farm dates from 1175 or later (**301**). Martin evidently held land of

Westminster in Denham in 1172 (*PR 18 Henry II*, 47). See also Harvey, *WA*, 338–9.

139. Confirmation by H II, at the petition of Richard of Ilchester, bp. of Winchester, to Alexander de Barentin and his sons Richard and Thomas, the bp.'s nephews, and to their heirs, of the gifts which the bp. made them, as his charter bears witness. These properties in London, include the messuage of John Burgundian, in the Fishmarket. Clarendon [(1181 ×) Feb. 1187)]

WAM 662 (with Great Seal).
Cal: *Acta H II and R I*, 28, no. H 7.
Date: Attested by Hugh of Morwick, d. 1187. His appearance, and that of Hugh Bardulf, as dapifers, suggests a date of 1181 or later (Eyton, *Itinerary*, 312, 330). Within the period 1181–1187, the king was abroad *c.* 10 March 1182–*c.* 10 June 1184; *c.* 16 April 1185–27 April 1186; and *c.* 27 Feb. 1187–30 Jan. 1188 (ibid., 246–56; 263–7; 277–84). A likely time of issue would be Feb. 1187 (cf. ibid., 277).

140.* Charter of liberties of Richard I (as in the spurious charters of liberties of H I, Stephen and H II). Westminster, 6 Oct. 1189.

WAM XLV (with Great Seal of Richard I); WAD, ff. 58v–59; F, ff. 80–81v; T, ff. 24v–25.
Cal: *Acta H II and R I*, 179, no. R 328.
Date: Cf. Landon, *Itinerary*, 10. The attestations are in order for the date given: Richard Fitz Nigel; Godfrey de Lucy and William Longchamps are correctly styled bp.-elect: all had been elected on 15 Sept. 1189 (Diceto II, 69).
Note: The wording of this charter, closely following the spurious charters of liberties ascribed to H I, Stephen and H II (above, **57, 111, 123**; cf. Flete, 55: *similiter et Ricardus rex eosdem sermones recitat in charta sua*), renders it highly suspect, although there is a possibility that the king was prepared to seal a document prepared by the recipient. The precision of the attestations is explicable in that Hugh du Puiset, Richard Fitz Nigel and William Longchamps all attested other charters for Westminster on 6–7 October 1189 (**141–2**). Prob. a genuine seal was taken from one of these (perhaps **141**, which has lost its seal), and attached to the fabrication at an early date. See also note to **141**.

141. Writ of Richard I ordering his sheriffs and officers throughout England, in whatever bailiwicks the abbey holds lands, that the abbey is to have its entire liberty, as conceded in his own charter and in those of his predecessors. No-one may exact more from them. Westminster, 6 Oct. 1189.

WAM XLVI (tongue and seal torn off); WAD, f. 59; F, f. 81v, omitting the dating clause; PRO, C52/22, m. 1d, no. 16 (enrolment).
Cal: Landon, *Itinerary*, 10, 149, no. 71 (his citation of F suggests that he followed an earlier foliation); *Acta H II and R I*, 178, no. R 327.

Date: Cf. Landon, *Itinerary*, 10, and no. 71.

Note: The text closely follows a similar writ of H II (**131**). The reference to liberties conceded in Richard's own charter might be taken to support the authenticity of **140**, although that itself may be based on some shorter, genuine grant of the same date. The other possible model would be **142**, dated 7 Oct., although its terms were prob. discussed when those of the present writ were being negotiated.

142. Writ of Richard I, ordering his justices, sheriffs and officers throughout England that the land and men of the abbey are to be quit of all pleas, gelds, Danegelds, murder-fines, sheriffs' aids and all other exactions, which he quitclaims for the souls of his parents. Westminster, 7 Oct. 1189.

WAD, f. 59; F, f. 82; PRO, C52/22, m. 1*d*, no. 17 (enrolment).
Cal: Landon, *Itinerary*, 10, 149, no. 76 (citing F, f. 81v).
Date: Cf. Landon, *Itinerary*, 10.
Note: The monks evidently fined a mark (13*s*. 4*d*.) for this charter (*PR 1 Ric. I*, 219, 221; cf. *PR 2 Ric. I*, 107, where the sum stands at half this amount). Henceforth, murder fines levied on the lands of the abbot and convent in various shires were pardoned *per libertatem carte regis* (*PR 1 Ric. I*, 219; *PR 2 Ric. I*, 107; *PR 3 and 4 Ric. I*, 31, 266), or *per cartam regis monachis de Westmonasterio* (*PR 3 and 4 Ric. I*, 303, 304; *PR 5 Ric. I*, 7, 127). Although no similar writ survives from John's reign, at its outset Geoffrey Fitz Peter instructed the sheriff of Worcs. not to exact the murder fine or other common demands from the abbot's lands in the shire (*Memoranda Roll 1 John*, 48), and subsequently Abbot Ralph was granted exemption of tallage and other dues *per libertatem carte regis* (*Rot. Canc. 3 John*, 132; *PR 3 John*, 117).

143. Confirmation by Richard I to Alexander de Barentin, butler (*pincerna*) of his father King Henry II, of all the tenements which he acquired in due form, including the seld in Dowgate, London. Westminster, 10 Nov. 1189.

WAM 657 (with Great Seal of Richard I).
Pd: *Formulare*, 51–52, no. XCV; *NPS Facsimiles*, plate 99, preceded by transcript.
Cal: Landon, *Itinerary*, 151, erroneously stating that the text printed in *Formulare* is **144**; *Acta H II and R I*, 182–3, no. R 336.
Date: Cf. Landon, *Itinerary*, 16. See also **139** above.

144. Confirmation by Richard I of the grant made by his father, H II, at the petition of Richard of Ilchester, bp. of Winchester, to Alexander de Barentin and his sons Richard and Thomas, nephews of the bp., ratifying the grants which the bp. made them of lands in London. Westminster, 10 Nov. 1189.

WAM 659 (with Great Seal of Richard I).

Cal: Cf. note to **143**.
Date: Cf. Landon, *Itinerary*, 16.

145. Writ of Richard I, generally addressed, ordering that the monks and their possessions are to be protected as though royal demesne. They are not to be disseised of any free tenement which they held on the day when the king last crossed from England into Normandy; and are not to be impleaded over any tenement except in the presence of the king, his chief justiciar, or the chancellor. Westminster, 16 Dec. [1189]

WAD, f. 59; F, f. 132.
Cal: G. V. Scammell, *Hugh du Puiset: a biography of a twelfth-century bishop of Durham*, (1956), 294.
Date: Attested by Hugh du Puiset, bp. of Durham. He was appointed co-justiciar at the beginning of the reign (Howden, *Chronica* III, 16; *Gesta Henrici* II, 87), but from March 1190 his justiciarship was confined to the region north of the Humber (ibid., 106).
Note: Richard crossed to Calais, 12 Dec. 1189 (Landon, *Itinerary*, 23). The present writ seems to be the only one issued solely on the authority of Hugh du Puiset (Scammell, 51, 294).

146. Writ of Richard I, informing those in whose bailiwicks the abbey holds lands or rents that he has received the abbey, its lands, rents, men and possessions into his protection. His officers are to protect these as though royal demesne; they are to cause the charters, which the abbot has from the king or his predecessors, to be seen and heard in their bailiwicks, and uphold the liberties and customary rights contained in these charters. No exaction is to be levied contrary to these charters. Westminster, 26 Jan. [1190]

WAM XLVII (fragment of seal), presumably the Exchequer seal used by William Longchamps in Richard's absence (Landon, *Itinerary*, 173); WAD, f. 59r–v; F, f. 82r–v; T, f. 33r–v.
Cal: Landon, *Itinerary*, Appendix, 183, no. 12; *Acta H II and R I*, 212, no. R 398.
Date: Attested by William Longchamps as bp. of Ely and chancellor. He ceased to hold the chancellorship 9 Oct. 1191 (Richard of Devizes, 48–52; *Gesta Henrici* II, 213–14). Despite its wording this writ was prob. one of those issued by Longchamps after Richard's departure, and in his name, in Jan. 1190 (West, *Justiciarship*, 67 and n. 4; Landon, *Itinerary*, 183).

147. Confirmation by King John, to his treasurer William of Ely, of the houses in Westminster held by Richard, the late bp. of London, and his whole messuage, which William holds of the grant of the bp., and the confirmation of Abbot William. Westminster, 20 April 1200.

WAD, f. 342; PRO, C53/2, m. 10 (enrolment).
Pd: *Rot. Chart.* 49a, m. 10, from enrolment: only the first two witnesses are given.
Cal: Cf. Richardson, 'William of Ely', 50.

Note: This royal charter was acquired as a result of William of Ely's subsequent grant of this property to the abbey (**439**).

148. Writ *praecipe* of King John, ordering Abbot Ralph to render justice without delay to William Southall and his wife Denise over forty acres of land with appurtenances in Pyrford which William claims that he holds of the abbot by free service of 5s. annually, and of which Walter de Reda dispossessed him. If the abbot fails to render justice, the sheriff of Surr. will do so. Portchester, 25 April [1200 (× 1206)]

WAD, f. 176v; LN, f. xlviij *verso*, *(Southaule)*; CAY, f. li.
Cal: Bentley, 24, no. 187, from CAY.
Date: Attested by Hugh Bardulf, who was d. by Michaelmas 1206 (*PR 8 John*, 4, 236). John was at Portchester on 25 April 1200 ('Itinerarium Johannis Regis', comp. T. Duffus Hardy, *Archaeologia* 22 (1829), 129).
Note: Cf. Harvey, *WA*, 359.

149. Charter of King John, restoring to Abbot Ralph and the monks their manor of Islip, Oxon., in which St Edward was born, and which he gave to the abbey at its dedication, since it was recognized in the king's court, by virtue of royal charters, and by the view of law-worthy men of that manor, that it belonged to Westminster and was wrongfully taken away. Abbot Ralph and the convent are to hold the manor peaceably, as their charters of King Edward and William the Conqueror bear witness. Westminster, 1 Nov. 1204.

WAM 15160 (Great Seal attached); WAM 15162 (duplicate, with Great Seal, and additional attestation of William Longsword, earl of Salisbury); WAD, f. 270r–v; F, ff. 82v–83 (from WAM 15162); PRO, C53/6, m. 8 (enrolment); CAY, f. lxxviii *verso* (memorandum).
Pd: *Rot. Chart.*, 139b, from enrolment.
Cal: Bentley, 40, no. 284 (item 4), from CAY.
Note: Westminster's claim that King Edward had granted Islip was prob. essentially true, although the manor was not held by the abbey after the Norman Conquest. In the twelfth century, Islip was acquired by the De Courcy family, whose English lands were forfeited when Robert de Courcy joined Philip Augustus of France in 1203 (Barbara Harvey, 'Islip', *VCH Oxon.*, VI, 208–9; Harvey, *WA*, 356), thus presenting the abbey with a belated opportunity of petitioning for King Edward's benefaction. The writs of King Edward (Sawyer, *Anglo-Saxon Charters*, nos. 1147, 1148) and the charter of William I (**3**), are all spurious. Whether or not this was apparent to the chancery staff, Westminster was obliged to pay heavily for the restoration of this manor. In November 1204 the abbot fined 200 marks (£133. 6s. 8d.) and two palfreys (*Rot. Litt. Claus.*, 15a, 32b; *PR 6 John*, 112; *Rot. de Oblat. et Fin.*, 222).

150. Notification by King John, generally addressed, that, at the request of James Salvage, royal clerk and rector of Oakham (Rutl.), he has conceded and confirmed that the tenants of All Saints' church, Oakham, and of its appurtenant chapels, are quit in perpetuity of suit of shire and hundred courts, and of sheriffs' aids and of those of their bailiffs and officers. Anyone disturbing the tenants will incur forfeiture. Lambeth, 28 April 1206.

WAM 20615 (seal now missing); WAD, f. 594r–v; F, f. 273v (attestations and dating clause omitted); PRO, C53/7, m. 1 (enrolment: the church is named as *Beati Petri de Hocham*).
Pd: *Rot. Chart.*, 165b, from enrolment.
Date: James Salvage, *alias* Savage, fined three palfreys for these exemptions in 1206 (*Rot. de Oblat. et Fin.*, 365; *PR 8 John*, 53).
Note: This royal charter presumably came to the abbey as a result of problems with the payment of an annual pension from Oakham church which James Salvage had earlier made to the abbey (**482**). See also Mason, 'Rutland Churches', 165; Harvey, *WA*, 404.

151. Letter patent of King John, ordering his knights, sergeants and other soldiers of his army that they are not to enter within the precincts of the abbey, the abbey church or its cemetery; nor permit others to enter; nor to cause, or permit others to cause, injury to the monks or to the king's men dwelling there, since the abbey, its men and all residents and goods are under the royal protection. Rochester, 24 Oct. 1215.

WAD, f. 650v; PRO C66/14, m. 10 (enrolment).
Pd: *Rot. Litt. Pat.*, 157v–158a, from enrolment.
Date: John was at the siege of Rochester by the date of this document (*Memoriale Fratris Walteri de Coventria*, ed. W. Stubbs (RS, 1873), II, 226).
Note: The monks, in petitioning the king, had presumably cited their earlier deeds of liberties and protection, since none survives in John's name. On the contrary, in 1205 the abbot had fined twenty marks (£13. 6s. 8d.) to have the king's *benevolencia* (*Rot. de Oblat. et Fin.*, 325). The rebels were in control of London in 1215, from mid-May (*Flores Historiarum*, ed. H. R. Luard (RS, 1890), II, 157).

152.* Letter of Pope Leo IX, granting to King Edward that, to obviate political dangers, he may commute his vow of making a pilgrimage to Rome, and instead found a monastery dedicated to St Peter. [1049]

Recited in full within the (spurious) Great Charter of King Edward: WAD, f. 44r–v; F, ff. 115–116v; BL Additional Roll 15895, no. 4 (excerpts).
Incipit: *Quoniam voluntatem tuam.*
Pd: *PUE* I, no. 2.
Recited, in abridged version ... *tibi indulgentia*: WAD, f. 39; and similarly abridged but with an additional variant ending: F, ff. 26v–27, in the (spurious) First Charter of King Edward.
Pd: Wilkins, *Concilia* I, 317; *PL* 143, col. 674; *PL* 195, col. 752, from F.
Date: Cf. *PUE* I, 217–18.

Note: Cf. *PUE* I, no. 2, note; Scholz, 'Sulcard of Westminster', 70.

153.* Letter of Pope Nicholas II, in response to a petition of King Edward, confirming and extending the privileges of the abbey, the repository of the royal regalia, and exempting it from episcopal jurisdiction. [1061]

> Recited in the Third Charter of King Edward (Sawyer, *Anglo-Saxon Charters*, no. 1041), itself a spurious document; WAD, ff. 41v–42; F, f. 42r–v; BL Additional Roll 15895, no. 7 (excerpts).
> Incipit: *Omnipotenti Deo referimus.*
> Pd: Wilkins, *Concilia* I, 319–20; Kemble IV, 183–5, no. DCCCXXV; *PL* 143, col. 1358–9, no. xxxvi; Mansi, 1054–58, no. xix.
> Note: King Edward's letter to Pope Nicholas is pd. Wilkins, *Concilia* I, 319; Kemble IV, 182–3, no. DCCCXXV; see also Scholz, 'Sulcard of Westminster', 70. On Edward's embassy to Rome in 1061, see Osbert de Clare, *Vita Edwardi*, *Analecta Bollandiana*, xli (1923), 87–8; Frank Barlow, *The English Church* 1000–1066, 2nd edn., 1974, 297, no. 4. On the strange greeting of this letter, see Chaplais, 'Original Charters', 93.

154.* Letter of Pope Paschal II, informing H I that the abbey is under the special protection of St Peter; that it is exempt from the jurisdiction of the bp. of London, and that he confirms its status as the coronation church, and its possession of all its lands and churches. Lateran, 28 June [1101 × 1114]

> F, ff. 157–158; C, f. 27v, extracts; BL Additional roll 15895, nos. 10 and 18 (extracts).
> Incipit: *Sollicitudinem filii karissimi.*
> Pd: *PUE* I, no. 9; Flete, 14, 17, 48 (extracts); *Gilbert Crispin*, 36 (extracts).
> Date: Cf. *PUE* I, 229.
> Note: Identified as a forgery by Chaplais, 'Original Charters', 92. See also Scholz, 'Two Forged Charters from Westminster', 468.

155. Pope Innocent II, authorizing H I to take the abbey under his protection, and excluding it from the jurisdiction of the bp. of London. Pisa, 30 Sept. [1133]

> WAD, f. 1v; F, f. 156v; T, ff. 53v–54; C, ff. 27v–28; PRO, C 81/193, no. 5768 (14C); BL Additional Roll 15895, no. 13.
> Incipit: *Presenti nostre fili.*
> Pd: *PUE* I, no. 17; Flete, 48–9.
> Date: Before the d. of Gilbert the Universal, bp. of London (*Fasti* I, 1); cf. *PUE* I, no. 17n.
> Note: Prob. the first genuine document of title concerned with the jurisdictional conflict between the abbey and the bp. of London.

156. Solemn privilege of Innocent II addressed to Abbot Gervase and his successors; takes the abbey under his protection as his predecessors, Nicholas II and Leo IX had done, and confirms the abbey's privileges and possessions. Lateran, 22 April 1139.

WAD, f. 1r–v; F, ff. 158–159 (subscriptions omitted); BL Additional Roll 15895, no. 12.
Incipit: *Licet omnibus ecclesiis.*
Pd: *PUE* I, no. 21.
Note: Accepted by Holtzmann as the first undoubted, specific papal privilege for Westminster (*PUE* I, no. 21).

157. Pope Innocent II, notifying Abbot Gervase and the convent that, at the request of Bp. H[enry (of Blois) of Winchester], he confirms and takes under his protection the lands which Gilbert of Hendon (Mddx.) and his predecessors held of the abbey. Lateran, 22 April [1139]

WAD, f. 124.
Incipit: *Justis desideriis assensum.*
Pd: *PUE* I, no. 20.
Date: Issued on the same occasion as **156**.
Note: Cf. Harvey, 'Fee Farms', 136. The pope had placed Bp. Henry in charge of the vacant bishopric of London in 1138 (Diceto I, 252) and the vacant see was filled only in July 1141 (*Fasti* I, 2).

158. Pope Innocent II, to Abbot Gervase and the monks, following the mission to the Curia of Prior Osbert de Clare. The canonization of King Edward would require more evidence than has been offered. Further evidence, and the petition for canonization, should be presented by the whole realm (of England). However, he has written to the legate, Henry (of Blois), bp. of Winchester, ordering the restitution to the abbey of those lands which have been misappropriated. Lateran, 9 Dec. [1139]

BL Cotton Vitellius A XVII, ff. 22v–23.
Incipit: *Quum religiosum virum.*
Pd: *Monasticon* I, 308, no. LIV (citing BL Donat. 4573, no. 2, which cannot be identified); *Letters of Osbert de Clare*, 87–8, no. 19; Wilkins, *Concilia* I, 419; *Epistolae Herberti de Losinga; Osberti de Clara et Elmeri*, ed. R. Anstruther (New York, 1846, rpt. 1969), 122–4, no. VII; *Foedera* I, i, f. 17; *PL* 179, col. 568, no. DII.
Cal: Jaffé, *RPR* I, 899, no. 8182.
Date: Osbert's mission is believed to have taken place in 1139 (Harvey, 'Fee Farms', 128).
Note: See Scholtz, 'Canonization', 38–49; Chaplais, 'Original Charters', 91. See also Harvey, 'Fee Farms', 128.

159. Pope Innocent II to Henry [of Blois], bp. of Winchester and papal legate. The pope has learned from [Prior] Osbert [de Clare] of the complaint of the monks of St Peter of Westminster that the possessions and goods of that church have been wrongfully seized and violently detained by many people. The pope orders Henry to hear the complaint of the monks; to render them justice, and not to permit anyone to do them further injury or harm. Lateran, 9 December [1139]

BL Cotton MS Vitellius A XVII, f. 17v.
Incipit: *Ex parte filiorum.*
Pd: *Letters of Osbert de Clare*, 88, no. 20; Wilkins, *Concilia*, I, 418; Anstruther, *Epistolae Herberti de Losinga*, 109–10, no. 1; *PL*, 179, cols. 567–8, no. DI.
Cal: Jaffé, *RPR*, 8181.
Date: See Harvey, 'Fee Farms', 128.

160. Pope Innocent II, requesting David I, king of the Scots, to confirm to the abbey the land which provides his annual donation of £1. 10s. supporting the anniversary of his late sister, Queen Matilda. Lateran, 9 Dec. [1139]

WAD, f. 158; F, f. 160 (date omitted); T, f. 53 (date omitted).
Incipit: *Dilectus filius noster.*
Pd: *PUE* I, no. 25; *Acts of Malcolm IV*, 290–1, no. 319.
Date: This is one of four letters, all dated 9 Dec., which Prior Osbert de Clare allegedly brought back from his mission to Rome in 1139 (Harvey, 'Fee Farms', 128). Holtzmann, *PUE*, and Barrow, *Acts of Malcolm IV*, date 1139 × 1142.
Note: This bull was perhaps requested by Westminster after the land had been granted to Eustace Fitz John by Henry, son of King David (*Acts of Malcolm IV*, no. 12, dated 1139 × 1141).

161.* Letter of Pope Innocent II, addressed to Abbot Gervase and the monks, ordering Abbot Gervase to get back lands alienated without the consent of the convent, and to keep safely the regalia of Edward the Confessor. Lateran, 9 Dec. [1139]

WAD, f. 1 (in part); F, ff. 159–60; C, f. 28 (extracts).
Incipit: *Sicut disponente Domino.*
Pd: Flete, 90–91, also 49 (extract); *PUE* I, no. 24; Harvey, 'Fee Farms', 128n.1 (extract).
Note: Dated to 1139 on the grounds that it was one of four letters supposedly brought back from Rome by Prior Osbert de Clare, but prob. a forgery composed by him (Harvey, 'Fee Farms', 128–9). Chaplais, 'Original Charters', 91, accepts as genuine. See also Richardson & Sayles, 416–17. On the regalia, see Barlow, *Edward the Confessor*, 269.

162. Pope Eugenius III to Abbot Gervase and his successors, confirming papal, royal and other privileges granted to the abbey. Trastevere, 8 March 1146.

BL Cotton Augustus II n. 50 (notarial copy); WAD, f. 2r–v; F, ff. 197v–199v; WA Mun. Bk. 12, f. 6 (précis).
Incipit: *Cum universis sancte.*
Pd: *Foedera* I, i, f. 14 (from BL Cotton Aug. II), *PL* 180, cols. 1115–17, no. XC (from F).

Cal: Jaffé, *RPR* II, 31, no. 8878.

Date: *Indictione ix^{na} Incarnationis Dominice anno m^o c^o xlv^o pontificatus vero domini Eugenii iij pape anno secundo.* The pope's second regnal year, and the subscription of Imar, cardinal bp. of Tusculum (Frascati) (for his travels in 1144–1145 see *Councils & Synods* I, 810–11). A. Morey and C. N. L. Brooke, 'The Cerne Letters of Gilbert Foliot and the Legation of Imar of Tusculum', *EHR* 63 (1948), 523–7.

163. Pope Eugenius III to Abbot Gervase and his successors, confirming the privileges earlier granted by popes, kings, Abp. Dunstan and other magnates. Ferentino, 27 March 1151.

WAD, ff. 2v–3; F, ff. 160v–161 (subscriptions omitted); T, ff. 49v–50 (subscriptions omitted but dating clause given).

Incipit: *Commisse nobis apostolice.*

Pd: *PUE* I, 286–88, no. 47, from cartularies; *Foedera* I, i, f. 14 (from F, T).

Date: '*vj Kal. Aprilis Indictione xiiij. Incarnationis Dominice anno m^o c^o l^o j^o. Pontificatus vero domini Eugenii iij^o pape vij^o*'. Indiction and year of grace, with subscriptions of Nicholas, bp. of Albano (cf. Jaffé, *RPR* II, 20), confirm a date of 1151, in contrast to the regnal year, which is incorrect. Most papal letters dated March 1151 were issued at Ferentino (Jaffé, *RPR* II, 71–72).

164. Pope Adrian IV to Abbot Gervase and the convent, confirming the abbey's jurisdiction over the priory of Great Malvern [Worcs.]. Lateran, 25 May [1157]

WAM 32627 (copy of 13C or later); WAD, f. 306; F, ff. 199v–200.

Incipit: *Quociens a viris.*

Pd: *PUE* I, no. 68.

Date: Adrian IV issued letters exclusively from the Lateran in May 1157 (Jaffé, *RPR* II, 121–127), but none were issued from there in May 1155, or 1156. See also *Letters of John of Salisbury* I, no. 45.

Note: Great Malvern was founded by the monk Aldwin, on land granted by Earl AEthelwine (or Odda), d. 1056 (cf. *De Gestis Pontificum*, 285–6; *Monasticon* III, 440), whose estates were later given by King Edward to Westminster (*Vita Wulfstani*, ed. R. R. Darlington, Camden Soc. third series, 40 (1928), xli-xlii; Harvey, *WA*, 30). By 1117, Great Malvern was a dependency of Westminster (*Gilbert Crispin*, 33–4; *Monasticon* III, 447–8). On the jurisdictional dispute which preceded the issue of this bull, see *Letters of John of Salisbury* I, no. 45; Saltman, *Theobald*, 88–9.

165. Pope Adrian IV to Abbot Gervase and the convent, confirming to the abbey its privileges, exemptions and lands. Lateran, 1 June 1157.

WAD, ff. 3v–4v; F, ff. 161v–164v; T, ff. 48v–49v (subscriptions omitted in both the latter).

Incipit: *Licet omnibus ecclesiis.*

Pd: *PUE* I, no. 69.

166. Pope Adrian IV to Abbot Gervase and the convent, confirming the cells of Great Malvern (Worcs.), Hurley (Berks.) and Sudbury (Suffolk), together with the abbey's churches and chapels (enumerated). Lateran, 1 June 1157.

WAM 12755 (a copy, early 13C, omitting church of Staines, chapels of Holwell (Herts., formerly Beds.) and Morton (Worcs.), and all attestations; abridged dating clause); WAD, ff. 4v–5v; F, ff. 164–167; T, ff. 47v–48v (both the latter abridge conclusion, and omit subscriptions and date); BL Additional Roll 15895, no. 18 (short extract).
Incipit: *Religiosis desideriis dignum.*
Pd: *PUE* I, no. 70.
Note: On Great Malvern cf. the pope's bull issued a week earlier (**164**). Hurley was founded, as a dependency of Westminster, by Geoffrey de Mandeville I in 1085–6 (**462**); Sudbury, given by the moneyer Wulfric, was confirmed by H I 1114 × 1116 (**72**).

167. Pope Alexander III to Abbot Laurence and the convent, proclaiming that King Edward is to be enumerated as a confessor. Anagni, 7 Feb. [1161]

WAD, f. 387v; F, ff. 169v–170v; C, ff. 48v–49; Vatican Library, MS Latin 6024, f. 151v.
Incipit: *Illius devotionis constanciam.*
Pd: Flete, 93, from WAD; Barlow, *Edward the Confessor*, 323–4, no. 14; J. v. Pflugk-Hartung, *Acta Pontificum Inedita* III (Stuttgart, 1886), 206, no. 196, from Vatican MS.
Cal: Jaffé, *RPR* II, 153, no. 10654.
Date: Barlow, *Edward the Confessor*, 309–10; Jaffé, *RPR* II, 153, no. 10654.
Note: See Scholz, 'Canonization', 38–59; Barlow, *Edward the Confessor*, 256–85; 309–27, an appendix of correspondence concerning Edward's canonization.

168. Pope Alexander III notifying the English clergy of the canonization of Edward the Confessor. Anagni, 7 Feb. [1161]

WAD, ff. 387v–388.
Incipit: *Illius devotionis constanciam.*
Pd: Mansi, XXI, col. 871, no. III, and col. 1047, no. XVII (identical texts, with different headings); Richard of Cirencester, *Speculum Historiale*, ed. J. E. B. Major, II, RS (London, 1869), 322–3; Migne, *PL*, 200, cols. 106–107, no. xxxiv; *Monasticon* I, 308b–309, no. LV; *AASS*, January 1, 302b–303, no. II; Wilkins, *Concilia*, I, 434; *Magnum Bullarium Romanum*, ed. E. Laertes Cherubini (new edn., Luxemburg, 1727), I, 40a–b; Widmore, 183–4, no. V.
Cal: Jaffé *RPR* II, 152, no. 10653 (7160).
Note: All pd. edns. belong to the same MS. tradition, and are prob. pd.

from one another, except Richard of Cirencester, whose text contains variants, although these are not significant for the content.

169. Pope Alexander III to Roger the infirmarer, confirming to the infirmary the churches of Battersea and Wandsworth (Surr.), granted by Abbot Laurence, at the request of Abbot Laurence and Roger. Anagni, 7 Feb. [1161]

WAD, f. 507v; F, f. 200r–v; WA Mun. Bk. 3, f. 19, omitting the abbot's initial.
Incipit: *Justis petentium desideriis.*
Pd: *PUE* I, no. 85.
Cal: Taylor, *Our Lady of Batersey*, 21.
Date: Prob. issued with **167–8** and **170**.
Note: Cf. Harvey, *WA*, 411–12.

170. Pope Alexander III to Walter the sacrist, confirming the church of Sawbridgeworth (Herts.) to provide lights for the sacristy altar, at the petition both of Walter and of Abbot Laurence. Anagni, 7 Feb. [1161]

WAD, f. 382; F, f. 169v.
Incipit: *Justis petentium desideriis.*
Pd: *PUE* I, no. 86.
Date: Prob. issued on the same occasion as **167–9**.
Note: Cf. Harvey, *WA*, 409.

171. Pope Alexander III to Abbot Laurence and the convent, confirming the privileges and possessions of the abbey, and especially the cells of Great Malvern (Worcs.), Hurley (Berks.) and Sudbury (Suffolk). Sens, 6 Oct. 1163.

WAD, ff. 6v–7; F, ff. 192–193v (omitting most of the subscriptions).
Incipit: *Commisse nobis apostolice.*
Pd: *PUE* I, no. 101.
Note: Cf. the bull of Pope Adrian IV confirming these cells (**166**).

172. Pope Alexander III to Abbot Laurence and the convent, confirming the privileges and possessions of the abbey, and particularly its exemption from the jurisdiction of the bp. of London. Tusculanum, 3 Dec. 1171.

WAD, f. 7r–v; F, ff. 168v–169v, omitting all subscriptions, but giving the dating clause; T, f. 47r–v, omitting subscriptions, dating clause incomplete; WA Mun. Bk. 12, f. 1 (précis).
Incipit: *Quotiens illud a.*
Pd: *PUE* I, no. 113.
Note: This papal confirmation was evidently sought, in part, to reinforce the exemption from episcopal jurisdiction earlier granted by Pope Innocent II (**155**). The personal relationship between the abbot and the bp. of London had been good in preceding years: cf. Laurence's letter to Pope Alexander in support of Gilbert Foliot, during the

Becket dispute (*Materials for the History of Thomas Becket, arch-bishop of Canterbury*, ed. J. C. Robertson and J. B. Sheppard (7 vols., RS, 1875–83), VI, 621–2, no. DXIX, dated by the editor to 1169).

173. Pope Alexander III, granting to Abbot Laurence and his successors the right to wear mitre and ring on Sundays and other solemn festivals, during mass and in processions within the abbey, and during papal and episcopal synods. Anagni, 18 April [1160 × 1173]

WAD, f. 7v; F, f. 200.
Incipit: *Cum monasterium tibi.*
Pd: *PUE* I, no. 118.
Date: Outer limits election of Pope Alexander (Sept. 1159) and d. of
    Abbot Laurence 9/10 April 1173. The pope was at Anagni in April
    1160; possibly in April 1161, and again in April 1173 (Jaffé, *RPR* II,
    149–266).

174. Pope Alexander III to Abbot Walter and the convent, granting to Walter and his successors that, since they already have papal permission to wear mitre and ring, they may also wear the dalmatic tunicle and sandals on solemn days within the monastery and its dependencies, in processions, in papal, legatine and episcopal synods. Anagni, 13 Sept. [1175 × 1180]

WAD, f. 8; F, ff. 170v–171; T, ff. 51v–52.
Incipit: *Largitione nostri muneris.*
Pd: *Monasticon* I, 311, no. LXX.
Cal: Jaffé, *RPR* II, 299, no. 12734, *sub an.* 1176.
Date: Outside limits the election of Abbot Walter and d. of Pope
    Alexander.

175. Pope Alexander III to Abbot [Walter] granting the right to wear gloves during solemn mass on festivals. Venice, Rialto, 2 April [1177]

WAD, f. 7v; F, f. 170v.
Incipit: *Hortatur nos et.*
Pd: *PUE* I, no. 143.

176. Pope Alexander III to Abbot Walter and the convent, confirming the possessions of the abbey, its exemption from the jurisdiction of the bp. of London, and prohibiting the alienation of the churches of Oakham (Rutl.), Ashwell (Herts.), Staines (Mddx.), Aldenham and Wheathamp-stead (Herts.), with their chapels. Ferrara, 18 April 1178 [*recte* 1177]

WAM 12732 (notarial copy of 15 Feb. 1302); WAD, f. 8r–v; F, ff. 167–
    168; T, ff. 46v–47 (subscriptions omitted in the two latter); WA
    Mun. Bk. 12, f. 1v (précis); BL Additional Roll 15895, no. 9
    (extracts).
Incipit: *In eo loco.*
Pd: *PUE* I, no. 144.

Date: Holtzmann, *PUE* dates 1177. The 'eighteenth year' of Pope
   Alexander ended 19 Sept. 1177, and whereas he was at Ferrara 2
   April 1177, he was at the Lateran in April 1178 (Jaffé, *RPR* II, 304,
   322).
Note: On the churches, see Harvey, *WA*, 403–5.

177. Pope Lucius III to the abbot and convent, confirming to the
infirmary the churches of Battersea and Wandsworth (Surr.), as the late
Abbot Laurence gave them. Verona, 17 March [(1182 ×) 1185]

WAD, f. 578v; F, f. 171; T, f. 51; C, f. 50; WA Mun Bk 3, f. 29, ending at
   omnino hominum, but giving dating clause.
Incipit: *Justis petencium desideriis*.
Pd: *PUE* I, no. 232; Flete, 95.
Cal: Taylor, *Our Lady of Batersey*, 21.
Date: Pope Lucius' only known visit to Verona in March, in 1185 (Jaffé,
   RPR, II, 486).

178. Pope Clement III to the abbot and convent, permitting them to
appropriate the tithes of the churches of which they were the patrons,
when vacancies occurred, for the support of the brethren, their guests,
and the poor, provided that vicarages were ordained and synodals paid.
Lateran, 5 July 1189.

F, f. 173v.
Incipit: *Fervor religionis et*.
Pd: *PUE* I, no. 261.
Note: See Harvey, *WA*, 48, 52, on the difficulties subsequently
   experienced by the abbey in securing extensive tithe income.

179. Bull of Pope Clement III, addressed to Abbot Walter and the
convent, confirming the abbey's possessions, and any which it might
subsequently acquire, and especially the churches of Oakham (Rutl.),
Ashwell (Herts.), Staines (Mddx.), Aldenham and Wheathampstead
(Herts.), with their appurtenances; prohibiting any bp. or abp. from
saying mass in St Margaret's, Westminster, or holding a synod there;
exempting the abbey from the bp. of London, and confirming all pensions
from churches which the abbey held before the [Third] Lateran Council.
Lateran, 20 July 1189.

WAM 1508; WAM 12754 (notarial copy of 15 Feb. 1302; only subscription that of the pope, but date given); WAM 12755 (copy of early
   14C); WAD, ff. 9v–10; F, ff. 171v–173 (omitting subscriptions, apart
   from that of the pope); T, f. 45r–v; LN, f. cxxviij *verso*; WA Mun.
   Bk. 12, f. 6, and f. 6r–v (both précis); BL Additional Roll 15895,
   no. 11.
Incipit: *Quotiens illud a*.
Pd: *PUE* I, no. 262.
Note: Prob. the knowledge that the chapter of St Paul's was lodging a
   complaint prompted a rival Westminster delegation to the *curia* to

counter-petition for exemption from episcopal control, and simultaneously request confirmation of various properties.

180. Pope Celestine III to Abbot William and the convent, confirming to the abbot and his successors the right to wear mitre and ring; gloves, dalmatic tunicle and sandals, together with priestly vestments of benediction, to be worn on all solemn days within the abbey and its dependencies; in processions in the abbey; in papal and legatine councils, and in episcopal synods. Rome, St Peter's, 13 Jan. 1192.

WAD, f. 12r–v; F, f. 175r–v; T, f. 52 (both the latter end at *paginum*, but give dating clause).
Incipit: *Largitione nostris muneris.*
Pd: *PUE* I, no. 301.

181. Pope Celestine III to the abbot, exempting the abbey from any ecclesiastical jurisdiction other than his own; prohibiting anyone from violently entering the church or despoiling its goods, and ordering the restitution of goods wrongfully taken. Rome, St Peter's, 13 Jan. 1192.

WAD, f. 12v; F, ff. 175v–176.
Incipit: *Ea que sunt.*
Pd: *PUE* I, no. 302 (abridged common form in final clauses).
Note: A second exemption obtained in the aftermath of the vacancy in the abbacy, and the attempted intrusion of Henry Longchamps (Ric. of Devizes, 39; Diceto II, 100), but worded so as to emphasize the abbey's exempt status, rather than those shortcomings which had been a pretext for the exercise of the diocesan's authority.

182. Pope Celestine III to the abbot and convent, excommunicating those who have stolen the goods of the abbey, or otherwise harmed it; granting leave to appeal against bps., but ordering the chapter to maintain good discipline, in order to avoid giving pretext for intrusion. Rome, St Peter's, 13 Jan. 1192.

WAD, f. 12; F, ff. 174v–175.
Incipit: *Licet ex iniuncto.*
Pd: *PUE* I, no. 300.
Note: Following the d. of Abbot Walter in Sept. 1190, the monks of Westminster came under heavy pressure from the justiciar, William Longchamps, to allow his brother Henry, a monk of Caen, to take up residence in the abbey, and to give a written and sealed undertaking that in due course they would elect him abbot. In Oct. 1191, the political movement against Longchamps permitted the monks to disregard their enforced promise, and instead to elect their prior, William Postard, as abbot (Ric. of Devizes, 25, 39, 54; Diceto I, 100–1). It is likely that this recent vacancy had both occasioned material loss to the abbey, and also prompted renewed jurisdictional claims on behalf of the bp. of London. Once again, episcopal petition was evidently countered by successful monastic counter-petition.

183. Pope Innocent III to the abbot and convent, confirming the liberties and immunities, and the ancient and reasonable customs of their church. Lateran, 23 April 1199.

WAD, f. 13; F, f. 176.
Incipit: *Cum a nobis*.
Pd: *Cal. Letters Innocent III*, 203, no. 104 (excluding common form), from WAD, with variants from F.
Cal: *Cal. Letters Innocent III*, 19, no. 104.
Note: Another bull of Innocent III, confirming to the abbot and convent all the privileges of the church and customs hitherto observed, is now known only from a memorandum dated 8 Jan., pontifical year unspecified (WA Mun. Bk. 12, ff. 7v, 15v, 19; cal. *Cal. Letters Innocent III*, 188–9, no. 1151).

184. Pope Innocent III to all English prelates, ordering that the privileges and indulgences granted to the abbey, by reason of its special relationship with the apostolic see, are to be observed. Lateran, 23 April 1199.

WAD, f. 13; F, ff. 200v–201.
Incipit: *Benignitas sedis apostolice*.
Pd: *Cal. Letters Innocent III*, 203, no. 105 (omitting common form of initial protocol).
Cal: *Cal. Letters Innocent III*, 19, no. 105.
Note: There survives a memorandum of a similar bull, dated 8 Jan., pontifical year unspecified, (WA Mun. Bk. 12, f. 15v; cal. *Cal. Letters Innocent III*, 189, no. 1153, as prob. identical with bull here above, but different dates show it must be distinct).

185. Pope Innocent III to the abbot and convent of Westminster. The pope has heard that benefices intended for the use of the chapter, and for the poor, have occasionally been assigned, at the instance of certain magnates, to their clerks. The pope orders that the chapter is not to divert to other uses the church of Sawbridgeworth (Herts.), assigned to the sacristy, or any other churches, assigned to hospitality or other pious uses. Lateran, 24 April 1199.

WAD, f. 380; F, f. 286; WA Mun. Bk. 12, f. 15v (memorandum only).
Incipit: *Ad audienciam apostolatus*.
Pd: *Monasticon* I, 312a, no. LXXIII.
Cal: *Cal. Letters Innocent III*, 19, no. 106; A. Potthast, *Regesta Pontificum Romanorum inde ab a. post Christum Natum MCXCVIII ad a. MCCCIV* (2 vols., Berlin, 1874–5), I, 64, no. 670.
Note: Cf. Harvey, *WA*, 388, 409; the confirmation by Pope Alexander III of the church to the sacristy (**170**); Abbot Laurence's charter to his clerk Maurice (**284**), and the assignment on the abbey's pension from this church for the anniversary of his parents (**283**). The bull was prob. issued, however, not in response to Laurence's earlier transactions, but to an appeal by the sacrist, and poss. others, against the methods used by Abbot William Postard to clear the obligations, perhaps personal as well as financial, arising from the crisis of 1190–

1191 (cf. **186**). There also survive memoranda of another bull, issued to the abbot and convent on 8 Jan., pontifical year unspecified, ordering them not to divert to other uses churches assigned to hospitality or to the infirmary (WA Mun. Bk. 12, ff. 9v, 14, 15, 15v: cal. *Cal. Letters Innocent III*, 189, no. 1152).

186. Pope Innocent III to the abbot, prohibiting the abbot from alienating the churches or other possessions pertaining to the whole community, without the consent of the chapter, or the greater and wiser part. Lateran, 30 April 1199.

WAD, f. 13; F, f. 176r–v; T, f. 50; C, f. 28 (extracts only); WA Mun. Bk. 12, ff. 1, 15v (memoranda).
Incipit: *Tua potissimum ad.*
Pd: *Cal. Letters Innocent III*, 203, no. 113 (from WAD, with selected variants from F and T): full text from *Tua potissimum*; omitting common form of initial protocol. Flete, 49–50 (extracts only, as in C).
Cal: *Cal. Letters Innocent III*, 20, no. 113.
Note: The unnamed abbot was William Postard, who, within a period of seven years, succeeded in discharging the abbey of a debt of 1,500 marks of silver, previously due for his 'confirmation' (Flete, 98), prob. a payment to the crown for free choice of abbot (Harvey, *WA*, 64n.). Financial solvency was perhaps achieved by an arbitrary rationalization of Westminster's assets but there was already a long-upheld papal view that monastic property was inalienable (H. G. Richardson, 'The Coronation in Medieval England', *Traditio* 16 (1960), 151–3). On the growing crisis in the abbey's finances at this period, see Harvey, *WA*, 84–6.

187.* The papal legate, Peter [Pierleoni], to Abbot Herbert and the convent: in commemoration of King Edward and Queen Matilda, who are buried in the abbey, he has granted an indulgence of forty days to those who visit the abbey on the feast of Saints Peter and Paul [29 June] or within the octave; and also on the feast of St Peter in Chains [1 Aug.]. [*post* 12 June × *ante* 2 Oct. 1121]

WAD, f. 387r–v.
Pd: *PUE* I, no. 13.
Date: Limits of the legate's visit to England (*Hist. Novorum*, 294–7).
Note: Authenticity questioned (*PUE* I, 237, no. 13; *Councils and Synods* I, pt. ii, 724; Brett, *English Church* 41, n. 4). If not an outright fabrication, interpolation may be strongly suspected in the clause relating to King Edward and Queen Matilda. The cult of St Peter was fostered at Westminster from the late 11C, perhaps as a counter-move against the growing cult of Edward the Confessor (Scholz, 'Sulcard of Westminster', 72; idem, 'Canonization', 40), and St Peter's Chains remained one of the principal feasts at the abbey throughout the Middle Ages (Scholz, 'Sulcard of Westminster', 73 and n. 58, 74). The cathedral of London had been dedicated

to St Paul since the episcopate of Bp. Mellitus, early in the 7C (Brooke & Keir, 16), and the forged legatine documents associating his cult with Westminster were perhaps intended to attract devotees from the episcopal seat. Westminster's energetic promotion of successive cults was perhaps the stimulus which prompted that of St Erconwald at St Paul's (Scholz, 'Canonization', 40–1).

188.* The papal legate, Peter [Pierleoni], to Abbot Herbert and his successors, and to the convent, confirming the abbey in all its possessions, present and to come; granting an indulgence of forty days to those who come to render their devotions to Saints Peter and Paul; and permitting the participation of five, or three, deacons, and the same number of subdeacons, at mass, or in processions, on seven especially solemn festivals. Anathema on anyone disturbing the abbey or its possessions. London [*post* 12 June × *ante* 2 Oct.] 1121.

WAD, f. 387.
Pd: *PUE* I, no. 12.
Date: The legate was forbidden to travel during his visit (Eadmer, *Historia Novorum*, 294–7).
Note: Authenticity queried (*PUE* I, 234–5; *Councils and Synods* I, pt. ii, 724; Brett, *English Church*, 41, n. 4).

189. The papal legate, John [of Crema]: at the request of Abbot Herbert and the convent for some benefaction, and since King Edward and Queen Matilda are buried in the abbey, he grants to all the faithful visiting the abbey on the feast of Saints Peter and Paul, or within the octave, an indulgence of forty days. [? Westminster (March × ? 8 Sept.) 1125]

WAD, f. 389v.
Date: John of Crema arrived in England by 29 March 1125, travelled throughout England and into Scotland, then on 8 Sept. held a legatine council at Westminster, shortly after which he left England (*Councils and Synods* I, pt. ii, 731–3).

190. The papal legate, Henry [of Pisa], to Hilary, bp. of Chichester, Robert [de Chesney], bp. of Lincoln, and Nigel, bp. of Ely: at the request of Abbot Laurence, he urges them to attend the celebrations at Westminster, following on the pope's decree that 'the holy father blessed Edward' is to be numbered among the saints. [1 Feb. 1161 × *ante* 13 Oct. 1163]

WAD, f. 388r–v.
Cal: Noted by Scholz, 'Canonization', 54 and n. 75.
Date: Issued between the publication of Pope Alexander III's bulls concerning the canonization of King Edward (**167–8**) and the Translation. Henry of Pisa was legate in France, 1160–1162, and Abbot Laurence visited him in Paris with evidence in support of the canonization (Barlow, *Edward the Confessor*, 311 and n. 1). The bps. of Chichester and Lincoln visited Normandy in the spring of 1162, when the cardinal was there (Eyton, *Itinerary*, 56).

Note: Cardinal Henry, and his associate, Cardinal Otto, had written urging the pope to accept the evidence in support of the canonization which Abbot Laurence had brought to them in Paris (Barlow, *Edward the Confessor*, 311–2). The onset of the Becket dispute at the Council of Westminster, a few days before the Translation, perhaps curtailed attendance at the ceremony, despite its 'official' character, more than later Westminster writers implied (Scholz, 'Canonization', 53–4, and n. 74).

191. The papal legate, John [of Salerno], to the abbot and convent, granting, in view of the abbey's special relationship with the Roman see, an indulgence for the solemn chanting of the angelic hymn *Gloria in Excelsis Deo* on the feast of the Purification of the Blessed Virgin (2 Feb.), if it falls after Septuagesima; on the feast of the Annunciation (25 March), and on the feast of St Benedict (21 March). [(London, Aug.) 1201]

WAM 12733; WAD, f. 11.

Date: Cardinal John [of Salerno] was in England in 1201, and in London in Aug. of that year (*Councils and Synods* I, ii, 1074–5).

Note: While all three feasts were major ones, the Purification might fall within Septuagesima (the pre-Lenten period) and the other two would (almost) invariably fall within Lent. The *Gloria* was not sung between Septuagesima Sunday and the night of Holy Saturday (*The Monastic Constitutions of Lanfranc*, transl. and ed. D. Knowles (1951), 17, but see also 30). On the angelic origin of this hymn, see Luke 2:13–14.

192. Proclamation by the papal legate, John [of Salerno] of an indulgence of forty days to those visiting the abbey on the feast of St Peter [in Chains] (1 Aug.). [(London, Aug.), 1201]

WAD, f. 390.

Date: As for **191**.

Note: The feast is prob. that of St Peter in Chains as in an earlier indulgence of doubtful authenticity ascribed to the legate Peter Pierleoni (**187**).

193. Grant by the papal legate, Nicholas [de Romanis], of an indulgence of twenty days to all those visiting the abbey on the feasts of St Peter; of Blessed King Edward, and of the Holy Relics. No abbot of Westminster, or anyone else of that church, may presume to claim a customary right in the offerings made on the feast of Saints Peter and Paul, or of St Peter in Chains, nor divert these offerings to any use other than that of the sacrist, who must faithfully administer these funds. Anyone infringing this ordinance will be excommunicated. Westminster, 11 Oct. 1213.

WAD, f. 390r–v.

Date: Nicholas de Romanis, cardinal bp. of Tusculum, was in England from *c.* Michaelmas (29 Sept.) 1213, and visited both Westminster and London (Roger of Wendover, *Flores Historiarum*, ed. H. G.

Hewlett (RS 1887), II, 93–4). He was in London 30 Sept.–2 Oct., and at Wallingford about the beginning of Nov. 1213 (*Councils and Synods*, II, i, 21). See also Angelo Mercati, 'La prima Relazione de Cardinale Nicolò de Romanis sulla sua Legazione in Inghilterra (1213)', in *Essays presented to R. L. Poole*, ed. H. W. C. Davis (1927), 274–89.

Note: Neither the feast of the Translation of St Edward (13 Oct.) nor that of his Deposition (5 Jan.), attracted popular support. The feast of the Relics (16 July) and that of St Peter in Chains (1 Aug.) were rather more successful, but not that of Saints Peter and Paul (29 June). Accounts of offerings at the major feasts, drawn up by the sacrist, are known only from the 14C (Harvey, *WA*, 43–5 and notes). In 1213, the legate investigated Abbot Ralph Arundel's alienation of the abbey's resources, and consequently deposed him in Jan. 1214 (Harvey, *WA*, 83–4).

194. Report by the papal judges-delegate, the prior of St Saviour, Bermondsey, and Nicholas, archdeacon of London, of the settlement between Geoffrey of Bedford, priest, and Geoffrey de Turre, clerk, over St Margaret's, Eastcheap (London). Geoffrey of Bedford resigned his right in the church, and the judges, on the presentation of the abbot and convent of Westminster, instituted Geoffrey de Turre as perpetual vicar. For the next three years, all offerings would be administered by Geoffrey de Turre, who would pay an annual pension of 5s. to the monks of Westminster, rendering it to the chamberlain in quarterly instalments, and 2s. annually to Geoffrey of Bedford. Within three years, the abbot and convent would provide Geoffrey of Bedford with a vicarage of equivalent value, but if none fell vacant, they would supply him with suitable food and clothing until they could assign one to him. [*c.* 11 March, 1184]

WAD, ff. 477v–478.

Date: The pensions were calculated from mid-Lent, i.e. the fourth Sunday in Lent, following the consecration of Walter of Coutances as bp. of Lincoln. This occurred 3 July 1183 (*Fasti* III. 2).

Note: The prior of Bermondsey is prob. Bertram, 1178–1184, but possibly Constantine, ?1184–?1186 (*Heads*, 115). The abbot of Westminster, at the time of the agreement, was Walter (*Heads*, 77).

195. Mandate of Abp. Theobald to Robert [de Chesney], bp. of Lincoln. The monks of Westminster have complained that A[lice] de Condet has violently withheld a rent pertaining to their clothing revenues; that John de Stuteville (Stutehilla) has seized their land of Uppingham (Rutl.), and Robert Foliot their manor of Sulby (Northants.). The abp. has written to these three as well as to Bp. Robert, whom he orders to bring severe ecclesiastical censure to bear on them. [Dec. 1148 × early 1150]

WAD, f. 649v.
Pd: Saltman, *Theobald*, 507–8, no. 277.
Date: Theobald not yet legate (cf. *Fasti* II, 4). Robert de Chesney

elected bp. of Lincoln, 13 Dec. 1148; consecrated at Canterbury, 19 Dec. (*Fasti* III, 2). The barony of Chipping Warden was 'conceded' to Robert Foliot by Henry II, 1154 × 1163 (F. M. Stenton, *The First Century of English Feudalism, 1066–1166* (2nd edn., 1961), p. 264, no. 8), but Robert perhaps held it earlier (cf. Sanders, 33).

Note: It was recorded in 1166 that the abbot held of Robert Foliot's barony of Chipping Warden one knight's fee of old enfeoffment (*Liber Niger Scaccarii*, 2313; *RBE*, 331). Foliot himself had difficulty in securing Sulby against Robert de Mowbray (*Charters of the Honour of Mowbray*, ed. D. E. Greenway (1972), no. 283). The abp.'s mandate prompted Foliot to issue a charter of confirmation (**479**). On the lands of Alice de Condet, see *The Registrum Antiquissimum of the Cathedral Church of Lincoln*, I, ed. C. W. Foster (Lincoln Rec. Soc., 1931), 282–90. On John de Stuteville, see *Early Yorkshire Charters*, IX, ed. C. T. Clay (Yorks. Archaeological Record Soc., Record Series, Extra Series VII), 23–27.

196. Notification by Abp. Theobald, papal legate, to his French and English men of Harrow, that he has confirmed to Edmund the physician, son of Osmar, the land which his father held in the abp.'s manor of Harrow (Mddx.) comprising 1½ hides, rendering 5s. annually. Witnesses. Lambeth [1150 × *ante* 28 Sept. 1152]

WAD, ff. 501v–502.
Pd: Saltman, *Theobald*, 345–6, no. 124.
Date: After Theobald appointed legate, early 1150 (*Fasti* II, 4). Attested by Richard de Belmeis [II], without a title, but presumably in his capacity as archdeacon of Middlesex (*Fasti* I, 15). He was elected bp. of London in the spring of 1152, and consecrated 28 Sept. (ibid., 2).
Note: This document was acquired by the abbey when Matilda [de Paris], daughter of Simon Fitz Osmar, granted the land to the abbey (**460–61**).

197. Confirmation by Abp. Theobald, papal legate, of King Stephen's quitclaims of geld on the manors of Westminster (6½ hides), and Battersea (Surr.) (44 hides), the remaining 28 hides to geld, and of his quitclaim of a virgate of land belonging to the church of Hanwell (Mddx.), according to the king's charters, which the abp. has inspected. [*c.* 1151 × 1154]

BL Campbell Charter XVI.1. (original); WAD, ff. 56v–57, and 162 (replacing concluding anathema by *valete*).
Pd: Saltman, *Theobald*, 505–6, no. 275; G. F. Warner and H. G. Ellis, *Facsimiles of Royal and other Charters in the British Museum* (1903), no. 28, with facsimile on plate XVIII facing; *Monasticon* I, 309, no. LVI.
Cal: Browning and Kirk, 236.
Date: Limits: Theobald's appointment as legate (*Fasti* II, 4) and d. of Stephen, whose charters concerning Battersea and Hanwell may be dated 1151 × 1152.
Note: Stephen's grants are **118–21**, all purportedly dating from 1150–52,

but only **118** is genuine. Theobald's attestation appears on all of them. His charter of confirmation would strengthen Westminster's title, in view both of doubts raised by these texts, and of the political uncertainty in the latter part of the reign. Given the variation in the conclusion of the WAD texts, Chaplais argued that the abbey received two charters on this subject from the abp. (Chaplais, 'Original Charters', 97, n. 2). The abp.'s confirmation should be compared particularly with **121**, which he evidently accepted as genuine.

198. Notification by Abp. Theobald, papal legate, of his judgement in the prolonged dispute between William of Ockendon and Abbot Gervase, concerning the church of Ockendon (Essex), which William relinquished to the abbey. Henceforth Gervase and his successors may appoint parsons to that church, saving the dignity of the diocesan bp. [1150 × *c*. 1157]

WAM LI; WAD, f. 506.
Pd: Saltman, *Theobald*, 507, no. 276; Flete, 88–9 (extracts).
Cal: *S.R.*, S.53.
Date: Issued between Theobald's appointment as legate and the deposition of Gervase.
Note: Ockendon was a demesne manor in 1086, but farmed from Herbert's abbacy onwards (Harvey, *WA*, 343), although the abbey had presumably retained the advowson.

199. Mandate of Abp. Theobald, papal legate, to Geoffrey Bataille and Richard de Fracheville, following the complaint by Abbot Gervase and the convent of their violent trespass on the manor of Kelvedon (Essex), held by the abbey TRE. Theobald orders them to relinquish that land to Westminster within fifteen days, under pain of anathema. [1150 × *c*. 1157]

WAD, f. 650.
Pd: Saltman, *Theobald*, 508–9, no. 278; *Gilbert Crispin*, 47 (abridged).
Date: Between Theobald's appointment as legate, and the deposition of Gervase.
Note: Cf. Harvey, *WA*, 342. The intrusion was prob. facilitated by the political unrest in Stephen's reign.

200. Notification by Abp. Theobald, papal legate, of his grant of an indulgence of forty days, together with participation in the prayers and spiritual benefits of the church of Canterbury, to those who visit the abbey at Christmas, Easter, Ascension, Pentecost, on the feast of the Holy Relics, and on all feasts of St Peter. [1150 × 1161]

WAD, f. 390v.
Pd: Saltman, *Theobald*, 509, no. 279.
Date: After Theobald was appointed legate. He d. 18 April 1161 (*Fasti* II, 4).

201. Notification by Richard [of Dover], abp. of Canterbury and papal legate, to his men of Harrow, both French and English, that he has confirmed to Simon s. of Osmar the land which his father held in the abp.'s manor of Harrow, comprising 1½ hides, as his father proved his title to it. Witnesses. [May 1177 × Sept. 1181]

WAD, f. 502.
Pd: *EEA* II, no. 69.
Date: Attested by William [of Northolt], archdeacon of Gloucester, who acquired that office 1177/8, presumably *post* 15 May 1177 (*Fasti* II, 107). The abp.'s legatine commission lapsed 30 Aug. 1181 (ibid., 4).
Note: Cf. Abp. Theobald's confirmation of this land to Osmar's son Edmund (**196**).

202. Notification by Richard [of Dover], abp. of Canterbury, to his French and English men of Harrow, that he has confirmed to Matilda, daughter of Simon s. of Osmar, her father's land which he held in the abp.'s manor of Harrow (Mddx.), comprising 1½ hides. Matilda and her heirs after her may hold this land freely, as the father of her father Simon proved his claim to it. Witnesses. [1182 × *ante* May 1183]

WAD, f. 502.
Pd: *EEA* II, no. 70.
Date: The attestation of Peter of Blois as archdeacon [of Bath] indicates a date no earlier than 1182 (*EEA* II, no. 70n.), while that of the abp.'s chaplain, Moses, is earlier than Jan. 1183, when he became prior of Coventry (*Heads*, 41).

203. Notification by R[ichard de Belmeis I], bp. of London, that he grants that the convent may hold the church of Sawbridgeworth (Herts.), with tithes and all other appurtenances, since H I gave it to them with his consent and advice, and as he, R[ichard] caused them to receive seisin by Roger the archdeacon. [*post* 25 Nov. 1120 × *ante* 16 Jan. 1127]

WAM 8588; F, f. 287.
Pd: *Formulare*, preface xix.
Date: H I's grant of the church of Sawbridgeworth, which formerly pertained to the honour of Otwel Fitz Count, d. 25 Nov. 1120 (Orderic VI, 304), is **86**. The bp. d. 16 Jan. 1127 (*Fasti* I, 1), and was predeceased by Roger Fitz Robert, archdeacon of Mddx., whose successor was installed 1121 × Jan. 1127 (ibid., 15).

204. Notification by Richard [de Belmeis II], bp. of London, of his grant of an indulgence of forty days, and of all benefits and prayers of the [cathedral] church, to those who visit the tomb of Edward, king of the English and most glorious confessor, canonized by Pope Alexander [III], on the feasts of the Deposition (5 Jan.) and Translation (13 Oct.), and from their vigils throughout their quindenes. [*post* 7 Feb. 1161 × *ante* 4 May 1162]

WAD, f. 393.
Date: Outside limits, bulls of canonization (**167–8**) and the bp.'s d. (*Fasti* I, 2).

Note: Clearly issued in anticipation of the Translation which, after careful planning, was postponed because of the king's absence abroad (Barlow, *Edward the Confessor*, 281).

205. Notification by Gilbert [Foliot], bp. of London, that, following a dispute between himself and the abbot and convent, concerning jurisdiction over the cell of Kilburn (Mddx.), he confirms to the abbot and his successors jurisdiction over that cell in spiritualities, rendering it permanently exempt from the jurisdiction of the bp. of London. The abbot and convent are empowered to administer the cell personally, and through proctors. [1163 × 1187]

WAD, ff. 636v–637; F, f. 239r–v; T, f. 41v.
Pd: *L. and C. Foliot*, no. 463; *Monasticon* III, 426–7, no. 3.
Date: Morey and Brooke comment: 'The nature of the case and the formulas suggest an early date, and it is not impossible that this is an act of Gilbert the Universal (1128–34)' (*L. and C. Gilbert Foliot*, no. 463n.).
Note: In 1231, a renewed agreement was made between Bp. Roger Niger and Abbot Richard of Barking (*Monasticon* III, 428, no. IX).

206. Confirmation by G[ilbert Foliot], bp. of London, of the foundation by Ralph Brito of St Laurence's hospital in *Bordwadestone* (Boston House in Brentford, Mddx.), for thirteen sick people, with church and cemetery attached, and endowment of rents in various places, for the salvation of King Henry II and his children; of his patron, Richard de Lucy, and of himself, his wife and children. The consent has been obtained of William of Northolt, parson of St Mary's, Hanwell (Mddx.), within the boundaries of which parish lies *Bordwadestone*. The consent has also been obtained of Abbot Walter and the convent, and the rights of the parish church are defined. [1176 × 1177/8]

WAD, f. 131r–v.
Pd: *L. and C. Foliot*, no. 464.
Date: Richard de Lucy appears to be alive; he d. 1179 (Howden, *Chronica*, II, 190). William of Northolt became archdeacon of Gloucester 1177/8, prob. *post* May 1177 (*Fasti* II, 107). Of those who attest as canons of St Paul's, Richard of Stortford attained this dignity in 1176, and Gilbert Foliot II in 1175 × 1179 (*Fasti* I, 51, 66). The unnamed abbot of Stratford [Langthorne] who attests, is prob. Ernald, occurs *c.* 1176 × 1181 (*Heads*, 144).
Note: The abbot and convent held the advowson of Hanwell at this period (cf. **210**). On the prob. identification of *Bordwadestone*, cf. *PN Mddx.*, 32.

207. Notification by G[ilbert Foliot], bp. of London, of his verdict, as papal judge-delegate, in the dispute between Abbot Walter and R[anulph] the clerk of Feering, alleged to have become a monk of Missenden (Bucks.), unjustly detaining the church of Feering (Essex).

Gilbert restored the church to the abbot, and at his request, bestowed it on the abbot's clerk, Mr Maurice. Witnesses. [*c.* 1176 × 1180]

WAM 1045; WAD, ff. 262v–263; F, f. 245r–v (no witnesses); WA Mun. Bk. 3, f. 28.
Pd: *L. and C. Foliot*, no. 465.
Date: Attestation of Mr Ralph de Alta Ripa, without a title (*Fasti* I, 19).

208. A second, more detailed notification of G[ilbert Foliot], bp. of London, of his verdict as papal judge-delegate in the dispute between Abbot Walter and Ranulph the clerk of Feering, over the church of Feering (Essex). Ranulph is identified as a brother of the late Pope Adrian IV. His son N. guaranteed his father's promise, and, lest he or his father should renege, pledged as surety the whole fee which he held of the abbot of St Albans. Witnesses. [*c.* 1176 × 1180]

WAM 1044; WAD, f. 262v; WA Mun. Bk. 3, ff. 27–28, omitting attestation of Robert de Bureswelle; also omitting *Johanne. Clerico* immediately follows *Agillun*.
Pd: *L. and C. Foliot*, no. 466; *NPS Facsimiles*, plate 986 (facsimile) and transcript (from WAM).
Date: Attestations identical to **207**; prob. the result of cautious after-thought, on the same occasion.

209. Notification by Gilbert [Foliot], bp. of London, of his verdict as papal judge-delegate in the dispute between Abbot Walter and the convent, and Mr Alexander, vice-archdeacon of Stow and canon of Lincoln, and Henry and Haket the clerks, over the churches of Doddington and Thorpe-on-the-Hill (Lincs.). Alexander, Henry and Haket renounced their claim to these churches, to which Bp. Gilbert, on the presentation of the abbot and convent, instituted Mr Nicholas the clerk. Nicholas, with the assent of the abbot and convent, granted half of the churches to Alexander, and to Robert Code, and the other half to Haket the clerk, for life, to be held of him for annual pensions. If Alexander and Robert relinquished [their share in] the churches, this would accrue to Haket, and *vice versa*, saving to Nicholas the sum total of the pensions, but if Nicholas d., or entered a religious order, the pensions would become due to the abbot and convent, or their assign. [1175 × *ante* 18 Feb. 1187]

WAD, f. 501r–v.
Pd: *L. and C. Foliot*, no. 467.
Date: Terms of office of Bp. Gilbert and Abbot Walter. Mr Alexander was promoted to archdeacon *c.* 1187, but prob. *post* 29 March (*Fasti* III, 45, 110), i.e. after the d. of Gilbert Foliot.
Note: Alexander alone held a perpetual vicarage in both churches when these were confirmed to Mr Nicholas by Hugh of Avallon, bp. of Lincoln, *c.* 1190 × *c.* March 1195 (**224**).

210. Notification by Gilbert [Foliot], bp. of London, that on the presentation of Abbot Walter and the convent, he has instituted Henry of

Bayeux as parson of Greenford and Hanwell (Mddx.). Witnesses
[*c.* 1183 × *c.* 1186]

WAD, f. 131; F, ff. 245v–246 (no witnesses).
Pd: *L. and C. Foliot*, no. 468.
Date: Before the d. of Bp. Gilbert, since Mr Walter of Witney is not
styled canon (*Fasti* I, 95–6). After appointment of Gilbert Foliot II as
archdeacon of Mddx. (ibid., 16), and Robert Foliot as a canon (ibid.,
86).

211. Confirmation by Gilbert [Foliot], bp. of London, to the convent, of
the following churches, all with their appurtenant pensions: St Martin,
Charing [i.e. St Martin in the Fields]; St Clement [Danes], near the
Temple; St Dunstan [in the West]; St Brigid [Bride]; St Martin, Ludgate;
St Alban [Wood Street]; St Agnes [within Aldersgate]; St Clement,
Candlewick Street; St James in the Vintry [Garlickhithe]; St Laurence
[Pountney] beside [London] Bridge; St Matthew [Friday Street], with the
appurtenant land adjacent to it; St Margaret [New Fish Street], beside the
Bridge; half of the church of St Magnus the Martyr [all the foregoing in or
near London]; Ockendon, Kelvedon, Feering (Essex); Sawbridgeworth
(Herts.), pertaining to the sacristy; Hendon (Mddx.); the chapel of Little
Tey, with a pension; and the tithes of [White] Roding (Essex), pertaining
to the precentor. Witnesses. [*c.* 1180 × *ante* 18 Feb. 1187]

WAD, f. 627; F, ff. 253v–254; T, f. 40r–v (attestations omitted from F and
T, but both supply *medietatem* (omitted WAD) before the church of
St Magnus the Martyr).
Pd: *L. and C. Foliot*, no. 462.
Date: Bp. Gilbert d. 18 Feb. 1187 (*Fasti* I, 2). Attestations, especially of
Gilbert Banastre and Roger of Worcester, suggest no earlier than
c. 1180 (ibid., 28, 43). Cf. *L. & C. Foliot*: 1163 × *c.* 1181; prob.
early.
Note: The confirmation by Pope Adrian IV of the abbey's churches,
dated 1 June 1157 (**166**) does not include those within the city of
London, so that Bp. Gilbert Foliot's confirmation is the first docu-
ment to provide a definitive list of these. See also Oxley, 'Medieval
Church Dedications', 117–25. Bp. Richard [Fitz Nigel]'s confirmation of these churches is **212**. At Michaelmas 1218, in a suit of darrein
presentment, the advowson of Kelvedon was claimed by Baldwin
Fillol, but awarded to the abbot, since the previous parson, Nigel of
Kelvedon, had been presented by Abbot Laurence (WAM 1007).

212. Confirmation by Richard [Fitz Nigel], bp. of London, to the
convent of Westminster, of their churches (unspecified) in his diocese, as
contained in an authentic charter of his predecessor, Bp. Gilbert [Foliot].
Witnesses [31 Dec. 1189 × *ante* Dec. 1196]

WAD, f. 627.
Date: Bp. Richard was consecrated 31 Dec. 1189 (*Fasti* I, 2). Attested by
Richard of Finchley, Alan the chaplain and John de Garland without
their later title of canon (ibid., 60, 62, 66).

Note: Bp. Gilbert's charter, listing the churches, is **211**.

213. Confirmation by Richard [Fitz Nigel], bp. of London, to the convent, of those churches previously confirmed by Bp. Gilbert [Foliot]. The churches and their pensions are identical with the list in Gilbert's confirmation. Witnesses. [31 Dec. 1189 × *ante* 30 Dec. 1196]

WAD, f. 627r–v.
Date: Outside limits as for Richard's generally-worded confirmation (**212**), but prob. issued shortly after that document, in order to obtain a detailed confirmation.
Note: The only marked amendment to Gilbert's list is a repetition of St Matthew's [Friday Street], after Ockendon, since the scribe had previously omitted to mention the appurtenant land and its rent.

214. Notification by Richard [Fitz Nigel], bp. of London, of his grant of the church of South Benfleet (Essex) to the convent, to augment the pittancer's office. The monks assigned to the chaplain of that church an annual vicarage, comprising the tithes due from four named individuals (as in **215**); the offerings of the altar; and the lesser tithes, with the assent of Ivo [of Cornwall], archdeacon of Derby, parson of the church. The chaplain and his successors would answer for all obligations due from that church to the bp. or his officials. Witnesses. [*c.* (1190 ×) 1192]

WAD, f. 617v; F, f. 254v; T, f. 40v (sealing clause and attestations omitted in both the latter); WA Mun. Bk. 3, f. 23 (only the first five witnesses).
Pd: *Monasticon* I, 309, no. LIX, from F.
Date: Ivo was archdeacon of Derby in 1191, and prob. 1190–1192 (*Councils & Synods* I, pt. ii, 1006, n. 1); on his surname, cf. **215**. Attestation of Peter de Waltham as archdeacon of London: appointed 1190 × 1192; in office in March 1194 × 1195 (*Fasti* I, 9–10); and of William of Ely, Roger the chaplain and John Witing without titles, whereas the first two became canons *c.* 1192 and Witing *c.* 1190 × 1192 (ibid., 35, 68, 75).

215. Notification by Richard [Fitz Nigel], bp. of London, to all throughout his bishopric, that, on the presentation of the convent of Westminster, and with the assent of Ivo of Cornwall, parson of the church of South Benfleet (Essex), he has admitted John of Thrapston, chaplain, to the perpetual vicarage of that church. John would receive the lesser tithes and the offerings of the altar, with the tithes due from four named persons (as in **214**), and would answer for all obligations due from that church to the bp. Witnesses. [Jan. 1190 × 1192]

WAD, f. 603v.
Date: Attestation of Peter of Waltham as archdeacon of London, and of William of Ely and Richard of Windsor without their later title of canon (*Fasti* I, 9–10, 35, 68). Evidently issued shortly after **214**.

216. Confirmation by Richard [Fitz Nigel], bp. of London, to the convent of Westminster, on account of the poverty of their sacristy, of a pension of £2 annually, payable from the church of Staines (Mddx.) by William of Stortford, clerk, to provide for the improved lighting of the abbey church. Witnesses. [1192 × *ante* 30 Dec. 1196]

WAM 16738; WAD, f. 374.

Date: Attestations of Alard of Burnham and William of Ely as canons, and Alan as chaplain, but all without the further titles they acquired by 30 Dec. 1196 (*Fasti* I, 10, 32, 35, 62). In 1177, Pope Alexander III had prohibited the alienation of the church of Staines (**176**).

217. Notification by Richard [Fitz Nigel], bp. of London, that, at the petition of Abbot William Postard and the convent, he has established a pension of two marks (£1. 6*s.* 8*d.*), payable annually by the rector of the church of Sunbury (Mddx.) to the abbey chamber. Witnesses. [21 April × 30 Dec. 1196]

WAD, f. 504v; F, ff. 287v–288 (no attestations).

Date: Attested by Alard [of Burnham], archdeacon of London, appointed 21 April × 30 Dec. 1196 (*Fasti* I, 10); by Alan the chaplain, who subsequently became a canon within that period (ibid., 62), and by Gilbert [Foliot II], archdeacon of Mddx., last occurs in those months (ibid., 16).

218. Notification by Richard [Fitz Nigel], bp. of London, that, on the presentation of Abbot William [Postard] and the convent, who hold the church of St Martin, Ludgate (London), he has instituted to this church Joseph the chaplain, who will render to the monks the pension formerly due from it. Witnesses. [22 April × 30 Dec. 1196]

WAD, f. 474; F, ff. 288r–v (no attestations).

Date: Attestations of Alard [of Burnham] as archdeacon of London, and Alan and Richard [of Finchley], the chaplains, without the style of canon (*Fasti* I, 10, 60, 62).

Note: St Martin's, Ludgate, had been confirmed to the convent by Bp. Gilbert [Foliot] (**211**).

219. Grant by Richard [Fitz Nigel], bp. of London, to his kinsman, William of Ely, the king's treasurer, of the houses which he had in Westminster, and the whole messuage, with buildings and tenements, in fee and inheritance, saving an annual payment to the abbey of a candle of 2 lbs weight at the feast of the Translation (13 Oct.). Witnesses. [*post* 20 April × 2 Sept. 1196]

WAD, ff. 341v–342; F, f. 248r–v (attestations omitted after those of the two archdeacons).

Pd: Richardson, 'William of Ely', 79–80, no. I, from both.

Cal: S. H. Philipot, *The Catalogue of the Lord Treasurers of England* (London, 1636), 5, from the original.

Date: *Factum est autem hoc anno pontificatus nostri septimo.* The dating clause of the original, as translated by Philipot, read: 'Anno 1196, being the seventh yeere of the raigne of Richard I, and the said number of yeeres of the government of the said Richard in the Bishoppricke of London' (quoted by F. M. Stenton, 'Acta Episcoporum,' *Cambridge Historical Journal* III (1929), 6n.–7n.). The king's regnal year concluded on 2 Sept. 1196. Attestations of Alard of Burnham as archdeacon of London, and of Alan the chaplain and Benedict of Sawston as canons, all date from *post* 20 April 1196 (*Fasti* I, 10, 62, 64).

Note: Cf. **147, 313**, and **439.**

220. Notification by William (de Ste Mère Eglise], bp. of London, that, at the presentation of the abbot and convent of Westminster, patrons of half the church of St Magnus [the Martyr] next to London Bridge, and at the presentation of the prior and convent of Bermondsey, patrons of the other half, he has instituted to that church Mr Simon de Valenciis, clerk, reserving to the abbot of Westminster and the prior of Bermondsey, and their convents, the pensions (unspecified) which they formerly received from that church. Simon will answer for all obligations due to the bp. or archdeacon. Witnesses. London, 14 April 1208.

WAD, f. 478r–v.

Note: Cf. the final concord of 23 April 1182, between Abbot Walter and the convent and Prior Bertram and the convent of Bermondsey (**287**) and a joint presentation made 1186 × 1189 by Abbot Walter and Prior Henry de Soilly and their respective convents (**368**).

221. Notification by R[obert de Chesney], bp. of Lincoln, of his grant of an indulgence of twenty days, and of participation in all spiritual benefits and prayers of the church of Lincoln, to all those who, on the feasts of the Deposition (5 Jan.) and Translation (13 Oct.), from their vigils and throughout their quindenes, visit the tomb of Edward, king of the English and most glorious confessor, canonized by Pope Alexander III. [*post* 7 Feb. 1161 × Dec. 1166; ? *c.* 13 Oct. 1163]

WAD, f. 393.

Pd: *EEA* IV, Appendix I, no. XIX.

Date: Robert de Chesney d. 25 × 27 Dec. 1166 (*Fasti* III, 2). Later than receipt of Pope Alexander's bulls concerning the canonization (**167–8**). The bp. attended the Translation (Richard of Cirencester, *Speculum Historiale de Gestis Regum Angliae*, ed. J. E. B. Mayor (RS, 1869), II, 326), when he possibly granted his indulgence, although a similar indulgence of Bp. Richard [de Belmeis II] of London, must antedate 4 May 1162 (**204**).

222. Notification by Robert [de Chesney], bp. of Lincoln, to Nicholas [de Sigillo], archdeacon of Huntingdon, and to all the clergy and laity of Huntingdon and Herts., that, at the request of his friends Abbot Laurence and Richard [of Ilchester], archdeacon of Poitiers, he has confirmed to Elias the clerk the perpetual vicarage of the church of

Datchworth, as set out in the charter of the abbot and convent. An annual payment of two besants [4s.] is due to Archdeacon Richard, and after his d., to the abbey. Witnesses. [c. 1164 × Dec. 1166]

WAD, f. 227.

Pd: *EEA* IV, Appendix I, no. XX.

Date: Robert de Chesney d. *c.* 25 × 27 Dec. 1166 (*Fasti* III, 2); Nicholas de Sigillo first occurs as archdeacon 1164 × 1166, prob. 1164 or early 1165 (ibid., 27).

Note: Richard of Ilchester had been appointed archdeacon of Poitiers by 1163 at latest (Diceto I, 312). Abbot Laurence's charter concerning Datchworth is now lost. Elias, *dilectus filius noster*, was prob. a member of the bp.'s *familia*: Elias son of Rannulf the clerk, Elias of Glemsford, and Elias de Ringesdon each attest one charter of the bp., of uncertain date (*EEA* I: Lincoln 1067–1185, ed. D. M. Smith (1980), nos. 119, 176, 188).

223. Notification by Hugh [of Avallon], bp. of Lincoln, that he has instituted his clerk, Mr Edmund, as parson of Deene (Northants.), at the presentation of the abbot and convent of Westminster, saving the perpetual vicarage held for life by Simon the clerk, all episcopal customs, and the dignity of the church of Lincoln. Witnesses. [21 Sept. 1186 × c. 1187]

WAM 16144; WAD, f. 242.

Pd: *EEA IV*, no. 209.

Date: The attestations of the *magistri* all appear without further title, whereas Mr Alexander was appointed archdeacon of Stow, prob. in the latter part of 1187 (*Fasti* III, 45) and Mr Robert of Bedford was precentor 1188 and at some date *post* 21 Sept. 1186 (ibid., 13, 116). Bp. Hugh was consecrated at Westminster 21 Sept. 1186 (ibid., 3).

Note: Mr Edmund is not otherwise recorded as a clerk of the bp. Deene was a demesne manor of the abbey TRE (Harvey, *WA*, 355). Simon the clerk is perhaps to be identified with the Simon of Deene who, at Michaelmas 1210, quitclaimed the advowson of Uppingham church to Abbot Ralph (**338**).

224. Confirmation by Hugh [of Avallon], bp. of Lincoln, to Mr Nicholas of Westminster, of the churches of Thorpe-on-the-Hill and Doddington (Lincs.), as he possesses them by grant of the abbot and convent of Westminster, for an annual pension of two besants [4s.], saving the perpetual vicarage held by Mr Alexander, archdeacon of Stow, who holds those churches for life, rendering a pension of £5 annually to Mr Nicholas, and saving the episcopal customs and the dignity of the church of Lincoln. Witnesses. [c. 1192 × c. March 1195]

WAD, f. 501v; F, f. 289r–v (attestations omitted).
Pd: *EEA IV*, no. 210.

Date: Attestation of Mr Roger de Rolleston as archdeacon of Leicester (*EEA* IV, nos. 11n and 188n).

Note: Since the institution of Mr Nicholas to these churches by the papal judge-delegate, Gilbert Foliot, Alexander had acquired the reversion of the subsidiary interests in them which had then been granted to Robert Code and Haket the clerk (cf. **209**).

225. Notification by Hugh [of Avallon], bp. of Lincoln; John [de Cella], abbot of St Albans, and Benedict, abbot of Stratford [Langthorne], papal judges-delegate, concerning the settlement of a dispute between Abbot William [Postard] and the monks of Westminster, and the nuns of Godstow, concerning the church of Bloxham [Oxon.]. The abbot and convent, pitying the poverty of the nuns, granted them the church in pure alms, except for a pension of five marks of silver [£3. 6s. 8d.], formerly due, which the nuns would render to the sacrist of Westminster, to illuminate the High Altar. Abbess Juliana and the nuns promised by the mouth and hand of their chaplain, Waleran, to pay the pension. This agreement was mediated, on behalf of Hubert [Walter], abp. and papal legate, by Hugh, abbot of Abingdon. Witnesses. 14 June 1197.

WAD, ff. 378v–379; Godstow Cartulary, PRO, E 164/20, f. xiij r–v.

Pd: Jane Sayers, *Papal Judges-Delegate in the Province of Canterbury 1198–1254: a study in Ecclesiastical Administration* (1971), App. B, 354–5, no. 5; *EEA* IV, no. 211.

Cal: Detailed transl., in Middle English: *The English Register of Godstow Nunnery near Oxford*, ed. A. Clark, 3 vols., EETS 129, 130, 142 (1906–1911), III, 229–30, no. 309; tabulated Sayers, *Papal Judges-Delegate*, 295, no. 117.

Note: King Henry II granted Bloxham church to Godstow 1173 × 1189. Roger de Clifford was to hold it for life, rendering one besant [2s.] annually, with reversion entirely to the nuns (Godstow Cartulary, f. xiij). Roger was prob. a kinsman of Henry's mistress, Rosamund Clifford, who d. *c.* 1176 and was buried at Godstow (*Monasticon* IV 366, nos. XIII, XV; *DNB* iv, 531–3). H II is said to have enriched the nunnery in consequence (*Gesta Henrici* II, 231–2; Howden, *Chronica*, III, 167–8). The king's grant of the church was confirmed by Walter of Godstow, archdeacon of Oxford (Godstow Cartulary, f. xiij) by Bp. Hugh of Lincoln (ibid., f. v *verso*); by Pope Celestine III in 1191 (ibid., f. clxxix *verso*); and included in a general confirmation by King Richard I (*Monasticon* IV, 364–5, no. VII). Bp. Hugh ordained the establishment of a perpetual vicarage there on 12 Dec. 1197 (Godstow Cartulary, ff. v verso–vj). See also *The English Register of Godstow*, 228–9, no. 308.

226. Confirmation by Hugh [of Avallon], bp. of Lincoln, to the abbot and convent, of the churches of Oakham and Hambleton (Rutl.), donated by W I, so that the monks receive annually from the incumbent a pension of thirty marks (£20), for the maintenance of a hospital, saving the customs and dignity of the church of Lincoln. Witnesses. [1197 × *c.* 1198]

WAD, f. 594; F, ff. 267v–268.
Pd: *EEA* IV, no. 212.
Date: Attested by Roger [de Rolleston] as dean of Lincoln: in office from 1195 × 1198 (*Fasti* III, 9–10); and by Richard [of Kent] as subdean: appointed to this office in 1197, and promoted to the archdeaconry of Northampton *ante* 19 Sept. 1200 (ibid., 22, 31). See also *Fasti* III, p. 167, Appendix 44.
Note: Cf. Abbot William's charter granting a pension from these churches to celebrate his anniversary (**321**); the subsequent charter of Abbot Ralph concerning them (**336**); charters of W I and W II concerning churches in Rutland (**46, 55–6**); two charters of James Salvage, 1204 × 1205, concerning pensions from these churches (**482–3**); Harvey, *WA*, 49–50, 389–90, 404. *The Registrum Antiquissimum of the Cathedral Church of Lincoln*, ed. C. W. Foster, Lincoln Record Soc., II (1933), 75–79, nos. 373–4; III (1935), nos. 1008–9.

227. Notification by Hugh [of Wells], bp. of Lincoln, that he has instituted Mr Simon of London to the church of Launton [Oxon.], on the presentation of the patrons, Abbot Ralph and the convent, reserving to Henry de Colwell, who holds that church, the perpetual vicarage, which he has, rendering an annual pension of two marks [£1. 6*s*. 8*d*.], saving the episcopal customs and the dignity of the church of Lincoln. Witnesses. London, 5 Oct. 1213.

WAM 15683; WAD, f. 275v.
Note: Launton was a demesne manor of the abbey TRE (Harvey, *WA*, 356). On 14 Oct. 1214, papal judges-delegate resolved a dispute between this rector and vicar, whereby Simon swore to leave Henry in peaceful possession of the vicarage in return for certain payments (WAM 15684; WAD, f. 276r–v; Cheney, *Selected Letters of Pope Innocent III*, 264, no. 901; C. R. and M. G. Cheney, *Calendar of Letters of Pope Innocent III*, 149, no. 901; tabulated Sayers, *Papal Judges Delegate*, 291, no. 76; 297, no. 5). Henry de Colwell still held the perpetual vicarage when Mr Robert s. of Robert, nephew of N[icholas de Romanis], bp. of Tusculum, was presented to Launton by the abbot and convent (*Rot. Hugh de Welles* I, 70).

228. Writ of Hilary, bp. of Chichester, ordering William s. of Gervase and Mr Serlo that they are not to exact any secular service from the virgate of land given by William s. of Odo to the church of St Peter's, Parham (Sussex), and to the bp.'s clerk, Alberic. [1147 × 1169]

WAM 4058; WAD, f. 582v.
Pd: *The Acta of the Bishops of Chichester 1075–1207*, ed. H. Mayr-Harting, C & Y Soc. (1964), 114–15, no. 55.
Date: Outside limits: the bp.'s term of office: consecrated 3 Aug. 1147 (Gervase of Canterbury I, 132); d. 1169 ('Tewkesbury Annals', *Ann. Mon.* I, 50; 'Winchester Annals', *Ann. Mon.* II, 59). Mr Serlo

was a clerk of Queen Alice who, with her second husband, William d'Aubigny, earl of Arundel, promised restitution of their exactions from churches in the diocese of Chichester (*The Chartulary of the High Church of Chichester*, ed. W. D. Peckham, Sussex Record Soc. XLVI (1961), no. 297; cf. *PUE* II, no. 57, dated 1148).

229. Notification by Hugh [du Puiset], bp. of Durham, of his grant to all those visiting the abbey on the feast of Saints Peter and Paul, and the feast of St Peter in Chains, of an indulgence of ten days, together with participation in all spiritual benefits and prayers of the church of Durham. [20 Dec. 1153 × 3 March 1195 (? × 1157)]

WAD, f. 390.
Date: Outside limits, the bp.'s term of office (*Fasti* II, 30), but prob. before the canonization of King Edward, and also before the deposition of Hugh's cousin, Abbot Gervase (Hugh was a nephew of King Stephen: *Fasti* II, 30). Cf. **145, 304**.

230. Notification by Henry [Marshall], bp. of Exeter, that, with the consent of the abbot and convent of Westminster, he has built a chapel, for the use of the church of Exeter, and for his successors, on the abbey's estate, in Longditch Street (Westminster), on land he bought from Geoffrey Picot. In this chapel, the divine office may be celebrated, although the chapel is not to function to the prejudice of the mother church of Westminster, nor to that of the chapel of St Margaret, in which parish the land is situated. [March 1194 × *ante* 10 Sept. 1198]

WAM 17312; WAD, f. 352v.
Date: Attested by Richard Fitz Nigel, bp. of London, d. 10 Sept. 1198 (*Fasti* I, 2). Henry Marshall was consecrated between 10 Feb. and 28 March 1194 (*HBC*, 246); profession of obedience *ante* 28 March 1194 (*Canterbury Professions*, ed. M. Richter, C & Y Soc. LXVII (1973), 57). Later than the confirmation of the land to the Lady Altar by William s. of William, whose tenant Geoffrey Picot was (**445**).

231. Notification by Richard [of Ilchester], bp. of Winchester, to all the faithful of his diocese, that, in honour of St Katharine he has granted to St Peter of Westminster and the convent the churches of Wandsworth and Battersea (Surr.) with all appurtenances, so that their tithes and offerings may support the monks of the Infirmary, adjacent to St Katharine's chapel. A vicarage is to be established, with perpetual vicars who, on the presentation of the abbot and convent, will be instituted by the bp. of Winchester, and answer for all obligations due to him. Witnesses. [*post.* 7 Nov. 1176 × 1188]

WAD, ff. 570v–571; WAD, f. 571 (confirmation, reciting in full); WAM 1816 (notarial copy, dated 28 Feb. 1306), which is torn and badly damaged by fungus, all attestations lost; WA Mun. Bk. 3, f. 20 (attestations defective); WA Mun. Bk. 12, f. 3v (memorandum).
Cal: Taylor, *Our Lady of Batersey*, 22.

Date: Bp. Richard d. 21/22 Dec. 1188 (*Fasti* II, 85); attestation of Peter [de Leia], bp. of St Davids (Gams, 186).
Note: See **18**, **166**, **169**, **177**, **232**. See also Harvey, *WA*, 411–12.

232. Notification by Godfrey [de Lucy], bp. of Winchester, to all the faithful throughout his diocese that, having inspected the charter of his predecessor, Bp. Richard [of Ilchester], concerning the concession and grant of the churches of Wandsworth and Battersea (Surr.) to the church of St Peter of Westminster and the convent, he has confirmed it. At the presentation of the abbot and convent, perpetual vicars may be instituted by the bp. of Winchester, answering for all obligations due to the bp., and to the monks for an annual pension of six marks [£4] from the church of Wandsworth, and two marks [£1. 6s. 8d.] from the church of Battersea, provided that these vicars answer for all episcopal burdens, and conduct themselves honestly, and that the episcopal rights, and the authority and dignity of the church of Winchester, are upheld. Witnesses. Southwark, 6 July 1193.

WAD, f. 580; WA Mun. Bk. 3, f. 21; WA Mun. Bk. 12, f. 3v (memorandum).
Cal: Taylor, *Our Lady of Batersey*, 22.

233. Notification by Mauger, bp. of Worcester, that he has instituted Mr Simon as parson of the church of Todenham (Gloucs.), at the presentation of Abbot Ralph [Arundel] and the convent, saving parochial and episcopal dues. Witnesses. [30 Nov. 1200 × late March 1208]

WAD, f. 324r–v; CAY, f. lxxii (memorandum).
Cal: Bentley, 37, no. 259 (item 3), from CAY.
Date: Bp. Mauger, 1200–1212 (*Fasti* II, 100), was one of the bps. ordered by Pope Innocent III to publish the Interdict (*Selected Letters of Pope Innocent III*, 102–3, no. 34). Consequently he fled into exile from the end of March 1208, and never returned, dying at Pontigny in 1212 (F. M. Powicke, *Stephen Langton* (1928), 76).
Note: The manor of Todenham had been acquired with Deerhurst, TRE, and was prob. always held in demesne (Harvey, *WA*, 345).

CHARTERS OF THE ABBOTS, PRIORS AND CONVENT

234. Grant by Abbot Vitalis to Gerald and his heirs of land called *Vuerc* in the city of London for £3 annual rent. [1076 × 1085]

Antique peritie crebris instructus ammonitionibus literarum serie in primi presentibus et futuris utillimum fore, censeo quod ego Vitalis abbas monasterii Sancti Petri quod Westmonasterium nominatur, cum consensu fratrum nostrorum, cuidam Giraldo, suisque heredibus, quandam terre mansionem quam Anglica lingua Vuerc appellatur apud Lundoniam civitatem concedo, ea ratione ut sexaginta solidos denariorum per tres Sancti Petri festivitates partitos annuatim solvant, quos quamdiu in arcuus [*sic*] monasterii intulerint, liberam possidendi habeant potestatem. Si autem desidie in commodo sibi inerti predictum censum reddere noluerint quicquid edificii terre cum pactum ab illis fuerit tollent, terra vero libera ecclesie remanebit. Herbertus de Curtono; Walterius de Valelia; Edricus de Deorhestria; Lambertus cocus; Willelmus et Rodgerius frater eius de Torsi; Willelmus frater Geraldi; Aelwinus cocus.

MS: WAD f. 462.
> Rubric: telligrafphus Vitalis abbatis Westmonasterii de quadam mansione terre apud London' vocata Vuerc.
Note: This obviously corrupt text is written on a slip of thin parchment 17.7 × 12.6 cm in the same hand as neighbouring folios which are headed by the rubric *Elemosinarius*. 'Vuerc' is not otherwise traceable, even in the Abbey indices.

235. Letter of confraternity of Abbot Vitalis with William of St Calais, bishop of Durham, and the cathedral priory. [1080 × 1085]

Hec est conventio[1] Willelmi Dunelmensis episcopi et domini Vitalis abbatis: si aliquid eorum obierit, fiat pro eo in utroque monasterio sicut pro eiusdem monasterii episcopo vel abbate; cum vero aliquis Dunelmensis monachus obierit fiant pro eo apud Westmonasterium vij plenaria officia in conventu et unusquisque sacerdos cantet pro eo unam missam; ceteri vero fratres cantent pro eo unusquisque unum salterium [*sic*]; laici vero qui salterium nesciunt cantent unusquisque centies et quinquagesies Pater Noster. Et hoc idem faciant Dunelmenses monachi pro monachis de Westmonasterio. Et huius conventionis[2] sit particeps Turstinus Dunelmensis archidiaconus.

MS: BL Cotton Domitian A VII, f. 52.
> 1. MS: *conditio*.
> 2. MS: *conditionis*.

Pd: *Durham Liber Vitae*, ed. A. H. Thompson, Surtees Soc. 136 (1923), f. 52, in facsimile.

Date: Accession of Bp. William and d. of Abbot Vitalis (*Fasti* II, 29; *Heads*, 76). Thurstan occs. May 1083 × June 1085 (*Fasti* II, 37).

Note: The agreement with Westminster was the model for Durham's similar agreement with Carlisle (*Liber Vitae*, f. 36v). Abbot Laurence of Westminster and Prior Alquin were commemorated at Durham (*Liber Vitae*, pp. 142 and 143 respectively). Also W[alterus] de R[okesbure], [sacrist] monk of Westminster: (ibid., f. 57, p. 94). Alquin and Walter were contemporaries of Abbot Laurence.

236. Grant by Abbot Gilbert to William Baynard of the berwick of Tothill in Westminster for one knight's fee, as it had been held by the thegn Wulfric Bordewate. He will hold it freely except for the aids, due as from the abbey's other knights, and for the tithes which are assigned to the almonry; after his death the land will revert to the abbey. 1083 [? error for 1086]

Anno Dominice Incarnationis millesimo lxxx°iij°¹ nos Gilbertus abbas et conventus Westmonasterii concessimus Willelmo Baynard quoddam berwicum de villa Westmonasterii nomine Totenhala, ad se hospitandum et tota vita sua tenendum pro servicio unius militis, cum omnibus rebus illi pertinentibus, ita bene et quiete sicut umquam Wlfricus Taynus, cognomine Bordewate, melius de ecclesia illud tenuerat. Consuetudines igitur et libertates quas nos in eodem habemus ipse Willelmus habebit, exceptis auxiliis nostris que inde sicut in aliis ecclesie terris de militibus nostris accipiemus, et exceptis decimis illius terre domui elemosinarie nostre constitutis. Hec vero sibi tenenda concessimus pro amore et servicio quod ecclesie nostre contulit eo tamen tenore ut post eius decessum terra illa predicta soluta ecclesie nostre maneat et quieta. Et super eo quidem affidavit nos predictus Willelmus quod nec terram prefatam vendet, nec in vadium ponet, nec alicui ad dampnum ecclesie nostre dimittet. Testibus: Roberto priore; Nicholao, Willelmo et Herberto monachis; Radulpho Baynard; Herlewyno fratre Grunzonis, et multis aliis.

MSS: (1) WAD, f. 79.
    Marginalia: (1) Carta cirographata Gilberti Westmonasterii de berewicu de Totenhale concessa Willelmo Baynard ad terminum vite pro servicio unius militis. (2) Fiat rubrica. (3) vij.
        1. *Sic*, MS. Possibly error for lxxxvj.
    (2) CAY, f. v (memorandum).
Pd: *Gilbert Crispin*, 38.
Cal: Bentley, 3, no. 13, from CAY.
Date: It is unlikely that Gilbert became abbot before 1085 (*Gilbert Crispin*, 38; Flete, 141; *Heads*, 77). The scribe made an error in copying the date, but, as he appears to have inserted the charter rather hastily this is not surprising. Note: See Harvey, *WA*, 354–5.

237. Grant by Abbot G[ilbert] and the convent to Robert son of Sweyn, of the land of Wheatley (Essex), which his father gave to the abbey for his soul, and which was confirmed by his mother on the day of his father's burial, in the presence of their barons Godobald, Turold and his brother William, and the abbot and convent, to hold at an annual rent of £3. [*c.* 1087]

G[ilbertus] abbas et conventus Westmonasterii concedunt Rotberto filio Suenonis ut ipse teneat de Sancto Petro et de abbate pro lx solidis per singulos annos terram, scilicet Wateleyam, quam pater suus dedit Sancto Petro pro anima sua, et de qua terra ipse Rotbertus cum sua matre fecit donacionem super altare Sancti Petri in eodem die quo sepultus est pater suus, videntibus baronibus suis Godobaldo, Turaldo et Willelmo fratre suo et multis aliis, in presencia abbatis et monachorum. Et tam diu sic eam teneat, donec pro predicta terra det cambium iii[1] libras quod abbas et monachi gratanter accipere debeant. Hii sunt termini denariorum: in Ramis Palmarum xxx solidos; in Festivitate Apostolorum Petri et Pauli xxx solidos.

MS: WAD, f. 502v.
    Rubric: Telligraphus G[ilberti] abbatis et conventus Westmonasterii de terra in Watelya. Reddendo per annum lx. solidos.
    Marginale: Wateleya.
       1. MS: *iiij.*
Pd: *Gilbert Crispin*, no. 8, p. 135.
Cal: Hart, no. 97.
Date: Prob. following on Robert's confirmation. Sweyn still held Wheatley 1086 (*DB* II, 43), although he was no longer sheriff.

238. Abbot Gilbert to Wymond, sheriff of Surrey, concerning the flight into sanctuary of Deorman de Clareton. [1086 × *c.* 1104]

Gisilberd abbod and ealle thage broth'a on Westmeynster gretad Wymond schearif on Suthreya Godes gretynge and ure. And we kythath that Theos Theorman of Clareton haefth gesoht to Criste and Sancte Petre and Eadwardes Kynges rste and eal thone haligdom that the innen thone halgan mynster ys. Nou biddeath we the for Godes lofan and for thaiere sokne that he gesouht haefth ther thu hine gemiltsie and forgif swa hwaet ge gilt he haefth. God the ge behealde. Amen.

MS: F, f. 259.
    Rubric: Littera testimonialis Anglica Gilberti Abbatis West-monasterii de eodem.
Pd: *Monasticon*, I, no. LXIV, 310.
Date: Wymond's tenure of office (*Sheriffs*, 135).
Note: On Westminster's sanctuary, see Honeybourne, 'Sanctuary boundaries'. The fugitive named in this writ has been identified as Deorman of Essex (Hart, no. 72 and note; cf. no. 109, which is also cal. in *Regesta* I, no. 399), but this argument is not convincing. This writ was evidently recorded in F as the oldest surviving documentation of the Westminster sanctuary, even though its grammar was scarcely intelligible by the time this cartulary was made. The copyist has consequently

experienced some confusion over minims, and although he tries to distinguish between the various English letter-forms, there is occasional misrepresentation, notably of the letters thorn and wyn, thus causing more mistakes. (The various obsolete letters, as he reproduces them, are transliterated in the present text). Both F and WAD contain several English-language writs of William I (**4–9**; **42**) and in recording these too, the cartulary scribes have experienced difficulties.

239. Writ of Abbot G[ilbert] informing N., sheriff of Essex, that R. has fled to sanctuary in Westminster Abbey. [1085 × 1117]

G[ilbert] abbod and alle tha brodera on Westmynstr' gretith N. schirere-fan on Estsex' Godesgretyng' and owr', and we kythath the that this man R. hafeth gesoht Crist and Seint Petr' and Edwarde Kynges reste and alle thon halidom th'inne thone halighan mynstr' is. Now bidde we the for Godes lofan and for thaer' sokne th' he gesoht' haueth th' thu hine gemyltsie and forgif swa what swa he gilt hafeth. God the ge behalde. Amen.

MS: WAD, f. 79v.
    Folio heading: De fugitivis visitantibus feretrum Regis Edwardi nondum canonizati.
Pd: *Gilbert Crispin*, 37.

240. Notification from Abbot Gilbert generally addressed, that Jordan has sought sanctuary. [1085 × 1117]

Gilbertus abbas et conventus Westmonasterii omnibus fidelibus Regis Anglie salutem. Sciatis quod iste Jordanus altare Sancti Petri et corpus Regis Edwardi requisivit, et ideo precamur ut libertatem sui corporis et pacem regis habeat. Valete.

MS: WAD, f. 79v.
Pd: *Gilbert Crispin*, 37.
Note: Presumably the last in the sequence of Gilbert's sanctuary writs, since English is now discarded.

241. Memorandum concerning a grant by Abbot G[ilbert] of the manor of Hendon (Mddx.) to his man Gunter in fee-farm for one week's farm every year. [1086 × 1107]

G[ilbertus] abbas Westmonasterii concessit Guntero homini suo et heredi illius manerium Hendon' in feudo firme pro una plenaria septi-mana firme quoquo anno. Testes: Milo Crispinus, Gislebertus Pipardus, Robertus prior et conventus monasterii in capitulo.

MS: WAD, f. 124.
    Rubric: Carta G. abbatis Westmonasterii de manerio de Hendon'.
Pd: *Gilbert Crispin*, no. 13, p. 138.
Date: Miles Crispin d. 1107 (*Gilbert Crispin*, 17). Gilbert Pipard was his dapifer (ibid., 138–9).
Note: This grant was confirmed by Herbert (**245**). Gervase (**263**) and

Henry II (**124**) issued confirmations for Gunter's son Gilbert. See also Harvey, *WA*, 352.

242. Grant in fee by Abbot G[ilbert] to William of Buckland of Cippenham and Burnham (Bucks.) for £2. 10*s.* a year and of Tetworth and of Tonge (Hunts.) for £3 a year for all service except the king's geld; also the courtyard in front of his house for 4*d.* He is to hold Chelsea (Mddx.) for life for £4 a year, but after his death it will revert to the Westminster demesne. When the king levies a scutage of £1, William will acquit the Abbey £1 from the fee of Tetworth and Tonge, and render £2 at Christmas and at Ascension for Chelsea, and £2. 15*s.* 2*d.* for his own fee at Annunciation and a week before Michaelmas. [1115 × 1117]

Hec est convencio inter G[ilbertum] abbatem et conventum Westmonasterii et Willelmum de Bocholanda, scilicet: G[ilbertus] abbas et conventus Westmonasterii dant et concedunt Willelmo de Bocholanda et heredibus suis in hereditate terram de Sipenham et de Burnham in feudo pro l solidis per singulos annos pro omni servicio preter commune geldum regis; et terram de Tetewrde et de Tunge similiter concedunt ei et heredibus suis pro lx solidis per singulos annos pro omni servicio preter commune geldum regis; et plateam que est ante domum suam similiter concedunt ei pro iiij^{or} denariis in feudo; similiter Celceiam tenebit in vita sua pro iiij^{or} libris quoquo anno pro omni servicio preter commune geldum regis. Et post mortem ipsius Willelmi remanebit Celceia in dominio ecclesie Westmonasterii. Et de feudo de Tetewrde et de Tunge, quando rex Anglie communiter accipiet xx solidos de milite, Willelmus de Bocholanda adquietabit ecclesiam Westmonasterii de xx solidis; et de Celceya in Nativitate Domini reddet xl solidos, et in die Ascencionis xl solidos; et de feudo suo in Annunciacione Sancte Marie lv solidos et ij denarios, et viij dies ante Festum Sancti Michaelis lv solidos et ij denarios. Hii sunt testes: Rotbertus episcopus Lincolniensis; Bernardus episcopus de Sancto David; Otuerus filius comitis; Clarebaldus medicus; Radulfus filius Algodi; Radulfus Diabolus; Ricardus de Rami Cur'; Ricardus de Magna Villa; Hugo de Monte; Asculius de Taneyo: Sagrinus; Osbertus de Bernivilla; Warinus de Hamesclape; Hugo de Midelton': de familia abbatis: Willelmus capellanus; Willelmus filius Fulconis; Gilebertus frater eius; Herbertus dispensator; Picotus; Rotbertus de Beslun; Willelmus camerarius; Willelmus Germinus; Ricardus filius Herberti; Oini et Tovius Ganet, et multi alii.

MS: WAD, f. 504.
> Rubric: Telligraphus abbatis et conventus Westmonasterii de terra in Burnham et Sippenham.
> Marginale: Burnham et Sippenham.

Pd: *Gilbert Crispin*, no. 37, pp. 154–5.
Date: Bernard became bishop of St Davids in 1115 and Abbot Gilbert died in 1117.
Note: See Harvey, *WA*, 338.

243. Grant by Abbot Herbert to the monks of Great Malvern (Worcs.)

of the manor of Powick (Worcs.) for £24 annually. They may hold this manor so long as they are obedient to the mother church, and the abbot will have those customary rights which he holds in other manors similarly at farm. [1121 × 1136]

Herbertus, abbas Westmonasterii, et totus conventus ecclesie omnibus successoribus suis pacem, prosperitatem et perpetuam salutem. Notum vobis fieri volumus nos concessisse fratribus et monachis nostris de Maluernia manerium nostrum de Powica ad firmam pro x^{ti}xiiij^{or} libris per annum. Hec pecunia per iiij^{or} terminos reddenda est, scilicet: vj libre in Natale Domini; sex in Pascha; sex[1] ad Festum Sancti Petri; sex ad Festum Sancti Michaelis. Et tamdiu teneant quamdiu obedientes fuerint et subjecti [sue m]^{1}atri ecclesie, et de hac obedientia fideliter servierint. Et illas consuetudines habeat abbas in eodem [mane]rio quas habet in omnibus aliis maneriis que similiter sunt ad firmam.

CYROGRAPHUM

MSS: (1) WAM XLIX.
    22 × 5.4 cm; step in top left-hand corner; slit but no t.u.
    Endorsed: (a) Carta Herberti abbatis (13C). (b) Poywika (14C).
      1. Supplied from WAD: WAM stained.
    (2) WAD, f. 293r–v.
    (3) F, f. 279v.
    (4) CAY, f. lxix *b*. (memorandum).
Pd: Chaplais, 'Original Charters', no. 1, p. 100, with partial facsimile, Plate VII(a); *Formulare*, xxii (abridged) (from original); *Monasticon*, III, 441, n.a, gives abstract of text, taken from *Formulare*.
Cal: Bentley, 33, no. 254 (item 36).
Note: See Harvey, *WA*, 363. Lands adjoining Powick are said to have been given to Great Malvern by Abbot Gilbert and the convent, and perambulated by the Westminster monks Hugh and Warner (*Monasticon*, III, 447–8), reciting two confirmatory charters of H I, one of them clearly spurious. Their texts are known only from the Patent Roll of 50 Edw. III: cf. *Cal. Pat. R. 1374–1377*, 282). A late source alleges that Gilbert's donations, made 18 W I (1083–4), included the manor of Powick (W. Thomas, *Antiquitates Prioratus Majoris Malverne* (London, 1725), iv, citing Placita Coram Rege, 12 Ed. II). Gilbert, however, prob. succeeded only in 1085 (*Heads*, 77). See also *Regesta* II, no. 1490.

244. Grant by Abbot Herbert, for the service of the High Altar, and for the needs of the whole church, both inside and outside, of £3 from St Margaret's Westminster; £1. 10s. from the church of Denham (Bucks.); 15s. due to Herbert from the High Altar on the two feasts of St Peter; the entire annual revenue from the Great Cross, and all the gelds of St Peter, of which alms are customarily offered to that church (the abbey), including those in Newchurch in London, when it can be recovered. [1121 × 1136]

Herbertus, Dei gratia abbas huius ecclesie Sancti Petri, omnibus successoribus suis, abbatibus et prelatis et magistris huius cenobii futuris, eternam salutem et perpetuam in Christo benedictionem. Sciat, reverenda paternitas et benigna fraternitas vestra, patres et fratres, peticione et consensu capituli huius, mee parvitati pro Christo subiecti devote et benigne et humili mente, ad honorem Dei et Sancti Petri, advocati nostri, et omnium reliquiarum in presenti ecclesia requiescentium, me concessisse perpetualiter ad servitia magni altaris et necessaria totius ecclesie intus et extra facienda, lx solidos de ecclesia Sancte Margarete in nostro cymiterio stante; et xxx^ta solidos de ecclesia de Deneham; et xv solidos qui mei esse solebant de duobus[1] festis Sancti Petri de magno altari; et totum apportatum magne crucis totius anni; et omnes gyldas Sancti Petri, quarum elemosine ad ecclesiam istam solite sunt deferri; et [in] Niwecirce in Lundonia, quando auxiliante Deo illa diracionnari poterit ad honorem et proficuum huius ecclesie. Hec omnia, karissimi, ad honorem Dei et domini nostri Apostoli Petri servitiis ecclesie fideliter concessi pro salute et quiete omnium fidelium defunctorum; et ut post obitum nostrum det nobis Deus regna celorum, et pro requie boni patroni nostri Regis Eadwardi huius ecclesie fundatoris devoti. Et hanc concessionem ante magnum altare, presente conventu, confirmavi, et desuper altare donationem posui, sicque omnes tam presentes quam futuros qui hec ab ecclesie servitio auferrent vel minuerent excommunicavi et maledixi, omnibus amen dicentibus qui aderant ibi. Nunc, igitur, karissimi patres et domini, estote fideles et amici Sancti Petri et ecclesie eius, et hanc donationem concedite [ex] partibus vestris, ut claviger paradysi introducat vos ad misericordiam Christi.

MSS: (1) BL Harleian Charter 84 F 46.
   10 × 18 cm.
   Seal: First seal of the convent: green; on tongue; St Peter seated, holding keys in left hand, right hand raised in blessing; legend: PETR. AP. XRI (*Cat. Seals BM*, 4299).
   Endorsed (a small step below the tongue): (a) H. abbatis ij^a (12C). (b) Carta de pensione de Denham facta ante consilium Lateranense: Sacrist' (in two hands of the early 14C). (c) Carta Herberti abbatis de lxs. de ecclesia Sancte Margarete in nostro cimiterio stante et de triginta solidis de Denham sacrist' Westmonasterii persol[vendis] (late 14C or early 15C).
      1. MS: *duabus*.
   (2) WAD, f. 384v.
   (3) WAM 3435 (15C, faded and stained).
Pd: *Monasticon*, I, No. L, 307 (from original); Chaplais, 'Original Charters', 100–101, with facsimile, Plate VII (b); Lathbury, *Denham*, 324 (from original).
Note: On St Margaret's, see Harvey, *WA*, 407–8. The unspecified feasts of St Peter were prob. *Petrus ad vincula* (1 Aug.) and *Petrus in cathedra in Antiochia* (22 Feb.).

245. Memorandum of the grant by Abbot H[erbert] to Gunter of

Hendon (Mddx.) and his heir of his land and manor as he held them of Abbot Gilbert (**241**). [1121 × *ante* Aug. 1134]

H[erbertus] abbas Westmonasterii concessit Guntero de Hendon terram suam et heredi suo, ita solidam et quietam sicut melius tenuit tempore Gisleberti Abbatis, et manerium ipsum, sicut melius tenuit eiusdem abbatis tempore et de conventu. Testibus: Eadwya priore; Philippo, Mauricio monachis; et Gaufrido; Paul Picot; Paul Osumul'; Rodberto, capellano Tovi; Richard de Eya, et multis aliis.

MS: WAD, f. 124.
    Rubric: Carta H. abbatis Westmonasterii de eodem.
Date: Gunter's son Gilbert succeeded his father during the reign of Henry I (**124**). Edwy was succeeded as prior by Osbert de Clare *ante* Aug. 1134 (**249**).
Note: See Harvey, *WA*, 352.

246. Agreement between Abbot Herbert and the convent, and Leofgar, whereby, with the common consent of the chapter, there was granted to Leofgar and his heirs, in fee-farm, the land of Coggeshall (Essex), and the land called Half-hide, which Norman holds, so that Leofgar may hold it freely, as the abbot specifically enjoined by an ensuing action in the halimote of the abbey's vill. [1121 × 1136]

Hec est conventio inter Abbatem Herbertum et monachos West-monasterii et Leouegarum: quod, communi consensu capituli, conces-sum est eidem Leouegaro et heredibus suis in feudo firma pro proficuo ecclesie terram de Coggeshal' pro xl solidis reddendo per annum pro omnibus serviciis et consuetudinibus, et terram illam quam Normanus tenet, que dimidia hida est appellata similiter, sibi concessa est et heredibus eius pro iij solidis per annum pro omnibus serviciis, ita ut libere et quiete et honorifice teneat, et ut hallimotum ville nostre placita sequentia nisi abbas nominatim asseruit et hoc sibi preceperit. Et ipse[1] Leouegarus, eodem die quo hec sibi concessa fuit, dedit Deo et Sancto Petro et fratribus ecclesie in elemosina, omnibus diebus vite sue, et heredes eius post eum, hoc idem dabunt. Testes sunt: Albericus de Vere; Goffridus de Colet', et Ricg' de Colet, et Alinus; Ricardus; Godefridus camerarius Alberici; Siricus; Widfarus; Adam de London; Randulfus de Plumsted.

MS: WAD, f. 266v.
    Rubric: Conventio inter abbatem et conventum Westmonasterii et Leouegarum de terra de Coggeshal' et de terra quam Normannus tenet qua dimidia hida appellata est.
        1. Interlineation begins: termini denariorum de Cogeshale: xx solidos ad Pascham et xx solidos ad Festum Sancti Michaelis; et de dimidia hida, xviij denarios ad Pascham et xviij denarios ad Festum Sancti Michaelis ad opus fratrum infirmorum.
Note: See Harvey, *WA*, 341–2.

247. Agreement between Abbot Herbert and the convent, and Henry son of Wilfred, whereby they granted to Henry, for life, the manor of Ockendon (Essex), for £10 annually. From his church of St Alphege, which Henry gave to God and St Peter, he will give £1 annually. Further provision in case Henry or his heir becomes a monk, and for succession to the manor and church. 1125.

Anno ab Incarnacione Domini M° centesimo XX°V° facta fuit hec conventio inter Herebertum abbatem et conventum Westmonasterii et Henricum filium Wluredi; videlicet quod Herebertus abbas et conventus Westmonasterii communi assensu tocius capituli concesserunt Henrico filio Wluredi manerium de Ochendon' in vita sua pro x libris dando per annum, et de ecclesia sua de Sancto Alfego, quam dedit Deo et Sancto Petro, dabit per annum xx solidos. Et post mortem ipsius Henrici heres eius tenebit supradictum manerium pro xj libris per annum et de ecclesia similiter xx solidis. Et si ipse Henricus monachus esse voluerit sine alia convencione recipietur, et unus heres eius tenebit sicut supradictum est. Et si heres eius monachus esse voluerit ea convencione recipietur qua et pater eius est receptus, et manerium et ecclesia postea soluta et quieta et libera cum omnibus incrementis suis remanebunt Deo et Sancto Petro. Terminis denariorum: ad Pascham c et x solidos; ad Festum Sancti Michaelis c et x solidos. Testibus: Albrico de Ver, Rogero de Ver, Rogero de Persora, Henrico Arbor, Godwino et Hachuno, et multis aliis.

MS: WAD, f. 446v.
   Rubric: Telligraphus Abbatis et conventus Westmonasterii de manerio de Wokindon' et de pensione xx solidorum de ecclesia Sancti Alfegi eisdem per Henricum filium Wluredi.
Note: Ockendon and Feering in Essex belonged to Harold II and were given by the Conqueror to the abbey in exchange for Windsor (**9–10**); Henry I confirmed the exchange (**67**); see also Harvey, *WA*, 343. The increasing revenues anticipated from the manor were evidently deemed sufficient payment in the event of Henry's heir wishing to become a monk.

248. Notification by Abbot Herbert that Jordan of Worcester has sought sanctuary. [1121 × 1136]

Herebertus abbas et conventus Westmonasterii omnibus fidelibus regis Anglie salutem. Sciatis quod Jordanus de Wygornia altare Sancti Petri Westmonasterii et corpus Regis E[dwardi] requisivit. Et ideo precamur ut libertatem sui corporis et pacem regis habeat. Valete.

MS: F, f. 258v.
   Rubric: Littera testimonialis Hereberti abbatis de eodem.
Pd: *Monasticon*, I, no. LXII, 310.

248A. Letter of Abbot Herbert and Prior Edwy to Warin, prior of Worcester, Uhtred the precentor and the monks. They are sending back a monk who absconded to Westminster from [Great] Malvern, since he had begun work on a missal for Worcester. They ask that he should be kindly received. [1124 × *ante* Aug. 1134]

Herbertus abbas Westmonasteriensis et Edwius prior eiusdem loci, venerabili priori Wigornie Warino et domino Uhtredo cantori, ceterisque fratribus ecclesie eiusdem, salutem in Christo et perpetuam pacem. Sciatis istum fratrem nostrum et monachum ad nos venisse, et causam recessurus sui de Malvernia, sicut nobis videtur rationabiliter, ostendisse. Nos rei veritatem ex integro necdum agnoscentes remittimus eum iterum ad vos a quibus ad nos venit, rogantes humiliter vestram pietatem et misericordiam ut illum fratrem et amicabiliter tractetis et diligatis, donec ego ipse ad provinciam veniam. Si illi bonum fuisset, sicut fratrem nostrum ecclesie nostre professum humiliter et benigne retineremus, sed dixit nobis quoddam opus, scilicet missale, apud vos incepisse, et antequam ad Malverniam rediret sua voluntate perficeret. Quoniam eum vestre pietati et caritati commendamus, donec causa eius recessionis a fratribus vestris Malvernie plenius per vos sciamus. Et si antequam ad provinciam iero vero illius cordi Deus inspiraverit do[ctrinamen]tum redire, precipio per sanctam obedientiam ut fraternaliter et amicabiliter recipiatur, laudando Creatorem qui ovem suam reduxit ad gregem. Valete.

MS: Cambridge: Corpus Christi College, MS 367, f. 52.
Pd: M. R. James, *A Descriptive catalogue of the Manuscripts in the Library of Corpus Christi College Cambridge*, 2 vols., 1912, II, 203 (abridged); Elizabeth A. McIntyre, 'Early Twelfth-Century Worcester Cathedral Priory, with special reference to the manuscripts there' (Oxford University D.Phil. thesis, 1978), 248.
Date: Terms of office of Herbert, Warin (*Heads*, 77, 83) and Edwy, who was succeeded as prior by Osbert de Clare before Aug. 1134 (**249**).
Note: On this MS, composed, in part at least, at Worcester, see James, *ut supra*; N. R. Ker, *Catalogue of Manuscripts Containing Anglo-Saxon* (1957), 110, no. 64.

249. Notification that Abbot Herbert, Prior Osbert de Clare and the convent, with the assent of Gilbert the Universal, bishop of London, gave the hermitage of Kilburn (Mddx.), which Godwin built, and its lands, to three maidens: Emma, Gunhild and Christine, to hold as King Ethelred gave Hampstead to the church of Westminster, and King Edward confirmed it. Godwin is to be master for life, followed by the senior maiden. The abbot and convent donated £1. 10s. of the alms given to the abbey by Sweyn, father of Robert of Essex, and Ailmar the priest donated land in Southwark (Surr.), which rendered 2s. annually. [27 Dec. 1127 × Aug. 1134]

Omnibus hominibus tam futuris quam presentibus, notum sit tempore Henrici Regis, qui tercius ex Normannis regnavit in Anglia, Herebertum abbatem Westmonasterii et Priorem Osbertum de Clara, una cum omni venerabili eusdem sancte ecclesie conventu, domino Gilberto Universali Lundonie sancte ecclesie presule annuente, dedisse tribus puellis, Emme, videlicet, et Gunilde et Cristine, heremetorium de Cuneburna, quod edificavit Godwynus, cum omni terra illius loci et omnibus illis que inibi eadem[1] sanctitatis vite norma fruendi causa future sunt. Concessu tamen atque precatu illius Godwyni heremite quatinus eundem locum, que ad illum pertinet, in elemosina pro redemptione animarum tocius predicti conventus fratrum, possideant, eadem condicione atque libertate qua Ethelredus, rex Anglorum pater Edwardi Regis, ad predictam Westmonasterii ecclesiam dedit Hamstedam. Post cuius obitum eciam predictus Edwardus, qui regni gubernacula suscepit, illud idem confirmavit, ad cuius ville possessionem ille prenotatus locus, antequam hec fierent, pertinebat, ut Deus Omnium Redemptor omnes illorum animas in celis inter sanctorum consorcia perseverare iubeat. Sit tamen semper locus ille sub custodia fratrum ne temerario quolibet iure peioretur aut sinistra regatur. Huic ergo loco concessit dari Dominus Abbas Herebertus et totus[a] conventus duo perpetua[b] beneficia, unum videlicet pro requie omnium animarum illius ecclesie fratrum et pro omnibus fratribus de Feschampa tam pro vivis quam pro defunctis, et aliud quod dederant Ailmaro omni tempore vite sue ut omnipotens Deus ab omni peste et clade omnes predictorum fratrum animas eripiat. Et sit ille prescriptus heremita Godwinus magister[2] loci illarumque puellarum quamdiu vixerit custos, et post eius obitum eligat conventus puellarum seniorem ydoneum qui earum ecclesie presit, abbatis tamen consilio. Et non habeat potestatem aliquam abbas priorve, aut quislibet alter aliquam intrare faciendi absque illarum voluntate et licencia que infra clause fuerint. Capellanus vero, qui in monasterio prefuerit de possessionibus vel ecclesie rebus, non se intromittat nisi illarum iussu, et omnes possessiones quas eis dominus donaverit, habeant libere sicut Sanctus Petrus habet suas. Et in principio omnium beneficiorum dedimus eis et concessimus imperpetuum xxx solidos de illa elemosina quam Sweno pater Roberti de Estsexa dedit Deo et Sancto Petro, scilicet lx solidos, quorum solidorum altera medietas in cena domui ad mandatum pauperum Christi faciendum constituta est. Hanc autem donacionem fecimus illis ancillis Dei pro statu ecclesie nostre in bonum et pro incolumitate et pace omnium seniorum, abbatum, et fratrum, et benefactorum nostrorum vivorum, et pro redempcione animarum a penis, ex quorum beneficio descenderunt, et pro animabus omnium abbatum nostrorum et fratrum ecclesie nostre defunctorum. Huic loco eciam Cuneburnie scilicet dedit Ailmarus sacerdos unam terram in caritate in Sowthwerk[3] que reddit per annum ij solidos. His testibus etc.

MSS: (1) F, ff. 325v–326v.
> Rubric: Primam fundacio monialium de Kylbourne per abbatem Westmonasterii Herebertum c[apitulu]m cxviij.
>> a. MS: *tocius totus.*
>> b. MS: *perpetue.*
> (2) LN, f. cxxv *recto.*
>> 1. *Illius loci et omnibus Dei ancillis que in eodem.*

118

2. Omits *magister*.
3. *Suthwrca*.

Pd: *Monasticon*, III, no. I, 426 (from F).

Date: Episcopate of Gilbert the Universal: *Fasti* I, 1.

Note: Westminster's association with Fécamp prob. originated in the time of Abbot Vitalis, who came from its cell of Bernay (*Gilbert Crispin*, 1). For King Ethelred's grant of Hampstead and Edward's confirmation, see Sawyer, *Anglo-Saxon Charters*, nos. 894, 1040, 1043, 1450. On Sweyn of Essex and his s. Robert, see Sanders, 139.

250. Grant by Abbot Herbert to the nuns of Kilburn of land in [Kensington] Gore, belonging to the manor of Knightsbridge (Mddx.), to make an assart. [*c.* 1130 × *c.* 1136]

Herebertus abbas ecclesie Sancti Petri Westmonasterii et totus eiusdem ecclesie conventus, tam futuris quam presentibus, salutem. Notum sit vobis nos, communi assensu tocius capituli et consilio, dedisse in elemosina pro anima regis nostri Edwardi, fundatoris ecclesie nostre, et pro animabus omnium fratrum et benefactorum nostrorum, ancillis Dei que sunt in ecclesia Beati Johannis Baptiste de Keneburna et omnibus que ibidem ad serviendum Deo future sunt, quandam terram ad sartandam in tenetura manerii nostri quod vocatur Cnithtebruga, et in loco qui Gara appellatur. Volumus eciam et firmiter precipimus ut in pace, et quiete, et libere, et sine omni servicio teneant illam predictam terram. Et si quis eis super hanc donacionem et donacionis libertatem aliquam inde violenciam vel dampnum vel contumeliam aut torturam aliquam fecerit, et elemosinam nostram violare vel auferre a predicta ecclesia presumpserit, nisi illis ancillis Dei citam et congruam satisfaccionem fecerit, ab omni conventu ecclesie nostre excommunicetur et a Christo pauperum suorum defensore perpetuo anathematis gladio feriatur. Amen. Hii sunt testes: Gregorius dapifer, Radulfus de Puntfret,[1] Ricardus prepositus, Ricardus cocus et multi alii.

MSS: (1) F, f. 326v–327v.
   Rubric: Carta H. abbatis de terra in Knyztbrigg' monialibus de Kybourne concessa. C[apitulu]m cxlviij.
   (2) LN, f. cxxv, r–v.
      1. *Pountfreit.*
   (3) CAY, f. cxxxiv *recto–verso*.

Pd: *Monasticon*, III, no. II, 426 (from F).

Cal: Bentley, 64, no. 527, from CAY.

Date: This charter is clearly later than **249**. It is uncertain when the hermitage of Kilburn was formally converted into a nunnery (the date of 1139, given by Knowles & Hadcock, 259, is clearly erroneous, since Herbert was dead by that year). The term *ancilla Dei* is usually translated as 'nun', and Kilburn's new status was prob. therefore achieved before the end of Herbert's abbacy, perhaps when the 'senior maiden' succeeded Godwin as head of the foundation.

251. Grant by Abbot Gervase to the preceptor of 8*s.* from the tithes of Roding (Essex) for the repair of books. [1138 × 1157]

Gervasius, abbas Beati Petri Westmonasterii, totusque conventus eiusdem ecclesie, omnibus hominibus suis, tam presentibus quam futuris, salutem. Manifestum vobis fieri volumus nos amore Dei, pro reparandis libris armarii, et pro ceteris negotiis que ad cantoris nostri pertine[n]t officium, communi assensu et consilio, concessisse et dedisse cantarie viij solidos de decima de Roinges, quam tenet Aluricus presbiter, et his terminis: ad Annuntiationem Sancte Marie iiij solidos, et ad Festivitatem Sancti Petri ad Vincula iiij solidos. Quapropter volumus et precipimus ut cantor ecclesie Beati Petri Westmonasterii, quisquis ille fuerit, predictos habeat solidos bene et honorifice et in pace. Ne quis eum super hac nostra donatione et predicta elemosina ullo modo inquietet.

MSS: (1) WAM 1172A.
    26 × 12.3 cm; t.u. 3.4 cm.
    Seals: (1) First seal of the convent: (*Cat. Seals BM*, 4299), red; attached by hemp cords inserted through a t.u. at the foot of the charter. (2) Seal of Gervase: pointed oval; 8.3 × 6 cm; monk presenting a church to the Virgin (seated) and Child: SIGILLUM GERVASII ABBATIS SANCTI PETRI [MON]ASTERII.
    Endorsed: (a) Confirmatio capituli de Alba Royn' (13C). (b) Carta Gervasii, abbatis Westmonasterii eiusdem loci conventus de viij solidis de decima de Roinges percipiendis concessa precentori dicte ecclesie Westmonasterii qui pro tempore fuerit pro reparacione librorum armarii et pro ceteris negotiis que ad cantoris pertinet officium. (14C). (c) Cantor (15C).
    (2) WAD, f. 648v.
Pd: Chaplais, 'Original Charters', no. 5, p. 102, with partial facsimile (Plate VII(c)); Robinson & James, 1 (from WAM).

252. Grant by Abbot Gervase of the manor of Kelvedon [Hatch] (Essex), for lights and other offices of the High Altar. [1138 × 1157]

Gervasius, Dei gratia abbas Beati Petri Westmonasterii, totusque eiusdem ecclesie conventus omnibus tam futuris quam presentibus Christi fidelibus, salutem et eternam felicitatem. Scire volumus fraternitatem vestram et caritatem que in Christo est, nos, uno et communi totius capituli nostri consilio propter honorem et reverentiam corporis Domini Nostri Jesu Christi, et Beati Petri Apostolorum Principis et advocati nostri, et omnium sanctorum quorum reliquie in nostra requiescunt ecclesia, ad luminare corporis Domini Nostri nominatim, et ad cetera altaris officia concessisse et dedisse necnon propriis manibus nostris Deo super altare Beati Petri advocati nostri manerium de Keleuedune sicut nostrum proprium cum omnibus rebus pertinentibus ad ipsum manerium optulisse. Volumus igitur ut ista donatio rata sit quia ab omnibus nobis ut ita sit confirmata est. Quicumque ergo hanc oblationem et hanc donationem temere violare et istud manerium ab illis officiis que supra nominavimus et sicut ordinavimus aliquo malo ingenio auferre vel

elongare aut distrahere conatus fuerit, nisi citius ad congruam emenda-
tionem venerit, perpetue maledictionis et anathematis gladio feriatur, sit
pars eius et portio cum Dathan et Abyron sit conversatio ipsius cum
diabolo et angelis eius in igne perpetuo. Amen.

MS: WAD, f. 377v.
Rubric: Carta Gervasii Abbatis et conventus Westmonasterii de
manerio de Keleuuedune.
Note: Kelvedon Hatch was given by Ailric the chamberlain in *c.* 1066
(Harmer, no. 74; *DB*, II., 14; Harvey, *WA*, 343).

253. Grant by Abbot Gervase for lights at the altar, of Bloxham (Oxon.)
church, held by Robert de Chesney: Robert is to pay five marks
(£3. 6*s.* 8*d.*) a year to the sacristy, and if he dies or enters a religious order
or is promoted to higher office, the church is to revert to the use of the
(high) altar of the Abbey. [1138 × 1148]

Universis sancte et catholice matris Ecclesie filiis, tam prelatis quam
subditis, tam presentibus quam futuris, Gervasius abbas Westmonasterii,
salutem. Sciant presentes et futuri me petitione et communi consensu
capituli nostri concessisse et dedisse luminari ceterisque officiis altaris
ecclesie nostre ecclesiam de Blokesham quam Rodbertus de Chaisn'
tenet de me et de ecclesia nostra. Qua propter volumus et precipimus ut
amodo predictus Rodbertus sacriste [*sic*] ecclesie nostre intendit et
recognitionem quam nobis inde facere debebat, sicilicet v marcas argenti
illi faciat: ad Pascha duas marcas et dimidiam; et ad Festum Sancti
Michaelis tantundem eundem. Si vero predictus Robertus obierit aut
vitam suam mutaverit aut ad dignitatis gradum promotus fuerit, predicta
ecclesia cum omnibus pertinentiis suis altari ecclesie nostre quieta et
libera permaneat. Qui vero hanc donationem aliqua perversitate inter-
upit sacrosancti corporis et sanguinis Christi reus sit, cui iniuriam inferre
presumit.

MS: WAD, f. 378r–v.
Rubric: Carta Gervasii abbatis et conventus Westmonasterii de
eodem.
Date: Robert de Chesney became archdeacon of Leicester in
1145 × 1146 (*Fasti* III, 33). The absence of this title is not necessarily
conclusive for the dating, but the charter was certainly issued before his
election as bishop of Lincoln, 13 Dec., 1148 (ibid.).
Note: Robert de Chesney belonged to an Oxfordshire family (*Eynsham
Cartulary*, ed. H. E. Salter, Oxford Historical Society 49 (Oxford, 1907),
411).

254. Grant by Abbot Gervase to William de Wenden and his wife
Adelaide, daughter and heir of Walter Stantus, of all Walter's tenements
and offices within and without the church. [1138 × 1157]

Gervasius, Dei gratia abbas Westmonasterii, omnibus probis hominibus
suis, Francis et Anglis, salutem. Sciant tam presentes quam futuri me
concessisse et dedisse Willelmo de Wendena[1] et Adelaidi uxori sue omnia

121

tenementa que fuerunt Walterii Stantus, et ministeria infra ecclesiam et extra, in domibus et terris, et omnibus aliis rebus, quia predicta Adelaidis filia fuit eiusdem Walteri, et iustissima heres ipsius. Quam ob rem volo et precipio quod predictus Willelmus uxorque eius Adelaidis et heredes eorum habeant et teneant omnia predicta tenementa et ministeria cum corrediis et consuetudinibus omnibus eisdem ministeriis pertinentibus, ita plenarie et quiete et libere et honorifice, sicut unquam Walterus Stantus vel aliquis antecessorum melius tenuerunt, et sicut Gaufridus frater sepedicte Adelaidis eis quieta clamavit omnia predicta a die desponsionis eorum usque in eternum, et heredibus illorum. Teste Osberto de Clara, priore; W. Capes; Rogero Branc'; Ricardo de Hair', monachis; Gregorio Dapifero; Ricardo de Furmonwill'; Hugone Bello; Elia de Mulesham; Hugone de Bifort; Gaufrido filio Godefridi; Rogero de Moretein; Johanne, armigero abbatis; multisque aliis.

MSS: (1) WAM L.
 16.8 × 8.9 cm; tongue 1.6 cm.
 Seals: (1) Seal of Gervase (as above, **251**); green; on tongue. (2) Counterseal: 3 × 2 cm, from an antique intaglio gem: helmeted goddess in front of an altar; legend: SIGILLUM GERVASII ABBATIS WESTM.
 Endorsed: Westmonasterium (14C).
  1. Corrected from *Wenduna*.
 (2) WAD, f. 87v.
 Rubric: Carta Gervasii Abbatis de seriantiis vestibuli et pincernarie de quibus subsequenter quieta clamantia per magistrum Willelmum de Wandene.
Pd: Chaplais, 'Original Charters', no. 6, p. 103.
Note: As the WAD rubric shows, these offices were identified as the serjeanties of the vestibule and the buttery, when the later William de Wenden relinquished them to Abbot Walter de Wenlock (1283–1307): cf. Flete, 117. See also Harvey, 'Fee Farms', 130, on Gervase's grant.

255. Confirmation by Abbot G[ervase] to Nicholas son of Clement of the agreement between him and Bertram the clerk, son of Leodbert, concerning the church of St Matthew in London, as a charter testifies. Nicholas is to pay 10*s.* a year towards the monks' clothing. [1141 × 1150]

G[ervasius], Dei gratia abbas Westmonasterii, totusque conventus eiusdem ecclesie episcopo Lundon[a] universisque sancte Dei ecclesie filiis, salutem. Sciatis nos concessisse et confirmasse Nicholao filio Clementis conventionem que facta est inter Bertramnium clericum filium Leodberti et prefatum Nicholaum super ecclesiam Sancti Mathei in London' cum pertinentiis suis sicut carta capituli Sancti Pauli testatur. Quare volumus et precipimus quod ipse Nicholaus predictam ecclesiam[b] teneat et habeat ita libere et quiete et honorifice sicut predictus Bertramius vel aliquis antecessorum suorum melius et liberius et honorificentius et quietius tenuit salvo jure ecclesie nostre. Reddendo inde x solidos per annum ad vesturam nostram in cathedra Sancti Pauli. Testibus hiis: Rodberto de Corneil; Roberto clerico de Turri;[1] Guillelmo sacerdote de sancto Audoeno; Bernardo sacrista Sancti Pauli; Henrico; Philomena; Amando clerico; magistro Herveo; Elia clerico; Jerino ingeniatore; Salomone de Sutbbeheda;[2] Hugone Bello et multis aliis.

MSS: (1) WAD, f. 476.
    Rubric: Confirmatio Abbatis et conventus Westmonasterii super conventione predicta, reddendo x solidos per annum.
    1. A short erasure follows.
    2. *Recte Stubbeheda* (Stepney).
    (2) F, f. 288 (omits witnesses).
    a. *London*
    b. *ecclesia*
Pd: Harvey, 'Fee Farms', no. 1, pp. 138–9 (from WAD).
Date: The agreement between Nicholas and Bertram (**380**) was made with the consent of Robert de Sigillo, bp. of London 1141 × 1150 (*Fasti*, I, 2).
Note: St Matthew's church in Friday Street paid £3. 19*s*. to the abbey in *c.* 1291 (*Taxatio Nicholai IV*, p. 9b).

256. Grant by Abbot G[ervase] and the convent to Azo and Alice, his maternal aunt, of the land held by his father Alfred in London, near the cemetery of St Laurence on Thames, for an annual rent of 2*s*. [1138 × 1157]

G[ervasius] abbas Westmonasterii et totus conventus eiusdem loci concedunt Azoni et Aliz' matertere sue et heredibus ipsius terram quam Alvredus pater ipsius Azonis tenuit in Lundonia prope cimiterium Sancti Laurentii super Tamisiam. Et volumus ut eam bene et in pace teneant eo tenore quo predictus Alvredus tenuit, scilicet ij solidos reddendo per annum: ad Pascha xij denarios, et ad Festum Sancti Michaelis xij denarios.[a] His testibus.[1]

MSS: (1) BL Egerton 3031, f. 48v.
    Rubric: Carta abbatis et conventus Westmonasterii super quadam terra in Londonia facta Azoni et Adelizie.
    (2) BL Harleian 1708, f. 113.
    1. MS ends *T.*
    (3) BL Cotton Vespasian E XXV, f. 60v.
    a. MS ends.
    Rubric (MSS (2) and (3)): Sigillum Sancti Petri Westmonasterii de terra Alueredi in London'.
Pd: B. Kemp, *Reading Abbey Cartularies* I, Camden 4th ser. XXXI (1986), 355, no. 462, from Egerton, Harley and Vespasian.
Date: Term of office of Abbot Gervase. On stylistic grounds, the charter appears more likely to be mid 12C than temp. Abbot Gilbert.
Note: The presence of this text in BL Egerton 3031 indicates that Reading held the land by 1193 at latest, although its transfer is not recorded. There is a possible link in the writ issued by Queen Eleanor as regent, Jan. 1156 × April 1157, ordering the sheriff of London to investigate a complaint by the convent of Reading that they had been unjustly

disseised of unspecified land in London donated, from the tenure of the abbot of Westminster, by Richard Fitz B. when he became a monk at Reading. If Reading's title is proved, the sheriff is to reseise its convent of the land, saving the right of the abbot of Westminster (*Reading Abbey Cartularies* I, no. 466).

257. Agreement whereby Abbot Gervase and the convent of Westminster granted to the chapter of St Martin [le Grand], London, at an annual rent of 7s., the church of St Agnes in London with its lands, as it was given to the abbey by Godric Lobbe when he became a monk. [1138 × 1157]

Hec est conventio inter ecclesiam Sancti Petri Westmonasterii et conventum eiusdem loci et ecclesiam Sancti Martini London' et capitulum eiusdem ecclesie: videlicet, ego Gervasius, abbas Sancti Petri Westmonasterii, et omnis conventus concedimus ecclesie Sancti Martini London' et toti capitulo eiusdem ecclesie tenendam de ecclesia nostra et conventu nostro ecclesiam Sancte Agnetis London' cum terris et omnibus rebus eidem ecclesie pertinentibus sicut Godricus Lobbe illas[1] tenuit melius, qui ecclesiam ipsam et teneduras suas donavit cum corpore suo die qua monachus effectus est ecclesie nostre. Volumus etiam quod honorabiliter et libere illas teneant inperpetuum[2] possessionem et quietam de omnibus consuetudinibus per vij solidos reddendo[3] ecclesie nostre per annum ad duos terminos: hoc est in Natale Domini xlij denarios, et infra septimanam Pasche xlij denarios. Quicumque vero aut ex conventu nostro aut de capitulo Sancti Martini hoc pactum infringere vel violare molitus fuerit, anethema sit et cum Juda proditore Dei infernales luat penes. Amen.

MSS: (1) WAD, f. 477.
    Rubric: Camerar' (rubric heading): Cirographus inter ecclesias Westmonasterii et Sancti Martini London' super ecclesiam Sancte Agnetis, reddendo per annum vij solidos.
    1. Reading taken from F.
    2. *Sic* for *perpetuam*.
    3. *Sic* in MS.
    (2) F, ff. 288v–289.
Pd: Harvey, 'Fee Farms', no. 8, p. 142 (from WAD).
Note: The dean of St Martin le Grand during the latter part of Stephen's reign was Henry of Blois, bp. of Winchester and uncle of Abbot Gervase (Brooke & Keir, 311), which possibly influenced the terms of this grant (Harvey, 'Fee Farms', 134).

258. Grant by Abbot Gervase to his clerk Elias son of Goldwin of land in London between the house of Baldwin son of Ingelric and that of Wlgar, for an annual rent of 2s. 8d. towards the clothing of the convent. [1138 × 1157]

G[ervasius], Dei gratia abbas Westmonasterii, omnibus baronibus et civibus London' et amicis et tenentibus suis, Francis et Anglis, salutem. Sciant presentes et futuri me firmiter concessisse et dedisse Helie clerico meo filio Goldewini et suis hereditario jure quandam terram de feodo Sancti Petri in London', que est inter mansionem que fuit Baldewini filii Ingelrici et inter mansionem Wlgari in feodo finabiliter tenendam. Reddendo inde per annum ij solidos et viij denarios libere pro omni servicio ad vestituram conventus Westmonasterii. Quare volo quod ipse eam habeat et teneat cum omnibus libertatibus eidem terre pertinentibus ita bene et in pace et libere et honorifice et quiete sicut aliquis melius et liberius et honorificentius et quietius terram tenet de ecclesia Sancti Petri Westmonasterii. Hiis testibus: Ansgodo monacho; Ricardo de Bissea, monacho; Hugone novicio' monacho; Ricardo preposito; Magistro Herveo; Gervasio Peverello; Salonone[1] de Stibbeta; Radulfo fratre abbatis; Amalrico fratre suo; Hugone Bello; Osmundo coco; Simone coco; Ricardo Blundo; Ricardo dispensatore, parente, et pluribus aliis.

MS: WAD, f. 493v.
    Rubric: Carta Gervasii abbatis Westmonasterii de quadam terra in London' reddendo ij solidos et viij denarios per annum.
    1. *Sic* in MS.
Pd: Harvey, 'Fee Farms', no. 2, p. 139.
Note: See Harvey, 'Fee Farms', 134, 138.

259. Grant by Abbot Gervase to Godwin Loffa of Bishopsgate for an annual rent of 4*s.* of the land in Langbourn ward (London), near the church of St Denis, which his grandfather Wlfward Grafte gave to the church of Westminster. [1138 × 1157]

Gervasius abbas Westmonasterii totusque conventus vicecomiti et omnibus baronibus Lundiniensibus, salutem. Notum sit presentibus et futuris nos concessisse Godwino Loffa de Bissopesgate et heredibus suis terram illam quam Wlfwardus Grafte, avus suus, dedit ecclesie Westmonasterii in custodia Langebort iuxta ecclesiam Sancti Dionisii, ad tenendum de nobis iiij solidos reddendo per annum, totum ad Pascha. Et ita volumus quod idem Godwinus predictam terram teneat bene et in pace et libere et quiete, sicut aliquis antecessorum suorum melius tenuit.

MS: WAD, f. 504v.
    Rubric: Telligraphus abbatis et conventus Westmonasterii de quadam terra in custodia de Langebort iuxta ecclesiam Sancti Dionisii.
Pd: Harvey, 'Fee Farms', no. 3, p. 139.
Note: In *c.* 1291 the abbey had 5*s.* rents in the parish of St Denis (*Taxatio Nicholai IV*, 10a). See also Harvey, 'Fee Farms', 136–7.

260. Confirmation by Abbot Gervase of the grant made by John son of Ralf to the church of St Pancras (Lewes) of the land Aluric Lambesheavod held in London, and two tenements which Wibert of Arras held of Westminster; St Pancras will hold all these for a total rent of 5*s.* a year. [1138 × 1157]

Gervasius abbas Westmonasterii et totus conventus vicecomiti et omnibus baronibus Lundonie, salutem. Sciant presentes et futuri nos concessisse et confirmasse donationem quam Johannes filius Radulfi dedit ecclesie Sancti Pancratii: videlicet, de terra quam AEluricus Lambesheavod tenuit in Lundonia et duas terras quas Wibertus de Arraz de nobis tenebat. Has terras concedimus ecclesie Sancti Pancratii de Leues ad tenendum de nobis, reddendo ecclesie nostre de terra AElurici Lambesheavod ii solidos per annum, et de terris Wiberti iij solidos. Et ita volumus ut bene et in pace predicta ecclesia Sancti Panchratii de ecclesia nostra teneat, quamdiu hos v solidos bene et legaliter reddiderit[1] his terminis: ad Pascha xxx denarios, ad Festum Sancti Michaelis xxx denarios. Hiis testibus: Petro Aldermanno, Alwardo presbitero, Radulfo de Arund', Rogero Pepercon, Ivone mercen[ario], AEadwardo Winpl', Willelmo filio Radulfi et aliis pluribus.

MSS: (1) PRO E 40/15564.
    26 × 7.6 cm; CIROGRAPHUM cut straight through.
    Endorsed: (a) Gervasii abbatis Westmonasterii. (b) Londoniensis diocesis de tenementis et terris in London'. (c) xvj. (d) [Illegible] in London.
    1. Corrected from *reddiderint* by expunging.
    (2) WAD, f. 476: variant, copied from Westminster's half of the cirograph. Text identical until the attestations, as follows: Willelmo de Coucham; Hugone filio Ulgeri; Johanne filio Radulfi filii Everardi; Roger Ganet; Salede; Estmundo, et aliis pluribus.
    Rubric: Carta abbatis et conventus Westmonasterii cirographata de donatione quam Johannes filius Radulfi dedit ecclesie Sancti Pancrati. Reddendo v solidos per annum.
Pd: Chaplais, 'Original Charters', no. 3, p. 101; partial facsimile (Plate IX(a).
Cal: *Cat. Ancient Deeds*, II, A.2389.

261. Grant by Abbot G[ervase] to Gerin the king's minister of the land of Endiff (near Charing in Westminster), which he bought from Walkelin, for 1lb. pepper annually at Michaelmas. Gerin gave 2s. to Walkelin's son and heir Robert for this concession. [1138 × 1157]

G[ervasius] abbas Westmonasterii omnibus hominibus suis et fidelibus, salutem. Sciatis me concessisse Gerino ministro regis, et homini meo, terram de AEnedetha, quam ipse emit de Walkelino et de heredibus suis, sibi et heredibus suis, dando per annum unam libram piperis abbati Westmonasterii ad Festivitatem Sancti Michaelis. Ad hanc conventionem hi fuerunt astantes et audientes ubi ipse Walkelinus, et Willelmus frater ipsius Walkelini, et Rodbertus filius Walkelini saisiaverunt ipsum Gerinum de terra illa, ita quod ipse Gerinus dedit Rodberto heredi ipsius Walkelini ij solidos pro una manca auri ut supradictam conventionem concederet: Helia prior; et Wimundus et Ricardus presbiteri; Ricardus prepositus; Salamon de Steb'; Rogerus de Meriend'; Herdewinus de AEnedeh'; Picotus cementarius; Rogerus de Curland'.

MSS: (1) WAM 17311.
    18 × 6 cm. Parchment tag, inserted through a t.u. at the foot of the charter, but seal lost.

Endorsed: (a) xv. (b) Celerarius (c) Terra de Anedehethe. (d) Carta G[ervasii] abbatis Westmonasterii de terra de Andehethe Gerino ministro regis concessa, reddendo inde annuatim abbati Westmonasterii unam libram piperis [in various 14C hands].
(2) WAD, f. 445.
Rubrics: (1) Celerarius. (2) Concessio G[ervasii] abbatis de terra de Andehethe.
Pd: Chaplais, 'Original Charters', no. 4, p. 101.
Date: Prior Elias, Picot *cementarius* and Salomon of Stepney all occur in documents of Gervase.
Note: Endiff lay on the Thames, between Westminster Abbey and Charing (*PN Mddx*, 168). On this grant, see Harvey, 'Fee Farms', 130, 138. Prior Osbert de Clare recorded the intercession of King Edward in the healing of a knight named Gerin, keeper of the royal palace at Westminster (*Vita AEdwardi Regis*, 126–7).

262. Grant by Abbot Gervase to his mother Damette of the manor of Chelsea (Mddx.) in fee farm for £4 a year. In return Damette has given £2 to the convent and a pall worth £5. [1138 × 1157]

Gervasius abbas Westmonasterii et totus conventus eiusdem loci omnibus hominibus suis Francis et Anglis, salutem. Sciant presentes et futuri nos concessisse manerium de Chelcheth' Damete, matri predicti abbatis, et heredibus suis ad tenendum in feudo et hereditate, cum omnibus eidem ville pertinentibus, in aqua et in terra, reddendo inde quatuor libras per annum, et defendendo erga regales consuetudines hiis terminis: ad Natale Domini xx solidos; ad Pascha xx solidos; ad Festum Sancti Johannis Baptiste xx solidos; ad Festum Sancti Michaelis xx solidos. Et ita volumus quod teneat bene et in pace, libere et honorifice, cum saca et soca et ceteris consuetudinibus liberis. Et pro hac concessione dedit predicta Dameta quadraginta solidos conventui et unum palleum centum solidorum.

MS: WAD, f. 114.
   Rubric: Dimissio manerii de Chelcheth'.
Pd: Flete, 89.
Note: See Harvey, 'Fee Farms', pp. 131 and no. 2, 138; **242** above.

263. Memorandum of the grant by Abbot Gervase to Gilbert son of Gunter of the manor of Hendon (Mddx.) in fee-farm for a rent of £20 a year. [Dec. 1154 × 1157]

Gervasius, Dei gratia abbas Sancti Petri Westmonasterii, et totus conventus ecclesie concederunt Gisleberto filio Gunteri et heredibus suis manerium[1] de Hendona in feudofirme cum omnibus rebus ad illud pertinentibus, pro xx[ti] libris reddendis inde per annum libere et honorifice et quiete, tenendum pro omnibus serviciis. Hiis testibus: Willelmo de Cuntevilla; Radulfo clerico; Mauricio clerico;[2] Godefrido presbitero fratre ipsius Gisleberti; Willelmo de Grest[ano]; Thomas pincerna; Willelmo de Mulesham; Stephano nepote Willelmi; Amalrico fratre abbatis; Radulfo Runt; Alexandro fratre eius; Ricardo preposito; Richerio filio eius; Richerio filio Evrardi et multis aliis.

MS: WAD, f. 124.
> Rubric: Carta Gervasii abbatis de eodem [i.e. de manerio de Hendon'].
>> 1. MS, *manenerium*.
>> 2. MS, *cleririco*.

Pd: Harvey, 'Fee Farms', no. 7, p. 142.
Date: Prob. issued in response to the mandate of H II (**124**).
Note: See Harvey, *WA*, 352, and 'Fee Farms', 135–6.

264. Confirmation by Abbot Gervase to the nuns of Kilburn (Mddx.) of the corrody held by Ailmar the hermit, the corrody of Abbot Gilbert and a third corrody which they held according to their charter (**249**). [1138 × 1157]

Notum sit omnibus ecclesie fidelibus tam presentibus quam futuris quod ego Gervasius abbas Westmonasterii dono et concedo, pro salute anime mee et pro anima Regis Edwardi, necnon et pro salute omnium successorum meorum, ancillis Christi de Keneburna unum plenarium moniale corredium: illud videlicet quod habuit Ailmarus heremita in pane et cervisia, in vino et medone, et in pitancia. Istud corredium prece ac petitione nostra communi consilio et consensu totius capituli nostri confirmari feci. Preterea, notum sit quod nos communiter et concordi voluntate corredium Gilberti abbatis illis concessimus, et tertium corredium quod secundum tenorem carte sue antea habuerunt, firmiter confirmo.[1] Volumus igitur et constanter precipimus ut hec tria beneficia in pane et cervisia et coquina, in vino, in medone et pitanciis, cum uno tantummodo clareto scilicet pro anima Gilberti abbatis, absque ulla contradictione et contrarietate et diminutione in perpetuam elemosinam habeant. Quincunque ergo hec beneficia manutenuerint et manutenendo pro Christo augere voluerint benedictionem Dei et nostram precipiant; qui vero diminuere presumpserit, semel et secundo ac tertio correptus, nisi digna emendatione satisfecerit iram Omnipotentis Dei et nostram maledictionem incurrat. Deus omnipotens sit testis et conservator ac susceptor huius donationis ac constitutionis nostre. Amen.

MSS: (1) F, ff. 327v–328.
> Rubric: Carta Gilberti abbatis de tribus corrediis monialibus de Kylborne concessis.
> (2) LN, f. cxxv *verso*.
>> 1. LN, *confirmavimus*.
> (3) CAY, f. cxxxiv *verso*.

Pd: *Monasticon*, III, no. IV, 427 (from F).
Cal: Bentley, 64, no. 527, from CAY.

265. Grant by Abbot Gervase to the nuns at Kilburn of land at Gore in the manor of Knightsbridge (Mddx.). They are to hold it free of service, as they were seised of it by Brother Osbert de Clare, and as it was measured by the men of the vill. [1138 × 1157]

Gervasius, abbas ecclesie Sancti Petri Westmonasterii, et totus eiusdem ecclesie conventus, tam futuris quam presentibus, salutem. Notum vobis sit nos, communi assensu totius capituli et consilio, dedisse in elemosina, pro anima regis nostri Edwardi, fundatoris ecclesie nostre, et pro animabus omnium fratrum et benefactorum nostrorum, ancillis Dei que sunt in ecclesia Beati Johannis Baptiste de Keneburna, et omnibus que ibidem ad serviendum Deo future sunt, quandam terram ad sartandum in tenetura, manerii nostri quod vocatur Knihtebruga, et in loco qui Gara appellatur. Volumus igitur et firmiter precipimus ut in pace et quiete et libere et sine omni servicio teneant illam predictam terram sicut eas inde saysivit frater noster Osbertus de Clara, et sicut meta et divisio illius terre facta est per respectum et considerationem et mensuram hominum illius ville. Et si quis eis super hanc donationem et donationis libertatem aliquam inde violentiam vel dampnum vel contumeliam aut torturam aliquam fecerit, et elemosinam nostram violare vel auferre a predicta ecclesia presumpserit, nisi ancillis Dei citam et congruum satisfactionem fecerit, ab omni conventu ecclesie nostre excommunicetur, et a Christo pauperum suorum defensore perpetuo anathematis gladio feriatur. Amen. Hii sunt testes: Gregorius dapifer; Radulphus clericus; Mauricius clericus; Ricardus prepositus; et Hathewy, qui idem manerium tenebat, et multi alii.

MSS: (1) F, f. 328r–v.
    Rubric: Carta Gervasii Abbatis et conventus Westmonasterii de terra de Gara in Knygthbrigge monialibus de Kylborne concessis.
    (2) LN, f. cxxv *verso.*
    (3) CAY, f. cxxxiv *verso.*
Pd: *Monasticon*, III, no. V, 427 (from F).
Note: See Harvey, *WA*, 353. See also **250** above.

266. Notification by Abbot Gervase to Earl Geoffrey [de Mandeville] that he has granted to Prior William of Hurley (Berks.) part of the pannage which the Abbey held in Edmonton (Mddx.), in the time of Geoffrey de Mandeville I. [1140 × 1157]

Gervasius, Dei gratia abbas, totusque conventus Sancti Petri Westmonasterii dilecto fratri et amico Comiti Gaufrido, et omnibus baronibus suis, salutem. Notum sit vobis omnibus quod, communi consensu totius capituli nostri, concessimus Deo et Beate Marie semper virgini, et Sancto Leonardo Confessori, et Willelmo Priori, cunctisque successoribus suis, et familie Christi monachis uidelicet Herleiensis monasterii, partem pasnagii nostri quod a diebus primi Gaufridi de Magnavilla possedit ecclesia nostra in Eadelmatona in porcis et denariis. Et precamur et volumus ut vos idem pro amore Dei et animarum vestrarum salute concedatis et faciatis et litteris vestris secundum quod in carta ista uidebitis ad ministros uestros confirmetis. Valete.

MS: WAM 3750*.

18.5 × 7.9 cm; tongue 2.5 cm.

Seal: Seal of Gervase (as above); red; on tongue.

Endorsed: (a) Gervasius abbas de pasnagio in Edelemantone (13C).
(b) 8v (15C).

Pd: Chaplais, 'Original Charters', no. 8, p. 104; Wethered, *Lands of Hurley*, 32–3 (trans., ibid., 33–4).

Cal: Wethered, *Lands of Hurley*, no. 564, p. 12.

Date: William was prior of Hurley from some uncertain date *post* 1140 (*Heads*, 92). The Geoffrey de Mandeville addressed was perhaps the first earl (1140–44), but more prob. his s. the second earl (*c.* Jan. 1156–Oct. 1166) (*HBC*, 460).

267. Grant by Abbot Gervase to Alger the clerk of the land which Puncelin his grandfather held in Ham (Essex), for an annual rent of £3. [? 1144 × 1156]

G[ervasius] abbas Westmonasterii et totus conventus eiusdem loci concedunt Algero clerico terram quam Puncelinus avus suus tenuit in Hamma, ipsi et heredibus suis ad tenendum de ecclesia Sancti Petri, bene et in pace, libere et quiete, reddendo per annum lx solidos: ad Natale xv solidos; ad Pascha xv solidos; ad Festum[1] Sancti Michaelis xv solidos.[2] Et ita teneat quamdiu[3] fideliter servierit. Hiis testibus: Willelmo priore Sancti Ivonis; Galfrido de Magna Villa; Warino filio Gerini; Henrico fratre suo; Alur[edo] clerico de Watham[stede]; Waltero de Lectona; Willelmo filio Alur[edi]; Simone filio Osberti; Radulfo de Querendona; Galure[do] Merc' et fratre suo, et multi alii.[4]

MS: WAD, f. 496v.

Rubric: Telligraphus[5] abbatis et conventus Westmonasterii de terra quam Puncelinus tenuit in Hamma, reddendo lx solidos.

Marginalia: Hamme.

1. *Festum* repeated, but struck out.
2. *Sic* in MS. The omitted term is presumably the feast of St John the Baptist.
3. *teneat quam*, written over an erasure; another *teneat* has been deleted after *quamdiu*.
4. *Sic*, MS, for *multis aliis*.
5. *Telligrahus*.

Pd: Harvey, 'Fee Farms', no. 6, p. 142.

Date: Since Geoffrey de Mandeville attests without a title, this witness is prob. Geoffrey III, attesting between the death of Geoffrey II in 1144, and 1156, when he himself was created earl of Essex (*G.E.C.*, v, 116–7). William, prior of St Ives, was in office in 1143, and he, or a later William, was prior in 1185 × 1187 (*Heads*, 95).

Note: See Harvey, 'Fee Farms', 135, and *WA*, 342.

268. Memorandum of an agreement between Abbot Gervase and Prior Robert of Merton. Land in Wandsworth (Surr.) was granted to Westminster, to facilitate the siting of [fulling-]mills, in exchange for other land in Wandsworth, granted to Merton priory, near the granges of Dunsfold (Surr.). [1138 × 1157]

Sciant presentes et futuri hoc convenisse inter ecclesiam Sancti Petri Westmonasterii et ecclesiam Beate Marie de Merton': quod ecclesia Beate Marie concessit ecclesie Sancti Petri quondam partem terre sue de Wendleswrth, ad assidendum molendina sua, iiij perticarum in lato[1] coram molendino, et octo in longo, secus viam. Et ecclesia Beati Petri, in recompensationem huius rei, concessit ecclesie Beate Marie duas acras de terra sua eiusdem ville coram grangiis de Dunesford. Hec transmutatio facta est auctoritate Gervasii abbatis Westmonasterii et Roberti prioris Mertonie, et assensu utriusque capituli.

MS: WAD, f. 370.
    Rubric: Cirographus inter ecclesiam Westmonasterii et ecclesiam de Merton de quadam parte terre pro molendinis fullenariis in Wendleswrth'.
    1. MS, *in lato* repeated.
Date: Robert de Tywe (1117–50) and Robert II (1150–67) were successively priors of Merton (*Heads*, 175).
Note: It is only in the rubric that these Wandsworth mills were described as fulling-mills during Gervase's abbacy, but the text is entered in WAD together with the confirmation to the convent by Abbot William d'Humez (1214–22) of a fulling-mill at Wandsworth, to maintain lights round the feretory of St Edward (WAD, f. 370). For the subsequent history of these mills, see Emma Mason, 'Westminster Abbey's fulling-mills at Wandsworth', *Bulletin of the Wandle Group*, no. 13 (December 1984), 4.

269. Grant by Abbot G[ervase] to Robert his marshal of three virgates and other lands, all waste, in Wheathampstead (Herts.) in fee-farm for an annual rent of 10s. [1138 × 1157]

G[ervasius], Dei gratia abbas Westmonasterii, et totus eiusdem ecclesie conventus concedunt Roberto marescallo suo et heredibus suis tres virgatas terre in manerio nostro de Watamsted' in feodo et hereditate: terram, videlicet, quam Willelmus de Couele in eadem villa ex utraque parte aque[1] tenuit, et eam postea pro v^que annorum servicii et monachorum victus defectu ecclesie voluntarie reddidit et quietam finaliter clamavit, et terram similiter quam Geroldus camberarius abbatis Hereberti tenuit, et postea pro viij° annorum servicii et monachorum victus defectu ecclesie quiete reddidit, que antea Leofwini magistri fuerat, quam et ipsi Leofwini[2] etiam heredes ecclesie et monachis quietam et sine calumpnia reddiderunt et solutam omnino clamaverunt. Et ideo volunt ut ipse Robertus et heredes eius terram istam ita bene et in pace, libere et quiete teneant, sicut prefatus Leofwinus umquam eam melius tenuit et sicut ullus homo Sancti Petri in tota villa melius. Concedunt eidem Roberto et heredibus suis etiam terram quam Ricardus de Osumull tenuit et pro servicii iii annorum et monachorum victus defectu ecclesie et monachis ipse et heredes eius omnino liberam reddiderunt et solutam et quietam clamaverunt, et unam similiter cotelondam que fuit Godwini porcarii ad se hospitandum et ad domos suas in ea faciendas. Omnes vero terre iste predicte vaste et deassise erant et eas versus regem de proprio illorum dominio singulis annis adquietari opportuit. Sed idem Robertus pro tribus virgatis amodo eas versus regem defendet. Hanc quidem donationem similiter et concessionem eidem Roberto et heredibus suis abbas et conventus Westmonasterii tam consilio et assensu totius capituli quam consideratione et iudicio proborum virorum illorum de Watamstede contulerunt et suo presenti scripto confirmaverunt et inde suum homagium in pleno capitulo susceperunt. Quare volunt et firmiter concedunt ut idem Robertus et eiusdem heredes terras teneant prenominatas bene et in pace, libere et quiete, in bosco et in plano, in terris et in aquis, cum omnibus consuetudinibus et libertatibus que in aliis terris Sancti Petri pertinent. Reddendo inde annis singulis x^{tem} solidos in firma manerii pro omni servicio hiis terminis: ad Natale xxx denarios; ad Pascha xxx denarios; ad Festum Sancti Johannis xxx denarios; ad Festum Sancti Michaelis xxx denarios. Et inde isti sunt testes: Radulfus clericus; Ricardus prepositus; Willelmus de Watamstede; Rogerus eiusdem[3] filius; Radulfus frater abbatis; Amalricus abbatis frater; Gerinus miles; Stephanus de Cuntav'; Willelmus[3] aurifaber; Hugo Bellus; Simon cocus; Radulfus eiusdem Roberti armiger, et multi alii.

MS: WAD, f. 205.

> Rubric: Carta G[ervasii] abbatis Westmonasterii et totus eiusdem ecclesie conventus de tribus virgatibus terre in manerio de Wathamstede.
> Marginalia: (1) supl' paucis gariantibus. (2) supl' paucis. (3) Gervasius abbas.
> 1. *aque* underlined.
> 2. *Sic* in MS.
> 3. MS. damaged and repaired after this word.

Pd: Harvey, 'Fee Farms', no. 5, p. 141.

Date: The lands were perhaps waste as a result of some incident during the civil war. Both Stephen and Matilda visited St Alban's, while Geoffrey de Mandeville had his headquarters not far away.

Note: See Harvey, *WA*, 347, and 'Fee Farms', 133.

270. Grant by Abbot G[ervase] to Elias the deacon of the church of Islip (Northants.) for an annual payment of half a mark (6*s.* 8*d.*), saving the rights of the church of Westminster and the holding of the sokemen of Islip who hold of that church. [1148 × 1157]

G[ervasius], Dei gratia abbas Westmonasterii, R[oberto] episcopo et toti clero episcopatus Lincolniensis, salutem. Sciant me in elemosinam canonice concessisse Helie, decano ecclesiam de Islepa, salvo iure ecclesie Beati Petri Westmonasterii, et salvo tenemento soccamanorum de Islepa, qui de ecclesia Beati Petri Westmonasterii tenent, reddendo michi per annum dimidiam marcam argenti. Hiis testibus: Ricardo de Bissea, monacho; Johanne monacho; Henrico, presbitero de Sudburgo;

Gaufrido, presbitero de Dena; Hugone capellano suo; Ricardo presbitero de Sudwica; Sueinone, presbitero de Stanerda;[1] Henrico, presbitero de Apetorp; Helia clerico; Radulfo de Septem Fontanis; Radulfo filio Nigelli; Willelmo de Grestano; Gaufrido fratre suo; Andrea de Hwath; Waltero de Sudburgo; Helia de Mulesham; Gaufrido filio Parentis; Ricardo Blundo.

MS: WAM 15183.
>16 × 6.5 cm. Step in left-hand corner.
>CIROGRAPHUM cut in two along bottom.
>Endorsed: Islepe. Scriptum G[ervasii], abbatis Westmonasterii, de ecclesia de Islepa. (14C)
>>1. Or *Stanertha*.

Pd: Chaplais, 'Original Charters', no. 7, p. 103, with facsimile (Plate VIII(a)).

Date: Limited by terms of office of Abbot Gervase and of Robert de Chesney, bp. of Lincoln (cf. *Fasti* III, 2).

Note: The Northamptonshire Survey, an early twelfth-century compilation, subsequently revised before the middle of the century (*VCH Northants.*, I, 357–8), stated that four of the King's sokemen held one hide of the fee of Westminster Abbey (ibid., I, 365). This estate was prob. the land, comprising 1 hide 1 virgate, which was held in 1086 by the bp. of Coutances (*DB* I, f. 220v.). The identification of the church as that of Islip, Northants (rather than of Islip, Oxon.), is confirmed by the attestations of local clergy, incl. those of Sudborough and Deene, in both of which Westminster held demesne manors (cf. Harvey, *WA*, 355).

271.* Grant by Abbot Gervase to William of Darnford in fee-farm of the manor of Deerhurst (Gloucs.) for an annual payment of £30; also the half hundred of Deerhurst with all its liberties as they were granted to the abbey by King Edward. [1138 × c. 1141]

G[ervasius], Dei gratia abbas Westmonasterii, omnibus amicis et tenentibus Sancti Petri Westmonasterii, tam clericis quam laicis, Francis et Anglis, salutem. Noverit universitas vestra nos unanimi consensu totius conventus nostri Sancti Petri Westmonasterii dedisse et concessisse et hac presenti carta nostra confirmasse Willelmo de Derneford in feodofirma manerium de Derhurst' cum omnibus pertinenciis suis. Tenendum et habendum de nobis et de successoribus nostris sibi et heredibus suis, libere et quiete, bene et in pace, jure hereditarie inperpetuum. Reddendo inde annuatim nobis et successoribus nostris xxx[ta] libras argenti ad duos anni terminos: scilicet, infra octabas Pasche xv libras, et infra octabas Sancti Michaelis xv libras pro omnibus serviciis, consuetudinibus et exactionibus secularibus ad nos vel ad successores nostros pertinentibus. Quare volumus et concedimus pro nobis et successoribus nostris quod predicti Willelmus et heredes sui habeant et teneant predictum manerium de Derhurste cum omnibus libertatibus et liberis consuetudinibus, in bosco et plano, in pratis et pasturis, in aquis et molendinis, in viis et semitis, in stagnis[1] et vivariis, in mariscis et piscariis, infra villam et extra, et in omnibus aliis locis ad predictum manerium de

133

Derhurst' pertinentibus. Concedimus etiam predictis Willelmo et heredibus suis dimidium hundredum de Derhurst cum duabus sectis visus franciplegii per annum, et cum omnibus aliis sectis et omnibus libertatibus: videlicet, in homagiis, releviis, herietis, eschaetis recipiendis et habendis, et in omnibus aliis ad predictum manerium de Derhurst pertinentibus. Et quod nos vel successores nostri vel nostri ballivi nullum ingressum habeamus infra libertatem predicti manerii de Derhurst ad districtiones vel ad aliquas submonitiones faciendas, nisi tantum pro firma nostra si forte retineatur ultra terminos predictos, et tunc namia que capta fuerint pro eadem non ducantur extra libertates predicti manerii de Derhurst'. Omnes vero alias districtiones et submonitiones infra predictum manerium faciendas predictis Willelmo et heredibus suis inperpetuum liberas concedimus et quietas. Concedimus etiam pro nobis et successoribus nostris quod, si predicti Willelmus vel heredes sui in comitatu, hundredo vel in aliqua alia curia per querimoniam de ipsis factam sint inplacitati et nos per libertates nostras curiam nostram exigerimus de ipsis sicuti de hominibus nostris, et curia nostra nobis per iudicium fuerit concessa, nos vel successores nostri curiam nostram alibi non tenebimus nisi infra predictum manerium de Derhurst, et tunc, si predicti Willelmus vel heredes sui vel homines nostri in predicto manerio de Derhurst sint amerciati coram nobis vel ballivis nostris pro quacumque causa vel forisfacto, predicti Willelmus vel heredes sui misericordiam illam absque alia contradictione habeant, tam de hominibus nostris quam de eorum hominibus propriis, ad firmam nostram predictam melius perficiendam et nobis reddendam. [Concedi]mus etiam predictis Willelmo et heredibus suis omnes libertates et liberas consuetudines quas gloriosus Rex Sanctus Edwardus nobis contulit et concessit. Et si no[s]² vel successores nostri in posterum aliquas libertates de aliis regibus seu aliis fidelibus Anglie perquisiverimus, nos easdem libertates eisdem concedimus et [confirm]amus, ita quod illis adeo libere et plenarie utantur sicuti nos melius et liberius illis utimur in dominicis maneriis nostris seu in aliis locis ubicumque libertates habuerimus. Nos autem et successores nostri predictis Willelmo et heredibus suis predictum manerium de Derhurst cum omnibus pertinentiis et omnibus libertatibus et liberis consuetudinibus predictis contra omnes homines et feminas pro predicto redditu inperpetuum warantizabimus, manutenebimus et defendemus. Et nos una cum conventu nostro predicte domus nostre Sancti Petri Westmonasterii ad hoc assensum probente et confirmante excomunicavimus omnes illos qui predictas libertates et liberas consuetudines de predictis Willelmo vel heredibus suis auferunt vel auferre nituntur, quoniam illis adeo specialiter et firmiter pro nobis et pro successoribus nostris illas concedimus et confirmamus sicuti nos specialius et liberius alicui illas dare possumus, concedere vel confirmare. Hiis testibus: Helia, priore Sancti Petri Westmonasterii; Ansgodo monacho; Ricardo de Bissea monacho; Adam monacho de Malvernia; Roberto Folet; Rogero de Stanton; Oliverio; Hugone Bello; Adam filio Godefridi de Persora, et pluribus aliis.

MSS: (1) WAM 32668.

26.5 × 19.5 cm; t.u. 1.5 cm; MS stained. Two vertical and three horizontal folds. Tag sur double queue. This charter is written in a 13C hand, and both the phraseology and the detailed legal provisions show that it cannot be a true copy of its putative original (Harvey, 'Fee Farms', p. 132 and n. 1).
Endorsed: (a) ij (13C). (b) Carta Gervasii abbatis Westmonasterii facta Willelmo Deneford' de manerio de Derestrt cum pertinentiis (13C). (c) Derherst (13C). (d) Derhurst' (13C).
   1. MS, *stangnis*.
   2. *West* interlined.
(2) WAD, f. 316r–v.
(3) CAY, f. lxxj *verso* (memorandum: payment given as £34).
Pd: Harvey, 'Fee Farms', no. 4, pp. 139–41 (from WAM), setting out grounds for its being a forgery.
Cal: Bentley, 36, no. 258 (item 2), from CAY.
Alleged date: The empress's confirmation is 1138 × 1148, prob. no later than 1141: cf. *Regesta* III, no. 259. Compare with the charter from the convent (**341**) confirming the grant made by 'Gervasius quondam abbas noster', and with Henry II's confirmation (**136**).
Note: Deerhurst (Gloucs.) was given to Westminster along with other former possessions of Pershore Abbey by the Confessor (Harmer, nos. 99–102, and pp. 290–294). It was assessed in *DB* at 50 hides (the half-hundred of Deerhurst was the only hundred possessed by the abbey and was worth £40 TRE and £41 in 1086). See also Harvey, *WA*, 344–5, and 'Fee Farms', 131–3.

272. Notification by Abbot Gervase to Aylwin the sheriff of Sussex that Turbern of the Weald has fled to sanctuary. [1138 × 1154]

Gervasius abbas et omnis congregatio Westmonasterii Aylwyno vice-comiti et omnibus baronibus de Southsexia, salutem. Sciatis quod Tur-bernus de Welda misericordiam Dei et altarem Sancti Petri atque sepulcrum Regis Edwardi ad liberacionem sui requisivit. Est autem consuetudo et privilegium et ab antiquis Anglie regibus dignitas ista ecclesie Sancti Petri donata ut amplius pro ea forisfactura de qua calumpniatus erat non perdat neque vitam, neque membra, neque omnino aliquid suarum rerum amittat. Valete.

MS: F, f. 258v.
   Rubric: Littera testimonialis antiqua de visitacione magni altaris Sancti Petri Westmonasterii et sepulcri Regis etc.
Pd: *Monasticon*, I, no. LXI, 310.
Date: No known sheriff of Sussex is named Aylwyn in the reign of Henry II, so that this writ antedates his accession.

273. Notification by Abbot G[ervase] to R sheriff of Sussex that — has fled to sanctuary. [1138 × 1157]

G[ervasius] abbas humilis et omnis congregacio Sancti Petri West-monasterii R vicecomiti et omnibus baronibus de Sussex, salutem. Sciatis quod iste [name erased] misericordiam Dei et altare Sancti Petri et sepulcrum Regis Edwardi ad liberacionem sui requisivit. Est autem consuetudo et privilegium et ab antiquis Anglie regibus dignitas ista ecclesie Sancti Petri donata, ut amplius forisfactum de quo calumpniatus erat non perdat neque vitam neque membra sua neque omnino aliquid suarum rerum amittat. Valete.

MS: WAD, f. 79v.
Date: Richard de Humez was sheriff of Sussex 1156 × 1157, and was succeeded by Ralph Picot 1157 × 1160 (*Sheriffs*, 141). However, R. was perhaps an otherwise unidentified sheriff in Stephen's reign, since before the end of Gervase's abbacy, and prob. before the end of Stephen's reign, there was a further development in the wording of the fugitive writ (**274**).

274. Notification by Abbot G[ervase] to N sheriff of Mddx. that H has fled to sanctuary because of a charge of theft. [1138 × 1157 (? × 1154)]

Domino N vicecomiti Midlesexie G[ervasius] humilis abbas et omnis congregacio Sancti Petri Westmonasterii, salutem. Iste H requisivit misericordiam Dei et Sancti Petri et sepulchrum Regis Edwardi propter reatum furti quod sibi imponitur. Scitote igitur talis est dignitas ecclesie nostre et Regis Edwardi postquam aliquis reus ibi misericordiam sicut supradiximus requisierit nec vitam nec membrum pro illo reatu debet amittere; precamur ergo vos et monemus ne contra domum et auxilium tanti patroni facere presumatis. Valete.

MS: WAD, f. 79v.
Date: There is no known N sheriff of Middlesex for the early years of Henry II, so this document almost certainly dates from Stephen's reign.
Note: This form of fugitive writ was prob. the latest issued during Gervase's abbacy, since Laurence's writ is a development of its format (**279**).

275. Confirmation by Abbot Laurence to Baldwin Crisp of the lands he holds of the abbey in London by hereditary right for the annual rent of £1. 19*s*. 3*d*.: the lands are specified in five parcels. [1158 × 1173]

Noverint ad quos littere iste pervenerint quod ego L[aurentius], Dei gratia abbas Westmonasterii, et conventus eiusdem loci concedimus et presenti carta confirmamus Baldewino Crispo omnes terras quas de nobis tenet[1] in London' jure hereditarie possidendas, reddendo inde annuatim xxxix solidos et tres denarios, videlicet: de terra que in foro est que fuit Stephani filii Walding viginti novem solidos et xj denarios; de terra que fuit Roberti presbiteri de Sumersete chirch' iiij solidos et vj denarios; de terra in qua Gaufridus Pinchehaste manet xxxij denarios, de sopa Derman carnificis, quam Walterus le Lutre eidem Baldewino vendidit, ij solidos; de terra que fuit Willelmi le Lutre ij denarios. Hiis testibus: Magistro Radulfo; Magistro Mauricio; Alano dapifero; Rogero clerico; Simone clerico; Rogero cubiculario; Gerardo; Gileberto; Radulfo de Mulesham; Roberto clerico; Everardo aurifabro; Simone fratre eius;

Johanne Thorneys; Osberto de Sutton; Johanne Blund; Alured de Westmonasterio; Aluredo filio Walteri.

MS: WAD, ff. 493v–494.
> Rubric: Cirographum L. abbatis et conventus Westmonasterii de terris in London. Reddendo xxxix solidos et iij denarios per annum.
> 1. MS *tenent*.

276. Notification by Abbot Laurence that he has remitted to Baldwin Crisp for life 3*s*. 3*d*. on the land in Cheap (*in foro*), (London), which belonged to Stephen son of Walding; and 8*d*. on the land where Geoffrey Pinchehaste lives. After Baldwin's death his heirs are to pay the usual rent, namely £1. 9*s*. 11*d*. on the former land and 2*s*. 8*d*. on the latter. [1158 × 1173]

Noverint ad quos littere iste pervenerint quod ego L[aurentius], Dei gratia abbas Westmonasterii, et conventus eiusdem loci remittimus Baldewino Crispo tantum in vita sua de terra que in foro est que fuit Stephani filii Walding, tres solidos et iij denarios; et de terra in qua Gaufridus Pinchehaste manet viij denarios. Post decessum vero Baldewini, heredes ipsius de prenominatis terris plenarie solitam censam persolvent, videlicet: de terra que in foro est xxix solidos et xj denarios, et de terra in qua Gaufridus Pinchehaste manet xxxij denarios, nisi forte a nobis impetrare possint ut eis inde aliquid condonetur. Hiis testibus: [none given]

MS: WAD, f. 493v.
> Rubric: Moderacio L. abbatis Westmonasterii super redditum in foro facta Baldewino Crispo tamen in vita sua.
Date: Later than **275**.

277. Grant by Abbot Laurence to Richard of Ilchester, archdeacon of Poitou, of the house in the Fishmarket, London, which the monk Peter of Windsor gave to the abbey; he is to hold it in fee for an annual rent of one pound of pepper at Easter. The archdeacon has paid ten marks (£6. 13*s*. 4*d*.) for this grant. [1158 × 1173]

Laurentius, Dei gratia abbas Westmonasterii, universis fidelibus ad quos presentes littere pervenerint, salutem. Notum sit omnibus quod nos provida deliberacione communicato fratrum nostrorum consilio concessimus et dedimus Ricardo archidiacono Pictavensi domum quam Petrus de Windesore monachus noster ecclesie nostre dedit London in piscaria; tenendam sibi et heredibus suis de ecclesia nostra inperpetuum in feudo et hereditate, reddendo michi j libram piperis annuatim in termino Pasche pro omni servicio. Quia ipse Petrus eandem domum sub ea condicione ecclesie nostre dedit ut predictus archidiaconus et heredes sui eam de ecclesia nostra hereditarie tenere deberent. Pro hac autem concessione et donacione dedit nobis idem archidiaconus decem marcas argenti. Testibus: Roberto de Burnham; Edwardo de Well'; Henrico de London'; Aluredo de Watm'; Magistro Gregorio; Elia capellano; Radulfo de Exonia; Willelmo de Sancta Fide; Johanne de Garlande;

Johanne Buccuinte; Gaufrido filio Sabelli; Johanne Burg'; Alexandro de Barent'; Osberto Quarel; Roberto filio Alani; Osberto de Kinet'; Radulfo Marisco.

MS: WAD f. 368.
Rubric: Carta Laurencii abbatis Westmonasterii de quadam domo in piscaria London'.

278. Confirmation by Abbot Laurence to John the Burgundian of the grant made to him by Richard of Ilchester, archdeacon of Poitou, of the house which Peter of Windsor had in the Fishmarket, London. John and his heirs will pay the archdeacon and his heirs one besant and one pound of pepper annually. [1158 × 1173]

Laurentius abbas Westmonasterii universis hominibus et fidelibus suis, salutem. Sciatis quod nos, communicato fratrum nostrorum consilio, concessimus, et hac carta nostra confirmavimus, Johanni Burgund' donationem quam Ricardus archidiaconus Pictavensis ei fecit de domo que fuit Petri de Windesor', London' in Piscaria, scilicet: ut Johannes et heredes sui teneant domum [de] ipso archidiacono et de suis heredibus in feodo et hereditate; reddendo inde eidem archidiacono et heredibus suis per annum unum bisantium et unam libram piperis, sicut ipse archidiaconus ei concessit et carta sua confirmavit. Testibus: Roberto de Burneham; Willelmo de Sancta Fide; Radulfo de Crout; Alano Senesc[allo]; Alexandro de Barent'; Osberto Quarel, et multis aliis.

MS: Royal Hospital of St Bartholomew Archives Hc. 1/1149.
13.8 × 8 cm; t.u. 2 cm.
Seal: Brown; 3.4 cm diameter, attached by tag; half-length figure of abbot; legend: SIGILLUM LAURENTII ABBATIS.
Pd: Moore, *Hist. St Bartholomew's* I, 76 (facsimile).
Cal: *Cart. St Bartholomew's*, no. 718.
Date: Later than **277**.
Note: Richard's grant to John is pd. Moore, I, 73–4; cal. *Cart. St Bartholomew's*, no. 722.

279. Notification by Abbot Laurence to Brithstan (? Brihmer de Haverhill), sheriff of Mddx., that Siward of Dunstable has sought sanctuary because of a charge of theft. [1158 × 1174]

Domino Brithstano vicecomiti de Middilsex' Laurentius abbas et omnis congregacio Sancti Petri Westmonasterii, salutem. Sciatis quod iste Sywardus de Dunstapell' requisivit misericordiam Dei et Sancti Petri et sepulcrum Regis Edwardi propter reatum furti quod sibi imponitur. Scitote ergo quia talis est dignitas nostre ecclesie et Regis Edwardi quod postquam aliquis reus ibi misericordiam sicut supradictum est requisierit nec vitam nec membra pro illo reatu debet amittere. Precamur vos ergo et monemus ne contra Deum et contra auxilium tanti patroni facere presumatis. Valete.

MS: F, ff. 258v–259.

138

Rubric: Littera testimonialis Laurentii abbatis de eodem.
Pd: *Monasticon* I, no. LXIII, 310.
Date: Brithstan is not listed among the sheriffs of London and Mddx., although the sheriff at Michaelmas 1159 is unnamed. Prob. his name is a corruption of Brihmer, i.e. Brihmer of Haverhill, in office at Michaelmas, 1157, 1158, 1174 (*Sheriffs*, 200).

280. Confirmation by Abbot Laurence of the grants (**249–50, 264–5**) of Abbots Herbert and Gervase to the nuns of Kilburn (Mddx.). [1158 × 1173]

Laurencius abbas Westmonasterii universis Sancte Matris Ecclesie fidelibus, salutem. Pium est ac religiosum ea que sanctis locis a fidelibus caritatis intuitu collata sunt confirmare et ne in posterum quorumlibet pravitate valeant auferri scriptorum munimine roborare; eapropter quecumque a predecessoribus nostris Hereberto et Gervasio abbatibus ancillis Christi de Kyneburna rationabiliter concessa sunt, nos auctoritate qua possumus ratum habemus et sigilli nostri impressione confirmamus. Hiis testibus: Radulfo fratre abbatis Westmonasterii; Magistro Mauricio, Symone clerico; Willelmo filio Isabelle; Radulfo de vij Fontibus, Hugone Bello et Roberto Testard.

MSS: (1) F, ff. 328v–329.
Rubric: Carta confirmacionis Laurentii abbatis de donacione predecessorum suorum ancillis de Kylborne c[apitulu]m clj.
Marginalia: (partially erased) Et confirma[cio] Laurentii [abbatis] de donatione predecessorum ancillis de Kelborne.
(2) LN, f. cxxv *verso* (omitting attestation of William fitz Isabel).
(3) CAY, f. cxxxiv verso.
Pd:*Monasticon* III, 427, no. VI.
Cal: Bentley, 64, no. 527.
Date: Possibly William Fitz Isabel attested in his capacity as sheriff: in office at Michaelmas 1162, and also in other years outside Laurence's abbacy (*Sheriffs*, 200).

281. Quitclaim made in the Exchequer at Westminster by Abbot Robert of St Albans and Robert Taileboys and his brothers to Abbot Laurence of charges in Aldenham (Herts.). In return, Abbot Laurence gave the brothers twenty-three marks (£15. 6s. 8d.) and quittance of pannage for twenty pigs in Aldenham wood yearly. 29 Sept. 1165.

Sciant omnes fideles, tam presentes quam futuri, quod Robertus abbas ecclesie Sancti Albani, pro se et conventu suo, et Robertus Tailleb[oys] et fratres eius Rogerus et Simon, pro se et heredibus suis, quietamclamaverunt Laurentio abbati et ecclesie Westmonasterii omnem calumniam quam Robertus abbas faciebat adversus ecclesiam Westmonasterii et abbatem pro Roberto Tailleb[oys] et fratribus eius Rogero et Simone in Aldenham, tam in bosco quam in plano. Pro hac autem quietatione dedit abbas Westmonasterii predictis fratribus xxiij marcas argenti consentiente Roberto abbate Sancti Albani. Concessit etiam abbas et conventus Westmonasterii supradictis fratribus et eorum heredibus quietationem pannagii xx porcorum in bosco de Aldenham singulis annis tempore glandis. Hec autem quietatio facta est ad scaccarium apud Westmonasterium anno xi regni Regis Henrici Secundi, in Festo Sancti Michaelis, assidentibus iusticiis regis: Nigello, episcopo Heliensi; Gaufrido archidiachono Cantuariensi; Ricardo, archidiacono Pictaviensi; Ricardo, thesaurario regis; Widone, decano de Waltham; Roberto, comite Legrensi; Ricardo de Luci; Henrico filio Geroldi, Willelmo Mald', camerariis regis: Symone filio Petri; Alano de Novilla; Gaufrido monacho; Willelmo filio Audel', mareschallo regis; Philippo de Daventr'.

MSS: WAM 4465, 4497. These have identical texts, apart from an occasional omission of a punctuation mark by one or the other, but are in different hands.

(1) WAM 4465.

18.1 × 13 cm; tongue (stub only): 2.6 cm; 12C hand. No seal.

Endorsed: (a) Quietaclamatio de calumnia Roberti Tayleboys et fratrum suorum de terra in Aldeham (13C). (b) facta ecclesie Westmonasterii (14C). (c) De calumnia Robertj Tailebois (12C).

(2) WAM 4497.

15.3 × 12.2 cm; t.u. 2.8 cm. Formal 12C bookhand.

Seal: red; on tag endorsed iiij; 8.5 × 6 cm; cleric standing; right hand raised in blessing; left hand holding crozier. Legend (worn): SIG . . . PISCOP

Counterseal: 3.6 × 3.3 cm. Classical figure; reclining against pillar to left; bird (?swan) to right. Legend: SIGILLA . . . NT. . . BATIS W. . .

Endorsed: (a) Transactio facta inter abbatem Westmonasterii et abbatem Sancti Albani pro calumpnia Roberti Tayleboys et fratrum suorum de terra in Aldenham (13C). (b) Transactio facta inter abbatem Westmonasterii et abbatem Sancti Albani de Aldenham (12C). (c) 113 (? 16C).

(3) WAD, f. 186r–v.

Pd: *Formulare*, p. xix (from *Hec autem quietatio* only) (from original).

Cal: Eyton, p. 85.

Note: Abbot Laurence was formerly a monk of St Albans (*Heads*, 77). Early in his abbacy, he is said to have received material support from Abbot Robert, but responded with ingratitude, prompting the onset of the dispute resolved by this present charter (*Gesta Abbatum* I, 112, 133–4). On its background, see ibid., 43–4; Harvey, *WA*, 345. Laurence's alleged offences included the admission to Westminster of Alquin, the deposed and absconded prior of St Albans (*Gesta Abbatum* I, 107–10), who became prior of Westminster during his abbacy (Pearce, *Monks of Westminster*, 44).

282. Agreement between Abbots Laurence of Westminster and Simon of St Albans concerning the dispute about land at Sandridge. They exchange eight acres near Sandridge and Wheathampstead (Herts.) respectively. [1167 × c. Easter 1169]

Hec est convencio inter monasterium Beati Petri Westmonasterii et monasterium Beati Albani super controversia[m] cuiusdam terre que iacet ex orientali parte strate que dirigitur ad Marford inter terram de Sandrug' et fluvium de Marford. Laurentius abbas Westmonasterii, assensu conventus sui, et consilio et assensu hominum suorum ad quos ius illius terre spectabat, in presentia Nicholai vicecomitis et multorum hominum de comitatu de Hereford,[1] concessit Symoni abbati et monachis ecclesie Sancti Albani totam illam terram de qua controversia erat inter pretaxata monasteria, et aliam eidem terre contiguam que iuris Beati Petri dinoscebatur esse, videlicet: octo acras plenarias et tantumdem amplius quantum spacium pedis et semis continet in latitudine, et in longitudine quadrantane unius. Symon vero abbas ecclesie Sancti Albani, assensu conventus sui et hominum suorum con-silio, in escambium predicte terre concessit Abbati Laurentio et monasterio Westmonasterii tantundem terre in Sandrugia que est conti-gua terre sue de Wathamest' scilicet: octo acras plenarias et tantundem amplius quantum spacium pedis et semis continet in latitudine, et in longitudine unius quadrantane, et hoc assensu Gregorii presbiteri de Sandrug', ad cuius ius illa terra spectabat. Tenebunt itaque prenominata monasteria predictas terras inperpetuum, liberas ab omni servicio et calumnia. Abbas quippe Westmonasterii warantizabit terram illam quam dedit abbati et ecclesie Sancti Albani contra omnes homines. Abbas similiter ecclesie Sancti Albani terram quam in escambium dedit abbati Westmonasterii warantizabit contra omnes homines. Hoc ergo factum est pro pace utriusque ecclesie et in scriptum redactum ne illius terre occasione de cetero possit inter eas litigium iterandi prompta haberi facultas.

MSS: (1) WAM 8956.
44.8 × 10.7 cm. Top edge has lower half of CIROGRAPHUM.
Seal (on tag): 7.8 × 5.5 cm; damaged. Seated figure holding object (? pastoral staff).
Endorsed: (a) Carta Aldenham (12C). (b) Cirographum inter monasterium Sancti Petri Westmonasterii et monasterium Sancti Albani de terra iuxta Marfford (13C). (c) de viij acris terre . . . (four and a half lines illegible: badly stained) pro terra iuxta Marford' (14C).
  1. *Hereford, sic*; WAD *Hertford.*
(2) WAD, f. 186.
Date: Abbot Laurence 1158 × 1173; Abbot Simon of St Albans 1167 × 1183 (*Heads*, 67, 77; Nicholas' term as sheriff (*PR 11 Henry II*, 15; *PR 15 Henry II*, 121).
Note: Cf. *Gesta Abbatum*, I, 133–4; Harvey, *WA*, 347.

283. Grant by Abbot Laurence to the Sacristy of the church of Saw-bridgeworth (Herts.), to provide lights for the altar, and wine and a pittance in the refectory on the Second Feast of St Agnes (28 Jan.), (to commemorate) the anniversary of the abbot's father and mother, and of the predecessors and benefactors of the monks. [1161]

Sciant [tam] presentes quam futuri quod ego Laurentius, Dei gratia abbas Westmonasterii, communi assensu et voluntate totius capituli nostri, donavi Deo et altari Sancti Petri ecclesie nostre, ad luminare ante corpus Christi et sanctorum reliquias que inibi continentur, ecclesiam de Sabrihteswrtha cum omnibus ad eam pertinentibus in perpetuum ius, ita quod per monachum qui prefuerit obedientie secretarii nostri, tanquam magister procuratorque, fiet omne ordinamentum ipsius ecclesie, videlicet de Sabrihteswrtha, et clericorum suorum et rerum et rectitudinum et omnes redditus venient ad manus ipsius quos fideliter expendet in usus necessarios predicti altaris et luminaris. Et preterea inde inveniet omni anno toti conventui in refectorio vinum et pitanciam die que dicitur Agnetis Secundo, videlicet quando sit anniversarium pro animabus patris et matris mee, omniumque predecessorum et benefactorumque fratrum huius loci. Hanc donationem L[aurentius] abbas, ut dictum est, donavit in capitulo Westmonasterii, et post capitulum statim super ipsum altare apostolorum principis Petri confirmavit. Ex Deo et eodem apostolo sanctissimo et ex potestate a Deo sibi tradita terribiliter eos anathematizans quicunque hanc donationem sive constitutionem suam infringeret. Et fracte scilicet huius donationis compotes quamdiu illam redintegrare nollent. Fecit autem hoc astante et unanimiter confirmante conventu.

MSS: (1) WAM 8579.
    19.7 × 11.2 cm; t.u. 2.8 cm. Tag but no seal.
    Endorsed: (a) Carta Domini Laurentii abbatis de Sabrithswrth' (12C). (b) ad sacristiam deputatur et ad inveniendum vinum et pitanciam conventui Die Sancte Agnetis. ij (13C). (c) Sacristarius.
    (2) WAD, f. 379v–380.
    (3) F, f. 286v–287.
Date: Pope Alexander III's confirmation of Sawbridgeworth church to the Sacristy is dated February 1161 (**170**).

284. Grant for life by Abbot Laurence to his clerk Maurice, perpetual vicar of Sawbridgeworth (Herts.), of the gifts and offerings made to that church, in return for the annual payment to the Sacristy of £15. Maurice would pay episcopalia and other burdens, and at appointed terms would render the stock. At his death everything would revert to the abbot. If Maurice died after making an annual payment, the abbot would recompense his assign or grant him custody down to the following Michaelmas. [? c. 1161]

Noverint ad quos littere iste pervenerint quod ego Laurentius, Dei gratia abbas Westmonasterii, et conventus eiusdem loci concessimus Mauricio clerico nostro, qui perpetuam ecclesie de Sabricheswrth vicariam habet, obvenciones et beneficia eiusdem ecclesie in vita sua, ita ut inde singulis annis persolvat ad officium sacriste et ad opera ecclesie nostre xv libras: dimidium, videlicet, ad Pascha et dimidium ad Festum Sancti Michaelis,

ita sane ut infra octavas utriusque termini totum persolvat. Episcopalia
ipse persolvet et cetera onera ecclesie sustinebit. Hec autem predicta ei
concedimus quamdiu legitime erga nos se habuerit et statutis terminis
bene reddiderit instauramenta que ibi recepta estimata sunt lxiij solidis et
x nummis. Beneficia ecclesie in terra eiusdem ecclesie collocabuntur et
ibidem ad voluntatem ipsius expendentur, opera etiam homines in
possessione ecclesie manentium eis invitis alias transferre non poterit.
Post mortem eius tota possessio libera et quieta et absque omni
calumpnia in manu nostra remanebit cum predictis instauramentis et cum
omnibus emendacionibus quas in ea fecerit. Si vero contigerit Mauricius
decedere post aliquam anni solucionem factam, aut quantum ab eo tunc
acceptum fuerit alicui pariter ipsius cum ipse diviserit de quo securi simus
restituemus, aut eidem possessionem usque ad proximum Festum Sancti
Michaelis dimittemus, et ipse totum acquietabit. Hiis testibus: Ysaac,
canonico de Walth[am], et Willelmo fratre eius; Philippo et Mauricio;
Simone clerico et Johanne nepote abbatis.

MS: WAD, ff. 648v–649.
    Rubric: Littera L. abbatis et conventus Westmonasterii cirographata
    de ecclesia de Sabrichewrth' et pensione xv librarum.
    Marginalia: Sabricheswrth'.
Date: Alexander III's confirmation of the church to the sacristy is dated
February 1161 (**170**).
Note: See Harvey, *WA*, 409.

285. Grant by Abbot Laurence to Prior William and the brethren of
Hurley of the church of Easthampstead (Berks.) to provide extra food on
the feast of St Edward. [1158 × 1174]

Laurentius abbas Westmonasterii omnibus Sancte Matris ecclesie
fidelibus, salutem. Ad pii patris spectat officium ut necessitatibus filiorum
tempestive provideat et discret[e], ea propter fratrum de Herleia neces-
sitati consulere satagens et utilitati ecclesiam de Iezthamesteda. Willelmo
eiusdem loci priori, et fratribus ibidem degentibus in perpetuam
elemosinam concedo, et hac presenti carta nostra eandem cum omnibus
pertinentiis suis eis confirmo, quatinus inde fratres in Festo Beati AEdwardi singulis annis ampliorem habeant refectionem, et huius intuitu
beneficii in predicti sancti veneratione ipsi se fratres devotiores exhibeant
ac promptiores. Testibus: Alano dapifero; Magistro Rogero de Lol-
leswurda; Simone clerico abbatis; Mauritio de Sancto Albano; Magistro
Waltero de Constant'; Willelmo de Mulesham et Radulfo fratre eius;
Radulfo de Coggeshala; Roberto de Cliveloride.

MS: WAM 2280.
    14.5 × 8.3 cm; tongue (torn): 1 cm.
    Endorsed: Yesthamsted (13C).
Cal: Wethered, *St Mary's, Hurley*, no. 25, 98–9.
Note: TRE Westminster held ten hides valued at 100*s.*, but in 1086 only
five hides valued at 50*s.* The reduction in value was prob. due to part of

the holding being incorporated into Windsor Forest. See also Harvey, *WA*, 337.

286. Grant by Abbot Laurence to Mr Ralph [de Beaumont] his physician, a royal clerk, of the church of Bloxham (Oxon.), for an annual payment of five marks (£3. 6s. 8d.) to the Sacristy. Ralph must not alienate the church, and if he died, or became a religious, or a bishop, the church would revert to the abbey. [1158 × 1170]

Universis Sancte Matris Ecclesie filiis L[aurentius], Dei gratia abbas Westmonasterii, et conventus eiusdem loci, salutem. Quos in ecclesiasticis negociis devotiores et fideliores intelligimus, eos ad ecclesiastica beneficia propentius et securius promovemus: hac usi consideracione Magistro Radulpho medico dilecto nostro, clerico domini nostri regis, ecclesiam de Blockesham cum omnibus ad eam pertinentibus in elemosinam concessimus, quam volumus eum libere et quiete et honorifice tenere. Reddendo inde annuatim officio sacriste ecclesie nostre, cui ab antiquo deputata est predicta ecclesia, v marcas argenti: ad Festum videlicet Sancti Michaelis ij marcas et dimidiam; ad Pascham ij marcas et dimidiam. Istud autem illi hoc tenore concedimus ne possit ecclesiam istam aut alii dare, aut aliquo modo a manu sua alienare, nisi per licenciam nostram. Si vero prefatus Radulphus aut decesserit, aut habitum religionis susceperit, aut ad gradum episcopatus promotus fuerit, ecclesia prenominata libera et quieta in manu nostra remanebit.

MS: WAD f. 378.
> Marginalia: Blockesham.
> Rubric: Carta Laurencii abbatis et conventus Westmonasterii de collacione ecclesie de Blockesham et de pensione v marcarum eiusdem ecclesie.

Date: Mr Ralph de Beaumont, *medicus et familiaris* of Henry II, was drowned in March 1170 when the king and his entourage were crossing from Normandy to Portsmouth (*Gesta Henrici*, I, 4).
Note: Ralph's influence at court perhaps prompted the abbot to present him to this church (J. E. Lally, 'Secular patronage at the court of Henry II', *BIHR*, 49 (1976), 173.

287. Final concord between Abbot Walter and Bertram, prior of Bermondsey, whereby the advowson of St Magnus Martyr, near London Bridge, was divided equally between them. Curia Regis, Westminster 23 April 1182.

Hec est finis et concordia facta in curia domini regis apud Westmonasterium ad scaccarium Pasche die Veneris in Festo Sancti Georgii Martiris anno xxviij regni Henrici Regis Secundi coram R[icardo] Wintoniensi episcopo et Rannulfo de Glanville justiciario domini regis, et Ricardo thesaurario, et Rogero filio Reinfridi, et Willelmo Basset, et Roberto de Wytefeld, et Alano de Furnell, et Michaele Belet, et Rannulfo de Gedding, et Willelmo Mauduyt camerario, et Gisleberto de Collevill, et Gervasio de Cornhell, et aliis baronibus domini regis qui tunc ibi aderant, inter Walterum abbatem et conventum ecclesie Beati Petri Westmonasterii et Bertramnum priorem et conventum ecclesie Sancti Salvatoris Bermundesseye, de advocationem ecclesie Sancti Magni Martiris juxta Pontem London', unde placitum fuerat inter eos in curia domini regis, scilicet: quod prenominatus abbas et conventus Westmonasterii habebunt et tenebunt inperpetuum medietatem prelibate advocationis liberam et quietam ab omni calumpnia et vexatione predicti prioris et conventus Bermundesseye, et idem prior et conventus de Bermundesseye habebunt et tenebunt inperpetuum aliam medietatem predicte advocationis liberam et quietam ab omni calumpnia et vexatione prelibati abbatis et conventus Westmonasterii. Et sepedictus abbas et conventus Westmonasterii libere et absque omni contradictione ecclesie de Bermundesseye presentabunt inperpetuum personam quem voluerint ad suam medietatem cum contigerit eam persona vacare. Et similiter prior et conventus de Bermundesseye libere et absque omni contradictione ecclesie Westmonasterii presentabunt inperpetuum personam quem voluerint ad suam medietatem cum contigerit eam persona vacare.

MS: WAD, f. 479.
> Rubric: (1) Ecclesia Sancti Magni. (2) Finalis concordia facta in curia domini regis inter abbatem et conventum Westmonasterii et priorem et conventum de Bermundesseye super advocatione ecclesie Sancti Magni prope Pontem London'.

Note: See **211**.

288. Grant by Abbot Walter to the hospital of St James of the church of St Alban (Wood Street), London. [1175 × 1190]

Sciant presentes et futuri quicumque has litteras viderint vel audierint, quod hec est conventio facta inter Walterum abbatem Westmonasterii et eiusdem loci conventum[1] et infirmas mulieres et fratres hospitalis Sancti Jacobi iuxta villam Westmonasterii, videlicet: quod infirme mulieres et fratres qui ibidem ad honorem et laudem Dei et earundem mulierum procurationem sunt congregati, tenebunt perpetuo ecclesiam Sancti Albani de London' de ecclesia Westmonasterii, sub pensione unius marce inde annuatim ad duos terminos anni camerario Westmonasterii reddende: dimidiam marcam, videlicet, ad Pascha, et dimidiam ad Festum Sancti Michaelis solvendo; quod si in solutione statute pensionis mulieres vel fratres cessaverint habebunt monachi de Westmonasterio regressum ad rem suam ecclesiam, videlicet Sancti Albani, donec per retentionem possessionis indempnitati sue fuerit prescriptum.[2] Hanc concessionem pietatis intuitu et misericordie consideratione predictus abbas et conventus Westmonasterii prefatis infirmis faciunt ut excepta marca quam in pensione solvent, quicquid emolumenti aut obvencionis residua ecclesie porcio ministraverit eis cedat ad usum et proficiat ad augmentum; fratres vero hospitalis in presentia capituli Westmonasterii, mulieres vero coram priore Westmonasterii ad eas misso sacramento corporaliter posito[3] iuraverunt quod hanc conventionem sicut prescripta est sine arte et malo ingenio firmiter tenebunt et fideliter observabunt et quod nullam querent machinacionem per quam statuta pensio ecclesie

Westmonasterii substrahatur aut aliquo modo minuatur.[4] Huius convencionis hii sunt testes, nominatim: Petrus sac[erdos] infirmarum mulierum, et Turoldus, et Bernardus, et Reginaldus, fratres hospitalis: iuraverunt Johannes sac[erdos]; Galfridus sac[erdos]; Roger et Thoma sac[erdotes]; Johannes de Coveham; Ricardus de Berking'; Rogerus Ganet; Helias; Edmundus pistor; Archboldus; Johannes de Sartrino; Odo; Adam, nepos abbatis; Robertus Palmer, et plures alii.

MSS: (1) WAD, f. 477r–v.
>   Rubric: Cirographum inter abbatem et conventum Westmonasterii et fratres hospitalis Sancti Jacobi super ecclesia Sancti Albani London, reddendo unam marcam per annum.
>   1. *Eiusdem loci conventum* repeated.
> (2) F, 290r–v.
>   2. *prospectum*.
>   3. *prestito*.
>   4. F breaks off at this point.

Note: The Hospital of St James was a leper hospital founded in the twelfth century; it has given its name to the Palace of St James and to St James's Park. From an early date, if not from its beginning, it was subject to Westminster (Knowles and Hadcock, 402; R. M. Clay, *The Medieval Hospitals of England* (Oxford, 1966), 305). Abbot Richard Berking (1222–46) successfully asserted his right to visit the hospital and this right was confirmed to his successor by the legate Ottobono in 1247 (Flete, p. 115). Matthew Paris noted that St Albans, Wood Street, was the chapel of a palace of King Offa, founder of the abbey of St Albans. The site was subsequently occupied by the little dwellings of neighbouring citizens, but retained its ancient liberty. Temp. Abbot Paul of St Albans (1077–93), the abbot of Westminster (i.e. either Vitalis or Gilbert Crispin) granted the church to the abbey of St Albans for alternating presentation (*pro patronatu alterius*), but it was not known for what consideration this was done (*Gesta Abbatum*, I, 55). The abbot of Westminster perhaps confirmed a donation by the resident priest. The St Albans 'Catalogus Benefactorum' of *c.* 1380 (Davis, 96) recorded, in a section comprising 11th and 12th century grants, that William, a clerk of London, gave to St Albans half the church of St Alban, and half that of St Michael, with his houses in the City, which (benefactions) render 14*s.* annually (BL Cotton Nero D.vii, f. 93r). Bishop Gilbert Foliot confirmed the (whole) church of St Alban to Westminster, with a pension of 1 mark (**211**).

289. Grant and confirmation by Abbot Walter to Nicholas, son of Randulf Duchet, of the abbey's land bordering the Thames (in London). [1175 × 1190]

Notum sit omnibus qui has litteras viderint vel audierint quod ego Walterus, Dei gratia abbas Westmonasterii, et eiusdem loci conventus dedimus et concessimus et presenti carta confirmavimus, Nicholao filio Randulfi Duchet terram nostram super Tamisiam, que iacet inter terram monialium de Halewelle et terram Radulfi fratris Jocii vinitarii, a fronte platee usque ad aquam, que nobis adiudicata fuit in pleno hustingo;

habendam et tenendam de nobis finabiliter pro suo servitio in feudo et hereditate sibi et heredibus suis bene et honorifice, libere et quiete, reddendo per annum sexdecim solidos pro omnibus servitiis ad quatuor terminos anni: ad Festum Sancti Michaelis vel infra quindecim dies quatuor solidos; ad Natalem Domini vel infra quindecim dies quatuor solidos; ad Pascha vel infra quindecim dies quatuor solidos; ad Festum Sancti Johannis vel infra quindecim dies quatuor solidos. Et sciendum quod nos debemus predictam terram warantizare prenominato Nicholao et heredibus suis contra omnes homines, nec plus poterimus ab eo exigere quam prenominatum servitium sexdecim videlicet solidorum per annum. Pro hac autem concessione et warantizatione et carte nostre confirmatione dedit nobis predictus Nicholaus quadraginta solidos in gersummam. Hiis testibus: Arnaldo de Arlave; Galfrido Pycot; Roberto filio Walchelini; Edwardo preposito; Jacobo presbitero de Holeb[or]n; Roberto presbitero de hospitali Sancti Egidii; Radulfo filio Ade; Willelmo de Sancto Michaele; Matheo sororio; Nicholao Peverello.

MS: WAD, f. 486r–v.
    Rubric: Cirographum abbatis et conventus Westmonasterii de terra sua super Tamisiam in parochia Sancti Martini. Reddendo per annum xvj solidos.

290. Grant by Abbot Walter to Norman Blund and his heirs of all the abbey's land in the parish of St Mary, Staining Lane (London), which belonged to Stephen the mercer. [1175 × 1190 (? 1187 × 89)]

Noverint presentes et futuri quod ego Walterus, Dei gratia abbas ecclesie Beati Petri Westmonasterii, et totus conventus eiusdem ecclesie concessimus et presenti carta capituli nostri confirmavimus Normanno Blundo et heredibus suis totam terram nostram in parochia Beate Marie in Stanningelane, cum omnibus pertinentiis suis, que fuit Stephani mercerii, quam emimus de Martino filio eius, habendam et tenendam de nobis et de ecclesia nostra inperpetuum libere et quiete et honorifice in feodo et hereditate; reddendo inde camerario nostro annuatim xij solidos pro omnibus rebus et pro omni servitio ad quatuor terminos anni, scilicet: infra octabis Pasche iij solidos; et infra octabis Sancti Johannis Baptiste iij solidos; et infra octabis Sancti Michaelis iij solidos; et infra xv dies Natalis Domini iij solidos. Et sciendum quod nos debemus warantizare prenominato Normanno et heredibus suis prenominatam terram cum omnibus pertinentiis suis contra omnes gentes per predictum servitium. Nec poterimus amplius exigere in predicta terra quam predictum servitium xij scilicet solidorum annuatim. Ipse autem Normannus fecit securitatem ecclesie nostre sacramento se conservaturum fidelitatem ipsi ecclesie et nobis de prenominato tenemento. Pro hac autem concessione et dimissione et presentis carte nostre confirmatione et warantizasione dedit prenominatus Normannus ecclesie nostre dimidiam marcam argenti in gersummam. Hiis testibus: Ricardo filio Reyneri; Henrico filio Ailwini; Michaele filio Johannis; Radulfo filio Ade; Henrico filio Reyneri; Henrico Blundo; Radulfo de Winton'; Waltero Gerino; Johanne filio Eldmandi; Andrea filio Radulfi filii Ade; Ada fratre eiusdem; et Nicholao fratre eorum; Ansello; Michaele clerico, et quampluribus aliis.

MS: WAD, f. 483.
> Rubric: Carta abbatis et conventus Westmonasterii de terra in parochia Beate Marie de Staningelane. Reddendo annuatim xij solidos.
> Marginalia: (1) Qwytt rent in Staninglane (17C). (2) Stannynglane.

Date: Richard Fitz Reiner was sheriff 1187–89 (Reynolds, 'Rulers of London', 355).

291. Confirmation by Abbot Walter and the chapter of Westminster to William Le Viel and his heirs of the abbey's land in Friday Street (London) which is in St Matthew's parish on the south side of the church. [1175 × 1190]

W[alterus], Dei gratia abbas Westmonasterii, et totus eiusdem loci conventus omnibus baronibus et hominibus London', Francis et Anglis, tam futuris quam presentibus, et omnibus qui litteras istas viderint, salutem. Noverit universitas vestra nos communi assensu concessisse et sigillo ecclesie nostre confirmasse Willelmo le Viel et heredibus suis terram nostram in Frydaystrat, que est parochia ecclesie Sancti Mathei ex parte australi sita, videlicet, inter terram que fuit Radulfi de Wodestrat et prenominatam ecclesiam Sancti Mathei, tenendam de nobis et de ecclesia nostra in feodo et hereditate pro xx solidis annuatim pro omni servitio camerario nostro solvendis ad duos terminos, scilicet: infra octabis Pasche x solidos, et infra octabis Sancti Michaelis x solidos. Testibus: Alexandro senescaldo; Johanne de Wellis; Henrico pincerna; Stephano de Bolonia; Johanne de Paltona; Thoma de Vaim; Willelmo Picot; Rogero Ganet; Waltero de Donitona nepote abbatis; Galfrido Bukeinte; Osberto Fergaunt; Johanne filio Herlichun; Radulfo le Bretun; Johanne Burguinnun; Alano de Norwega; Pentec[oste] Sparewe; Willelmo filio Aluffi; Aimero le Fustan'; Roberto filio Galfridi et pluribus aliis.

MS: WAD, f. 484v–485.
> Rubric: Carta abbatis et conventus Westmonasterii de terra in Fridaystrate, reddendo xx solidos annuatim.

292. Grant by Abbot Walter to the nuns of Clerkenwell, of the house which Alulf, son of Fromond, gave them in the abbey fee in Bread Street (London), between the house of Ralph Quatremars and that of Warin the turner, and another tenement in Eastcheap next to that of Simon of Paris, which Osbert Becche gave them in the abbey fee. Husting Court, London, 1184.

Omnibus Christi fidelibus ad quorum noticiam littere iste pervenerint Walterus, Dei gratia abbas Westmonasterii, et eiusdem loci conventus, eternam in Domino salutem. Universitati vestre notum facimus nos concessisse monialibus de Fonte Clericorum domum quam Alulfus filius Fromundi eis dedit in Bredstrate, que de nostro feodo est, que inter domum Radulfi de Quatremars et domum Gwarini tornatoris sita est, tenendam de nobis perpetuo pro xxx denariis annuatim camerario nostro[1] solvendis ad duos terminos anni: xv,[2] videlicet, denarios ad Pascha et xv ad Festum Sancti Michaelis. Preterea concessimus eis aliam terram de feudo nostro in Estchep proximam terre Simonis de Parys quam Osbertus Becche eis dedit, tenendam de nobis pro duobus solidis camerario nostro ad prescriptos terminos annuatim solvendis. Et ut nostra concessio firma permaneat eam sigilli nostri testimonio confirmavimus. Hiis testibus: Willelmo vicecomite London'; Ricardo filio Reineri; Henrico filio Ailwini; Johanne filio Herlichun; Rogero filio Alani; Willelmo filio Brithmari[3] et multis aliis. Et hoc factum est in pleno hustingo Lundon' anno Regis Henrici Secundo xxx°.

MSS: (1) WAD, f. 485r–v.
  Rubric: Cirographum abbatis et conventus Westmonasterii de quadam domo in Bredstrate reddendo xxx denarios. Et de alia terra in Estchepe reddendo duos solidos.
  1. Supplied from Clerkenwell MS.
  (2) BL Cotton Faustina B II (Clerkenwell Cartulary), f. 66.
  2. *videlicet xv d.*
  3. Remainder omitted.
Pd: *Cart. Clerkenwell*, no. 235. Dating clause omitted.
Note: The sheriff may be William, son of Sabelina: cf. **293**.

293. Grant by Abbot Walter to St Bartholomew's Hospital, London, of the tenement of Terric son of Albric, which Terric held of the abbey in Friday Street, with a house which Andrew, son of Terric, held of the abbey and the tenement which Ralph de Quatremars held of the abbey in Bread Street (London). [1184]

Sciant presentes et futuri quod ego Walterus, Dei gratia abbas Westmonasterii, et conventus eiusdem loci concessimus hospitali Sancti Bartholomei de Lundon et fratribus eiusdem hospitalis, totum tenementum Terrici filii Albrici, quod predictus Terricus de nobis tenuit in Fridaystrate, preter unam domum de eodem tenemento quam Andreas filius predicti Terrici[1] de nobis tenet; tenendum de nobis iure perpetuo, reddendo annuatim camere monachorum vij solidos ad duos terminos, scilicet: ad Purificationem Sancte Marie iij solidos et vj denarios; [et][2] ad Festum Sancti Petri ad Vincula iij solidos et vj denarios. Similiter eis concessimus totum tenementum quod de nobis Radulfus de Quatremars tenuit in Bredstrat, solvendo inde annuatim camere monachorum v solidos et x denarios ad Festum Sancti Petri ad Vincula. Ut autem conventio ista perpetuetur sigilli nostri auctoritate et sigilli hospitalis Sancti Bartholomei testimonio roboratur. Facta est vero hec conventio anno regni Henrici Regis Secundo xxx°, depositionis autem Ricardi Cantuariensis archiepiscopo primo, Willelmo filio Sabell' tunc existente vicecomite London'. Hiis testibus: Willelmo filio Isabel'; Johanne Buchunte; Henrico filio Ailwini; Ricardo filio Reineri; Willelmo filio Brithmari.

MSS: (1) WAD, f. 485.

Rubric: Cirographum abbatis et conventus Westmonasterii de quodam tenemento in Fridaystrate. Reddendo vij solidos et de alio tenemento in Bredstrat. Reddendo v solidos et x denarios.
    2. Inserted from St Bartholomew's Cartulary.
    (2) Cartulary of St Bartholomew's Hospital Hc 2/la, f. 202a.
    1. *Albrici.*
Pd: Moore, *Hist. St Bartholomew's*, I, 136 n. 1 (from Cartulary)
Cal: *Cart. St Bartholomew's*, no. 735, p. 77.
Date: The king's regnal year further limited by the death of the archbishop (*Fasti* II, 5).
Note: Richard Sporley in his version of *Flete* blames Abbot Walter for making this grant (BL Claudius A VIII, f. 50); it is not mentioned in *Flete* itself. 'The house of Ralph Quatremars was in the southern part of Bread Street . . . and next door towards the river, was a stone house which belonged to Alulf the father of Constantine who was sheriff in 1197' (Moore, *Hist. St Bartholomew's*, 211; cf. **292** above).

294. Grant by Abbot Walter to John son of Robert son of Herlichun and his heirs, of land in Friday Street (London), which belonged to Reymund and the land in the same street which belonged to Ralf Blund. [1175 × 1190]

Noverint et presentes et futuri quod ego Walterus, Dei gratia abbas ecclesie Beati Petri de Westmonasterio, et totus conventus eiusdem ecclesie concessimus et dimisimus et presenti carta capituli nostri confirmavimus Johanni filio Roberti filii Herlichun et heredibus suis terram nostram in Friday Strete que fuit Reymundi, cum pertinentiis suis, habendam et tenendam de nobis et de ecclesia nostra in perpetuum libere et quiete et honorifice in feudo et hereditate; reddendo inde ecclesie nostre annuatim quindecim solidos pro omnibus rebus et pro omni servicio ad duos terminos anni, scilicet: [infra octabas Pasche septem solidos et sex denarios, et]¹ infra octabas Sancti Michaelis septem solidos et sex denarios, sine omne occasione et miskenninga. Concessimus etiam et dimisimus et presenti carta confirmavimus prefato Johanni et heredibus suis in eodem vico terram nostram, que fuit Radulfi Blund, que prius fuerat Turstini, tenendam de nobis et de ecclesia nostra in perpetuum libere et quiete et honorifice, in feudo et hereditate; reddendo inde ecclesie nostre annuatim quinque solidos et quinque denarios ad Festum Apostolorum Petri et Pauli, vel infra octabas, pro omnibus rebus et pro omni servicio, sine occasione et misckeningia. Et sciendum quod nos debemus warantizare prenominato Johanni et heredibus suis prenominatas terras cum omnibus pertinentiis suis contra omnes gentes per predictum servicium. Nec poterimus amplius exigere in prenominatis terris quam prius nominatum servicium, scilicet: de terra que fuit Reimundi xv solidos annuatim et de terra que fuit Radulfi Blund, que prius [fuit] Turstini, v solidos et v denarios annuatim sicut prescriptum est. Ipse autem Johannes fecit ecclesie nostre securitatem per sacramentum se conservaturum fidelitatem nobis et ecclesie nostre de prenominato tenemento. Pro hac autem concessione et dimissione et carte nostre confirmatione et warantizatione dedit nobis prefatus Johannes unum bisantium auri in gersumam. Hiis testibus: Henrico filio Ailwini; Ricardo filio Reyneri; Radulfo de Cornhull'; Rogero filio Alani; Willelmo filio Sabile; Willelmo de Haverhell'; Galfrido le Blund; Stephano le Blund, Johanne nepote Sancti Thome; Benedicto sentario, et multis aliis.

MS: WAD, f. 484.
> Rubric: Carta indentata abbatis et conventus Westmonasterii de tota terra in Frydaystrete que fuit Reymundi, reddendo xv solidos annuatim. Et de terra que fuit Radulfi Blund, reddendo annuatim v solidos et v denarios in eadem vico.
> 1. Omitted in MS.

295. Grant by Abbot Walter to John son of Robert son of Herlichun of a third part of the seld in Cheap which belonged to William le Leutre, also of land outside Aldersgate which belonged to Wyburg (both in London). [1175 × 1190]

Noverint et presentes et futuri quod ego Walterus, Dei gratia abbas Westmonasterii Beati Petri de Westmonasterio, et totus conventus eiusdem ecclesie, concessimus et dimisimus et presenti carta capituli nostri confirmavimus Johanni filio Roberti filio Herlichun et heredibus suis terciam partem selde in foro que fuit Willelmi le Leutre, que tota est de feudo nostro, habendam et tenendam de nobis et de ecclesia nostra in perpetuum, libere et quiete et honorifice in feudo et hereditate; reddendo inde ecclesie nostre annuatim dimidiam marcam argenti pro omnibus rebus et pro omni servicio ad duos terminos anni, scilicet: infra octabas Sancti Michaelis xl denarios et infra octabas Pasche xl denarios, sine omni occasione et mischeningia. Concessimus etiam et dimisimus et presenti carta confirmavimus prefato Johanni et heredibus suis terram nostram extra Aldredesgate que fuit Wyburg', tenendam de nobis et ecclesia nostra in perpetuum libere et quiete et honorifice in feudo et hereditate. Reddendo inde ecclesie nostre annuatim duos solidos pro omnibus rebus et pro omni servicio ad duos terminos anni, scilicet: infra octabas Sancti Michaelis xij denarios, et infra octabas Pasche xij denarios, sine omni occasione et mischenningia. Et sciendum quod nos debemus warantizare prenominato Johanni et heredibus suis prenominatam terciam partem selde in foro et predictam terram extra Aldredesgate contra omnes gentes per predictum servicium, nec poterimus amplius exigere in prenominatis terris quam prenominatum servicium. Ipse autem Johannes fecit ecclesie nostre securitatem per sacramentum se conservaturum fidelitatem nobis et ecclesie nostre de prenominatis tenementis. Pro hac autem concessione et dimissione et carte nostre confirmatione et warantisione dedit nobis prefatus Johannes unum bisantium auri in gersummam. Hiis testibus: Henrico filio Ailwini; Ricardo filio Renn[fridi]; Radulfo de Cornhull'; Rogero filio Alani; Jordano de Turre; Willelmo filio Sabile; Willelmo filio de [sic] Haverhell; Galfrido le Blunt; Stephano le Blunt; Johanne nepote Sancti Thome; Benedicto sentario, et multis aliis.

MS: WAD, f. 484r–v.

Rubric: Cirographum eorundem abbatis et conventus de tercia parte selde in foro que fuit Willelmi Lutre, reddendo dimidiam marcam, et de terra extra Aldredesgate que fuit Wiburg', reddendo duos solidos.

296. Final concord between Abbot Walter and the brothers Richard and William of Paddington concerning their holding in Paddington (Mddx.). Curia Regis, Westminster 31 May, 1185.

Hec est finalis concordia facta in curia domini regis apud West-monasterium die Veneris proximam post Ascensionem Domini, anno xxx°i° regni Regis Henrici Secundi, coram J[ohanne] Norwicense episcopo et Rannulfo de Glanvill', justiciariis domini regis, et Ricardo tesaurario et Godefrido de Luci[1] et Huberto Walter et Willelmo Basset et Nigello filio Alexandri et aliis fidelibus domini regis ibi tunc presentibus, inter Walterum abbatem de Westmonasterio et Ricardum et Willelmum fratres de Paddinton' de toto tenemento quod ipsi tenuerunt in Padinton' de ecclesia de Westmonasterio unde pla[citum fuit inter] eos in curia domini regis, scilicet: quod prefati Ricardus et Willelmus cla[maverunt quietum] in perpetuum de se et omnibus suis successoribus et heredibus totum prefatum tenementum et quicquid juris in eo habebant, sine ullo retinemento, prefate ecclesie de Westmonasterio et abbati, et terram cum omnibus pertinentiis suis ei reddiderunt. Et pro hac recognitione prefatus abbas dedit eis xl marcas argenti et quatuor conredia in ecclesia de Westmonasterio, quorum duo sunt ad opus predicti Ricardi et Willelmi usque xij[2] annos sequentes, et alia duo sunt ad opus uxorum predictorum Ricardum et Willelmi cum caritatibus et pitanciis quamdiu ipse mulieres uixerint.

MSS: (1) WAM 16194.
   16 × 18.8 cm. Top indented: Cirographum. Words from missing corner supplied from WAD.
   Endorsed: (a) Elemos (14C). (b) de Padinton' (12C). (c) Quietaclamantia facta per Ricardum de Padington' et fratrem eius de terris suis in Padinton ecclesie Westmonasterii concessis (14C).
   (2) WAD, f. 470v.
      1. *Lucy.*
      2. Omits *usque, duodecim* in place of *xij.*
Pd: *Formulare*, 217–8, no. CCCLVIII, from WAM.

297. Grant by Abbot Walter to Henry Sumer his sergeant of the mill which was obtained from Gilbert of Wandsworth, together with thirty acres of land in Sutton (Surr.). [1175 × 1190]

[Noverint omnes qui litteras istas viderint] vel audierint, quod ego [Walterus] abbas Westmonasterii, Dei gratia,[1] et ei[usdem loci conventus concessimus et dedimus et hac presenti carta nostra confirm]avimus Henrico Sumer, [servienti] nostro, et heredibus suis iure [hereditario pro servicio suo molendinum illud, quod adepti sumus de Gilleberto] de Wandleswrth, cum [triginta acr]is terre de Suddun quas [prenominatus

Gillebertus tenuit; reddendo inde annuatim ad altar]e Beati Petri in Die Trans[lationis Sanc]ti Aedwardi libram incensi [et elemosinario nostro dimidiam marcam argenti quatuor statut]is terminis, scilicet: ad [Natalem Domini] viginti denarios; ad Pascha [totidem; ad Festum Sancti Johannis totidem; ad Festum Sancti Michaelis to]tidem, ut honorificentius et plen[ius ide]m elemosinarius anniversarium [nostrum et parentum nostrorum, quod inperpetuum fieri] procuret.[2] Si vero prefatus Henricus sex solidatas terre, quas prenominatus [Gillebertus nobis iniuste detinet que spectant ad predictum] molendinum, perquirere poterit, ipse quidem et heredes sui decetero libram ince[nsi ad altare elemosinario vero nostro ad anniversarium nostru]m decem solidos annuatim persolvent. Hanc autem conventionem se fideliter observaturum [iuravit in capitulo nostro prefatus Henricu tactis s]acrosanctis evangeliis. Hiis testibus: Galfrido Picot senescallo; Magistro[3] Galfrido [de Norwyc'; Arnoldo de Herlave; Willelmo Picot milite]; Roberto filio Walkelini; Waltero clerico nepote abbatis;[4] Thoma clerico; Johanne de Palto[   ]; Willelmo de Colevill'; Adam camerario; Roberto de Schireburn'; Ricardo de Berching'; [Pente]cost[o]; Thoma filio Barbelote'; Ricardo janitore et Johanne fratre suo; Johanne aurifabro; Galfrido [   ]re; [   ] serviente; Rogero Enganet, et aliis quampluribus.

MSS: (1) WAM 1767.
    20 × 13.5 cm. Cut as for cirograph. Very damaged: missing phrases supplied from copy.
    Endorsed: Carta Henrici Sumer de molendino de Wandleswirth.
    (2) WAD, f. 470v.
      1. *Ego Walterus Dei gratia abbas Westmonasterii.*
      2. *instituimus.*
      3. *Magistro* omitted.
      4. MS lists no further witnesses, but concludes *et aliis multis.*

298. Grant by Abbot Walter to William son of Ernis, of land at Penge (Surr.), for thirty years. Chapter, Westminster 29 Sept. 1176.

Sciant omnes ad quos littere iste pervenerint quod ego Walterus, Dei gratia abbas Westmonasterii, et conventus eiusdem loci, communi assensu concessimus Willelmo filio Ernisii terram illam que est extra nemus nostrum de Pange, sicut aqueductus designat usque ad propriam terram prefati Willelmi, et a nemore archiepiscopi Cantuariensis usque ad parcum de Becham; tenendam de nobis pro xx solidis per annum, scilicet: x solidis ad Pascha et x ad Festum Sancti Michaelis, usque ad xxx annos. Post illum vero terminum, remanebit terra illa ecclesie nostre in eo statu in quo fuit die qua eam predictus Willelmus suscepit, nisi heres ipsius Willelmi obtinere possit apud abbatem et conventum ut deinceps teneat sicut antecessor tenuit. Si vero infra prefatum terminum decesserit sepedictus Willelmus, heres ipsius tenebit usque ad memoratum terminum. Hanc autem conventionem fideliter tenendam juravit idem Willelmus in capitulo nostro, tactis sacrosanctis evangeliis. Facta est autem hec conventio inter nos anno vi coronationis Regis Henrici iunioris, et martirii Beati Thome, ad Festum Sancti Michaelis. His testibus: Magistro Nicholao et Jordano, clericis abbatis; Gilleberto de Wandelesuurtha; Ricardo de Berching'; Radulfo camerario abbatis; Henrico de Winton; Henrico de Limeseia; Eudone filio Ernisii; Hugone Carbunel; Roberto de Martinivilla; Radulfo de Bruhill'; Ricardo Aguillun; Roberto clerico de Becham et Osberto fratre eius; Willelmo presbitero de Beccham et multis aliis.

MS: WAM LII.
    10.5 × 9.3 cm. Seal missing.
    Endorsed: Penge (15C).
Note: No copy because the transaction would have been out of date before any cartulary was made.

299. Confirmation by Abbot Walter to the convent of the church and manor of Benfleet with Fanton and Paglesham (Essex), which manors were anciently assigned to the pittancer. [1175 × 1190]

Walterus, Dei gratia abbas Westmonasterii, omnibus Sancte Matris Ecclesie filiis ad quos presens carta pervenerit, eternam in Domino salutem. Justis petentium desideriis facilem nos convenit impertiri consensium et vota que a rationis tramite non discrepant effectu sunt prosequente complenda. Noverit itaque universitas vestra nos divine pietatis intuitu, et pro salute anime mee et patris et matris mee, concessisse et confirmasse, sine ullo retinemento, conventui nostro ecclesiam de Benflet, cum ipso manerio et cum omnibus terris et maneriis sibi adiacentibus, scilicet: Fantun' et Pakelesham cum omnibus pertinenciis suis, que scilicet maneria ab antiquis temporibus pia largitione antecessorum meorum venerabilium abbatum Westmonasterii ad officium pitanciarie semper pertinuisse dinoscuntur quatinus eadem maneria libere, quiete et honorifice in propria habeant dispositione, et in usus suos ad utilitates quicquid ex eis poterit provenire, ita quod per eos fiat omne ordinamentum predictorum maneriorum in ponendis autem vel removendis pitanciariis utar consilio conventus prout expedierit. Contestor igitur omnes successores meos abbates ne ipsi faciant vel fieri sinant ullam infractionem huius nostre concessionis immo augeant, confirment et stabiliant. Hanc autem concessionem promta voluntate feci in capitulo nostro, et sigillo proprio roboratam super ipsum altare Beati Petri apostolorum principis devotus optuli ex auctoritate Dei et Beati Petri et ex potestate mihi tradita terribiliter eos anathematizans, quicumque hanc concessionem nostram ausu temerario infringere, seu diminuere, aut irritam facere presumpserint. Hoc autem factum est toto conventu Westmonasterii assistente, et sentenciam latam confirmante, et pro beneficio isto nobis omnimodas gracias referente.

MS: WAD, f. 603; also recited in full in confirmation of Abbot Richard, WAD, f. 603r–v.
    Rubric: Carta Walteri abbatis Westmonasterii de ecclesia de Benflete cum manerio et hamlettis adiacentibus.
Note: See Harvey, *WA*, 340, 341, 343; and **339** below.

300. Grant by Abbot Walter to Nicholas of Paglesham and his heirs of the vill of Paglesham, a member of Benfleet (Essex), except for the church. Curia Regis, Westminster [Jan.–Sept. 1190]

Sciant tam presentes quam futuri quicunque has litteras viderint vel audierint quod ego Walterus, Dei gratia abbas Westmonasterii, et eiusdem loci conventus concessimus et hac presenti carta nostra confirmavimus Nicholao de Paklesham et heredibus suis villam nostram de Pakelsham, membrum de Benflete, cum omnibus pertinenciis suis, excepta ecclesia cuius donationem et ius patronatus in manu nostra retinemus, habendam et tenendam de nobis finabiliter libere et quiete et honorifice; reddendo inde annuatim novem libras pitanciario nostro ad quatuor statutos terminos, videlicet: infra octo dies Pasche quadraginta quinque solidos; infra octo dies Nativitatis Sancti Johannis Baptiste totidem; infra octo dies Festivitatis Sancti Michaelis totidem; infra octo dies Natalis Domini totidem. Preterea idem Nicholaus vel heredes sui ad placita nostra de Benflet tanquam capitalis manerii ad summonitionem nostram venient. Sciendum itaque est quod Nicholaus vel heredes sui predictam villam aut aliquam eiusdem ville porcionem absque consensu nostro dare aut vendere aut invadiare non poterunt. Juravit itaque predictus Nicholaus in capitulo nostro quod hanc conventionem et concessionem sicut prescripta est sine dolo et machinatione tenebit et de hoc tenemento abbati et ecclesie Westmonasterii fideliter existet nec artem aut ingenium queret ut prenominatos redditus ecclesie Westmonasterii ullo unquam tempore substrahatur aut minuatur. Hoc autem eis concedimus quamdiu bene reddiderint et inde erga nos se fideliter habuerint. Facta est autem hec conventio anno primo regni Regis Ricardi apud Westmonasterium in curia domini regis coram Willelmo Eliensis episcopo, domini regis cancellario, et Hugone Dunelmensi et Hugone Cestrensi episcopis, et coram aliis baronibus scaccarii domini regis. Hiis testibus: Henrico de Cornhull'; Willelmo filio Nigelli; Willelmo de Cusinton'; Willelmo de Cherintona; Roberto Revel; Willelmo filio Johannis; Rogero presbitero de hospitio domine regine; Gaufrido Pycot senescallo abbatis; Johanne filio Tureb'; Reginaldo filio Serlonis; Laurentio filio Jordanis; Johanne filio Osberti; Henrico de Baioc'; Waltero nepote abbatis; Thoma filio Philippi et aliis multis.

MS: WAD, f. 613v.
> Rubric: Cirographus Walteri abbatis et conventus Westmonasterii de villa de Pakelesham. Reddendo annuatim novem libras.
> Marginalia: Pakelesham.

Date: 1 Ric. is 3 Sept. 1189 to 2 Sept. 1190. William Longchamps was consecrated bp. of Ely on 31 Dec. 1189 (*Fasti* II, 45); therefore the limits of this document are Jan. to Sept. 1190. Abbot Walter d. 27 Sept. 1190.

Note: As this charter is dated from the last year of Abbot Walter's life, it is probably later than **299**, by which Abbot Walter returned Benfleet with Fanton and Paglesham to the convent; here he was presumably acting on their behalf, as the rent was to be paid to the pittancer, to whom the manor was assigned by previous abbots as well as by Walter himself.

301. Confirmation by Abbot Walter to Martin de Capella of the manor of Denham (Bucks.), except the church and tithes. Each year he is to prepare hospitality for the abbot at fifteen days' notice. [*c.* 1182]

Walterus, Dei gratia abbas Westmonasterii, et conventus eiusdem loci omnibus hominibus Sancti Petri, salutem. Noverit universitas vestra nos communi assensu concessisse et hac presenti carta nostra confirmasse Martino de Capella manerium nostrum de Deneham cum omnibus pertinentiis suis, tenendum de nobis et ecclesia nostra iure hereditario, preter ecclesiam eiusdem manerii cum decimis, oblationibus et omnibus aliis ad eam pertinentibus, quam in manu nostra et donatione retinemus. Reddet autem predictus Martinus inde annuatim ecclesie nostre quindecim libras ad quatuor statutos terminos anni, videlicet: in Natali Domini; in Pascha; in Nativitate Sancti Johannis Baptiste; in Festo Sancti Michaelis; singulis terminis sexaginta et quindecim solidos; et preterea singulis annis domino abbati ad suam summonitionem quindecim diebus ante factam conveniens hospicium preparabit. Quare volumus et precipimus quatinus prenominatus Martinus et heredes sui teneant prefatum manerium libere et quiete et honorifice, cum omnibus ad feudofirmam suam pertinentibus, sicut alii feudofirmarii de terra Sancti Petri melius et liberius tenent. Hiis testibus: Gileberto de Cranford; Ricardus de Balie; Asculfo de Cranford; Willelmo de Suthall; Johanne Vautort; Rogero de Norh[amp]t[on]; Waltero de Greneford; Willelmo de Ykeham; Johanne Cabus; Radulfo de Tochintun'; Radulfo Deire; Ada de Sunnebyr; Magistro Willelmo de Actun; Samsone Deirel; Philippo et Gileberto de Sancto Michaele fratribus; Johanne Nikel; Elia de Settesb'; Thoma de Norhamtun' et multis aliis.

MSS: (1) BL Harleian Charter III c.38.
    18 × 25 cm; top indented for cirograph.
    Seal: on tag; orange; 4.9 cm diameter (chipped); mounted man holding sword; legend: + SIGILLUM [MAR]TINI D. . . (*Cat. Seals BM*, II, no. 5795, p. 262).
    (2) WAD, ff. 178v–179r.
    (3) LN, ff. xxxiij *verso*–xxxiiij *recto*.
    (4) CAY, f. xxxvi *verso*.
Pd: Lathbury, *Denham*, p. 27 (from Harl. Ch.).
Cal: Bentley, 14, no. 138, from CAY.
Date: Cf. **138**. Martin held land of Westminster in Denham in 1172 (*PR 18 H II*, 47).
Note: Cf. **138**. See also Harvey, *WA*, 338–9. In the reign of King Henry III, the service of hospitality was remitted to Henry de Capella, in return for an additional annual payment of £3 (BL Harleian Charter 85 A 11).

302. Grant by Abbot Walter to 'our brethren' of Hurley of the church of Easthamstead (Berks.). [1175 × 1190]

Universis Christi fidelibus, Walterus, Dei gratia abbas Westmonasterii, et eiusdem loci conventus, salutem in Domino. Noverit universitas vestra nos unanimi assensu et concordi voluntate dedisse et concessisse Deo et ecclesie Sancte Marie de Herleia et fratribus nostris ibidem Deo servientibus ecclesiam de Iezamstede, cum omnibus pertinentiis suis libere et quiete, pacifice et perpetue, habendam et tenendam sine aliquo retenemento, quatinus eam in libera habeant disposicione et in usus suos et utilitatem ecclesie sue quicquid ex ea possunt deducere convertant et ob hoc beneficium Festivitatem Beati Regis Edwardi et devotius celebrent et honorabilius peragant, sicud eandem ecclesiam sancte recordacionis Laurentius abbas ob hanc causam eis liberaliter contulit, et sua carta confirmavit. Hiis testibus: Willelmo priore; Rogerio capellano; Gaufrido capellano; Gaufrido Picot senescallo; Radulpho Bereng'; Waltero Coce; Alano et Gaufrido servientibus, et aliis.

MS: WAM 2270.
> 16.2 × 13.1 cm; t.u. 2.7 cm.
> Endorsed: (a) Ecclesia Yestamstede (13C). (b) xxxij (13C).

Cal: Wethered, *St Mary's, Hurley*, 98–9, no. 25.

Date: Prob. issued towards the end of Walter's abbacy, during which Prior William (Postard) succeeded Richard in office (**306**).

303. Grant by Abbot W[alter] to Mr Nicholas his clerk of the tithe of Bulby and Elsthorpe (Lincs.). [1175 × 1190]

W[alterus], Dei gratia abbas Westmonasterii, et conventus eiusdem loci, omnibus Sacrosancte Ecclesie filiis ad quos littere iste pervenerint, salutem. Noverit universitas vestra nos concessisse et caritatis intuitu donasse Magistro Nicholao clerico nostro decimam nostram de Bolebi et Hellestorp in perpetuam elemosinam, solvendo singulis annis elemosinario nostro iiij^{or} solidos: duos ad Festum Sancti Michaelis, et duos ad Pascha. Et ut nostra hec donatio rata et illibata infuturum perseveret eam scripti nostri attestatione et sigilli nostri munimine confirmamus. Testibus hiis: Alexandro fratre abbatis; Galfrido Picot; Ricardo clerico; Edwardo preposito, Ricardo de Berkinges et aliis pluribus.

MSS: (1) WAM 573.
> 15.5 × 7 cm; t.u. 1.5 cm.
> Seal: on tag; white wax. Obverse: 6.5 × 4.5 cm; abbot, standing, crozier in right hand, left hand raised in blessing; legend (worn): [SI]GILLV. . .
> Reverse: circular, 1.5 cm diameter; classical head, facing right; legend (worn): TM EVM. . .
> Endorsed: (a) Carta W abbatis [scriptum] (scripta)^c de iiij solidis anno pensione de ecclesia de Bolebi Hellesthorp' ecclesia ad Westmonasterium pertinente (13C). (b) ffacto elemosinario Westmonasterii (13C). (c) Bolebi iiij^{or} solidi pro decimis (14C). (d) De Boleby et Hellestorp (12C).
> (2) WAD f. 470v.

Date: W is Abbot Walter because Geoffrey Picot was Walter's seneschal.

Note: This grant from vills on the border between Lincs. and Rutland may represent part of the tithes of Rutland given to the Abbey by the Confessor and William I (Harvey, *WA*, 47).

304. Grant by Abbot Walter to Hugh de Nunant, bp. of Coventry, of the manor of Perton in Staffs., restored by King Richard, to be held for life. Westminster, 2 Feb. 1190.

Sciant presentes et futuri quod ego Walterus, Dei gratia abbas Westmonasterii, et eiusdem loci conventus concessimus et tradidimus Hugoni de Nunant' Coventrie episcopo manerium nostrum de Pertune quod est in Statfordescira quod Dominus Rex Ricardus, inspectis cartis antecessorum suorum, nobis plenarie reddidit, tenendum de nobis tota vita sua pro quadraginta solidis ad duos terminos inde annuatim solvendis, videlicet: ad Festum Sancti Johannis Baptiste viginti solidos; et ad Natale Domini viginti solidos, ita ut predictum manerium cum omni integritate sua et omnibus pertinenciis suis et emendacionibus cunctis quas in eo fecerit ad nos post decessum ipsius absque reclamatione ullius persone vel alicuius ecclesie libere revertatur. Facta est autem hec concessio apud Westmonasterium in presentia Willelmi Eliensis episcopi, domini regis cancellarii, et Hugonis Dunelmensis episcopi, justiciarii domini regis, et multorum aliorum baronum qui tunc ibi aderant, anno regni Regis Ricardi primo in Purificatione Sancte[1] Marie. Hiis testibus: Roberto de Witefeld; Michaele Belet; Hugone Bardulf; Rogero filio Reinfridi; Galfrido Picot; Willelmo Picot nepote eius; Magistro Gaufrido de Norwic'; Magistro Henrico[2] medico; Ricardo filio Gaufridi Picot; Roberto de Scribab'; Roberto del Broch; Thoma clerico; Radulfo de Saresbiria; Gregorio filio Herwicun.

MSS: (1) WAD, f. 648r–v.
> Rubric: Cirographum inter inter [*sic*] abbatem et conventum Westmonasterii et Hugonem de Nunant' Coventrie episcopum, de manerio de Perton' eidem tradito ad terminum vite.
> Marginalia: Pertune.
> (2) WAM Book 12, f. 152.
>> 1. *Beate.*
>> 2. *Mr Henry Belet medico.*

305. Grant by Abbot Walter to Robert of Wick of the vill of [Upton] Snodsbury, the vill of Bricklehampton and three virgates in Wick, all of which were held by his father of Abbot Laurence, for the annual rent of £10. 8*s.* 4*d.* to the farm of Pershore (Worcs.). [1175 × 1190]

Walterus, Dei gratia abbas Westmonasterii, et conventus eiusdem loci omnibus qui istas litteras viderint vel audierint, salutem. Noverit universitas vestra nos unanimiter concessisse et presenti carta confirmasse Roberto de Wycha et heredibus suis villam nostram que dicitur Snoddesbury, cum omnibus pertinentiis suis in feodo et hereditate de nobis tenendam, quam Laurentius abbas et conventus Westmonasterii Petro de Wicha, patri suo, per cartam suam concesserunt, et idem Robertus solvet inde annuatim ad firmam de Pershore vj libras ad iiij[or] statutos terminos.

Preterea concedimus ei villam nostram de Brythelmeton, tenendam de nobis in feodo et hereditate cum omnibus pertinentiis suis, quam pater suus ex concessione Laurentii abbatis et conventus Westmonasterii per cartam suam tenuit, et idem Robertus reddet inde annuatim iiij libras ad firmam de Pershore, ad iiij^{or} statutos terminos. Et notum sit omnibus, tam presentibus quam futuris, quod ego Walterus abbas Westmonasterii et totus conventus eiusdem ecclesie concessimus Roberto filio Petri de Wycha tres virgatas terre in villa nostra de Wycha hereditario iure libere de nobis tenendas, sicut Laurentius abbas Westmonasterii et totus conventus concesserunt Petro de Wycha, patri eius, per cartam suam, et idem Robertus reddet inde annuatim ad firmam de Pershore pro omni servicio viii solidos iiij denarios ad iiij^{or} statutos terminos, scilicet: unam virgatam de nostro dominio; unam virgatam que fuit Leswardi, et unam virgatam terre que fuit Gunteri et Sweni, etc.

MS: WAM 22476 (early 14C copy).
  16.2 × 15.1 cm.
Note: See Harvey, *WA*, 361, 364.

306. Grant by Abbot Walter and the convent to Ralph Fitz Stephen, the king's chamberlain, of land between their respective vills of Todenham and Wolford (Gloucs.) where he can strengthen his mill-pond, and in return he would have the abbot's demesne corn ground in readiness for his arrival and during his stay. [1175 × 1190]

Sciant presentes et futuri, quicunque has literas viderint vel audierint, quod ego Walterus abbas Westmonasterii et eiusdem loci conventus concessimus et sigilli nostri appositione confirmavimus Radulfo filio Stephani, camerario domini regis, tam terre nostre quam est in marisco inter villam nostram de Todeham et Wleward villam suam ubi possit firmare unum stagnum ad molendinum suum; et ipse in compensatione huius nostre liberalitis concessit nobis quod in eodem molendino bladum nostre dominice curie contra adventum abbatis et quamdiu ibi moram fecerit moletare absque prestatione moliture. Hi[i]s testibus: Priore Ricardo; Alexandro monacho; Martino monacho; Radulfo de Arundel; Magistro Nicholao; G[alfrido] filio Petri; Willelmo Bastard; Ricardo de Berking; Radulfo de Saresberia et multis aliis.

MSS: (1) WAD, f. 324.
  Rubric: Carta abbatis et conventus Westmonasterii de terra in quodam marisco ad stagnum cuiusdam molendini.
  (2) CAY, f. lxxii.
Cal: Bentley, 37, no. 259, from CAY.
Date: Prob. issued in the earlier part of Walter's abbacy, since Prior Richard was succeeded by William (Postard) before Walter's death (**302**).
Note: Todenham and Wolford adjoin each other near Moreton-in-Marsh, Gloucs. See also Harvey, *WA*, 345. On Ralph Fitz Stephen, see *Cart. Darley*, I, xxii–xxiii; T. F. Tout, *Chapters in the Administrative History of Medieval England*, 6 vols. (Manchester, 1928–37), I, 111.

307. Agreement whereby Abbot William and the convent demised to Alfwin the dyer the house which William de Camera and Elfgiva Lombard his wife gave to the abbey, to hold for eight years at a yearly rent of 9s. [c. 21 April 1196]

Hec est conventio facta inter + Abbatem + Willelmum Westmonasterii et eiusdem loci conventum et Alfwinum teintere, videlicet: quod idem abbas et conventus dimiserunt ei domum suam quam Willelmus de Camera et Elfgiva Lumbard' uxor eius eis dederunt, tenendam de eis usque ad viij annos completos; reddendo inde annuatim predicto abbati et conventui pro omni servicio ix solidos, videlicet: quatuor solidos et vj denarios in Festo Sancti Michaelis, et totidem ad Pascham. Completis itaque octo annis dicta domus quieta et absoluta remanebit predicto abbati et conventui. Terminus autem octo annorum predictorum inceptus ad proximam[1] Pascham post mortem abbatis de Cadamo qui venit cum Magistro Philippo Dunelmensi electo in Anglia. Hiis testibus: Willelmo de Camera; Magistro Ernaldo; Magistro Simone de Bareswrth; Simone camerario; Jacobo hostiario; Roberto marescallo, et aliis.

MS: WAD, f. 486.
> Rubric: Cirographum inter abbatem et conventum Westmonasterii et Alfwinum teinterer de quadam domo ad terminum octo annorum.
> 1. MS: *proximum.*
Date: Robert, abbot of St Stephen's, Caen, d. 11 April 1196 (William of Newburgh, *Historia Rerum Anglicarum*, in vols. I and II of *Chronicles of the Reigns of Stephen, Henry II and Richard I*, ed. R. Howlett (4 vols., RS, 1884–9), Newburgh II, 465; Howden, *Chronica* IV, 5). Easter 1196 fell on 21 April.

308. Assignment by Abbot William to the abbey chamberlain of 9s. from land which Elfgiva Lombard gave, and 1s. from our headland, to be paid to Godfrey de St Martin until he receives one of our churches within the walls of the City of London. [1196 × 1200]

Sciant presentes et futuri quod ego Willelmus abbas Westmonasterii assignavi camerario conventus nostri quo pro tempore fuerit, novem solidos de terra quam Elfgiva Lumbarda ecclesie nostre in elemosinam dedit, et duodecim denarios de caputio nostro, per manum suam annuatim recipiendos, et Godefrido de Sancto Martino solvendos, donec idem Godefridus unam ecclesiarum nostrarum inter muros civitatis London', quam ei promisimus, habeat. Cum autem iamdictus G[odefridus] ecclesiam a nobis receperit et habuerit, camerarius conventus nostri prefatos decem solidos amplius non percipiet, sed sicut fuerunt prius in (libera)[c] nostra libera disposicione erunt. Et ut hec nostra assignacio stabilis interim perseveret, huic scripto nostro sigilli nostri munimentum apposuimus. Testibus: Philippo, et Adam, et Gilebert, capellanis et monachis nostris.

MS: WAD, f. 650.

Rubric: Littera Willelmi abbatis Westmonasterii de ix solidis assignatis camerario Westmonasterii.

Date: Later than **307** and **353**.

309. Quitclaim by Abbot William and the convent to Henry Fitz Reygner of 3*s.* rent at the gate of his house, which he holds of the abbey's chamber, in exchange for certain land near the white monastery of the Holy Innocents towards the Thames. [1191 × 1200]

Noverint omnes ad quos presens scriptum pervenerit quod ego Willelmus, Dei gratia abbas Westmonasterii, et totus eiusdem loci conventus relaxavimus et quietum clamavimus Henrico filio Reygneri et heredibus suis inperpetuum tres solidatas redditus ad portam domus sue quas de camera nostra tenuit et warantizabimus in escambium cuiusdam terre prope album monasterium Sanctorum Innocentium ex altera parte, scilicet versus Tamisiam. Que terra versus vicum habet in latitudine xxxj aune; in medio xxxvij aunes, et versus Tamisiam xxxiiij aunes; in longitudine centum et deus[1] aunes. Predictus autem Henricus warantizabit nobis terram predicti escambij contra omnes homines et contra omnes feminas. Et ut hoc ratum et firmius permaneat sigilli nostri apposicione roboravimus. Hiis testibus: Thebabaldo senescallo nostro; Magistro Waltero de London', Penthecoste de Wanleswrth'; Rogero Enganeth; Ricardo portario; Stephano de Berkinge; Jacobo hostiario abbatis; Johanne pincerna abbatis, et multis aliis. Et hec sunt nomina illorum qui terras predicti escambii tenuerunt et quietas clamaverunt in curia domini regis cum uxoribus et heredibus suis inperpetuum pro octo marcis quas propter predictam terram acceperunt, scilicet, Ansgod le corveser et Bertelmeu le fiz Godwine.

MS: WAD, f. 472v.

Rubric: Escambium abbatis et conventus Westmonasterii de quoddam redditu iij solidorum iuxta portam Henrici filii Reygneri pro quoddam terram iuxta album monasterium Sanctorum Innocentium.

1. *Sic* in MS for *deux*. The scribe employs the French word for ell, and is seemingly counting in French.

Note: For the Holy Innocents (St Mary le Strand), see Brooke and Keir, 140.

310. Final concord between Walter, son of Thurstan of Colham, and Abbot William and the convent of Westminster, whereby Walter quitclaimed his right in the seneschalcy of the abbey, in return for an annual payment of five marks from the abbey's chamber, until they recompensed him with £10 worth of rents for his lifetime, or less if it should be acceptable. Curia Regis, Westminster 27 Aug. 1198.

Hec est finalis concordia facta in curia domini regis apud Westmonasterium die Jovis proxima post Festum Sancti Bartholomei anno regni Regis Ricardi ix°, coram H[uberto] Cantuariensi archiepiscopo, G[alfrido] filio Petri, Ricardo Eliensi archidiacono, Magistro Thoma de

Husseborne, Ricardo de Herierd, Willelmo de Warenn', Osberto filio Hervei, Johanne de Gestling', justiciariis, et aliis baronibus et fidelibus domini regis ibidem tunc presentibus, inter Walterum filium Thurstani de Coleham, petentem, et Willelmum abbatem de Westmonasterio et conventum eiusdem loci, tenentes, de senescaucia abbatie de Westmonasterio, unde placitum fuit inter eos in prefata curia, scilicet: quod predictus Walterus remisit et quietum clamavit predictis abbati et successoribus suis totum ius et clamium suum quod habuit in predicta senescaucia, de se et heredibus suis in perpetuum. Et pro hoc fine et concordia et quieto clamio, predictus abbas et conventus concesserunt dare predicto Waltero annuatim quinque marcas argenti, ad duos terminos anni, scilicet: ad Festum Sancti Michaelis duas marcas et dimidiam, et ad Pascham duas marcas et dimidiam, de camera ipsius abbatis donec ei satisfecerint de decem libratis redditus in tota vita sua, vel de minus quo pacatus fuerit. MIDDELSEX'

MSS: (1) PRO, C.P.25(1) 146/1, no. 13.
    (2) WAD, f. 91v.
Pd: *Fines 9 Ric I*, no. 206, p. 159.
Cal: *Fines London & Mddx*, I, 2 no. 14.
Note: The phrase *in tota vita sua* has been given its usual translation in the heading. However, in this instance it might be translated as 'in the course of his life', since it is not otherwise clear why the sum due to Walter should initially be only £3. 6s. 8d. per annum, if there is an eventual obligation to render him £10 annually. For the preceding lawsuit, see *Rot. Curiae Regis*, I, 138.

311. Confirmation by Abbot William to the king's chamberlain, Robert Mauduit [II], and his heirs, of the abbey's houses in Longditch in Westminster, with the lands which William, the usher of Abbot Walter, gave to the abbey. [Oct. 1194 × May 1200]

Noverint presentes et futuri quod ego Willelmus, Dei gratia abbas Westmonasterii, et totius eiusdem loci conventus, communi assensu et voluntate concessimus, et presenti hac carta nostra confirmavimus Roberto Mauduit, camerario domini regis, et heredibus suis, in villa Westmonasterii domos nostras de Langedich; habendas et tenendas de nobis libere et quiete, cum omnibus terris et pratis, quas scilicet Willelmus, hostiarius Abbatis Walteri, ecclesie nostre concessit et dedit; reddendo inde singulis annis finabiliter infirmario nostro qui pro tempore fuerit undecim solidos ad duos terminos: ad Pascha, videlicet, v solidos et vj denarios, et ad Festum Sancti Michaelis v solidos et vj denarios, pro omni servicio. Et est sciendum quod predictus Robertus et heredes sui reddent annuatim pro prefata terra ad firmam ville Westmonasterii duodecim denariorum; et Johanni filio Eadwardi et heredibus suis octo denariorum; et Ricardo filio Eadmundi et heredibus suis octo denariorum. Ut autem hec nostra concessio futuris temporibus stabilis et rata permaneat, eam presentis scripti testimonio et sigilli nostri appositione roboravimus. His testibus: Willelmo de Hely, thesaurario domini regis; Simone de Pateshill'; Johanne de la Wike; Andrea de Scaccario; Thoma de Windlesour'; Willelmo filio Roberti; Rogero Enganet; Albino computatore; Roberto de Rokingham'; Hugone de Fonte; Galfrido de Cruce; Johanne filio Eadwardi; Stephano de Berking'; Alexandro de Eie; Roberto de Fraxineto; Willelmo de Avenay; Johanne filio Willelmi filii Roberti; Normanno Borel'; Ludovico clerico de Rokingham', qui hanc cartam scripsit, et multis aliis.

MSS: (1) WAM 17614.
   23.8 × 15.2 cm; t.u. 3.5 cm. Slit, slotted tag. Top edge cut: Cirographum.
   Seal: green; fragment; 3 × 2 cm. Obverse: hand with bow, pointing right; legend: T … C..
   Reverse: classical motif: man leaning on a staff, facing right; legend: SIG[ILLUM] R[OBERTI M]ALDVT.
   Endorsed: (a) Carta Willelmi abbatis et conventus Westmonasterii facta Roberto Maudut, camerario domini regis, et heredibus suis, de domibus nostris de Langedich cum omnibus terris et pratis quondam Willelmi hostilarii Abbatis Walteri in villa Westmonasterii (13C).
   (b) Carta Willelmi abbatis Westmonasterii Roberto Mawdit reddendo xj solidorum et xij et xvj denariorum Longditch (16C). (c) Non registratur con…. (d) Carta (16C).
   (2) BL Add. MS 28024, ff. 46v–47.
Pd: Richardson, 'William of Ely', 83 (from WAM and BL Add. MS); *Beauchamp Cartulary*, no. 190 (from WAM).

312. Confirmation by Abbot William to the king's chamberlain, Robert Mauduit [II], of licence to have a chapel in his house adjacent to Longditch, Westminster, without prejudice to the parish church of St Margaret. [*c.* 1195 × 1200]

Omnibus Sancte Matris Ecclesie filiis ad quos presens carta pervenerit Willelmus, Dei gratia abbas Westmonasterii, et eiusdem loci conventus, eternam in Domino salutem. Noverit universitas vestra nos, ad peticionem et instanciam baronum domini regis, concessisse et hac presenti carta nostra confirmasse Roberto Mauduit, domini regis camerario, et heredibus suis ut habeant capellam suam in villa Westmonasterii in curia sua iuxta Langedich, absque omni dampno et detrimento parrochiane ecclesie, videlicet: ut nullum de parochianis in capella sua admittant, unde parochialis ecclesia detrimentum aliquod paciatur. Tali quidem conventione quod ipse Robertus et heredes sui singulis annis finabiliter de predicta capella ad magnum altare nostrum ij bisantias persolvent, unum scilicet ad Pascha et alterum ad Festum Sancti Michaelis. Si autem contigerit purificaciones in capella predicta fieri, non aliter fient nisi in presentia parochiani sacerdotis, qui omnes oblaciones ibi recipiet, quod quidem ita statuimus, ut de nullo vel de nulla fiant ibi sponsalia nuptie vel purificaciones qui sint de parochia Sancte Margarete. Si vero contigerit aliquem de familia sua infirmari, confessionem, unccionem, communionem, et ea que Christiani sunt, a capella Sancte Margarete percipiet, et que debita sunt eccl[es]iastica eidem capelle Sancte Margarete persolvet. Et si forte prefatus Robertus et uxor eius de villa recesserint, quamdiu absentes erunt, serviens eius qui ibidem domos suas et curiam suam custodiet, ad parrochialem ecclesiam divinum audiet officium, et que debita sunt ecclesiastica ibidem persolvet. Si autem contigerit quod prefatus Robertus vel heredes sui a solutione prenominate pensionis quandoque cessaverint, liberam habebit potestatem abbas qui pro tempore fuerit in predicta capella divinum prohibendi officium. Juravit etiam predictus Robertus in capitulo nostro, tactis sacrosanctis evangeliis, quod predictam pensionem sicut prelocutum est solvet, nec artem vel ingenium committeret, unde prenominata pensio ecclesie Westmonasterii umquam ullo tempore subtrahatur aut minuatur. Et ut hec nostra concessio futuris temporibus stabilis et rata permaneat, eam presentis scripti testimonio et sigilli nostri apposicione roboravimus. Hiis testibus: Willelmo de Aubeygni; Simone de Pateshull'; Ricardo de Heriet; Willelmo thesaurario; Magistro Willelmo de Neket'; Magistro Ernulfo, fratre abbatis; Theobaldo, senescallo nostro; Johanne de la Wike; Andrea de Scaccario; Willelmo filio Roberti; Willelmo Borel; Thoma de Windlesor; Ricardo janitore; Rogero Enganet; Roberto de Rokingham; Albino computatore; Henrico Sumer; Alexandro de Eya; Johanne [filio] Edwardi; Lodovico *clerico qui hoc cirografphum scripsit,* et multis aliis.

MS: WAD, f. 352r–v.
  Rubric: Carta W. abbatis et conventus Westmonasterii de quadam capella constituenda in curia Roberti Mauduit, *reddendo per annum ij bisantias.*
Pd: Mason, 'The Mauduits and their Chamberlainship', 19.
Date: William Postard d. 4 May 1200 (Flete, 44). William of Ely became treasurer *c.* 1195 × 1197 (Richardson, 'William of Ely', 48).

313. Confirmation by Abbot William to William of Ely, the king's treasurer, of lands and houses in Westminster given to him by Richard, bp. of London. [*post* 20 April 1196, prob. later 1196]

Universis Sancte Matris Ecclesie filiis, Guilielmus, Dei gratia abbas Westmonasterii, et totus eiusdem loci conventus, salutem eternam in Christo. Quos ecclesiarum necessitatibus utiliores futuros esse conicimus, eis in beneficiis prompcius et devocius providere debemus. Eapropter karissimo nostro et speciali amico Guilielmo de Ely, thesaurario domini regis, terras et domos quas tenuit venerabilis pater noster Ricardus Lundoniensis episcopus in villa Westmonasterii, ab eodem episcopo dicto thesaurario donatas, ipsi et illi cui ipse eas assignare voluerit, et heredibus illius, de nobis hereditario iure tenendas concedimus, et sigillorum nostrorum attestacione confirmamus. Quas volumus eum tenere quiete, honorifice, pacifice, sicut unquam memoratus Lundoniensis episcopus melius et liberius eas possedit, ita sane ut singulis annis in Translacione Beati Regis Edwardi cereum unum duarum librarum inde persolvat ecclesie nostre pro omnibus serviciis, sectis, consuetudinibus et exactionibus. His testibus: Magistro Ernulpho; Theobaldo de Fering', senescallo; Alano, capellano domini Lundoniensis episcopi; Rogero Enganet; Ricardo portario; Thoma de Niewegate, scriptore; Johanne de Storteford; Willelmo, capellano thesaurarii; Willelmo de Castello; Albino; Henrico Sumer; Roberto filio Gerini; Ada de Esenden'; Guillielmo de Wand', et pluribus aliis.

MSS: (1) WAM 17313

18.3. × 11.5 cm; t.u. 2 cm. Two slits but tag and seal missing.

Endorsed: (a) Carta Gervasii (*sic*) abbatis Westmonasterii de quadam terra et domibus quas R. episcopus London' tenuit et concessit Guillielmo de Ely thesaurario regis, pro redditu j° [cerei duarum] librarum in Festo Translationis Sancti Edwardi coram dicto sancto inveniendo (13C). (b) Sacrist' (14C).

(2) WAD, f. 363r–v.

Pd: Richardson, 'William of Ely', 80–81 (from WAD).

Date: cf. **219**.

314. Final concord between Stephen of Turnham and Edelina his wife, claimants, against Abbot William. Stephen and Edelina quitclaimed their rights in one and a half virgates and two hides in Battersea (Surr.) and the abbot granted them a piece of land in Westminster by the Thames next to the church of the Holy Innocents. Curia Regis, Westminster 11 Nov. 1198.

Hec est finalis concordia facta in curia domini regis apud Westmonasterium die Mercurii in Festo Sancti Martini anno regni Regis Ricardi x°, coram E[ustachio] Eliensi, P[hilippo] Dunelmensi, episcopis; G[aufrido] filio Petri; Willelmo de Sancte Marie[1] Ecclesie; Willelmo Brawer;[2] Ricardo de Heriet; Reginaldo de Argentom', et aliis domini regis fidelibus ibidem tunc presentibus, inter Stephanum de Turnham et Edelinam uxorem eius, petentes, per ipsum Stephanum positum loco eiusdem[a] Edeline ad lucrandum vel perdendum, et abbatem de Westmonasterio, tenentem, de una virgata terre et dimidia et duabus hidis terre cum pertinentiis in Patricheseye. Unde recognitio de Morte Antecessoris summonita fuit inter eos in prefata curia, scilicet: quod predictus Stephanus et Edelina remiserunt et quietum clamaverunt de se et heredibus suis totum ius et clamium quod habuerunt in predicta terra eidem abbati et eius successoribus in perpetuum: et pro hac remissione et quieta clamantia predictus abbas dedit predictis Stephano et Edeline quandam terram in Westmonasterio contra ecclesiam Sanctorum Innocentium, cuius latitudo versus[b] vicum continet xxxj ulnas et in medio continet xxxvij ulnas et versus Thamisam continet in latitudine xxxiiij[c] ulnas et in longitudine quicquid continetur inter vicum de Westmonasterio et Thamisam, tenendam eiusdem Stephano et Edeline et heredibus eorum de predicto abbate et eius successoribus in perpetuum; reddendo inde annuatim in Festo Sancti Michaelis eidem abbati vel eius successoribus unam libram piperis vel sex denarios pro omni servitio. Et predictus abbas et successores eius debent warantizare predictam terram predictis Stephano et Edeline et heredibus eorum contra omnes homines.

Surr'[3]   Middelsex[3]

MSS: (1) PRO, C.P.25(1), 282/3, no. 62.

1. Error for *Matre*.
2. Error for *Briwer*.
3. In different hands and inks.

(2) WAD, f. 168v.
Rubric: (1) Batricheseye'. (2) Concordia inter Stephanum de Turnham et Edelinam uxorem eius et abbatem Westmonasterii de una
virgata terre et dimidia et duabus hidis terre in villa de Bat[ri]ch'.

   a. *ipsius*.
   b. *usque*.
   c. *xxxciij*.

Pd: *Fines 10 Ric. 1*, no. 126, pp. 84–85.
Cal: *Fines Surrey*, 212; Browning & Kirk, 239.
Note: On the correct style of William de Ste-Mère-Eglise at this date, cf.
Fasti I, 2. On Battersea, cf. Harvey, *WA*, 357–8.

315. Grant by Abbot William of the church of Sunbury (Mddx.) to
Gilbert of Cranford, at the request of Mr Adam of Cranford, for an
annual pension payable to the chamberlain. [1191 × 1200]

Omnibus Sancte Matris Ecclesie filiis ad quos presens scriptum
pervenerit, Willelmus, Dei gratia abbas Westmonasterii, et eiusdem loci
conventus, salutem in Domino. Noverit universitas vestra quod nos de
communi consensu et voluntate tocius capituli nostri, ad instanciam et
petitionem Magistri Ade de Cramford, dedimus et concessimus Gilleberto de Cramford, clerico, ecclesiam de Sunnebury cum omnibus
pertinentiis suis, in liberam et perpetuam elemosinam, solvendo
camerario nostro annuatim nomine pensionis duas marcas argenti ad
duos terminos anni, scilicet: ad Festum Sancti Michaelis unam marcam,
et ad Annunciacionem Sancte Marie unam marcam. Quod ne tractu
temporis possit in dubium vel in irritum revocari hanc nostram concessionem et donacionem presentis scripti attestacione et sigilli nostri
appositione corroborare et communire curavimus. Hiis testibus: Ada de
Sunnebiry; Martino de Capella; Thoma pincerna; Asculfo de Cramford;
Philippo de Sancto Michaele, et multis aliis.

MS: WAD, f. 506.
   Rubric: Littera abbatis et conventus Westmonasterii super dona-
   cione ecclesie de Sunneburi, salva pensione duarum marcarum.
   Marginalia: Sunnebury.
Date: The abbot is almost certainly William Postard: cf. the earlier
attestation of Adam of Sunbury (**301**).
Note: Cf. Harvey, *WA*, 354.

316. Final concord between Ailward of Charing and Hawise his wife,
plaintiffs, and Abbot William, tenant, who acknowledged their right in
three virgates of land in Teddington (Mddx.). Curia Regis, Westminster
26 Nov. 1197.

Hec est finalis concordia facta in curia domini regis apud Westmonasterium in crastino Sancte Katerine anno regni Regis Ricardi ix^m,

coram Domino H[uberto] Cantuariensi archiepiscopo, Radulfo Here-
fordense, Ricardo Eliensi archidiacono, Magistro Thoma de Husseburn',
Willelmo de Warenna, Ricardo de Herierd', Osberto filio Hervei,
justiciariis, et aliis baronibus et fidelibus domini regis tunc ibi presentibus, inter Ailwardum de Cherringe et Hawissam uxorem suam, petentes, et abbatem Westmonasterii, tenentem, de iij^bus virgatis terre cum
pertinenciis in Tudinton', unde recognicio de Morte Antecessoris summonita fuit inter eos in prefata curia, scilicet: quod predictus abbas
recognovit predictis Ailwardo et Hawisse predictas tres virgatas terre
cum pertinenciis in Tudinton' esse ius eorum et hereditatem; tenendas de
se et de successoribus suis sibi et heredibus suis in perpetuum, per
liberum servicium j marce argenti per annum pro omni servicio, salvo
forinseco servicio. Et pro hoc fine et concordia et recognicione predictus
Ailward et uxor eius Hawissa dederunt predicto abbati xx solidos
esterlingorum. Middelsex'

MS: PRO, C.P.25(1), 146/1, no. 11.
Pd: *Fines 9 Ric. I*, 68, no. 97.
Cal: *Fines Lond & Mddx, I*, no. 9, p. 1.
Note: cf. Harvey, *WA*, 354.

317. Confirmation by Abbot William to the convent of the church of
Benfleet with the manor of Benfleet, and appurtenant Fanton and
Paglesham (Essex). Chapter, Westminster [? 1191 × 1200]

Willelmus, Dei gratia abbas Westmonasterii, omnibus Sancte Matris
Ecclesie filiis ad quos presens carta pervenerit, eternam in Domino
salutem. Justis petentium desideriis facilem nos convenit inpertiri consensum et vota que a rationis tramite non discrepant: effectu sunt
prosequente complenda. Noverit itaque universitas vestra nos, divine
pietatis intuitu et pro salute anime mee et patris et matris mee, concessisse et confirmasse sine ullo retinemento conventui nostro ecclesiam de
Benflet cum ipso manerio et cum omnibus terris et maneriis sibi adiacentibus, scilicet Fanton' et Pakelesham, cum omnibus pertinentiis suis, que
scilicet maneria ab antiquis temporibus pia largitione antecessorum
meorum venerabilium abbatum Westmonasterii ad officium pitanciarie
semper pertinuisse dinoscuntur, quatinus eadem maneria libere, quiete
et honorifice in propria habeant dispositione, et in usus suos et utilitates
quicquid ex eis poterit provenire, ita quod per eos fiat omne ordinamentum predictorum maneriorum, inponendis autem vel removendis
pitanciariis, utar consilio conventus, prout expedierit. Contestor igitur
omnes successores meos abbates ne ipsi faciant aut fieri sinant ullam
infractionem huius mee concessionis immo augeant et confirment, et
stabiliant. Hanc autem concessionem promta voluntate feci in capitulo
nostro et sigillo proprio roboratam super ipsum altare Beati Petri
apostolorum principis devotus obtuli ex auctoritate Dei et Beati Petri et
ex potestate michi tradita, terribiliter eos anathematizans quicumque
hanc concessionem nostram ausu temerario infringere seu diminuere aut
irritam facere presumpserint. Hoc autem factum est toto conventu

Westmonasterii assistente et sententiam latam confirmante et pro beneficio isto nobis omnimodas gratias referente.

MS: WAD, ff. 602v–603.
    Rubric: Carta Domini Willelmi abbatis Westmonasterii de ecclesia
    de Benflete cum manerio et terris et omnibus aliis rebus sibi
    adjace[n]tibus.
Date: The attribution of this charter to William Postard is likely, because
Benfleet was appropriated 1189 × 1198 (Harvey, *WA*, 405).
Note: See **214–15, 299, 339**.

318. Agreement between Abbots Warin of St Albans and William of
Westminster about the view of frankpledge in Aldenham (Herts.) and the
suit of the hundred court. [6 June × 17 July 1194]

Sciant tam presentes quam futuri hanc esse formam firme pacis inter
Abbatem Warinum de Sancto Albano et Abbatem Willelmum de Westmonasterio de controversia que fuit inter illos de visu francplegiorum de
Aldenham et de secta hundredi, videlicet: quod Abbas Sancti Albani
Warinus premissa summonicione congrua mittet quem voluerit de
bailivis suis ad videndum francplegium in Aldenham, ita quod suscepto
ab eodem bailivo abbatis Sancti Albani iuramento hominum de Aldenham et audito vero dicto de his unde requisiti fuerint, ipse bailivus abbatis
Sancti Albani vadia ab his qui in misericordia fuerint recipiet, et ipsa
vadia et omnes forisfacture que illa die de visu francplegiorum
pervenient, remanebunt quieta abbati Westmonasterii in manu bailivi
sui. Per sic quod singulis annis in die visus francplegiorum bailivus abbatis
Sancti Albani recipiet per manum bailivi abbatis Westmonasterii duos
bisancios vel quatuor solidos sterlingorum sive fuerint forisfacture sive
non fuerint, nec poterit amplius exigi ab abbate Westmonasterii vel
bailivo suo vel hominibus de Aldenham pro visu francplegiorum, salva
secta hundredo sicut antiquitus fieri solebat et salvis placitis corone. Et ut
hec forma pacis stabilis sit et firma, sigillorum munimine utriusque partis
roboratur. His testibus: Willelmo de Sisavern', senescallo Sancti Albani;
Laurentio de Theobrug'; Gaufrido de Childew'; Waltero Blancfrunt';
Rollando Blancfront; Nicholao dispensatore; Roberto de Lenn'; Aed-
wardo preposito Westmonasterii; Thoma pincerna; Alano filio Aedwardi; Ada de Winton'; Joseph servienti; Jacobo ostiario; Roberto
marescallo.

MSS: (1) WAM 4502.
    17.7 × 16 cm; t.u. 1.6 cm. Cirographum on top edge. Tag but no seal.
    Endorsed: (a) Cirographum inter abbatem Westmonasterii et
    abbatem Sancti Albani de Aldenam (12C). (b) de visu franciplegii et
    secta hundredi (13C). (c) vij (16C).
    (2) WAD, f. 186v–187.
Date: *Rolls K.C. 1194–95*, 7, 28.

319. Grant by Abbot William to Geoffrey Picot and his heirs of two virgates of assart between his houses and the abbot's wood at Aldenham (Herts.). [1191 × 1200]

Noverint omnes qui litteras istas viderint vel audierint quod ego Willelmus, Dei gratia abbas Westmonasterii, et eiusdem loci conventus concessimus et hac presenti carta nostra confirmavimus Galfrido Picot et heredibus suis duas virgatas terre de essartis que jacent inter domos suas et nemus nostrum in villa de Aldenham jure hereditario, de nobis tenendas pro una marca argenti in firma de Aldenham, singulis annis reddenda pro omni servicio: ad Pascham, scilicet, sex solidos et octo denarios, et ad Festum Sancti Michaelis totidem. Volumus itaque et precipimus quatinus prefatus Galfridus et heredes sui predictas virgatas terre de nobis libere et honorifice per prenominatum servicium teneant, ut autem hec nostra concessio stabilis et rata permaneat, eam sigilli nostri appositione communivimus. Hiis testibus: Stephano camerario; Arnaldo Herlave; Theobaldo senescallo; Laurentio de scaccario; Thoma pincerna; Rogero de Merden; Ada camerario; Albino clerico; Ricardo janitore; Simone Calvo, et multis aliis.

MS: WAD, f. 187.
  Rubric: Cirographum Galfridi Picot de duabus virgatis terre in Aldenham.
Date: The witnesses attest charters of William Postard's abbacy.
Note: See Harvey, *WA*, 345.

320. Final concord between Abbot William and the convent of Westminster, and Hugh of Buckland, concerning the advowson of Datchworth (Herts.). The abbot and the convent quitclaimed this to Hugh, with the proviso that before the clerk whom he presented was instituted to the church or gained admission, he would swear in the chapter at Westminster to pay the abbot and convent and their successors £1 yearly at Michaelmas when he was instituted. Curia Regis, Westminster 4 Dec. 1192.

Hec est finalis concordia facta in curia domini regis apud Westmonasterium die Veneris proxima post Festum Sancti Andree anno regni Regis Ricardi quarto, coram Domino Waltero Rothomagensi archiepiscopo, et Rogero filio Reinfridi, et Roberto de Wittefeld', et Osberto filio Hervei, et Symone de Patteshill', et Hugone de Chaucumbe', et Magistro Thoma de Husseburn', justiciariis domini regis, et aliis fidelibus domini regis ibi tunc presentibus, inter Willelmum abbatem et conventum de Westmonasterio, et Hugonem de Bocland' de advocatione ecclesie de Dachewrth', unde placitum fuit inter eos in curia domini regis per breve recognicionis, scilicet: quod predicti abbas et conventus quietam clamaverunt in perpetuum de se et de successoribus suis prefato Hugoni et heredibus suis prefatam advocationem ecclesie de Dachewrth', per sic: quod clericus quem Hugo vel heredes sui presentabunt ad prefatam ecclesiam antequam institutionem vel ingressum habuerit in prefatam ecclesiam de Dachewrth' jurabit in capitulo de Westmonasterio quod solvet annuatim prefatis abbati et conventui et eorum successoribus viginti solidos sterlingorum ad Festum Sancti

Michaelis, cum institutus fuerit. Hec autem concordia facta fuit inter predictos abbatem et conventum et Hugonem asensu, et voluntate Willelmi de Bocland', qui fuit homo abbatis de Westmonasterio de villa de Dachewrth', qui fuit dominus prefati Hugonis de prefata villa de Dachewrth'.

MS: PRO, C.P. 25(1), 84/1, no. 1.
Pd: *Fines HII & Ric. I*, no. 14, pp. 13–14.

321. Grant by Abbot William to the infirmary of twenty-one marks (£14) from the churches of Oakham and Hambleton (Rutl.) in perpetuity, in return for the celebration of his anniversary. [1191 × 1200]

Willelmus, Dei gratia abbas Westmonasterii, omnibus Sancte Matris Ecclesie filiis ad quos presens carta pervenerit, eternam in Domino salutem. Noverit universitas vestra me divine pietatis intuitu, concessisse et pro salute mea et patris et matris et antecessorum meorum dedisse et hac presenti carta mea confirmasse dilectis in Christo fratribus et filiis nostris conventui, videlicet Westmonasterii, viginti et unam marcam argenti ad infirmariam eorum sustentandam singulis annis percipiendas et inperpetuum possidendas, de residuo ecclesiarum de Ocham et de Hameledone, per manum infirmarii qui pro tempore fuerit, ita ut in usus et necessitates fratrum infirmorum prout expedierit fideliter expendantur, et idem infirmarius anniversarium nostrum singulis annis in perpetuum decenter et honeste[1] procuret. Obtestor autem omnes successores meos abbates per tremendum Dei iudicium[2] ne ipsi ullam infractionem huic mee concessioni faciant vel fieri permittant. Si quis vero hanc nostram concessionem et donacionem[3] in magno vel in minimo infringere voluerit vel alios ad hoc quolibetmodo conduxerit indignationem Omnipotentis Dei nisi resipiscat incurrat; ut autem hec nostra concessio perpetuum[4] robur optineat, eam presentis scripti testimonio et sigilli nostri apposicione roboravimus. Hiis testibus: Tedbaldo senescallo nostro; Arnulfo fratre meo; Nicholao nepote meo; Robert Mauduyt; Willelmo de Rochingeham; Andrea et Albino de scaccario; Lodouico clerico; Rogero Enganet; Willelmo filio Roberti; Odone aurifabro, et multis aliis.

MSS: (1) WAD, f. 578.
    Rubric: Carta Domini Willelmi abbatis Westmonasterii de eodem.
    Marginalia: Anniversarium Willelmi abbatis Postard (erased) Humez.
    (2) F, f. 268r–v: attestations omitted.
      1. *honeste et decenter*.
      2. *judicium Dei*.
      3. *donacionem et concessionem*.
      4. *inperpetuum*.
Pd: Flete, 98–99, from F.
Date: The abbot is William Postard, not withstanding WAD marginalia, as shown by the attestations, notably Theobald of Feering as seneschal.

Note: Cf. Harvey, *WA*, 404; Mason, 'Rutland Churches', 164–5; **226, 336**.

322. Grant by Abbot William to his knight William Picot of the manor of Doddington (Lincs.), except the advowson of the church, in fee and inheritance. [1191 × 1200]

Omnibus qui litteras istas viderint vel audierint, Willelmus abbas West-monasterii et totus eiusdem loci conventus, salutem. Noverit universitas vestra nos unanimi assensu tocius capituli nostri concessisse et hac presenti carta nostra confirmasse Willelmo Picot militi nostro manerium nostrum de Dodinton' cum omnibus pertinentiis suis, excepta advoca-cione ecclesie quam in manu nostra plenarie retinemus; habendum et tenendum de nobis in feudo et hereditate, libere, quiete et honorifice; reddendo inde singulis annis camerario nostro quicumque fuerit duode-cim libras ad quatuor terminos, videlicet: infra quindecim dies Natalis Domini sexaginta solidos; infra quindecim dies Pasche sexaginta solidos; infra quindecim dies Nativitatis Sancti Johannis sexaginta solidos; et infra quindecim dies Festi Sancti Michaelis sexaginta solidos. Si autem pre-fatus Willelmus vel heredes sui aliquo tempore ad defendendum predic-tum manerium consilio et auxilio nostro indiguerint, tale eis auxilium et manutenentum prestabimus quod cartas nostras et munimenta per aliquem ex nostris ad defensionem prefati manerii quando et ubi oport-unum fuerit sumptibus et expensis illorum mittemus. Et ut hec nostra concessio stabilis et rata permaneat, eam presenti scripto et sigilli nostri apposicione roborare curavimus. Hiis testibus: Waltero de Heselton'; Fulcone de la Hule; Henrico de Meleford'; Gaufrido Pycot; Waltero Pycot; Teobaldo senescallo; Alexandro filio Radulfi; Simone de Buketon'; Ricardo janitore; Edwardo qui fuit prepositus; Alano filio eius; Thoma pincerna; Magistro Johanne Wincestr', et multis aliis.

MS: WAD, f. 501.
> Rubric: Scriptum indentatum abbatis et conventus Westmonasterii de manerio de Dodinton', excepta advocacione ecclesie, reddendo per annum xij libras.

Note: Cf. Harvey, *WA*, 348. In 1205, William Picot claimed the advow-sons of Doddington and Thorp [on the Hill]. Abbot Ralph produced a charter, in form of a cirograph, of Abbot William and the convent, which granted the vill of Doddington and Thorp [on the Hill] to William Picot, at farm for £12 annually, excepting the advowsons. Ralph identified the appendant seal as that of his predecessor, but Picot challenged the authenticity of this document (*Curia Regis Rolls*, IV, 13, 45–6, 48).

323. Grant by Abbot William to the nuns of Godstow, of Bloxham church (Oxon.), and quitclaim of the whole right of the abbot and convent in the church, saving an annual pension of five marks (£3. 6s. 8d.) to the sacrist for altar lights. Westminster, 14 June 1197.

Universis Sancte Matris Ecclesie filiis ad quos presens scriptum pervenerit, Willelmus, Dei gratia abbas Westmonasterii, et totus eiusdem loci conventus, salutem in Domino. Ad universitatis vestre noticiam volumus pervenire nos a lite que vertebatur inter nos et sanctimoniales de Godestow super causa ecclesie de Blokesham, cuius cognicio Lincolniensis episcopo, et de Sancto Albano, et de Stratford abbatibus ab apostolica sede fuit delegata, per amicabilem composi-tionem recessisse sub hac forma: Nos attendentes religionem et honestatem sanctimonialium predicte domus, scilicet de Godestow, et earundem paupertati compatientes, unanimi assensu concessimus et dedimus in perpetuam elemosinam prefatis sanctimonialibus ecclesiam de Blokesham cum omnibus pertinenciis suis plenarie, integre, perpetuo; habendam et possidendam et totum ius quod in eadem ecclesia habuimus ecclesie Beati[1] Johannis Baptiste de Godestow et sanctimonialibus ibidem Deo servientibus quietum clamavimus, salva nobis pensione quinque marcarum quas de eadem ecclesia antiquitus percipere solebamus, quam pensionem prefate moniales annuatim reddere debent sacriste ecclesie nostre ad luminare altaris ad duos anni terminos, scilicet: infra octavas Festivitatis Omnium Sanctorum duas marcas et dimidiam, et infra octavas Pentecost' duas marcas et dimidiam. Facta est autem hec transactio inter nos et predictas sanctimoniales anno Verbi Incarnati millesimo centesimo nonagesimo septimo, anno Regis Ricardi octavo, die tercia post Festum Sancti Barnabe apostoli apud Westmonasterium, mediante ex parte Domini Huberti, Cantuariensis archiepiscopi et apost-olice sedis legati, viro venerabili Hugone, abbate Abendon', et hinc compositionis opem et operam adhibente. Et ut hec nostra concessio rata inposterum perseveret, nos eam presente carta et sigillorum nostrorum appositione roboravimus. Hiis testibus: Domino Hugone abbate Abendon'; et Nicholao et Ricardo monachis et capellanis eius; Waleranno capellano; Johanne de Kensinton et Henrico de Kensinton fratre eius; Martino clerico domine regine; Godefrido de la Dene; Willelmo de Haggehurste; Roberto de Clere; Magistro Earnulfo Postard; Magistro Simone de Bareswrd; Teodbaldo senescallo Westmonasterii; Radulfo de Septem Fontibus; et Henrico fratre eius, et multis aliis.

MS: Godstow Cartulary: PRO E164/20, f. xiiij.
    Rubric: Carta de Bloxham facta abbati Westmonasterii.
      1. MS: *beate*.
Cal: Full translation in Middle English, *The English Register of Godstow Nunnery near Oxford*, ed. Andrew Clark, E.E.T.S., O.S. 142 (1911), 208–9, no. 308.
Note: Although Abbots Gervase (**253**) and Laurence (**286**) had held the advowson of Bloxham, evidently a valuable living, in view of the important clerics whom they appointed to the church, Abbot William was unable to uphold his title after H II's grant of this church to Godstow, followed by the verdict of the papal judges-delegate (**225** and note). See R. A. R. Hartridge, *A History of Vicarages in the Middle Ages*, Cambridge Studies in Medieval Life and Thought (1930), 209.

324. Final concord in the king's court at Northampton between Abbot William, claimant, and William of Darnford, defendant, about right of hospitality at Deerhurst (Gloucs.), which the abbot quitclaimed to William. Curia Regis, Northampton, 22 Jan. 1192.

Hec est finalis concordia facta in curia[1] domini regis apud Norhamton, anno tercio regni Regis Ricardi, die Sancti Vincencii coram H[ugone] episcopo Coventrenci et Willelmo Marescallo et Galfrido filio Petri et Hugone Bardulf et Roberto de Wicef[eld][2] et Othone filio Willelmi et Osberto filio Hervici et Ricardo del Pec', iusticiis domini regis, et aliis baronibus et fidelibus domini regis tunc ibidem presentibus, inter Willelmum abbatem de Westmonasterio, petentem, et Willelmum de Derneford, tenentem, de uno hospicio quod prefatus abbas clamavit habere consuetudine annuatim ad se et suos hospitandum in villa de Derherst'. Unde placitum fuit inter eos in curia domini regis, scilicet: quod prefatus abbas quietum clamavit prefatum hospicium prefato Willelmo et heredibus suis in perpetuum, et pro hoc fine et quieta clamantia et concordia prefatus Willelmus et heredes sui dabunt quolibet anno prefato abbati xl solidos ad duos terminos per annum: ad octabas Sancti Michaelis xx solidis, et ad octabas Pasche xx solidos.

MSS: (1) WAM 32671 (formerly 32653).
      15.5 × 8.7 cm. Indented at top: CIROGRAPHUM.
      Endorsed: (a) Finalis concordia in curia Regis Ricardi . . . (illegible) Will de Derneford (13C). (b) Derherst (13C).
      1. MS: *in curia in curia.*
      2. Supplied from WAD.
    (2) WAD, f. 318v.
Note: cf. **271** and note.

325. Final concord made between Baldwin of Parham, plaintiff, and Abbot William concerning the advowson of Parham (Sussex), which Baldwin quitclaimed. Curia Regis, Westminster, 4 Nov. 1199.

Hec est finalis concordia facta in curia [domini regis] apud Westmonasterium, die Jovis proxima post Festum Omnium Sanctorum, anno regni Regis [Johannis primo,] coram G. filio Petri, Magistro Thoma de Husseburn', Willelmo de Warenn', R[icardo de Her'], Simone de Pateshill', Johanne de Gestlinges, justiciis, et aliis baronibus domini [regis tunc ibi] presentibus, inter Baldewinum de Perham, petentem, et Willelmum abbatem de Westmonasterio, [tenentem,] per Jacobum celerarium, positum loco predicti abbatis ad lucrandum vel perdendum, [de advo]cacione ecclesie de Perham, unde recognicionem summonitum fuit inter eos in prefata curia, scilicet: quod predictus Baldewinus remisit et quietum clamavit predicto abbati et successoribus suis totum ius et clamium quod habuit in advocacione predicte ecclesie de se et heredibus suis in perpetuum. Et pro hac fine et concordia et quieta clamancia predictus abbas dedit predicto Baldewino unam marcam argenti.

MSS: (1) WAM 4036 (Abbot's copy).
      13.2 × 9.8 cm. Top and sides cut CIROGRAPHUM. Torn down centre: missing words supplied in square brackets from WAD and foot of fine. Small slits; seal missing.

Endorsed: (a) Quieta clamancia facta Willelmo de Perham (13C).
(b) Perham deracionatione . . . (stained) (13C). (c) Infirmarius
(15C).
(2) WAD, f. 578.
(3) PRO CP 25(1), 233/2, no. 14 (variant).
Note: WAM 4058 (copy on WAD, f. 582v) was evidently acquired by
Westminster as a result of this agreement: pd.: *The Acts of the Bishops of
Chichester 1075–1207*, ed. H. Mayr-Harting, Cant. and York Soc. 55
(1964), 114–5.

326. Grant by Abbot William to the convent of the vill of Parham
(Sussex), except the advowson of the church. They are to pay £8 a year to
the convent kitchener. If homage is rendered, the abbot will receive it in
person, but any relief is to be rendered to the convent. Chapter,
Westminster [(1191 ×) 1200]

Omnibus Sancte Matris Ecclesie filiis ad quos presens carta pervenerit,
Willelmus, Dei gratia abbas Westmonasterii, eternam in Domino
salutem. Noverit universitas vestra nos, divine pietatis intuitu et pro
salute anime mee et antecessorum et successorum meorum, concessisse
et hac presenti carta mea confirmasse, sine ullo retinemento, placiti vel
relevii, et sine omni exactione tailagii, vel cuiuscumque rei, conventui
nostro Westmonasterii villam nostram de Perham cum terris sibi adiacentibus et cum omnibus pertinentiis suis, excepta solummodo advocatione
ecclesie, cuius donationem in manu nostra retinemus, quatinus idem
manerium libere, quiete et honorifice in propria habeant dispositione, et
in usus suos et utilitates quicquid ex prefato manerio poterit provenire,
ita quod per eos fiat omnis dispositio predicti manerii. Solvent igitur
annuatim vice mea octo libras argenti coquinario conventus qui pro
tempore fuerit quatuor statutis terminis, videlicet: infra octavas Natalis
Domini quadraginta solidos; infra octavas Pasce xl solidos; infra octavas
Sancti Johannis Baptiste quadraginta solidos; infra octavas Sancti
Michaelis quadraginta solidos, absque omni infestatione mei vel successorum meorum. Quod si fortassis aliquo tempore contigerit de eodem
tenemento homagium debere fieri, ego vel successores mei qui pro
tempore fuerint, in persona nostra homagium recipiemus: relevium vero
conventui nostro in usus suos quietius remanebit. Contestor igitur omnes
successores meos abbates per tremendum Dei iudicium ne ipsi faciant,
vel fieri permittant, ullam infractionem vel diminutionem huic nostre
concessioni in maximo vel in minimo, immo augeant et confirment. Hanc
autem concessionem promta voluntate feci in capitulo nostro Westmonasterii, et sigillo proprio roboratam super ipsum altare Beati Petri
apostolorum principis devotus optuli, ex auctoritate Dei et Beati Petri et
ex potestate michi tradita terribiliter anathematizans quicumque hanc
nostram concessionem ausu temerario quolibet modo infringere seu
diminuere vel irritam facere presumpserint. Hoc autem factum est toto
conventu Westmonasterii assistente et sententiam latam confirmante et
pro beneficio isto gratias omnimodas nobis referente.

MSS: (1) WAM 4064

7.7 × 24.3 cm; t.u. 1.9cm.
Seal: green; 7.8 × 5.2 cm; on obverse a standing abbot holding a book in left hand; Legend: SIG . . . (worn).
Counter seal: 4.3 × 3cm; bust of King Edward with sceptre in right hand: Legend: SANCTE EDWARD . . .
Endorsed: (a) Carta Willelmi abbatis Westmonasterii de villa de Perham conventui suo concessa (13C). (b) Perham (14C).
(2) WAD, f. 572.
Date: Prob. after **325**.
Note: The more elaborate grant by Abbot Ralph of Parham to the convent (**335**) was made without prejudice to the existing endowment of the kitchen, viz. 8*s*. per day (*sic*), but included the right to present to the church. The £8 per annum assigned by Abbot William [Postard] is not mentioned in Abbot William d'Humez's definitive assignment to the kitchen (*Documents illustrating the rule of Walter de Wenlok, abbot of Westminster, 1283–1307*, ed. B. F. Harvey (Camden 4th ser., ii, 1965), 215–6). On Parham see also Harvey, *WA*, 359–60.

327. Grant by Abbot Ralph and the convent to their clerk, Alexander of Swerford, of their houses in London, between Ludgate and Fleet Bridge, formerly belonging to William Turpin, to hold in perpetuity for an annual rent of 8*s*. due to the proctor of the Lady Altar, for lights, saving the service due to the chief lords. [*c.* Sept. 1206 × *ante* Jan. 1214]

Omnibus Sancte Matris Ecclesie filiis ad quos presens scriptum pervenerit, Radulfus, Dei gratia abbas Westmonasterii, et eiusdem loci conventus, salutem in Domino. Noverit universitas vestra nos concessisse et hac presenti carta nostra confirmasse Alexandro de Swereford, clerico nostro, domos nostras in London', inter Ludgate et Pontem de Flete, scilicet domos que fuerunt Willelmi Turpin, tenendas et habendas sibi et heredibus suis de nobis libere et quiete inperpetuum, reddendo inde singulis annis, ad luminaria altaris Beate Dei Genetricis Marie, ei qui pro tempore predictum altare procuraverit octo solidos ad quatuor anni terminos, scilicet: ad Natale Domini duos solidos; et ad Pascha duos solidos; et ad Festum Sancti Johannis Baptiste duos solidos; et ad Festum Sancti Michaelis duos solidos, pro omni servitio ad nos pertinente, salvo servicio capitalium dominorum. Et ut hec concessio et carte nostre confirmatio rata sit et stabilis permaneat, eam sigilli nostri appositione corroboravimus. Hiis testibus: Willelmo Eliensi, domini regis thesaurario; Willelmo archidiacono Huntingdon'; Roberto Mauduit, domini regis camerario;[1] Magistro Jocelino Marescallo; Willelmo de Boveneya; Willelmo de Castell; Ricardo ,de Dol; Odone aurifabro; Henrico Sumer; Richardo Testard; Johanne fratre eius; Richardo filio Edmundi; Stephano de Berking', et multis aliis.

MS: WAD, f. 561.
Rubric: Cirographus abbatis et conventus Westmonasterii de eodem.
Marginalia: j nova.

1. MS: *camerarii*.

Date: Attestation of William of Cornhill as archdeacon of Huntingdon (*Fasti* III, 28), limited by term of office of Abbot Ralph (*Heads*, 77).

Note: The recipient is almost certainly the well-known Exchequer officer of that name (Matthew Paris, *Chron. Majora*, ed. H. R. Luard, IV (R.S. 1877), 587–88; F. M. Powicke, *King Henry III and the Lord Edward* (1947), 90–91; R. C. Stacey, *Politics, Policy and Finance under Henry III 1216–1245* (1987), 41–2, 257). The 'chief lords' of the property were prob. the nuns of Clerkenwell, Roger de Friville and Ralph de Rosei, as listed in **386–7**.

328. Notification by Abbot Ralph that, with the assent of the chapter, he has confirmed to Ralph Fitz Stephen of Boulogne, and his heirs in perpetuity, the land in Longditch Street, Westminster, between the land of Walkelin of the almonry and that of the fee of Stephen of Barking, which Thomas brother of Pancras, sergeant of the sacristy, granted to the high altar, to hold at an annual rent of 7s. due to the high altar, and saving the forinsec service pertaining to the vill. This concession, made by the convent in full chapter, has been written in their martyrology to preserve it for posterity, and the cirograph of this charter has been deposited in the treasury. [1200 × 1203]

Omnibus ad quos presens scriptum pervenerit Radulfus, divina miseratione abbas Westmonasterii, salutem in Domino. Noveritis nos assensu et voluntate totius capituli nostri dedisse et concessisse et hac presenti carta nostra confirmasse Radulfo filio Stephani de Bolonia totam terram nostram in villa Westmonasterii quam Thomas frater Pancracii, serviens de sacrista ecclesie nostre, ad magnum altare ecclesie nostre dedit et concessit, que videlicet terra iacet in vico de Langedich, inter terram Walkelini de elemosinaria ex una parte, et inter terram que est de feodo Stephani de Berkinges ex alia parte; habendam et tenendam cum omnibus pertinentiis suis ipsi Radulfo et heredibus suis inperpetuum in feodo et hereditate, libere et quiete, integre et plenarie, honorifice et pacifice; reddendo inde annuatim ad magnum altare ecclesie nostre septem solidos ad quatuor terminos anni, videlicet: ad Natale Domini viginti et unum denarios; et ad Pascham viginti et unum denarios; et ad Festum Sancti Johannis viginti et unum denarios; et ad Festum Sancti Michaelis viginti et unum denarios pro omni servitio et exactione, salvo servicio forinseco pertinente ad villam. Ut autem hec donatio et concessio firma sit et stabilis eam presenti scripto et sigilli mei appositione roboravimus. Et concessionem istam in pleno capitulo a conventu nostro factam redigi fecimus in scripturam in martirologio nostro ut ad noticiam perveniat posterorum, et cirographum presentis carte, in thesauro ecclesie nostre reponi fecimus in testimonium. Hiis testibus: Ricardo de Dol, senescallo Westmonasterii; Uliano Chendedut; Magistro Simone de London'; Odone aurifabro, tunc preposito Westmonasterii; Roberto de Rockingeham; Henrico Sumer; Ricardo filio Edmundi; Stephano de Berking'; Roberto de Krokesleg'; Walkelino de elemosinario; Galfrido de Cruce; Wymundo pistore; Willelmo pistore; Willelmo de

Scardeburg'; Michaele filio eius; Ricardo Ospinel; Willelmo Noel, et multis aliis.

MS: WAD, f. 355r–v.
  Rubric: Carta Radulfi abbatis Westmonasterii de tota terra quam Thomas frater Pancracii ecclesie (nostre)ᶜ (Westmonasteri)ⁱ dedit in villa Westmonasterii.
Date: Ralph Fitz Stephen, perhaps to be identified with the recipient, d. 1202 × 1203 (*Cart. Darley*, I, xxiii).
Note: Ralph Fitz Stephen held another, less valuable, tenancy in Longditch, of Odo the goldsmith (**442**). The *curialis* Ralph Fitz Stephen would prob. need premises in Westminster. He did not normally style himself 'of Boulogne', but his first wife had been vicomtesse of Rouen (*Cart. Darley*, I, xxiii).

329. Confirmation by Abbot Ralph, at the petition of the king's chamberlain, Robert Mauduit II, and his wife Isabel, of gifts made to provide lights for St Mary's altar in the abbey. The names of the donors are to be entered in the abbey's martyrology and they will share in the spiritual benefits of the abbey. [Nov. 1200 × Jan. 1214]

Omnibus Christi fidelibus ad quos presens scriptum pervenerit, Radulfus, divina miseratione abbas Westmonasterii, et eiusdem loci conventus, salutem in Domino. Noverit universitas vestra nos ad petitionem Roberti Mauduit, domini regis camerarii, et Isabelle uxoris sue, et aliorum bonorum virorum, concessisse et hac presenti carta nostra confirmasse quod omnia bona collata vel conferenda altari Beate Marie eiusdem ecclesie Westmonasterii, sive in redditibus, sive in terris, sive in quibuscumque elemosinarum largitionibus, rata sint et stabilia ad luminaria eiusdem altaris ministranda, et alias elemosinas provisas ibidem faciendas. Et preterea concessimus quod nomina omnium illorum qui bona sua predicto altari contulerint vel collaturi sunt in martyrologio nostro conscribantur, et omnium bonorum que in ecclesia nostra fient, in orationibus, in jejuniis, in vigiliis, in missis, in disciplinis, et in omnibus aliis elemosinis, sint participes. Nos autem excommunicav[er]imus in pleno capitulo solempniter accensis candelis omnes quicumque in alios usus predicta bona absque communi consilio abbatis et conventus eiusdem loci transferent. Teste Deo, et Beata Maria, et omnibus sanctis Dei.

MSS: (1) WAM LIII.
  18.3 × 11.5 cm; t.u. 2.5 cm.
  Seals: attached by tags. (1) Green; damaged; 6.5 × 8 cm; abbot standing with crozier in left hand; right hand raised; legend: [SIGILLUM] RAD[ULPHI D]EI GR[ATIA ABBATIS WEST-[MONASTERII]: on reverse: counter-seal, 2.5 cm diameter; two fishes; legend worn. (2) Green; fragmentary; obverse, seated cleric: reverse, seated figure.
  Endorsed: (a) Confirmatio abbatis et conventus de redditibus Sancte Marie (another hand but contemporary with charter). (b) Parti-

cipatio beneficiorum capelle Beate Marie Westmonasterii (14C). (c)
Scriptum Radulfi abbatis (14C).
(2) WAD, ff. 507v–508.
Pd: Mason, 'The Mauduits and their Chamberlainship', 21–22.

330. Final concord between Abbot Ralph, plaintiff, and William de
Ginnes and his wife Matilda, defendants, concerning a carucate of land in
Battersea (Surr.), and the wood and land of Penge (Surr.). Curia Regis,
Westminster. Easter term 1204.

Hec est finalis concordia facta in curia domini regis apud Westmonasterium a die Pasche in j mensem, anno regni Regis Johannis
quinto, coram Gaufrido filio Petri, Ricardo de Her[iet'], Simone de
Pat[es]hull, Eustachio de Faucunb[er]g, Johanne de Gestling, Osberto
filio Hervei, Godefrido de Insula, Waltero de Creping', justiciariis, et
aliis baronibus domini regis tunc ibi presentibus, inter Radulfum
abbatem Westmonasterii, petentem, et Willelmum de Ginnes, et
Matildem uxorem suam, tenentem, de una carucata terre cum pertinentiis in Batricheseya sicut aquaductus designat usque ad propriam terram
predicti Willelmi, et a nemore archiepiscopi Cantuariensis usque ad
parcum de Beke[n]ham. Unde placitum fuit inter eos in prefata curia,
scilicet: quod predicti Willelmus et Matildis recognoverunt totam predictam terram cum pertinentiis esse ius ipsius abbatis et ecclesie Sancti Petri
de Westmonasterio. Et pro hac recognitione et fine et concordia predictus abbas concessit predicto Willelmo et Matildi et heredibus ipsius
Matildis totam predictam terram cum pertinentiis, tenendam de ipso
abbate et successoribus suis inperpetuum per liberum servicium viginti
solidorum per annum pro omni servicio, reddendo ad duos terminos
anni, scilicet: ad Pascha decem solidos, et ad Festum Sancti Michaelis
decem solidos. Et pro hac concessione predicti Willelmus et Matildis
remiserunt et quietum clamaverunt predicto abbati et successoribus suis
totum ius et clamium quod habuerunt in bosco et in terra de Pange de se
et heredibus ipsius Matildis inperpetuum, ita quod predictus abbas et
successores sui possint facere voluntatem suam de predicto bosco et terra
sine contradictione predictorum Willelmi et Matildis et heredum ipsius
Matildis: ita tamen quod predictus abbas concessit predicto Willelmo et
Matildi et heredibus ipsius Matildis communam herbagii in bosco suo de
Pange de omnibus propriis averiis de Bekenham, exceptis capris et alienis
averiis, quamdiu boscum clausum non fuerit. Et preterea idem abbas
concessit predictis Willelmo et Matildi et heredibus ipsius Matildis
triginta porcos in predicto bosco quietos de pannagio et omnes alii porci
et omnia averia de Bekenham removeantur de predicto bosco de Pange
quamdiu pessio durat, scilicet: inter Festum Sancti Michaelis et Festum
Sancti Martini. Et si forte contigerit quod predictus abbas vel successores
sui predictum obscum de Pange clauserunt predicti Willelmus et Matildis
et heredes ipsius Matildis habebunt in predicto bosco pasturam ad
quadraginta animalia et ad centum oves et predictos triginta porcos
quietos de pannagio. Et si forte contigerit quod idem abbas vel successores sui de predicto bosco essartare voluerint licet bene facere eis hoc

sine contradictione predictorum Willelmi et Matildis vel heredum ipsius Matildis sed tamen remanebit de predicto bosco et herbagio non sartato quod idem Willelmus et Matildis et heredes ipsius Matildis habeant sustentacionem ad predictos triginta porcos et ad quadraginta animalia et ad centum oves. Et idem abbas cepit homagium ipsius Willelmi de predicta terra in eadem curia.

MS: WAD, f. 168r–v.
> Rubric: Concordia inter abbatem Westmonasterii et Willelmum de Ginnes et Matildem uxorem suam de una carucata terre in Batricheseya.

Pd: English transl., in full, Browning and Kirk, 240–41.
Cal: *Fines Surrey*, 6.

331. Final concord between Aubrey de Vere, plaintiff, and Abbot Ralph, tenant, concerning the manor of Feering (Essex), following a plea between them. Aubrey quitclaimed the manor, and in return the abbot granted and conceded to him Little Coggeshall (Essex), pertaining to Feering, to hold in perpetuity, for an annual rent of 2*s.* and saving the forinsec service. Curia Regis, Westminster, Michaelmas term 1201.

Hec est finalis concordia facta in curia domini regis apud Westmonasterium a die Sancti Michaelis in unum mensem, anno regni Regis Johannis tercio, coram G. filio Petri, Ricardo de Her', Simone de Pateshill', Johanne de Gestling', Eustacio de Faucunberg', Godefrido de Insula, Waltero de Creping', justiciariis, et aliis baronibus domini regis tunc ibi presentibus, inter Albricum de Ver, petentem, et Radulfum abbatem Westmonasterii, tenentem, de toto manerio de Feringes cum omnibus pertinenciis. Unde placitum fuit inter eos in prefata curia, scilicet: quod predictus Albericus remisit et quietum clamavit predicto abbati et successoribus suis totum ius et clamium quod habuit in predicto manerio cum omnibus pertinenciis, de se et heredibus suis imperpetuum; et pro hac quieta clamia et fine et concordia, predictus abbas dedit et concessit predicto Albrico et heredibus suis totam terram que vocatur Parva Coggeshale, que pertinet ad predictum manerium de Feringes; habendam et tenendam de se et successoribus suis imperpetuum, per servicium duorum solidorum per annum pro omni servicio, salvo forinseco servitio, reddendum ad Festum Sancti Michaelis.

MSS: (1) WAM 1043.
> 26 × 9.8 cm; top and left side indented for cirograph; no tag or seal.
> Endorsed: Albrico de Ver (13C).
> (2) WAD, f. 266.
> (3) PRO, CP25(1), 52/6, no. 53 (variant).

Cal: *Fines Essex*, I, 24, no. 53.
Note: Cf. Harvey, *WA*, 341; *Curia Regis Rolls* I, 464–5.

332. Notification by Abbot Ralph to the men of Benfleet that he has granted the manor of Benfleet (Essex) to the prior and convent, as it had belonged to their pittancer from ancient times and which the abbot had held from them for a term. [1200 × 1214]

Radulphus, divina miseratione abbas Westmonasterii, universis hominibus de Benflet, tam liberis quam aliis, salutem. Noverit universitas vestra nos reddidisse et quietum clamasse inperpetuum dilectis filiis nostris priori et conventui Westmonasterii totum manerium suum de Benflet, cum omnibus possessionibus et redditibus et omnibus pertinentiis suis sine aliquo retinemento, quod scilicet manerium ad pitanceriam eorum pertinet, et ad eandem antiquitus fuit assignatum, quod videlicet manerium ad terminum de eis tenuimus per eorum voluntatem et concessionem. Iccirco vobis mandamus quatinus sicut nobis fuistis intendentes, decetero predictis priori et conventui intendatis. Mittimus autem ad vos latores presentium monachos nostros ut predicti manerii loco predicti prioris et conventus saisinam recipiant et ut vobis viva voce dicant et ostendant quod litteris testamur presentibus. Valete.

MSS: (1) BL Additional Charter 8474.
19.1 × 3 cm; bottom left-hand corner torn where a step might have been.
Endorsed: Cives . . . Benfleta . . . (legible remains of three lines, very faded and rubbed, and partially overwritten with modern notes).
(2) WAD, f. 602v.
Note: Cf. Harvey, *WA*, 340; **299**, **317**, **344**.

333. Settlement between Abbots John of St Albans and Ralph of Westminster of the dispute about view of frankpledge in Aldenham (Herts.) and suit of the hundred court. The abbot of St Albans will send his bailiff to view frankpledge in Aldenham and take the pledges and escheats, which will belong to the abbot of Westminster through his bailiff, who is to pay each year to the abbot of St Albans two besants or 4*s.*, whether or not there are any escheats. This is saving suit of the hundred court as it was formerly rendered, and the pleas of the Crown. [1200 × 1214]

Sciant tam presentes quam futuri hanc esse formam firme pacis inter Abbatem Johannem de Sancto Albano et Abbatem Radulphum de Westmonasterio de controversia que fuit inter illos de visu francplegiorum de Aldenham et de secta hundredi, videlicet: quod Abbas Sancti Albani Johannes premissa summonitione congrua mittet quem voluerit de baillivis suis ad videndum francplegium ad Aldenham, ita quod suscepto ab eodem baillivo abbatis Sancti Albani iuramento hominum de Aldenham et audito vero dicto de his unde requisiti fuerint, ipse baillivus abbatis Sancti Albani vadia ab his qui in misericordia fuerint recipiet, et ipsa vadia et omnes forisfacture que illa die de visu francplegiorum pervenient remanebunt quieta abbati Westmonasterii in manu baillivi sui, per sic quod singulis annis in die visus francplegiorum baillivus abbatis Sancti Albani recipiet per manum baillivi abbatis Westmonasterii duos bizancios, vel iiij^{or} solidos sterlingorum, sive fuerint forisfacture, sive non fuerint. Nec poterit amplius exigi ab abbate Westmonasterii, vel baillivo suo vel hominibus de Aldenham pro visu francplegiorum, salva secta hundredi sicut antiquitus fieri solebat, et salvis placitis corone. Et ut hac forma pacis stabilis sit et firma, sigillorum munimine utriusque partis roboratur. His testibus: Willelmo de Sisseverna, senescallo abbatis Sancti Albani; Ricardo de Dol, senescallo abbatis Westmonasterii; David de Jarpenvill'; Philippo de Oxehai; Uliano Cheneduit; Laurentio de Theburg'; Roberto de Mikelefeld; Rogero de Muriden'; Rogero filio Simonis; Nicholao dispensatore; Ricardo Testard'; Bartholomeo pincerna; Jacobo ostiario; Waltero marescallo, et multis aliis.

MSS: (1) WAM 4501.
> 17.5 × 19.4 cm; t.u. 2.6 cm; top indented: CIROGRAPHUM.
> Seal: brown; 7 × 4.8 cm; mitred abbot, crozier in left hand, right hand raised in blessing; legend: [SIG]ILLUM . . . SANCTI AL[BANI].
> Counterseal: head and shoulders of a man, classical style, profile to right; legend: [SE] CRETORU[M] SIGNACULUM.
> Endorsed: (a) Carta inter abbatem Westmonasterii et abbatem Sancti Albani (contemporary with MS). (b) de visu francplegiorum de Aldenham et secta hundredi (13C). (c) vj (13C).
> (2) WAD, f. 186v.

Note: Cf. **318**. On the exchange rate of the besant to sterling, cf. *H. Med. Exch.*, 295.

334. Final concord between Thomas de Preston, plaintiff, and Abbot Ralph, defendant, concerning the advowson of Parham, (Sussex) following an assize of darrein presentment summoned between them. Thomas quitclaimed the advowson, and the abbot and convent admitted him to their spiritual benefits and prayers. Curia Regis, Westminster, Easter term 1208.

Hec est finalis concordia facta in curia domini regis apud Westmonasterium a Die Pasche in unum mensem, anno regni Regis Johannis nono, coram ipso domino rege, Simone de Pateshull', Jacobo de Poterne, Henrico de Ponte Audemar, justiciis, et aliis fidelibus domini regis tunc ibi presentibus, inter Thomam de Preston', petentem, per Alexandrum Walensem, positum loco suo ad lucrandum vel perdendum, et Radulfum abbatem Westmonasterii, deforciantem, de advocacione ecclesie de Perham. Unde recognitio ultime presentacionis summonita fuit inter eos in prefata curia, scilicet: quod predictus Thomas recognovit advocacionem predicte ecclesie esse ius ipsius abbatis et conventus, et ecclesie Sancti Petri de Westmonasterio, et eam remisit et quietam clamavit de se et heredibus suis eidem abbati et conventui et eorum successoribus et ecclesie Sancti Petri de Westmonasterio imperpetuum; et predictus abbas et conventus receperunt eum in singulis beneficiis et orationibus que fuerint in ecclesia sua de Westmonasterio imperpetuum.

MSS: (1) WAM 4035.
> 19.7 × 6.9 cm; top and left side indented: cirograph.

Endorsed: (a) Quieta clamancia Thome de Prestun' de advocacione ecclesie de Perham capitulo Westmonasterii concessa (14C). (b) Infirmarius (15C). (c) 92 (?16C).
(2) WAD, f. 578.
(3) PRO C.P.25 (1), 233/5, no. 7 (variant).
Pd: *Formulare*, 220, CCCLXIV, from WAM.
Note: Cf. *Curia Regis Rolls*, V, 111, 188.

335. Grant and confirmation by Abbot Ralph to the convent in perpetuity, of the vill of Parham (Sussex) with the advowson of the church, for his own soul and those of his predecessors and successors. This grant is without prejudice to the existing grant of 8*s.* per day to the kitchen. The abbot is to receive any homage due from the manor but the convent will receive any relief. The convent may appoint any monk or layman as warden, and he cannot be dismissed by the abbot—similarly with any parson whom the convent present to the church. Chapter, Westminster [*c.* Sept. 1206 × Jan. 1214]

Omnibus Sancte Matris Ecclesie filiis ad quos presens carta pervenerit, Radulfus, divina miseratione abbas Westmonasterii, eternam in Domino salutem. Noverit universitas vestra me, divine pietatis intuitu et pro salute anime mee et antecessorum meorum et successorum, dedisse et concessisse et hac presenti carta mea confirmasse, sine ullo retinemento placiti vel relevii et sine omni exactione tallagii, vel cuiuscumque rei, conventui Sancti Petri Westmonasterii villam de Pereham, cum terris sibi adiacentibus et cum advocatione ecclesie et cum omnibus pertinentiis suis quatinus idem manerium in propria habeant dispositione et in perpetuum possideant, et in usus suos et utilitates redditus prefati manerii et exitus cum auxiliis et tallagiis convertant et assignent ubi assignare voluerint et quicquid de prefato manerio poterit provenire, sine calumpnia et illatione iniurie vel molestie, mei vel successorum meorum, in perpetuum habeant et possideant. Ita quod occasione concessionis prefati manerii de servitiis coquine prefati conventus cotidianis, videlicet octo solidis diebus singulis de abbate qui pro tempore fuerit, vel ballivo loco ipsius posito, percipiendis: nichil omnino in modico vel in maximo ullo tempore minuatur, nec occasione predicti manerii in usus prefati conventus confirmati aliquid auxilium a prefato conventu aliquando ego vel successores mei poterimus exigere vel accipere. Quare si fortasse aliquo tempore contigerit de aliquo tenemento prefati manerii homagium debere fieri, ego vel successores mei in persona nostra homagium recipiemus; relevium vero conventui nostro in usus suos quietum remanebit. Custodem vero poterit prefatus conventus licite et libere in dicto manerio monachum seu laicum quem voluerint apponere et cum voluerint ammovere sine contradictione mei vel successorum meorum. Nec poterimus ego vel successores mei custodem prefati manerii qui pro tempore fuerit amovere vel distringere aut aliquid nobis de prefato reddat manerio. Si vero ecclesia prefati manerii vacaverit, conventus prefatus quem voluerint ad personatum dicte ecclesie per se libere presentabit, absque contradictione mei vel successorum meorum. Contestor igitur omnes successores meos abbates Westmonasterii per[1] tremendum Dei iudicium ne ipsi faciant vel fieri permittant ullam infractionem seu diminucionem huic mee donacioni et concessioni in maximo vel minimo immo augeant et confirment. Hanc autem concessionem spontanea voluntate feci in capitulo Westmonasterii et sigillo proprio roboratam super ipsum altare Beati Petri apostolorum principis devotus optuli. Augmentatores et conservatores commendans Deo Patri ut sint heredes Dei et coheredes autem Christi; infractores vero sue diminutores huius beneficii et omnes qui hanc meam concessionem consilio, consensu vel auxilio vel etiam ausu temerario infringere vel diminuere vel irritam facere presumpserint ex auctoritate Dei Patris Omnipotentis et Filii et Spiritus Sancti, et ex auctoritate Beatorum Apostolorum Petri et Pauli, et Beati Regis Edwardi et omnium sanctorum Dei, et ex potestate michi tradita, terribiliter anathematizans portas celi eis claudens et portas inferni referans excommunicationis vinculo innodavi et eterne dampnationis ignibus deputavi, ubi vermis non moritur et ignis non extinguitur. Hoc autem factum est toto conventu Westmonasterii assistente et accensis candelis summam latam confirmante, et pro beneficii istius collatione et confirmatione gratias omnimodas Deo referente. Hiis testibus: Domino Willelmo Eliensi, domini regis thesaurario; Willelmo archidiacono Huntindon'; Magistro Roberto de Gloucestria; Magistro Jocelino Marescallo; Roberto Mauduit; Henrico Foliot; Willelmo de Buveneya; Johanne filio Willelmi; Thoma de Chimili; Willelmo de Castell'; Gaufrido de Say; Johanne de Sterteford; Roberto de Rasingburn'; Alexandro clerico; Lodovico clerico; Ricardo de Dol, tunc senescallo Westmonasterii; Uliano clerico; Magistro Simone de London'; Odone aurifabro; Willelmo filio Andree; Roberto de Rokingeham; Henrico Somer; Thoma de camera; Bartholomeo filio Hugonis; Stephano de Berking'; Roberto de Crokesleg'; Thoma de Dol, et multis aliis.

MS: WAD, ff. 572–573.
    Rubric: Carta Radulfi abbatis de eodem.
        1. MS: *pro*. The whole sentence, Contestor igitur . . . confirment, is reminiscent of the language of spurious charters of W I, H II and Ric I: e.g. *Cal. Ch. Rolls 1321–41*, 335. The elaborate anathema is also reminiscent of dubious older documents.
Date: Attestation of William of Cornhill as archdeacon of Huntingdon (*Fasti* III, 28), limited by term of office of Abbot Ralph. See also **487**.

336. Confirmation by Abbot Ralph to the convent for his own soul, and those of his parents and ancestors, and for the support of their infirmary, of twenty-one marks (£14) a year from the churches of Oakham and Hambleton (Rutl.). His successors are exhorted to maintain and augment the donation. [1200 × 1214]

Omnibus sancte Matris Ecclesie filiis ad quos presens carta pervenerit, Radulphus, Deo disponente abbas Westmonasterii, eternam in Domino salutem. Hostiam Deo satis immolat acceptabilem qui pietatis affectu confirmatur infirmis et super miseros affluit misericordie visceribus. Hinc est quod consolationi fratrum nostrorum infirmorum pie sollicitudinis oculo providere desiderans et multiplicem quam[1] egrotantes patiuntur miseriam compaciendo cupiens relevare, divine miserationis intuitu concessi, et pro salute anime mee, et animarum patris et matris mee et antecessorum meorum, dedi et hac carta mea confirmavi dilectis in Christo filiis et fratribus nostris conventui, videlicet Westmonasterii, ad infirmariam eorum sustentandam viginti et unam marcas argenti singulis annis de ecclesiis de Ocham et de Hameledon' percipiendas, et inperpetuum quiete possidendas, ita quod per consilium conventus et per manum infirmarii qui pro tempore fuerit, in usus et necessitates fratrum infirmorum prout expedierit fideliter expendantur. Obtestor autem omnes successores meos abbates per tremendum Dei judicium, ne ipsi ullam infractionem huius nostre concessionis faciant vel fieri permittant, set eam potius augeant, confirment et conservent. Scituri quod particeps mercedis efficitur qui bonam alterius constitutionem pro salutem favore prosequitur. Si quis vero hanc nostram concessionem et donationem in magno vel in minimo infringere voluerit, vel alios ad hoc quolibet modo induxerit, indignacionem Omnipotentis Dei, nisi resipiscat, incurrat. Ut autem hec nostra concessio perpetuum robur optineat, eam presentis scripti testimonio et sigilli mei appositione roboravi. Hiis testibus: Hugone filio Ricardi; Ernulfo Postard; Ricardo janitore; Stephano de Berking'; Willelmo de Bukingham; Andrea et Albino de Scaccario; Gaufrido camerario meo; Rogero Engan[et]; Willelmo filio Roberti; Odone aurifabro, et multis aliis.

MSS: (1) WAD, f. 577v–578.
> Rubric: Carta Radulfi abbatis Westmonasterii de pensione xxj marcarum de ecclesiis de Ocham et Hameldon'.
> Marginalia: Ocham et Hameldon'.
> (2) F, f. 268v: ends at *Obtestor*.
>> 1. *multiplice quod*.

Date: The confirmation was probably made early in Ralph's abbacy, since seven of the witnesses also attested the original grant of Abbot William (**321**). Bishop Hugh of Lincoln confirmed these churches 1196 × 1200 (**226**).

Note: On these churches, see Harvey, *WA*, 404; Mason, 'Rutland Churches', 163–5. Abbot Ralph's grant perhaps implies that an anniversary should be kept for his kindred, although if so, it is not otherwise recorded.

337. Confirmation by Abbot Ralph and the convent of the grant by Robert of Ardre, parson of the church of Oakham (Rutl.), to William de Remis of two virgates in Thorp, to hold of their church in Oakham at an annual rent of 2*s*. [1200 × 1214]

Sciant presentes et futuri quod ego R[adulfus], Dei gratia abbas Westmonasterii, et eiusdem loci conventus ratam habemus et presenti carta confirmamus Willelmo de Remis et heredibus suis donacionem illam quam Robertus de Ardre, persona ecclesie de Okham, eis fecit, de duabus scilicet virgatis terre in villa de Thorp, habends et tenendis de ecclesia nostra de Okham; reddendo eidem ecclesie annuatim duos solidos pro omni servicio, sicut carta predicti Roberti de Ardre testatur. Ut autem hec nostra concessio stabilis et rata permaneat, eam presentis scripti testimonio et sigilli nostri appositione roboravimus. Hiis testibus: Ricardo de Dol.

MS: WAD, f. 600r–v.
> Rubric: Confirmatio R. abbatis Westmonasterii super donationem quam Robertus de Ardre fecit de duabus virgatis terre in Thorp.
Date: Attestation of Richard de Dol, seneschal of Abbot Ralph.

338. Final concord between Abbot Ralph, plaintiff, and Simon of Deene, defendant, following a recognition concerning the advowson of Uppingham (Rutl.). Simon quitclaimed the advowson to the abbot and convent, who received him and his heirs into the spiritual benefits and prayers of the abbey. Curia Regis, Northampton, Michaelmas term 1210.

Hec est finalis concordia facta in curia domini regis [apud] Norhtanton' a Die Sancti Michaelis in quinque septimanis, anno regni Regis Johannis xij^{mo}, coram ipso domino rege, Simone de Patshull', Jacobo de Poterna, Henrico de Ponte Aldemer', Roberto de Aumar', Rogero Huscarl', justiciariis, et aliis fidelibus domini regis tunc ibi presentibus, inter Radulfum abbatem de Westmonasterio, petentem per Odonem aurifabrum positum loco suo ad lucrandum vel perdendum, et Simonem de Den, deforciantem per Ivonem filium suum positum loco suo ad lucrandum vel perdendum, de advocatione ecclesie de Huppingeham'. Unde recognitio ultime presentacionis summonita fuit inter eos in eadem curia, scilicet: quod predictus Simon recognovit advocationem predicte ecclesie cum pertinentiis esse ius ipsius abbatis et conventus et ecclesie Sancti Petri de Westmonasterio et eam remisit et quietam clamavit de se et heredibus suis predicto abbati et successoribus suis inperpetuum; et idem abbas recepit ipsum Simonem et heredes suos in singulis beneficiis et orationibus que fient de cetero in ecclesia sua de Westmonasterio inperpetuum.

MSS: (1) WAM 20616.
> 14 × 10.5 cm; indented CIROGRAPHUM top and right-hand side. Endorsed: (a) Finalis concordia inter Radulphum abbatem Westmonasterii et Simonem de Deen de advocatione ecclesie de Yppyngham (13C). (b) Yppingeham (15C). (c) Yppinkeam (contemporary with muniment).
> (2) WAD, f. 242v.
> (3) PRO, C.P. 25(1), 192/2, no. 21 (variant).
Note: See Mason, 'Rutland Churches', 163–5.

339. The weekly farm of the monks: specified foodstuffs; 1 mark for the servants; £8. 10s. from the more remote manors; for allowances and pittances £32 from Benfleet, Fanton, Paglesham and Wennington (all in Essex) and Comberton (Worcs.); £15 for firewood; for the chamber and all necessaries: all rents from London; Doddington (Lincs.); Chollington (Suss.); Cippenham (Bucks.) and Sulby (Northants.). One mill at Stratford (Essex), and at Parham (Suss.). Total £70. For servants in specified offices: from Hanworth £1.10*s*.; from Cowley £1.10*s*. (both in Mddx.); from Titeburst 10*s*.; from Mardley 15*s*. (both in Herts.); from Ilteney £1.4*s*.; from Ockendon 5*s*. (both in Essex); from tenants of the vineyards, with exceptions, £1; for the Lord's Supper £3 from Wheatley (Essex) and 7*s*. from Knightsbridge (Mddx.). [temp. H.I, *c*. 1118 × 1120?]

Hec est firma monachorum in septimana: ad panem: vj cumbas et lx et vij solidos ad coquinam; et xx hops de brasio; et x de gruto; et iij cumbas avene; et ad servientes j marcam argenti. Et illa maneria que longinqua sunt et hoc reddere non poterint reddent pro tota septimana viij libros et x solidos. Ad karitates et pitancias: xxxij libri de Bienflet, de Fantone, de Pakelesam, et Winetona, et de Cumbritona; ad ligna xv libri; ad cameram et ad omnia que necessaria sunt omnes redditus Lundonie, et Dodintuna, et Cillentuna, et Sippeham, et Sulebi, et j molendinum apud Stretfort et Perham. Hec est summa: lx et x libri. Ad servientes coquine et pistrini et bracini et orti et vinee et infirmatorii, et portarii: de Hanewrde xxx solidi; de Coveley xxx solidi; de Titebirste x solidi; de Merdeleya xv solidi; de Elteneya xxiiij solidi; et v solidi de Okkenduna; et xx solidi de illis qui tenent terras vinearum, exceptis illis qui habent terrulas pro solidatis suis. Ad servicium cene Domini lx solidi de Wateleya; et vij solidi de Knichtebrigge.

MSS: (1) WAM 5670.
    20.3 × 8.3 cm; no t.u.
    Endorsed: (a) Extenta conventus Westmonasterii (12C). (b) Com-
    positiones (15C).
    (2) WAD, f. 629.
Pd: *Gilbert Crispin*, 41, from WAM.
Date: Later than the recovery of Comberton (**66**; **488**), and of Dod-dington (**61**, **475**). It has been suggested that the document represents the allowance made to the monks when the abbey was in the hands of H I, between the death of Abbot Gilbert and the appointment of Abbot Herbert (*Gilbert Crispin*, 44), but that would not explain why it was copied into WAD so long afterwards.
Note: Discussed in *Gilbert Crispin*, 42–50; Harvey, *WA*, 80.

340. Notification by the convent of Westminster to the citizens of London that they have conceded to Eorlwin, brother of Wlfwin, in fee and inheritance, the land with the building on it which Godric Catepol held of their chamberlain in Eastcheap, to hold at an annual rent of 7*s*., whether or not there is an outbreak of fire (which destroys the building). [1136 × 1138]

Conventus ecclesie Sancti Petri Westmonasterii omnibus civibus London', Francis et Anglis, salutem. Sciatis quod, communi consensu et concordi voluntate totius capituli, concessimus Eorlewino fratri Wlfwini terram et totum edificium quod super terra est, quam Godricus Catepol tenuit de camerario nostro in Eastceapa, in feudum et in hereditatem, tam sibi quam heredibus suis, ardeat civitas necne, unoquoque anno per redditionem vii solidorum in die Ramarum Palmarum. Hii sunt testes: Gregorius dapifer; Reinaldus Barill; Radulphus de Ponte Fracto; Willelmus de Winter; Tovius Ganet; Tovius corveisarius; Durandus Duredent, Wisgarus de Pirifo', et multi alii.

MS: WAD, f. 504v.
> Rubric: Telligraphus conventus Westmonasterii de quadam terra in Estchepe.
> Marginalia: London'.

Date: Gregory was dapifer under Abbots Herbert (**250**) and Gervase (**254, 265**), so this document was possibly issued during the vacancy between them.
Note: It is remarkable that the rent is due on Palm Sunday, rather than at the usual quarterly terms.

341. Notification by the convent of Westminster to their tenants and friends, that they have confirmed to William of Darnford the manor of Deerhurst (Gloucs.), to be held of the current abbot and of his heirs, at an annual rent of £30, as the former abbot, Gervase, granted that manor in fee-farm. William and his heirs may hold the manor with all liberties, as Abbot Gervase granted in the charter which William holds. [1158]

Omnibus amicis et tenentibus Sancti Petri Westmonasterii, tam clericis quam laicis, Francis et Anglicis, totus eiusdem loci conventus, salutem. Noveritis nos concessisse et confirmasse Willelmo de Derneford manerium de Derhurst cum omnibus suis pertinentiis; tenendum et habendum de abbate nostro qui pro tempore fuerit sibi et heredibus suis libere et quiete, integre et pacifice, iure hereditario inperpetuum; reddendo inde annuatim abbati nostro qui pro tempore fuerit xxx^{ta} libras argenti ad duos terminos, scilicet: infra octabas Pasche xv libras, et infra octabas Sancti Michaelis xv libras, pro omnibus serviciis, consuetudinibus et exactionibus secularibus ad ipsum abbatem qui pro tempore fuerit pertinentibus, sicuti Gervasius quondam abbas noster illud manerium de Derhurst in feodo firma illis dedit et concessit. Unde concedimus et confirmamus quod predicti Willelmus et heredes sui habeant et teneant predictum manerium de Derhurst cum omnibus suis pertinentiis adeo libere, quiete et integre, sicuti predictus Abbas Gervasius melius et liberius illis dedit et concessit cum omnibus libertatibus et liberis consuetudinibus in carta sua quam predictus Willelmus de Derneford de ipso habet plene contentis et specificatis. Nos autem, predictus conventus Sancti Petri Westmonasterii, uno cum abbate nostro qui pro tempore fuerit predictum manerium de Derhurst, cum omnibus suis pertinentiis et cum omnibus libertatibus [et liberis consuet]udinibus, a predicto Abbate Gervasio predictis Willelmo et heredibus suis datis et concessis pro predicto redditu, [in perpetuum warant]izabimus. Et nos excommunicationis sententiam a predicto abbate nostro Gervasio in omnes illos illatam qui libertates [et liberas con]suetudines predicto manerio de Derhurst pertinentes auferrent de

Willelmo de Derneford vel de heredibus suis, firmiter concedimus et confirmamus. Hiis testibus: Helia priore Sancti Petri Westmonasterii; Osberto de Clare; Roberto Fol[et]; Rogero de Stant[on]; Willelmo de Mulas; Helia clerico; Gregorio senescallo, et pluribus aliis.

MSS: (1) WAM 32670.
    23.5 × 11.5 cm.
    Seal very damaged; fragments on tag.
    Endorsed: (a) Derhurst (12C). (b) Carta . . . Willelmo de Derhurst
    . . . Derhurst (badly stained) (14C).
    (2) WAD, ff. 316v–317.
Date: The vacancy following the deposition of Abbot Gervase.
Note: The related charter of H II confirms the manor in similar terms (**136**), as granted by the convent, and by the former Abbot Gervase (**271**). The existing text of the abbot's charter has been amplified in the thirteenth century (Harvey, 'Fee Farms', 131–3).

342. Final concord made between the Chapter of Westminster and Peter of Sutton and his wife Margaret, concerning land in Dowgate (London), of which she is co-heiress, formerly belonging to Sermann and now occupied by Robert of Marlborough, from which the monks used to receive 8s. annually. Mirabel, daughter of Oger the dapifer, will hold the land for life, without payment. After her d., or her entry into religion, or her vacating the land for any other reason, Peter and his wife will render 4s. annually in alms, payable to the monks' chamber, for that part of the land which they hold. The other 4s. rent will be rendered by John Tresgod and his wife Amy and their heirs, as their cirograph bears witness. Husting Court, London [1179–81]

Hec est finalis concordia inter monachos Westmonasterii et Petrum de Sutton' et Margaretam uxorem eius, facta apud London' in Hustingo, existentibus tunc vicecomitibus Willelmo filio Sabel et Reginaldo veteri, et aliis baronibus Lundon' presidentibus, de una terra in Duvegate, que fuit Sermanni, in qua mansit Rob[ertus] de Marlebergia, de qua solebant idem [*sic*] monachi antiquitus viij solidos percipere per annum, videlicet: quod Mirable, que fuit filia Ogeri dapiferi, tenebit eandem terram tota vita sua libere sine censu. Post decessum autem ipsius Mirable, aut si forte ad religionem se transtulit, vel quocumque modo terra illa de manu ipsius exierit, memoratus Petrus et uxor eius, et heredes eorum, vel quicumque eam tenuerint, reddent annuatim pro parte illius terre quam tenebunt iiij solidos inperpetuum camere prescriptorum monachorum in elemosinam, scilicet: ad Pascham ij solidos; ad Festum Sancti Michaelis ij solidos. Nec amplius poterunt monachi de parte Petri et uxoris sue sive heredum suorum exigere quam illos quatuor solidos per annum, sed Johannes Tresgod et uxor eius Amia et heredes eorum alios quatuor solidos monachis persolvent, sicut cirographum eorum testatur. Et illu actum est consilio et assensu Margarete uxoris [sue] supradicti Petri, que est heres ipsius terre. Hiis testibus: Gilleberto, constabulario Turris London'; Johanne Buchunte; Edwardo Blundo; Henrico filio Ailwini;

Radulpho Brand; Rogero filio Alani; Ricardo filio Reyneri; Andrea Bucherel; Willelmo filio Sabel'; Johanne de Coveham; Willelmo de Haverhell; Walerammo; Johanne Burguinun; Radulfo Britone; Petro, Johanne, clericis vicecomitis, et toto Hustingo.

MS: WAD, f. 486v.
> Rubric: Concordia facta in Hustingo London' inter monachos Westmonasterii et Petro de Suttun' et Margaretam uxorem eius de una terra in Duuegate. Reddendo iiij solidos.

Date: William Fitz Sabelina and Reginald le Viel as sheriffs: cf. Reynolds, 'Rulers of London', 355, where Reginald's colleague is listed as William Fitz Isabel. The Westminster charters distinguish clearly between these two men.

343. Final concord made between the Chapter of Westminster and John Tresgod and Amy his wife, concerning land in Dowgate (London), of which she is co-heiress, formerly belonging to Serman, and now occupied by Robert of Marlborough, from which the monks used to receive 8*s.* annually. Mirabel, daughter of Oger the dapifer, will hold the land for life, without payment. After her d., or her entry into religion, or her vacating the land for any other reason, John and his wife and their heirs will render 4*s.* annually in alms to the monks' chamber, for that part of the land which they hold. The other 4*s.* rent will be rendered by Peter of Sutton and his wife Margaret and their heirs, as their cirograph bears witness. Husting Court, London [1179–81]

Hec est finalis concordia inter monachos Westmonasterii et Johannem Tresgod et Amiam uxorem eius facta apud London' in Hustingo, existentibus tunc vicecomitibus Willelmo filio Isabell' et Reginaldo veteri, et aliis baronibus London' presidentibus, de una terra in Duvegate que fuit Sermani, in qua mansit Robertus de Marlebergia, de qua solebant idem monachi antiquitus viij solidos percipere per annum, videlicet: quod Mirable, que fuit filia Ogeri dapiferi, tenebit eandem terram tota vita sua libere sine censu. Post decessum autem ipsius Mirable, aut si forte ad religionem se transtulit, vel quocumque modo terra illa de manu ipsius exierit, memoratus Johannes et uxor eius et heredes eorum, vel quicumque eam tenuerit, reddent annuatim pro parte illius terre quam tenebint quatuor solidos inperpetuum camere prescriptorum monachorum in elemosinam, scilicet: ad Pascham duos solidos; ad Festum Sancti Michaelis duos solidos; nec amplius poterunt monachi de parte Johannis et uxoris sue, sive heredum suorum, exigere quam illos iiij^{or} solidos per annum. Sed Petrus de Suttuna et uxor eius Margareta et heredes eorum alios iiij^{or} solidos per annum monachis persolvent, sicut cirographum eorum testatur. Et istud actum est consilio et assensu Amie uxoris supradicti Johannis, que est heres ipsius terre. Hiis testibus: Gilleberto, constabulario Turris London'; Johanne Buchunte; Edwardo Blundo; Henrico filio Ailwini; Radulpho Brand; Rogero filo Alani; Ricardo filio Reinerii; Andrea Bucherel; Willelmo filio Sabel'; Johanne de Coveham; Willelmo de Haverhell'; Walerammo; Johanne Burguinun;

Radulpho Britone; Petro, Johanne, clericis vicecomitibus, et toto Hustingo.

MS: WAD, ff. 486v–487.
> Rubric: Concordia inter monachos Westmonasterii et Johannem Tresgod et Amiam uxorem eius de predicta terra in Duvegate. Reddendo iiij solidos annuatim.

Date: See **342**.

344. Record of a payment to the Exchequer by the prior [William Postard] and convent for the enrolment on the Pipe Roll of a memorandum that William of Eynsford III quitclaimed to them his vill of Benfleet (Essex), which he held of them for life, at a farm of £24, and that he restored the charter concerning this, in the Curia Regis in presence of the Barons of the Exchequer. 29 Sept. 1189.

Prior Ecclesie Beati[1] Petri de Westmonasterio et conventus eiusdem loci redd[iderun]t compotum de j marca ut scribatur in Magno Rotulo quod Willelmus de Einesford tertius clamavit eis villam suam de Benflet[2] cum pertinentiis suis quietam, quam debuit tenere de eis tantum in vita sua ad firmam pro xxiiij libris, et quod reddidit eis cartam suam quam habuerat de hac conventu[3] in Curia Regis coram Baronibus de Scaccario. In thesauro liberaverunt.[4] Et quieti sunt.[5]

MSS: (1) PRO, E372/35, membr.25 (dorse).
> (2) WAD f. 602v (insertion in margin of folio).
> Marginale: Bemflete.
> 1. MS: *sancti*.
> 2. MS: *Bemflete*.
> 3. MS: *conventione*.
> 4. MS: *In thesauro liberaverunt* omitted.
> 5. WAD concludes: *Q[uaer]e in Primo Rotulo regni regis Ricardi in tergo in Midd' in fine*.

Pd: *Pipe Roll 1 Ric. I*, 230.
Cal: *Formulare*, xxi.
Date: The Pipe Roll records the Michaelmas audit of the Exchequer.
Note: Although William Postard's dates as prior are uncertain, he was in office during Walter's abbacy (**302**) and also during the vacancy, which concluded in his own election (Ric. of Devizes, 54; Diceto, II, 100–01). On Benfleet see Harvey, *WA*, 340.

345. Notification by Prior Robert of Moulsham and the convent of the celebration, at the request of Abbot Ralph Arundel, of four feasts with copes and processions and with wine and pittances. The abbot in return has given the convent their manor of Benfleet (Essex), which he held at farm from them for some years. [1200 × 1214]

Omnibus Sancte Matris Ecclesie filiis ad quos presens scriptum pervenerit, R[obertus] dictus prior Westmonasterii, et eiusdem loci conventus, salutem eternam in Domino. Noverit universitas vestra nos bono animo et unanimi assensu et voluntate et divini amoris obtentu concessisse et carta nostra in pleno capitulo nostro confirmasse venerabili et dilecto patri et abbati nostro, Radulfo de Arundel, ad petitionem et voluntatem ipsius, incrementa quatuor festorum per anni revolutionem celebranda in cappis et processionibus cum vinis et pitanciis honorabiliter in eisdem festis inveniendis, videlicet: Festum Beati Laurentii, Festum Beati Vincentii, Festum Beati Nicholai, et Festum Translationis Beati Benedicti, que omnia prius cum cervisia et pitancia simpliciter statuta, cum vinis et pitanciis et processionibus statuimus honorabiliter celebranda. Statuimus etiam quicquid fiat de pitanceria nostra vel festivitatibus similibus ut, scilicet aliter disponantur et mittentur ne aliquid de predictis quatuor festivitatibus minuatur aut mittetur si possibilitas assit, ut modo prenominato possint celebrari. Huius autem auctoritate confirmationis et caritative assensu concessionis, concessit et reddidit et confirmavit nobis idem venerabilis pater noster et abbas ad petitionem et voluntatem nostram manerium nostrum de Bainflete[1] per aliquot annos ab eodem ad firmam possessum cum omnibus pertinentiis, emendationibus, instauris, possessionibus, consuetudinibus, et omnibus rebus quecumque fuerint ad idem manerium pertinentibus. Ut autem hec confirmatio et concessio nullatenus a posteris abbatibus, videlicet, seu prioribus, vel quicumque alii fuerint, possit infringi eam auctoritate Beati Petri et omnium sanctorum et nostra confirmamus, eiusque infractores in pleno capitulo nostro data sententia vinculo anathematis innodantes. Sigilli nostri appositione eam roboravimus.

MSS: (1) BL Add. Charter 8473.
     16.6 × 12.1 cm; t.u. 2.2 cm.
     Seal: on tag; brown; 6.5 cm diameter. Obverse: seated figure in habit, ? bearded; right hand raised in benediction. Reverse: ? coronation of the Virgin (seriously damaged). No surviving legend. *Cat. Seals BM*, I, no. 4303, p. 801.
     Endorsed: (a) De iiij festis in capis celebrandis ad instantiam Radulphi abbatis, videlicet Sanctorum Laurentii, Vincentii, Nicholai et Translationis Sancti Benedicti abbatis. (b) Dupplicatur xiiij. (c) Pitanciarius.
     (2) WAD, f. 602v.
     (3) F, f. 246v–247.
      1. *Bemflete.*
Pd: Flete, 99–100.

346. Confirmation made in form of a cirograph by Prior Robert of Moulsham, with the assent of the convent, to William English of Westminster and his heirs, of a messuage in the vill of Westminster, lying between the land of Geoffrey Smith and that of William parmenter, which messuage William English and his wife Isabel received in fee and inheritance from the aforesaid Geoffrey son of Jocelin Smith and his heirs, by service of 3s. annually, which rent Geoffrey and his heirs granted to provide lights for the Lady Altar. William English and his heirs were assigned to render this rent to Prior Robert, or to anyone else who might be warden of the altar, as Geoffrey's charter testifies. William and Isabel, in presence of the better and more lawworthy men of the vill of Westminster, constituted the Blessed Virgin and the warden of the altar their heirs. Prior Robert, as chief lord, on behalf of the Blessed Virgin, and in his capacity as warden, has confirmed the messuage to William and his heirs, at an annual rent of 4s. 6d. due to him (Prior Robert) or to anyone who is warden for the time being. [c. 1199 × 1207]

Sciant presentes et futuri quod ego Robertus de Mullesham, prior Westmonasterii, assensu et voluntate tocius conventus nostri, dimisi et concessi et hac presenti carta confirmavi Willelmo Anglico de Westmonasterio et heredibus suis unum masuagium cum pertinentiis in villa Westmonasterii; quod masuagium iacet inter terram Gaufridi fabri ex una parte, et terram Willelmi parmentarii ex altera, et quod masuagium predictus Willelmus Anglicus et Isabella uxor eius receperunt in feudo sibi et heredibus eorum de predicto Gaufrido filio Jocilini fabri et heredibus suis per servitium trium solidorum per annum pro omni servitio et per gersummam quattuordecim solidorum. Redditum quorum trium solidorum predictus Gaufridus et heredes sui dederunt et concesserunt ad administrationem luminaris altaris Beate Marie in ecclesia nostra pro xl solidis. De quibus tribus solidis predictus Willelmus et heredes sui assignati fuerunt reddere mihi, vel alii qui pro tempore esset custos predicti altaris, sicut carta ipsius Gaufridi testatur. Unde sciendum est quod predictus Willelmus ante decessum Isabelle uxoris, eius assensu et voluntate utriusque, de predicto masuagio cum pertinentiis Beatam Mariam et custodem altaris ipsius qui pro tempore fuerit, coram melioribus et legalioribus hominibus ipsius ville Westmonasterii, heredes fecerunt et constituerunt. Ego autem vice gloriose Virginis et nomine ipsius altaris custodis tamquam capitalis dominus concessi et dimisi et presenti scripto confirmavi predicto Willelmo et heredibus suis predictum masuagium cum pertinentiis vel cui assignare vel dare voluerit; reddendo inde singulis annis mihi vel alii qui pro tempore fuerit custos predicti altaris iiij^{or} solidos et vj denarios, unde prius reddidit nisi tres solidos tantummodo. Habendum et tenendum sibi et heredibus suis, vel assignatis, libere et quiete, integre et plenarie, per liberum servitium predictorum iiij^{or} solidorum et vj denariorum reddendorum ad iiij^{or} anni terminos, videlicet: ad Natale Domini tresdecim denarios et obolum; et ad Pascha tresdecim denarios et obolum; et ad Festum Sancti Johannis Baptiste tresdecim denarios et obolum; et ad Festum Sancti Michaelis tresdecim denarios et obolum. Ut autem hec omnia securam firmitatem futuris temporibus obtineant ego Robertus, vice gloriose Virginis et nomine altaris ipsius tunc temporis custodis, sigillum meum apposui parti carte cyrographate quam remanet ipsi Willelmo et heredibus vel assignatis suis, et ipse Willelmus sigillum suum apposuit parti carte cyrographate que remanet penes me vel alium tunc temporis ipsius altaris custodem. Hiis testibus: Domino Willelmo Eliensi, domini regis thesaurario; Domino Roberto Mauduit; Johanne de Sterteford; Willelmo de Castell; Alexandro clerico; Ludovico clerico; Odone aurifabro; Henrico Sumer; Ricardo filio Edmundi; Roberto de Claigate; Stephano de Berking; Roberto de Crokesl'; Laurentio Muschat, et toto alimoto Westmonasterii.

MSS: (1) WAM 17326.
> 20.3 × 17 cm; t.u. 2.3 cm. Indented CYROGRAPHUM at top.
> Seal: on tag; red; 4 × 3.5 cm. Obverse: fleur-de-lys; legend: + S. WILL LE ANGLEIS DE CHECCER.
> Endorsed: (a) Convencio inter capellam et Willelmum Anglicum de Westmonasterio de tribus solidis annui redditus solvendis eidem capelle ad luminaria sustentanda pro quodam mesuagio in villa Westmonasterii. (b) Westmonasterii capella lvj.
> (2) WAD, ff. 547v–548.

Pd: Richardson, 'William of Ely', 86–7, no. VI.

Date: William English, sergeant of the Exchequer, transported treasure in the early years of John's reign (*Rot. Litt. Claus.* I, 12, 13, 16). He was active on Exchequer business in the latter part of H II's reign and was prob. a brother of Richard of Ely, royal treasurer and subsequently bp. of London, and a kinsman of his successor as treasurer, William of Ely; he is last mentioned in 1207 (Richardson, 'William of Ely', 47 and n. 2; 86–87n.).

Note: Geoffrey son of Jocelin's charter is **433**. Walter, a later proctor of the Lady Altar, granted this messuage to Robert son of Maurice and his heirs, *c.* 1225 × 1235 (WAM 23638(d)).

347. Confirmation by Prior Robert of Moulsham, in his capacity as warden of the Lady Altar, and with the assent of the convent, to Mr Geoffrey Pic[ot] and his heirs, of a messuage in Westminster [formerly held by] Gilbert [   ] and his wife Alice, which messuage lies between the house of Roger Enganet and that of Agnes of Claygate. Gilbert [   ] gave this messuage to the Lady Altar when he set out for Jerusalem, [the grant to take effect] after the d. of his wife, since it was their purchased and acquired land. Mr Geoffrey [Picot] would hold this land, rendering 8*d.* annually to the Lady Altar, and the service of 3*s.* 4*d.* due to [the chief lord] of that fee. [? Temp. John]

Sciant tam presentes quam futuri quod ego Robertus de Molesham, prior Westmonasterii, tunc custos altaris Beate [Marie] [concessi et dedi] et hac presenti carta mea confirmavi, consilio et assensu tocius conventus eiusdem loci, Magistro Gaufrido [   ] et heredibus suis, et illi cuicumque dare vel vendere, vel assignare voluerit mesuagium illud in Westm[onasterio   ] [   ] Aliz uxoris eius; quod mesuagium iacet inter domum Rogeri Henganet, et domum Agnetis de Cleigat', ex[   ]; et quod mesuagium predictus Gilebertus, quando iter arripuit Ierosolimam, dedit altari Beate Marie predicti loci [   ] uxoris sue, scilicet post decessum eiusdem uxoris sue sicut eorum empcionem, et adquisicionem. Prefatus vero Magister [Galfridus   ], vel alii qui custos efficietur predicti altaris ad opus luminaris Beate Marie predicti loci octo denarios: ad [Festum Sancti] Michaelis duos denarios; et ad Nathale Domini duos denarios; et ad Pascham duos denarios; et ad [Festum Sancti Johannis

Baptiste] duos denarios. Hoc vero mesuagium tenebit predictus Magister
Gaufridus Pic[ot], vel heredes sui, vel ille cuilibet m[   ] de
predicto altari, libere et pacifice et quiete, ab omni exactione et consuetudine per predictum serv[icium   ] eiusdem feodi, scilicet:
quadraginta denarios[1] qui reddendi de predicto mesuagio annuatim per
quatuor [terminos] loci. Ego vero Robertus de Molesham, prior predicti
loci, tunc custos, altaris Beate Marie, vel ille qui custos eiusdem [altaris]
predicto Magistro Gaufrido Pic[ot] et heredibus suis, vel illi cuicumque
hoc mesuagium dederit, vel vendiderit, vel [   ] servicio contra
omnes homines et feminas inperpetuum. Et ut hec donacio et concessio et
presentis carte [   ] permaneat, eam istius sigilli mei munimine
roboravi. Hiis testibus: Roberto capellano; Willelmo [   ]
clerico; Willelmo filio Andree; Ricardo Testard; Odone aurifabro, tunc
preposito;   Henrico   Sumer;   R[a   ][1]   Willelmo   pistore,
e[   ].

MS: WAM 23638(e).
    15.5 × 10.7 cm (as muniment survives). The text has been cut away
    at the right-hand side and also covered at the lower edge to form a
    membrane of a compotus roll on the reverse.
    Annotated: Quaere registratur.
    1. MS: *denarii*.
Date: Gilbert's grant to the Lady Altar was prob. made *c.* 1189, when
the contingent from England was preparing to embark on the Third
Crusade. The attestations to Prior Robert's grant suggest a date about the
middle of King John's reign.
Note: Despite the cavalier treatment of this charter, it had not been
entered into any cartulary.

348. Grant by Prior Robert of Moulsham to Adam sergeant of the
church of Westminster of that land in Westminster which the prior bought
from Peter Fauset. The land is in the fee of Hamund de Hotot next to the
holding John Pimerich once had in the same fee. Adam is to hold it freely
in perpetuity of the proctors of the Lady Altar for 2*s.* a year, saving only
the forinsec service of the abbot. [Temp. John]

Sciant presentes et futuri quod ego Robertus de Mulesham, prior Westmonasterii, voluntate et assensu conventus eiusdem loci, concessi et
dimisi et hac presenti carta confirmavi Ade servienti de ecclesia Westmonasterii, totam terram illam cum pertinentiis in villa Westmonasterii
quam emi de Petro Fauset, que fuit de feodo Hamundi de Hotot: que
videlicet terra jacet iuxta terram quam Johannes Pimerich aliquando
tenuit que fuit de eodem feodo. Habendam et tenendam ipsi Ade et
heredibus suis de nobis et successoribus nostris altaris Beate Virginis
Marie in eadem ecclesia procuratoribus libere et quiete, integre,
inperpetuum: reddendo inde singulis annis de predicta terra duos solidos
procuratori prefati altaris qui pro tempore fuerit ad quatuor principales
anni terminos pro omni servitio, salvo tamen forinseco servitio abbatis.
Hanc autem terram predicto Ade et heredibus suis warantizabimus
contra omnes homines et feminas per predictum servitium. Ut autem hec

concessio et carte presentis confirmatio rata sit et stabilis eam sigilli mei
appositione corroboravi. Hiis testibus: Odone aurifabro; Ricardo
Testard; Gaufrido de Cruce; Wimund pistore; Johanne filio Alani;
Gaufrido de Ecclesia; Gervasio portitore; Ivone de Medmeham; Wil-
lelmo filio Herberti; Nicholao de cellario; Helia parmentario; Gervasio
Tatin; Laurentio Muschat, et multis aliis.

MSS: (1) WAM 17329.
    14.3 × 12.3 cm; t.u. 2 cm.
    Seal: green; on tag; 4.8 × 3.3 cm; obverse: standing angel:
    SIG[   ]ERT DE MVLESHAM
    Endorsed: (a) Robertus de Molesham prior Westmonasterii dimittit
    Ade servienti de ecclesia Westmonasterii quandam partem terre in
    Westmonasterio predicto . . . (13C). (b) reddendo inde annuatim
    custodi capelle Beate Marie ecclesie Westmonasterii ij solidos per
    annum (14C). (c) Westmonasterii capelle redditus lv (14C).
    (2) WAD, f. 547r–v.
Note: Peter Fauset's grant is **430**. This and related documents refer only
to a Lady Altar. A special fund was apparently set up under Abbot Ralph
to raise money for the building of a new Lady Chapel: building was
actually begun during the abbacy of his successor, William d'Humez
(*History of the King's Works*, ed. H. M. Colvin, 6 vols. (1963–1973), I,
131). At least forty documents in the abbey muniments concern properties in Westminster assigned to the fund, and endorsed 'Westm' capell''.

349. The form of the oath to be taken by those fleeing to sanctuary at
Westminster. [Early 13C]

Forma juramenti confugientium ad sanctuarium Westmonasterii.
In primis: jurabit quilibet ad dicendum veram causam adventus sui et
condiciones eiusdem et adversus quales personas.
Item: jurabit quod fideliter et honeste se habebit dum infra sanctuarium
manserit, jura quoque et privilegia ac consuetudines eiusdem loci
sustinebit, pro posse suorum defendet.
Item: jurabit quod omnem correctionem et jurisdictionem presidentis
ibidem, necnon judicia et precepta licita, justicia et equitate suadentibus
obedienter subibit et tollerabit, et contra eam non veniet quovismodo
directe vel indirecte, salvis provocationibus et appellationibus ad sedem
apostolicam licite directis.
Item: jurabit quod pacta et contractus que et quos infra dictum sanctuarium fecerit fideliter observabit.
Item: jurabit, si propter debitum ad prefatum sanctuarium confugerit,
quamcito comode poterit satisfaciet creditoribus suis ac adversus eosdem
in colloquiis et tractatibus honeste et modeste ac sine garula et probosis
verbis se habebit.
Item: jurabit quod panem unum, serviciam ac alia victualia in dicto
sanctuario non vendet communiter, sine licencia speciali domini archidiaconi[1] Westmonasterii vel ipsius locumtenentis petita et optenta.
Item: jurabit quod non recipiet aliquem fug[i]tivum[a] seu aliquos fugitivos

aut alios suspectos in domum suam vel mensam ad hospitandam sine licencia supradicta.[b]

Item: jurabit quod arma defensiva non portabit infra sanctuarium sine predicta licencia sed ipso[c] ad immun[i]tatem recepto, illa si que habet, dicto archidiacono[2] vel eius locumtenenti sine contradictione liberabit cum fuerit requisitus.

Item: jurabit quod non exibit sanctuarium die vel nocte postquam receptus sine licencia predicta, nisi fecerit finem cum adversariis suis.

Item: jurabit quod false, subdole, aut maliciose aliquem fugitivum non diffamabit, nec quovismodo defraudabit.

Item: jurabit quod violenciam voluntariam in dicto sanctuario non faciet nec alicui illicite fieri videbit qui illud pro posse suo impediet. Hoc omnia fideliter observari promittet, sicut Deus se adiuvet et Sancta Dei Ewangelia etc.

MSS: (1) LN, f. cxxxix *verso*.
    1. MS: *archani* (also in CAY).
    2. MS: *archno'* (*archano*, CAY).
    (2) CAY, f. cxlviii *verso*.
    (a) *fugitivum aliquem*.
    (b) *antedicta*.
    (c) *sed ipso sed ipse*
(3) WAD f. 37; memorandum inserted in lower margin: forma juramenti confugiencium ad sanctuarium Westmonasterii querentium in novo Registro Nigri paperio et . . . [faded] articulo (late 14C hand).

Date: The earliest documented (monastic) archdeacon is Richard de Crokesley, but all that is known of his term of office is its termination on his election to the abbacy in Dec. 1246 (Pearce, *Monks of Westminster*, 4, 212). It is not known when the office originated. The style and content of the oath suggest a date early in the thirteenth century, while the clause referring to appeals to the papal curia probably post-dates the Concordat of Avranches (23 May, 1172).

Note: On the sanctuary precincts, see Honeybourne, 'Sanctuary Boundaries'. From the customary compiled under the direction of Abbot Richard de Ware (1259–83), it is clear that the daily allocation of bread in a monastic corrody was generous (*Customary of the Benedictine Monasteries of Saint Augustine, Canterbury, and Saint Peter, Westminster*, ed. E. M. Thompson, Henry Bradshaw Society, XXIII and XXVIII (1902–4), II, 103; on the corrody see also 102, 180, 244), hence the temptation of the fugitive to sell his surplus to pilgrims who remained in the church overnight. The duty of maintaining good order in the church itself fell upon the sacrist, who was particularly enjoined to maintain adequate lighting (ibid., 42 ff. and especially 47–8, 61, 268).

DONORS' CHARTERS

350. Grant by Geoffrey de Mandeville, earl of Essex, to the bishop and barons of London, and all clerks and laymen, French and English, that he has confirmed to St Peter and the convent of Westminster, for the souls of his parents and ancestors, and for his own body and soul and those of his wife and heirs, £1's worth of land in London towards the anniversary of his mother for the use of the monks in refectory—namely the land held by Fulco Bruningi paying one mark (13s. 4d.); the land of Ernulf orphan paying 5s.; the land of Wuluric Trace paying 10d., and the land of Wuluric his neighbour paying 10d. [1140 × 1144 (? summer 1141)]

Gaufridus comes Essexie episcopo et omnibus baronibus London', clericis et laycis, Francis et Anglis, salutem. Sciatis me firmiter concessisse et in perpetuum dedisse Deo et Sancto Petro et conventui Westmonasterii, pro anima patris et matris mee et antecessorum meorum, et pro salute corporis et anime mee et uxoris mee et heredum meorum, xx solidatas terre de redditibus meis London' ad anniversarium matris mee ad opus monachorum in refectorio, solutas et quietas de me et de heredibus meis sine aliquo retinemento et liberas ab omnibus servitiis michi et heredibus meis pertinentibus, scilicet: terram quam Fulco Bruningi tenet que reddit j marcam argenti; et terram Ernulfi Orbi que reddit v solidos; et terram Wulurici Trace que reddit x denarios; et terram Wulurici, vicini sui, que reddit x denarios. Quare volo et firmiter precipio quod ipsi eas teneant ita libere et quiete et honorifice, cum omnibus consuetudinibus et libertatibus cum quibus eas unquam liberius et quietius et honorificentius tenui vel aliquis antecessorum meorum una die et una nocte. Et prohibeo ne super hoc aliquis [ei]s[1] inde iniuriam vel contumeliam faciat. Hiis testibus: Gilberto comite; Roheisa comitissa; Gregorio dapifero; Ernulfo de Magna Villa; Pagano de Templo Salamonis; Warino filio Geroldi; Willelmo, priore de Waledene; Fulcone de Nodar'; Gaufrido de Querendon; Hamelino, et pluribus aliis.

MSS: (1) WAD, f. 492v–493.
Rubric: Carta Galfridi comitis Essex' de xx solidis redditus in London' ad anniversarium matris mee faciendum.
Marginalia: Anniversarium matris Gaufridi comitis
Essex'.
1. Hole in MS.
(2) F, f. 282.
Date: Geoffrey II was created earl of Essex Dec. 1139 × Dec. 1140. The address to the bishop and barons of London suggests a date post mid 1141 when the Empress granted Geoffrey control of the Tower. Saffron Walden was granted to him about the same time (*Regesta* III, nos. 273–6; Hollister, 'The Misfortunes of the Mandevilles', 27). On the attestation

of William prior of Walden, see *Heads*, 75; Knowles and Hadcock, 79. It may suggest a date *c.* 1141, even though Earl Geoffrey and his wife Countess Rose took preliminary steps towards the foundation of Walden Priory *c.* 1136 (*Heads*, 75). While the bp. of London is not named, Robert de Sigillo was nominated July 1141 (*Fasti* I, 2).

Note: Geoffrey's parents were William de Mandeville I and Margaret de Ria (Hollister, 'Mandevilles', 26).

351. Confirmation, in pure and perpetual alms, by Henry Fitz Ailwin of London to St Peter of Westminster and the monks, for the soul of H II, for his own soul, those of his ancestors and successors, and of all the faithful departed, of 5s. quit-rent which Laurence the plumber held of him, between the land which Henry Toltric held towards the east, and the land which William Bukelar held towards the west. The monks will intercede annually for the souls of all those named, on the anniversary of his obit. [*ante* 1212 (? 1189 × 1191)]

Sciant presentes et futuri quod ego Henricus filius Ailwini de London' dedi et concessi et presenti carta mea confirmavi Deo et ecclesie Sancti Petri de Westmonasterio et monachis ibidem Deo servientibus, pro salute anime Regis Henrici et anime mee et antecessorum et successorum meorum et omnium fidelium defunctorum, in puram et perpetuam elemosinam quinque solidatas quieti redditus de terra quam Laurentius plumbarius tenuit de me inter terram quam Henricus Toltric tenuit versus orientem, et terram quam Willelmus Bukelarus tenuit versus occidentem. Habendas et tenendas predicte ecclesie Sancti Petri et monachis ibidem Deo servientibus inperpetuum, libere, quiete, integre et finabiliter, et ad faciendum servitium pro anima predicti Regis Henrici et pro anima mea et animabus omnium fidelium defunctorum in die anniversarii obitus mei annuatim quando evenerit. Ut autem hec mea donatio et concessio perpetua firmitate consistat, presentem paginam sigilli mei munimine roboravi.

MS: WAD, f. 485v–486.
Rubric: Carta Henrici filii Ailwini de London' de v solidis redditus pro anniversario suo faciendo.
Marginalia: Anniversarium Henrici filii Ailwini.
Date: Since Henry Fitz Ailwin (d. 1212) appears without his title of mayor, his grant is prob. earlier than Oct. 1191. Mention of H II suggests that this king was already d.

352. Grant by Andrew Bucherel to St Peter of Westminster and the monks on the occasion of his pilgrimage to Jerusalem, of a rent of 8s. from land in London of their fee, which he bought, and held of them at a rent of 2s. Moreover, he bequeathed them fifteen marks (£10) to buy 15s. worth of rent. In return, the monks would celebrate the anniversary of his death and those of his ancestors. Nothing would be retracted if he returned. [Late 12C × *ante* 29 Sept. 1192]

Omnibus Christi fidelibus ad quorum noticiam littere iste pervenerint,

Andreas Bucherel salutem in Domino. Quam ea secura et Deo accepta est peregrinatio quam religiose viventium vota prosequ[u]ntur et commendant orationes, iccirco noveritis me cum ad visitandum sepulcrum Domini Jerusalem essem profecturus, dedisse, et hac presenti carta mea confirmasse Deo et Beato Petro Westmonasterii, et monachis ibidem Deo servientibus, octo solidatas redditus in London' in una terra de feudo suo, quam emi, et de eis pro duobus solidis annuatim tenui si me in hoc itinere decedere contigerit. Dedi etiam et legavi, et in testamentaria rerum mearum dispositione assignavi, quindecim marcas ad quindecim solidatas reddituum emendas, ut ex hiis viginti et tribus solidis anniversaria singulis annis et perpetuo, tam mei quam meorum antecessorum, sollempniter die obitus mei fiat memoria, et exinde honesta conventui procuretur refectio. Et hoc sciendum quod concessio ista sub tali firmitate concepta est, ut licet ego rediero, nulla posteriore voluntate retractetur, quin semper eo modo eo tenore quo in hac carta descripta est post mortem meam firma et illibata perseveret. Hiis testibus: Roberto filio Brictrici; Andrea fratre eiusdem; Andrea; Gaufrido Picot; Magistro Samsone; Ricardo clerico; et Phillippo nepote abbatis; Ricardo de Berking; et Willelmo hostiario, Henrico filio Levestoni, Ricardo filio Reineri, Henrico Albo, civibus London'; Philippo presbitero, et multis aliis; Rogero filio Alani, et Rogero Ganet.

MS: WAD, f. 493r–v.

    Rubric: Carta Andree Bucherel de octo solidatas (*sic*) redditus et de xv marcis datis ad xv solidatas redditus emendas ad anniversarium suum faciendum.

    Marginalia: (on f. 493) Anniversarium Andree Bucherel (14C).

Date: Andrew Bucherel I was sheriff 1172–1174, and probably alderman (Beaven, *Aldermen*, I, 365). Richard Fitz Reiner d. before 29 Sept. 1192 (*Cart. Clerkenwell*, no. 284, pp. 186–187; *PR 4 Ric. I*, 279).

Note: It might be suspected that this grant represents a disguised sale, intended to finance the donor's travels, but there are contemporary charters in numerous collections which reflect the genuine fears of intending crusaders about the perils of their journey, and the consequent need to make adequate spiritual provision.

353. Grant in pure and perpetual alms by William de Camera and Eluva Lombard his wife to St Peter and the convent of Westminster, for their souls, and those of their ancestors and successors, of the land which they bought from Hawise daughter of Rumin, lying between the wharf of Godard le Tanner and the land of Ralf the shipwright, with buildings and a wharf and other appurtenances. [*c.* 1191 × *ante* 21 April 1196]

Willelmus de Camera and Eluva Lumbard' uxor eius omnibus Christi fidelibus ad quorum notitiam presens scriptum pervenerit, salutem. Noverit universitas vestra nos, pro salute animarum nostrarum et omnium antecessorum et successorum nostrorum, dedisse et concessisse et presenti carta confirmasse Deo et Beato Petro apostolorum principi et conventui Westmonasterii terram nostram quam emimus de Hawisa filia Rumin, videlicet: illam que iacet inter sharvam Godardi le Tannur et

terram Radulfi qui facit naves, cum edificiis et cum sharva et cum
omnibus ad eandem terram pertinentibus, in puram et perpetuam
elemosinam, liberam et absolutam, ab omni exactione seculari. Nos et
heredes nostri prefatam terram warantizabimus et adquietabimus prefato
conventui versus omnes homines inperpetuum. Hiis testibus: Henrico,
maiore London'; Rogero Duc[et]; Rogero filio Alani; Willelmo de
Haverhell; Magistro Ern[ulfo]; Theob[aldo] senescallo; Jord[ano]
Esperlenos; Magistro Simone de Bareswic; Henrico Sumer; Jacobo
hostiario; Ricardo janitore; Eustachio pincerna; Roberto marescallo;
Gerardo coco; Willelmo Albo, presbitero, et pluribus aliis.

MS: WAD, f. 486.
> Rubric: Carta Willelmi de Camera et Eluve uxoris sue de terra quam
> emerunt de Hawisa filia Rumin apud sharvam Godardi.

Date: Theobald of Feering as seneschal (of Abbot William Postard).
William and the convent subsequently demised this land to Alfwin the
dyer, *c.* 21 April 1196 (**307**); cf. **308**.

354. Grant by William de Newham, master of the Templars in England,
with the assent of their whole chapter, to Ralph goldsmith and his heirs,
of their land below Baynard's Castle (bounds given), which Walter son of
Robert and his heirs gave to their house in alms, and confirmed by their
charters. Ralph will render 1*s.* annually. [1185 × 1200]

Omnibus Sancte Matris Ecclesie filiis presentibus et futuris ego Willelmus
de Neuham, Militie Templi in Anglia minister humilis, salutem. Noveritis
nos, communi consilio et assensu totius capituli nostri, concessisse et hac
carta nostra confirmasse Radulfo aurifabro et heredibus suis terram
nostram sub Castello Bainardi, habentem in longitudine quinquies xx^{ti}
pedes, in latitudine xlij pedes: illam videlicet quam Gauterus filius
Roberti et heredes sui domui nostre in elemosinam dederunt et cartis suis
confirmaverunt. Habendam et tenendam libere et quiete; reddendo inde
annuatim domui nostre xij denarios pro omnibus servitiis et exactionibus.
His testibus: Fratre Thoma de Tanton'; Fratre Willelmo, preceptore
London'; Fratre Roberto de Fliethe; Fratre Henrico; Fratre Gar[ino];
Gaufrido Halderman; Henrico parmentario; Goldhauet pessunerio; Willelmo Franco; Stephano aurifabro; Haimaro pessunerio.

MSS: (1) WAM 13436.
> 13.8 × 11.8 cm.; t.u. 1.8 cm.
> Seal: on tag; green; 3 × 2.5 cm; Agnus Dei, facing right; legend:
> + SIGILLVM TEMPLI.
> Endorsed: (a) Carta Fratris Willelmi de Neuham Militie Templi in
> Anglia de quadam terra sub Castello Baynardi London' (13C). (b)
> Infirmaria, et registratur in officio camerarii (14C).
> (2) WAD, f. 480v.

Pd: *Records of the Templars in England in the Twelfth Century*, ed. B. A.
Lees, Records of the Social and Economic History of England and Wales
(1935), 170–1, no. 15, from WAM.
Date: William de Newham was master of the Order in England within

the period 1185 × 1200 (M. Reddan, 'Houses of Military Orders', *V.C.H. London* I (1909), 490a). He had been replaced by 1200 (Lees, *Records of the Templars*, xvii–xviii).

355. Notification by William son of Brichtmar of Haverhill, that, for the souls of his parents, his own, his wife and children, and all kinsfolk, both ancestors and successors, he has granted to St Peter of Westminster and the monks, in free and perpetual alms, 14*s.* rent from certain land in West Cheap, between the shop of Walter Travers and that shop of Nigel goldsmith which he holds of the [lepers] of St Giles, which land Nigel and his heirs hold in fee of William and his heirs. The monks will receive this rent annually, by the hand of Nigel or his heirs, or any other tenant. At William's petition, the monks assigned this rent to the sacristy, to buy wine, and for oblations at masses. The monks granted to William and his wife that their anniversary would be celebrated like those of their bretheren. William's son James witnessed and assented to this grant. [*c.* 1190/91 × 1212]

Sciant presentes et futuri quod ego Willelmus de Haverhulle, filius Brihmari de Haverhull', dedi et concessi, pro anima patris mei et matris mee, et mea, et uxoris mee, et liberorum meorum, et consanguineorum meorum, tam antecessorum quam successorum, Deo et Beato Petro Westmonasterii, et monachis ibidem Deo servientibus, in liberam et perpetuam elemosinam, quatuordecim solidatas redditus de quadam terra mea, que jacet in Westchep, inter sopam Walteri Travers et sopam Nigelli aurifabri, quam idem Nigellus tenet de infirmis Sancti Egidii; quam videlicet terram prefatus Nigellus aurifaber et heredes eius tenent in feodo de me et de heredibus meis. Percipient autem prefati monachi Westmonasterii has predictas quatuordecim solidatas redditus per manum eiusdem Nigelli vel heredum suorum, vel per manum alterius qui tenuerit predictam terram, quicumque ille fuerit, singulis annis ad quatuor terminos, videlicet: infra quindecim dies Natalis Domini tres solidos et sex denarios; infra octavas Pasche tres solidos et sex denarios; infra octavas Sancti Johannis Baptiste tres solidos et sex denarios; infra octavas Sancti Michaelis tres solidos et sex denarios. Et hanc meam elemosinam totam prenominati monachi Westmonasterii per meam petitionem assignaverunt ad sacristariam suam, videlicet ad emendum vinum et oblata ad missas. Idem vero monachi, caritatis intuitu, michi et uxori mee concesserunt quod anniversarium nostrum sicut pro uno fratrum suorum facient singulis annis celebrari. Hanc autem donationem meam feci Thoma filio meo et herede presente, et hoc idem concedente, que videlicet donatio mea ut futuris temporibus stabilis et firma permaneat, eam presenti scripto et sigillo meo confirmavi. Hiis testibus: Henrico maiore London'; Johanne filio Herlicunni; Nigello aurifabro; Hugone canonico; Adam, clerico Henrici maioris; Thoma Gandeshider; Helia, presbitero de Hunilane; Henrico Bonehaie; Nicholao Duchet; Roberto le Blund; Johanne Buchement, et aliis.

MS: WAD, f. 368r–v.

Rubric: Carta Willelmi de Haverhulle, filii Brihtmari de Haverhull',
de quatuordecim solidatis redditus de terra que jacet in Westchep.
Marginalia: (1) que iacens. (2) Anniversarium Willelmi Harvill et
uxoris sue.
Date: During the mayoralty of Henry Fitz Ailwin.
Note: See Harvey, *WA*, 373n., 386, 388 no. 6.

356. Confirmation, in pure alms, by Mr Simon, son of Walter Black of
London, to the Blessed Virgin, St Peter and the monks of Westminster,
for his soul and those of his parents and kindred, of 2s. quit-rent in the
Fishmarket of London, near St Paul's. The rent is due from a shop which
Stephen de Syen holds, between the shop formerly belonging to Turold
the Fishmonger and that of Hugh Palmer, measuring 8½ feet in each
direction and rendering 2s. to the king, and 3s. to the nuns of Ankerwyke.
The quit-rent is due to the warden of the Lady Altar, to provide lights.
[Temp. John]

Notum sit omnibus presentibus et futuris quod ego Magister Simon, filius
Walteri Nigri, London', concessi et dedi et hac carta mea confirmavi Deo
et Beate Marie et beato Petro Westmonasterii et monachis ibidem Deo
servientibus, pro anima mea, patris et matris mee et parentum meorum,
duas solidatas redditus quieti in piscenaria London' que est prope
ecclesiam Sancti Pauli, videlicet: de scopa illa quam tenet Stephanus de
Syen, que est inter scopam que fuit Turoldi piscenarii et scopam Hugonis
palmerum; que quidem scopa continet octo pedes et dimidium in
latitudine, et totidem in longitudine; et inde solvuntur domino regi duo
solidi, et monialibus de Ankerwik' tres solidi; in puram et perpetuam
elemosinam solvendas custodi altaris Beate Marie in eadem ecclesia ad
luminaria invenienda qui pro tempore fuerit, ad Festum Beati Michaelis,
et non in alios usus. Et ut hec mea donatio et concessio rata sit et stabile
permaneat, eam sigilli mei appositione corroboravi. Hiis testibus:
Ricardo de Dol, tunc senescallo Westmonasterii; Alano de Baalun;
Willelmo de Westmonasterio; Hugone le Taillur; Odone de Westmonasterio; Adam de Westmonasterio; Gaufrido de Cruce; Ricardo filio
Edmundi; Stephano de Berking'; Nicholao de celario; Adam de ecclesia;
Willelmo Sticael; Laurentio Muschat, et multis aliis.

MSS: (1) WAM 13879.
    23.3 × 10 cm; t.u. 3.1 cm.
    Seal: on tag; black; 3.3 cm diameter; classical figure framed in oval,
    facing right, ? Heracles, with cusps in which are: (a) crescent moon;
    (b) fleur de lys; (c) sun; (d) star; legend: SECRET . . ILAT ORSVS
    SIMONIS . . . [? NIGRI].
    Endorsements: (a) Willelmus Kelsuhul alias dictus W. Conc' (13C).
    (b) Magister Simon de London' dat capelle duos solidos redditus de
    quadam schopa in veteri piscenaria (13C). (c) Piscaria London'
    capella, ix (14C).
    (2) WAD, f. 561v.

357. Confirmation by Gilbert Rufus to his son Geoffrey Rufus of a shop in the New Fishmarket, which he bought from Bauderic the clerk who became a canon at St Mary's church beyond London Bridge (i.e. priory of St Mary Overy, Southwark), to hold by hereditary right at an annual rent of 2*s*. due to the king. [?12C]

Sciant presentes et futuri quod ego Gilebertus Rufus dedi et concessi et hac carta mea confirmavi Gaufrido Rufo filio meo unam soppam in Nova Peschuneria, sicut rectam emptionem meam, et adquisitionem meam, scilicet illam soppam quam ego emi de Bauderico clerico qui devenit canonicus ad ecclesiam Sancte Marie ultra Pontem Lundon'. Habendam et tenendam illi et heredibus suis, libere et quiete, jure hereditario; reddendo inde singulis annis domino regi duos solidos pro omni servitio et consuetudine et exactione. Pro hac vero donatione et concessione predictus Gaufridus dedit michi xl solidos sterlingorum. His testibus: Johanne, capellano de Sancto Nicholao; Ricardo, capellano de Sancta Maria Magdalena; Gernua, subvicecomite Lundon'; Godsalmo pessunier; Johanne Blundo; David Blundo; Symone le pessunier; Roberto de Marisco; Henrico Blundo; Nicholao tinctore; Ricardo Crasso, et multis aliis.

MSS: (1) WAM 13878.
    17.3 × 8.5 cm; t.u. 2 cm.
    Seal: On tag; black; 4 cm diameter; fish; legend: SIG[ILLUM] GILLEBERT[I] . . . (worn).
    Endorsed: (a) Gilbertus Ruffus dat Gauffrido Rufo quandam schopam in Nova Piscenaria London' (13C). (b) Piscaria London' capella viij (14C).
    (2) WAD, f. 561v.

358. Confirmation by Laurence of Stanstead, surnamed 'the Devil', son of William, surnamed 'the Devil', to his nephew, Joseph son of Peter, of all his land in London, which is situated within the gate of Ludgate, next to St Martin's chapel, together with that chapel, which is founded on his fee, to hold of him and his heirs at an annual rent of 4*s*. [mid 12C]

Sciant presentes et futuri quod ego Laurentius de Stanstede cognomine Diabolus, filius Willelmi cognomento Diaboli, dedi et concessi et hac mea carta confirmavi Joseph filio Petri, nepoti meo, totam terram meam quam teneo in London', que scilicet terra est infra portam de Hludgate juxta capellam Sancti Martini, cum eadem capella, que est super feudo meo fundata apud australem partem; tenendam et habendam de me et heredibus meis sibi, quamdiu vixerit, libere, quiete et honorifice. Reddendo annuatim pro omnibus serviciis mihi et heredibus meis iiij solidos ad iiij terminos, scilicet: ad Pascham xij denarios; et ad Festum Sancti Johannis Baptiste xij denarios; et ad Festum Sancti Michaelis xij denarios; et ad Natale Domini duodecim denarios. Ego autem Laurencius et heredes mei warantizabimus predicto Joseph predictam terram et capellam contra omnes homines. Hii sunt testes: Petrus sacerdos; Robertus capellanus; Ricardus diaconus; Willelmus clericus; Augustinus calic[erius]; Willelmus calic[erius]; Stephanus calic[erius];

Ricardus calic[erius]; Robertus faber; Stephanus aurifaber; Walterus aurifaber; Marcus carpentarius; Johannes Morin; Adam sermonicinarius; Willelmus plumbarius; Rogerus carpentarius; David parmentarius, et multi alii.

MS: WAD, f. 474v.
Rubric: Carta predicti Laurentii de tota terra sua in London juxta capellam Sancti Martini infra portam de Ludegate.

359. Concession and resignation by Laurence, surnamed 'the Devil', son of William, of his claim to the patronage of St Martin's Church, Ludgate, to St Peter and the monks of Westminster, for his soul and those of his ancestors, and for confraternity, both in life and in death. [Temp. Henry II, *ante* 1187]

Sciant presentes et futuri quod ego Laurentius, cognomento Diabolus, filius Willelmi, concessi et resignavi totum jus quod clamabam in patronatu ecclesie Sancti Martini de Ludegate, cum pertinentiis suis, Deo et Beato Petro et monachis de Westmonasterio, liberum et solutum de me et heredibus meis inperpetuum, pro salute anime mee et antecessorum et successorum meorum, et pro fraternitate domus, tam in vita quam in morte habenda, et ne hec concessio revocetur in irritum, sigilli mei appositione illam corroboravi. Hiis testibus: Johanne, filio meo et herede, presente et hoc annuente; Roberto, capellano Sancti Martini de Ludgate; Johanne Lovegold, Johanne de Sterteford, Osberto de Sancto Audoeno, Willelmo de Sancto Martino de Ludgate, capellanis; Magistro Ricardo de Lirling', Magistro Simone, clericis; Stephano aurifabro; Augustino calicerio; Jacobo parmentario; Adam sermocinario, et multis aliis.

MS: WAD, f. 474.
Rubric: Carta Laurencii filii Willelmi de resignatione et concessione juris sui in prenominatu ecclesie Sancti Martini de Ludegate.
Date: Before 211.

360. Confirmation by Laurence, surnamed 'the Devil', son of William, surnamed 'the Devil', with the assent of John, his son and heir, to St Peter of Westminster and the convent, of the lordship of his whole fee in Ludgate, so that he and his heirs will hold the land of the church and convent, rendering annually 1lb. of pepper on the Feast of the Translation of St Edward. [*c.* 1191 × 1200]

Sciant tam presentes quam futuri quod ego Laurencius cognomento Diabolus, filius Willelmi cognomento Diaboli, dedi et concessi et hac presenti carta mea confirmavi Deo et Beato Petro Westmonasterii et eiusdem loci conventui dominium totius feudi mei in Ludgate cum omnibus pertinentiis suis, ita quod ego et heredes mei tenebimus idem tenementum de ecclesia Beati Petri et conventu Westmonasterii reddendo annuatim unam libram piperis in Die Translationis Beati Regis Edwardi. Hoc autem factum est Johanne, filio meo et herede, presente et hoc annuente; et Jordano filio meo; Joseph, persona ecclesie Sancti

Martini de Ludgate; Roberto, eiusdem ecclesie capellano; Osberto de Wanci; Willelmo Revel; Stephano aurifabro; Augustino le Calicer; Tedbaldo de Feringes; Rogero Enganet; Eustachio pictore; Petro de Wenden; Henrico de Hertford; Willelmo de infirmaria; Galfrido, Ada, Radulfo et Willelmo, servientibus ecclesie, et multis aliis.

MS: WAD, f. 474v.
> Rubric: Item carta Laurencii predicti de domino totius feodi sui in Ludgate.

Date: Attestations, in particular that of Theobald of Feering, suggest a date temp. Abbot William Postard.

361. Acknowledgement by Osbert abbot of Bec, and the convent, that they are bound to render in perpetuity, to the chamberlain of Westminster, 15s., for land and a house of the fee of the church of Westminster, namely *Musterlingebur*, which Richard, prior of Ruislip, obtained from the wife of Stephen the healer and his heirs in London, with their assent. Husting Court, London, 1183–1184.

Sciant presentes et futuri quod ego Osbertus abbas Beccensis et eiusdem loci conventus perpetuo tenemur solvere camerario Westmonasterii singulis annis quindecim solidos ad duos statutos terminos anni: septem, scilicet, solidos et vj denarios ad Pascha, et tantundem[1] ad Festum Sancti Michaelis, pro terra et domo de feudo ecclesie Westmonasterii, scilicet: Musterlingebur quas Ricardus prior de Ruislep de uxore Stephani sanitarii et heredibus eius in London' per assensum eorum comperavit; quindecim autem solidos de quibus prediximus pensionem ad prefatos terminos prior de Ruislep, vel quicumque eandem possessionem servabit, nostra assignatione camerario Westmonasterii reddere tenetur. Facta est autem hec mutua[2] concessio anno Regis Henrici Secundi tricesimo nostro sigillo confirmata et in hustingo London' plenius recordatur.[3] Hiis testibus: Ricardo Wintoniense episcopo; Magistro Ricardo medico; Willelmo filio Sabel, vicecomite; Ricardo filio Reineri; Henrico filio Ailwini; Rogero filio Alani; Johanne filio Erlicun, et multis aliis.

MSS: (1) WAD, f. 493.
> Rubric: Recognitio cirographata abbatis et conventus Beccensis de xv solidis annui redditus.
> 1. Amended from F; MS *tantmdem*.
> 2. MS: *mutua* repeated.
> 3. *Recordatur* supplied by F.

(2) F, ff. 289v–290 (attestations omitted).
Note: Ruislip was an alien priory dependent upon Bec. Prior Richard de Coleliva prob. held office 1176–1198 (*Heads*, 107). On *Musterlingebur*, see Keene & Harding, no. 267.

362. Notification by Thomas de Haverhill that he has granted to the church of St Peter of Westminster 2s. quit-rent from the land which John

Blund, goldsmith, held of him in the parish of St Alphege, Cripplegate, and 3*s*. 6*d*. rent from the land which Bruming son of Stephen held of him towards the Tower of London. These rents are to be held in free, pure and perpetual alms, to provide a lamp in perpetuity at the Lady Altar. [1205 × 1218 (? 1213 × 1214)]

Omnibus Christi fidelibus ad quos presens scriptum pervenerit, Thomas de Haverell' salutem in Domino. Noverit universitas vestra me divine caritatis intuitu concessisse et dedisse Deo et ecclesie Sancti Petri de Westmonasterio duas solidatas quieti redditus de terra quam Johannes Blundus aurifaber tenuit de me in parochia Sancti Alfegi apud Crepelgate, percipiendas ad quatuor terminos anni; et quadraginta et duos denarios redditus de terra quam Bruming filius Stephani tenuit de me versus Turrim London', recipiendum ad quatuor terminos anni. Habendos et tenendos in liberam et puram et perpetuam elemosinam ad inveniendam unam lampadem in eadem ecclesia coram altari Beate Marie Virginis inperpetuum. Hanc vero concessionem et donationem ego Thomas de Haverell' et heredes meos warantizabimus predicte ecclesie Sancti Petri de Westmonasterio contra omnes homines et feminas inperpetuum. Et ut hec mea concessio et donatio stabilis maneat et firma, eam presenti scripto et sigilli mei appositione confirmavi. Hiis testibus: Petro, priore Sancte Trinitatis London'; Martino priore Sancte Marie de Suwerk'; Godefrido, priore Novi Hospitalis extra Bissopesgate; Magistro Waltero London'; Roberto filio Reygneri, canonico Sancte Marie de Suwerk'; Alexandro de Langhal', canonico Sancte Trinitatis; Johanne de Eggeswere; Galfrido de Sancta Elena, canonico Sancti Bartholomei; Willelmo capellano; Simone capellano novi hospitalis; Willelmo filio Reyneri; Henrico de Sancto Albano.

MS: WAD, f. 483v.
  Rubric: Carta Thome de Haverell de duobus solidis et de xlij denariis annui redditus in parochia Sancti Alphegi apud Crepelgate, et versus Turrim.
Date: Attestations of Priors Martin of Southwark, 1205 × 1218 (*Heads*, 184); Peter of Holy Trinity Aldgate, 1197 × 1221 (*Heads*, 174) and Godfrey of Bishopsgate Hospital, by *c*. 1218 (*VCH London*, I, 534a). Mr Walter of London perhaps attested in his capacity as archdeacon of London 1213 × 1214 (*Fasti* I, 10, 56).

363. Notification by Anselm son of Hakon of London that, for his soul and those of all his kinsfolk, he has quitclaimed to Abbot Ralph and the convent all his claim to the advowson of St Clement within the walls of London. The abbot and his successors may present freely to that church, when it is vacant, without further objection by Anselm or any of his kinsfolk. [London, 1200 × Jan. 1214]

Omnibus ad quos presens scriptum pervenerit Anselmus filius Haconis de London, salutem in Domino. Noverit universitas me, pro redemptione anime mee et omnium parentum meorum, quietum clamasse inperpetuum Abbati Radulpho et conventui Westmonasterii totum clamium meum quod habui de advocatione Sancti Clementis infra muros London' site, ita quod ego vel aliquis parentum meorum nunquam aliquo tempore poterimus aliquam querelam movere adversus dictum abbatem vel successores suos et conventum dicti loci vel eis molestiam inferre super advocatione dicte ecclesie, sed libere eam conferrant cui voluerint cum vacaverit absque alicuius reclamatione vel impedimento meo vel meorum. Hiis testibus: Domino Henrico, maiore London'; Rogero filio Alani; Alano filio Petri; Willelmo de Haverell, et filio suo Thoma; Willelmo filio Reigneri; Henrico fratre suo; Petro filio maioris, et Thoma fratre suo; Laurentio, capellano de Abbechurch; Magistro Hugone de Cornhull', et multis aliis.

MS: WAD, f. 487v.
  Rubric: Quieta clamancia Anselmi filii Haconis de advocatione ecclesie Sancti Clementis infra muros London'.
Date: During the mayoralty of Henry Fitz Ailwin (Beaven, *Aldermen*, 364) and the abbacy of Abbot Ralph.
Note: St Clement, 1C pope martyred by the Romans, is said to have been particularly favoured by Scandinavians, as borne out by his other London dedication, St Clement Danes (Brooke & Keir, 141, n. 4). Anselm's patronymic is prob. significant in this respect. Cf. **211**, **213**.

364. Confirmation, in pure and perpetual alms, by John Corner to St Peter of Westminster and the monks, for his soul; those of all his ancestors and heirs, and of all the faithful departed, to provide lights for the Lady Altar, of 4*s.* quit-rent in London, from his capital mansion in the parish of St Faith in the crypt of St Paul's. [*c.* 1191 × 1214]

Sciant presentes et futuri quod ego Johannes Cornerius dedi, concessi et presenti carta mea confirmavi Deo et ecclesie Sancti Petri apud Westmonasterium et monachis ibidem Deo servientibus et servituris, pro anima mea et pro animabus omnium antecessorum et heredum meorum, et pro animabus omnium fidelium defunctorum, quatuor solidatas quieti reditus in London', in liberam et puram et perpetuam elemosinam de capitali managio meo, quod est in parochia Sancte Fidis in criptis Sancti Pauli. Habendas et tenendas et percipiendas easdem monachis libere, quiete, integre, finabiliter de predicto managio ad duos terminos anni, scilicet: infra octabis Pasche duos solidos; et infra viij dies Festi Sancti Michaelis duos solidos, ad invenienda luminare inperpetuum coram altari Beate Marie in predicta ecclesia Sancti Petri. Has autem quatuor solidatas quieti reditus integre ego Johannes predictus et heredes mei finabiliter warantizabimus et quietas faciemus prenominatis monachis de Westmonasterio contra omnes homines et feminas sicut liberam et puram et perpetuam elemosinam. Et quia volui hanc donationem et concessionem meam ratam et inconcussam esse inperpetuum, presentem cartam sigillo meo confirmavi. Hiis testibus: Henrico filio Ailwini, tunc maiore London'; Thoma filio Johannis, aldermanno; Willelmo de Haverill'; Thoma filio eius; Willelmo filio Reineri; Willelmo de Berking';

Roberto filio Aliz; Willelmo et Martino fratribus eius; Johanne filio Vitalis; Willelmo Longo, aurifabro.

MSS: (1) WAM 13763.
28 × 9 cm; t.u. 1.7 cm.
Brown and cream corded tag (fragment).
Endorsed: (a) Johannes Cornerius dat capitulo quatuor solidos quietius redditus in London' (14C). (b) Sancte Fidis apud Sanctum Paulum London' capelle London'. vij (14C). (c) Capella iiij solidi (14C).
(2) WAD, f. 561r–v.

365. Notification by Froger, bp. of Séez, that, with the consent of the convent of Westminster, he has granted the church of St James on the Thames to John, nephew of the late Thomas [Becket], abp. of Canterbury. John will render £1 annually to the chamber of the abbey. [March 1173 × 1175/9]

Froger, Dei gratia Sagiensis episcopus, omnibus Sancte Matris Ecclesie filiis ad quos littere iste pervenerint, salutem. Noverit universitas vestra me concessisse, cum assensu conventus monachorum Sancti Petri de Westmonasterio, Johanni, nepoti beate memorie Thome Cantuariensis[1] archiepiscopi, ecclesiam Sancti Jacobi super Tamisiam, cum pertinenciis suis, in perpetuam elemosinam. Ita quod idem Johannes solvet annuatim de eadem ecclesia xx solidos camerario de Westmonasterio ad Festum Sancti Michaelis. Ne quis autem hanc concessionem meam in irritum revocare presumat, presentis scripti attestatione et sigilli mei auctoritate eam corroborare dignam[2] duxi. Testibus: Johanne archidiacono Sag[iensis]; Maria abbatissa de Berking'; Theb[aldo] nepote archiepiscopi; Magistro Gregorio; Magistro Henrico de London'; Thoma capellano; Stephano cognato archiepiscopi; Rogero cancellario.

MSS: (1) WAD, f. 476.
Rubric: Scriptum Frogeri Sagiensis episcopi de concessione ecclesie Sancti Jacobi super Tamisiam solvendo xx solidos per annum.
1. *Cantuariensis* omitted; supplied from F.
2. MS: *dignum*.
(2) F, f. 289 (attestations omitted).
Date: Mary [Becket], abbess of Barking, *soror beate* [*sic*] *Thome Martiri*, appointed 1173 (Gervase of Canterbury, I, 242; *Cal. Charter Rolls* V, 285); successor appointed 1175/9 (*Heads*, 208). Papal bulls announcing the canonization of Thomas Becket reached England in March 1173 (Anne Duggan, *Thomas Becket, a textual history of his letters* (1980), 54).
Note: In 1167 and again in 1170, Froger of Séez acted on behalf of H II as a negotiator in the Becket dispute (*Letters of John of Salisbury* II, 110, 686, 695; *Materials for the history of Thomas Becket*, ed. J. C. Robertson and J. B. Sheppard, VII (R.S. 1885), 224–5, no. 637). Perhaps, therefore, his grant to John was intended to expiate any offence incurred in the eyes of Becket's supporters. Cf. **211**, **213**.

366. Confirmation by Simon the forester and his wife Emma, daughter of Ralph Sumery, to Joyce the weigher, of all their land in St Laurence's parish towards the Thames, between the cemetery of St Laurence's church towards the south, and the land formerly belonging to the alderman Matthew Blund towards the north (measurements given). Joyce will hold in fee and inheritance, rendering 6*d.* annually to Simon and Emma, and, on behalf of them and their heirs, 4*s.* annually to the canons of Holy Trinity [Aldgate], London. Prohibition of dislodgement; gersum of 7 marks (£4. 13*s.* 4*d.*). [29 Sept. 1207 × 29 Sept. 1208]

Sciant presentes et futuri quod ego Simon forestarius et ego Emma filia Radulphi de Sumeri, uxor predicti Simonis, concessimus et dimisimus et presenti carta nostra confirmavimus Joceo ponderatori totam illam terram quam habuimus in parochia ecclesie Sancti Laurentii versus Tamisiam, inter cimiterium ipsius ecclesie versus austrum et terram que fuit Mathei Blundi aldermanni versus aquilonem. Que etiam terra continet in fronte secus vicum reg[is] orientalem undecim ulnas et dimidiam de ulnis ferreis Regis Johannis Anglie, et in capite occidentali xj ulnas de eisdem ulnis, et in longitudine ex utraque parte viginti et septem ulnas de eisdem ulnis, scilicet: quicquid ibidem habuimus in longitudine et latitudine, in ligno et lapido, et in rebus cum omnibus pertinentiis suis. Habendam et tenendam eidem Joceo et heredibus suis de nobis et heredibus nostris in feodo et hereditate, libere, quiete, honorifice, bene et in pace, integre et finabiliter. Reddendo inde annuatim nobis et heredibus nostris pro omni servitio et exactione et rebus cuntis sex denarios esterlingorum duobus terminis anni, scilicet: infra octabis Pasche tres denarios; infra octo dies [Festi] Sancti Michaelis tres denarios, sine c[avilatione] et miskenninga; et pro nobis et pro heredibus nostris canonicis ecclesie Sancte Trinitatis London' quatuor solidos annuatim duobus terminis anni, scilicet: infra octabis Pasche duos solidos; infra octo dies Festi Sancti Michaelis ij solidos pro omnibus serviciis et omnibus rebus. Et sciendum quod ego predictus Simon et ego prefata Emma uxor predicti Simonis et heredes nostri nullo modo poterimus nec debemus prenominatum Joceum neque heredes suos de predicta terra nec pertinentiis dehospitari, causa nos vel heredes nostros vel aliquem alium hominem vel feminam ibidem hospitandi; nec amplius inde exigere ne[c] habere debemus quam predictos sex denarios per annum terminis statutis. Hanc autem terram predictam integre in longitudine et latitudine et in rebus cuntis cum omnibus pertinentiis suis ego predictus Simon et ego Emma uxor predicti Simonis prenominato Joceo et heredibus suis contra omnes homines et feminas finabiliter debemus warantizare. Pro hac igitur concessione et dimissione et warantia et presentis carte nostre confirmatione, predictus Joceus dedit nobis septem marcas argenti in gersummam. Hiis testibus: Henrico filio Ailwini, tunc maiore London'; Roberto Wint[on'], Willelmo Hardell, tunc vicecomitibus London'; Jacobo ald[ermanno]; Matheo ald[ermanno]; Nicholao Duk[et]; Nicholao Wint'; Goc[elino] filio Willelmi; Godwino marescal[lo]; Waltero Sue'; Laurentio Duket; Rogero de Cornhull'; Roberto pistore; Waltero clerico; Rogero Waleys; Johanne

Sperling; Willelmo, Martino, fratribus eius; Thoma filio Hodierne; Simone Bat; Edwardo de Honilane, et pluribus aliis.

MS: WAD, f. 487r–v.
    Rubric: Carta Simonis forestarii et Emme uxoris sue de predicta terra.
Date: Prob. issued on the same occasion as Emma's grant of this land (**367**).

367. Confirmation by Emma, daughter of Ralph de Sumery, to Joyce the weigher, of all that land which she had, and which belonged to her father Ralph, in St Laurence's parish towards the Thames, between the cemetery of St Laurence's towards the south, and the land formerly belonging to Matthew Blund the alderman towards the north (measurements given), to hold in fee and inheritance of Emma and her heirs, at an annual rent of 6*d*.; and also, on her behalf, 4*s*. to the canons of Holy Trinity Aldgate; dislodgement prohibited; gersum of 7 marks (£4. 13*s*. 4*d*.). [29 Sept. 1207 × 29 Sept. 1208]

Sciant presentes et futuri quod ego Emma filia Radulphi de Sumeri concessi et dimisi et presenti carta mea confirmavi Joceo ponderatori totam illam terram quam habui et que fuit predicti Radulphi patris mei in parochia ecclesie Sancti Laurentii versus Tamisiam inter cimiterium ipsius ecclesie versus austrum et terram que fuit Mathei Blundi aldermanni versus aquilonem: que etiam terra continet in fronte versus vicum regalem orientali[a] undecim ulnas et dimidiam de ulnis ferreis Regis Johannis Anglie; et in capitem occidentalem[b] duodecim ulnas de eisdem ulnis; et in longitudine ex utraque parte viginti et septem ulnas de eisdem ulnis, scilicet: quicquid ibidem habui in longitudine et latitudine, in ligno et lapide et in rebus cuntis[c] cum omnibus pertinentiis suis.[d] Habendam et tenendam eidem Joceo et heredibus suis de me et heredibus meis in feodo et hereditate, libere, quiete, honorifice, bene et in pace, integre et finabiliter. Reddendo inde[e] annuatim michi et heredibus meis pro omni servicio et exaccione et rebus cuntis sex denarios esterlingorum duobus terminis anni, scilicet: infra octabis Pasche tres denarios; infra octo dies Festi Sancti Michaelis tres denarios, sine ca[usa] et miskenninga; et pro me et pro[f] heredibus meis canonicis ecclesie[g] Sancte Trinitatis London' quatuor solidos annuatim duobus terminis anni, scilicet: infra octabis[h] Pasche duos solidos; [et][i] infra octo dies Festi Sancti Michaelis duos solidos pro omnibus serviciis et omnibus rebus.[j] Et sciendum quod ego prenominata Emma et heredes mei nullo modo poterimus nec debemus predictum Joceum neque heredes suos de predicta terra nec pertinentiis dehospitari causa me vel heredes meos vel aliquem alium hominem vel feminam ibidem hospitando; nec amplius inde exigere nec habere debemus quam predictos sex denarios per annum terminis statutis. Hanc autem terram predictam, integre in longitudine et latitudine et in rebus cunctis, cum omnibus pertinentiis suis, ego predicta Emma et heredes mei predicto Joceo et heredibus suis contra omnes homines et feminas finabiliter debemus warantizare. Pro hac igitur concessione et dimissione et warantisione et presentis carte mee confirmatione predictus Joceus dedit michi Emme septem marcas argenti in gersummam. Hiis testibus: Henrico filio Ailwini, tunc maiore London'; Roberto Winton', Willelmo Hardell, vicecomitibus London'; Jacobo ald[ermanno]; Nicholao Duk[et]; Matheo aldermanno; Nicholao Wint'; Johanne Sperling, aldermanno; Willelmo, Martino, fratribus eius; Laurentio Duk[et]; Goc[elino] filio Willelmi; Godwino marescallo; Rogero de Cornhull'; Waltero fratre; Thoma filio Hodierne; Roberto Prell; Simone Bat; Edwardo de Hu[n]ilane; Rogero Waleys; Walter clerico.

MSS: (1) WAD, f. 487.
> Rubric: Carta Emme filie Radulphi de Sumery de tota terra que fuit predicti Radulphi patris sui in parochia Sancti Laurencii versus Tamisiam.
> (2) Univ. of Glasgow U.2.6 (microfilm deposited at Guildhall Library), f. 79 (incomplete).
> a. *orientalem.*
> b. *occidentali.*
> c. *latitudine, et lapidibus et rebus cunctis.*
> d. (continues erroneously): *et rebus cunctis.*
> e. *inde* omitted.
> f. *pro* omitted.
> g. *ecclesie* omitted.
> h. *octo die.*
> i. *et* supplied from Aldgate MS.
> j. *serviciis et rebus cunctis etc.* Aldgate MS. ends here.

Cal: *Cart. Aldgate*, no. 402.
Date: Attestations of Henry Fitz Ailwin as mayor, and of William Hardel and Robert of Winchester as sheriffs (*Sheriffs*, 200). Although Emma's marital status is not mentioned, the attestations indicate that the document was issued on the same occasion as **366**.
Note: On the earlier history of this land, see *Cart. Aldgate*, nos. 399–401. The date there ascribed to no. 400 is clearly incorrect, and Ralph de Sumery prob. acquired his lease from Prior Ralph (1147–67). Joyce's daughter Bola later granted the land to William de Cheynduit, rector of St Laurence, who gave it to St Peter and the monks of Westminster (*Cart. Aldgate*, no. 401).

368. Notification by Nicholas, archdeacon of London, that on the presentation of Abbot Walter and the convent of Westminster, to whom belongs half the advowson of the church of St Magnus the Martyr, and at the presentation of Prior Henry de Soilli and the convent of Bermondsey, to whom belongs the other half of the church, he has inducted his nephew Mr Nicholas as parson. [1186 × 1189]

Universis Sancte Matris Ecclesie filiis ad quos presens scriptum pervenerit, Nicholaus archidiaconus London' salutem in Domino. Vestre notificamus universitati nos ad presentacionem Walteri abbatis West-monasterii et conventus eiusdem loci, ad quorum donationem medietas ecclesie Sancti Magni Martiris de Ponte pertinet, et ad presentationem

Henrici de Soliaco, prioris Bermundeseye, et eiusdem loci conventus, ad quos alia medietas prefate ecclesie cum iure donationis pertinet, Magistrum Nicholaum, nepotem nostrum, in personam ecclesie predicte recepisse et ipsum per officialem nostrum in corporalem possessionem eiusdem induxisse, unde ut ea que a nobis gesta sunt firma habeantur hoc presenti scripto cum sigilli nostri appositione roboranda duximus. Hiis testibus: Nicholao, capellano nostro; Ricardo de Sancto Johanne; Helia de Honilane; Gaufrido de Sancta Margareta de Ponte; Waltero de Sancto Botulpho de Ponte; Gregorio capellano; David filio eius; Swenone capellano nostro; Johanne capellano eiusdem ecclesie; Willelmo filio Alexandri; Radulfo de Ulla; Hudone de Sancto Georgio.

MSS: (1) WAD, f. 478v.
>Rubric: Scriptum archidiaconi London' de institutione rectoris in eadem ecclesia.
>(2) F, f. 246r–v (omits attestations).
>Rubric: De admissione presentati ad ecclesiam Sancti Magni London'. Capitulum xxiiij.

Date: Term of office of Henry de Soilli, prior of Bermondsey (*Heads*, 115).

Note: Cf. final concord between Abbot Walter and Prior Bertram of Bermondsey and their convents, 23 April 1182 (**287**). Half of the church of St Magnus was confirmed to Westminster by Bp. Gilbert Foliot (**211**).

369. Notification by Nicholas, archdeacon of London, that on the presentation of Abbot Walter and the convent of Westminster, he has instituted Geoffrey of Bedford to the church of St Margaret near London Bridge. Geoffrey is to pay a pension of 10*s*. a year to the abbey chamber. [1175 × 1189]

Omnibus Sancte Matris Ecclesie filiis ad quos presentes littere pervenerint, Nicholaus, Dei gratia London' archidiaconus, eternam in Domino salutem. Universitati vestre notum[1] facimus nos, ad presentationem venerabilis viri Walteri, abbatis Westmonasterii, et eiusdem conventus, recepisse et nullo contradicente in generali capitulo instituisse Galfridum de Bedeford capellanum in ecclesia Sancte Margarete de London' prope Pontem, quia ad prefati abbatis et conventus donationem pertinere dinoscitur. Ita ut nomine pensionis x solidorum camerario Westmonasterii singulis annis ad duos terminos anni reddere debeat: ad Pascha, videlicet, quinque solidos, et ad Festum Sancti Michaelis v solidos eodem modo; et sub eadem pensione Galfridus clericus memoratam ecclesiam ex donatione abbatis et conventus et ex nostra concessione ante tenuerat et in ea ad presentationem abbatis et conventus cum debita sollempnitate per nos institutus fuit. Ne igitur que in presentia nostra gesta sunt decetero possunt in dubium revocari, ea sigilli nostri testimonio roboravimus. Hiis testibus: Radulfo cantore; Stephano camerario; Magistro Ricardo, fratre Nicholai archidiaconi; Magistro Nicholao, eiusdem nepoti; Nicholao, capellano archidiaconi; Magistro Silvestro; Roberto eius capellano; Johanne, capellano del Baille; Johanne de Sancta Margareta; Rogero de Sancto Edmundo; Ernisio

Bissope; Willelmo Aldelmanno ad Camberletk'; Andrea le Blunt; Jacobo le Want', et multis aliis.

MSS: (1) WAD, f. 477v.

> Rubric: Littera Nicholai archidiaconi London' de institutione Galfridi de Bedeford' in ecclesia Sancte Margarete London' prope Pontem. Reddendo x solidos per annum.
> Marginalia: Nota for x^s payable by the parson of St Margarettis London (17C).
> (2) F, f. 290v–291.
> 1. MS: *notum notum*.

Date: Terms of office of Abbot Walter, and of Archdeacon Nicholas (*Fasti* I, 9).
Note: Cf. **211**.

370. Notification by Richard son of William Fitz Reinger that he has confirmed to William son of Henry Fitz Gerard his stone house which Hugh of Stanning' held of him in the parish of St Margaret towards London Bridge, which house faces Richard's chief dwelling towards the East, and also confirms his stone cellar beneath that house, which John son of Pain held of him. These are to be held by William and his heirs of Richard and his heirs in fee and inheritance, at an annual rent of 1 lb. of cumin. Dislodgement prohibited; gersum of £10. [*c.* 1180 × 1200]

Sciant presentes et futuri quod ego Ricardus filius Willelmi filii Reingeri concessi et dimisi et presenti carta mea confirmavi Willelmo filio Henrici filii Gerardi quandam domum meum lapideam quam Hugo de Stanning' de me tenuit in parochia Sancte Margarete versus Pontem London'; que domus est in fronte capitalis managii mei versus orientem, et quoddam cellarium meum lapideum quod est subter domum illam in eadem parochia, quod scilicet Johannes filius Pagani de me tenuit, scilicet quicquid in predicta domo et cellario habui in longitudine et latitudine, in lignis et lapidibus et in rebus cuntis, integre. Habendam et tenendam dicto Willelmo et heredibus suis de me et heredibus meis in feudo et hereditate, libere et quiete, bene et in pace, inperpetuum; reddendo inde annuatim michi et heredibus meis pro omni servitio et exactione et rebus cuntis unam libram cimini infra octabis Pasche, sine omni occasione. Et sciendum est quod ego Ricardus et heredes mei nullo modo poterimus nec debemus predictum Willelmum nec heredes suos de predicta domo nec cellario dehospitari causa me vel heredes meos, vel aliquem alium hominem vel feminam ibidem hospitandi, nec amplius inde exigere nec habere nec clamare debemus inperpetuum quam predictam libram cimini per annum termino statuto. Et ego Ricardus et heredes mei predictam domum et cellarium dicto Willelmo et heredibus suis contra omnes homines et feminas inperpetuum debemus warantizare et aquietare. Pro hac igitur concessione, dimissione, warantizatione, acquietatione et presentis carte mee confirmatione, dictus Willelmus dedit michi Ricardo decem libras sterlingorum in gersummam.[1]

MS: WAD, f. 490.

Rubric: Carta Ricardi filii Willelmi filii Reingeri de quadam domo lapidea quam Hugo de Stanning' de se tenuit in parochia Sancte Margarete.

1. Text ends.

Date: The grantor is prob. the Richard Fitz Reiner who was sheriff of London in 1187 × 1189 (cf. Reynolds, 'Rulers of London', 355).

371. Confirmation, in pure and perpetual alms, by Matilda de Paris to the church of St Peter of Westminster, and the convent, for the souls of her parents and all her ancestors, of a certain piece of land which she had in London, in St Margaret's parish towards the Thames, with half a stone wall, concerning which wall she caused an assize of the city to be held. The land lies between that which belonged to William Fisher, to the north, and that which belonged to Stephen Blund, mercer, to the south (measurements given), to hold at an annual rent of 6*d.*; dislodgement prohibited. [1199 × 1213]

Sciant presentes et futuri quod ego Matillis de Paris dedi et concessi et presenti carta mea confirmavi ecclesie Sancti Petri de Westmonasterio et conventui eiusdem ecclesie, pro anima patris et matris mee et omnium antecessorum meorum, quandam partem terre quam habui in London in parochia ecclesie Sancte Margarete versus Pontem London', cum medietate muri lapidei, unde assisam civitatis tradidi ad murum faciendum; que terra jacet inter terram que fuit Willelmi Fisher versus aquilonem, et terram que fuit Stephani Blund mercerij versus austrum, et continet in fronte secus vicum regis orientali sex ulnas de ulnis ferreis Regis Johannis Anglie; et in profunditate triginta v ulnas de eisdem ulnis; et in capite versus occidentem sex ulnas de eisdem ulnis, scilicet: quicquid ibidem habui in longitudine et latitudine, in lignis et lapibus, et in rebus cuntis, cum omnibus pertinentiis suis integre. Habendum et tenendum ecclesie predicte et eiusdem conventui in pura et perpetua elemosina, libere, quiete, honorifice, bene et in pace, integre, finabiliter. Reddendo inde annuatim michi et heredibus meis pro omni servitio et exactione et rebus cuntis sex denarios infra octabis Pasche. Et sciendum quod ego Matillis vel heredes mei nullatenus poterimus predictam ecclesiam neque conventum de predicta terra dehospitari causa me vel heredes meos vel aliquem alium hominem vel feminam per nos ibidem hospitandi, nec amplius inde exigere vel habere debemus, quam predictos sex denarios per annum termino statuto, et de omnibus servitiis versus capitalem dominum debemus acquietare per predictum servitium. Hanc autem terram predictam integre cum omnibus pertinentiis suis ego Matillis et heredes mei predicte ecclesie et conventui contra omnes homines et feminas finabiliter debemus warantizare per predictum servitium sex denariorum. Et ut hec donatio et concessio rata sit et stabilis, presentis sigilli mei inpressione confirmavi. Hiis testibus: Henrico maiore London'; Rogero filio Alani; Alano filio Petri; Constantino filio Alulfi; Thoma de Haverrell'; Willelmo filio Reinerii; Henrico filio Reinerii; Nicholao Duket.

MS: WAD, ff. 489v–490.

Rubric: Carta Matillis de Parys de quadam parte terre in predicta parochia, cum medietate cuiusdam muri lapidei.

Date: 'Ells of King John' and attestation of Henry Fitz Ailwin as mayor.

Note: An early instance of the invocation of the Assize of Buildings. See *London Assize of Nuisance 1301–1431: a calendar*, ed. Helena M. Chew and William Kellaway (LRS 10, 1973), ix–x.

372. Confirmation by Matilda de Paris, daughter of Simon de Paris, to Richard son of Willam Fitz Reinger of certain land which she had in St Margaret's parish towards the Thames, lying between the land which belonged to William Sig' and that, towards the south, which she gave to St Peter of Westminster (measurements given); to hold to Richard and his heirs in fee and inheritance of Matilda and her heirs, at an annual rent of 5*s*. sterling; dislodgement prohibited; gersum of £10. [Temp. John]

Sciant presentes et futuri quod ego Matillis de Paris, filia Simonis de Paris', concessi et dimisi et presenti carta mea confirmavi Ricardo filio Willelmi filii Reing[eri] quandam terram quam habui in parochia ecclesie Sancte Margarete versus Pontem London'; que terra jacet inter terram que fuit Willelmi Sig' et terram quam ego Matillis dedi ecclesie Sancti Petri de Westmonasterio versus austrum; que etiam continet in fronte secus vicum regis oriente in latitudine sex ulnas et tres quartas de ulnis ferreis Regis Johannis Anglie; et in medio viginti et unam ulnas de eisdem ulnis; et in capite occidentali viginti ulnas et dimidiam de eisdem ulnis; et in longitudine quinquaginta et duas ulnas de eisdem ulnis: scilicet quicquid ibidem habui in longitudine et latitudine, in ligno et lapido, et in rebus cuntis cum omnibus pertinentiis integre, sine aliqua exceptione. Habendam et tenendam eidem Ricardo et heredibus suis de me et de heredibus meis in feodo et hereditate, libere, quiete, honorifice, bene et in pace, integre et finabiliter. Reddendo inde annuatim michi et heredibus meis pro omni servitio et exactione et rebus cuntis quinque solidos esterlingorum ad quatuor terminos anni, scilicet: infra octabis Nativitatis Domini quindecim denarios; infra octabis Pasche xv denarios; infra octabis Nativitatis Sancti Johannis Baptiste xv denarios; infra octo dies Festi Sancti Michaelis xv denarios, sine c[avilatione] et meskenninga. Et sciendum quod ego Matillis et heredes mei nullo modo poterimus nec debemus prenominatum Ricardum nec heredes suos de predicta terra nec pertinentiis dehospitari causa me vel heredes meos vel aliquem alium hominem vel feminam ibidem hospitandi; nec amplius inde exigere nec habere debemus, quam predictos quinque solidos per annum terminis statutis. Hanc autem terram predictam integre cum omnibus pertinentiis suis ego Matillis et heredes mei predicto Ricardo et heredibus suis contra omnes homines et feminas finabiliter debemus warantizare, et de omnibus servitiis et exactionibus et rebus cuntis versus capitales dominos ipsius feodi et versus omnes gentes aquietare. Pro hac igitur concessione et dimissione et warantisione et aquietatione et presentis carte mee confirmatione predictus Ricardus dedit michi Matilli decem libras esterlingorum in gersummam. Hiis testibus: Rannulpho sacerdote; Willelmo Wylikyn, aldermanno; Matheo aldermanno; Nicholao

Duk[et]; Johanne Walran; Johanne Blundo; Roberto de Turr'; Ada camerario; Warino filio Nicholai; Petro Bukerel; Willelmo viro Sar'; Roberto Blund carnifice; Jordano filio Reng[eri]; Godino ferratorio; Simone Blund, pisconerio; Galfrido Lageman; Thoma pisconerio; Willelmo Bat; Joceo ponderatore; Hugone de London'; Waltero clerico, et pluribus aliis.

MS: WAD, f. 490r–v.
　　Rubric: Carta Matillis de Paris de quadam terra in eadem parochia. Date: 'Ells of King John'. Robert Blund was sheriff of London 1196–1197, and alderman (Reynolds, 'Rulers of London', 356); Nicholas Ducket was sheriff 1191–1192 and 1196–1197, and prob. alderman (ibid., 355–6). Later than **371**.

373. Notification by Richard son of William Fitz Reinger of a rent that he is bound to render to Matilda de Paris: £2 for that land which she granted and confirmed to him by charter, for her lifetime, in the parish of St Margaret towards London Bridge. After Matilda's d., Richard and his heirs will render only 5*s.* annually to the Chamber of the church of SS. Peter and Paul of Westminster, as her charter bears witness. Matilda is empowered to distrain on that fee for non-payment of the rent. [Temp. John]

Sciant presentes et futuri quod ego Ricardus filius Willelmi filii Reingeri annuatim reddere debeo Matildi de Parys' quadraginta solidos esterlingorum de terra quam eadem Matildis michi Ricardo concessit et carta sua confirmavit in parochia ecclesie Sancte Margarete versus Pontem London' quamdiu ipsa Matillis vixerit ad quatuor anni terminos: infra octabis Nativitatis Domini decem solidos; infra octabis Pasche x solidos; infra octabis Sancti Johannis Baptiste decem solidos; infra octo dies Sancti Michaelis x solidos. Ita quod post obitum eiusdem Matildis ego Ricardus vel heredes mei nichil amplius reddere debemus de predicta terra quam quinque solidos per annum ad cameram ecclesie beatorum apostolorum Petri et Pauli de Westmonasterio, sicut carta testatur, quam michi Ricardo inde fecit. Preterea sciendum quod si ego Ricardus vel heredes mei predictum censum predicte Matildi quamdiu vixerit ad terminos statutos non solverimus, concessi pro me et heredibus meis quod ipsa Matildis namium inde capiat super ipsum feodum ad predictum censum percipiendum quamdiu ipsa vixerit. Et ut hec conventio rata et inconcussa permaneat, presens scriptum mutuo munimine sigilli nostri roboratur. Hiis testibus: Willelmo aldremanno; Roberto Blundo; Galfrido Firherde; Warino filio Nicholai; Simone piscatore; Galfrido Lagemann'; Wigod mercerio; Ernaldo Bedello; Ricardo Blundo; Roberto de Turri; Johanne de Elbegate, et multis aliis.

MS: WAD, f. 490v–491.
　　Rubric: Recognitio indentata Ricardi filii Willelmi filii Reingeri de xl
　　solidis ad vitam Matillis de Paris t[ame]n pro quadam terra et de v
　　solidis post obitum eiusdem Matillis ad cameram Westmonasterii.

Date: cf. **372**.

374. Notification by Serlo son of Hugh of Kent of his grant to Robert son of Edward of that land adjacent to *Prestbure* in London, in the parish of St Martin Outwich, to hold in inheritance, at an annual rent of 5*s*. Gersum of 1*s*. [*c*. 1190 × 1200]

Serlo filius Hugonis de Kent universis ad quos presens scriptum pervenerit, salutem in Domino. Noscat universitas vestra quod ego concessi Roberto filio Edwardi terram illam que jacet juxta Prestebure in London in parochia Sancti Martini de Otteswich'; tenendam ipsi et heredibus suis de me et heredibus meis singulis annis pro quinque solidis pro omni servitio, scilicet: ad Pascham duos solidos et sex denarios, et duos solidos et sex denarios ad Festum Sancti Michaelis. Et ego et heredes mei ipsi Roberto et heredibus suis predictam terram contra omnes homines warantizabimus. Et pro hac concessione dedit iamdictus Robertus mihi duodecim denarios in gersummam. Ut autem hac mea concessio rata permaneat et firma, ipsam presenti scripto et sigilli mei apposicione corroborare curavi. Hiis testibus: Nicholao, persona ecclesie Sancti Martini; Petro, tunc capellano eiusdem ecclesie; Clemente clerico; Abraham et Martino, fratribus; Wlnardo pistore; Randulfo, Mauricio, Edwardo, Rogero, Simone, et Willelmo, fratribus; et Asketino, et multis aliis, scilicet: Laurentio Ruffo; Osberto Nigro; Gileberto Ferur; Waltero Illevost[er], Roberto Nigro; Waltero filio Roberti; Petro Want'; Waltero pistore.

MS: WAD, f. 369v.
    Rubric: Carta eiusdem Serlonis de terra illa que jacet juxta Prestebury.
Date: Prob. early in Serlo's career, since he is not surnamed 'the mercer', a style ascribed to him in 1207, when he was one of the farmers of London and Middlesex (*PR 9 John*, 49).
Note: Serlo was mayor 1216–22 (Beaven, *Aldermen* I, 337). The parish of St Martin Outwich included Bishopsgate and Broad Street.

375. Grant by Serlo son of Hugh to Martin son of Kenewald, with the assent of Robert son of Edward, of the land which Robert held of him in fee and inheritance in St Martin's parish, to be held by Martin and his heirs of Serlo and his heirs at an annual rent of 5*s*. Gersum of 1*s*. [*c*. 1200]

Sciant tam presentes quam futuri quod ego Serlo filius Hugonis dimisi et concessi Martino filio Kenewaldi, assensu et voluntate Roberti filii Edwardi, totam terram quam idem Robertus de me tenuit in feodo et hereditate in parochia Sancti Martini. Tenendam finabiliter ipsi et heredibus suis de me et heredibus meis; reddendo inde annuatim michi et heredibus meis quinque solidos pro omni servicio, scilicet: ad Pascham duos solidos et sex denarios, et duos solidos et sex denarios ad Festum Sancti Michaelis. Pro hac autem dimissione et concessione dedit mihi iamdictus Martinus xij denarios in gersummam. Et ego Serlo et heredes mei ipsi Martino et heredibus suis contra omnes homines et feminas predictam terram waranti[za]bimus. Testibus: Radulfo filio Simonis, aldremanno; Nicholao, persona ecclesie Sancti Martini; Udone, custode soche domini episcopi London'; Albino mercerio; Laurentio Ruffo; Ricardo Blundo; Gilleberto ferun[erio]; Roberto filio Edwardi; Radulfo Flahun; Rogero pistore; Waltero Wolmongere; Silvestrio Abraham; Ricardo filio Rogeri; Clemente clerico; Ailwardo et Waltero Pethet; Duranto; Mauricio; Wluardo, et multis aliis.

MS: WAD, f. 369v.
    Rubric: Carta Serlonis filii Hugonis de tota illa terra quam Robertus filius Edwardi de ipso tenuit in parochia Sancti Martini.
Date: Later than **374**, although also issued during Nicholas's occupancy of St Martin's. Richard Blund was sheriff in 1198–9 (Reynolds, 'Rulers of London', 356); Odo the soke-reeve attested a grant of land in the parish of St Mary Woolnoth, *ante* 1210 (*Cart. Clerkenwell*, no. 236).

376. Quitclaim by Pain Tabur, son of Pain Tabur, and Agnes his wife, to Serlo the mercer, of their land with houses and appurtenances in the parish of St Martin Outwich, of Serlo's fee, lying between the land of John Beggy to the north, and Serlo's land to the south. Gersum of four marks (£2. 13s. 4d.). [Temp. John]

Sciant presentes et futuri quod ego Paganus Tabur, filius Pagani Tabur, et ego Agnes uxor eiusdem vendidimus, quietum clamavimus et forisaffidavimus extra nos et heredes nostros Serloni mercerio totam terram cum domibus et pertinentiis quam habuimus in parochia Sancti Martini de Otteswich' de feodo ipsius Serlonis. Que jacet inter terram que fuit Johannis Beggy versus aquilonem, et terram eiusdem Serlonis versus austrum, videlicet: quicquid ibidem habuimus vel habere potuimus in terris, in domibus, in lignis et lapidibus, in longitudine et latitudine, in rebus cuntis, cum omnibus pertinentiis suis, integre sine aliquo retinemento. Habendum et tenendum ipsi Serloni et cuicumque dare, dimittere, legare vel assignare voluerit, et heredibus suis libere, quiete, bene et in pace, extra nos et heredes nostros inperpetuam et finalem venditionem. Ita etiam quod ego Paganus Tabur sive ego Agnes uxor eiusdem predicta, sive heredes nostri, sive aliquis per nos vel pro nobis, nullo modo poterimus neque debemus aliquid inde habere, exigere, capere nec clamare inperpetuum. Et ut hec nostra venditio, quieta clamatio, et forisfidatio perpetuam firmitatem obtineat, presentem cartam sigillis nostris roboravimus. Pro hac igitur venditione, quieta clamatione et forisaffidatione et sigillorum nostrorum appositione, dedit nobis dictus Serlo quatuor marcas esterlingorum. Hiis testibus: Waltero de Insula, tunc aldermano;[1] Elia mercerio; Petro, filio Laurentii de Burton'; Roberto de Wrotham; Rogero de Cardvill'; Johanne de Solio; Ricardo Cobold; Roberto pistore; Andrea ferunario; Willelmo de Bradestrate; Waltero serviente; Rogero clerico, et aliis.

MS: WAD, f. 369r–v.

Rubric: Carta Pagani Tabur, filii Pagani Tabur, et Agnetis uxoris sue de tota terra sua in parochia Sancti Martini de Otteswich'.

1. MS: *aldermanum*.

Date: Serlo the mercer was one of those accounting for the farm of London at Michaelmas 1207 (*PR 9 John*, 49) and he was mayor 1216–1222 (Beaven, *Aldermen*, I, 366). Walter de Insula was alderman of St Martin, Outwich (i.e. Bishopsgate and Broad Street) at some uncertain date (ibid. I, 237). He was still active *c.* 1227–30 (ibid. I, 336; *PR 14 Henry III*, 108).

377. Confirmation by William son of Alulf to the prior and convent of St Peter of Westminster of the whole of his land with an appurtenant wharf in the parish of St Mary at Hill, between the land formerly belonging to Richard son of Oswant and the lane opposite Billingsgate, of the fee of Henry de Bohun. This land measures in length, towards the lane, 18¼ of the ells of King John, and in width, 14⅛ of those ells. The prior and convent will render 2*s.* annually. Dislodgement prohibited; gersum of £20 sterling to William, and ½ mark to his son Peter. [29 Sept. 1201 × 29 Sept. 1202]

Sciant presentes et futuri quod ego Willelmus filius Alulfi concessi et dimisi et presenti carta me[a] confirmavi priori et conventui ecclesie Sancti Petri de Westmonasterio totam illam terram meam cum caio ad eandem terram pertinente in parochia Sancte Marie de la Hulle, inter terram que fuit Ricardi fili Oswanti et venellam que est contra Billingesgate, que est de feodo Henrici de Bohun;[b] que etiam terra continet in longitudine versus predictam venellam decem et octo ulnas et unum quarterum unius ulne de ulnis Johannis Regis Anglie; et in[c] latitudine versus Tamisiam quatuordecim[d] ulnas et dimidium quarterium unius ulne de predictis ulnis,[e] scilicet quicquid in illa terra et illo caio habui in ligno et lapide, in longitudine et in latitudine et in rebus cuntis. Habendam et tenendam predictis priori et conventui de me et de heredibus meis in feodo et hereditate, libere, quiete, integre, finabiliter; reddendo inde annuatim michi et heredibus meis pro omnibus servitiis et exactionibus et pro omnibus rebus duos solidos esterlingorum ad duos terminos anni, scilicet: infra octo dies Festi Sancti Michaelis xij denarios, et infra octabis Pasche xij denarios, sine omni occasione et forisfactura. Preterea ante sciendum est quod nec ego Willelmus predictus nec heredes mei poterimus hospitari[1] aliquem hominem nec feminam qui hospitati fuerint ibidem per predictos priorem et conventum causa me vel heredes meos sive aliquem alium hominem vel feminam ibidem hospitandi. Hanc autem terram predictam, cum edificiis suis et cum caio ad eandem terram pertinente, in longitudine et latitudine et in rebus cuntis, ego Willelmus predictus et heredes mei finabiliter warantizabimus predictis priori et conventui contra omnes homines et feminas, et de omnibus servitiis versus seinuragios feodi finabiliter acquietabimus per predictum servitium, scilicet per duos solidos esterlingorum terminis statutis solvendos. Pro hac igitur concessione et dimissione et warantizatione et acquietatione et presentis carte mee confirmatione predicti prior et conventus dederunt mihi Willelmo prenominato viginti libras esterlingorum in gersummam, et Petro filio meo dimidiam marcam. Hiis testibus: Henrico filio Ailwini, tunc maiore London'; Rogero filio Alani; Normanno Blundo draperio, tunc vice[comite] London'; Alano filio Petri; Thoma de Haverella; Willelmo filio Sabeline; Roberto filio Ricoldi.

MSS: (1) WAD, f. 491r–v.
> Rubric: Cirographum Willelmi filii Alulfi de tota terra sua cum caio in parochia Sancte Marie de la Hulle.
>> 1. MS: *schospitari*. The text of the original muniment prob. read *dishospitari*.
> (2) Cartulary of Holy Trinity Aldgate (Univ. of Glasgow MS U.2.6, microfilm deposited in Guildhall Library), f. 47 (incomplete).
>> a. *me* omitted.
>> b. *que est de feodo Henrici de Bohun* omitted.
>> c. *in* omitted.
>> d. *xiij*.
>> e. text concludes: *ulnis Regis etc.*
> Marginalia: *Hec carta sigillata remanet in Westmonasterium.*

Cal: *Cart. Aldgate*, no. 231, p. 44.
Date: Norman Blund was sheriff of London 29 Sept. 1201 × 29 Sept. 1202 (*Sheriffs*, 200).

378. Confirmation by Walter son of Ralph Oter, in pure and perpetual alms, to the Blessed Virgin and the church of St Peter of Westminster, of all his land in the City of London, in the parish of St Mary at Hill, with both the wooden and the stone buildings (measurements given). The annual rent of 2*d.* is due to the socage of Henry de Bohun or his heirs. [1191 × 1199]

Sciant presentes et futuri quod ego Walterus filius Radulfi Oter dedi et concessi et hac presenti carta mea confirmavi, in puram et perpetuam elemosinam Deo et Beate Marie et ecclesie Beati Petri Westmonasterii totam terram meam in civitate London' que jacet in parochia Sancte Marie de Hulle, cum edificiis tam ligneis quam lapideis. Que terra continet in longitudine versus austrum et aquilonem triginta et tres ulnas et tres quartarios de ulnis Regis Ricardi; et in latitudine versus aquilonem tresdecim ulnas; et iterum versus austrum ex alia parte in latitudine decem et octo ulnas. Habendam et tenendam ecclesie eidem libere et quiete, integre et plenarie, inperpetuum. Reddendo inde annuatim duos denarios de socagio Henrico de Boun vel heredibus suis ad unum anni terminum, scilicet in medio Quadragesime. Et ut hec mea donatio et concessio et carte mee confirmatio rata sit et stabilis permaneat, eam sigilli mei appositione corroboravi. Hiis testibus: Radulfo capellano; Henrico maiore London'; Rogero filio Alani; Johanne le alderman; Radulfo fratre eius; Britio cordario; Johanne de Garlande; Gaufrido piscario; Willelmo de Einesford; Benedicto lingedraper; Willelmo de Sandewico; Wibardo le Bedel; Hugone le Flameng'; Waltero filio Alexandri Sperleng; Nicholao de celario; Laurentio Muschat; Gaufrido,

Adam, Willelmo, Johanne, servientibus ecclesie Westmonasterii, et multis aliis.

MSS: (1) WAM 13858.
12.5 × 17.5 cm.
Seal: On tag; black; 5 cm diameter; wild boar, facing right; legend: + SIGILL' WALTERI FIL. RADULFI OTER.
Endorsed: (a) Walterus Oter dat [c]apelle quandam partem terre in London' in parochia Sancte Marie de Hull (13C). (b) Capella London' x (14C).
(2) WAD, f. 561v–562.
Date: Attestations and the hand are late 12C; references to ells of King Richard, and mayoralty of Henry Fitz Ailwin. Henry de Bohun succeeded his father, Humphrey III, *c.* 1187, and attained his majority before 1200. Despite the reference to his heirs, he lived until 1220 (Sanders, 91–2).

379. Grant, with warranty, by Marona, widow of Martin Sperling, to the Blessed Virgin and the convent, of 2*s.* rent in the City of London, formerly rendered to her by Bryce the corder for land in the parish of St Mary at Hill; between that which Bryce holds of the abbey and that which she holds of the canons of Holy Trinity (Aldgate), London. In return, the convent gave her two marks (£1 6*s.* 8*d.*) for the support of her sons. [Late 12C]

Sciant presentes et futuri quod ego Marona, quondam uxor Martini Sperling, dedi et concessi et hac presenti carta mea confirmavi, in puram et perpetuam elemosinam, Deo et Beate Marie et conventui ecclesie Westmonasterii, duas solidatas redditus in urbe London', quas Bricius cordarius solebat michi reddere de quadam terra que est in parochia Sancte Marie de la Hulle. Et est inter terram quam idem Bricius tenet de predicta ecclesia Westmonasterii, et terram quam ego teneo de canonicis Sancte Trinitatis de London'. Habendas et possidendas et percipiendas libere et quiete inperpetuum per manus eiusdem Bricii, vel heredum suorum, vel eius quicumque eandem terram in feudo tenuerit, ad duos terminos anni, scilicet ad Pascham duodecim denarios, et ad Festum Sancti Michaelis duodecim denarios. Et ego Marona et heredes mei warantizabimus predictum redditum duorum solidorum predicto conventui contra omnes homines et feminas. Et pro hac donatione et concessione et carte mee confirmatione, dedit mihi predictus conventus duas marcas argenti ad pueros meo[s] consulendos. Et ut hec mea donatio et concessio et carte mee confirmatio rata sit et stabilis permaneat, eam sigilli mei appositione corroboravi. Hiis testibus: Johanne Sperling; Johanne de Garlande; Bricio cordario; Martino le Ferun; Gileberto le seutrer; Edwardo de Tolleshunte; Willelmo filio Edrici; Waltero de Fuleham; Ricardo filio Reginaldi; Rannulpho Sprot; Ricardo Dod; Roberto Wedertot; Willelmo de Eynesforde, et multis aliis.

MS: WAD, f. 491.

Rubric: Carta Marone quondam uxoris Martini Sperling' de duabus solidatis redditus in parochia Sancte Marie de la Hulle.

Date: John Sperling and Gilbert le Seutrer attested a charter dated *c.* 1170 × 1197 (*Cart. Aldgate*, no. 236). John de Garland is prob. the prebendary of St Paul's, and royal justice, of that name (*Fasti* I, 66).

Note: John Sperling, the leading witness, was a tenant of Holy Trinity Aldgate, *c.* 1170 × 1197 (*Cart. Aldgate*, no. 76).

380. Agreement between Bertram, and Nicholas son of Clement, concerning the church of St Matthew, Friday Street. Bertram would render 5*s.* annually to Nicholas from that church, but if Nicholas d. first, or entered the religious life, Bertram would be quit of this payment. If Bertram d. first, or entered the religious life, then Nicholas would hold the church freely, quit of any claim by Bertram or anyone on his behalf. Robert [de Sigillo], bp. of London, assented to this agreement. Chapter, St Paul's [1141 × 1151]

Hec est conventio inter Bertramium et Nicholaum filium Clementis de ecclesia Sancti Mathei. Concessione clementis facta est inter Bertramium et Nicholaum hoc modo, scilicet: Bertramius reddet singulis annis Nicholao v solidos de eadem ecclesia: xxx denarios in Nativitate Sancte Marie, et xxx denarios in media Quadragesima. Et si prior mortuus fuerit Nicholaus, vel vitam suam mutaverit relinquens seculum, quietius erit exinde Bertramius nec postea alicui aliquid reddet, set quiete eam ulterius tenebit de omni calumpnia Nicholai et suorum, quantum ad ipsum Nicholaum pertinet. Si vero Bertramius prior mortuus fuerit, vel seculum relinquendo vitam mutaverit, in pace et quiete deinde semper tenebit Nicholaus sicut suam propriam liberam de omni calumpnia Bertramii et omnium suorum, ita quod inde nichil clamare poterit nec Nicholaus ullo modo impedire, quantum ad ipsum Berthramium pertinet. Hec conventio facta est in capitulo Sancti Pauli concessione Roberti episcopi London' et fide firmata ex utraque parte, scilicet: Nicholaus fide firmavit sine malo ingenio quod ex sua parte hoc tenebit, et Bertramius similiter. Hiis testibus: Ricardo archidiacono; Magister Radulphus;[1] Robertus Catamo; Robertus Auco; Gaufridus cunestabulus; Odo canonicus; Nicholaus canonicus; Walterus; Theodoricus; Rannulphus; Nicholaus; Hubertus; Magister Henricus; Hugo; Baldewinus; Gaufridus; Hamo; Hunfridus presbiter; Radulphus presbiter; Rogerus filius Billehold; Thiwoldus canonicus; Robertus filius Nebulari.

MSS: (1) WAD, ff. 475v–476.
    Rubric: Conventio inter Bertramium et Nicholaum filium Clementis de ecclesia Sancti Mathei in Friday Strete.
        1. Attestations change to the nominative case, indicating that in the original they opened with *Testes sunt hii.*
(2) F, f. 249r–v (which concluded: *hiis testibus* etc.).
Rubric: Confirmatio ecclesie Sancti Mathei in Frydaystret London' per capitulum Sancti Pauli. Capelum xxxiij.
Marginalia: Cyrogr[aphum].

Date: Within the limits of Robert de Sigillo's term as bishop of London (*Fasti* I, 2). Mr Nicholas Clement became a canon of St Paul's 1138 × 1150, and occurs as such down to 1183 × 1184, and perhaps later (ibid., 39, 90).

Note: On Nicholas son of Clement, see also *E.C. St Paul*, nos. 72, 134, 169. Abbot Gervase's confirmation to Nicholas son of Clement required him to pay 10*s.* annually towards the monks' clothing (**255**). The rubric in F suggests that the income of the church was assigned to the Lady Chapel of Westminster. The church of St Matthew, with a pension of 10*s.* (cf. **255**), and the adjacent and appurtenant land rendering 14*s.*, was confirmed to Westminster by Bp. Gilbert Foliot (**211**). Richard the archdeacon (Richard Ruffus I), was archdeacon of Essex, not of London (*Fasti* I, 12–13).

381. Confirmation by Adam son of Alulf, in the presence of the whole parish, to the church of St Matthew, Friday Street, to its rector, the priest Philip, and to all his successors, of all his land beside the gable of that church towards the west; in length, including the wall towards the west, it measures 22 of the feet of St Paul's; in width, with the walls towards the south and the north, it contains 24 of those feet. The church and its rectors will hold this land quit of all secular service. Adam received 7 marks (£4. 13*s.* 4*d.*) from Philip who, at Adam's request, pronounced an anathema on anyone who alienated this land. London 1200.

Sciant presentes et futuri quod ego Adam filius Alulfi dedi, concessi et hac presenti carta mea confirmavi Deo et ecclesie Sancti Mathei in Fridaistrat, et Philippo sacerdoti tunc tempore in eadem ecclesia ministranti, et omnibus successoribus suis in predicta ecclesia Deo servientibus, totam terram meam proximam iuxta gabulum predicte ecclesie Sancti Mathei versus occidentalem partem jacentem, que terra continet in longitudine cum muro versus occidentalem partem viginti et duos pedes de pedibus Sancti Pauli; in latitudine vero cum muris versus australem partem et borialem partem viginti et quatuor pedes de eisdem pedibus. Habendam et tenendam predicte ecclesie et rectoribus eiusdem ecclesie, libere, quiete, integre, finabiliter, absque omni servitio seculari. Ita quod ego predictus Adam vel heredes mei de predicta terra nichil habere vel capere vel exigere, sive minuere poterimus imperpetuum. Et sciendum est quod ego predictus Adam et heredes mei terram sepedictam predicte ecclesie et rectoribus eiusdem ecclesie contra omnes homines et feminas debemus warantizare et acquietare. Pro hac igitur donatione et concessione et warantizatione, et presentis carte mee confirmatione, ego predictus Adam filius Alulfi recepi de predicta ecclesia septem marcas argenti, scilicet per manum Philippi sacerdotis tunc tempore in eadem ecclesia ministrantis. Ita videlicet quod predictus Philippus sacerdos, et omnes successores eius in eadem ecclesia ministrantes, et Deo servientes, predictam terram integre, honorifice, et inconcusse inperpetuum habeant et possideant. Preterea sepedictus Philippus sacerdos, per consensum et assensum et petitionem predicti Ade, excommunicavit atque anathematizavit omnes homines et feminas qui hanc predictam terram a predicta ecclesia vel a rectoribus predicte ecclesie seperabunt vel alienabunt. Hec donacio et concessio fuit facta et hec sententia data anno ab Incarnatione Domini Nostri Jhesu Christi M°CC° coram presentia omnium parochianorum. Hiis testibus: Henrico filio Ailwini, tunc tempore maiore London'; Rogero filio Alani; Jordano de Turre; Johanne filio Herlizun, tunc tempore aldermanno nostre guade; Thoma, Johanne, Willelmo, Bartholomeo, filiis suis; Constantino filio Alulfi, et Arnaldo fratre suo; Rogero le Duc; Petro filio eius; Willelmo, Roberto, Martino, filiis Aliz; Andrea Albo; Henrico filio eius; Laurencio filio Gregorio; Ricardo, Johanne, Thoma, Willelmo, filiis eius; Johanne Olivant; Petro filio eius; Henrico filio Henrici cum capillis; Laurencio filio eius; Radulfo Olivant; Richero de selda domini regis; Michaele Potel; Waltero le seuer; Johanne Mauger; Radulfo Oxon'; Godefrido aurifabro; Everardo auri-fabro; Rogero fratre suo; Nicholao aurifabro; Martino aurifabro; Johanne le Corner, aurifabro; Abel aurifabro; Willelmo de Berking', aurifabro; Gauger Gernoun; Galfrido aurifabro; Thoma aurifabro, multisque aliis.

MS: WAD, ff. 483v–484.
>Rubric: Carta Ade filii Aluffi de tota terra sua iuxta gabulum ecclesie Sancti Mathei in Fridaystrete.

Note: The witnesses, in addition to the mayor, comprise a combination of leading Londoners and parishioners of St Matthew's.

382. Confirmation by Roger Bursar (le Borser), mercer, to Jocelin son of Jocelin of Cornhill that neither he nor his heirs will sell or otherwise alienate the land which he holds of Jocelin in the parish of St Michael, Cornhill, lying between the land of William son of Nicholas the goldsmith, and that of Agnes, sister of St Thomas [Becket]. The land will revert to Jocelin or his heirs in the event of the failure of heirs. Roger has sworn to uphold this undertaking in the soke of Dom William de Sainte Mère Eglise [London, Dec. 1189 × *ante* 7 Dec. 1199]

Sciant presentes et futuri quod ego Rogerus le Borser, mercennarius, concessi et huic scripto meo specialiter confirmavi Jocelino filio Jocelini de Cornhill' quod ego nec heredes mei poterimus ullo tempore terram illam quam ab eo teneo in parochia Sancti Michaelis de Cornhill', que est inter terram Willelmi filii Nicholai aurifabri et terram Agnetis sororis Beati Thome, numquam vendere, invadiare, legare, neque aliquo[1] alio modo alienare debemus a dicto Jocelino et heredibus suis. Sed forte si ego vel heredes mei aliquo tempore sine herede de me vel de meis heredibus legittime exeuntibus obierimus, dicta[1] terra[1] cum edificiis et pertinentiis eidem Jocelino et suis heredibus libere, quiete revertat. Hanc vero concessionem[1] sine fraude et dolo tenendam[1] et observandam tactis sacrosanctis Ewangeliis pro me et pro heredibus meis, juravi in soca Domini Willelmi Sancte Marie [*sic*] Ecclesie. Hiis testibus: Galfrido Aldreman; Magistro Hugone, capellano; Waltero de Stebbeheth'; Henrico de Chesewik, soquereve; Oliuero, clerico de Turrim; Admundo filio Girardi; Willelmo Foberd; Willelmo Wilequin; Johanne filio Danielis; Johanne Jacob; Main drapario; Hosmundo cordewaner;

Johanne Begi; Waltero Lardor; Matheo Pistree; Willemo de Estchep; Galfrido de Estchep; Ada le Gost; Johanne le Gos; Ada diacono, et multis aliis.

MS: (1) WAM 13899.
  13.6 × 12.2 cm; t.u. 1.2 cm.
  Slots for cords, now missing.
  Endorsed: (a) Carta Rogeri le Borser de quadam terra in parochia Sancti Michaelis de Cornhulle Jocelino filio Jocelini de Cornhill concessa (13C). (b) Sacrist' (14C).
    1. MS stained: word supplied from copy.
  (2) WAD, f. 368v.
Date: Prob. issued between William de Sainte Mère Eglise's appointment as Dean of St Martin le Grand and his election to the bishopric of London (*Fasti* I, 2, 48).
Note: See Honeybourne, 'Sanctuary Boundaries', 316–33.

383. Notification by John Buccuinte of his grant to Jocelin of Cornhill and his heirs of that land lying between the land of Reginald and that of William son of Nicholas, to hold of John and his heirs in fee and inheritance for 6s. annually. Dislodgement prohibited; and neither can John or his heirs alienate the land except for [? non-payment of] the rent. Jocelin and his heirs may sell or alienate the fee of that land as they please, except to churches or Jews, saving the right of his lord, John Buccuinte. Jocelin gave a gersum of 2lb. of pepper. [Later 12C]

Sciant presentes et futuri quod ego Johannes Bucc' concessi Gocelino de Cornelle et heredibus suis terram illam que est inter terram Reginaldi et inter terram Willelmi filii Nicholai; tenendam de me et de heredibus meis sibi et heredibus suis in feudo et hereditate finabiliter pro vj solidis reddendis inde per annum pro omni servitio ad duos terminos, scilicet: infra octo dies Pasche iij solidos, et infra octo dies Sancti Michaelis iij solidos. Ita quod ego predictus Johannes non possum disherbergare predictum Gocelinum vel heredes suos propter me herbergare vel heredes meos; nec ego predictus Johannes neque heredes mei non possimus de predicta terra vendere nec dare neque dispendere vel invadiare nisi predictum censum terre, scilicet sex solidos. Et ego predictus Gocelinus et heredes mei possimus feudum prenominate terre et vendere atque invadiare ubi voluerimus, nisi ecclesiis vel Judeis, salvo jure domini mei Johannis Bucc' et heredum suorum. Et pro hac concessione atque conventione predictus Gocelinus dedit michi Johanni Bucc' duas libras piperis in gersumam.[1] Hiis testibus:[2] Helias capellanus; Henricus clericus; Philippus scriptor; Radulfus filius Roberti; Johannes Burguillun; Jacobus Drapier; Willelmus Norreis; Hamo nepos; Hamo filius Radulfi Brant; Alanus clericus, et satis aliorum.[3]

MS: WAD, f. 368v.
  Rubric: Carta Johannis Bucc' de terra que est inter terram Reginaldi et terram Willelmi filii Nicholai.

1. MS: *gersume*.
2. Attestations in nominative, suggesting that in the original the preceding phrase was *testes sunt*.
3. MS: *alios*.

384. Confirmation by Alice, daughter of John Buccuinte and widow of Henry Naget, to Jocelin son of Jocelin of Cornhill, of her whole land in the parish of St Michael, Cornhill, between the land which William of Pontefract held of the nuns of Clerkenwell, and that of William son of Nicholas, goldsmith. She also confirmed her whole land between that of the aforesaid William son of Nicholas and that of Agnes, sister of St Thomas [Becket] the martyr, which lands her father John Buccuinte gave her. Jocelin may hold or alienate these lands as he pleases, rendering 11*s.* annually. Dislodgement prohibited; gersum of 16*s.* 4*d.* [Late 12C]

Sciant presentes et futuri quod ego Athelicia filia Johannis Bocuinte, quondam uxor Henrici Naget, in viduitate mea et in ligia potestate mea, concessi et dimisi et presenti carta mea confirmavi Jocelino filio Jocelini de Cornhull' totam terram meam cum pertinentiis suis quam habui in parochia Sancti Michaelis de Cornhull' inter terram quam Willelmus de Ponte Fracto tenuit de monialibus de Clerkenewell', et terram Willelmi aurifabri filii Nicholai. Preterea concessi et dimisi et hac presenti carta mea confirmavi eidem Jocelino totam terram meam cum omnibus pertinentiis suis, que est inter terram Willelmi filii Nicholai prefati et terram Agnetis sororis Beati Thome martiris. Quas videlicet terras cum pertinentiis suis predictus Johannes Bocuinte pater meus mihi dedit ac dimisit, scilicet, quicquid in hiis terris habui, in longitudine et latitudine et in rebus cunctis. Habendas et tenendas eidem Jocelino et heredibus suis vel quibuscumque illas dare, vendere, legare, aut assignare voluerit et heredibus eorum, de me et de heredibus meis finabiliter, in feodo et hereditate, libere, quiete, integre, bene, in pace; reddendo inde annuatim mihi vel heredibus meis pro omni servicio et exaccione et rebus cunctis undecim solidos sterlingorum ad quatuor terminos anni, videlicet: infra quindenam Festi Sancti Michaelis triginta et tres denarios; infra quindenam Natalis Domini triginta et tres denarios; infra quindenam Pasche triginta et tres denarios; et infra quindenam Festi Nativitatis Sancti Johannis Baptiste triginta et tres denarios, sine omni occasione et meskenning'. Et sciendum est quod ego Athelicia predicta, vel heredes mei, vel aliquis alius per nos, vel pro nobis, nullatenus poterimus dehospitare eundem Jocelinum sive heredes suos sive assignatos suos de predictis terris, vel de suis pertinenciis, causa nos vel aliquem alium hominem vel feminam ibidem hospitandi, nec amplius inde poterimus habere, exigere, capere vel clamare imperpetuum quam predictos undecim solidos per annum statutis terminis. Has quoque terras prenominatas cum omnibus pertinentiis suis integre ego Athelicia predicta et heredes mei finabiliter warantizabimus predicto Jocelino et heredibus suis vel quibuscumque illas dare, vendere, legare aut assignare voluerit, et heredibus eorum; et de omnibus demandis acquietabimus; pro eis per omnia respondebimus contra omnes homines et feminas per predictum servitium undecim solidorum per annum pro omnibus rebus. Pro hac igitur dimissione, concessione, warantizatione, acquietatione, et sigilli mei appositione, et presentis carte mee confirmatione, dedit prenominatus Jocelinus mihi Athelicie sexdecim solidos et quatuor denarios sterlingorum[1] in gersumam. Hiis testibus: Domino Simone, capellano de Sancto Michaele de Cornhill'; David, capellano de Sancto Christoforo; Willelmo de Ripa, capellano; Roberto Justice; Philippo de Wint'; Radulfo Perer; Petro de Braking'; Radulfo Palmer, cuteler; Willelmo pictore; Hugone fabro; Gilberto Ferrun; Ricardo Sobuld'; Roberto de Hakene, fruit[ario]; Reginaldo Cuteler, et aliis.

MSS: (1) WAM 13900.
     19.4 × 16 cm; t.u. 1.5 cm.
     Slot with tag; seal missing.
     Endorsed: (a) Carta Athelicie filie Johannis Bocuinte de quadam terra in parochia Sancti Michaelis de Cornhulle Jocelino filio Jocelini concessa (13C: last four words added in a second hand). (b) Sacristarius (14C).
     (2) WAD, f. 369.
     1. Adds *premanibus*.
Date: William of Pontefract attested grants made to Clerkenwell priory in the 1180s and 1190s (*Cart. Clerkenwell*, nos. 41, 61, 85, 87, 92, 96, 98, 199).

385. Notification by Richard Blund of London that, for the health of his soul, those of his parents, wife, children, his nephew Robert, of all their ancestors and benefactors, and of all the faithful departed, he has confirmed in perpetual alms, to St Peter of Westminster and the convent, for pittance, one of his stalls in the parish of St Nicholas Shambles, lying towards the west, in front of the house formerly belonging to Geoffrey of Arden. He asks that his name should be inscribed in the martyrology. [Mid 12C]

Ricardus Blundus de London' omnibus Francis et Anglicis hoc scriptum audientibus, salutem in Christo. Notum sit vobis quod ego, pietatis intuitu et pro salute anime mee, et pro anima patris mei et matris, et pro anima uxoris mee et meorum infantium, et pro anima Roberti nepotis, et pro animabus omnium antecessorum nostrorum et nostrorum benefactorum, et pro animabus omnium fidelium defunctorum, dedi et concessi et hac mea confirmavi carta ecclesie Sancti Petri de Westmonasterio et toti conventui ibidem Deo servienti, unum de stallis meis quos habui in parochia Sancti Nicholai ad Mazatriam, scilicet illum qui jacet apud occidentalem partem et qui est ante domum que fuit Galfridi Darden', in perpetuam elemosinam finabiliter, sine ullo retenemento michi vel heredibus meis, ad illorum pitanciam sine fine, scilicet unum illorum quem Willelmus Hiberniensis tenuit de me. Et omnes illi qui hanc elemosinam alibi ponent nisi ad predictam pitanciam excomunicati sunt. Et ego peto quod nomen meum scriptum sit in martilogio. Hiis testibus: Petro capellano de Colcherch'; Walerammo filio Meilla'; Huberto nepote Galfridi; Willelmo filio Roberti; Roberto fratre suo; Alexandro filio Fauk[alsio]; Galfrido de Soam; Margareta, et multis aliis.

MS: WAD, f. 602.
> Rubric: Carta Ricardi Blundi de London' de uno stallo in parochia Sancti Nicholai ad Mazatriam.
> Marginalia: London'.

Date: The grantor's nephew is possibly the Robert Blund who was sheriff 1196–7 (Beaven, *Aldermen*, 364).

386. Grant by William Turpin of King Henry's chamber to Rose his wife of all his land outside Ludgate, with its stone houses and appurtenances, which was held by Osmund the carter and Ermengard his wife and of which they made him heir in the King's Court. Rose is to have the land freely by paying 1s. 6d. a year to the nuns of Clerkenwell and 4s. to Roger de Friville and his heirs at Michaelmas and 2s. to Ralph de Rosei at two terms. Rose can give this to any church she pleases for the souls of herself, of her husband and of King Henry. [c. 1177]

Sciant presentes et futuri quod ego Willelmus Turpin de camera Domini Regis Henrici dedi et concessi et hac presenti carta mea confirmavi Roesie uxori mee pro servitio suo totam terram meam extra Ludgate cum domibus lapideis et omnibus pertinentiis suis: quam videlicet terram Osmundus caretarius et Ermengarda uxor eius tenuerunt, et de qua terra me fecerunt heredem in curia domini mei Regis Henrici, de predicta terra cartas quas habuerunt michi resignantes. Habendam et tenendam predicte Roesie libere et quiete, integre et honorifice, absque reclamatione omnium heredum meorum, reddendo scilicet de prefata terra: monialibus de Clerchenewelle decem et octo denarios per annum pro omni servitio; et Rogero de Frivile et heredibus suis iiij solidos ad Festum Sancti Michaelis singulis annis; et Radulfo de Rosei et heredibus suis duodecim denarios ad Pascha et duodecim denarios ad Festum Sancti Michaelis singulis annis pro omni servitio. Predicta vero Roesia, cum in fata decesserit vel in vita sua, si ei placuerit, secundum promissionem et conventionem inter nos factam, pro animabus nostris et pro anima domini mei Regis Henrici, ecclesie cui voluerit ad honorem Dei et Beate Virginis Marie predictam terram cum pertinentiis suis et in puram et perpetuam dabit elemosinam, absque omni calumpnia et reclamatione heredum meorum. Ut autem hec mea concessio et donatio rata et stabilis permaneat, eam presentis scripti testimonio et sigilli mei appositione roboravi. His testibus: Willelmo filio Radulfi, senescallo de Normannia; Stephano, senescallo de Andegavia; Mansero Biset; Willelmo Crevequor; Willelmo de Hastinges; Willelmo Malet; Sahero de Quenci; Ricardo Giffard; Philippo de Windlesores; Roberto de Broc; Radulfo Purcel; Bernardo coco, et multis aliis.

MSS: (1) WAM 13844.
> 16 × 11.2 cm; t.u. 1.1 cm.
> Seal: fixed by tag of brown tape; orange; 4.3 × 2.6 cm; key on obverse; legend: + SIGILL WILLELMI TURPIN.

Endorsed: (a) Willelmus Turpin dat Roesie uxori sue totam terram suam cum pertinentiis extra Lutgate (14C). (b) Ludgate: capella iiij (14C).
(2) WAD, f. 560v.

Date: Manasser Biset d. 1176 × 1177 (Sanders, 5). William Fitz Ralph's term as seneschal of Normandy had prob. begun by that date (C. H. Haskins, *Norman Institutions*, Harvard Historical Studies XXIV (1925), 180). The attestation of Stephen seneschal of Anjou is that of Stephen de Tours *alias* de Marzai, known to have been in office *c.* 1180–1189 (Eyton, *Itinerary*, 235, 297. No predecessors are listed).

Note: *Cart. Clerkenwell*, no. 306, dated by the editor 'shortly before 1187', must in fact antedate this charter.

387. Confirmation to the Lady Altar in the church of St Peter of Westminster, in pure and perpetual alms, to provide lights, by Rose the cushion-maker, widow of William Turpin of King Henry's Chamber, for her soul, that of 'her lord' [William] and of all their ancestors, of all her land outside Ludgate, with its stone houses, which William confirmed to her by charter. This land was held by Osmund carter and Ermengarde his wife, who made William their heir in the court of H II and gave him the deeds. The proctor of the Lady Altar will hold the land freely, saving the service due to the nuns of Clerkenwell, and to Roger de Friville and Ralph de Rosei and their respective heirs. Rose has offered upon the Lady Altar this present charter and those of 'her lord'. [Temp. John, *ante* Jan. 1214]

Sciant presentes et futuri quod ego Roesia la custurere, que fui uxor Willelmi Turpin de camera Domini Regis Henrici, pro salute anime mee et pro anima domini mei et omnium antecessorum nostrorum, dedi et concessi et hac presenti carta mea confirmavi Deo et altari Beate Virginis Marie in ecclesia Beati Petri Westmonasterii in puram et perpetuam elemosinam ad luminaria eiusdem altaris administranda, totam terram meam extra Ludgate, cum domibus lapideis et omnibus pertinenciis suis, quam scilicet terram predictus dominus meus Willelmus Turpin mihi pro servicio meo dedit et carta sua confirmavit; illam videlicet terram quam Osmundus caretarius et Ermengarda uxor eius tenuerunt; et de qua terra predictum Willelmum dominum meum fecerunt heredem in curia Domini Regis Henrici, cartas et munimenta omnia que de predicta terra habuerunt illi resignantes. Habendam et tenendam procuratori predicti altaris Beate Virginis Marie, libere, quiete, integre et honorifice, absque omni reclamatione omnium heredum meorum vel domini mei, sicut carta predicti domini mei testatur, salvo servicio monialium de Clerchenewelle, et Rogeri de Frivile et heredum suorum, et Radulfi de Rosei et heredum suorum. Hanc autem cartam meam et cartas et munimenta predicti domini mei de prefata terra super altare Beate Virginis Marie obtuli, et prefate ecclesie in perpetuum resignavi. Ut autem hec mea donatio stabilis et rata permaneat eam presentis scripti testimonio et sigilli mei appositione roboravi. Hiis testibus: Symone, Alexandro et Ricardo, capellanis; Odone aurifabro; Stephano de Berkinges; Ada,

nepote episcopi; Galfrido de Cruce; Thoma vinitore; Ivone de Medmeham; Nicholao de cellario; Laurentio Muschat; Ricardo filio Ranulfi;
Ada, Galfrido, Johanne, Willelmo Stutel, servientibus de ecclesia; Elia
parmentario, et multis aliis.

MSS: (1) WAM 13845.
    20.6 × 13.7 cm; t.u. 1.7 cm.
    Seal: on tag; green; 5.3 × 3.3 cm; standing female figure facing left,
    holding a fleur-de-lys; legend: + SIGILL. ROHE.I.S DE BLAIS.
    Endorsed: (a) Ludgate capella v (14C). (b) Carta Roysie la custerere
    de quadam parte terre cum pertinentiis data capelle ad luminario-
    rum sustentationem extra Ludgate London'.
    (2) WAD, f. 560v–561.
Date: Attestations and hand; later than **386** but within the term of office
of Abbot Ralph Arundel, who granted this land to Alexander of Swerford (**327**). William Turpin was still active *c.* Michaelmas 1199 (*PR 1
John*, 225), and possibly as late as 1206 (*PR 8 John*, 120), but became a
monk before 29 Sept. 1209 (*PR 11 John*, 152). Already, in 1204, a
plaintiff named Cecily claimed as dower land in Dorset, conferred on her
by William Turpin, formerly her husband, but this was contested on the
grounds that the couple had never been married (*Curia Regis Rolls* III,
150).

388. Notification by Brichtmar of Haverhill that, with the assent of his
son and heir, William, he has confirmed to St Peter of Westminster, in
perpetual alms, 6*s.* annual rent from the land which Robert hosier holds
of the fee of William Matel outside Ludgate. Robert and his heirs, or
whoever holds that land, will pay the rent to the sacrist, to buy wine for
masses. Brichtmar has willingly and devoutly granted these poor alms to
the abbey for his soul and that of his wife Denise, who is buried there; for
those of his son William and his wife Alice and their children, and for all
his (Brichtmar's) ancestors and descendants, so that the monks may
remember them in their prayers, and they may participate in all spiritual
works of that church, as Abbot Walter and the convent granted in full
chapter, and received them into confraternity. [1175 × 1190]

Noverint omnes tam presentes quam futuri qui litteras istas viderint vel
audierint quod ego Brichtmarus de Haverhulla, voluntate et assensu
Willelmi filii et heredis mei, donavi et presenti carta confirmavi Deo et
Sancto Petro Westmonasterii in perpetuam elemosinam vj solidos
singulis annis de terra quam Robertus caliciarius tenet de feudo Willelmi
Matel extra portam Lundon' que dicitur Ludgate. Hos vero vj solidos
predictus Robertus caliciarius et heredes sui, vel quicumque terram illam
tenuerint, solvent annuatim sacriste Westmonasterii duobus terminis
anni ad emendum vinum ad missas, scilicet: tres solidos ad Nativitatem
Sancti Johannis Baptiste, et tres solidos ad Natale Domini. Hanc autem
mee parvitatis elemosinam voluntarie et devote donavi prenominate
ecclesie pro salute anime mee et Dionisie uxoris mee, que ibi honorifice
sepulta est, et Willelmi filii mei; et A[   ] uxoris sue, et filiorum
suorum, necnon et omnium antecessorum et posteriorum meorum, ut

fratres inibi Deo servientes memores nostri sint iugiter in orationibus suis, et ut participes simus a modo omni tempore missarum, psalmorum, orationum, elemosinarum, et omnium beneficiorum ecclesie illius, sicut Dominus Walterus, abbas eiusdem loci, et totus conventus, in plenario capitulo nobis unanimiter concesserunt, et in fraternitatem et societatem suam nos tam in vita quam in morte susceperunt.

MS: WAD, f. 367v.
> Rubric: Carta Brichtmari de Haverhulla de sex solidis redditus extra Ludegate.

Date: Temp. Abbot Walter.
Note: See Harvey, *WA*, 373n., 386n.

389. Grant, in fee and inheritance, by Roger de Friville to Augustine Fitz Ailwin of his whole land outside Ludgate, next to the house of Osmund, to hold at an annual rent of 5*s*. Dislodgement prohibited; gersum of 5*s*. [Late Henry II]

Sciant tam presentes quam futuri quod ego Rogerus de Frivilla concedo Augustino filio Ailwini totam terram meam extra Ludgate que jacet juxta domum Osmundi in feodo et hereditate et finabiliter; tenendam illi et heredibus suis de me et heredibus meis, reddendo annuatim pro omni servitio quinque solidos ad Festum Sancti Michaelis sine omni occasione. Ita quod ego Rogerus nec heredes mei non poterimus predictum Augustinum vel heredes suos deherbergare propter me vel aliquem alium herbergandum. Pro hac autem concessione dedit mihi predictus Augustinus v solidos in gersummam. Et ego Rogerus et heredes mei warantizabimus totam predictam terram prefato Augustino et heredibus suis contra omnes homines. Hiis testibus: Johanne filio Nigelli aldermanno; Augustino calicier; David parmenter; Folchmaro pistore; Osmundo; Galfrido de Wycumbe; Johanne Oysel; Johanne Morin; Adam de Waltham; Ricardo de Hereford; Willelmo Macon; Willelmo B[er]engier; Gervasio centurier; Godefrido Palmer; Roberto fabro; Roberto Palmer; Radulfo fruitario; Thurstano Franciger; Petro senario; Willelmo de Writele; Willelmo Orpedeman, et pluribus aliis. Tota autem hec predicta terra erit quieta hoc anno presenti de predicto censu, et ad Festum Sancti Michaelis proximum intrabit prefatus Augustinus ad censum suum reddendum de prefata terra.

MS: WAD, ff. 474v–475.
> Rubric: Carta Rogeri de Frivilla de tota terra sua extra Ludgate.

Date: Cf. others in series (**386** ff.). John Fitz Nigel was sheriff of London in 1177–78 (Reynolds, 'Rulers of London', 355. See also Beaven, *Aldermen*, I, 364).

390. Notification from Reginald, baker of Richard bp. of London, and Emma his wife that they have confirmed to the Lady Altar of Westminster, in pure and perpetual alms, to provide lights a rent of 6*s*. from the land they hold of the canons of St Osith in the parish of Ludgate, lying between the land Reginald holds of the Hospital of St James near Charing and the land which was William Turpin's of King Henry's chamber. [Temp. John]

Sciant presentes et futuri quod ego Reginaldus, pistor Ricardi London' episcopi, et Emma uxor mea dedimus et concessimus et hac presenti carta nostra confirmavimus Deo et altari Beate Marie Virginis West-monasterii, in puram et perpetuam elemosinam ad invenienda luminaria coram prefato altari, sex solidatos redditus de terra nostra quam tenemus de canonicis Sancte Osithe in parochia de Ludgate: que videlicet terra iacet inter terram nostram quam tenemus de Hospitali Sancti Iacobi prope la Cherringe et inter terram que fuit Willelmi Turpin de camera Regis Henrici; percipiendos de nobis et heredibus nostris in perpetuum de prefata terra ad duos terminos anni, scilicet: ad Purificationem Beate Marie tres solidos; et ad Vincula Sancti Petri tres solidos, solvendos custodi predicti altaris qui pro tempore luminaria ibidem ministraverit. Ego autem Reginaldus et Emma uxor mea et heredes nostri prefatos sex solidatos redditus prefato altari warantizabimus contra omnes homines et omnes feminas. Ut autem hec nostra donatio et concessio firma sit et stabilis, eam presentis scripti testimonio et sigilli nostri appositione roboravimus. Hiis testibus: Roberto capellano; Johanne filio Willelmi; Odone aurifabro, tunc preposito; Thoma filio Emme; Reinerio pistore; Ricardo filio Heimundi; Stephano de Berking'; Roberto de Crokesl'; Roberto de Cleygate; Laurentio Muscat; Ada de ecclesia; Willelmo de Scardebuith; Helya parmentario; Galfrido de ecclesia; Waltero clerico, et multis aliis.

MSS: (1) WAM 13846.
    20 × 11.7 cm; t.u. 1.6 cm.
    Seals: green; on tags. (1) 4 × 3.7 cm; fleur de lys; legend: SIGILL.
    REGINALDI PISTORIS. (2) 4 cm diameter; floriated square cross:
    legend: EME LA FEME ARM . . . (broken) DLES.
    Endorsed: (a) Reginaldus pistor et Emma uxor sua . . . [hole and
    stain] tandum . . . in parochia de . . . (b) . . . capella ij.
    (2) WAD, f. 560.
Date: Attestations; Odo the goldsmith as reeve.
Note: Abbot William d'Humez (1214–22) and the convent granted to Richard the fruiterer, in fee and inheritance, the land acquired from Reginald and Emma, to hold at a rent of 15s. due to the Abbey, and a further 2s. due annually in alms to St Martin's church, Ludgate (WAD f. 475v.).

391. Confirmation by Roger de Friville, for his soul and those of his ancestors, to St Peter and the convent of Westminster, of the whole land outside Ludgate lying next to the house which formerly belonged to Osmund. This land, with its buildings and other appurtenances, was given to St Peter and the convent by Augustine Fitz Ailwin, and later by Reginald, baker of Richard [Fitz Nigel], bp. of London, and his wife Emma. The convent will render 5s. annually. Dislodgement prohibited.

Roger and his wife received a gersum of 2 besants (4*s.*) and 2 marks (£1. 6*s.* 8*d.*). [Temp. John]

Sciant presentes et futuri quod ego Rogerus de Frivilla, pro salute anime mee et antecessorum meorum, dedi et concessi et hac presenti carta mea confirmavi Deo et Sancto Petro et conventui Westmonasterii totam terram illam extra Ludegate que jacet juxta domum que fuit Osmundi, quam scilicet terram cum edificiis et pertinentiis suis Augustinus filius Ailwini, et postea Reginaldus pistor Ricardi London' episcopi et Emma uxor ipsius Reginaldi, Deo et Sancto Petro dederunt et predicto conventui. Habendam et tenendam prefato conventui de me et heredibus meis finabiliter, libere et quiete, integre et plenarie, solvendo michi et heredibus meis annuatim quinque solidos ad Festum Sancti Michaelis sine omni occasione pro omni servitio. Ita quod nec ego Rogerus nec heredes mei poterimus illum qui loco conventus tenebit predictum tenementum deherbergare pro me vel alio herbergando. Et ego Rogerus de Frivilla et heredes mei totam predictam terram warantizabimus predicto conventui contra omnes homines. Pro hac autem donatione, concessione et warantizatione et carte mee confirmatione, dedit mihi predictus conventus in gersummam et uxori mei duos bisantios et duas marcas. Hiis testibus: Willelmo de Bukingham'; Rogero Enganet; Henrico Sumer; Ricardo Testard; Nicholao filio Galfridi; Odone aurifabro; Johanne filio Edwardi; Petro de Wanden'; Stephano de Berking'; Ada de Westminster; Wimundo pistore; Pagano Dolbe; Gaufrido de Cruce, et multis aliis.

MS: WAD, f. 475.
    Rubric: Carta eiusdem Rogeri cirographata de tota terra que fuit Osmundi extra Ludgate.
Date: Attestation of Roger Enganet, with those of Henry Sumer and Richard Testard (cf. Rosser, 'Medieval Westminster', 360).
Note: Prob. the convent was systematically acquiring property outside Ludgate, temp. John, since this land, granted by Reginald and Emma (**390**) and confirmed by Roger de Friville, adjoined that acquired from Rose, widow of William Turpin, which itself owed service to Roger (**386–7**). Early in the reign of Henry III, Roger s. of Roger de Friville quitclaimed to the prior and convent 5*s.* annual rent which they formerly rendered for land outside Ludgate, which had been granted to them by Augustine Fitz Ailwyn and by Reginald, the baker of Bp. Richard, and by Emma his wife (WAD, f. 475).

392. Confirmation by Turold, master of the Hospital of St James near Charing, and the brethren and sisters of that house, that he has confirmed the grant made by Reginald, baker of Richard bp. of London, to the church of St Peter of Westminster and the convent of the land that he holds of the fee of the hospital in Fleet Street; this land lies between that of Geoffrey of Wycombe and that of the canons of St Osyth. The convent is to pay 3*s.* a year to the hospital, as Reginald did. [Temp. John]

Sciant presentes et futuri quod ego Turoldus, magister Hospitalis Sancti

Jacobi iuxta Cherringe, et fratres et sorores eiusdem loci, concedimus et hac presenti carta nostra confirmamus ecclesie Sancti Petri West- monasterii et eiusdem loci conventui donum et elemosinam quam Reginaldus, pistor Ricardi episcopi London', eidem ecclesie et conventui fecit et concessit de terra que de feodo nostro est in Flietestrate, quam predictus Reginaldus de nobis tenet. Que videlicet terra jacet inter terram Gaufridi de Wicumba et inter terram canonicorum Sancte Osithe. Predictus vero conventus Westmonasterii donum prefati Reginaldi et elemosinam libere et quiete et honorifice, sine calumpnia et exactione, finabiliter, possidebit reddendo inde singulis annis ecclesie Sancti Jacobi et successoribus nostris tres solidos pro omni servitio; quos prius prefatus Reginaldus nobis de predicta terra persolvit ad duos terminos anni, scilicet: infra octo dies Natalis Domini decem et octo denarios, et infra octo dies Sancti Johannis Baptiste decem et octo denarios. Ut autem hec nostra concessio et confirmatio rata permaneat et stabilis eam presentis scripti testimonio et sigilli nostri appositione roboravimus. Hiis testibus: Simone capellano; Alexandro capellano; Odone aurifabro; Henrico Sumer; Stephano de Berking'; Wimundo pistore; Petro de Wandene; Gaufrido de Cruce; Gaufrido Cuttelebatte, et multis aliis.

MSS: (1) WAM 13847.
 19.6 × 9.6 cm; t.u. 1.5 cm.
 Seal: green; 6.7 × 4.6 cm; standing cleric holding a cross in left hand; legend: . . . SIGILL . . . SAN[CT]I IA[COBI] INF. . .
 Endorsed: (a) Confirmatio magistri et fratrum Sancti Jacobi de donatione cuiusdam partis terre facta capelle in Fletestret (14C). (b) Ludgate: capella iij (14C).
 (2) WAD, f. 560r–v.
Date: Later than Reginald's grant to the abbey of rent from adjacent land (**390**). Turold was in office in the reign of Richard I, and in the mayoralty of Henry Fitz Ailwin, although, since the earliest known appearance of the next master is 1218 × 1219, Turold may have continued in office for some time after 1212 (*VCH London*, I, 545b and n. 45).

393. Grant by Henry of Ely, clerk, to the abbot and convent of a messuage which Robert Crutgeorne held in St Clement's parish towards London. Gersum of £1. [Temp. John]

Sciant presentes et futuri quod ego Henricus de Ely clericus concessi et hac presenti carta mea confirmavi abbati de Westmonasterio et eiusdem loci conventui unum mesuagium cum omnibus pertinentiis, scilicet: illud quod Robertus Crutgeorne tenuit in parochia Sancti Clementis versus Londoniam; *tenendum bene et in pace, absque omni calumpnia mei vel heredum meorum inperpetuum.* Pro hac autem concessione et carte mee confirmatione dederunt mihi predictus abbas et predictus conventus viginti solidos esterlingorum. Ego vero Henricus et heredes mei waran- tizabimus predictum mesuagium cum pertinentiis prefatis monachis con- tra omnes gentes. Et ut hec concessio mea stabilis et inconcussa permaneat, presenti scripto confirmavi, et sigilli mei testimonio cor- roboravi. Ego etiam Henricus et Walterus filius meus et heres, tunc presens, affidavimus in pleno halimoto de Westmonasterio firmiter tenere prescriptum pactum predictis monachis absque omni dolo et fraude. Hiis testibus: Ricardo Testard; Henrico Sumer; Johanne filio Edwardi; Nicholao summonitore; Petro de Wend'; Thoma vinitore; Ricardo filio Randulfi; Galfrido fabro; Pagano Dolbe, et multis aliis.

MS: WAD, f. 473.
> Rubric: Carta Henrici de Ely de uno mesuagio in parochia Sancti Clementis versus London.

Date: The first two witnesses were reeves *c.* 1197 × 1217 (Rosser, 'Medieval Westminster', 360).

394. Notification by Walter son of Cecily that he has confirmed to Robert, son of Robert of Rockingham, in fee and inheritance, part of his land which he holds of the abbot of Westminster in the parish of St Clement Danes for an annual rent of 2*s.* Dislodgement prohibited; gersum of 1*s.* 6*d.* [Late 12C]

Notum sit omnibus presentibus et futuris quod ego Walterus filius Cecilie concessi et hac carta mea confirmavi Roberto filio Roberti de Rugingeham' unam partem terre mee quam teneo de abbatia Westmonasterii in parrochia Sancti Clementis Dacorum, tenendam in feodo et hereditate de me et de meis heredibus sibi et heredibus suis finabiliter; reddendo per annum duos solidos ad quatuor terminos pro omnibus servitiis, scilicet: infra octo dies Sancti Michaelis sex denarios; infra octo dies Natalis Domini sex denarios; infra octo dies Pasche sex denarios; et infra octo dies Nativitatis Beati Johannis Baptiste sex denarios. Nec ego Walterus nec heredes mei poterimus predictum Robertum vel heredes suos desherbergare, propter nos nosmet ipsos herbergare. Hanc predictam terram ego Walterus et heredes mei warantizabimus predicto Roberto et heredibus suis contra omnes homines et feminas. Pro hac autem concessione et confirmatione et warantizatione, dedit mihi predictus Robertus decem et octo denarios in gersumam. Hiis testibus: Johanne, persona de Sancto Clemente; Ingeleramo sacerdote; Willelmo, fratre persone; Henrico, fratre suo; Turoldo medico; Roberto, filio suo; Sabrino; Rogero filio Ace; Ansegodo; Christiano; Willelmo fabro; Ordmaro; Henrico Parur; Waltero, filio Nicholai; Rogero Judas; Roberto de Norhamton', et multis aliis.

MSS: (1) WAM 17078.
> 17.7 × 12.7 cm; t.u. 1.5 cm; tag, seal missing.
> Endorsed: (a) Westmonasterium. Carta Walteri filii Cecilie de quadam terra in parrochia Sancti Clementis Dacorum . . . reddere . . . (13C). (b) Celerarius (14C).
> (2) WAD, f. 444r–v.

Date: Earlier than Walter's grant to Abbot William Postard (**395**) with which this charter was prob. acquired by the abbey.
Note: On Robert of Rockingham, cf. *Beauchamp Cartulary*, xxxij.

395. Confirmation by Walter son of Cecily, to [William Postard] abbot of

Westminster and his successors, and to the convent, of 13*s.* worth of rents [from tenements] behind the church of St Clement beyond the bar, between the land of Fichet and that of Roger de la Rie: comprising 1*s.* from Simon of the Gaol; 1*s.* from Ordmar son of Edward; 2*s.* from Robert of Rockingham; 3*s.* from Osbert le Warang; 3*s.* from Robert of the Temple and 3*s.* from William carter. The abbot and convent will render 3*s.* annually to the farm of Westminster for those rents, but retain the surplus. The abbot and convent gave him a gersum of 8 marks (£5. 6*s.* 8*d.*). If Walter cannot warrant the rents, he will make an exchange of equal value, by view of the neighbours. Westminster Halimote, Sept. 1197 × Sept. 1198.

Sciant presentes et futuri quod ego Walterus filius Cecilie dedi et concessi et presenti carta mea confirmavi abbati de Westmonasterio et successoribus suis et conventui eiusdem loci xiij solidos redditus qui iacent retro ecclesiam Sancti Clementis extra barram, inter terram Fichet et terram Rogeri de la Rie, quos Simon de Gaolia et Ordmarus filius Edwardi et Robertus de Ruckingeham et Osbertus de Warang et Robertus de Templo et Willelmus caretarius tenent, scilicet: de Simone de Gaolia xij denarios; et de Ordmaro xij denarios; et de Roberto de Ruckingeham [ij] solidos; et de Osberto le Warang iij solidos; et de Roberto de Te[mplo] iij solidos; et de Willelmo caretario iij solidos. Pro hac autem donatione et carte mee confirmatione predicti abbas et conventus dederunt mihi octo marcas argenti. Et ego Walterus et heredes mei prenominato abbati et successoribus suis et predicto conv[entui] predictos xiij solidos redditus warantizabimus contra omnes h[omines et omnes] feminas. Et si forte contigerit quod ego uel hered[es mei] prenominato abbati et conventui predictos xiij solidos redditus warantizare non poterimus, dabimus eis escambium ad [valentiam] predictorum xiij solidorum reditus vel visu vicinorum catallum [predict]orum abbatis et conventus persolvemus. Et sciendum est quod ego [Walterus] remisi et quietum clamavi predictis abbati et conventui totum ius quod habui in predictis xiij solid[atis] redditus de me et heredibus meis inperpetuum. Ita quod prefati abbas et conventus reddent [in] firma de Westmonasterio iij solidos per annum pro omni servicio pro [illis] xiij solid[at]is redditus, et superplussagium remanebit predicto [abbati] et successoribus suis et sepedicto conventui de Westmonasterio. Et ut hec concessio stabilis et inconcussa permaneat ego eam [presen]ti scripto confirmavi et sigilli mei testimonio co[r-oboravi]. Hoc autem pubblice factum est in pleno halimoto predicti [abbatis] de Westmonasterio, anno regni Regis Ricardi ix°, coram: [Theobaldo] de Feringes, tunc temporis predicti abbatis senescallo; Rogero Enganet, tunc temporis preposito de Westmonasterio; Albino clerico; [Henrico Sumer]; Ricardo janitore; Hugone de Fonte; Galfrido de [Cruce]; Ada de Westmonasterio; Petro de Wandene; Johanne filio Edwardi; Nicholao filio Galfridi; Stephano de Berkinges; Ricardo de Claigate; Galfrido fratre suo; Roberto de Claigate, et multis [aliis] fidelibus domini abbatis de Westmonasterio ibidem tunc presentibus.

MSS: (1) WAM 17080.

    18 × 17 cm; damaged at edge and down centre fold; missing words

supplied from WAD; t.u. 3 cm, with slit and tag in centre; seal missing.

Endorsed: (a) Carta Walteri filii Cecili[e] de xiij solidis annui redditus que iacent retro ecclesie . . . . . . sas extra barra ecclesie Westmonasterii preterea concom' clamat se de . . . et clamium quod habuit in dictis xiij^{cim} . . . (13C). (b) Celera et regist (?14C). (c) . . . xiij^s what granted to abbot of Landys (16C).

(2) WAD, ff. 472v–473.

396. Confirmation in fee and inheritance by Matilda widow of Jospe to Walter of Winchester, spicer, and his heirs, of a house which she had in the parish of St Clement Danes, between the land of Reginald goldsmith to the east, and that of Reginald carpenter to the west (measurements given); to hold at an annual rent of 1*d.* to Matilda, and 8*s.* to 'St Mary of Westminster', dislodgement prohibited; gersum of 13*s.* 4*d.* to Matilda, and 4*d.* to her daughter Margery. [Late 12C]

Sciant presentes et futuri quod ego Matilda que fui uxor Jospe concessi et dimisi et hac presenti carta mea confirmavi Waltero de Winton' lespicer et heredibus suis quandam domum quam habui in parochia Sancti Clementis Dacorum, videlicet: illam que est inter terram Reginaldi aurifabri versus orientem, et terram Reginaldi carpentarii versus occidentem, et continet in latitudine in capite versus cheminum regale octo ulnas uno quarterio minus de ulnis ferreis Domini Henrici regis Anglie; et in latitudine in parte posteriori versus aquilonem novem ulnas et duos pedes de eisdem ulnis; et in longitudine quinquaginta et octo ulnas et duos pedes de eisdem ulnis, scilicet: quicquid ibidem habui in longitudine et latitudine sine aliquo retinemento integre. Habendam et tenendam predicto Waltero et heredibus suis de me et heredibus meis in feodo et hereditate, libere et quiete, bene et in pace in perpetuum. Reddendo inde annuatim mihi et heredibus meis pro omni servicio et exactione et rebus cunctis unum denarium ad Festum Sancti Michaelis, et ad opus Sancte Marie Westmonasterii octo solidos per annum ad quatuor terminos, scilicet: ad Nathale Domini duos solidos; et ad Pascham duos solidos; et ad Festum Sancti Johannis Baptiste duos solidos; et ad Festum Sancti Michaelis duos solidos, sine omni occasione. Et sciendum est quod ego dicta Matilda vel heredes mei vel aliquis per nos vel pro nobis nullatenus poterimus nec debemus dehospitare predictum Walterum vel heredes suos, causa me vel heredes meos vel aliquem alium hominem vel feminam ibidem hospitandi, nec plus exigere, clamare, vel habere in predicta domo cum pertinentiis quam unum denarium per annum termino statuto. Hanc autem predictam domum integre cum omnibus pertinentiis suis ego dicta Matilda et heredes me debemus warantizare predicto Waltero et heredibus suis contra omnes homines et feminas in perpetuum per predictum servicium unius denarii per annum solvendi mihi et heredibus meis ad Festum Sancti Michaelis pro omni servicio, salvis octo solidis per annum solvendis ad opus Sancte Marie West- monasterii sicut predictum est. Pro hec concessione et dimissione et warantizatione, et presentis carte mee confirmatione et sigilli mei appositione dedit mihi predictus Walterus unam marcam argenti in gersumam, et Margerie, filie mee, quatuor denarios. Hiis testibus: Domino Johanne, tunc persona Sancti Clementis Dacorum; Domino Thoma, tunc capellano Sancti Clementis Dacorum; Hamone Brand; Stephano de Stranda; Benedicto le Capel[er]; Normanno Alutar'; Reginaldo aurifabro; Ricardo filio Alwredi; Gileberto carpentario; Roberto aur[ifabro]; Ewerardo de Fonte; Johanne filio Ewerardi; Willelmo le Franceis; Willelmo le Provencal, et multis aliis.

MSS: (1) WAM 17079.
  17.7 × 15.5 cm; t.u. 2 cm.
  Seal: on tag labelled Carta Walteri le Spicer (13C); green; 4 × 2.8 cm; fleur de lys; legend: SIGILL. MATILDIS IOPE.
  Endorsed: (a) Matildis que fuit uxor Jospe dat Waltero de Wynton' le espicer unam domum in parochia Sancti Clementis Dacorum (13C). (b) Capella (14C). (c) Charta iij^a (16C).
  (2) WAD, ff. 553v and 555r (f. 554 is an insertion).
Date: The first witness, John, parson of St Clement Danes, also attests Walter Fitz Cecily's related grant to Robert son of Robert of Rockingham (**394**).

397. Confirmation by Simon of Fleet Bridge and his wife Agnes to Ailnoth de la Ruding of all their land in the parish of St Clement, lying between the land of Ranulph Fiket and that of Godiva Cruke, with a house, two chambers and a lead (? gutter), to hold in inheritance at an annual rent of 5s. Prohibition of dislodgement and of alienation to the Church or to a Jew. Gersum of £1. [Late 12C]

Sciant presentes et futuri quod ego[1] Simon de Ponte Flete et Agnes uxor mea concessimus et dedimus et confirmavimus Ailnotho de Larudenge et heredibus suis totam terram nostram que est in parochia Sancti Clementis, scilicet: terram illam que jacet inter terram Ranulfi Fiket et inter terram Godeve Cruke in longitudine et in latitudine, cum una domo et cum duabus cameris et cum omnibus pertinentiis suis, cum uno plumbo. Tenendam et habendam sibi et heredibus suis de nobis et de heredibus nostris libere, quiete, finabiliter, jure hereditario. Reddendo nobis et heredibus nostris per annum quinque solidos pro omni servicio, scilicet: ad Pascha xv denarios; et ad Festum Sancti Johannis Baptiste xv denarios; et ad Festum Sancti Michaelis xv denarios; et ad Natale Domini xv denarios. Et sciendum est quod ego Simon de Ponte Flete et Agnes uxor mea non poterimus dehospitari predictum Ailnothum de Larudenge vel heredes suos causa nos hospitandi; et predictus Ailnothus vel heredes sui non poterunt vendere vel invadiare predictam terram ecclesie vel Judeo. Preterea, ego Simon de Ponte Flete et Agnes uxor mea et heredes nostri warantizabimus predicto Ailnotho de Larudenge et heredibus suis predictam terram contra omnes homines et feminas. Pro hac autem concessione et donatione et warantisione sepedictus Ailnothus de Larudenge dedit predicto Simoni de Ponte Flete et Agneti uxori sue viginti solidos sterlingorum in gersumam. His testibus: Johanne, persona de Sancto Clemente; Willelmo capellano, fratre eius; Roberto filio

238

Toroldi; Roberto de Ruggingeham; Roberto filio eius; Ansegod de Barra; Benedicto capeler; Waltero filio Cecilie; Eustachio clerico; Willelmo forestario; Gileberto filio eius; Willelmo filio eius; alio Willelmo filio eius; Roberto de Stanmere; Simone filio eius; Roberto de Wambele; Ailuuardo fratre eius; Roberto filio Roberti de Wambele; Alano de Tripelawe; Willelmo fratre eius; Ailuuino Godmar; Stephano de Heia; Johanne bucher; Gileberto Godmar; Willelmo Peitevin; Rogero fabro; Gileberto de Walda, et multis aliis.

MSS: (1) WAM 17077.

> 19 × 17 cm; t.u. 3.8 cm, on which is written: Carta Symonis de Ponteflete quam fecit Ailnotho de Larudenge.
>
> Seals: on tags; natural wax. (1) 4.5 × 3.4 cm; standing figure with right arm extended: legend: + SIGILL' AGNETIS DE PONTE FLETE. (2) 5 × 3.5 cm; fleur de lys; legend: + SIGILL' SIMONIS DE PONTE FLETE.
>
> Endorsed: (a) Simon de Ponte Flet' et Agnes uxor eius dant Aylnotho de Larudeng' totam terram suam (13C). (b) pro Westmonasterii capella lxxxxj lxxxx—depositum et duplicatum—v vj (14C) (c) in parochia Sancti Clementis (14C).
>
> 1. Supplied from WAD.

(2) WAD, ff. 556v–557r.

Date: Hand is later 12C; also attestations of Robert of Rockingham, Walter Fitz Cicely; John, parson of St Clement Danes.

Note: At Michaelmas 1208, land in the parish of St Clement Danes, owned by Rannulf Fichet, but held by a tenant, rendered 2s. 2d. annually to the abbot of Westminster, and 3s. annually to the gardener of Westminster (*PR 10 John*, 170 n. 11).

398. Confirmation by Richard son of William Noloth, to Richard, chaplain of the Holy Innocents, of a full half of his land which he holds of the fee of Mohun, near the land of Peter son of Richard, in St Martin's parish (boundaries given), to hold in fee and inheritance at an annual rent of 1s., dislodgement prohibited. If Richard [Noloth] wants to alienate the other half of his land, or to enfeoff anyone, then Richard the chaplain may have it at a price of 1s. less than anyone else. Gersum of one mark (13s. 4d.) to Richard Noloth, and one besant (2s.) to his wife. [Temp. John]

Sciant presentes et futuri quod ego Ricardus, filius Willelmi Noloth, concessi et dedi et hac carta mea confirmavi Ricardo, capellano de Innocentibus, totam medietatem terre mee cum pertinentiis quam teneo de feodo de Moun, scilicet: illam que jacet propinquior terre Petri filii Ricardi in parochia Sancti Martini, et habet longitudine usque ad fossatum marescalli; et in latitudine decem et novem pedes et dimidiam pedem. Habendam et tenendam de me et de heredibus meis illi et cui assignaverit libere, quiete, pacifice, in feodo et hereditate, finabiliter. Reddendo inde annuatim pro omni servicio et exactione duodecim denarios ad quatuor terminos: ad Nativitatem Domini iij denarios; ad Pascham iij denarios; ad Festum Sancti Johannis iij denarios; ad Festum

Sancti Michaelis iij denarios. Nec ego Ricardus nec heredes mei poterimus prefatum Ricardum, vel illum cui assignare voluerit, aliquo modo dehospitari causa nosmet ipsos ibidem hospitandi; et si ita contigerit quod ego Ricardus alteram medietatem predicte terre cum pertinentiis alicui invadiare vel inde aliquem feffare voluero; predictus Ricardus propinquior erit inde de duodecim denariis quam aliquis alius. Hanc autem prenominatam terram cum pertinentiis ego Ricardus et heredes mei warantizabimus prefato Ricardo vel cui assignare voluerit contra omnes gentes. Pro hac autem concessione et presentis carte mee confirmatione, dedit mihi prefatus Ricardus unam marcam argenti de gersuma, et uxori mee unum bizantum. Hiis testibus: Roberto de Rokingham; Johanne de Abbendon; Willelmo filio Willelmi; Willelmo filio Arnulfi; Petro filio Ricardi; Thoma vinitore; Ailwardo Hut.

MSS: (1) WAM 17141.
19.5 × 12.8 cm; t.u. 2 cm; tag, seal missing.
Endorsed: (a) Carta Willelmi Noloth facta Ricardo capelle de Innocentibus de medietate terre sue de feodo Moun (13C). (b) In parochia Sancti Martini reddendo inde annuatim dicto Willelmo et suis heredibus xij denarios (13C). (c) Westmonasterii infirmaria: non registratur (14C). (d) Suthhus. (e) lij. (f) Alienum.
(2) WAD, f. 472.
Date: Attestations: earlier than **399**.

399. Confirmation by Richard son of William Noloth to Richard, chaplain of the Holy Innocents, of the whole of the land which he held of the fee of William de Mohun in St Martin's parish, to hold of him and his heirs in fee and inheritance, at an annual rent of 1*d*., and 1*s*. 8*d*. to the chief lords of the fee. Gersum of £1 8*s*. [Temp. John; ? *ante* 1206]

Sciant presentes et futuri quod ego Ricardus, filius Willelmi Noloth, dedi et concessi et hac carta mea confirmavi Ricardo, capellano de Innocentibus, vel cui assignare voluerit, totam terram illam cum pertinentiis quam tenui de feodo Willelmi de Moun in parochia Sancti Martini et quicquid ibidem habui in rebus cunctis, sine aliqua excepcione, et sine aliquo retinemento. Tenendam et habendam de me et heredibus meis ipsi Ricardo et quibus assignare voluerit in feodo et hereditate, libere, quiete, finabiliter. Reddendo inde annuatim mihi vel heredibus meis j denarium ad Natale Domini pro omni servicio ad me vel heredes meos pertinente; et preterea reddendo inde capitalibus dominis predicti feodi xx denarios: ad Natale Domini v denarios; ad Pascha v denarios; ad Festum Sancti Johannis Baptiste v denarios; et ad Festum Sancti Michaelis v denarios, pro omni servitio et exactione. Hanc [autem][1] terram cum omnibus pertinentiis ego prefatus Ricardus et heredes mei warantizabimus predicto Ricardo capellano, vel cui assignare voluerit, contra omnes homines. Pro hac autem concessione et dimissione et presentis carte mee confirmatione dedit mihi predictus Ricardus xxviij[2] solidos esterlingorum in gersumam. Hiis testibus: Roberto de Rokingham; Johanne de Abendon'; Willelmo filio Willelmi; Willelmo filio Arnulfi; Petro filio Ricardi; Thoma vinitore; Ailwardo Hut; Eustachio filio Willelmi;

Gladewino parmentario; Gaufrido de Cruce; Alexandro filio Willelmi, et multis aliis.

MSS: (1) WAM 17142.
    22.5 × 9.2 cm; t.u. 1.2 cm.
    Seal: on tag; white; 4 cm diameter; fleur de lys; legend: + SIGILL'
    RICARDI FIL WIL[LELMI].
    Endorsed: (a) Carta Ricardi filii Willelmi Noloth de terra sua in
    parochia Sancti Martini de feodo Moun (13C). (b) Concessa
    Ricardo, capellano de Innocentibus, reddendo inde annuatim dicto
    Ricardo unum denarium et capitalibus dominis xx^{ti} denariis (13C).
    (c) S. Martyni (16C). (d) Non registratur (16C). (e) Westmonasterii
    (16C). (f) Infirmaria (14C).
      1. MS torn: word supplied from copy.
      2. MS: *octo* written above *xxviij*.
    (2) WAD, f. 472.
Date: Later than **398**. William IV de Mohun d. 1193. His son Reginald I came of age in 1206 and d. 1213, leaving Reginald II, who came of age only in 1227 (Sanders, 114). These charters were prob. acquired by the convent following a grant made to them, *c.* 1225 or later, by Robert, son of Richard the chaplain, of rent due from a tenement of the fee of Reginald de Mohun (WAM 17445).

400. Notification by Abbot G[uerin] and the convent of St Victor, Paris, that they have entered into confraternity with the prior and chapter of Westminster, and will commemorate their deceased brethren annually, on 1 May. [Paris, 1173 × 1175 (or 1190 × 1191]

Dominis et amicis in Christo dilectissimis . . . priori et capitulo Westmonasterii, G[uerinus] cenobii Sancti Victoris Paris' dictus abbas totusque conventus unitatem spiritus in vinculo pacis. Sanctorum docemur serie scripturarum ac sincere caritatis debito provocamur ut studeamus alter alterius onera portare et orare proinvicem ut salvemur. Nos autem licet in hac parte cunctis Christi fidelibus simus communiter debitores vobis tamen specialem intendimus fraterne societatis unitatem perpetuo deinceps conservare ut et vos in Christi visceribus carius amplectamur, et pro salute vestra Domino nostre devotionis et orationis sacrificium immolemus. Ad petitionem igitur G[uerini] venerabilis abbatis et patris nostri spiritualis a nobis unanimiter in capitulo statutum est, ut annis singulis vestrorum commemorationem fratrum defunctorum Kal. Maij celebriter recolamus vespertinis ix lectionum vigiliis et missa matutinali sollempniter celebrata. Proinde rogamus attentius dilectionem vestram ut intuitu divine pietatis nobis quoque vestris orationibus caritatis vicem rependere studeatis.

MS: F, ff. 262v–263.
    Rubric: Confederatio Sancti Victoris Paris' et Westmonasterii. Clxj.
Date: Apparently issued during a vacancy at Westminster. Stylistically, it appears to date from late 12C. The vacancy therefore either that between d. of Laurence, 10/11 April 1173 and election of Walter, *post* 8

July 1175, or that between d. of Walter, 27 Sept. 1190, and election of William Postard, 9 Oct. 1191 (*Heads*, 77). It is unlikely that Westminster would have entered into confraternity with St Victor *post* 1204.

Note: The obituary list of St Victor includes members of the Order of Sempringham, and some individual clerics in England, but makes no mention of the convent of Westminster, nor of any of the abbey's personnel, either under 1 May or any other day of the year (*Obituaires de la Province de Sens*, tome I (Dioceses de Sens et de Paris), ed. A. Molinier (Recueil des Historiens de la France, Academie des Inscriptions et Belles-Lettres, Paris, 1902), (i), 531–608; cf. *Repertoire des Documents Necrologiques Français*, ed. P. Marot avec J.-L. Le Maitre (Recueil des Historiens de la France, Academie des Inscriptions et Belles-Lettres I, Paris, 1980, 591–4). Abbot Laurence of Westminster has been suggested as the author of a report of lectures given by Hugh of St Victor, while the title *magister*, ascribed to him by St Bernard, implies that he taught in the schools (F. E. Croydon, 'Abbot Laurence of Westminster and Hugh of St Victor', *Medieval and Renaissance Studies* II, ed. R. Hunt and R. Klibansky (1950), 169–71; cf. Flete, 91). Laurence, when abbot of Westminster, wrote to his kinsman, Abbot *Ervisius* (? Hervey) of St Victor, commending to him a certain John, a kinsman of the prior of Westminster, who wanted to study in the schools (*PL* 196, col. 1385, no. VII). A similar letter, written *c.* 1166, commended Laurence's own nephew, another John (Croydon, 'Abbot Laurence', 170). The unsatisfactory Ervisius was reputedly English (Fourrier Bonnard, *Histoire de . . . St Victor de Paris* (Paris, 1904–8), I, 227; *PL* 196, col. xiv), and numerous English exiles were at his abbey during the Becket dispute (*PL* 196, col. xv). The confraternity agreement was prob. made during the vacancy following Laurence's d., and perhaps negotiated by one or other of his protégés commended to the abbey of St Victor.

401. Notification by Walter [of Coutances], abp. of Rouen, of his grant of an indulgence of twenty days, with participation in the prayers and spiritual benefits of the church of Rouen, to all those who visit the abbey at Christmas, Easter, Ascension and Pentecost; at the Feast of the Holy Relics, on all feasts of St Peter and of all the Apostles, and on the two feasts of Blessed Edward, king and confessor. [Nov. 1184 × 16 Nov. 1207 (? Oct. 1191 × *ante* 25 Dec. 1193)]

Walterus, Dei gratia Rothomagensis archiepiscopus, universis Sancte Ecclesie fidelibus salutem. Condignum est, et Deo amabile, sicut novit vestra discretio, ut illis qui sanctam ecclesiam fideli devotione veneran- tur, et bonis sibi a Deo prestitis eam sustentant, spiritualia remedia benigne conferamus. Noverit ergo, universitas vestra, nos, pro Dei et Beate Marie matris eius, et Beati Petri apostolorum principis venera- tione, omnibus fidelibus qui ecclesiam Beati Petri de Westmonasterio in Natali Domini, et in Pascha, et in Domini Ascensione, et in Pentecostem, et in festivitate sanctarum reliquiarum[1] que in illa ecclesia gloriose continentur, et in omnibus festivitatibus Beate Marie, et in omnibus festivitatibus Beati Petri et omnium apostolorum, et in duabus festivitatibus Beati Edwardi, regis et confessoris, votive adierint et elemosinis suis illam ecclesiam honoraverint, de penitentiis eis injunctis suffragiis Jhesu Christi et Beati Petri confisi viginti dies relaxamus, et orationum et beneficorum Rothomagensis ecclesie eos participes esse concedimus amodo. Valete.

MS: WAD, f. 390v.
>Rubric: Indulgencia W. Rothomagensis archiepiscopi de xx diebus injuncte penitentie concessis venerantibus et benefactoribus ecclesie Westmonasterii in festis suprascriptis.
>1. MS: *relilicquiarum*.

Date: Walter's term of office (Gams, 640) but papal confirmation of his elevation was received at Rouen only on 3 March 1185, and he was still styled bp. Lincoln at Christmas 1184 (*Fasti* III, 2). The indulgence was prob. requested while he was justiciar, early Oct. 1191 × 25 Dec. 1193 (West, *Justiciarship*, 75–78; *HBC*, 71).

Note: Walter, a Cornishman, was successively archdeacon of Oxford and bp. of Lincoln before his elevation to Rouen (*Fasti* III, 2).

402. Agreement in the form of a cirograph, between Nicholas son of Geoffrey and Robert of Croxley, by which Nicholas granted to Robert, his heirs or assigns, his office of summoner in the abbey, with a monastic corrody and all appurtenances, besides the land pertaining to that office, for twelve years, in return for £2. 10*s*. [*c.* 24 June 1209]

Hec est conventio facta inter Nicolaum filium Gaufridi et Robertum de Crokesleia, scilicet: quod idem Nicolaus dimisit et concessit predicto Roberto et heredibus suis, vel cui idem Robertus assignare voluerit, totum ministerium suum quod habuit in Abbacia Westmonasterii, scilicet ministerium summonitionis, cum corredio monacali et cum omnibus pertinentiis, preter terram que pertinet ad predictum ministerium summonitionis, usque ad terminum duodecim annorum pro quinquaginta solidis quos idem Robertus dedit predicto Nicolao pre manibus. Et idem Nicolaus et heredes sui warantizabunt predicto Roberto et heredibus suis, vel cui assignare voluerit, predictum ministerium cum pertinentiis,[1] contra omnes gentes usque ad predictum terminum; ita tamen quod predictus Robertus et heredes sui, vel ille cui idem Robertus predictum ministerium assignaverit, facient ea que ad predictum ministerium pertinent infra predictum terminum; ita quod idem Nicolaus vel heredes sui non sint perdentes de predicto ministerio. In fine vero predictorum duodecim annorum predictum ministerium cum pertinentiis revertetur ad ipsum Nicolaum et ad heredes suos quietum de ipso Roberto et heredibus suis inperpetuum sine omni calumnia. Huius vero convencionis terminus incepit ad Festum Sancti Johannis Baptiste proximum post electionem Hugonis de Well', Lincolniensis electi, anno regni Regis Johannis undecimo et anno nono benedictionis Radulfi abbatis Westmonasterii. Hanc autem convencionem fideliter tenendam utraque affidavit et sigillum suum apposuit. Hiis testibus: Ricardo de Dol; Odone aurifabro; Henrico Sumer; Gaufrido camerario; Ada de Westmonasterio; Stephano de Berking'; Waltero Marescallo; Eustacio pictore; Berth' hostiario; Nicolao de celario; Thoma vinitore, et multis aliis.

MS: WAM 5788.
>14.5 × 15 cm; t.u. 2.5 cm; top intended CYROGRAPHUM.
>Seal: Green; 3 cm diameter; obverse: eagle facing right; legend: SIGILL NICOL FIL GALFRID +.
>Endorsed: Hec conventio facta inter Nicholaum filium Galfridi et Robertum de Crokesl' de ministerio [summonitore . . .] in Abbatia Westmonasterii (14C).
>>1. *cum pertinentiis* repeated in MS.

403. Confirmation by Nicholas son of Geoffrey to Robert of Croxley for his homage and service, of his whole office of summoner in the abbey, with a monastic corrody and all other appurtenances, to be held by Robert and his heirs of Nicholas and his heirs in perpetuity, by service of 4*d.* annually. Gersum of £5. [Temp. John; *post* 24 June 1209]

Sciant presentes et futuri quod ego Nicolaus filius Gaufridi dedi et concessi et hac presenti carta mea confirmavi Roberto de Crokesle pro homagio et servicio suo totum ministerium meum quod habui in Abbacia Westmonasterii, scilicet ministerium summonicionis cum corredio monacali et cum omnibus aliis pertinenciis sine aliquo retenemento; habendum et tenendum de me et heredibus meis ipsi Roberto et heredibus suis bene et in pace, libere et quiete, integre et plenarie inperpetuum, per liberum servicium quatuor denariorum per annum pro omni servicio, reddendum ad duos terminos anni, scilicet: ad Pascham duos denarios, et ad Festum Sancti Michaelis duos denarios. Et ego Nicolaus et heredes mei warantizabimus predicto Roberto et heredibus suis totum predictum ministerium cum omnibus pertinenciis contra omnes homines et feminas per predictum servicium. Et pro hac donatione et concessione et warantizatione et carte mee confirmatione predictus Robertus dedit mihi in gersumam centum solidos esterlingorum. Et ut hec mea donatio et concessio rata sit et stabilis permaneat, eam sigilli mei appositione roboravi. Hiis testibus: Ricardo de Dol; Odone aurifabro; Ricardo Testard; Adam de Westmonasterio; Galfrido camerario; Stephano de Berkinge; Roberto de Rokingeham; Henrico Sumer; Johanne de Abendona; Ricardo filio Edmundi; Gaufrido de Claigate; Roberto de Claigate, et multis aliis.

MS: WAM 5789.
>20 × 9.8 cm; t.u. 1.7 cm.
>Seal: on tag; green; 3.3 × 3.8 cm; eagle, facing right; legend: + SIGILL' NICOL' FIL' GAUFRIDI.
>Endorsed: Carta Nicholai filij Gaufridi de toto ministerio suo quod habuit in Abbatia Westmonasterii, scilicet ministerium summonicionis cum corrodio monacali et omnimodis alijs pertinenciis, Roberto de Crokesle concesso (14C).

404. Notification by Leofwine Kepe that, for his soul and those of his parents and ancestors, he has granted to St Peter and the convent all his lands and rents in the vill of Westminster, and has placed his sealed charter on the High Altar. 29 June [Temp. H II]

Notum sit tam presentibus quam futuris quod ego Leffewine Kepe, pro salute anime mee et patris et matris mee et antecessorum meorum, concessi et dedi Deo et Beato Petro et conventui Westmonasterii omnes terras meas et omnes redditus meos quos habui in villa Westmonasterii, et presentem cartam sigillo meo proprio sigillatam in die apostolorum Petri et Pauli super magnum altare eiusdem ecclesie optuli. Hiis testibus: Ricardo, filio et herede meo hoc annuente et presente; Radulfo, fratre Abbatis Laurencii; Simone de Denham, clerico abbatis; Alano de Seperton; Hugone le Bel; Roberto Testard; Willelmo filio Ordrici; Henrico Colepouch'; Willelmo de Benflet; Roberto de Bemflet; Radulfo de Molesham; Willelmo, capellano de Sancto Martino; Alexandro, Salomono, filiis[1] suis; Willelmo pictore; Simone et Burchardo filiis suis; Aschetillo de Sartrin; Willelmo filio eius; Johanne nepote Rogeri camerarii; Radulfo pistore; Willelmo de Scardeburth; Edmundo de Eya; Radulfo de Eya; Johanne filio eius, et multis aliis. Hanc cartam scripsit Vivianus clericus.

MS: WAD, f. 443r–v.
   Rubric: Carta Leffwine Kepe de omnibus terris cum redditibus quas habuit in villa Westmonasterii.
      1. MS: *filiis filiis*.
Date: Attestation of Ralph, brother of Abbot Laurence. Simon and Burchard the painters were active 1182 × 1186 (*Beauchamp Cartulary*, no. 183).

405. Notification by Baldwin son of Baldwin of his confirmation to Geoffrey the chaplain of Tothill, of half a messuage in Westminster, to hold by service of 1*s.* 6*d.* annually, due to Baldwin, and by the free service of finding one man for the abbot of Westminster, for mowing or reaping, one day a year in that vill, for the abbot's food. Gersum of 2*s.* [Late 12C]

Universis ad quos presens carta pervenerit, Baldwinus filius Baldwini, salutem. Noveritis me dedisse et hac mea carta confirmasse Galfrido capellano de Tothill' dimidium masagium in Westmonasterio cum pertinentiis suis, habendum et tenendum de me et heredibus meis libere et quiete et integre, per servitium xviij^{to} denariorum per annum, scilicet: ix denariorum ad Festum Sancti Michaelis, et ix denariorum ad Pascha, pro omni servitio quod ad me vel heredes meos pertineat, et per liberum servitium inveniendi quendam hominem abbati Westmonasterii ad fenum suum levandum, vel blada sua colligendum, uno die per annum in eadem villa ad cibum ipsius abbatis, pro omni servitio. Hanc autem donationem et concessionem et carte huius confirmationem feci ego Baldwinus ipsi Galfrido et heredibus suis vel cuicumque idem Galfridus illud dimidium masagium cum pertinentiis suis dare voluerit. Et ego et heredes mei warantizabimus illis omnibus prenominatis prefatum dimidium masagium cum pertinentiis suis contra omnes. Et inde dedit mihi idem Galfridus duos solidos in gersuma. Testibus: Johanne sacerdote, filio Moysi; Johanne, capellano de Curia Regis; Rogero capellano; Edwardo preposito; Willelmo hostiario; Willelmo filio Ordrici; Galfridio filio Fredesenti; Warino Hareng'; Elia Hodin; Willelmo Chanterel; Ricardo pictore; Ricardo de Berking', et multis aliis.

MS: BL Harleian Charter 50 A 10.
  28 × 14 cm.
  Endorsed: Westmonasterii (modern).
  Seal: green; 4 cm diameter; lion passant; legend: SIGILL BALDEWINI FIL BALDE.
  Counterseal: very worn, with indistinct figure; legend: [GRAT]IA DEI VIVO CUM ALIIS.
Pd: *Facsimiles of Charters in the British Museum*, ed. Warner and Ellis, no. 73, and plate XLVII.
Date: Attestations of Edward the reeve, who was in office in 1190 (*PR 1 Ric. I*, 227) but was d. in 1202–3 (*Fines London and Mddx*, 7) and prob. in 1198 (*Fines 10 Ric. I*, 90); of William Fitz Ordric, who warranted land in Westminster in 1197–8 (*Fines London and Mddx*, 2); and of William the usher (*alias* William of Hurley), who was d. by Jan. 1203 and prob. before May 1200 (*Beauchamp Cartulary*, nos. 190–193).

406. Notification by Edward, reeve of Westminster, that he has confirmed to Ralf Clerk and his heirs that messuage which Sawal the clerk bought from Brungar the champion and later demised to Ralph Hurel, from whom Edward bought it. The messuage lies between the land of William Fiz and that of Ralph of Seven Fountains, which Albin the clerk holds of him, and is to be held of Edward and his heirs in perpetual inheritance, at an annual rent of 3s. 4d. Ralph Clerk, so called not from his office, but as his cognomen, gave a gersum of 3s. [Late 12C, *ante* 1197]

Sciant tam presentes quam futuri quicumque hanc cartam viderint vel audierint, quod ego Aedwardus [prepositus Westmonasterii concessi et hac pre]senti carta mea confirmavi Radulfo Clerico et heredibus suis masagium illud quod olim Sawal[us clericus emerat de Brungaro Athleta], quod etiam ille Sawalus clericus postea dimisit Radulfo Hurel, de quo ego illud masagium emi, quod iacet [inter terram Willelmi Fiz' et terram Radulfi de] Septem Fontibus, quam Albinus clericus tenet de eo, tenendum de me et de heredibus meis perpetua heredita[te; reddendo inde annu]atim pro omni servitio xl denarios ad quatuor statutos terminos anni, scilicet: ad Natale Domini x denarios; et ad Pascha x denarios; [et ad Nativitatem Sancti] Johannis Baptiste x denarios; et ad Festum Sancti Michaelis x denarios. Pro hac autem concessione et huius carte mee confirmatione, predictus Radulphus Clericus, non officio ita vocatus sed cognomine, dedit michi ad gersummam iij solidos. His testibus: Rogero capellano; Albino clerico; Gocelino fabro; Alano et Johanne, filiis meis; Randulfo Fiz', coco, et Ricardo filio eius; Willelmo filio [Asketini];

Wimundo pistore; Hugone filio Richeri de Fonte, et Galfrido de Cruce, fratre eius; Willelmo Chanterel, Willelmo Albo [presbitero, qui hanc cartam] scripsit, et multis aliis.

MSS: (1) WAM 17314 (damaged).
  24 × 10 cm; t.u. 2.7 cm.
  Fold with slit, tag and seal missing.
  Endorsed: (a) Capella (13C). (b) Carta Edwardi prepositi de uno mesuagio dato Radulfo Clerico (12C). (c) Westmonasterii capella lxxxiij (14C).
  (2) WAD, f. 555, from which the gaps in the original are filled.
Date: Edward styled himself as 'formerly reeve' in 1197 (**446**; Richardson, 'William of Ely', 84–85). He was in office in 1190 (*PR 2 Ric. I*, 157).
Note: Brungar the champion was perhaps a professional duellist, employed in judicial duels (cf. *The Treatise on the laws and customs of the realm of England commonly called Glanvill* ed. G. D. G. Hall (1965), 23–5, 28).

407. Confirmation, in pure alms, by John son of Edward, for his soul and those of all his ancestors, to the Lady Altar and the convent, to provide lights for this altar, of the whole land which Ralf Clerk held of his father Edward in the vill of Westminster, lying between the land formerly belonging to William Fiz and the land of Ralph of Seven Fountains, which Albin the clerk held of Ralph, to hold in perpetuity for 1*s.* annually. Moreover, he granted, to provide lights for that altar, an annual rent of 1*s.* which Roger Fot rendered for land adjacent to Tothill, with the whole service of land. [Temp. John]

Sciant presentes et futuri quod ego Johannes filius Edwardi, pro salute anime mee et omnium antecessorum meorum, in perpetuam elemosinam dedi et concessi et hac presenti carta mea confirmavi Deo et altari Beate Virginis Marie Westmonasterii et eiusdem loci conventui, ad luminaria prefati altaris administranda, totam terram quam Radulfus clericus tenuit de Edwardo patre meo in villa Westmonasterii, quam jacet inter terram que fuit Willelmi Fiz et terram Radulfi de Septem Fontibus, quam Albinus clericus tenuit de ipso Radulfo. Habendam et tenendam de me et heredibus meis bene et in pace, libere et quiete, inperpetuum per liberum servicium duorum denariorum per annum pro omni servicio reddendorum, scilicet: unum denarium ad Pascham, et j denarium ad Festum Sancti Michaelis. Preterea concessi ad luminaria eiusdem altaris administranda xij denarios redditus singulis annis inperpetuum, quos Rogerius Fot michi reddere consuevit de quadam terra iuxta Tothul, et totum servicium terre illius liberum et quietum inperpetuum de me et heredibus meis. Hanc autem donationem et (concessionem)^c elemosinam ego Johannes et heredes mei warantizabimus predicto conventui versus omnes homines et feminas per predictum servicium. Hiis testibus: Odone aurifabro; Rogero Enganet; Henrico Sumer; Lodovico clerico; Ricardo Testard; Ada de Westmonasterio; Nicholao filio Galfridi; Stephano de Berking'; Galfrido de Cruce; Wimundo pistore; Ada,

Johanne, Galfrido, Radulfo, servientibus ecclesie; Laurentio Muschat, et multis aliis.

MS: WAD, f. 557.
> Rubric: Carta Johannis filii Edwardi de terra quam Radulfus clericus tenuit de Edwardo patre predicti Johannis in Westmonasterio.
> 1. MS: *redditum*.

Date: John had succeeded his father before 30 Oct. 1197, when he quitclaimed to Ralph of Seven Fountains an acre of land in Westminster adjacent to St James's Hospital (*Fines 9 Ric. I*, 55, no. 79; cal: *Fines London and Mddx*, I, 2, no. 10). Attestations of Roger Enganet, Henry Sumer and Richard Testard, one or more of whom was prob. currently reeve (cf. Rosser, 'Medieval Westminster', 360).

408. Confirmation by John son of Edward of Westminster to Prior Robert of Moulsham, of 8*s.* quit-rent in the vill of Westminster, to put to whatever use he wishes, comprising 1*s.* in Aldwych which Paulinus of Aldwych rendered for half an acre in the Fields; 4*s.* which Henry son of Humphrey of Aldwych rendered for five acres; and 3*s.* which William of the Garden rendered for two acres. The prior gave John a gersum of five marks (£3. 6*s.* 8*d.*). [Temp. John]

Sciant presentes et futuri quod ego Johannes filius Edwardi de Westmonasterio dedi et concessi et hac presenti carta mea confirmavi Roberto de Mulesham, priori de Westmonasterio, octo solidatas quieti redditus in villa Westmonasterii in quibuscumque usibus assignare vel dare voluerit, scilicet: in Aldewich duodecim denarios quos Paulinus de Aldewich solebat michi reddere de dimidia acra terre in Campis, ad Pascham et ad Festum Sancti Michaelis; et quatuor solidos quos Henricus filius Humfridi de Aldewich solebat michi reddere de quinque acris terre ad eosdem terminos; et tres solidos quos Willelmus de Gardino solebat michi reddere de duabus acris terre ad quatuor principales anni terminos, scilicet singulis terminis ix denarios. Habendas et percipiendas eisdem terminis per manus predictorum Paulini et Henrici et Willelmi, vel heredum suorum vel aliorum quicumque predictas terras tenuerint, eidem Roberto vel ipsi[1] cuicumque vel quibuscumque usibus assignare vel dare voluerit. Ego vero Johannes et heredes mei warantizabimus predictum redditum predicto Roberto vel illi qui loco suo assignaverit. Pro hac autem donatione et concessione et carte mee confirmatione dedit mihi predictus Robertus quinque marcas argenti. Et ut hec mea donatio et concessio et carte mee confirmatio rata sit et stabilis permaneat, eam sigilli mei appositione corroboravi. Hiis testibus: Odone aurifabro de Westmonasterio; Ricardo Testard; Henrico Sumer; Ricardo filio Edmundi; Gaufrido de Cruce; Stephano de Berking'; Roberto de Crokesl'; Thoma vinitore; Willelmo de la Barre, Edrico de Gardino; Nicholao de celario; Gervasio de Coquina; Laurentio Muschat; Adam de Ecclesia, et multis aliis.

MS: WAD, f. 557v.

Rubric: Carta eiusdem Johannis de viij solidis redditus in villa Westmonasterii.
  1. MS: *idem Robertus vel ipse.*
Date: Attestations of Richard Testard and Henry Sumer. One, or both, prob. still reeve (cf. Rosser, 'Medieval Westminster', 360).

409. Confirmation by John son of Edward to Adam the chamberlain, his heirs or assigns, of a messuage which he held of John's father Edward, next to that of Mr William of Hanslope towards the east, to hold at a rent of 4*s.* 2*d.* annually. Gersum of 10*s.* [*c.* 1197 × 1200]

Sciant presentes et futuri quod ego Johannes filius Edwardi concessi et hac carta mea confirmavi unum mesagium cum pertinentiis, quod est proximum mesagio Magistri Willelmi de Hamsslepe versus orientem, Ade camberario et heredibus suis vel cui ipse assignare voluerit, quod ipse Adam tenuit de patre meo Edwardo; tenendum de me et heredibus meis libere et quiete; reddendo inde pro omni servitio quatuor solidos per annum et duos denarios ad duos terminos, scilicet: ad Annunciationem Beate Marie duos solidos et unum denarium; et ad Festum Sancti Michaelis duos solidos et unum denarium. Hoc predictum mesagium predicto Ade et suis heredibus ego et heredes mei warantizabimus. Pro hac concessione et carte mee confirmatione, dedit michi predictus Adam decem solidos. Et ego ei affidavi hanc conventionem fideliter observandam. Hiis testibus: Willelmo de Ely; Roberto Mauduyt; Magistro Jocelino; Andrea de Scaccario; Magistro Willelmo de Hameslep; Johanne de Wicha; Albino clerico; Theobaldo senescallo; Arnaldo de Herlaue; Galfrido Picot; Henrico Sumer; Ricardo portario; Stephano de Berking'; Martino de Halbendon', et multis aliis.

MS: WAD, f. 556.
  Rubric: Carta Johannis filii Edwardi de uno mesuagio in Westmonasterio.
Date: John succeeded his father some time before 30 Oct. 1197 (*Fines 9 Ric. I*, 55, no. 79; cal. *Fines London and Mddx*, I, no. 10). The attestation of Theobald of Feering, as seneschal, indicates a date within the abbacy of William Postard. The absence of the official titles of William of Ely and Robert Mauduit is not significant, since this text is not the original.

410. Confirmation by Richard son of Ranulf to the Lady Altar of Westminster of 4*d.* rent, which John son of Edward the reeve rendered him for two acres, with all liberties, free customs, reliefs or escheats due to Richard or his heirs. [Early 13C]

Sciant presentes et futuri quod ego Ricardus filius Ranulfi dedi et concessi et hac presenti carta mea confirmavi, pro salute anime mee et omnium antecessorum meorum, altari Beate Marie Westmonasterii quatuor denarios redditus quos Johannes filius Edwardi prepositi mihi solebat reddere annuatim ad Natale Domini de duabus acris terre quas ipse Johannes tenuit de me cum omnibus libertatibus et liberis consuetudinibus et releviis, et eschaetis, et cum omnibus pertinenciis mihi vel heredibus meis pertinentibus. Et ut hec mea donatio et concessio rata sit et stabilis et inperpetuum permaneat, presentem cartam meam fieri feci, et sigillo meo communivi. Hiis testibus: Odone aurifabro, tunc preposito; Galfrido de Cruce; Ricardo filio Edmundi; Willelmo Dod; Roberto de Crokesl'; Stephano de Berking'; Laurentio Muscat; Ivone filio Ricardi de Medmeham; Martino fratre suo; Gervasio Bachel'; Ricardo de celario; Gervasio Tatin, et multis aliis.

MS: WAD, f. 557.
> Rubric: Carta Ricardi filii Ranulphi de iiij denariis redditus pro duabus acris terre.

411. Quitclaim by Simon of the Gaol to the Blessed Virgin and the church of St Peter of Westminster of his whole land in the vill of Westminster, lying between the land of Randulf Siket and that of Reginald carpenter, to provide lights for the Lady Altar. The proctor of this altar is to render 1s. annually to the custodian of the anniversary of Edward, formerly reeve of Westminster. In return for this quitclaim and charter, Simon received 5 marks (£3. 6s. 8d.) from Robert of Moulsham, precentor and proctor of the altar. [Oct. 1197 × c. 1200]

Sciant presentes et futuri quod ego Simon de Gaiola dedi et concessi et quieteclamavi Deo et Beate Marie et ecclesie Beati Petri Westmonasterii totam terram quam habui in villa Westmonasterii, que terra est inter terram Randulfi Siket et terram Reginaldi carpentarii: in longitudine et latitudine cum domibus et edificiis et omnibus pertinentiis, ad luminaria invenienda altari Beate Dei Genitricis Marie in eadem ecclesia. Quam scilicet terram omnino quietam clamavi de me et heredibus meis sine omni retinemento mei vel heredum meorum. Reddendo inde annuatim per manus procuratoris eiusdem altaris, qui pro tempore fuerit, duode-cim denarios ad quatuor terminos anni ei qui pro tempore procuraverit anniversarium Edwardi, quondam prepositi Westmonasterii, scilicet: ad Natale Domini tres denarios; et ad Pascham tres denarios; et ad Festum Sancti Johannis Baptiste tres denarios; et ad Festum Sancti Michaelis tres denarios. Pro hac autem donatione et concessione et quietaclamatione et carte mee confirmatione recepi quinque marcas argenti per manus Roberti de Mulesham, tunc precentoris eiusdem ecclesie, et pretaxati altaris procuratoris. Et ut hec mea donatio et quietaclamatio rata sit et stabilis permaneat, eam sigilli mei appositione corroboravi. Hiis testibus: Ricardo de Dol, tunc senescallo Westmonasterii; Odone aurifabro West-monasterii; Ricardo Testard; Adam de Westmonasterio; Johanne de Abbendon'; Gaufrido de Cruce; Stephano de Berking'; Ricardo filio Edmundi; Johanne pincerna; Nicolao de celario; Willelmo Stuttel; Laurentio Muschat; Gaufrido Fabro, et multis aliis.

MSS: (1) WAM 17323.
> 17.7 × 14.5 cm; t.u. 2.2 cm.
> Seal: on tag; green; surviving fragment 3.8 × 2.8 cm; fleur de lys; legend: + SI[   ]C

Endorsements: (a) Simon de Gayola dat et quieteclamat capelle totam terram suam ad luminaria sustentanda quam habuit in villa Westmonasterii (13C). (b) Westmonasterii capella lxxv (14C).
(2) WAD, f. 552.

Date: Edward the reeve succeeded by son 30 Oct. 1197 (*Fines, 9 Ric. I*, 55, no. 79); Robert of Moulsham as precentor; Richard de Dol as seneschal.

412. Grant by Adam of Westminster, with the assent of Matilda his wife, and for the soul of her mother Scolastica, of 1*s*. rent in Westminster, to provide lights for the Lady Altar. [Temp. John]

Sciant presentes et futuri quod ego Adam de Westmonasterio, assensu et voluntate Matildis uxoris mee, dedi et concessi et hac presenti carta confirmavi, in puram et perpetuam elemosinam pro anima Scolastice matris predicte Matildis et animabus nostris et parentum nostrorum, Deo et altari Beate Dei Genitricis Marie in ecclesia Westmonasterii ad luminaria invenienda duodecim denariatas redditus in villa Westmonasterii quas Ricardus Testard solebat mihi reddere de terra que fuit quondam Roberti de Baignorio in eadem villa cuius homagium inde recepi. Habendas et tenendas eidem altari inperpetuum, et percipiendas per manus eiusdem Ricardi, vel illius quicumque illam terram tenuerit, ad eosdem terminos quibus ego Adam percipere solebam, videlicet: ad Pascha et ad Festum Sancti Michaelis. Et quia predictus redditus annuus predicte Matildi uxori mee fuit hereditarius, sub utroque nomine hanc cartam predicto altari ego Adam sigillo meo confirmare feci et corroborare. Hiis testibus: Ricardo de Dol, tunc senescallo Westmonasterii; Odone aurifabro Westmonasterii; Ludovico clerico; Ricardo Testard; Ricardo filio Edmundi militis; Roberto de Crokesle; Stephano de Berkinges; Gerardo coco; Nicholao de celario; Ivone filio Ricardi; Gaufrido, Adam, Willelmo, Johanne, servientibus eiusdem ecclesie; Laurentio Muschet; Willelmo Noel; Ricardo de celario; Gervasio Tatin, et multis aliis.

MSS: (1) WAM 17437 (formerly 17687).
　　　17 × 8.9 cm; t.u. 1.7 cm.
　　　Three slits: (a) Tag with seal, green; broken; 4.5 × 3.1 cm; fleur de lys; legend: SIGILL' MATILD' FIL ROBERTI . . . (b) Tag and seal missing. (c) Tag only.
　　　Endorsed: (a) Adam de Westmonasterio et Matildis dant capelle ad luminaria sustentanda xij denariatas annui redditus in Westmonasterio. (b) Westmonasterii capella lvij.
　　　(2) WAD, f. 548.

413. Confirmation by William Little to Alexander son of Henry, and Edith daughter of Geoffrey de Barra, and their sons, of the whole plot of land in the vill of Westminster which Osmund son of Roger Ursel gave him and confirmed by charter, to hold in inheritance of William and his heirs, at an annual rent of 1*s*. Alexander and Edith may designate as their heirs whichever of their sons they please, to hold this land in inheritance. Gersum of three and a half marks (£2. 6s. 8d.). Halimote, Westminster [c. 1200 × 1210]

Sciant tam presentes quam futuri[1] quod ego Willelmus Parvus dedi et concessi et hac presenti carta mea confirmavi Alexandro filio Henrici et Edithe filie Galfridi de Barra et eorum pueris totam illam partem terre quam Osmundus filius Rogeri Ursel michi dedit, et carta sua confirmavit, in villa Westmonasterii: habendam et tenendam hereditarie sibi et heredibus suis, de me et heredibus meis, libere. pacifice et quiete per servicium duodecim denariorum annuatim, reddendorum ad quatuor terminos anni pro omni servicio et omni exactione, scilicet: ad Festum Sancti Michaelis tres denarios; ad Natale Domini tres denarios; ad Pascha tres denarios; ad Festum Sancti Johannis Baptiste tres denarios. Ego autem Willelmus et heredes mei warantizabimus predicto Alexandro et predicte Edithe et eorum pueris predictam partem terre, cum omnibus pertinenciis et liberis consuetudinibus eidem parte terre pertinentibus, per predictum servicium contra omnes gentes. Et sciendum quod predictus Alexander et Editha possunt facere heredes suos de quibuscumque puerorum suorum voluerint ad tenendum istam partem terre hereditarie, sicut predictum est. Et pro hac donatione et concessione et presentis carte mee confirmatione, dedit michi predictus Alexander tres marcas argenti et dimidiam in gersummam. Hiis testibus: Willelmo de Herlauia, domino meo; Roberto de Rokingham; Mauricio de Herlauia; Odone aurifabro, tunc preposito; Ricardo filio Eadmundi; Henrico Sumer; Alexandro de Heya;[2] Johanne de Aqua; Ricardo Alto; Willelmo filio Andree; Johanne fusore; Gaufrido de Cruce; Ada, nepote episcopi; Stephano de Berking; Magistro Gaufrido Pirone, et toto halimoto cum multis aliis.

MSS: (1) WAM 17321.
  15.2 × 21.5 cm; t.u. 2.3 cm.
  Seal: 4.5 × 4.0 cm; eagle, facing right; legend: + SIGILL. WILL. PARVI DE [E]IA.
  Endorsed: (a) Westmonasterii capella lxv (14C). (b) Willelmus Parvus dat Alexandro filio Henrici et Edithe filie Galfridi quandam partem terre in Westmonasterio.
  (2) WAD, f. 549v.
    1. MS: *Sciant presentes et futuri*.
    2. MS: *Ely*.
Date: Attestations of William of Hurley (*Beauchamp Cartulary*, no. 191), and Adam 'nephew of the bp.' (ibid., nos. 185–186n); Odo the goldsmith as reeve.

414. Confirmation by Alexander, clerk of the Exchequer, to provide lights for the Lady Altar, of a messuage with a curtilage in Westminster. The custodian of the altar would render him a rent of 1s. annually. [c. 1200 × 1210]

Omnibus ad quos presens scriptum pervenerit, Alexander clericus de

Scaccario, salutem. Sciatis me divine caritatis intuitu, et pro salute anime mee et omnium parentum meorum, et pro salute Edithe filie Gaufridi de la Barre, et omnium parentum et puerorum suorum, dedisse et concessisse et hac presenti carta mea confirmasse Deo et altari Beate Marie in ecclesia Westmonasterii ad administrationem luminaris inveniendi, in puram et perpetuam elemosinam unum mesuagium cum curtillagio in villa Westmonasterii: quod masuagium est inter terram meam ex una parte versus aquilonem et terram Reginaldi pistoris ex altera versus austrum, continens in latitudine in capite versus regale chiminum duodecim pedes et dimidium, et predictum curtillagium cum totidem pedibus in latitudine extendens se, in longitudine usque infollatum meum ante capitale masuagium meum. Habendum et tenendum de me et heredibus meis bene et in pace, libere et quiete; reddendo inde michi et heredibus meis ille qui pro tempore fuerit custos predicti altaris annuatim duodecim denarios ad quatuor anni terminos, scilicet: ad Festum Sancti Michaelis tres denarios; et ad Natale Domini tres denarios; et ad Pascham tres denarios; et ad Festum Sancti Johannis Baptiste tres denarios, pro omni servitio ad me vel heredes meos pertinente. Ego vero Alexander et heredes mei warantizabimus predictum masuagium cum predicto curtillagio custodi predicti altaris qui pro tempore fuerit contra omnes homines et feminas per predictum servicium. Ut autem hec mea donatio et concessio et carte mee confirmatio rata sit et stabilis permaneat, eam sigilli mei appositione corroboravi. Hiis testibus: Willelmo de Castellis, Lodovico, clericis de Scaccario; Odone aurifabro, tunc preposito Westmonasterii; Ricardo filio Eadmundi; Adam nepote episcopi; Johanne fusore; Roberto de Claygat'; Stephano de Berking'; Roberto de Crokell'; Gaufrido de Cleygat'; Reginaldo pistore; Thoma vinitore; Willelmo parvo de Eya; Willelmo Noel; Nicolao de celario; Ricardo de celario, Laurentio Muschat, et multis aliis.

MSS: (1) WAM 17416.
　　　16.8 × 18.4 cm; t.u. 3 cm.
　　　Seal (on tag): green, 3 × 2 cm; classical head facing to right; legend: + SIGILL' ALEXANDRI CLERICI.
　　　Endorsements: (a) Alexander clericus dat capella ad luminaris sustentationem unum mesuagium cum curtilagio in villa Westmonasterii (13C). (b) Westmonasterium lxvj (14C). (c) Capella (14C).
　　　(2) WAD, ff. 549v–550.
Date: Attestation of Adam *nepos episcopi*.
Note: Alexander of Swerford, who became in due course a senior official of the Exchequer, was, early in his career, employed by Abbot Ralph (**327**). Among his contemporaries there were, however, other Exchequer clerks named Alexander (Richardson, 'William of Ely', 88).

415. Confirmation, in pure and perpetual alms, by Geoffrey de Cruce, at the petition and with the assent of his wife Edith and Geoffrey his son and heir, to the Lady Altar, for the souls of his parents and of all their ancestors, of a rent of 2*s.* 8*d.* which Alan of Aldwych rendered them annually from a curtilage. The younger Geoffrey, assenting, placed the charter on the Lady Altar. [Temp. John]

Sciant presentes et futuri quod ego Galfridus de Cruce, peticione, concessione et voluntate Edithe uxoris mee et Galfridi filii et heredis mei, dedi et concessi, et hac presenti carta mea confirmavi Deo et altari Beate Marie de Westmonasterio, pro animabus patrum et matrum et omnium antecessorum nostrorum, triginta duorum denariorum redditum, quos Alanus de Aldewiche nobis solebat reddere per annum pro uno curtillagio quod de nobis tenuit; habendum et tenendum bene et in pace, libere et quiete, in puram et perpetuam elemosinam, sine aliquo retenemento nostri vel successorum nostrorum. Et sciendum est quod ego Galfridus et heredes mei predictos triginta duorum denariorum redditus conventui de Westmonasterio warantizabimus contra omnes gentes. Hanc vero elemosinam et donacionem Galfridus filius et heres meus ex parte sua concessit et dedit et presentem cartam super ipsum altare Beate Marie posuit et optulit. Hiis testibus: Rogero Enganet; Albino clerico; Henrico Sumer; Ricardo Testard; Nicholao filio Galfridi; Stephano de Berking'; Johanne filio Edwardi; Wimundo pistore; Petro de Wandena; Johanne filio Willelmi filii Ordrici; Edmundo filio Wimundi; Johanne filio Hugonis de Fonte; Pagano Dobbe, et multis aliis.

MSS: (1) WAM 17081.
    21 × 13 cm; t.u. 1.8 cm.
    Two tags bearing dark green seals.
    (1) 5 × 2.5 cm; fleur de lys; legend: SIGILL: EDIT: DE: CRUCE.
    (2) 6 × 4 cm; legend: SIGILLVM GALFRIDI DE CRUCE.
    Endorsed: (a) Carta Galfridi de Cruce et Edithe uxoris sue (early 13C). (b) de redditu xxxij denariorum dato capelle (13C). (c) Aldewich' capella iij (14C).
    (2) WAD, f. 557v.
Date: Attestations and the hand.
Note: The petition of the donor's family, and the action of the younger Geoffrey, would suggest that the donor was incapacitated, and perhaps gravely ill.

416. Confirmation by Hugh de Fonte to his daughter Margaret of William son of Herbert, with the whole tenement which he holds of Hugh in Westminster, and an acre of land adjoining that acre which William holds of him, to be held by Margery at an annual rent of 1*s.* 6*d.* and half a pound of cumin annually, for all services. [Late 12C]

Sciant presentes et futuri quod ego Hugh de Fonte dedi et concessi et hac presenti carta mea confirmavi Margarete filie mee Willelmum filium Herberti cum toto tenemento quod de me tenet in Westmonasterio, et unam acram terre que iacet iuxta acram quam predictus Willelmus de me tenet; tenendum de me et heredibus meis illa et heredibus libere et quiete, integre, plenarie. Reddendo mihi et heredibus meis illa et heredes sui xviij denarios et dimidiam libram cimini per annum pro omni servicio, scilicet: ad Natale Domini iiij denarios et obolum; et ad Pascha iiij denarios et obolum et dimidiam libram cimini; et in Festo Sancti Iohannis Baptiste iiij denarios et obolum; et in Festo Sancti Michaelis iiij denarios et obolum. Hiis testibus: Rogero, Salomone, capellanis; Rogero Enganet, tunc preposito; Albino clerico; Henrico Sumer; Ricardo Testard; Nicholao filio Gaufridi; Gaufrido de Cruce; Iohanne filio Eadwyd; Adam nepote episcopi; Petro de Wendene; Iohanne filio Willelmi; Ordrico; Stephano de Berking'; Pagano Dobbe; Ricardo de Cleigate; Roberto fratre eius, et multis aliis.

MSS: (1) WAM 17320.
    17.5 × 13 cm; t.u. 3.5 cm.
    Seal: green; on tag; 4.5 cm diameter (broken); eagle facing right and legend: SIGILL HUGONIS FIL . . .
    Endorsed: (a) Westmonasterii capella l (14C). (b) Carta Hugonis de Fonte dat' Margerie filie sue Willelmum filium Herberti cum quodam tenemento et unam acram terre in Westmonasterio (13C). (2) WAD, f. 546r–v.
Date: The hand, and the attestation of Adam, nephew of the bishop; also that of Roger Enganet as reeve (Rosser, 'Medieval Westminster', 360).

417. Confirmation, for their souls and those of their predecessors, by Simon Hurel and his wife Margaret, to the Lady Altar of the church of St Peter of Westminster, to provide lights, of 2*s.* rent in pure and perpetual alms, which William son of Herbert and Edric of the Garden hold of them in the vill of Westminster. [Temp. John]

Sciant presentes et futuri quod ego Simon Hurel et Margareta uxor mea et heredes mei dedimus et concessimus et presenti carta nostra confirmavimus Deo et altari Sancte Marie ecclesie Sancti Petri Westmonasterii ad lumen inveniendum, pro salute anime nostre et predecessorum nostrorum, duos solidatos redditus in puram et perpetuam elemosinam, scilicet quos Willelmus filius Hereberti et Edricus de Gardino tenent de nobis in villa Westmonasterii. Et ego predictus Simon et Margareta uxor mea et heredes mei debemus warantizare Deo et altari Sancte Marie illos duos solidatos redditus contra omnes gentes. His testibus: Eudone aurifabro; Ricardo Testard; Henrico Sumer; Petro de Wandena; Gaufrido de Claigate; Walkelino de elemosinaria; Willelmo Noel de Porta; Herwardo scriptore; Adam de monasterio; Gaufrido de monasterio; Elya parmentario; Roberto de Claigata, et multis aliis.

MSS: (1) WAM 17432.
    17.2 × 9.2 cm; t.u. 1.8 cm.
    Seals: green; on tags: (1) 3.3 cm diameter; dog, left forepaw raised; legend: + SIGILL SIMONIS HUREL. (2) 5 × 3 cm; bird soaring; legend: SIGILL MARGARIA FILIE HUGONIS.
    Endorsed: (a) Carta Symonis Hurel et uxoris sue (early 13C). (b) de duobus solidis redditus datis capelle (13C). (c) Westmonasterii capella lij (14C).

(2) WAD, f. 546v.

Date: Attestations of Richard Testard and Henry Sumer (cf. Rosser, 'Medieval Westminster', 360).

418. Confirmation, in pure and perpetual alms, by Margery, daughter of Hugh de Fonte, to the monks of Westminster, to provide lights for the Lady Altar, for her soul and those of her predecessors, of 2*s.* rent in the vill of Westminster, which William son of Herbert and Edric of the Garden rendered to her former husband, Simon Hurell, and to her, for the tenement in that vill which she had of the gift and confirmation of her father Hugh. The rent is to be paid annually to the proctor of the altar. [Early 13C]

Sciant presentes et futuri quod ego Margeria filia Hugonis de Fonte dedi, concessi et hac presenti carta mea confirmavi Deo et monachis West-monasterii ad invenienda luminaria coram altari Beate Marie in eadem ecclesia duos solidatos redditus in villa Westmonasterii, in puram et perpetuam elemosinam pro salute anime mee et omnium predecessorum meorum: illos videlicet quos Willelmus filius Hereberti et Edricus de Gardino solebant reddere Simoni Hurell', quondam viro meo, et michi, de quodam tenemento in eadem villa, et quos ego Margeria habui ex dono et confirmatione predicti Hugonis patris mei. Habendos et tenendos libere et quiete, integre et plenarie inperpetuum, et percipiendos per ipsum qui pro tempore fuerit prenominati altaris con-stitutus procurator ad duos terminos anni, videlicet ad Pascha et ad Festum Sancti Michaelis. Ego vero Margeria et heredes mei waran-tizabimus predictis monachis et procuratori memorati altaris qui pro tempore fuerit predictum redditum duorum solidorum contra omnes homines et feminas. Ut autem hec mea donatio et concessio et carte mee confirmatio rata et stabilis permaneat, eam presenti scripto et sigilli mei appositione corroboravi. Hiis testibus: Odone aurifabro, tunc preposito Westmonasterii; Ricardo filio Edmundi; Roberto de Claigate; Roberto de Crokesl'; Stephano de Berkinge; Petro de Wandene; Gaufrido de Claigate; Walkelino de elemosinario; Willelmo Nohel; Gervasio port-itore; Adam de ecclesia; Gaufrido de ecclesia; Johanne de ecclesia; Elia parmentario; Laurentio Muschat; Gervasio Tatin; Willelmo le Palmer, et multis aliis.

MSS: (1) WAM 17413.
    17.8 × 13 cm; t.u. 1.8 cm.
    Seal: on tag; green; 4.8 × 3.2 cm; soaring bird; legend: SIGILL MARGA. . . FILIE H. . .
    Endorsed: (a) Carta Margerie [filie Hugonis de Fonte]ⁱ Hurrell' de duobus solidis redditus datis capelle in Westmonasterio (13C). (b) Westmonasterii capella lj (14C).
    (2) WAD, f. 546v.

419. Confirmation by Richard de Dol to Ralph Testard of his land in the vill of Westminster, lying between that formerly belonging to William son of Ordric, and that of Simon Poitevin, in length 29 of the iron ells of King

Richard, and in width 6 of those ells, less 4 inches, to hold of Richard and his heirs in fee and inheritance at an annual rent of 3*s*. Gersum of a besant (2*s*.). [Early 13C]

Sciant presentes et futuri quod ego Ricardus de Dol dedi et concessi et hac presenti carta mea confirmavi Radulfo Testard terram meam cum pertinentiis suis in villa Westmonasterii; que videlicet terra jacet inter terram que fuit Willelmi filii Ordrici ex una parte, et inter terram Simonis Peitevin ex alia parte; et que terra continet in longitudine viginti et novem ulnas et dimidiam de ulnis ferreis Regis Ricardi, et in latitudine versus vicum regium sex ulnas de eisdem ulnis, quatuor pollices minus, et in latitudine versus occidentem quinque ulnas de eisdem ulnis. Habendam et tenendam de me et heredibus meis sibi et heredibus suis in perpetuum, in feodo et hereditate, libere et quiete, integre et plenarie, pacifice et honorifice; reddendo de prefata terra singulis annis michi et heredibus meis tres solidos ad quatuor terminos anni, pro omni servitio et exactione, videlicet: ad Pascha novem denarios; et ad Festum Sancti Johannis novem denarios; et ad Festum Sancti Michaelis novem denarios; et ad Natale Domini novem denarios, salvo forinseco servitio. Et ego Ricardus de Dol et heredes mei warantizabimus predictam terram cum pertinentiis suis predicto Radulfo et heredibus suis, et aquietabimus versus omnes homines et omnes feminas. Pro hac autem donatione et concessione et carte mee confirmatione, dedit mihi prefatus Radulfus unum bizantium in gersumam. Et ut hec mea donatio et concessio firma sit et stabilis, eam presentis scripti testimonio et sigilli mei appositione roboraui. Hiis testibus: Odone aurifabro, tunc preposito Westmonasterii; Henrico Sumer; Ricardo Testard; Ricardo filio Edmundi; Roberto de Crokesleg'; Stephano de Berking'; Gaufrido de Cruce; Wimundo pistore; Willelmo pistore; Willelmo de Scardeburg'; Gaufrido Cuttelebatte; Thoma filio Pavie; Ivone de Coquina; Rogero coco; Alexandro de Eia; Ricardo Alto; Willelmo Parvo; Johanne de Aqua; Ricardo de cellario; Nicholao de cellario; Walkelino de elemosinario; Willelmo Noel; Willemo, serviente de ecclesia; Laurentio Muschet; Gervasio Tatin, et multis aliis.

MSS: (1) WAM 17316.
    17.5 × 12.5 cm; t.u. 2.8 cm.
    Seal: on pink cord; 5 × 2.8 cm; fleur de lys; legend: + SIGILL[V]M RICARDI DE DOL.
    Endorsed: (a) Ricardus de Dol dat Radulfo Testard totam terram suam cum pertinentiis in villa Westmonasterii (13C). (b) Westmonasterii capella xxxvij (14C).
    (2) WAD, f. 543r–v.
Date: Attested by Odo the goldsmith as reeve, although the following attestation of Henry Sumer should be noticed (cf. Rosser, 360). The measurements in 'ells of King Richard' could be taken from an earlier deed or description of the plot.

420. Confirmation by Richard de Dol, for his soul and for those of his ancestors, to St Peter of Westminster, in pure and perpetual alms, to provide lights for the high altar, of 2*s*. rent from land which Ralph Testard holds of him and his heirs in the vill of Westminster, lying between the land formerly belonging to William son of Ordric and that of Simon Poitevin. The rent is due to the sacrist, who is empowered to distrain for non-payment. [Early 13C]

Sciant presentes et futuri quod ego Ricardus de Dol dedi, concessi et hac presenti carta mea confirmavi, pro salute anime mee et pro salute animarum omnium antecessorum meorum, Deo et ecclesie Sancti Petri Westmonasterii, in puram et perpetuam elemosinam ad invenienda luminaria coram magno altari in eadem ecclesia duos solidos de terra quam Radulfus Testard de me et heredibus meis tenet in villa Westmonasterii: que videlicet terra jacet inter terram que fuit Willelmi filii Orderici ex una parte, et inter terram que fuit Simonis Peytevin ex alia parte. Ita quod sacrista quis pro tempore fuerit predictos duos solidos singulis annis percipiet inperpetuum ad quatuor terminos anni; quolibet scilicet termino vj denarios de prefata terra quicumque illam teneat. Et ego et heredes mei warantizabimus predicte ecclesie prefatam elemosinam duorum solidorum contra omnes homines et omnes feminas. Nec poterimus ego vel heredes mei predictam elemosinam in aliquo minuere vel detinere. Quod si aliquod detineatur sacrista qui pro tempore fuerit liberam habebit potestatem distringendi prefatam terram et catalla in eadem terra inventa retinendi donec predicta[1] elemosina duorum solidorum integre persolvatur. Ut autem hec mea donatio et concessio firma sit et stabilis inperpetuum, eam presentis scripti testimonio et sigilli mei appositione roboravi. Hiis testibus: Odone aurifabro; Magistro Simone de London'; Lodovico clerico; Henrico Sumer; Galfrido de Cruce; Stephano de Berking'; Ricardo filio Edmundi; Willelmo pistore, et multis aliis.

MS: WAD, f. 357.
    Rubric: Carta Ricardi de Dol de ij solidis de terra quam Radulfus Testard de se tenuit in villa Westmonasterii.
    1. *predicta* repeated.
Date: Prob. issued soon after **419**.
Note: Discrepancy between the rent mentioned in **419** and that in this charter.

421. Confirmation by John Testard to Isabel, wife of Robert Mauduit the king's chamberlain, of two messuages with appurtenances in Westminster, which are of the fee of Herbert bp. of Salisbury, and situated between the land of Thomas the vintner and that of Peter of Ely. Isabel will render 2*s*. 2*d*. annually, and may dispose of the messuages as she chooses, even to a religious house. Peter Lek retains a life interest in the house where he now dwells, rendering Isabel 1*s*. 6*d*. annually. Gersum of two and a half marks (£1. 13*s*. 4*d*.). [Temp. John, *ante* Jan. 1214]

Sciant presentes et futuri quod ego Johannes Testard dedi et concessi et hac presenti carta mea confirmavi Ysabelle, uxori Roberti Maudut domini regis camerarii, duo masagia cum pertinentiis in villa Westmonasterii: que sunt de feudo Herberti Sarresberiensis episcopi et jacent inter terram Thome vinitoris et terram Petri de Ely. Habenda et tenenda de me et heredibus meis ipsi Ysabelle et heredibus suis bene et in pace, libere et quiete, integre et plenarie, inperpetuum, per liberum servicium viginti et sex denariorum per annum pro omni servicio et exactione, reddendorum ad duos terminos anni, scilicet: ad Festum Sancti Michaelis xiij denariorum; et ad Pascha xiij denariorum. Et sciendum quod predicta Ysabella poterit facere heredem suum de quocumque vel de quacumque voluerit de predictis duabus masagiis, aut illa dare vel assignare ubicumque voluerit, sive in religionem sive extra religionem. Et ego Johannes et heredes mei warantizabimus predicte Ysabelle et heredibus suis vel ubicumque predicta masagia dederit vel assignaverit contra omnes gentes per predictum servicium, salvo Petro Leko tota vita sua domum suam in qua manet, tenendam de ipsa Ysabella et heredibus suis per servicium decem et octo denariorum per annum pro omni servicio. Hanc vero donationem et concessionem et presentis carte mee confirmationem feci predicte Ysabelle pro servicio suo et pro duabus marcis et dimidia argenti quas in manum dedit in gersumam. Hiis testibus: Henrico Foliot; Thoma de Windlessore'; Roberto de Bassingeburn'; Willelmo filio Roberti; Odone aurifabro; Henrico Sumer; Roberto de Rokingeham; Laurentio hostiario; Petro de Ely; Thoma vinitore; Stephano de Berking'; Gaufrido de Cruce; Wimundo pistore; Johanne filio Edwardi; Martino King; Nicolao de celario; Ada de ecclesia; Gaufrido de ecclesia; Nicolao filio Gaufridi, qui hanc cartam scripsit, et multis aliis.

MSS: (1) WAM 17328.

    15.8 × 16.1 cm; t.u. 1.7 cm.

    Seal: on tags; green; 2.8 cm diameter; man's head, full face; legend: + SIGILL' IOHANNIS TESTARD.

    Endorsed: (a) Johannes Testard dat Isabelle uxori Roberti Mauduit duo mesuagia in villa Westmonasterii pro servitio xxvj denariorum per annum (13C). (b) Westmonasterii capelle lxxxiiij (14C).

    (2) WAD, f. 555v.

Date: Earlier than **422**.

Note: The wording of John's charter indicates that Isabel's purchase was made with the intention of subsequently granting the messuages to the Lady Altar (see **422**).

422. Confirmation, in pure and perpetual alms, by Isabel [Basset], wife of Robert Mauduit [II], the king's chamberlain, for her soul and those of her predecessors, to the Lady Altar, to provide lights, of two messuages in the vill of Westminster which she bought from John Testard, lying between the land of Thomas the vintner and that of Peter of Ely, which are of the fee of Herbert, bp. of Salisbury, as John's charter testifies. The proctor of the altar will receive an annual rent of 2*s*. 2*d*. from those messuages, as stated in John's charter, which she gave to the altar. [Temp. John, *ante* Jan. 1214]

Universis Sancte Matris Ecclesie filiis ad quos presens carta pervenerit, Isabel uxor Roberti Mauduit, domini regis camerarii, salutem. Noverit universitas vestra me, pietatis Dei intuitu, et pro anime mee salute, et animarum predecessorum meorum, dedisse et concessisse et hac presenti carta mea confirmasse Deo et altari Beate Marie de Westmonasterio duo masuagia cum pertinentiis in villa Westmonasterii: illa videlicet duo masuagia que emi de Johanne Testard, et jacent inter terram Thome vinitoris, et terram Petri de Ely, et sunt de feodo Herberti Sarresberiensis episcopi, in puram et perpetuam elemosinam; et sicut carta prenominati Johannis testatur, quam modo habui, et quam eidem altari Beate Marie in testimonium dedi, ad luminaria eiusdem altaris inperpetuum administranda. Ita tamen quod quicumque monachorum Westmonasterii predictum altare custodierit, reddet annuatim de predicta terra prenominato Johanni viginti et sex denarios ad duos terminos, scilicet: ad Pascha xiij denarios, et ad Festum Sancti Michaelis xiij denarios, secundum tenorem carte prenominati Johannis quam eidem altari dedi, ut predictum est. Et ut hec mea donatio et concessio et presentis carte mee confirmatio prenominato altari Beate Marie rata et stabilis in perpetuum permaneat, eam presentis sigilli mei munimine roboravi. Hiis testibus: Ricardo de Dol, tunc temporis senescallo Westmonasterii; Henrico Foliot; Thoma de Windlesor'; Johanne filio suo; Willelmo filio Roberti; Johanne filio suo; Odone aurifabro; Roberto de Rokingham'; Johanne de Abendonn'; Willelmo filio Andree; Rogero Enganet; Henrico Sumer; Adam nepote episcopi; Stephano de Berkinges; Ricardo Testard; Galfrido de Cruce; Wimone pistore; Thoma vinitore; Nicholao filio Galfridi; Willelmo de Escardebr'; Nicholao de celario; Martino King; Lodovico clerico, qui hanc cartam scripsit, et pluribus aliis.

MSS: (1) WAM 17327.
    15.2 × 19.2 cm; t.u. 2.9 cm.
    Seal: green; 4.3 × 3.3 cm; Basset arms; legend: SIGILL' ISABELE BASSET.
    Endorsed: (a) Isabella uxor Roberti Mauduit dat capelle duo mesuagia in villa Westmonasterii apud Endhuth (13C). (b) Westmonasterii capella (14C). (c) l (14C; on tag).
    (2) WAD, f. 508v.
Pd: Mason, 'The Mauduits and their Chamberlainship', 20.
Date: Earlier than Abbot Ralph's grant of spiritual benefits to benefactors of the Lady Altar, made at the request of Isabel and Robert (**329**).
Note: In the reign of H III, John Testard granted to the abbey a rent of 2*d.* which he formerly received from the proctor of the Lady Altar for land held of the fee of the bp. of Salisbury in Westminster (WAM 17430; copy WAD, f. 548v).

423. Confirmation by Richard Testard, in pure and perpetual alms, to the Lady Altar, for lights, of 1*s.* rent in the vill of Westminster, which he claimed by royal writ in the abbot's court from Robert of Bagnor and Derewenn his wife, namely the 1*s.* which Odo the goldsmith of Westminster is bound to him (Richard) for that land. [Temp. John]

Sciant presentes et futuri quod ego Ricardus Testard dedi et concessi et hac presenti carta mea confirmavi, in puram et perpetuam elemosinam Deo et altari Beate Marie in ecclesia Westmonasterii ad luminaria

invenienda eidem altari, duodecim denariatas redditus in villa Westmonasterii de terra quondam Roberti de Baignorio et Derewenne uxoris
sue; quam terram ego Ricardus disrationavi in curia abbatis Westmonasterii per breve domini regis super eosdem Robertum et Derewen-
nam, unde placitum fuit[1] inter nos in prefata curia. Habendas et tenendas
et percipiendas ad duos anni terminos, scilicet: ad Pascha sex denarios, et
ad Festum Sancti Michaelis sex denarios; illos scilicet duodecim denarios
quos Odo aurifaber de Westmonasterio et heredes sui tenentur reddere
mihi et heredibus meis singulis annis de predicta terra. Ego autem
Ricardus et heredes mei warantizabimus procuratori prefati altaris qui
pro tempore fuerit predictum redditum duodecim denariorum contra
omnes homines et feminas. Ut autem hec concessio et donatio et carte
mee confirmatio rata sit et stabilis permaneat eam sigilli mei appositione
corroboravi. Hiis testibus: Ricardo de Dol; Ludovico clerico; Alexandro
clerico; Odone, tunc preposito Westmonasterii; Henrico Sumer; Ricardo
filio Edmundi; Adam de Westmonasterio; Roberto de Crokesl';
Stephano de Berking; Gerardo coco; Thoma vinitore; Willelmo Noel;
Ivone filio Ricardi; Laurento Muschat; Nicholao de celario; Adam,
Gaufrido, Willelmo, servientibus de ecclesia, et multis aliis.

MSS: (1) WAM 17330.
     14 × 10.7 cm; t.u. 1.5 × cm.
     Seal: on tag; green; 2.5 × 2 cm; mounted figure, facing right; legend:
     SIGILL RICARDI TESTARD.
     Endorsed: (a) Ricardus Testard dat capelle ad luminaria susten-
     tanda in villa Westmonasterii xij denariatas annuatim redditus
     (13C). (b) Westmonasterii capelle lix (14C).
       1. *fuit* repeated in MS.
     (2) WAD, f. 548r–v.

424. Confirmation by Richard Testard, in pure and perpetual alms, to
the Lady Altar, to provide lights, of 1*s.* quit-rent which Odo the
goldsmith holds of him in Westminster, and which formerly belonged to
Andrew of the Exchequer. Odo will now pay the rent to the proctor of the
Lady Altar, who may distrain for non-payment. [Temp. John]

Sciant presentes et futuri quod ego Ricardus Testard dedi et concessi et
hac presenti carta mea confirmavi Deo et Altari Beate Marie in ecclesia
Westmonasterii, in puram et perpetuam elemosinam, ad inven[i]enda
luminaria coram predicto altari duodecim denariatas quieti redditus de
terra quam Odo aurifaber de me tenet in villa Westmonasterii et que fuit
Andree de Scaccario. Ita quod custos prefati altaris qui pro tempore
fuerit percipiet singulis annis per manum Odonis prefati vel heredum
suorum de predicta terra absque contradictione et sine retinemento vel
calumpnia mei vel heredum meorum prefatos duodecim denarios ad duos
terminos anni in perpetuum, scilicet: ad Pascham vj denarios, et ad
Festum Sancti Michaelis vj denarios; et libere et quiete, integre et
plenarie, pacifice et sine diminutione predictum quietum redditum
duodecim denariorum recipiet tanquam ex dono meo puram et

261

perpetuam elemosinam. Si vero predictus Odo vel heredes sui prefatum redditum xij denariorum custodi predicti altaris non reddiderit, licebit predicto custodi altaris prefati predictam terram distringere et namas retinere, donec ei totus prefatus redditus duodecim denariorum integre persolvatur. Ego vero Ricardus Testard' et heredes mei prefato altari Beate Marie totum predictum quietum redditum duodecim denariorum ut puram et perpetuam elemosinam warantizabimus in perpetuum contra omnes homines et omnes feminas. Ut autem hec mea donatio et concessio rata sit et stabilis in perpetuum eam presenti scripto et sigilli mei appositione roboravi. Hiis testibus: Uliano Chendedut; Magistro Simone de Londoniis; Ludovico et Alexandro, clericis de Scaccario; Odone aurifabro, tunc preposito Westmonasterii; Henrico Sumer; Petro de Ely; Eduuardo filio Odonis; Ricardo filio Edmundi; Roberto de Crokesleg'; Stephano de Berking'; Gerardo coco; Wimundo pistore; Galfrido de Cruce; Gaufrido Cuttelebatte; Willelmo pistore; Nicholao de cellario; Thoma filio Pavie; Willelmo Noel; Johanne cancellario, et multis aliis.

MSS: (1) WAM 17433.
17 × 9.8 cm; t.u. 1.8 cm.
Seal: on tag; green; 2.7 × 2.2 cm; worn; legend: . . . RICARDI . . .
Endorsed: (a) Carta Ricardi Testard' de xij denariis (13C). (b) quieti redditus datis capelle ad luminaria sustentanda in villa Westmonasterii (13C).
(2) WAD, f. 548v.

425. Confirmation, by Odo the goldsmith, to the Lady Altar, of an annual rent of 1s. 8d. from a messuage which he holds in the vill of Westminster, lying between the messuage of Andrew of the Exchequer and the house which belonged to Richard of Medmenham. In return, Robert of Moulsham, the precentor, gave a gersum of £2. Halimote, Westminster [late 12C]

Sciant presentes et [futuri quod ego Odo aurifaber] dedi et concessi [et hac presenti] carta mea confirmavi Deo et altari Sancte Marie de Westmonasterio viginti denariorum redditum per annum de mes[agio] meo quod teneo in villa Westmonasterii; et jacet inter masagium Andree de Scaccario et domum que fuit Ricardi de Medmeham, scilicet: ad Pascham [quinque] denarios; et ad Festum Sancti Johannis Baptiste quinque denarios; et ad Festum Sancti Michaelis quinque denarios; et ad Natale Domini quinque denarios. Et e[go] Odo et heredes mei warantizabimus predictum redditum predicto altari contra omnes homines et omnes feminas; et si warantizare non poterimus, faciemus rationabile [escambium predicto altari] ad valentiam [predicti redditus. Et pro hac don]atione, concessione et warantizatione et carte mee confirmati[one Robertus de Mulesham pre]centor Westmonasterii dedit [mihi quadraginta solid]os esterlingorum. Hiis testibus: Ricardo de Dol; Rogero Enganet; Henrico Sumer; Ricardo Testard; Ada de Westmonasterio; Nicholao filio Gaufridi; Johanne filio Edwardi; Stephano [de Ber]king'; Petro de Wandene; Wimundo pistore; Gaufrido de Cruce; Thoma vinitore; Willelmo Noel; Pagano Dobbe, et toto halimoto de Westmonasterio.

MSS: (1) WAM 17414: badly stained; missing words supplied from WAD.
17.2–18 × 6.7 cm; t.u. 1.3 cm; slits; tag missing.
Endorsed: (a) Odo aurifaber dat capelle annuatim xx denarios de mesuagio . . . (stained) duplicatur (13C). (b) Westmonasterii capella (13C). (c) vij dupplicatur (13C).
(2) WAM 17452 (duplicate, in a hand of *c.* 1190 × 1200, not identical with hand of WAM 17414 but of approximately same date); badly stained top left and bottom left corners.
16.8 × 11.4 cm; t.u. 2.3 cm; seal and tag cut out.
Endorsed: (a) Odo aurifaber dat capelle . . . (word stained) annum xx denarios de masuagio s . . . (stained) in Westmonasterio (13C).
(b) Westmonasterii capella vij (14C). (c) Duplicatur (MS cut).
(3) WAD, ff. 532v–533.
Date: Robert of Moulsham as precentor; attestations, especially precedence taken by Dol; Enganet (prob. still a reeve); Sumer and Testard.

426. Confirmation by Richard Testard, for his soul and those of his father and all his kinsfolk, to provide lights for the Lady Altar, of 2*s*. rent in the vill of Westminster, from the land which Odo the goldsmith holds of William de Legha in fee, which rent Richard used to receive from Odo, who will now render it to the proctor of the Lady Altar. [Temp. John]

Sciant presentes et futuri quod ego Ricardus Testard dedi et concessi et hac presenti carta mea confirmavi, pro anima patris mei et salute anime mee et omnium parentum meorum, Deo et altari Beate Marie in ecclesia Westmonasterii ad luminaria invenienda duas solidatas redditus in villa Westmonasterii de terra quam Odo aurifaber tenet de Willelmo de Legha in feodo, quas ego Ricardus percipere solebam a predicto Odone. Habendas et tenendas et percipiendas a sepedicto Odone et heredibus suis ille qui pro tempore fuerit custos eiusdem altaris ad duos anni terminos, scilicet: ad Pascham duodecim denarios, et ad Festum Sancti Michaelis duodecim denarios. Et ut hec mea donatio et concessio et carte mee confirmatio rata sit et stabilis permaneat, eam sigilli mei appositione corroboravi. Hiis testibus: Ricardo de Dol; Uliano Chesned'; Ludovico, Alexandro, clericis de Scaccario; Henrico Sumer; Ricardo filio Edmundi; Adam de Westmonasterio; Stephano de Berking'; Roberto de Crokesl'; Thoma vinitore; Willelmo pistore; Martino filio Ricardi; Laurentio Muschat, et multis aliis.

MSS: (1) WAM 17435.
13.8 × 10.9 cm; t.u. 2.2 cm; slit, but tag and seal missing.
Endorsed: (a) Ricardus Testard dat capelle ad luminaria sustentanda ij solidos redditus in Westmonasterio (13C). (b) Westmonasterii capelle lviij (14C).
(2) WAD, f. 548.
Date: Attestation of Adam of Westminster, and the hand.

Note: The genealogy of the Testard family is recited in a lawsuit held in Trinity Term 1231, when Richard is described as the son of Juliana (*Curia Regis Rolls* XIV, 339, no. 1584). Her husband was Robert Testard (*Beauchamp Cartulary*, no. 199).

427. Confirmation by Richard Testard, in pure and perpetual alms, for his soul and those of his ancestors, to the Lady Altar of a rent of 2*s.* 2*d.* in the vill of Westminster, to provide lights: namely that rent which Robert Mauduit the king's chamberlain and his heirs rendered Richard and his heirs for three acres of land which lie between the road of Tothill (in Westminster) and the road which runs from Tothill towards the Hospital of St James, as far as the meadow, and for one acre of meadow which Robert and his heirs hold of Richard and his heirs, for the aforesaid 2*s.* 2*d.* annually, which Robert and his heirs will render the proctor of the Lady Altar. [Temp. John]

Sciant presentes et futuri quod ego Ricardus Testard dedi et concessi et hac presenti carta mea confirmavi, pro salute anime mee et animarum antecessorum meorum, Deo et altari Sancte Marie Westmonasterii redditum viginti sex denariorum in villa Westmonasterii, in puram et perpetuam elemosinam ad luminaria predicti altaris administranda: illum videlicet redditum quem Robertus Mauduit, domini regis camerarius, et heredes sui mihi et heredibus meis solvere tenentur pro tribus acris terre que jacent inter viam de Tothull' et viam que extendit de Tothull' versus Hospitalem Sancti Jacobi usque in pratum; et pro una acra prati quam predictus Robertus et heredes sui tenent de me et heredibus meis pro prefatis xxvj denariis per annum, solvendis ad duos terminos anni, scilicet: ad Pascha xiij denarios; et ad Festum Sancti Michaelis xiij denarios. Quos xxvj denarios custos prenominati altaris Beate Marie qui pro tempore fuerit recipiet de predicto Roberto et heredibus suis ad prefatos terminos ad luminaria prefati altaris administranda liberos et quietos ab omni seculari servitio et exactione. Hos autem predictos xxvj denarios annuatim percipiendos ego prefatus Ricardus Testard et heredes mei warantizabimus prenominato altari Beate Marie contra omnes gentes. Hanc vero donationem et concessionem et presentis carte mee confirmationem feci predicto altari Sancte Marie pro salute anime mee et animarum predecessorum meorum. Hiis testibus: Roberto Mauduit, domini regis camerario; Willelmo Mauduit, filio eius; Lodovico clerico; Johanne filio Willelmi; Odone aurifabro; Henrico Sumer; Stephano de Berchengis; Ada de Westmonasterio; Ricardo filio AEdmundj; Roberto de Crochelle; Gerardo coco, et multis aliis.

MSS: (1) WAM 17318.
    15.6 × 6.5 cm; t.u. 1 cm.
    Seal: on tag; green; 3 × 2.4 cm; man on horseback, facing right; legend: + SIGILL RICARDI TESTARD.
    Endorsed: (a) Ricardus Testard dat capelle redditum xxvj denariorum in Westmonasterio apud Tothull' (13C). (b) Tothull: capella vj (14C). (c) Carta 7a (16C). (d) W. Mauduit canc[ellavit?] (13C).
    (2) WAD, f. 516r–v.

Date: Attested by Adam of Westminster; also the hand.

428. Confirmation by Hamo de Hotot to William de Hobruge of his whole land and tenement which he held of the fee of the abbot of Westminster in the vill of Westminster, comprising the land and tenement which William son of Richer, John Pimeriche and Peter Fausard held of him, saving 1*s.* and half a pound of cumin annually. Hamo has attorned William to render the service of 1*s.* which he owes the abbot of Westminster in quittance of that fee. [*c.* 1200]

Sciant presentes et futuri quod ego Hamo de Hotot dedi et concessi, et hac presenti carta mea confirmavi Willelmo de Hobruge totam terram meam et totum tenementum meum quod habui in villa de Westmonasterio de feudo abbatis de Westmonasterio sine aliquo retenemento, scilicet totam terram illam et totum tenementum quod Willelmus filius Richeri et Johannes Pimeriche et Petrus Fausard' tenuerunt de me in eadem villa. Habenda et tenenda illi et heredibus suis, vel cuicumque ipse eam dare voluerit, et heredibus suis, de me et heredibus meis, salva tenura tenencium per liberum servicium duodecim denariorum et dimidium librum cymini per annum pro omni servitio; reddendo ad duos terminos anni, scilicet: ad Pascham dimidiam libram cymini et sex denarios, et ad Festum Sancti Michaelis vj denarios. Et ego Hamo atornavi ipsum Willelmum ad faciendum servicium per manum suam quod debeo abbati de Westmonasterio, scilicet duodecim denarios in aquietamentum eiusdem feudi. Et ego Hamo et heredes mei warantizabimus predicto Willelmo et heredibus suis, vel cuicumque eam dare voluerit et heredibus suis, totam predictam terram et tenementum predictum cum omnibus pertinentiis suis contra omnes homines et feminas. Et pro hac donacione et concessione et carte mee confirmacione predictus Willelmus dedit michi in gersumam unam marcam argenti et devenit inde affidatus meus. Quare volo et firmiter precipio quod predictus Willelmus et heredes sui, vel cui illam dare voluerit et heredes sui, habeant et teneant totam predictam terram et tenementum cum omnibus pertinentiis suis de me et heredibus meis bene et in pace, libere et quiete, integre et plenarie inperpetuum per predictum servicium. Et ut hec mea donatio et concessio rata sit et stabilis permaneat, eam sigilli mei apposicione roboravi. Hiis testibus: Ricardo de Dol; Ricardo Testard; Henrico Sumer; Odone aurifabro; Nicholao filio Gaufridi; Stephano de Berkinge; Radulfo de Setfonteines; Theobaldo de Feringes; Johanne filio Edwardi; Gaufrido de Cruce; Gaufrido de Claigate; Roberto de Claigate; Nicholao de Braie, et multis aliis.

MSS: (1) WAM 17324.
    13.7 × 30.5 cm; t.u. 2.1 cm.
    Seal: on tag; green; 3.7 cm diameter; peacock?; body facing left but head twisted to right; legend: SIGILLV[M H]AMO . . .
    Endorsed: (a) Hamo de Hotot dat Willelmo de Hobrig' totam terram et tenementum que habuit in Westmonasterio (13C). (b) Capella (14C).

(2) WAD, ff. 545v–546.

Date: Attestations of Richard Testard and Henry Sumer, prob. as reeves (cf. Rosser, 'Medieval Westminster', 360). See also **429**.

Note: 'Hobruge' may be Hoe Bridge, Shepperton, Mddx. (*PN Mddx*, 18), where the abbey held a demesne manor (Harvey, *WA*, 354).

429. Confirmation by William de Hobregge, for his soul and those of his parents and ancestors, to the Blessed Virgin, to provide lights for the Lady Altar, of his whole land and tenement which he had from Hamo de Hotot in the vill of Westminster, of the abbot's fee, comprising the land and tenement which William, son of Richer, John Pimerich and Peter Fausard held of William in that vill. The Altar will hold this land in perpetuity of William and his heirs, saving the tenancies of the tenants, by service of 1*s*. annually, which the proctor of the Altar will render the abbot; and 1 lb cumin to William or his heirs. William has restored to Robert [of Moulsham] the precentor his charter which he had from Hamo de Hotot concerning that tenement. [*c*. 1200]

Sciant presentes et futuri quod ego Willelmus de Hobregge dedi et concessi et hac presenti carta mea confirmavi Deo et Beate Marie ad luminaria invenienda altari Beate Marie in ecclesia Beati Petri Westmonasterii, pro animabus patris et matris mee, et antecessorum meorum, et pro salute anime mee, totam terram et totum tenementum illud quod habui in villa Westmonasterii de dono Hamonis de Hotot de feodo abbatis Westmonasterii, scilicet: totam terram illam et totum tenementum illud quod Willelmus filius Richeri et Johannes Pimerich' et Petrus Fausard tenuerunt de me in eadem villa. Habendum et tenendum de me et heredibus meis inperpetuum, libere et quiete, salva tenura tenentium per liberum servitium duodecim denariorum per annum quos ille qui pro tempore fuerit eiusdem altaris procurator reddet abbati eiusdem loci ad duos terminos anni, scilicet: ad Pascham sex denarios, et ad Festum Sancti Michaelis sex denarios, et pro dimidia libra cymini reddenda annuatim mihi vel heredibus meis ad Pascham pro omnibus servitiis et exactionibus. Ita quod nec abbas nec aliquis successorum eiusdem loci ulla tempore illum prenominatum redditum ad nullum aliud officium nisi ad prenominatum servitium predicti altaris assignare possit. Et ego Willelmus reddidi in manu Roberti cantoris eiusdem ecclesie cartam meam quam habui de Hamone de Hotot de prenominato tenemento in loco warantizationis. Et ut hec mea donatio et concessio rata sit et stabilis permaneat, eam sigilli mei appositione corroboravi. Hiis testibus: Hugone de Bella Aqua; Ricardo de Dol, tunc senescallo Westmonasterii; Odone aurifabro; Ludovico clerico; Ricardo Testard; Johanne fratre eius; Henrico Sumer; Ricardo filio Edmundi; Adam de Westmonasterio; Johanne Pimerich'; Stephano de Berkinges; Roberto de Crokesle; Gaufrido de Cruce; Ivone de Medmeham; Nicholao de celario; Laurentio Muschat, et multis aliis.

MSS: (1) WAM 17325.
    19.3 × 15 cm; t.u. 3 cm; tag (marked Hotot).

Seal: green; 3.5 cm diameter; shield with two horizontal bands; legend: SIGILLUM WILL[ELM]I DE HOBRUCI +.
Endorsed: (a) Willelmus de Hobregg' dat capelle totam terram et tenementum que habuit in villa Westmonasterii de dono H[am]onis Hetot (13C). (b) Carta xxxvj^a (16C). (c) Capella (14C).
(2) WAD, f. 546.
Date: Attestations, including Richard Testard and Henry Sumer; Robert of Moulsham as precentor.

430. Quitclaim by Peter Fauset, for his soul, those of his parents and all his ancestors, to the Lady Altar of his whole land in the vill of Westminster, which he held of the precentor, Robert [of Moulsham], to provide lights for that altar. Robert gave him a gersum of 7*s.* 2*d.*, and Peter placed the charter on the altar. [*c.* 1200]

Sciant presentes et futuri quod ego Petrus Fauset, pro salute anime mee et patris et matris mee et omnium antecessorum meorum, concessi et dimisi et quietum clamavi de me et omnibus successoribus et heredibus meis Deo et altari Beate Virginis Marie ecclesie Westmonasterii totam terram meam in villa Westmonasterii quam tenui de Roberto precentore, ad luminaria predicti altaris inperpetuum administranda. Pro hac autem concessione et dimissione et carte mee confirmatione dedit mihi prefatus Robertus septem solidos et duos denarios. Hanc autem cartam super predictum altare Beate Marie optuli ad invenienda eiusdem altaris luminaria inperpetuum. Hiis testibus: Ricardo Testard; Gaufrido de Cruce; Stephano de Berking'; Thoma vinitore; Nicholao de celario; Ricardo filio Randulfi; Laurentio Muschet; Adam, Gaufrido, Johanne, servientibus ecclesie Westmonasterii, et multis aliis.

MSS: (1) WAM 17417.
    14.3 × 10.3 cm; t.u. 2.6 cm.
    Slit, tag with seal fragment; broken and worn; floral device; legend: . . . ETR . . .
    Endorsed: (a) Petrus Fauset quietum clam[avit] capelle ad luminaria sustentanda ius suum et clamium in quadam parte terre apud Westmonasterium (14C). (b) Carta xxiiij^a. (c) Westmonasterii capella lxxiij.
    (2) WAD, f. 551v.
Date: Robert of Moulsham as precentor.
Note: This land was subsequently leased by Robert of Moulsham, when prior, to Adam the sergeant (**348**). See also **429**.

431. Confirmation by Mr Simon of London, son of Walter Niger, for his soul and those of his parents and all the faithful, to the church and monks of Westminster, in pure and perpetual alms, of all the land, with houses, which he held in fee and inheritance of Stephen son of Osbert in the vill of Westminster, to provide candles for the altar of the Holy Trinity in the abbey, saving 2*s.* rent due from that land to the Lady Altar, payable by the proctor of the Holy Trinity altar. The proctor will also render 1*d.* annually to Stephen son of Osbert and his heirs, and 1*s.* 6*d.* to the chief lords of the fee. Simon has handed over to the monks a charter concerning those services which he had from Stephen and his heirs. [Temp. John]

Sciant presentes et futuri quod ego Magister Simon de London', filius Walteri Nigri, dedi et concessi et hac presenti carta mea confirmavi Deo et ecclesie Westmonasterii et monachis ibidem Deo servientibus, in puram et perpetuam elemosinam, totam terram cum domibus et omnibus pertinentiis suis quam tenui in feodo et hereditate de Stephano filio Osberti in villa Westmonasterii ad inveniendos cereos qui constituti sunt ad altare Sancte Trinitatis in ecclesia Westmonasterii; salvis duobus solidis reddendis de predicta terra ad altare Beate Marie in eadem ecclesia per procuratorem altaris Sancte Trinitatis. Procurator vero altaris Sancte Trinitatis totum redditum qui provenire poterit de predicta terra et domibus et pertinentiis suis integre percipiet et per manum eius custos altaris Beate Marie annuatim percipiet duos solidos memoratos, quolibet termino anni sex denarios. Reddet etiam predictus procurator de prefata terra et suis pertinentiis Stephano filio Osberti et heredibus suis unum denarium ad Pascham pro omni servitio et rebus cunctis et capitalibus dominis feodi illius decem et octo denarios per annum, scilicet: ad Festum Sancti Michaelis novem denarios, et ad Pascham novem denarios. Unde cartam de predictis servitiis, quam de prefato Stephano et heredibus suis habui, reddidi monachis memoratis. Hanc autem donationem et concessionem feci pro salute anime mee et patris et matris mee et omnium fidelium, interdicens in nomine Sancte Trinitatis Patris et Filii et Spiritus Sancti, ad cuius honorem prefatum redditum assignavi ne redditus terre memorate in alios usus transferatur, sed sicut est distinctum in presenti carta altari Sancte Trinitatis et altari Beate Virginis tribuatur. Ut autem hec mea concessio firma sit et stabilis eam presenti scripto et sigilli mei appositione roboravi. Hiis testibus: Gaufrido capellano; Johanne de London' capellano; Henrico capellano de Stanes; Magistro Nicholao de Humet; Magistro Thoma fisico; Gaufrido de Eton'; Waltero de Huppinore; Hugone Underore; Roberto Trenchevent; Gervasio Tatin, et multis aliis.

MSS: (1) WAM 17436.
    16.5 × 12 cm; t.u. 2 cm.
    Slit, but tag and seal missing.
    Endorsed: (a) Carta Simonis de London' de tota terra sua in Westmonasterio procuratori Sancte Trinitatis concessa a qua dictus procurator [erasure follows] solvat annuatim ij solidos custodi capello Beate Marie pro eisdem (13C). (b) Procurator altaris Sancte Trinitatis haberet hanc terram que est modo in manum sacristarii reddendo capelle Beate Marie ij solidos (14C).
    (2) WAD, f. 349v.
Date: The second witn. is prob. the Mr John of London who became a canon of St Paul's 1201 × 1203, and d. prob. *ante* May 1212 (*Fasti* I, 46).
Note: Stephen son of Osbert confirmed this grant temp. Abbot William d'Humez (WAM 17439; WAD, ff. 349v–350), and about the same time, made a further grant of 8*s.* rent in Tothill (WAM 17319; WAD, f. 350).

The dating of Stephen's confirmation suggests that Mr Simon was father of the Walter Niger, *alias* of London, canon of St Paul's in the 1230s (*Fasti* I, 76).

432. Confirmation to the Lady Altar by Laurence Muschet, for his soul, and those of his parents and ancestors, of a rent of 6*d.*, payable to the proctor, from the tenement which he holds of Roger Paschar' in the vill of Westminster, from a curtilage pertaining to that tenement. [Temp. John]

Sciant presentes et futuri quod ego Laurentius Muschet, divine pietatis intuitu, et pro redemptione animarum patris et matris mee, et omnium antecessorum meorum, dedi et concessi et hac presenti carta mea confirmavi Deo et altari Beate Virginis Marie de Westmonasterio redditum sex denariorum de tenemento quod teneo in villa de Westmonasterio de Rogero Paschar', videlicet: de curtilagio quod est in mora quod pertinet ad predictum tenementum, ex quo curtilagio debent predicti sex denarii provenire. Solvendum ei qui pro tempore dicti altaris custos fuerit, ad duos terminos anni a me et heredibus meis inperpetuum, videlicet: ad Pascham tres denarios, et ad Festum Sancti Michaelis tres denarios. Et ut hec donatio firma et stabilis futuris temporibus perseveret, presentis scripti testimonio et sigilli mei appositione eam corroboravi. Hiis testibus: Lodovico, clerico de Scaccario; Odone aurifabro; Ricardo Testard; Roberto de Crokesle; Stephano de Berking'; Galfrido de Cruce; Gervasio Purs'; Ricardo de celario; Nicholao de celario; Gerardo coco; Rogero Fot, et multis aliis.

MS: WAD, f. 562v.
Rubric: Carta Laurentii Muschet de redditu sex denariorum in Eye.

433. Confirmation, in pure and perpetual alms, by Geoffrey son of Jocelin the smith to the Lady Altar, for his soul and for those of his kinsfolk, of a rent of 3*s.* in the vill of Westminster, which William English rendered for a messuage which he holds in fee of Geoffrey and his heirs in that vill. The rent is due annually to the proctor of the Lady Altar, by the hands of William English, or whoever holds that tenement. [Temp. John]

Sciant presentes et futuri quod ego Gaufridus filius Gocelini fabri dedi et concessi et hac presenti carta mea confirmavi Deo et altari Beate Dei Genetricis Marie Westmonasterii, pro salute anime mee et parentum meorum, in puram et perpetuam elemosinam tres solidatos redditus in villa Westmonasterii quod Willelmus le Engleis solebat reddere mihi de masuagio quod tenet de me et heredibus meis in feudo in eadem villa Westmonasterii, reddendos annuatim custodi predicti altaris qui pro tempore fuerit ad eosdem terminos ad quos predictum redditum recipere solebam, scilicet ad quatuor anni terminos, videlicet: ad Natale Domini novem denarios; et ad Pascham novem denarios; et ad Festum Sancti Iohannis Baptiste novem denarios; et ad Festum Sancti Michaelis novem denarios, per manus eiusdem Willelmi le Engleis vel cuiuscumque predictum tenementum tenuerit. Ego autem Gaufridus et heredes mei warantizabimus predicto altari predictum redditum contra omnes homines et omnes feminas. Et ut hec mea donatio et concessio et carte mee confirmatio rata sit et stabilis permaneat, eam sigilli mei appositione corroboravi. Hiis testibus: Ricardo de Dol, tunc senescallo Westmonasterii; Odone aurifabro; Adam de Westmonasterio; Roberto de Rokingham'; Henrico Sumer; Gaufrido de Cruce; Ricardo filio Edmundi; Thoma vinitore; Stephano de Berking; Nicolao de celario; Ricardo de celario; Laurentio Muschat; Adam, Gaufrido, Willelmo Stuttel, Iohanne, servientibus ecclesie Westmonasterii, et multis aliis.

MS: WAM 17322.
> 14.8 × 10.9 cm; t.u. 2.2 cm.
> Seal: green; on tag; 3.8 cm diameter; eagle, facing right; legend: SIGILL GALFRIDI FAB FIL GOCELIN FAB.
> Endorsed: (a) Westmonasterii (16C). (b) Capella lxij (14C). (c) Galfridus filius Gocelini fabri dat capelle tres solidatas redditus in villa Westmonasterii (13C).

Date: William English is last recorded in 1207 (Richardson, 'William of Ely', 86, 87).
Note: Cf. **346**.

434. Confirmation by Geoffrey de Hanley to Peter of Ely, his heirs or assign, for his homage and service, of his messuage in the vill of Westminster, between the messuage of Robert Marinlli and that of Peter le Cho, which Geoffrey bought from William Cretun, chamberlain of Richard [Fitz Nigel], former bp. of London, to hold of Geoffrey and his heirs in inheritance, rendering him an annual rent of 1 lb. of cumin, and 2s. to the bp. of Salisbury. Peter gave him a gersum of 4 marks (£2. 13s. 4d.) [Temp. John]

Sciant presentes et futuri quod ego Gaufridus de Hanleia dedi et concessi et hac carta mea confirmavi Petro de Ely et heredibus suis vel cui assignare, vendere vel legare voluerit, pro homagio et servicio suo, mesuagium meum cum pertinentiis in villa de Westmonasterio quod est inter mesuagium Roberti Marinlli' et mesuagium Petri le Cho, quod emi de Willelmo Cretun, camerario Ricardi quondam London' episcopi, tenendum de me et heredibus meis libere, quiete et hereditarie. Reddendo michi et heredibus meis annuatim unam libram cimini ad Natale, et duos solidos episcopo Saresbiriensi reddendos ad duos anni terminos, videlicet duodecim denarios ad Pascha, et duodecim denarios ad Festum Sancti Michaelis. Et ego Galfridus et heredes mei warantizabimus predicto Petro et heredibus suis vel cui eam dare, vendere vel legare voluerit, predictum mesuagium cum pertinenciis contra omnes homines, Judeos et Christianos. Et pro hac donatione et concessione et carte mee confirmatione, dedit michi predictus Petrus quatuor marcas argenti de gersoma. Et in huius rei testimonio huic scripto sigillum meum apposui. Hiis testibus: Willelmo domini regis thesaurario; Magistro Gocelino Mareschallo; Willelmo filio Andree; Odone, tunc preposito; Henrico Sumer; Stephano de Berching'; Ricardo filio Edmundi, milite; Martino

King'; Roberto de Cleigate; Thoma vinitario; Galfrido filio Galfridi de Cruce; Martino de Medmeham; Petro de Leone, et multis aliis.

MSS: (1) WAM 17443.
    14.5 × 9.8 cm; t.u. 2.4 cm.
    Seal: on tag; 4 × 2.6 cm; stag's head facing left: legend: + SIGILL G[AU]FRIDI.
    Endorsed: (a) Gaufridus de Henleya dat Petro de Hely quoddam mesuagium in villa Westmonasterii (13C). (b) Westmonasterii capelle lxxxv (14C).
    (2) WAD, f. 555v–556.
Date: Attestations of William of Ely, and of Mr Jocelin Marshall.
Note: The recipient is prob. the Peter of Ely who was a sergeant of the royal treasurer (William of Ely): cf. Richardson, 'William of Ely', 89n.–90n. Peter granted his messuage 'in the vill of Westminster, in the street leading to Charing, opposite Endiff', *c.* 1225, to Richard, a merchant of St Paul's, London, and his wife Sabina (WAM 17317).

435. Confirmation, to take effect after their deaths, by Rose the cushion-maker and Ralph Mauduit, to provide lights for the Lady Altar, for the soul of H II and for their own, of a messuage in the vill of Westminster which they held of Gerard of Mitcham, and which he granted and confirmed to them by charter, lying between the stone house of Roger Enganet and the land of Peter of Wenden, to be held by the Lady Altar at an annual rent of 4s. due to Roger Enganet. Rose and Ralph will render to the altar 1s. 2d. annually. [Temp. John]

Sciant [presentes et futuri] quod ego Roe[isia la custerere et ego Radulfus Mauduit dedi]mus et conc[essimus et presenti] carta nostra confirma[vimus, post decessum nostrum, Deo et altari Beate Marie] ecclesie W[estmonasterii ad lu]minarium inveniendum, pro anima [Regis Henrici et pro salute animarum] nostrarum, unum masagium cum pertinenciis in villa Westmonasterii quod t[enuimus de Gerardo de Miggeham,] scilicet: masagium quod est inter domum lapideam Rogeri Engan[et, et terram Petri de Wand]ene, et quod idem Gerardus nobis dedit et concessit, et carta sua confirmavit [pro donatione] sex marcarum in gersummam. Habendum et tenendum Deo et eidem altari, libere et [quie]te, integre et plenarie, in perpetuum, sine omni calumpnia nostri vel heredum nostrorum, per liberum servicium [quatuor] solidorum reddendorum Rogero Enganet ad iiij^{or} terminos anni, scilicet: ad Natale Domini xij^{cim} denarios; et ad Pascham xij^{cim} denarios; et ad Festum Sancti Johannis Baptiste xij^{cim} denarios; et ad Festum [Sancti M]ichaelis xij^{cim} denarios. Et de predicto me[sagio sin]gulis annis persolvemus predicto altari quatuordecim [denarios], ad duos anni terminos, scilicet: ad Pascham septem denarios, et ad Festum Sancti Michaelis septem denarios. [Hanc autem d]onationem et concessionem donavimus et concessimus pro salute anime Regis Henrici [et animarum nostrarum]. Et ut hec nostra dona[tio et con]cessio rata sit et stabilis permaneat, [eam sigillorum nostrorum] appositione corroboravimus. Hiis testibus: Henrico Sumer; Od[one aurifabro]; Ricardo Testard; Stephano de Berking'; Gaufrido de

271

Cruce; Wimundo pistore; [Johanne filio Edw]ardi; Nicholao filio Gaufridi; Petro de Wandene; Thoma vinitore; [Ricardo filio Edmundi, et mult]is aliis.

MSS: (1) WAM 17438.
    17.4 × 12.9 cm; remains of slit; severely damaged; missing text supplied from WAD.
    (2) WAD, f. 550r–v.
    Rubric: Carta Roeysie la custere et Radulfi Mauduyt de uno mesuagio in villa Westmonasterii.
Pd: Mason, 'The Mauduits and their Chamberlainship', 23, from WAD.
Note: Ralph was prob. a kinsman of the royal chamberlain, Robert Mauduit (cf. Mason, 'The Mauduits and their Chamberlainship', 6–7, 9), and was in the royal service towards the end of H II's reign (*PR 34 H II*, 17).

436. Notification by Geoffrey de Mandeville [I], that for his soul and that of his [first] wife, Alice, who is buried in the cloister, where he is to be buried, and for the souls of his sons and daughters, he has granted, in perpetual inheritance, to St Peter of Westminster his little manor of Ebury next to the abbey. His wife Lesceline and his son and designated heir, William, are associated with this grant, made in presence of Abbot Gilbert and the monks, and many of their respective knights. Ralph de Hairun has delivered seisin. [1085 × 1100]

Ego Goffridus de Magna Villa, pro anima mea et pro anima coniugis mee Athelais in claustro Sancti Petri sepulte, que etiam iuxta eam sepeliendus sum, pro animabus quoque filiorum filiarumque mearum, dedi Sancto Petro Westmonasterii maneriolum quod iuxta ecclesiam eius habebam, scilicet Eye, in perpetuam hereditatem sicut illud umquam melius tenui. Et hoc donum Deo et Sancto Petro, cum uxore mea Lecselina, concessione filii mei Willelmi, quem mihi heredem facere disposui, quos etiam huius elemosine participes fieri per omnia volo, super altare predicti Apostoli Petri presentavi, in presentia Gisleberti abbatis et monachorum et multorum militum meorum et suorum, et continuo per Radulfum de Hairun de predicto manerio Sanctum Petrum saisiri feci. Huius igitur concessionis testes sunt: Hugo Maskereal; Rogerius frater eius; Willelmus filius Martelli; Richerius; Radulfus de Hairun; Goiffridus nepos eius; Willelmus nepos Turaldi; Goffridus miles eius; Leuricus Cnivet; Goffridus, et multi alii.

MSS: (1) WAD, f. 100.
    Rubric: Carta Gaufridi de Magna Villa.
    Marginalia: (a) Pro animabus Domini G. de Magna Villa, comitis Essex' et Domine Athelaidis, consortis sue ac liberorum suorum. (b) Mandeuile dedit Eye.
    (2) F, ff. 281v–282.
    (3) LN, f. v *verso*.
    (4) CAY, f. 5 *verso*.

Pd: *Gilbert Crispin*, 139, no. 15, from WAD, F and LN; *Mon. Ang.* 1, 309, no. LVIII, from F (attestations omitted).
Date: Geoffrey de Mandeville [I] d. *c.* 1100 (Hollister, 'Mandevilles', 19). Alice d. before W I (*Gilbert Crispin*, 32–3).
Cal: Bentley, 4, no. 15, from CAY.
Note: See Harvey, *WA*, 350. King W II's confirmation of this grant is **52**. The cloister was completed by Abbot Gilbert, *ante* 1100 (*Gilbert Crispin*, 37).

437. Notification by Marwanna daughter of William, that she has sold to William of Ely, the king's treasurer, for two marks (£1. 6*s.* 8*d.*), her messuage at Endiff [in Westminster], adjacent to that of John Pymerich. She has done this at the petition, and with the assent, of her son William, as she was seized of that messuage by right and inheritance. William had never had seisin of it, even though he and his wife Alice might dwell there at Marwanna's pleasure, so that neither William nor any heir of his may claim right in that messuage. Marwanna and William warrant this sale to the treasurer and his heir or assign. In return, he gave £1 to William and 1*s.* to Alice, who witnessed and assented to the sale, and confirmed that she had no dower rights in that messuage, her dower comprising only one-third of his acquisitions and a gold ring. Halimote, Westminster [*c.* 1196 × 1212]

Sciant presentes et futuri quod ego Marwanna filia Willelmi vendidi masagium meum cum pertinentiis, salvo servitio quod inde debetur, quod est juxta masagium Johannis Pymerich, quod habet apud Ane de Heia, Willelmo de Ely, domini regis thesaurario, pro duobus marcis, et hoc feci voluntate Willelmi filii mei et heredis mei et petitione et assensu eius, sicut quod seysita fui masagio illo sicut jure meo et hereditate mea, et de quo masagio predictus filius meus nunquam saysinam habuit, licet ipse et A[delicia] uxor eius ex gratia mea per aliquot tempus, scilicet quamdiu michi placeret, in masagio illo hospitarentur, ita quod nec predictus Willelmus heres meus nec aliquis heres eius post eum aliquid juris poterit vendicare ullo tempore in predicto masagio. Hanc autem venditionem ego et predictus Willelmus heres meus et heres eius warantizare debemus contra omnes homines et omnes feminas ipsi thesaurario et heredi eius, vel ei cui predictum masagium dare vel legare vel vendere voluerit. Pro qua warantizatione predictus thesaurarius dedit Willelmo heredi meo viginti solidos, et Adelicie uxori sue xij denarios, quod eidem venditioni presens interfuit et assensum prebuit, quam etiam in pleno halimoto recognovit quod nunquam hoc masagium, vel in toto vel in parte, tanquam dotem suam petet, quam ut cognovit idem quando predictus filius meus eam desponsavit nichil ei concessit vel nominavit in dotem quod ad masagium istud pertineat, set sicut tunc concessa est bene contenta fuit in desponsatione sua dote quam ei dedit, et nominavit, scilicet tertia parte perquisitionum suarum que ad predictum mesagium non pertinent, et uno anulo aureo. Juravit etiam predicta Adelicia in pleno halimoto quod nunquam calumpniam ponet vel aliquid juris petet in eodem masagio. Ego etiam et predictus Willelmus heres meus juravimus quod nunquam nos, vel heredes nostri vel aliquis per nos, contra venditionem istam veniet vel calumpniam ponet in jamdicto mesagio, contra predictum thesaurarium vel contra eum qui per ipsum masagium illud habuit. Ut autem hec mea venditio robur obtineat inposterum ipsum ne posset in dubium futuris temporibus venire scripto presenti et sigilli mei appositione testificor. Hiis testibus: Henrico Sumer et Ricardo Testard, prepositis; Rogero Enganet; Adam nepote Ricardi episcopi Wintoniensi; Nicholao summonitore; Johanne filio Edwardi; Odone aurifabro; Girardo coco; Galfrido de Cruce; Wimundo pistore; Edmundo filio suo; Willelmo filio Avive; Ailwardo Hutte; Pagano Duble; Petro de Wandene, et multis aliis.

MS: WAD, f. 342r–v.

    Rubric: Carta Marwanne filie Willelmi de masagio suo quod est juxta masagium Johannis Pimerich.

Date: Adam [of Westminster], nephew of Richard [of Ilchester], bp. of Winchester, d. in or shortly after 1212 (*Beauchamp Cartulary*, no. 186). Also within the limits of William of Ely's term as royal treasurer (Richardson, 'William of Ely', 82). Henry Sumer and Richard Testard as reeves (cf. Rosser, 'Medieval Westminster', 360).

438. Acknowledgement by William, son of Absalon and Marwenna, together with his wife Alice, that he was present at the sale which Marwenna made to the king's treasurer, William of Ely, of her messuage, saving the service due. It is next to the messuage of John Pimerics, which he has at Endiff; of which messuage Marwenna was seized as her right and inheritance, when she sold it. William was never seised of that messuage, although he and Alice lodged there at his mother's pleasure. William and his wife assented to the sale, which he, his mother and his heirs warranted to the treasurer and his heirs. In return, the treasurer gave him £1, and 1*s.* to his wife, who acknowledged in the halimote that she would never claim this messuage in dower, since it formed no part of the dower assigned at her marriage. When the messuage was sold, William had no children by his wife, nor any hope of any. Halimote [Westminster], [*c.* 1196 × 1212]

Sciant presentes et futuri quod ego Willelmus, filius Absalonis et Marwenne, cum Alicia uxore mea, presens interfui venditioni quam ipsa Marwenna mater mea fecit Willelmo de Ely, domini regis thesaurario, de masagio suo cum pertinentiis, salvo servitio quod exinde debetur, pro duabus marcis, quod masagium est iuxta masagium Johannis Pimerics, quod habet apud Anedeheie, de quo masagio ipsa saisita fuit sicut jure et hereditate sua quando eam vendidit, et de quo masagio ego nunquam saisinam habui, licet ego et A[licia] uxor mea ex gratia matris mee per aliquod tempus quam diu ipsi placeret in illo masagio hospitaremus. Ita quod nec ego nec aliquis heres post me aliquid juris ullo tempore poterit vendicare in predicto masagio. Huic autem venditioni ego et predicta uxor mea voluntatem et concessionem et assensum prebuimus, quam etiam venditionem ego et predicta mater mea et heredes mei warantizare debemus predicto thesaurario et heredibus eius, vel ei cui predictum masagium dare, legare, vel vendere voluerit, contra omnes homines et omnes feminas. Pro qua warantizatione predictus thesaurarius dedit michi viginti solidos et predicte uxori mee xij denarios, que etiam in pleno halimoto recognovit quod nunquam hoc masagium vel in toto vel in parte tanquam dotem suam petet, quam, quod et verum est, ibidem recognovit, scilicet quod quando eam desponsavi nichil ei concessi vel nominavi in dotem quod ad masagium illud pertineat, sed sicut tunc concessa est bene contenta fuit in desponsatione sua dote quam ei dedi et nominavi, scilicet tertia parte perquisitionum mearum que ad predictum masagium non pertinent, et preterea uno anulo aureo. Juravit etiam in predicto halimoto quod nunquam calumpniam ponet, vel aliquid juris petet occasione alicuius dotis in predicto masagio. Predicta etiam mater mea et ego juravimus quod nunquam nos vel heredes nostri contra venditionem istam veniemus, nec aliquis per nos contra predictum thesaurarium, vel contra eum qui per ipsum masagium illud habuerit calumpniam ponet in eodem masagio. Et sciendum est quod quando hec venditio facta est, nullam prolem ex predicta uxore mea susceperam, nec suscepturum sperabam. Ut autem mea concessio et meus assensus quem feci in hac venditione robur optineat inposterum, et ut hoc quod a me et a predicta uxore mea actum, concessum, vel recognitum est, non decidat a memoria hominum, ea presenti scripto et sigilli mei appositione testificor. Hiis testibus: Henrico Sumer et Ricardo Testard, prepositis; Rogero Enganet; Adam, nepote R[icardi] episcopi Wintoniensi; Nicholao sumonitore; Johanne filio Edwardi; Odone aurifabro; Girardo coco; Galfrido de Cruce; Wimundo pistore; Edmundo filio suo; Willelmo filio Avive; Ailwardo Hutte; Pagano Dolbe; Petro de Wandene, et multis aliis.

MS: WAD, f. 342v.
Rubric: Carta Willelmi filii Absolonis et Marwenne de eodem.
Date: Within the limits of William of Ely's term as royal treasurer (Richardson, 'William of Ely', 82), and those of Henry Sumer and Richard Testard as reeves (Rosser, 'Medieval Westminster', 360). The latter were still in office after the d. of Adam [of Westminster] nephew of Richard [of Ilchester] bp. of Winchester, which occurred in or soon after 1212 (*Beauchamp Cartulary*, no. 186).

439. Notification by William of Ely, formerly treasurer of the kings of England, that he has confirmed to the monks of Westminster, for the souls of Henry, Richard and John, kings of England, for that of Richard [Fitz Nigel], bp. of London, and for his own soul, all his houses, a courtyard and an unattached stable in the vill of Westminster, which he had of the gift of Richard, bp. of London, and which are of the fee of Westminster. So long as he remains domiciled in that property by licence of the monks, he will render them, in addition to the candle of 2 lbs weight which he formerly rendered, 1 lb of incense on the Feast of the Ascension. [*post* 1 Sept. 1218 × *ante* 25 Feb. 1221]

Universis Christi fidelibus ad quos presens scriptum pervenerit, Willelmus de Heli, quondam regum Anglie thesaurarius, salutem. Noverit universitas vestra me dedisse et hac presenti carta mea confirmasse Deo et monachis Westmonasterii, pro animabus Henrici, Ricardi et Johannis, regum Anglie, et pro anima Ricardi London' episcopi, et pro salute anime mee, omnes domos meas, et curiam cum pertinentiis, simul cum quodam stabulo quod non est de ipsa curia, in villa Westmonasterii, quas habui ex donatione Ricardi London' episcopi, et que sunt de feodo Westmonasterii, habendas et possidendas inperpetuum; et totum jus quod in eadem curia vel domibus memorati habui, ipsis monachis (inperpetuum^c) quietum clamavi inperpetuum de me et heredibus meis, solvam autem predictis monachis quamdiu per licenciam ipsorum in ipsis domibus mansero, preter cereum duarum librarum quem pro eisdem domibus reddere consuevi, unam libram liberi incensi in Ascensione Domini ratione huius mee donationis et concessionis quam ipsis monachis feci de domibus et terris et curia cum pertinentiis suis, et ut hec mea donatio et concessio firma et stabilis perseveret, eam presenti scripto et sigilli mei appositione roboravi. Hiis testibus: Domino Pandulfo Norwycensi electo, apostolice sedis legato; Domino Huberto de Burgo, justiciario Anglie; Domino Eustachio de Faucunberge, domini regis thesaurario; Roberto de Nova Villa; Thoma de Chimilli; Willelmo de Castell'; Johanne filio Willelmi; Alexandro clerico; Roberto capellano; Uliano Chesneduit, senescallo Westmonasterii; Odone aurifabro; Johanne fusore; Roberto de Cleygate; Magistro Phillipo; Ricardo Muschat; Petro de Ely; Radulpho de Chesewik; Magistro Alano coco, et multis aliis.

MS: WAD, ff. 342v–343.
    Rubric: Carta Willelmi de Ely, quondam regum Anglie thesaurarii, de domibus et curia predictis, cum quodam stabulo adjacente.
Pd: Richardson, 'William of Ely', 89, no. VIII.
Date: Attested by the legate Pandulf, as bp.-elect of Norwich, therefore *post* 1 Sept. 1218 (*Fasti*, II, 56), and by the royal treasurer Eustace de Fauconberg, who held this office from the autumn of 1217 (*Rot. Litt. Claus.*, I, 340b), and was elected bp. of London 25 Feb. 1221 (*Fasti*, I, 2).
Note: Bp. Richard's grant to his kinsman William is **219**. See also Richardson, 'William of Ely', 59–60. The attestations indicate that William had been reconciled with the regency government, following his defection during the civil war (Richardson, ibid., 56–60). The land recorded in this charter was later acquired by the justiciar Hubert de Burgh, *c.* Nov. 1222 × April 1224 (ibid., 90, no. IX). On the location of this property (in Endiff) and its extension by William, see Rosser, 'Medieval Westminster', 21–3.

440. Confirmation by Robert son of Gerin of Westminster to Geoffrey the roofer, for his homage and service, of a messuage in Westminster, located between the gate of the messuage which Robert holds of Geoffrey de Neville in Westminster, and the land of William parmenter. Geoffrey and his heirs will hold in inheritance of Robert and his heirs, for an annual rent of 1s. 8d. Geoffrey gave a gersum of 4s. [*c.* 1200 × *ante* 24 June 1209]

Sciant omnes presentes et futuri quod ego Robertus filius Gerini Westmonasterii dedi et concessi et hac presenti carta mea confirmavi Gaufridi cohopertori, pro homagio et servicio suo, unum masuagium cum pertinentiis in Westmonasterio, illud scilicet quod jacet inter portam meam masuagii mei, quod teneo de Gaufrido de Nevill', in Westmonasterio et terram Willelmi parmentarii. Habendum et tenendum prefato Gaufrido et heredibus suis de me et heredibus meis, libere, quiete, pacifice, honorifice et hereditarie, reddendo mihi annuatim xx^{ti} denarios, scilicet: quinque denarios ad Natale; et quinque denarios ad Pascham; et ad Nativitatem Sancti Johannis Baptiste quinque denarios; et ad Festum Sancti Michaelis quinque denarios, pro omni servicio ad me vel ad meos pertinente. Et pro hac donatione et concessione et carte mee confirmatione dedit mihi memoratus Gaufridus quatuor solidos de gersuma. Et ut hec donatio mea stabilis perseveret, hoc scriptum sigilli mei munimine roboravi. Hiis testibus: Salamon capellano; Willelmo capellano; Rogero Enganet; Ada nepote episcopi; Adwardo Hutte; Wimundo pistore; Edmundo filio eius; Willelmo filio Andree; Hugone Noting' clerico; Henrico Sumer'; Thoma vinitore; Gaufrido fabro; Roberto fratre eius; Ricardo filio Ranulfi; Roberto molendinario; Alexandro de Heia; Hereberto de Heia; Roberto Nadler'; Gaufrido de Cruce; Willelmo filio Gaufridi; Henrico fratre eius; Petro de Wenden'; Nicolao summonitore, et multis aliis.

MSS: (1) WAM 17331.
    17.7 × 11.8 cm; t.u. 2.4 cm; slit; tag and seal missing.
    Endorsed: (a) Robertus filius Gerini dat Gaufrido cohopertori terram Willelmi parmentarii (13C). (b) Westmonasterii capella lxxxvj (14C).
    (2) WAD, f. 556.
Date: Attestation of Nicholas [Fitz Geoffrey Fitz Fredesent] as summoner (cf. **402**).
Note: Abbot Gervase had granted to Gerin the king's minister land in Endiff (**261**), perhaps the site of Robert's messuages mentioned here.

441. Quitclaim by John son of Edward of Westminster to the Blessed Virgin and the church of St Peter of Westminster of 7s. 8d. worth of rents in the vill of Westminster, comprising 5s. which the brethren of St James rendered for one and a half acres of land enclosed within their churchyard; 2s. for a meadow, which Hugh son of Robert, the smith, rendered when he was a layman, and rendered by the brethren when he became a brother there; and 8d. which Robert of Croxley rendered for land which he bought from Mr Ernald Postard in that vill. The grant is made to provide lights, or other necessities, for the Lady Altar, as its proctor decides. Robert of Moulsham, the precentor, gave him a gersum of six and a half marks (£4. 6s. 8d.). [Temp. John]

Sciant presentes et futuri quod ego Johannes filius Edwardi de Westmonasterio dedi et concessi et omnino quiete clamavi de me et heredibus meis Deo et Beate Marie et ecclesie Sancti Petri Westmonasterii septem solidatas et octo denariatas redditus in villa Westmonasterii, scilicet: quinque solidatas quas fratres de Sancto Jacobo solebant mihi reddere de una acra terre et dimidia que includitur intra atrium ipsorum fratrum; et duas solidatas de uno prato per manus eorundem fratrum quas Hugo filius Roberti fabri solebat michi reddere cum secularis esset postea factus frater eiusdem loci; et octo denariatas quas Robertus de Crokeslega solebat mihi reddere de terra quam emit de Magistro Ernaldo Postard in eadem villa. Habendas et tenendas eidem ecclesie libere et quiete de me et heredibus meis ad luminaria invenienda, vel ad alios usus utiles et necessarios altaris Beate Dei Genitricis Marie in eadem ecclesia juxta quod procurator eiusdem altaris melius vel utilius disposuerit, et percipiendas ad eosdem terminos quos ego Johannes percipere solebam, scilicet, septem solidatas de predictis fratribus ad quatuor terminos anni: ad Natale Domini viginti et unum denarios; et ad Pascham viginti et unum denarios; et ad Festum Sancti Johannis Baptiste viginti et unum denarios; et ad Festum Sancti Michaelis viginti et unum denarios; et octo denarios de Roberto de Crokesleg' vel heredibus suis ad duos terminos anni, scilicet: ad Pascham quatuor denarios, et ad Festum Sancti Michaelis quatuor denarios. Ego autem Johannes et heredes mei warantizabimus predictum redditum septem solidorum et octo denariorum procuratori predicti altaris qui pro tempore fuerit et ei solvendum juxta terminos suprascriptos. Et pro hac donatione et concessione et quieta clamacione recepi per manus Roberti de Mulesham, tunc eiusdem ecclesie precentoris, sex marcas et dimidiam argenti. Et ut hec mea donatio et concessio et quieta clamatio rata permaneat, eam sigillo meo corroboravi. Hiis testibus: Ricardo de Dol; Odone aurifabro; Ludovico clerico; Henrico Sumer; Ricardo filio Edmundi; Gaufrido de Cruce; Roberto de Crokesl'; Stephano de Berking'; Gervasio portitore; Nicholao de celario; Ada de Ecclesia; Laurentio Muschat, et multis aliis.

MS: WAD, ff. 520v–521.
> Rubric: Quieta clamantia Johannis filij Edwardi de vij solidatis et viij denariatis redditus in Westmonasterio.

Date: Robert of Moulsham as precentor.

Note: In 1201, John son of Edward the reeve, by his attorney Albin the clerk, claimed against Mr Ernald Postard a messuage in Westminster between the land of Gervase Bacheler and that of Wlint the laundress (*Fines London and Mddx*, I, 4, no. 5).

442. Grant by Odo the goldsmith to the Lady Altar of a rent of 3*s.* 6*d.* in Longditch, Westminster, comprising 2*s.* from the land which Ralf Fitz Stephen of Boulogne holds of him in fee, and 1*s.* 6*d.* from the messuage formerly held by John the clerk, and now rendered by Thomas son of Pavia or his heirs. If the messuage is destroyed by fire or other misfortune, Odo and his heirs will answer for the rent from their other lands or tenements to the proctor of the altar, who is also empowered to distrain for non-payment. Odo assigned Thomas and Ralph to render their rents direct to the proctor, if he himself should be absent in distant lands. Robert of Moulsham, the precentor, gave him a gersum of three marks (£2). [*c.* 1200]

Sciant presentes et futuri quod ego Odo aurifaber Westmonasterii dedi et

concessi et hac presenti carta mea confirmavi Deo et altari Beate Dei
Genitricis Marie in ecclesia Beati Petri Westmonasterii tres solidatos
redditus et sex denariatos in villa Westmonasterii in vico de Langedich',
scilicet: duos solidos de terra et masuagio quod Radulfus filius Stephani
de Bolonia tenet de me in feudo; et decem et octo denarios de terra et
masuagio quod [*sic*] fuit Johannis clerici in eodem vico, quos Thomas
filius Pavie vel heredes sui annuatim persolvent. Ita tamen quod ego Odo
vel heredes mei respondebimus et persolvemus per manus nostras predictum redditum trium solidorum et sex denariorum procuratori prescripti
altaris qui pro tempore fuerit, ad quatuor anni terminos, scilicet: ad
Pascha decem denarios et obulum; et ad Festum Sancti Johannis Baptiste
decem denarios et obulum; et ad Festum Sancti Michaelis decem
denarios et obulum; et ad Natale Domini decem denarios et obulum. Si
autem contigerit predicta mesuagia per combustionem, vel per aliquod
aliud infortunium, consumi vel adnichilari, ego Odo et heredes mei
respondebimus de predicto redditu trium solidorum et sex denariorum de
aliis terris nostris vel tenementis prefato procuratori eiusdem altaris.
Concedo etiam et bono animo consentio predicto procuratori qui pro
tempore fuerit quod pro defectu predicti redditus ad terminos nominatos
solvendi nisi voluntario respectu ab eo dato et concesso, poterit super
predicta tenementa vel super alia que in eadem villa habuerim rationabiliter namiare. Assignavi etiam predictos Thomam et Radulfum quod
si forte absens fuerim vel in remota patria ut ipsi vel heredes eorum
predictum redditum predicto procuratori persolvant ad terminos suprascriptos ne me vel heredes meos injuste de solutione predicti redditus
possit calumpniari. Pro hac autem donatione et concessione et carte mee
confirmatione, dedit mihi Robertus de Mulesham tunc precentor Westmonasterii et eiusdem altaris procurator tres marcas argenti. Et ut hec
mea donatio et concessio et carte mee confirmatio rata sit et stabilis
permaneat, eam sigilli mei appositione corroboravi. Hiis testibus:
Ricardo de Dol, tunc senescallo Westmonasterii; Ricardo Testard;
Ludovico clerico; Henrico Sumer; Ricardo filio Edmundi; Gaufrido de
Cruce; Roberto de Crokesle; Stephano de Berking'; Nicholao de celario;
Thoma filio Pavie; Willelmo Stuttel; Laurentio Muschat; Radulpho de
Bolonia, et multis aliis.

MS: WAD, f. 509r–v.
    Rubric: Carta Odonis aurifabri Westmonasterii de tribus solidatis et
    sex denariatis annui redditus in vico de Langedich'.
    Marginalia: Robertus Mulesham precentor.
Date: Robert of Moulsham as precentor; attestions of Richard Testard
and Henry Sumer, prob. reeves.

443. Confirmation, in pure and perpetual alms, by Nicholas son of
Geoffrey son of Fredesent of Westminster, for his soul and those of his
predecessors, to the Lady Altar and the convent, to provide lights for that
altar, of an annual rent of 1*s*. 8*d*. in the vill of Westminster by the hand of
the proctor of St James's Hospital. He also confirms to the convent, to

provide lights for that altar, a rent of 1*s.* 2*d.*, which the proctor of St James's Hospital rendered him. Gersum of 11*s.* 6*d.* [Temp. John]

Sciant presentes et futuri quod ego Nicholaus filius Galfridi filii Fredesent de Westmonasterio dedi et concessi et hac presenti carta mea confirmavi, pro salute anime mee et animarum predecessorum meorum, Deo et altari Beate Marie Westmonasterii et eiusdem loci conventui, ad luminaria eiusdem altaris administranda, in puram et perpetuam elemosinam, redditum viginti[1] denariorum, singulis annis percipiendum finabiliter in villa Westmonasterii per manum procuratoris Hospitalis Sancti Jacobi qui pro tempore fuerit. Preterea concedo predicto conventui, ad luminaria prefati altaris administranda, redditum quatuordecim denariorum, quos idem procurator Hospitalis Sancti Jacobi mihi reddere consuevit, et eisdem terminis, quibus prefatus procurator Hospitalis Sancti Jacobi michi reddere consuevit, scilicet: ad Pascha quinque denarios, et ad Nativitatem Sancti Johannis Baptiste quinque denarios et ad Festum Sancti Michaelis quinque denarios, et ad Natale Domini quinque denarios. Et est sciendum quod prenominatus conventus Westmonasterii nichil poterit exigere a procuratore vel a fratribus predicti Hospitalis Sancti Jacobi pro tenemento illo quod de me tenent nisi predictos viginti denariorum annuatim. Et ego Nicholaus et heredes mei warantizabimus prenominato conventui prefatum redditum viginti denariorum contra omnes gentes. Pro hac autem donatione et concessione et presentis carte mee confirmatione, dedit mihi predictus conventus undecim solidos et sex denarios de gersumma. His testibus: Henrico Sumer; Adam nepote episcopi; Johanne filio Aedwardi; Odone aurifabro; Wimone pistore; Petro de Wendena; Galfrido Cuttelebat'; Nicholao de celario; Eustachio pictore; Adam, Johanne, Galfrido, Radulfo, servientibus ecclesie Westmonasterii; Lodovico clerico de Rokingham', qui hanc cartam scripsit, et pluribus aliis.

MS: (1) WAM 17108.
19 × 21.3 cm; t.u. 3.5 cm; tag, seal missing.
Endorsed: (a) Nicholaus filius Galfridi dat capelle annuum redditum xx denariorum ad luminaria sustentanda, percipiendum de procuratore Sancti Jacobi (14C). (b) De Sancto Jacobo capella, ij carte (14C). (c) Westmonasterii (16C). (d) Fitz Fredecent (16C).
(2) WAD, f. 530.
1. *sex*, in error.

444. Confirmation by Nicholas son of Geoffrey son of Fredesent, in pure alms to the Lady Altar, to provide lights, for his soul and those of his ancestors, of an annual rent of 1*s.*, whether he lives or dies, payable at Longditch, in the vill of Westminster, by the hand of Walkelin, sergeant of the almoner, or his heirs. Moreover, Nicholas has granted to the Lady Altar and the convent the whole fee which Walkelin holds of him near Longditch, including aid, relief or homage. [Temp. John]

Sciant presentes et futuri quod ego Nicholaus filius Galfridi filii Fredesent dedi et concessi et hac presenti carta mea confirmavi, pro salute anime mee et animarum antecessorum meorum, Deo et altari Beate Marie Westmonasterii ad luminaria eiusdem altaris administranda, in puram et perpetuam elemosinam, redditum duodecim denariorum, sive vixero sive moriar, singulis annis finabiliter, percipiendum in villa Westmonasterii apud Langedic' per manum Walkelini servientis elemosinarii vel heredum suorum eisdem terminis quibus prefatus Walkelinus annuatim mihi reddere consuevit, scilicet: ad Pascham sex denarios et ad Festum Sancti Michaelis sex denarios. Sciendum est preterea quod totum feudum illud quod prefatus Walkelinus de me tenet juxta Langedich et quicquid de predicto feudo provenire poterit, in auxilio vel relevio vel homagio vel in omnibus aliis rebus, hoc totum Deo et altari Beate Marie et conventui Westmonasterii inperpetuum concessi, absque omni contradictione vel retenemento mei vel heredum meorum. Ut autem hec mea donatio et concessio stabilis et rata permaneat, eam presentis scripti testimonio et sigilli mei appositione roboravi. Hiis testibus: Alexandro et Salomone presbiteris; Ada nepote episcopi; Lodovico, clerico de Rokingham; Odone aurifabro; Eustachio pictore; Nicholao de cellario; Ada, Galfrido, Radulfo et Johanne, servientibus ecclesie; Johanne filio Edwardi; Willelmo de infirmario; Herewardo scriptore; Galfrido de Cruce, et multis aliis.

MS: WAD, f. 509v.
    Rubric: Carta Nicholai filii Galfridi filii Fredesent de redditu duodecim denariorum apud Langedich'.
Date: Attestation of Adam [of Westminster] the bishop's nephew.

445. Confirmation, in pure and perpetual alms, by William son of William of Westminster to the Lady Altar of 4*d.* rent, to provide lights for this altar. The rent is due annually from Geoffrey Picot, from land which he holds of William in Longditch Street, and which the bp. of Exeter and his successors hold of Geoffrey and his heirs. The proctor of the Lady Altar is to receive the rent annually from Geoffrey and his heirs. [*c.* 1194 × 1198]

Sciant presentes et futuri quod ego Willelmus filius Willelmi de Westmonasterio dedi et concessi et hac mea presenti carta confirmavi Deo et altari Beate Marie in ecclesia Westmonasterii quatuor denariatos redditus in puram et perpetuam elemosinam ad invenienda luminaria coram prefate Dei Genitricis Marie altari, quos videlicet quatuor denariatos redditus Galfridus Pycot et heredes sui tenentur michi solvere per annum, et heredibus meis, de terra quam prefatus Galfridus Picot de me tenet[1] in Langedich'strate, quam videlicet terram episcopus Exoniensis et successores sui de prefato Galfrido tenent et heredibus suis. Custos vero predicti altaris, qui pro tempore ibidem luminaria administraverit, prefatos quatuor denariatos redditus integre et plenarie, sine diminutione, de prefato Galfrido et heredibus suis percipiet singulis annis absque calumpnia vel reclamatione aut etiam prohibitione mei vel heredum meorum. Ego vero Willelmus et heredes mei prefatam elemosinam quatuor denariorum predicto altari contra omnes homines warantizabimus, et contra omnes feminas. Hiis testibus: Salomone capellano; Simone capellano; Odone aurifabro; Henrico Sumer; Roberto de Rokingham; Ailwardo Hutt; Livingo mercatore; Johanne de Abindon'; Gladewino parmentario; Rogero le Fraunceys; Willelmo filio eius; Willelmo de Scardeburg'; Galfrido Cuttlebatte; Nicholao de cellario; Willelmo Coc; Walkelino de elemosinaria, et multis aliis.

MS: WAD, f. 510.
> Rubric: Carta Willelmi filii Willelmi de Westmonasterio de quatuor denariatis redditus in vico de Langedich'.
> 1. MS: *tenenet.*

Date: Henry Marshall, bp. of Exeter, had 'bought' the land from Geoffrey Picot *c.* 1194 × *ante* 10 Sept. 1198 (**230**).

446. Notification by Edward, former reeve of Westminster, that he has granted, in inheritance, to William of the Temple, clerk of the king's chamberlain, Robert Mauduit, the half messuage that Geoffrey the priest held in Westminster. William and his heirs will render 2*s.* annually to Edward, and on one day in the year they will provide a man to mow or reap in that vill for the abbot of Westminster. The said half messuage lies toward Tothill, between the other half of the same messuage, which is held by Adam of Sunbury, and the land of Wlvuna the laundress. Edward has also granted William all the land which Geoffrey the priest held of Avice of Longditch, to hold in inheritance, at an annual rent of 6*d.* Gersum of one besant (2*s.*). [Oct. 1194 × *ante* 1197]

Sciant presentes et futuri quod ego Edwardus, quondam prepositus ville Westmonasterii, dedi et concessi et hac carta confirmavi Willelmo de Templo, clerico Roberti Mald[uit], domini regis camerarii, dimidium illud masagium quod Galfridus presbiter tenuit in villa de Westmonasterio; habendum et tenendum sibi et heredibus suis de me et heredibus meis cum pertinentiis suis hereditarie reddendo michi annuatim duos solidos pro omni servitio quod ad me vel ad heredes meos pertineat, scilicet: ad Pascha xij denarios, et ad Festum Sancti Michaelis xij denarios. Preterea idem Willelmus et heredes sui post ipsum invenient singulis annis abbati Westmonasterii unum hominem per unum diem ad fenum suum levandum vel ad blada sua colligenda ad cibum ipsius abbatis in eadem villa pro omni servitio quod ad ipsum pertineat. Illud vero dimidium masagium iacet in vico versus Tothill' inter aliam medietatem eiusdem masagii quam Adam de Sunebir' tenet et inter terram quam Wlvuna locrix tenet. Concessi etiam et dedi predicto Willelmo et heredibus suis totam terram illam quam predictus Galfridus presbiter tenuit de Avicia de Langedich', tenendam de me et heredibus meis hereditarie per servicium sex denariorum annuatim reddendorum pro omni servicio, scilicet: ad Pascha tres denarios; et ad Festum Sancti Michaelis tres denarios. Ego vero Edwardus et heredes mei warantizabimus predicto Willelmo et heredibus suis totum prenominatum tenementum integre contra omnes homines et feminas inperpetuum. Quare volo quod predictus Willelmus et heredes sui post ipsum habeant et teneant totum predictum tenementum cum omnibus pertinentiis suis de me et heredibus meis bene et in pace, honorifice, quiete et libere ab omnibus placitis et querelis, et ab omni seculari exactione per prescriptum servitium. Et pro hac donatione et concessione et huius carte confirmatione predictus Willelmus dedit michi unum bisantum de gersuma. Hiis testibus: Guillelmo de Heli, domini regis thesaurario; Jocelino Marescallo; Gaufrido filio Stephani, clerico domine regine; Johanne de la Wich'; Andrea de Scaccario; Thoma de Windleshor'; Guillelmo filio Roberti; Stephano de Heketona; Hugone de Winton'; Willelmo de Walda; Willemo de Castell'; Rogero Enganet; Albino computatore; Gervasio scriptore; Alano et Petro computatoribus; Ricardo funditore; Ricardo Testard; Johanne fratre suo; Nicholao filio Galfridi; Adam nepote episcopi; Thoma de Rocheford', et multis aliis.

MS: BL Harleian Charter 49 G 30.
    18 × 24 cm; t.u. 6.5 cm.
    Seal: green; elliptical; 4 × 2.8 cm; ? sacrifice of Isaac: larger figure holds down head of smaller one with right hand, left hand raised over own shoulder with sword pointing down; legend: SIGILLUM SECRETI +.
    Endorsed: (a) Concessio facta Willelmo de Templo, clerico Roberti Malduit Westmonasterii. (b) Edward' de Totehull' Berkynge. (c) (Running under tag) Masgarum . . . Homo ad . . . . . . cibum.
Pd: Richardson, 'William of Ely', 84–86n, no. V.
Date: Attestation of Gervase *scriptor*: cf. Richardson, ibid., 85n. Robert Mauduit succeeded his father as royal chamberlain on 2 Oct. 1194 (*Beauchamp Cartulary*, xxx; *Waverley Annals, Ann. Mon.* II, 249–50).
Note: Cf. **448**.

447. Confirmation by Simon son of William of Hanslope, with the assent of Clarice his mother, to Lucy, widow of Richard of Barking, of all his land in the vill of Westminster, in Tothill Street and the curtilage adjoining it, which is of the fee of Avice of Longditch, namely the land formerly belonging to Geoffrey the priest of Tothill, which William of Hanslope held of John son of Edward, as half a messuage and lying between the land of Wlveva the laundress and that of Adam of Sunbury. Simon has restored to Lucy the charters concerning that land. Lucy will render 1 lb cumin annually to Simon, and 2*s*. 6*d*. to John Fitz Edward as chief lord of the fee, for the curtilage, concerning which Simon has restored the cirograph to Lucy, who will also provide for the abbot, one day in the year, a man to cut hay or gather fodder. Dislodgement prohibited. Lucy may designate as her heir any man or woman she chooses. Gersum of 6 marks (£4). [Temp. John]

Sciant presentes et futuri quod ego Simon filius Willelmi de Hamslape, assensu et voluntate Claricie matris mee, dedi et concessi et hac mea presenti carta confirmavi Lucie que fuit uxor Ricardi de Berkinges totam terram meam quam habui in villa Westmonasterii in vico de Tothulle, cum omnibus pertinentiis suis et edificiis, et cum quodam curtilagio predicte terre adiacente que est de feodo Avicie de Langedich, videlicet; totam terram illam que fuit Galfridi presbiteri de Tothull', et quam Willelmus pater meus de Johanne filio Edwardi tenuit pro medietate unius mesagii, et que terra iacet inter terram que fuit Wlveve la lavendere ex una parte, et inter terram Ade de Sunnebur' ex alia parte, quam de eodem feodo tenet pro medietate unius mesagii, de qua videlicet terra prefate Lucie cartas reddidi. Habendam et tenendam de me et heredibus meis sibi et heredibus suis in perpetuum in feodo et hereditate, bene et in pace, libere et quiete, integre, plenarie, et honorifice. Reddendo de prefata terra annuatim mihi et heredibus meis unam libram cumini in villa Westmonasterii in termino Pasche pro omni servitio et exactione, et Johanni filio Edwardi et heredibus suis triginta denarios tamquam capitali domino feodi illius ad duos terminos anni, scilicet ad Pascha xij denarios ex una parte, et tres denarios ex alia parte, pro prefato curtillagio, unde prefate Lucie cyrographum reddidi; et ad Festum Sancti Michaelis prefato Johanni et heredibus suis xij denarios ex una parte, et tres denarios ex alia parte, pro prefato curtilagio pro omni servitio et exactione, salvo servitio domini abbatis, scilicet: inveniendi unum hominem uno die tantummodo in anno ad fenum illius levandum, vel segetes colligendas ad cibum abbatis. Et sciendum quod nec ego Simon nec heredes mei aliquid amplius de prefata terra poterimus exigere nisi tantum prefatam libram cumini singulis annis termino statuto. Hec poterimus prefatam Luciam aliquo modo de prefata terra dehospitari causa nos, vel aliquem alium ibidem hospitandi. Prefata vero Lucia de prefata terra libere poterit de quocumque homine vel de quacumque femina voluerit heredem sibi constituere aut ubi voluerit assignare absque reclamatione vel contradictione mei vel heredum meorum, salva predicta libra cumini quam mihi solvet vel cui assignavero. Et ego Simon et heredes mei prefatam terram cum omnibus pertinentiis suis predicte Lucie et heredibus suis finabiliter warantizabimus contra omnes homines et omnes feminas per predictum servitium. Pro hac autem donatione et concessione et carte mee confirmatione dedit mihi prefata Lucia sex marcas argenti in gersumam. Ut autem hec mea donatio et concessio firma sit et stabilis, eam presentis scripti testimonio et sigilli mei appositione roboravi. Hiis testibus: Ricardo de Dol, tunc senescallo; Odone aurifabro, tunc preposito; Radulfo Rufo; Radulfo le Chauv; Henrico Sum[er]; Galfrido camerario; Roberto de Crokesleg'; Adam nepote episcopi; Wimundo pistore; Alexandro de Eya; Ricardo filio Eadmundi; Alexandro le Fundur; Thoma de Sancto Johanne de Eya; Simone pictore; Hugone Chanterel; Nicholao de cellario; Roberto de Cleigate; Galfrido fabro; Johanne parmentario, et multis aliis.

MS: BL Harleian Charter 51 C 47.
    22.1 × 14.8 cm; t.u. 2 cm.
    Seals: green: (1) 4 cm diameter; eagle; legend: SIG[ILLUM SIMONI]S FIL WILL DE HAMSL. (2) Fragment.
    Endorsed: (a) Berkinges Tothull' (13C). (b) Westmonasterii (modern).
Date: Attestation of Adam the bishop's nephew.
Note: By comparison with the related charter of Edward the reeve (**446**) it is clear that William of Hanslope was *alias* William 'of the Temple'.

448. Notification by John, son of Edward the former reeve of Westminster, that he has confirmed to Lucy, wife of Richard of Barking, the half messuage that Geoffrey the priest held in Westminster, for an annual rent of 2*s*. Lucy and her heirs are to provide yearly for the abbot a man for one day's reaping or mowing. The said half messuage lies in the street towards Tothill between the other half of the same messuage, held by Adam of Sunbury, and the holding of Wlviva the laundress. He has also granted Lucy all the land that Geoffrey the priest held of Avice of Longditch, for an annual rent of 6*d*. Gersum of one besant. [Temp. John]

Sciant omnes gentes quod ego Johannes filius Edwardi, quondam prepositi ville Westmonasterii, concessi et presenti carta mea confirmavi Lucie uxori Ricardi de Berking' dimidium illud mesuagium quod Galfridus presbiter tenuit in villa de Westmonasterio cum pertinentiis suis; habendum et tenendum sibi et heredibus suis de me et heredibus meis libere et quiete, bene et in pace et honorifice in perpetuum. Reddendo inde annuatim mihi et heredibus meis duos solidos pro omni servitio quod ad me vel heredes meos pertinet ad duos terminos anni: ad Pascha, videlicet, xij denarios, et ad Festum Sancti Michaelis totidem, salvo servitio abbatis, scilicet: quod predicta Lucia et heredes sui invenient singulis annis predicto abbati unum hominem per unum diem ad fenum suum levandum, vel ad blada sua colligenda, ad cibum ipsius abbatis in eadem villa, pro omni servitio et exactione. Et sciendum est quod prefatum dimidium mesuagium iacet in vico versus Tothell', inter aliam medietatem eiusdem mesuagii quam Adam de Suneber' tenet, et terram quam Wlviva lotrix tenuit. Concessi et confirmavi predicte Lucie et heredibus suis totam terram illam quam predictus Galfridus presbiter tenuit de Avicia de Langedich; tenendam de me et heredibus meis hereditarie per servicium sex denariorum annuatim reddendorum pro omni servitio, scilicet: ad Pascha tres denarios; et ad Festum Sancti Michaelis tres denarios. Ego vero Johannes et heredes mei warantizabimus predicte Lucie et heredibus suis totum prenominatum tenementum contra omnes homines et omnes feminas. Pro hac autem concessione et confirmatione mea dedit mihi predicta Lucia unum bisanzium de gersuma. Et ut hec mea concessio et confirmatio stabilis et rata futuris permaneat temporibus, eam presenti scripto cum sigilli mei appositione roboravi. Hiis testibus: Ricardo de Dol, tunc senescallo; Odone aurifabro, tunc preposito; Henrico Sumer; Galfrido camerario; Roberto de Crockesl'; Adam nepote episcopi; Wimundo pistore; Alexandro de Eia; Galfrido de Cruce; Ricardo filio Eadmundi; Alexandro Fundur; Simone pictore; Galfrido de Claig', et Roberto Claig'; Hugone Chanter'; Nicholao de Cellario; Johanne Parmentario, et multis aliis.

MS: BL Harleian Charter 50 A 32.
    19.1 × 12.9 cm; t.u. 2.4 cm; seal missing from tag.
    Endorsed: (a) Totehull' Berkynge. (b) Concessio facta Lucie uxori Ricardi de Berking. (c) Westmonasterii.
Date: Attestation of Adam the bishop's nephew.

449. Confirmation by John son of Edward to Isabel, wife of the king's

chamberlain Robert Mauduit, and her heirs, of 7*s*. 8*d*. rent in the vill of
Westminster, comprising 4*s*. 2*d*. from Juliana, widow of Adam of
Sunbury, for the fee which she held in Tothill Street, between the land
formerly belonging to Mr William of Hanslope and that of William the
palmer; and 3*s*. 6*d*. rent, of which William le Wallere rendered 1*s*. 6*d*.,
Edric of the Garden rendered 1*s*. 6*d*., for the fees they held of him in
Tothill Street, Westminster, between the land of Robert Mauduit and
that of Roger Fot, and Martin Smud rendered 6*d*. for his fee in Tothill
Street, between the land of Roger Fot and that of Gervase of the Kitchen.
Isabel might dispose of that land as she pleased, even to a religious
[house], saving to him only a rent of 2*d*. If Isabel suffers loss because of
the 1*s*. 5*d*. rent which John is bound to render the almoner of Westminster annually for those rents, he concedes that Isabel or her heirs may
receive from the fee which Lucy of Barking holds of him in Tothill Street
as much of that 1*s*. 5*d*. as they render the almoner through his default.
Gersum of six marks (£4). [Temp. John]

Sciant presentes et futuri quod ego Johannes filius Edwardi dedi et
concessi et hac presenti carta mea[1] confirmavi Isabelle, uxori Roberti
Mauduit domini regis camerarii, septem solidatos et octo denariatos
redditus in villa Westmonasterii. Illos videlicet septem solidos et octo
denariatos de quibus Juliana, que fuit uxor Ade de Sunneburia,
tenebatur, solvere michi et heredibus meis annuatim quatuor solidos et
duos denarios ad quatuor anni terminos pro feodo quod tenuit de me in
Westmonasterio, et quod iacet in vico de Tothull', inter terram que fuit
Magistri Willelmi de Hameslape et terram Willelmi palmarij; et illos tres
solidos et sex denarios de quibus Willelmus le Wallere tenebatur solvere
mihi et heredibus meis annuatim decem et octo denariatos ad quatuor
terminos; et de quibus Edricus de Gardino tenebatur solvere michi et
heredibus meis annuatim decem et octo denariatos ad quatuor terminos;
et de quibus Martinus Smud tenebatur solvere michi et heredibus meis
annuatim sex denariatos ad quatuor terminos pro feodis que predicti
Willelmus le Wallere et Edricus de Gardino tenuerunt de me in Westmonasterio, et jacent in eodem vico de Tothull' inter terram predicti
Roberti Mauduyt et terram Rogeri Fot; et pro feodo quod predictus
Martinus Smud tenuit de me in eodem vico, et iacet inter terram predicti
Rogeri Fot et terram Gervasii de Coquina. Quos septem solidos et octo
denariatos predicta Isabella et heredes sui tenebunt de me et heredibus
meis, plene et integre, libere et quiete, pacifice et honorifice, reddendo
inde annuatim michi et heredibus meis duos denariatos ad duos anni
terminos scilicet: ad Pascham unum denariatum, et ad Festum Sancti
Michaelis unum denariatum, pro omni servicio et exactione. Et sciendum
est quod predicta Isabella poterit facere heredem suum de quocumque
vel de quacumque voluerit de prenominatis septem solidis et octo
denariatis per annum, aut illos dare vel assignare ubicumque voluerit,
sive in religione, sive extra religionem, salvo servitio predictorum
duorum denariatorum michi et heredibus meis. Hunc autem predictum
redditum ego Johannes et heredes mei warantizabimus prenominatis
Isabelle et heredibus suis vel ubicumque dederit vel assignaverit et contra

capitales dominos et contra omnes gentes per predictum servicium. Et si forte contigerit quod predicta Isabella vel heredes vel assignati sui in dampnum inciderint pro decem et septem denariatis quos ego Johannes et heredes mei solvere tenemur annuatim elemosinario ecclesie Westmonasterii pro predictis feodis, concedo quod predicta Isabella vel assignati sui recipiant de feodo quod Lucia de Berking' tenet de me in eodem vico de Tothull' quantum predicto elemosinario de predictis decem et septem denariatis per defectum mei vel heredum meorum reddiderint. Hanc vero donationem et concessionem et presentis carte mee confirmationem feci prenominate Isabelle pro servicio suo et pro sex marcis argenti quas in gersummam michi dedit. Hiis testibus: Roberto Mauduit, domini regis camerario; et Henrico Foliot; Radulfo Basset; Johanne filio Willelmi; Ricardo de Dol, tunc temporis senescallo; Odone aurifabro; Henrico Sum[er]; Ricardo Testard; Johanne fratre eius; Roberto de Rokingham; Gaufrido de Cruce; Stephano de Berking'; Ricardo filio Edmundi, et multis aliis.

MS: WAD, f. 520r–v.
    Rubric: Carta Johannis filii Edwardi de septem solidatis et octo denariatis redditus in Tothull'.
    1. MS: *mea mea*.
Date: Prob. Henry Sumer, Richard Testard, or both, still reeve.

450. Confirmation to the Lady Altar, to provide lights, by Isabel [Basset], wife of Robert Mauduit [II], the king's chamberlain, for her soul, that of her husband, and of all their ancestors and successors, of 7s. 8d. rents in the vill of Westminster, of the fee of John son of Edward, which he confirmed to her by charter. The rents are due from Juliana, widow of Adam of Sunbury; William le Wallur, Edric of the Garden and Martin Smud, their heirs or assigns, for tenements which they held of John in Tothill Street, as stated in John's charter which she assigned to the proctors of the altar. [1200 × 1214]

Omnibus Sancte Matris Ecclesie filiis ad quos presens scriptum pervenerit, Isabella uxor Roberti Mauduyt, domini regis camerarii, salutem in Domino. Noverit universitas vestra me, caritatis intuitu et pro salute anime mee et domini mei et omnium antecessorum et successorum nostrorum, dedisse et concessisse et hac presenti carta mea confirmasse Deo et altari gloriose Virginis Marie in ecclesia Westmonasterii, ad luminarium administrandum, septem solidatos et octo denariatos redditus in villa Westmonasterii, de feodo Johannis filii Edwardi: illos scilicet quos predictus Johannes michi dedit, concessit et carta sua confirmavit pro sex marcis argenti; de quo redditu Juliana que fuit uxor Ade de Sunnebur', et Willelmus le Wallur, et Edricus de Gardino, et Martinus Smud et heredes [suorum et] eorum assignati fuerunt mihi et heredibus meis vel assignatis respondere, de tenementis qua de memorato Johanne tenuerunt in eadem villa, in vico scilicet de Tothull', sicut in carta predicti Johannis continetur et distinguatur. Quam cartam procuratoribus memorati altaris quam sepedictus Johannes michi fecit liberam ob maiorem securitatem predicti redditus percipiendi, assignavi enim procuratores prefatos qui pro tempore fuerint, ad prefatum redditum percipiendum de suprascriptis tenentibus et eorum heredibus, ad eosdem terminos in carta ipsius Johannis statutos et assignatos, libere et quiete, integre et plenarie, sine omni reclamatione vel calumpnia mei vel heredum meorum, salvis predicto Johanni et eius heredibus duobus denariis ad Pascham et ad Festum Sancti Michaelis per manus predictorum procuratorum persolvendis. Ut autem hec mea donatio et concessio et carte mee confirmatio rata et stabilis perseveret, eam presenti scripto et sigilli mei appositione corroboravi. Hiis testibus: Domino Roberto Mauduyt, viro meo; Willelmo Mauduyt, filio meo; Johanne filio Willelmi; Matheo filio Thome; Odone aurifabro, tunc preposito Westmonasterii; Roberto de Cleygate; Stephano de Berkinge; Roberto de Crokesle; Laurentio Muschat, et multis aliis.

MS: WAD, f. 520v.
> Rubric: Carta Isabelle uxoris Roberti Mauduit, domini regis camerarii, de eodem.

Pd: Mason, 'The Mauduits and their Chamberlainship', 20–1.

Date: Earlier than **329**.

451. Confirmation by John son of Edward, at the petition, and with the assent, of his mother Cecily, for the souls of his parents and all his ancestors, to the Lady Altar, to provide lights, of an annual rent of 4*s.* in the vill of Westminster, near Tothill, due from William the palmer, with the service he owes. The proctor of the altar should render John 6*d.* annually for this rent. [Temp. John]

Sciant presentes et futuri quod ego Johannes filius Edwardi, petitione et assensu Cecilie matris mee, pro anima patris et matris mee et omnium antecessorum meorum, dedi et concessi et hac presenti carta mea confirmavi Deo et altari Beate Virginis Marie Westmonasterii ad luminaria eiusdem altaris administranda singulis annis quatuor solidorum redditum in villa Westmonasterii juxta Tothell' de Willelmo palmario, et totum servitium eiusdem Willelmi quod ad me pertinet, absque omni reclamatione mei, vel omnium heredum meorum liberum, in perpetuum. Ita quod custos predicti altaris de hiis iiij^{or} solidis sex denariis mihi singulis annis pro omni servitio reddet. Et sciendum quod ego Johannes et heredes mei prefatum redditum prefato altari warantizabo contra omnes homines et omnes feminas. Ut autem hec donatio mea stabilis et rata permaneat eam presenti scripto et sigilli mei appositione roboravi. Hiis testibus: Alexandro capellano; Ricardo Testard; Adam nepote episcopi; Galfrido de Cruce; Ivone de Medmeham; Laurencio Muschet; Ricardo filio Ranulfi; Stephano de Berking'; Nicholao de cellario; Adam, Galfrido, Radulfo et Johanne, servientibus ecclesie, et multis aliis.

MSS: (1) WAM 17393.
16.5 × 9 cm; t.u. 2 cm.
Seal: on tag; green, but was perhaps in office by early 1161 (*Fasti* III, 33). The second witn. may be his predecessor, Hugh Barre, who resigned 1157 × 1159 (ibid.). Gervase of Cornhill prob. attests as sheriff of

London and Mddx. He held office in 1160–1 (Reynolds, 'Rulers of London', 335.
Endorsements: (a) Carta Johannis filii AEdwardj de terra Willelmi palmerii (contemporary with charter). (b) De redditu iiij solidorum (13C). (c) Tothull: capella: xxij (14C). (d) Uxor Radulfi cementarii tenet (nearly contemporary with charter).
(2) WAD, f. 521.

452. Memorandum of the attestations to a quitclaim by Hugh son of Warner of land in Sunbury and Teddington (Mddx.), and of a compensatory grant of three virgates of land by Abbot L[aurence], in fee and inheritance, formerly belonging to Hamund, in Teddington. Hugh restored to the abbot the king's writ concerning his claim, and swore to Alan the dapifer to uphold the agreement. Curia, Westminster [*c.* 1161 × 1173] (?1161 × 1162)

Isti fuerint presentes in curia Westmonasterii quando Hugo filius Guarnerii clamavit calumpniam suam quietam de tota terra quam calumpniabatur in Sunnebury et in Todington', et Abbas L[aurentius] pro hac quietatione concessit ei in feodo et hereditate tres virgatas terre que fuerunt Hamundi in Todington'. Ita quod ipse H[ugo] reddidit in manu abbatis breve regis super eadem calumpnia et affidavit in manu Alani dapiferi pactionem istam finabiliter tenendam: Baldricus, archidiaconus Legrensis; Hugo, Lexon'[1] archidiaconus; Alwredus, clericus de Wathamstede; Magister Mauricius; Simon clericus; Gervasius de Cornhull'; Alanus; Radulfus [d]e Septem[2] Fontibus; Henricus de Cara Movilla; Gralent de Tany; Rogerus filius Willelmi de Wathamstede; Walterus le Har'; Robertus de Bosco; Ailmer de Wandleswrth' et Gilebertus; Robertus[3] de Derhurst; Gaufridus filius Godefridi: ex parte sua: Paganus et Radulphus de Immurtha; Hugo de Weston'; Hamundus, clericus de Kingeston', et multi alii.

MS: WAD, f. 156.
    Rubric: Renunciacio Hugonis filii Guarnerii de calumpnia predicte terre.
    1. MS: *sic,*? for *quondam Legrec'.*
    2. MS: *VII Septem.*
    3. MS: *Roberto.*
Pd: Van Caenegem, 43, n. 1, *Isti fuerint . . . Todington'* only, where it is dated 1171 × 1176.
Date: Abbot Laurence d. 10/11 April 1173 (*Heads,* 77). Baldric de Sigillo, archdeacon of Leicester, first occurs as archdeacon *c.* 1162/3 4 cm. diameter; eagle facing right; legend: + SIGILL. IOHANNIS FIL. EDWARDI.
Note: Cf. **133.** See also Harvey, *WA,* 354.

453. Notification by William of Northolt, archdeacon of Gloucester, to his friends, French and English, that he has confirmed to his sergeant, Robert Simple, two hides in Cowley (Mddx.) of his inheritance, formerly belonging to William's grandfather, Hugh of Colham, and to his son

Richard son of Hugh, to hold in fee and inheritance of William and his heirs, rendering the service due from that land to the abbot and convent of the church of St Peter of Westminster, and rendering to William, and his heirs, in recognition of his right in that land, one besant (2*s.*) annually. [1177 × May 1186]

Willelmus de Norhall', archidiaconus Gloecestrie, omnibus amicis suis tam Francis quam Anglis, salutem. Notum vobis facio me dedisse et hac presenti carta mea confirmasse Roberto Simplici, servienti meo, pro servitio suo duas hidas terre in Coueleia de hereditate mea, que fuerunt Hugonis de Coleham avi mei, et Ricardi filii eiusdem Hugonis, avunculi mei, in feudo et hereditate, ei et heredibus suis post eum, de me et heredibus meis, tenendas ita libere et quiete et honorifice, in bosco et plano, in viis et semitis, in pratis et pascuis, in aquis et in omnibus aliis locis, sicuti predecessores mei unquam melius et liberius[1] tenuerunt. Faciendo inde omne servitium quod de eadem terra debetur abbati et conventui ecclesie Beati Petri de Westmonasterio; et preterea persolvet idem Robertus et heredes sui mihi et heredibus meis in recognitionem iuris mei quod habeo in predicta terra, singulis annis unum bisantium infra octabis Sancti Michaelis. His testibus: Hugone de Ov'; David de Jarponvill'; Osberto de Senleia; Rogero de Messendene; Angot' Duredent; Godefrido de Tokinton'; Waltero de Greneford; Rogero de la Dune; Radulfo de Tokinton'; Waltero Duredent; Godefrido de Benchesham; Hamone de Roxeie; Hugone fratre eius; Radulfo de P[re]stune; Godefrido de Prestune; Adam de Greneford'; Jacobo, Ranulfo, Ada de Essexe, Alexandro, Waltero et Ligerio, servientibus meis, et multis aliis.

MSS: (1) WAM 381.
     17.8 × 13.2 cm; t.u. 2.4 cm.
     Seal: on plaited cords; black; 5.8 × 3.8 cm; Virgin and Child with kneeling suppliant; legend: + SIGILLUM WILLELMI ARCHIDIACONI GLOEC.
     Endorsed: (a) Covele (13C). (b) Carta Willelmi de Norhale, archidiaconi Gloucestrie, Roberto Simplici concessa (13C). (c) Duplicatur j (13C). (d) Celararia (14C).
     (2) WAM 371.
     Paper; 16C; 28.5 × 15.4 cm; no seal.
     1. . . . tenuerunt. Reddendo inde xxx solidis pro omnibus servitiis abbati et conventui ecclesie Beati Petri Westmonasterii; et preterea persolvent idem Robertus et heredes sui michi et heredibus meis in recognitionem juris mei quod habeo in predicta terra singulis annis unum bizantium vel duobus solidis octavas Sancti Michaelis. Hiis testibus: Hugo de Ov'; Daude de Gerponvill'; Osberto de Senleya' Rogero de Messinden'; Angot de Tokinton'; Waltero Duredent; Godefrido de Benchesham; Hamone de Roxeie; Hugone fratre Radulfi de Prestune; Ada de Greneforde; Jacobo, Ranulpho, Ada de Essex', Alexandro, Waltero et Ligerio, servientibus meis, et multis aliis.

Heading: Carta Willelmi de Norehale, archidiaconi Gloucestrie, de duabus hidis in Covele.
(3) WAD, f. 446.
Variant text as WAM 371, but attestations as in the original, apart from . . . Hugone fratre . . . Prestune, as in 371. Spellings are as in 371, suggesting that the latter was copied from WAD.
Date: Mr William of Northolt was archdeacon of Gloucester 1177–1186, and was elected bp. of Worcester *c*. 25 May 1186 (*Fasti* II, 100).
Note: On Cowley cf. Harvey, *WA*, 124, 350.

454. Notification by Walter of Greenford that he has confirmed to Robert Simple that he and his heirs may hold in fee and inheritance of Walter's uncle, William of Northolt, those lands which William granted and confirmed to him by charter, comprising two hides in Cowley (Mddx.), formerly belonging to Richard of Cowley, and an assart in Northolt (Mddx.) once held of William of Northolt by Derwin of Roxeth. [1177 × 1186]

Walterus de Greneford' omnibus Sancte Matris Ecclesie filiis ad quos presentes littere pervenerint, salutem. Noverit universitas vestra me concessisse et presenti carta mea confirmasse Roberto Simplici quod ipse et heredes sui post ipsum teneant in feodo et hereditate de Willelmo de Norhalle, avunculo meo, et heredibus suis post eum terras illas quas prenominatus Willelmus, avunculus meus, ei pro servitio suo dedit, ita libere et quiete et honorifice sicut predictus Willelmus, avunculus meus, ei dedit et carta sua confirmavit, scilicet: duas hidas terre in Coueleya que fuerunt Ricardi de Coueleya, et unum essartum in Norhallia quod aliquando tenuit Derwynus de Roxeheya de supradicto Willelmo de Norhalle, avunculo meo. Hiis testibus: Magistro Ada de Craneford; Magistro Petro de Lecche; Radulfo et Johanne capellanis; Rogero de Messendene; Godefrido de Tokinton'; Ansgoto Duredent; et Augustino Malet; et Radulfo de Tokinton'; et Hamone de Roxheya; Godefrido de Benchesham; et Godefrido de Preston'; et Radulfo de Preston; Roberto de Wambeleya; Ada de Greneford'; Jacobo; Ada Marescallo; Alexandro; Osberto, et aliis multis.

MS: WAD, f. 446.
Rubric: Carta Walteri de Greneforde de eodem.
Date: Issued later than **453** but before William of Northolt had been elected to the bishopric of Worcester in May 1186 (*Fasti* I, 64; II, 100, 107).
Note: Following a lawsuit brought against him in 1204 by Roger de la Dune and Godfrey son of Ralph, concerning two parts of two hides of land in Cowley, Robert Simple undertook sole responsibility for the service due to the abbot and convent of Westminster, while the plaintiffs would warrant the land against Walter of Greenford (*Fines London and Mddx.*, I, 8, no. 35).

455. Confirmation by Roger of Missenden to Robert Simple and his heirs, that they may hold in fee and inheritance, of his uncle William of

Northolt, and his heirs, those lands which William gave him (Roger); comprising two hides of land in Cowley (Mddx.) which belonged to Richard of Cowley, and an assart in Northolt (Mddx.) which Derwin of Roxeth once held of William of Northolt. [1177 × 1186]

Rogerus de Messindene omnibus Sancte Matris Ecclesie filiis ad quos presentes littere pervenerint, salutem. Noverit universitas vestra me concessisse et presenti carta mea confirmasse Roberto Simplici quod ipse et heredes sui post ipsum teneant in feodo et hereditate de Willelmo de Norhalle avunculo meo, et heredibus suis post eum, terras illas quas prenominatus Willelmus avunculus meus ei pro servitio suo dedit, ita libere et quiete et honorifice sicut predictus Willelmus avunculus meus ei dedit et carta sua confirmavit, scilicet: duas hidas terre in Coueleya que fuerunt Ricardi de Coueleya; et unum essartum in Norhall' quod aliquando tenuit Derwinus de Roxeheya de supradicto Willelmo de Norhall' avunculo meo. Hiis testibus: Magistro Ada de Cranford; Magistro Petro de Lecche; Radulfo et Johanne capellanis; Godefrido de Tokinton'; Ansgoto Duredent; et Augustino Malet; Waltero de Grene-ford; et Radulfo de Tokinton'; et Hamone de Roxeheie; Godefrido de Benchesham; et Godefrido de Preston'; et Radulfo de Preston'; Roberto de Wambeleye; Ada de Greneford; Jacobo; Ada Marescallo; Alexandro; Osberto, et aliis multis.

MS: WAD, f. 446r–v.
Rubric: Carta Rogeri de Messinden' de eodem.
Date: The attestations suggest this was issued on the same occasion as **454**.

456. Confirmation by Earl Aubrey de Vere III to the almonry of Westminster, to sustain the poor, of two parts of his tithe in Kensington (Mddx.) which his forbears formerly gave the almonry. [*c.* 1191 × 1194]

Sciant presentes et futuri quod ego Comes Alb[ricus] de Uer, pro salute mea, et pro animabus patris et matris mee et antecessorum meorum, concessi et hac presenti carta mea confirmavi Deo et elemosinarie Beati Petri Westmonasterii ad sustentationem pauperum, duas partes totius decimationis de dominico meo in Kensint', quas antecessores mei eidem elemosinarie antiquitus dederunt; tenendas et habendas libere et quiete, sicut umquam temporibus antecessorum meorum predicta elemosinaria melius et liberius illas habuit. His testibus: Willelmo filio Fulconis; Galfrido Grosso; Huberto Manant; Tedbaldo de Fering'; Magistro Helia; Ranulfo Lupo; Willelmo Grosso; Willelmo Talemasche; Eustachio; Willelmo clerico, et pluribus aliis.

MSS: (1) WAM 5041.
14.5 × 8. cm; t.u. 1.5 cm.
Tag but seal missing.
Endorsed: (a) Kensiton' (15C) (b) Littera Comitis Oxoniensis de decimis dominicis (15C). (c) In Kensinton' ecclesie Westmonasterii ad sustentacionem pauperum concessis (16C).
(2) WAD, f. 469v.

Date: Attestation of Theobald of Feering, who was seneschal of Westminster temp. Abbot William Postard (**309**). The grantor must therefore
be Aubrey de Vere III, earl of Oxford, 1142 × 1194 (Sanders, p. 52;
G.E.C., X, 201–207).

457. Quitclaim by Herbert [le Poer], archdeacon of Canterbury, to the
abbot and convent, of land at Staines (Mddx.), called New Court, which
his father took from the abbey and treated as his own demesne, and which
Herbert himself held of the abbot for 10*s*. [1191 × 1194]

Herebertus, Dei gratia Cantuariensis archidiaconus, omnibus ad quos
presentes littere pervenerint, salutem in Domino. Noverit universitas
vestra me reddidisse et inperpetuum omnino clamavisse abbati et conventui Westmonasterii totam terram quietam de Stanes, que dicitur Nova
Curia, quam pater meus extraxit et occupavit de proprio dominio abbatis
et monachorum Westmonasterii, contra voluntatem et assensum eorum,
quam scilicet tenui de predicto abbate et conventu pro decem solidis. Et
nunc, quia amplius contra rationem et voluntatem predictorum
monachorum terram prefatam et Novam Curiam tenere nolo, eis sicut
iustum est supradictam terram et curiam, in pace et cum bona voluntate,
etiam voluntarie, pro liberatione anime patris mei, reddo. His testibus:
Osberto filio Hervei; Othone filio Willelmi; Magistro Johanne de Bride-
port; Magistro Thoma de Husburne; Teobaldo senescallo abbatis;
Andrea de Scaccario; Albino clerico; Rogero Enganet, et multis aliis.

MSS: (1) WAM 16737.
     19 × 10 cm; t.u. 2 cm.
     Seal: on tag; white; 4 × 3 cm; classical figure enthroned (right);
     attendant offering a cup; trees in background; legend: + SVM
     CVSTUS . . . TEST . . . SIGILLUM.
     Endorsed: (a) Quietaclamantia Herberti Cantuariensis archidiaconi
     de terra in Stanes que dicitur Nova Curia . . . (13C). (b) et idem
     Westmonasterio concessit (13C). (c) iiij (13C).
     (2) LN, ff. xij *verso*–xiij. Rubric identifies the donor as *Herebertus*
     although text begins *Henricus*.
     (3) CAY, f. xiv: *Hereberti*, *Henrici* variation, as in LN.
Cal: Bentley, 6, no. 48, from CAY.
Date: Theobald of Feering was seneschal of Abbot William (**309**).
Herbert le Poer was appointed archdeacon of Canterbury 1175 × 1176
(*Fasti* II, 14; Ralph de Diceto I, 403), and remained in office until he
became bp. of Salisbury in 1194 (*Fasti* II, 14).
Note: Richard of Ilchester, formerly a senior royal officer, and bp. of
Winchester, d. Dec. 1188 (*Fasti* II, 85). He was prob. the father of
Herbert le Poer (C. Duggan, 'Richard of Ilchester, Royal Servant and
Bishop', *TRHS* 5th ser., 14 (1966), 3 and n. 3).

458. Notification by Matthew of Staines, of his confirmation, in pure and
perpetual alms, for his soul and those of all his kinsfolk, to St Edward,
patron of the church of Westminster, of 6*d*. rent in in the vill of Staines
(Mddx.), from the tenement which Ralph Swift holds of him, lying

between the messuage of Elias Scad and that of Milicent. The tenement renders 1*s*. 6*d*., of which 6*d*. is to be paid annually by Ralph to St Edward on the Feast of his Translation (13 Oct.). [Temp. John]

Sciant presentes et futuri quod ego Matheus de Stanes dedi et concessi et hac presenti carta mea confirmavi, pro salute anime mee et omnium parentum meorum, in puram et perpetuam elemosinam Deo et Beato Edwardo, patrono ecclesie Westmonasterii, sex denarios redditus in villa de Stanes de tenemento quod Radulphus Swift tenet de me in eadem villa, scilicet: de uno masuagio cum pertinentiis, quod masuagium est inter masuagium Helie Scad et masuagium Milisent. Percipiendos per manus dicti Radulphi, vel heredum suorum, qui de me tenent et tenere debent per liberum servitium decem et octo denariorum, de quibus predictus Radulphus solvet annuatim Beato Edwardo sex denarios Die Translationis eiusdem. Ut autem hec donatio et concessio rata sit et stabilis permaneat, cum sigilli mei apposicione predictus Radulfus sigillo suo eam corroboravit. Hiis testibus: Johanne filio Johannis de Stanes; Hereberto filio Ricardi le palmer; Willelmo filio Ricardi de Stanes; Elia Scad'; Johanne vinitore; Thoma de Haverhulle; Rogero Blundo; Ate le draper; Roberto de Cantuaria; Petro de Mimes; Odone aurifabro de Westmonasterio; Ludovico clerico; Henrico Sumer; Ricardo filio Edmundi; Adam, Gaufrido, Willelmo, servientibus ecclesie, et multis aliis.

MSS: (1) WAD, f. 136.
> Rubric: Carta Mathei de Stanes de vj denariis annui redditus in eadem villa.
> (2) LN, f. xv *verso*.
> (3) CAY, f. xvij.
Cal: Bentley, 7, no. 60, from CAY.
Date: Attestations. Thomas of Haverhill was mayor of London 1203–1204 (Reynolds, 'Rulers of London', 356).
Note: See Harvey, *WA*, 354.

459. Notification by Stephen the parson of Hendon that after the death of Ralph his father, who had held the church of Hendon (Mddx.) for many years by gift of Abbot Laurence and the convent of Westminster, they, as true patrons, presented him to it on payment of an annual pension of two marks (£1. 6*s*. 8*d*.) to the abbey sacristy. The right of presentation to Hendon church belongs to the abbot and convent and he, Stephen, had possessed it on the institution of Gilbert, Bp. of London, for 43 years. [1206 × 1216]

Omnibus Sancte Matris Ecclesie filiis ad quos presens scriptum pervenerit, Stephanus persona de Hendon' salutem in Domino. Ad universitatis vestre noticiam volo pervenire quod, cum Radulfus pater meus ecclesiam de Hendon' ex dono Domini Laurentii abbatis West-monasterii et eiusdem loci conventus per aliquot annos pacifice possedis-set ipsoque decedente prefatam ecclesiam vacare contingerit, predicti abbas et conventus prefatam ecclesiam ut veri patroni mihi karitatis intuitu contulerunt, salva sibi et ecclesie sue annua et debita pensione duarum marcarum ad sacristiam memorate ecclesie pertinencium. Ut autem posteris successuris de iure patronatus dicte ecclesie veritas manifesta elucescat, litteris presentibus et patentibus innotesco quod memoratam ecclesiam de Hendon ex dono et collatione et presentatione predictorum abbatis et conventus, necnon et institutione viri venerabilis Gileberti London' episcopi, per xliij annos in confectione presentis scripti, et me etiam tunc prospere agente pacifice possedi et obtinui. Et ne aliquis in jure prefato contra dicti loci abbatem qui pro tempore fuerit et conventum aliquo tempore aliquid vendicare vel in eorum preiudicium attemptare poterit. Huius rei testimonium confirmans litteris presentibus sigillum meum apposui, et ad plenam veritatis noticiam litteras presentes sigillo meo munitas eidem ecclesie commisi. Valeatis omnes in Domino.

MS: WAD, f. 376v.
  Rubric: Scriptum Stephani, persone de Hendon', de pensione duarum marcarum eiusdem ecclesie.
Date: Calculated from the terms of office of Abbot Laurence, *c.* 1158–1173 (*Heads*, 77), and Bp. Gilbert Foliot, 1163–1187 (*Fasti* I, 2), and the duration of Stephen's tenure of the church.
Note: Cf. **211**, **213**.

460. Confirmation, in pure and perpetual alms, by Matilda de Paris, for her soul and those of her kinsfolk, to St Peter of Westminster and the monks, of the whole land, comprising one and a half hides, which she held in the vill of Harrow (Mddx.), to hold as her father Simon and her grandfather Osmar held it, rendering annually 5*s.* to the abp. of Canterbury. [Temp. John]

Sciant presentes et futuri quod ego Matilda de Paris, pro salute anime mee et parentum meorum, dedi et concessi et hac presenti carta mea confirmavi Deo et Sancto Petro Westmonasterii et monachis ibidem Deo servientibus totam terram meam quam habui in villa de Herghes, scilicet hidam unam et dimidiam cum omnibus pertinentiis suis, in liberam et perpetuam elemosinam, habendam et tenendam in perpetuum tam libere, honorifice et quiete ut Simon pater meus et Osmarus avus meus umquam melius et liberius eam tenuerunt, in bosco et plano, et prato et pascuis et pasnagio. Reddendo inde annuatim domino archiepiscopo Cantuariensi qui pro tempore fuerit quinque solidos pro omni servitio. Et ut hec mea donatio rata et in[con]cussa permaneat, eam sigilli mei testimonio corroboravi. Hiis testibus: Alexandro presbitero; Ricardo presbitero; Odone aurifabro; Stephano pincerna; Galfrido de Cruce; Rogero Cnokethald; Gervasio Tatyn, et multis aliis.

MS: WAD, f. 502v.
  Rubric: Carta eiusdem Matilde de eadem.
Date: As for **461**.
Note: Cf. **201–2**.

461. Notification by Matilda [de Paris], daughter of Simon son of Osmar, that, for her soul and those of her ancestors and successors, she has confirmed, in pure and perpetual alms, to the church of St Peter of Westminster and to the convent, for their clothing, all her land in the vill of Harrow (Mddx.), comprising one and a half hides, to hold in perpetuity, rendering 5s. annually to the abp. [of Canterbury] and his successors. In return, the convent would provide her honourably with all necessities, both in clothing and food. For greater security, she has delivered to the convent those charters of her ancestors which she had concerning that land. [Temp. John (late 1206 × May 1213)]

Omnibus Sancte Matris Ecclesie filiis ad quos presens scriptum pervenerit, Matillis filia Simonis filii Osmari, salutem. Noverit universitas vestra me, caritatis intuitu et pro salute anime mee et omnium antecessorum et successorum meorum, dedisse et concessisse et hac presenti carta confirmasse, in puram et perpetuam elemosinam, Deo et ecclesie Beati Petri Westmonasterii et eiusdem loci conventui, ad vestituram suam, totam terram meam quam habui in villa de Herghes, scilicet unam hidam et dimidiam, cum pertinentiis: habendam et tenendam libere et quiete, integre et plenarie, inperpetuum; reddendo inde singulis annis domino archiepiscopo et eius successoribus pro tempore existentibus, quinque solidos pro omni servitio. Pro hac autem donatione et concessione et carte presentis confirmatione, memoratus conventus omnia necessaria, tam in vestitu quam in victu, mihi honorabiliter ministrabit. Et ut conventus pretaxatus prefatam terram pacifice et honorifice et integre, cum omnibus pertinentiis suis, sine aliqua reclamatione vel calumpnia cuiuscumque hominis, habeat, teneat, et possideat, presens scriptum sigilli mei appositione communivi. Et in huius rei warantizatione et firmiori securitate, cartas antecessorum meorum quas habui de prenominata terra, memorato conventui liberavi. Hiis testibus: Ricardo de Dol, tunc senescallo Westmonasterii; Uliano Chesneduit; Johanne filio Willelmi; Odone aurifabro de Westmonasterio; Ludovico clerico; Stephano (clerico)^c de Berking'; Ricardo filio Edmundi; Roberto de Crokesl'; Thoma vinitore; Ada et Johanne servientibus de ecclesia; Gervasio Tatyn; Laurentio Muschat, et multis aliis.

MS: WAD, f. 502r–v.
  Rubric: Scriptum Matildis filie Simonis filii Osmari de predicta terra.
Date: Attestations. The unnamed abp. is Stephen Langton, in exile from his appointment late in 1206 until May 1213 (*Fasti* II, 6).
Note: Matilda is clearly identified in the related charter concerning this land which she granted to the abbey (**460**). The ancestral deeds which she relinquished included **196** and **201–2**.

462. Grant by Geoffrey de Mandeville [I] to St Peter and the church of Westminster, for his soul, that of his wife Lesceline, who counselled this benefaction, and for his deceased wife, Alice, the mother of his sons, of the church of St Mary of Hurley, in Berks., with the whole vill of Hurley and the surrounding wood, except for the land of Edric the reeve and that of the rustics of Little Waltham, which he retained. Osmund, bp. of

Salisbury, was present at the dedication of the church of Hurley, and confirmed further specified endowments. Geoffrey obtained from W I a confirmation of these endowments, and Abbot Gilbert declared anathema on all who infringed this gift. [1085 × 1086]

Sciant presentes et futuri quod ego Gosfridus de Magnavilla concessi et donavi Deo et Sancto Petro et ecclesie Westmonasterii, pro salute et redemptione anime mee et uxoris mee Leceline, cuius consilio hoc bonum inchoavi, et pro anima Athelaise prime uxoris mee, matris filiorum meorum jam defuncte, ecclesiam Sancte Marie de Hurleya in Barrocscire cum tota predicta villa de Herleya et cum toto circumjacenti nemore, sine partitione aut divisione aliqua, vel alicuius hominis in ipsa parochia aliquid tenentis, excepta terra AEdrici prepositi et excepta terra rusticorum de Parva Waltham, quas retinui in manu mea. Concessi, dico, et firmiter donavi cum toto dominio meo in campis et pratis, silvis, pascuis, molendinis, aquis, piscariis atque piscationibus et omnibus appendiciis suis: id est ecclesiam de Waltham cum una hida terre et dimidia que sibi subjacent, et cum socna capelle de Remenham et cuntis consuetudinibus illi antiquitus debitis. Dedi etiam predicte ecclesie de Herleya ea die qua feci eam dedicari, Osmundo episcopo Saresberiensi presente, terram AEdwardi de Hwatetecumba in dotalicium. Qua die supradictus episcopus, pontificali auctoritate, confirmavit omnes donationes meas quas eidem sancto loco contuli, scilicet: in omnibus maneriis meisque in dominio meo eo tempore erant, tertiam partem decime totius annone mee, et duas partes decime totius pecunie maneriorum meorum, et totam decimam pasnagiorum meorum, et totam decimam caseorum, et totam decimam lini et lane, et totam decimam vinearum mearum, et totam decimam omnium aliarum rerum mearum, de quibus juste et recte debet Deo decima reddi. Insuper itaque in unoquoque manerio dominii mei dedi predicte ecclesie de Herleya unum rusticum qui octo acras habeat, et in parco unam porcariam cum terra porcarii. Hiis etenim addidi adhuc in insula[1] de Heli unam piscarium que reddit unum millearium et dimidium siccarum anguillarum et unum presentum anguillarum, quadraginta videlicet grosas anguillas, et in villa que Mosa vocatur tria millearia siccorum allecium. Turoldus vero dapifer meus concessit et dextera sua super altare confirmavit, cum oblatione Radulphi filii sui, duas partes decime totius annone sue de Wokendona et totam decimam totius pecunie sue et in Berdena totam decimam totius annone et totius pecunie sue. AEdricus quoque prepositus meus totam decimam annone et totius pecunie sue ibidem donavit. Ego vero ad expletionem huius tanti boni et ad sustentationem monachorum in eadem ecclesia Deo servientium, feci a domino meo Rege Willelmo hec omnia confirmari et ab eodem episcopo et Abbate Gileberto Westmonasterii omnes infractores sive diminutores hujus mee elemosine feci excomunicari, ut sit habitatio eorum cum Juda, Domini proditore, et viventes descendant in eterne perditionis Baratrum cum Dathan et Chore, nisi emendaverint digna satisfactione. Contestor autem filios, heredes scilicet, et omnes posteros meos per tremendum Dei judicium ne ipsi faciant aut fieri sinant ullam infractionem huic mee donationi, immo augeant et stabiliant illam, ita ut

Deus stabiliat dies et vitam illorum in eterna beatitudine et habeant partem in hac mea elemosina mecum in celesti requie. Testes:[a] Lecelina uxor ipsius Gosfridi; Willelmus de Magnavilla; Walterus de Magnavilla; Ricardus de Magnavilla; Hugo Mascherel; Harnulf de Greneford; Rodolfus de Hairun; et Turoldus de Wokendone; Richerius; Rogerus Blundus, et multi alii.

MSS: (1) WAD, f. 159r–v.
 Rubric: Carta Goffridi de Magna Villa de ecclesia Sancte Marie de Hurlea cum tota villa et toto nemore circumiacenti et omnibus aliis in carta contentis.
 1. MS: *insule*.
 (2) F, 280v–281v.
  a. MS: *Hiis testibus* etc.
Pd: Chaplais, 'Original Charters', 105–8.
Date: After the appointment of Gilbert Crispin (*Heads*, 77), and following the d. of Geoffrey de Mandeville's first wife (cf. **23**, **436**; *Gilbert Crispin*, 32), and his remarriage. Geoffrey is believed to have d. *c.* 1100 (Hollister, 'Mandevilles', 19).
Note: On this text, see Chaplais, 'Original Charters', 98; on the foundation of Hurley, Harvey, *WA*, 43; *Gilbert Crispin*, 32–3; Knowles & Hadcock, 54, 68; on Westminster's acquisition of Hurley's possessions, Harvey, *WA*, 337–8. A forged version of Geoffrey's charter is printed by Chaplais, 'Original Charters', 105–8.

463. Letter of Bartholomew [de Vendôme], abp. of Tours, addressed to Richard [of Dover], abp. of Canterbury, and all prelates; Ranulf [de Glanville] the seneschal, and all justices throughout England. Asked to give evidence in the dispute between Abbot Walter and a certain knight, over the advowson of Ockendon church (Essex), he declares that, at the request of Queen [Eleanor] of the English, the late Abbot Laurence presented him to that church, to which he was inducted. [1175 × Feb. 1184 (? 1180 × 1184)]

Venerabili Domino Ricardo, Dei gratia Cantuariensi archiepiscopo, et universis prelatis, et Domino Ranulfo senescallo, et omnibus justiciis per Angliam constitutis, Bartholomeus, divina clemencia Turonensis ecclesie humilis minister, salutem in vero salutari. Litteras Domini Walteri abbatis de Westmonasterio recepimus, ad nos directas, quatinus cum suborta sit controversia inter eundem abbatem et quendam militem, de patronatu ecclesie de Wochendona, nos qui ad eandem ecclesiam aliquando recepti fuimus super huius rei veritate prout nobis cognita erat testimonium perhiberemus. Nos vero inquisitioni tanti viri satagere et ad sapiendam controversiam quod super hoc verum novimus in medium proferre volentes vos decetero super hoc nolumus dubitare. Notum sit igitur discretioni vestre quod, ad preces domine regine Anglorum, Laurentius, vir laudabilis memorie, quondam abbas de Westmonasterio, prefatam ecclesiam de Wokendona, omni contradictione cessante, nobis dedit et concessit, et ad eius presentationem ad eandem ecclesiam recepti fuimus, super quo vos nostro credere testimonio quantum expediens fuerit postulamus. Valete.

MS: WAD, f. 506.
    Rubric: Littera Bartholomei Turonensis episcopi testimonialis super jure patronatus ecclesie de Wokindon'.
Date: Terms of office of Abp. Richard and Abbot Walter (*Fasti* II, 5; *Heads*, 77), but Ranulph the seneschal is almost certainly the justiciar Glanville. The earliest date would then be 1179, but more prob. 1180, when Glanville was regent (West, *Justiciarship*, 55–6).
Note: Cf. **198, 211, 213**.

464. Notification by William de Mandeville, earl of Essex, to his men and his friends, French and English, that he has confirmed to Geoffrey Fitz Walter the whole of Roding (Essex), to hold in fee and inheritance by the service of the fee of one knight, as the charter of Earl Geoffrey his brother bears witness, to hold as Aubrey de Vere, William's grandfather, or Earl Geoffrey his father held it. [1166 × 1189]

Willelmus de Mandavilla, comes de Essex', omnibus hominibus suis et amicis, Francis, Anglis, clericis, laicis, futuris et presentibus, salutem. Sciatis universi me donasse et concessisse et hac carta mea presenti confirmasse Galfrido filio Walteri totam Roinges: tenendam sibi et heredibus suis de me et heredibus meis in feodo et hereditate, per servicium feodi unius militis, sicut carta Comitis Galfridi fratris mei illi testatur. Quare volo et firmiter concedo quod illam terram habeat et teneat, libere, quiete, integre et honorifice, cum omnibus libertatibus et liberis consuetudinibus illi tenemento pertinentibus, in bosco et plano, in pratis et pascuis, in semitis et viis et aquis et omnibus locis, sicut unquam Albericus de Ver avus meus, vel comes Galfridus pater meus, vel aliquis alius antecessorum meorum illam terram melius vel plenius vel quietius vel honorificencius aliquo tempore tenuit, per prenominatum servicium. His testibus: Comite Alberico; Radulfo de Berineres; Ricardo de Rocella; Johanne de Rocella; Savale de Osenwilla'; David de Gerpunvilla'; Osberto filio Ricardi; Viscardo Laidet; Gilleberto de Ver; Ricardo de Levini; Asculfo capellano; Radulfo de Setfuntaines; Willelmo de Gramavilla; Waltero camerario; Alexandro clerico, et multis aliis.

MS: WAM 1231.
    17.4 × 15.5 cm; t.u. 2.6 cm.
    Seal: on tag; white; 7.7 cm diameter; earl on horseback, facing right, brandishing a sword (worn).
    Endorsed: Willelmus de Mandavilla Waltero filio Galfridi (*sic*) totam Rodiynges (13C).
Date: William's tenure of the earldom (G.E.C. V, 116–19).
Note: Geoffrey de Mandeville I held six estates in Roding in 1086, although the various Rodings were not differentiated then (*DB* II, 57b, 60b–62a). The *carta* of Geoffrey earl of Essex does not list Geoffrey Fitz Walter among the tenants of the earldom in 1166, although Geoffrey

Gernet then held one fee of old enfeoffment, and Geoffrey de Jarpenville held one of new enfeoffment (*Liber Niger Scaccarii*, 229; *RBE*, I, 346). The tithes of (White) Roding, which pertained to the precentor's office, were confirmed to the abbey by Gilbert Foliot, bp. of London (**211**).

465. Notification by Geoffrey, count of Perche, that, with the assent of his wife Matilda, he has confirmed the gift which Sweyn of Essex, grandfather of Henry of Essex, made to St Peter and the abbot and convent of Westminster, comprising an annual rent of £3 in the vill of Wheatley (Essex), payable by his bailiffs, which the convent are to hold as honourably as they ever did. [1191 × 1202]

Sciant tam presentes quam futuri quod ego Gaufridus, Dei gratia comes de Pertico, divine pietatis intuitu, concessi et hac presenti carta mea confirmavi, consensu Matildis uxoris mee, donationem illam quam Swanus de Essexa, avus videlicet Henrici de Essex', dedit et concessit Deo et Sancto Petro et abbati et conventui Westmonasterii, videlicet sexaginta solidatas redditus in villa de Wateleya finabiliter, singulis annis percipiendas a baillivis meis, qui pro tempore fuerint, Dominica scilicet in Ramis Palmarum ad mandatum pauperum faciendum proxima die Jovis. Volo autem et firmiter precipio quatinus prefatus conventus Westmonasterii libere et quiete et honorifice prefatum redditum habeant, sicut unquam alicuius tempore melius et liberius habuerunt. Precor vero et obtestor omnes successores meos ne ipsi ullam infractionem huic mee concessioni faciant vel fieri permittant. Ut autem hec mea concessio futuris temporibus stabilis et rata permaneat eam presentis scripti testimonio et sigilli mei attestatione roboravi. Hiis testibus: Hugone de Taber', senescallo meo; Ricardo filio Willelmi; Johanne de Rokesford; Rogero de Longo Ponte; Odone de Lormar'; Hugone de Polestede; Hugone filio eiusdem; Johanne del Fliet; Laurentio de Pakelesham; Johanne de Perdiz, et pluribus aliis.

MS: WAD, ff. 496v–497.
    Rubric: Carta Gaufridi comitis de Pertico de sexaginta solidatis redditus in villa de Wateleya.
Pd: *Gilbert Crispin*, 50 (extracts).
Date: Tenure of title of Geoffrey III, count of Perche, 1191 × *ante* 1202 (V. de Saint-Allais, *L'Art de Vérifier les Dates des Faits historiques, des Chartes, des Chroniques, et autres anciens Monuments*, XIII (Paris, 1818), 180–181).
Note: The lands of Henry of Essex escheated to H II in 1163 (Sanders, 121, 139). The king's daughter Matilda, wife of Henry the Lion, duke of Saxony and Bavaria, had a daughter, another Matilda, who married the future Count Geoffrey in 1189 (Saint-Allais, ibid.). As her marriage portion, the younger Matilda conveyed to the count of Perche part, at least, of the lands formerly held by Henry of Essex (Sanders, 121).

466. Notification by Celestria, former wife of Daniel de Aqua of Aldenham, that, with the consent of Thomas her son, she has quitclaimed to Thomas de Camera a messuage and five acres in Aldenham (Herts.). She and her son have abjured this land before the court of Westminster [Abbey] and Thomas de Camera has given them £3. 5*s*. [*c*. 1200 × *ante* 1214]

Sciant presentes et futuri quod ego Celestria que fui uxor Danielis de Aqua de Aldeham, assensu et uoluntate Thome filii mei, concessi et quiete clamavi de me et heredibus meis sine omni retenemento Thome de Camera et heredibus suis unum mesagium et quinque acras terre cum pertinentiis in Aldeham, scilicet: tres acras que iacent ante portam predicti mesagii et duas acras que jacent a latere predicti mesagii, et totum ius et clamium quod habui in predicta terra: habendum et tenendum ipsi Thome et heredibus suis bene et in pace, libere et quiete, integre et plenarie inperpetuum, sine omni retenemento vel calumpnia de me vel heredibus meis, et sine omni servitio reddendo quod pertineat ad me vel heredes meos. Ego autem totam predictam terram coram tota curia Westmonasterii abjuravi cum Thoma filio meo. Pro hac autem concessione et quieta clamantia inperpetuum predictus Thomas dedit mihi et Thome filio meo sexaginta et quinque solidos esterlingorum. Et ut hec concessio et quieta clamantia rata et stabilis permaneat eam sigilli mei appositione corroboravi. Hiis testibus: Ricardo de Dol, tunc senescallo Westmonasterii; Gaufrido Picot; Alexandro capellano de Aldeham; Waltero de Grenef'; Odone aurifabro de Westmonasterio; Gaufrido camerario; Roberto de Krokel'; Waltero Marescallo; Bartholomeo hostiario; Roberto de Bosco de Aldeham; Phylippo de Camera; Ada de Bosco; Radulfo clerico, et multis aliis.

MSS: (1) WAM 4461.
    18.6 × 11 cm; t.u. 1.4 cm.
    Seal: on long green cords; red; 4.8 × 3.3 cm; fleur de lys; legend: + SIGILL . . . UXOR DANIELIS.
    Endorsements: (a) Quieta clamantia Celestrine que fuit uxor Danielis de Aqua de Aldenham facta Thome de Camera de uno mesuagio et V acris terre in Aldenham (14C). (b) xvij (14C).
    (2) WAD, ff. 187v–188.
Date: Attestation of Richard de Dol as seneschal.
Note: This deed is in the same hand and the same words as 467 (apart from two necessary changes of name). On Aldenham, cf. Harvey, *WA*, 345.

467. Notification by Thomas son of Daniel de Aqua of Aldenham that, with the consent of Celestria his mother, he has quitclaimed to Thomas de Camera a messuage and five acres in Aldenham (Herts.). He and his mother have abjured this land before the court of Westminster [Abbey] and Thomas de Camera has given them £3. 5*s*. [*c*. 1200 × *ante* 1214]

Sciant presentes et futuri quod ego Thomas filius Danielis de Aqua de Aldeham, assensu et uoluntate Celestrie matris mee, concessi et quiete clamavi de me et heredibus meis, sine omni retenemento, Thome de Camera et heredibus suis unum mesagium et quinque acras terre cum pertinentiis in Aldeham, scilicet: tres acras que iacent ante portam predicti mesagii et duas acras que iacent a latere predicti mesagii, et totum ius et clamium quod habui in predicta terra; habendum et tenendum ipsi Thome et heredibus suis bene et quiete et libere et in pace, integre et plenarie, in perpetuum, sine omni retenemento vel calumpnia de me vel heredibus meis, et sine omni servitio reddendo quod pertineat ad me vel heredes meos. Ego autem totam predictam terram coram tota curia Westmonasterii abiuravi cum Celestria matre mea. Pro hac autem concessione et quieta clamantia inperpetuum predictus Thomas dedit mihi et Celestrie matri mee sexaginta et quinque solidos esterlingorum. Et ut hec concessio et quieta clamantia rata sit et stabilis permaneat eam sigilli mei appositione corroboravi. Hiis testibus: Ricardo de Dol, tunc senescallo Westmonasterii; Gaufrido Picot; Alexandro capellano de Aldeham; Walter de Grenef'; Odone aurifabro Westmonasterii; Gaufrido Cam'; Roberto de Krokel'; Waltero Marescallo; Bartholomeo hostiario; Roberto de Bosco de Aldeham; Phylippo de Camera; Ada de Bosco; Radulfo clerico, et multis aliis.

MSS: (1) WAM 4460.
    18.4 × 9.6 cm; t.u. 1.4 cm.
    Cord: pink and green; seal missing.
    Endorsements: (a) Quieta clamantia Thome filii Danielis de Aqua de Aldenham de uno mesuagio et v acris terre Thome de Camera concessis (14C). (b) xiiij (14C).
    (2) WAD, f. 188.
Date: As **466**.
Note: Cf. Harvey, *WA*, 345.

468. Confirmation by Nicholas [de Sigillo], archdeacon of Huntingdon, of the perpetual vicarage of the church of Datchworth (Herts.) to Elias the clerk at the request of Abbot Laurence of Westminster and of Richard [of Ilchester], archdeacon of Poitiers, rector of that church. Elias is to pay two *aurei* a year to Richard and if Richard leaves the said church or dies Elias is to pay the two *aurei* to the abbey. No more is ever to be asked of him. [*c.* 1164 × Dec. 1166]

Nicholaus Huntend' archidiaconus omnibus ad quos littere presentes pervenerint, salutem. Dilecto clerico nostro Elie utiliter in posterum providere cupientes venerabilium amicorum nostrorum Laurentii abbatis Westmonasterii et Domini Ricardi Pictaviensis archidiaconi petitione, perpetuam ecclesiam de Dachwrth vicariam in perpetuam elemosinam ei concedimus et presentis scripti testimonio confirmamus; ita scilicet quod predictus Elyas ecclesiam illam possideat cum omnibus pertinentiis suis et cum omni integritate fructuum, et reddet annuatim predicto Ricardo Pictaviensi archidiacono, qui eiusdem ecclesie persona constitutus est, duos aureos tantum; si vero Ricardus Pictaviensis archidiaconus eidem ecclesie cesserit vel decesserit prescripto tenore et conditione idem Elias ecclesie Westmonasterii annuatim reddet illos duos aureos et ecclesiam illam habebit, cum omnibus pertinentiis suis et cum omni illa fructuum integritate quam prius eam possidebat, et ita quod ab eo quamdiu vixerit nichil preter hos duos aureos de jure exigi possit. Hec itaque conventio, scripto et sigillo abbatis et conventus Westmonasterii confirmata est. Hiis testibus: Willelmo filio Martini; Magistro Jordano; Magistro Hugone; et Thoma, clerico et tornato, et Radulfo, clerico Exonensi.

MS: WAD, f. 380v.
    Rubric: Scriptum Nicholai archidiaconi Huntingdon' super redditum duorum aureorum de ecclesia de Dachwurth.
Date: As for **222**, which is related.
Note: In **222**, the pension is of two besants. The term *aureus* (a gold coin) was frequently used to denote the besant (R. E. Latham, *Revised Medieval Latin Word List* (1965), 38. See also *H Med Exch.*, 294–5).

469. Writ of William d'Aubigny the Breton ordering his officers in Sawbridgeworth (Herts.) not to harass the monks serving the church there. Any plea concerning them is to be heard in his court. [*c.* (Nov. 1120 ×) 1130]

Willelmus de Alb[ini] Br[ito] omnibus ministris suis et hominibus Francis et Anglis de Sebriht', salutem. Sciatis quod ecclesia de Sabriht' et omnia ad eam pertinentia sunt in manu mea, et ideo volo ut monachi qui ibidem Deo serviunt et omnia sua sint in pace, et nullus eis iniuriam vel torturam faciat. Et si quid ortum fuerit de eis unde calumniari vel implacitari debeant, volo ut remaneat donec coram me querela fiat. Et de monachis et de hominibus eorum, et de decimis et de aliis rectitudinibus que iuste ecclesie facere debetis, volo ut faciatis nec aliquid remaneat. Sic me diligitis et ut pro vobis faciam et grates sciam. Valete.

MS: WAM 8580.
    16.7 × 4.1 cm.
    Tongue, with pink silk bag; seal missing.
    Endorsed: Sebrichieswrth (13C).
Date: This church was granted to Westminster by Henry I, *c.* Nov. 1120 × 1127, following the death of Otwel Fitz Count (**86**). William d'Aubigny the Breton accounted for the lands of Otwel Fitz Count in 1130 (*PR 31 Henry I*, 133–4).
Note: It should be noted that the monks of Westminster undertook some pastoral duties in the earlier part of the twelfth century (cf. Marjorie Chibnall, 'Monks and pastoral work: a problem in Anglo-Norman history', *Jnl. of Ecclesiastical History*, 18 (1967), 165–72, and Brett, *English Church*, 221).

470. Confirmation by William [de Mandeville] earl of Essex, in perpetual and free alms, for his soul, for that of H II, and those of his parents and ancestors, to the church of St Peter of Westminster, of the church of Sawbridgeworth (Herts.) to the abbey. [1166 × 1189]

Willelmus comes Essexie omnibus Sancte Matris Ecclesie filiis, salutem. Noverit universitas vestra me concessisse et hac presenti carta mea confirmasse ecclesie Sancti Petri Westmonasterii ecclesiam de Sabrihceswrthe cum omnibus pertinentiis suis in perpetuam et liberam elemosinam, pro salute mea et domini mei Regis Henrici, et pro animabus patris et matris mee et antecessorum meorum. Quare volo et firmiter precipio ut teneant eas bene, quiete, libere et honorifice, sicut unquam melius, quietius et liberius tenuerunt temporibus antecessorum meorum. Hiis testibus: Willelmo de Ver; Asculfo capellano; Ricardo de Vercoroli; Willelmo de Lisoris; David de Jarpovilla; Symone fratre eius; Osberto filio Ricardi; Osberto de Sancto Claro; Willelmo de Norhala; Johanne de Rochella; Eustachio camerario; Rogero et Symone, clericis abbatis Westmonasterii.

MSS: (1) BL Cotton Charter X.I.
16.3 × 10.2 cm; t.u. 2 cm.
Seal: on tag; yellow; 8.2 cm diameter; earl on horseback, facing right, right arm raised brandishing sword; legend: SI. . .MI . . .OM. . . .E ESSE. . . (see *Cat. Seals BM* II, 318, no. 6200).
Endorsed: (a) Illegible, on fold: . . .swea. (b) Carta W. comitis Essex' de ecclesia de Sabricheswrth concessa e. . . (stained). (c) iii.
(2) F, f. 287 (attestations end with Asculf capellanus).
Pd: J. H. Round, *Geoffrey de Mandeville* (New York, 1892), 231 n. 3 (witnesses only).
Date: The witness William de Norhala is prob. William of Northolt whose name recurs in the Westminster charters (e.g. **453–5**). He was elected bp. of Worcester *c.* 25 May 1186 (*Fasti* II, 100), having been a prebendary of London, and archdeacon of Gloucester 1177–1186 (*Fasti* I, 64; II, 107). His attestation without any title would suggest a date *ante* 1177.
Note: This church, which prev. pertained to the honour of Otwel Fitz Count, was granted to the abbey by King Henry I (**86**) on the advice of Richard de Belmeis I, bp. of London (**203**). Otwel or Othuer (d. Nov. 1120) was the second husband of Margaret de Ria, who had prev. married William de Mandeville I (Hollister, 'Mandevilles', 21, 26), the grandfather of Earl William. Pope Alexander III confirmed the church, prob. in 1161 (**170**). Bp. Gilbert Foliot also confirmed this church, pertaining to the sacrist's office, with a pension of £15 (**211**).

471. Grant by Alan de Hull to Beatrice daughter of Iseult, daughter of Gilbert of Stevenage, of two acres in the fields of Stevenage (Herts.), to hold in inheritance, at an annual rent of 6*d.*; gersum of 18*s.* [Temp. John]

Sciant presentes et futuri quod ego Alanus de Hulla dedi, concessi et hac presenti carta mea confirmavi Beatricie filie Ysoude, filie Gilberti de Stythenach', pro homagio et servitio suo, duas acras terre mee in campis de Stithenache: illas scilicet duas acras que abuttant super pratum domini abbatis de Westmonasterio juxta dumum ex parte austr[al]i, et vocantur Gosiacre, integre in longitudine et latitudine sicut jacent. Tenendas et habendas de me et heredibus meis, sibi et heredibus suis, vel cui dare vel assignare voluerit, libere et quiete et hereditarie. Reddendo inde annuatim mihi et heredibus meis vj denarios ad quatuor terminos, scilicet: ad Festum Sancti Andree iij obulos; ad Annunciationem Beate Marie iij obulos; ad Festum Sancti Johannis Baptiste iij obulos; et ad Festum Sancti Michaelis iij obulos, pro omni servitio, consuetudine et exactione.

Pro hac autem donatione et carte confirmatione dedit mihi predicta Beatricia xviij solidos in gersummam. Et ego Alanus de la Hulla et heredes mei warantizabimus etc. Hiis testibus etc.

MS: F, f. 284v.
Date: Earlier than **473**.
Note: There follow in F, on this folio, brief memoranda of the following:
(1) Grant by Alan de Hull to Robert Fitz Iseult of two acres which the prior of Wymondley later had.
(2) Grant of half a virgate to W. de Hairum in Stevenage.
(3) Grant by Alan de Hull to the prior of Wymondley.
(4) Agreement between the abbot and convent of Westminster and Osbert le palmer of Stevenage.
And at the top of f. 285:
(5) Brief memorandum of a grant by Henry, heir of Alan de Hull, of land which Thomas de Mapaz had. This item possibly represents a confirmation to the abbey of the lands which Alan had granted to Thomas son of Gilbert of Mappershall, and which were later granted by Alan to the Abbey (**472–3**).

472. Confirmation by Alan de Hull to Thomas son of Gilbert of Mappershall of the messuage formerly held by his mother Christine; a garden; one croft with a rent of 1s. 5d.; ten acres; a little grove and another croft (Stevenage, Herts.). [Temp. John]

Sciant presentes et futuri quod ego Alanus de Hulle dedi, concessi et hac presenti carta mea confirmavi Thome filio Gileberti de Maperteshale, pro homagio et servitio suo, totum illud mesuagium quod Christiana mater mea tenuit de feodo meo in Stithenach'; et gardinum cum omnibus suis pertinentiis, sicut fossatum circuit; et croftam similiter cum omnibus pertinentiis suis, que jacet inter predictum mesuagium et domum Ingoldi filii Rogeri; et redditum septemdecim denariorum cum omnibus pertinentiis suis, quem mihi idem Ingoldus reddidit annuatim; et duas acras juxta viam ecclesie que abutant in Livdane; et illas duas acras cum pertinentiis suis que abutant super brueram, et vocantur Longe Acre; et sex acras in cultura que est inter Cureswell' et Slittemere; et totam parvam gravam cum pertinentiis, que est ante portam meam, que vocatur Rodingge; et totam illam croftam que vocatur Songerescroft, cum omnibus pertinentiis suis, scilicet de divisa que tendit versus predictam gravam apud austrum. Habendum et tenendum de me et de heredibus meis sibi et heredibus suis, vel cuicumque iamdictum tenementum cum prefato redditu assignare voluerit, libere et quiete et hereditarie. Reddendo inde annuatim mihi vel heredibus meis duodecim denarios ad duos terminos anni, scilicet: ad Pascha sex denarios, et ad Festum Sancti Michaelis sex denarios, pro omni servitio et exactione et consuetudine, salvo tamen modo servicio domini regis, quantum pertinet ad tantum tenementum eiusdem feodi in villa de Stithenach'. Pro hac etiam donatione et confirmatione, dedit mihi predictus Thomas decem marcas argenti in gersumam. Et ego predictus Alanus de la Hulle et heredes mei warantizabimus predicto Thome filio Gileberti et heredibus suis, vel

305

cuicumque assignare voluerit, totam prenominatam terram cum pertinentiis suis, et cum predicto redditu contra omnes homines et omnes feminas. Et ut carta ista firma sit et stabilis, sigillo meo corroboravi. Hiis testibus: Domino Johanne de Meperteshale; Domino Petro de Well'; Henrico filio Gileberti; Deodato de Pullehangre; Roberto Taylepast; Galfrido de Pullehangre; Hugone de la Mote; Nicholao filio Rogeri; Jordano filio Albrici; Osberto palmero; Nicholao Hachel'; Henrico de Brant'; Thoma fratre eius; Amaurico de Boxe; Helia de Stent'; Roberto filio eius; Galfrido de Mand'; Deodato le Charpenter; Ada de Pettesho, et multis aliis.

MS: WAD, f. 215.
> Rubric: Carta Alani de la Hulle de uno mesuagio in Stithenach', cum gardino et una crofta, et de redditu septemdecim denariorum cum suis pertinenciis.

Date: Earlier than **473**.

473. Confirmation, in pure and perpetual alms, by Alan de Hull, for the souls of his ancestors and successors, to the church of St Peter of Westminster and the monks, of the messuage which his mother Christine held of his fee in Stevenage (Herts.), with a garden; a croft; a rent of 1*s.* 5*d.*; and a total of ten acres; a little grove and a croft, to hold at an annual rent of 10*d.* [Temp. John]

Sciant presentes et futuri quod ego Alanus de Hulla dedi, concessi et hac presenti carta mea confirmavi ecclesie Sancti Petri de Westmonasterio et monachis ibidem Deo servientibus, pro animabus antecessorum et successorum meorum, in puram et perpetuam elemosinam totum illud messagium quod Cristina mater mea tenuit de feodo meo in Stithenache cum pertinentiis suis; et gardinum cum suis pertinentiis, sicut fossatum circuit; et croftam similiter cum suis pertinentiis, que jacet inter predictum messagium et domum Ingoldi filii Rogeri, et redditum decem et septem denariorum quos ab eodem Ingoldo recipere consuevi; et duas acras juxta viam ecclesie que se habotant in Linden', cum suis pertinentiis, et illas duas acras cum suis pertinentiis que se habotant super Brueriam, et vocantur Longe Acre; et sex acras in cultura que est inter Cureswell et Flittemere cum suis pertinentiis; et totam parvam gravam que jacet ante portam meam, et vocatur Ruddinge, cum suis pertinenciis; et totam illam croftam que vocatur Sangerescroft, scilicet de diversa que se extendit versus predictam gravam versus austrum, cum suis pertinenciis. Habenda et tenenda predictis monachis inperpetuum, libere et quiete, reddendo inde annuatim michi et heredibus meis duodecim denarios per manum Ingoldi prenominati et heredum suorum, scilicet: ad Festum Annunciationis Beate Marie sex denarios et ad Festum Sancti Michaelis sex denarios pro omni servicio et seculari demanda. Ego vero Alanus et heredes mei warantizabimus predictis monachis totum predictum tenementum cum suis pertinentiis contra omnes homines et feminas. Ut autem hec donatio et concessio rata et stabilis perpetuo permaneat, presens scriptum sigillo meo roboravi. Hiis testibus: Ricardo de Doll, tunc senescallo de Westmonasterio; Yvone de Hamleg'; Johanne de

Stanes; Nicholao filio Avice; Nicholao Bacheler; Johanne de Brokesburene; Johanne Butillir'; Helia de Niweton; Gwidone serviente, et multis aliis.

MSS: (1) WAD, f. 215r–v.
> Rubric: Carta eiusdem Alani de predictis messuagiis, gardino et una crofta et de redditu predicto cum pertinenciis in Stithenache.
> (2) F, f. 283v–284 (attestations end with Ivo de Hamleg').

474. Grant by Robert Fitz Ralph of Watton, to his wife Katherine, of half the vill of Watton (Herts.) in dower. [(1141 × 1142) × 1158]

Sciant presentes et futuri quod ego Rodbertus de Wattuna, filius Radulfi de Wattuna, concessi et donavi Katerine sponse mee medietatem tocius ville mee de Wattuna in dotalicium et hac karta[1] mea confirmavi, cum omnibus pertinentiis suis et redditibus et libertatibus: in bosco; in plano; in agro; in pratis; in pascuis; in aquis; in rivis; in viis; in semitis, et in omnibus locis, absque ullo retenemento, sicut ego vel pater meus eam liberius et magis quiete et pacifice ullo tempore possedit et habuit. Testibus his: Petro de Valoniis; Rodberto de Val'; Ricardo de Chaune; Radulfo de Lattune; Waltero de Nevile; Radulfo de Huvile; Willelmo de Bosco; Andrea[2] Revel; Philippo Revel; Reginaldo de Thanet; Ricardo capellano; Wigero preposito; Henrico preposito, et multis aliis.

MS: WAM 4737.
> 19 × 6.8 cm; t.u. 2.2 cm; tag; seal missing.
> Endorsed: (a) Carta Roberti de Wattune (13C). (b) 119 (modern).
> 1. MS: *karte*.
> 2. MS: *Andreae*.

Date: Hand is mid-12C. Peter de Valognes succeeded as lord of Bennington, Herts., 1141 × 1142, and d. 1158, when he was succeeded by his brother Robert (Sanders, 12).

Note: In 1166, Robert Fitz Ralph held one fee of old enfeoffment of Robert de Valognes (*Liber Niger Scaccarii*, 245; *RBE* I, 361). The attestations of Peter and Robert de Valognes to this charter indicate that Robert Fitz Ralph's land was the manor of Woodhall in Watton, which in turn was held of the Valognes fee (*VCH Herts.*, III, 161). Katherine's dower was presumably later acquired by Westminster, and augmented the abbey's demesne land in Watton (cf. Harvey, *WA*, 346).

475. Notification by Hugh de Euremou to his lord, Bp. R[obert Bloet] and the barons of Lincs., that he has restored to St Peter of Westminster the manor of Doddington (Lincs.), since King [Henry I] took the manor which Hugh gave to St Peter [in exchange] for it, and restored it to Count Eustace. [? 1102 × 1103]

Domino Suo Episcopo R[oberto] et baronibus [de] Lincolnscira, Hugo de Euremou, salutem. Sciatis me reddidisse Sancto Petro Westmonasterii manerium de Dotinton'; quia manerium quod pro illo

307

dederam Sancto Petro rex a me accepti, et Comiti Eustachio reddidit, nec volo ut causa mei Ecclesia Dei ullo modo dampnum habeat.

MS: WAD; f. 501.
> Rubric: Carta Hugonis de Euremou de manerio predicto.
> Marginalia: Ista carta debuit precedere cartam Willelmi regis ad istud signum (f. 500v, in margin of **31**).

Pd: *Gilbert Crispin*, 144, no. 25.
Date: Cf. **61**.
Note: The exchanged manor was Duxford, Cambs.: **61**.

476. Notification by Geoffrey Fitz Peter, earl of Essex, that Abbot Ralph and the convent of Westminster have, at the earl's petition, confirmed to the nuns of Shouldham, and their brethren, all tithes pertaining to them in Clakelose Hundred (Norf.), in return for £1. 10s. due annually to the almoner of Westminster. [1200 × 1213]

Galfridus filius Petri, comes Essex', omnibus ad quos presens scriptum pervenerit, salutem. Noverit universitas vestra Dominum R[adulphum] abbatem de Westmonasterio et eiusdem loci conventum ad petitionem nostram concessisse et carta sua confirmasse sanctimonialibus de Suld-ham et fratribus earum omnes decimas que ad eos pertinent in Clakelose hundredo, tenendas de eis inperpetuum, solvendo annuatim elemosinario Westmonasterii triginta solidos ad duos terminos, videlicet: infra octabas Pasche xv solidos, et infra octabas Sancti Michaelis xv solidos. Hoc autem eis concesserunt predictus abbas et conventus quamdiu erga ecclesiam Westmonasterii predicte moniales legittime se habuerint et bene reddiderint predictos xxx solidos. Testibus hiis: Galfrido de Bocl'; Ricardo de Heriet'; Ricardo de Dol; Jordano Peverel; Radulfo aurifabro; Ricardo ianitore; Bartholomeo pincerna; Roberto de Croch'; Jacobo hostiario, et multis aliis.

MSS: (1) WAM 1717*.
> 19.3 × 6.8 cm; t.u. 2 cm.
> Seal: on tag; 6.8 cm diameter; brown; obverse: earl on horseback, brandishing a sword; SI[GILLUM GAUFRIDI COMITI]S EXIE +.
> Counterseal: 3.2 cm diameter; six-petalled flower (worn); legend: . . .IL . . . ETRI . . .
> Endorsed: (a) Littera comitis Essex' pro xxx solidis de Schuldham' (14C). (b) solvendis ecclesie Westmonasterii pro decimis in Clakelose hundredo elemosinarie (14C).
> (2) WAD, f. 469v.

Date: Abbot Ralph succeeded in 1200 and Earl Geoffrey d. in 1213.
Note: Shouldham (Norf.) was a Gilbertine house founded by Geoffrey Fitz Peter in the reign of Richard I (Knowles & Hadcock, 194, 196). These tithes are not listed in the detailed confirmations of Pope Adrian IV, nor in subsequent confirmations. They were perhaps granted to Westminster by one of Geoffrey Fitz Peter's tenurial predecessors, such

as William de Mandeville II, but any charter was prob. surrendered when Westminster confirmed Geoffrey Fitz Peter's donation to Shouldham.

477. Acknowledgement by the nuns and brethren of Shouldham that they have received from Abbot Ralph and the convent of Westminster all tithes which pertained to them in Clakelose Hundred (Norf.), to hold in perpetuity at an annual rent of £1. 10*s*. due to the almoner. [1200 × 1213]

Omnibus ad quos presens scriptum pervenerit, sanctimoniales de Suldha[m] et fratres earum salutem in Domino. Noverit universitas vestra nos accepisse a Domino Abbate Radulfo et conventu Westmusterii omnes decimas que ad eos pertinent in Clakelose hundredo tenendas de eis inperpetuum. Reddendo annuatim elemosinario Westmusterii xxx solidos ad duos terminos, videlicet: infra octabas Pasche xv solidos, et infra octabas Sancti Michaelis xv solidos. Hoc autem nobis concesserunt predictus abbas et conventus Westmusterii quamdiu nos habuerimus legittime erga predictam ecclesiam Westmusterii et bene reddiderimus. Hiis testibus: Gaufrido filio Petri, comite Essex'; Gaufrido de Bocland; Rogero de Crampesham'; Rogero de Stradessete; Petro de Bekeswelle; Ricardo de Dol; Jurdano Peverel; Ricardo Testard; Johanne Testard; Alano Herun; Roberto de Crokesl'; Jacobo hostiario, et multis aliis.

MSS: (1) WAM 1718.
 17.4 × 8.2 cm; seal and tag torn off.
 Endorsed: (a) Mon[iales] de Suldham de annuo redditu xxx solidis pro decimis (13C) (b) in Clackelose hundredo etc Westmonasterio solvendis (14C). (c) Elemosinarius (14C).
 (2) WAD, ff. 469v–470.
Date: Geoffrey Fitz Peter as earl of Essex.
Note: The absence of any mention of the head of house may indicate that this document was issued during a vacancy. Prior J. was in office 1197 × 1199, perhaps to be identified with Jocelin, in office 1203–4 (*Heads*, 205).

478. Notification by Richard Fitz William to the English and French men of his fee that he confirms to the almonry of the church of St Peter of Westminster two-thirds of the tithes of his fee of *Buchetuna* [? Buckton, Heref.] which it holds of Richard by hereditary right of the realm, both from the demesne and the villein land, in everything which may be tithed, as the abbey held it by the gift of Richard's father William. [mid 12C]

Notum sit omnibus tam presentibus quam futuris, tam Anglis quam Francis, totius feudi mei quod ego Ricardus filius Willelmi concedo et carta mea confirmo Deo et elemosinarie domui ecclesie Beati Petri Westmonasterii duas partes decimacionis feudi mei de Buchetuna quod tenet de me iure hereditario regni tam de dominio quam de villatia in omnibus que decimari possunt tam honorifice et libere et quiete sicut unquam melius possedit et tenuit domus predicta donatione patris mei Willelmi. Hiis testibus: Hamone clerico[1] Herfordiensi; Willelmo filio meo; Willelmo de Fernar'; Ilberto filio Hamonis; Goscelino fratre eiusdem.

MS: WAM LV.
> 17.4 × 7 cm.
> Seal: red; on tongue from bottom left-hand corner and a tie; 6.2 cm diameter; figure on horseback, facing right, holding a falcon in right hand.
> Endorsed: (a) Carta Ricardi filii Willelmi de ij[bus] partibus feodi sui decimationis in Buchetuna ecclesie Westmonasterii concessis (13C).
> (b) Elemosinarie (14C). (c) Bouketon' pro decimis (14C).
>> 1. MS: *clereco*.

Date: An early date is indicated by the wording of this document.
Note: The name of the first witness supports the identification of Richard's fee with Buckton, Heref., which in 1086 pertained to the barony of Ralph de Mortimer (*VCH Heref.* I, 345).

479. Notification by Robert Foliot that he and his wife Margaret granted to St Peter of Westminster and the monks the manor of Sulby (Northants.), to hold for the service of one knight, as they rendered to the grantors' predecessors, in the reign of H[1]. [Dec. 1148 × early 1150]

Robertus Foliot omnibus Sancte Dei Ecclesie filiis per Angliam constitutis, et omnibus hominibus et amicis suis, tam Francis quam Anglicis, salutem. Sciatis me et Margaretam uxorem meam concessisse Deo et Sancto Petro Apostolo Westmonasterii, et monachis ibidem Deo famulantibus manerium de Suleby cum omnibus eidem manerio pertinentibus, ad tenendum de nobis et heredibus nostris inperpetuum eodem servicio quo faciebant predecessoribus nostris tempore Regis Henrici, videlicet servitium unius militis. Quare volo et firmiter precipio quod dicti monachi teneant supradictum manerium bene et in pace, et libere et quiete, intus et extra, sicuti ipsi unquam melius et liberius tenuerunt tempore alicuius antecessorum nostrorum. Et super hoc nullus se inde[1] intromittat nisi per eos. Hiis subscriptis testibus ex parte Roberti Foliot: Waltero priori [de] Sancto Neoto; Marcho monacho; Ivone Tailleboys; Osberto de Maisi; Willelmo, clerico de Burtoria; Radulfo de Pottona; Willelmo de Maiscu'l; Willelmo Francigeno; Ernulfo fratre Roberti Foliot; Roberto filio Egenulphi; Elia filio [Ivonis] Taileboys: ex parte monachorum: Rogero de Wenberga; Absolon et Willelmo filio suo, et Johanne fratre eius; Sampson filio Haconis.

MS: WAD, f. 499r–v.
> Rubric: Carta Roberti Foliot de manerio de Sulebi.
> Marginalia: Sulebi.

Date: Term of office of Prior Walter of St Neots was *c.* 1145 × 1152/8 (*Heads*, 108), but the charter was presumably issued in response to the mandate of Abp. Theobald (**195**).
Note: Robert Foliot held the barony of Chipping Warden, Northants., from an uncertain date in the mid 12C. His wife Margery (or Margaret)

was daughter of Richard de Reinbuedcurt, son of Guy de Reinbuedcurt, the DB holder of this barony (Sanders, 33). In 1086, the abbey was not a tenant of the barony. The only land of the barony in Sulby comprised two and a half hides and one third of a virgate (*DB* I, f. 227). In 1166 the abbot held one fee of old enfeoffment of the barony of Robert Foliot (*Liber Niger Scaccarii*, 213; *RBE*, 331).

480. Confirmation in pure and perpetual alms by Henry Sumer for his soul and those of all his predecessors and heirs, to St Peter and the convent, to provide lights for the Lady Altar, of a virgate of land in the vill of Deene (Northants.), which Simon of Deene and Ivo his son confirmed to him by their charters, in hereditary right, to hold at an annual rent of 1 lb pepper. The land comprised half a virgate which Modiva held and half a virgate which Simon and Ivo gave him from their demesne. The convent would acquit him of the pepper rent. [Temp. John]

Sciant presentes et futuri quod ego Henricus Sumer dedi, concessi, et hac presenti carta mea confirmavi, pro salute anime mee et omnium predecessorum et heredum meorum, Deo et Beato Petro et conventui Westmonasterii, ad administracionem luminarium altaris Beate Virginis Marie, unam virgatam terre in villa de Dien, quam Simon de Dien et Ivo filius eius michi dederunt et cartis suis confirmaverunt, pro homagio et servicio meo. Tenendam et habendam de eis et heredibus suis iure hereditario pro una libra piperis eis in Natali Domini annuatim solvenda: dimidiam scilicet virgatam terre quam Modiva tenuit in eadem villa, et dimidiam quam predictus Simon et Ivo michi dederunt de dominico suo. Habendam et tenendam de me et de heredibus meis cum omnibus pertinentiis suis in puram et perpetuam elemosinam, liberam, quietam ab omnibus querelis, placitis et auxiliis et ab omni seculari consuetudine per predictum servicium. Et ut hec donacio mea stabilis et rata permaneat, eam presentis scripti testimonio et sigilli mei apposicione roboravi, et cartas predictorum Simonis et Ivonis dominorum meorum super altare Beate Marie optuli. Predictus vero conventus prefatam libram piperis michi et heredibus meis persolvent. Et ego et heredes mei warantizabimus eis predictam terram pro posse nostro contra omnes homines et omnes feminas, et acquietabimus eos versus predictos Simonem et Ivonem et heredes eorum. Hiis testibus: Simone et Alexandro capellanis; Roberto Mauduit; Andrea de Scaccario et Willelmo filio eius; Willelmo de Hanslape; Rogero Enganet; Alexandro clerico; Magistro Michaele; Odone aurifabro; Wimundo pistore; Petro de Wandene; Stephano de Berking'; Gileberto le Brac[us]; Herewardo scriptore; Gaufrido, Ada, Radulfo, servientibus ecclesie; Gileberto Trepingar, et multis aliis.

MS: WAD, f. 567v–568.
    Rubric: Carta Henrici Sumer de una virgata terre in villa de Dien.
Note: The manor of Deene was given to Westminster by King Edward (Harvey, *WA*, 355). A final concord which terminated a lawsuit brought by Abbot William d'Humez early in 1215 shows that Simon of Deene held the manor by a service of hospitality (F. M. Stenton, *The First Century of*

English Feudalism (2nd edn., 1961), Appendix no. 17, 267–9). Henry Sumer prob. acquired his tenancy either through favour of the abbot or through contacts acquired in his capacity as a reeve of Westminster.

481. Notification by Juliana, abbess of the church of St John the Baptist, Godstow, that the convent, with the assent of the whole chapter, has promised to the abbot and convent of Westminster, to render annually to their sacrist, a pension of five marks (£3. 6s. 8d.) from the church of Bloxham (Oxon.), to provide lights for the High Altar. The oath to observe this has been sworn by the nuns' chaplain, Waleran. 14 June 1197.

Omnibus Sancte Matris Ecclesie filiis ad quos presens scriptum pervenerit, Juliana abbatissa ecclesie Sancti Johannis Baptiste de Godestowe, et totus eiusdem loci conventus eternam in Domino, salutem. Quia malignantis mundi calumpnie multipliciter excrescunt, et mendaces plerumque ut nec vera dicentibus credatur, promissionem quam viris venerabilibus abbati et conventui Westmonasterii fecimus super pensione ecclesie de Bloccesham nobis a prefato conventu in perpetuam elemosinam concesse, scripto duximus corroborandam. Noverit itaque universitas vestra nos, unanimi assensu totius capituli nostri, spontanea voluntate concessisse et firmiter ac fideliter in vera fide et Christiana securitate promisisse predicto abbati et conventui West-monasterii quod de ecclesia de Bloccesham, quam ipsi nobis in perpetuam elemosinam caritative concesserunt, singulis annis sacriste Westmonasterii ad luminare magni altaris eiusdem ecclesie nomine pensionis quinque marcas argenti persolvemus ad duos terminos, videli-cet: infra octavas Festivitatis Omnium Sanctorum duas marcas et dimidiam; et infra octavas Pentecostes duas marcas et dimidiam. Promis-imus etiam eis in bona fide, pura et simplici conscientia coram Deo, prestito etiam iuramento per os et manum Waleramni capellani nostri, in verbo veritatis, in animas nostras sacrosanctis evangeliis ab eodem inspectis, quod nunquam apud aliquem vel aliquos per nos vel per interpositam personam artem aliquam fraudis vel ingenii queremus ut predicta ecclesia Westmonasterii prenominate pensionis ecclesie de Bloccesham diminutionem aliquam incurrat vel alienacionem vel quo minus prefatus conventus per manum sacriste sui predictum redditum ad statutos terminos integre et absque detentione et occasione percipiat, sed omnem operam dabimus quatinus pacis et concorde bonum, quod inter nos et prenominatam ecclesiam Westmonasterii consilio magnorum virorum initiatum est, debita semper in Domino stabilitate subsistat. Et ut hec nostra promissio debita fide et omnimoda securitate compleatur, eam presenti scripto et sigillo ecclesie nostre communivimus. Hiis testibus: Domino Hugone abbate Abbendonie; et Nicholao et Ricardo monachis et capellanis eius; Waleramno capellano, qui hanc promis-sionem iuramento firmavit; Johanne de Kensinton'; et Henrico de Kensinton', fratre eius; Marino, clerico domine regine; Godefrido de la Den'; Willelmo de Haggehurst'; Roberto de Clere; Magistro Ernulfo Postard; Magistro Simone de Bareswrde; Teodbaldo, senescallo Westmonasterii; Radulfo de Septem Fontibus et Henrico fratre eius, et multis aliis.

MS: WAD, f. 379.
   Rubric: Scriptum indentatum Juliane abbatisse et conventus de Godestowe super pensione predicta.
Date: Attestions identical with **225**.
Note: Cf. **225**, **323**.

482. Notification from James le Salvage that he has sworn in chapter, before the whole convent, to pay an annual pension of thirty marks (£20) from the church of Oakham (Rutl.) to Westminster. He will try to secure confirmation from the pope and the diocesan bp. for payment of this pension, but if permission is refused, he will grant in lieu thirty marks from his churches of Swanscombe and Stockbury (Kent). Westminster Abbey [1193 × *ante* July 1205]

Omnibus Sancte Matris Ecclesie filiis ad quos littere iste pervenerint, Jacobus le Salvag' salutem. Sciatis me, sacramento corporaliter prestito in pleno capitulo Westmonasterii coram toto conventu ipsius ecclesie, bona fide iurasse me quo advixero de ecclesia de Ocham triginta marcas nomine pensionis predicto conventui redditurum ad quatuor statutos terminos, videlicet: ad Natale Domini centum solidos; ad Pascham centum solidos; ad Natale Sancti Johannis Baptiste centum solidos; ad Festum Sancti Michaelis centum solidos. Juravi etiam quod si a solucione predicte pensionis aliquando cessavero, predictus conventus West-monasterii omnes fructus ecclesie de Ocham illius absque cuiuscumque reclamatione libere percipiet. Preterea iuravi me omnem operam quam potero adhibiturum ut prenominata pensio triginta marcarum a domino papa et a diocesano episcopo confirmetur. Adieci quoque sub eadem religione iuramenti quod si dominus papa vel diocesanus episcopus solucionem predicte pensionis michi aliquando interdixerint, triginta marcas de ecclesiis meis de Swenescam et de Stockingebire predicto conventui ad supradictos terminos annuatim persolvam, quas videlicet ecclesias eidem conventui ad hoc ipsum faciendum bona fide obligavi. Et ut hec mea promissio stabilis et firma permaneat, nec aliqua umquam mutabilitate possit infringi, hanc presentem cartam meam inde factam sigilli mei appositione consignavi. Hiis testibus: Domino H[uberto], Cantuariensi archiepiscopo; Roberto, archidiacono de Huntindon'; Magistro Simone de Suwell'; Magistro J. de Tinemue; R[anulpho] thesaurario Saresberiensi; Magistro Willelmo de Neketon'; Magistro Helia de Derham; Thoma et Helia, clericis; Ricardo de Dol, senescallo abbatis Westmonasterii; Ricardo janitore; Gaufrido camerario, et multis aliis.

MSS: (1) WAD, f. 649r–v.
   Rubric: Scriptum eiusdem de xxx marcis annue pensionis de ecclesia de Ocham.
   Marginalia: Ocham.
   (2) F, f. 267v: detached rubric only: Carta Jacobi le Salvage de xxx

marcis nomine annue pensionis pro ecclesiis [*sic*] de Oakham ecclesie Westmonasterii a solvendis.

Date: Attestations of Abp. Hubert, 1193–13 July 1205, when d. (*Fasti* II, 5); Robert de Hardres, archdeacon of Huntingdon, April 1192 × (1204 × 1207) (*Fasti* II, 27).

Note: See Harmer, 323, 514–5; Harvey, *WA*, 404; Mason, 'Rutland Churches', 164–5. Evidently James was only perpetual vicar of Stockbury (*EEA*, II, no. 150; III, 518).

483. Notification by James Salvage, parson of Swanscombe (Kent), that, for his soul, those of his parents and all his ancestors, he has confirmed to the convent a payment of twenty marks (£13. 6*s*. 8*d*.) as alms to the abbey from Hambleton church (Rutl.) so long as he remains in the clerical habit. He has sworn to keep this promise. [Temp. John]

Universis Sancte Matris Ecclesie filiis ad quos presens carta pervenerit, Jacobus Salvage, persona de Sweneschans [*sic*], eternam in Domino salutem. Qui ecclesiarum utilitatibus specialiter deserviunt ecclesiastica specialius merentur remuneratione gaudere: ad omnium itaque noticiam pervenire desidero quod, considerata religione et honestate fratrum ecclesie Westmonasterii et elemosinarum largicione que in ea geruntur mora et gratuita liberalitate, pro salute anime mee et patris et matris mee et omnium antecessorum meorum, dedi et concessi et hac presenti carta mea confirmavi conventui Westmonasterii viginti marcas argenti de ecclesia de Hameldon nomine elemosine quamdiu in clericali habitu permansero, singulis annis percipiendas ad tres terminos anni: ad Natale, videlicet, Domini quinque marcas; et ad Pascham decem marcas; et ad Natale Sancti Johannis Baptiste quinque marcas. Ego autem prefatus Jacobus Salvage hanc donacionem caritative faciens coram predicto conventu Westmonasterii in capitulo suo, spontanea voluntate tactis sacrosanctis evangeliis, me in hac donatione fidelem permansurum iuravi, atque eidem conventui statutis terminis singulis annis predictas viginti marcas absque omni occasione vel fraude redditurum. Ut autem hec mea donatio et concessio nulla ratione vel occasione meis temporibus adnichilari valeat, sed stabilis et rata permaneat, eam presentis scripti testimonio et sigilli mei apposicione roboravi.

MSS: (1) WAD, f. 649.
    Rubric: Carta Jacobi Salvag', persone de Sweneschams de viginti marcis annue pensionis de ecclesia de Hameldon'.
    Marginalia: (1) Pitanciarius. (2) Hameldon'.
    (2) F, f. 267v: detached rubric only, apparently referring to this charter: Item carta eiusdem [Jacobi le Salvage] de pensione xx marcarum de ecclesia de Hameldon.

Date: James Savage was a member of Abp. Hubert's *familia* (K. Major, 'Familia of Archbishop Stephen Langton', *EHR* 48 (1933), 530; *EEA*, III, 307). In 1206 he was a royal clerk (**150**).

484. Notification by Geoffrey Fitz Peter, earl of Essex, that he has received from Abbot Ralph and the convent their vill of Claygate (Surr.)

to hold of them for his lifetime, at an annual rent of £3 to the almonry. He received the vill devoid of stock, whether of corn or cattle. After his d., the vill will revert to the abbot and convent, with the improvements he makes, whether in buildings, ploughs, cultivated and uncultivated land, and all growing corn, although corn in the barn is at his disposal, but he undertakes to conserve the woodland. [1200 × 1213]

Sciant presentes et futuri quod ego Gaufridus filius Petri, comes Essex', recepi de Radulfo abbate et conventu Westmonasterii villam eorum de Claygate cum omnibus pertinentiis suis, tenendam de eis tantummodo in vita mea pro sexaginta solidis ad quatuor terminos anni elemosinarie eorum reddendis, videlicet: ad Natale Domini quindecim solidis; ad Pascha quindecim solidis; ad Festum Sancti Johannis Baptiste quindecim solidis; et ad Festum Sancti Michaelis quindecim solidis, et ita singulis annis quamdiu tenuero de illis predictam villam. Et sciendum quod recepi predictam villam absque omni stauro, sive bladi sive pecunie. Post decessum vero meum prefata villa ad abbatem et conventum Westmonasterii quieta et soluta redibit, absque omni reclamatione heredum meorum vel aliquorum ad me pertinentium, cum emendationibus quas in eadem villa fecero: sive in edificiis, sive in carrucis, in terris cultis et incultis, cum omni blado seminato. Bladum autem predicte ville quod in horreo erit, in mea erit dispositione, cui voluero dare vel relinquere absque aliqua contraditione. Boscum autem predicte ville faciam custodiri ut non wastetur. Et ut hec conventio stabilis sit et firma, eam sigilli mei appositione et testium subscriptione confirmavi. Hiis testibus: Domino Willelmo, archidiacono de Tautune; Rogero, constabulario Turris; Gerardo de Kayli; Johanne de Kauz; Ricardo de Dol, senescallo abbatis; Ricardo de Stapelek' clerico; Uliano Cheneduit; Jordano Peverel; Gaufrido camerario; Jacobo hostiario; Gerardo coco; Roberto de Krokel', et aliis pluribus.

MS: WAM 1842.
    19.7 × 10.3 cm; t.u. 1.4 cm.
    Seal: on tag; 5.8 cm diameter; obverse: equestrian figure, facing right.
    Counter seal: now missing.
    Endorsed: (a) Kleygate (14C). (b) Firma non renovatur.
Date: Geoffrey Fitz Peter as earl.
Note: Claygate had been granted to the abbey in the mid eleventh century, and was confirmed by King Edward (Harvey, *WA*, 358).

485. Confirmation by Roger son of Edward to the Blessed Virgin and the abbot and convent, for the use of the almonry, of six acres of land in the vill of Claygate (Surr.), which Hubert held there, and which lie to the west of the land which the almoner holds in that vill, of the fee which was Gilbert's. The land will be held in perpetuity, at an annual rent of 1s. 6d. The abbot and convent gave him a gersum of £1. 5s. 8d., by the hands of Peter, the almoner. [Temp. John]

Sciant presentes et futuri quod ego Rogerus filius Eduuardi dedi et concessi et hac presenti carta mea confirmavi Deo et Beate Marie et abbati et conventui Westmonasterii, ad usus et utilitatem elemosinarie eiusdem ecclesie, sex acras terre cum omnibus pertinentiis suis in villa de Claigate, quas Hubertus tenuit in eadem villa. Que scilicet sex acre iacent a terra quam elemosinarius tenet de feodo quod fuit Guleberti in eadem villa versus occidentem. Habendas et tenendas de me et heredibus meis inperpetuum, libere et quiete, integre et plenarie, absque alicuius reclamatione; reddendo inde michi vel heredibus meis elemosinarius qui pro tempore fuerit singulis annis octodecim denarios pro omni servicio et exaccione seculari ad duos terminos anni, scilicet: ad Festum Sancti Michaelis novem denarios, et ad Pascha novem denarios. Ego autem predictus Rogerus et heredes mei warantizabimus predictam terram cum omnibus pertinentiis predictis abbati et conventui et eorum elemosinario, qui pro tempore fuerit, per predictum servicium octodecim denariorum contra omnes homines et feminas inperpetuum. Pro hac autem donatione et concessione et huius carte mee confirmatione dederunt michi predicti abbas et conventus per manus Petri monachi, tunc temporis elemosinarii, viginti quinque solidos sterlingorum et octo denarios in gersummam. Et ut hec donatio et concessio et presentis carte mee confirmatio rata et stabilis permaneat inperpetuum eam sigilli mei appositione roboravi. Hiis testibus: Ricardo de Dol, tunc senescallo Westmonasterii; Willelmo de Brademere; Willelmo Pichot; Odone aurifabro de Westmonasterio; Stephano de Berkinge; Ricardo filio Edmundi; Roberto de Crokesl'; Hamundo de Laburgh'; Roberto le Brutun; Hugone Stuth; Alano de Drapier, et multis aliis.

MSS: (1) WAM 1855.

    19.3 × 9.8 cm; t.u. 2.4 cm.

    Seal: on tag; green; 4 × 6.5 cm; bird (? eagle) with raised wings, head looking across its back, to the left: legend: + SIGILL' ROGERI FILII EDWARDI.

    Endorsed: (a) Carta Rogeri filij Edwardi de sex acris terre cum pertinenciis in villa de Cleygate ecclesie Westmonasterii ad utilitatem elemosinarie concessis, reddendo inde annuatim per manus elemosinarii dicto Rogero et suis heredibus octodecim denariis (13C). (b) Cleygat' de sex acris terre (14C).

    (2) WAD, ff. 465v–466.

486. Confirmation, in pure and perpetual alms, by Hugh son of Ingulf to the church of Westminster and the monks, of half an acre in South Lambeth (Surr.), next to the land of Walter the brewer, in the land called Hide, in order to link up the water-course of the Winterburn with the Thames. The abbot and convent gave him a gersum of two marks (£1. 6s. 8d.). [Temp. John]

Sciant presentes et futuri quod ego Hugo filius Ingulfi dedi et concessi et hac presenti carta mea confirmavi Deo et ecclesie Westmonasterii et monachis ibidem Deo servientibus, in puram et perpetuam elemosinam, dimidiam acram terre in Sudlamhee que jacet iuxta terram Walteri le bracur, in terra que vocatur Hida, ad entrahendum cursum aque de

Winterburne usque ad Tamisiam. Habendam et tenendam de me et heredibus meis bene et in pace, libere et quiete, integre et plenarie inperpetuum, absque omni seculari servicio et exactione. Et ego Hugo et heredes mei warantizabimus et aquietabimus predictam dimidiam acram [versus]¹ dominum fundi et versus omnes homines. Et pro hac donatione et concessione et carte mee confirmatione, abbas et conventus dederunt michi duas marcas argenti. Hiis testibus: Willelmo Eliensi, domini regis tesaurario; Magistro Benedicto; Gocelino marescallo; Willelmo de Neketon; Reginaldo de Cronhull'; Thoma de Chimilli; Rogero Foliot; Uliano Cheinduit; Pentecoste de Wendlswrth'; Amauricio; Jacobo ostiario; Nicolao filio Galfridi, et multis aliis.

MSS: (1) WAD, f. 164r–v.
    Rubric: Carta Hugonis filii Ingulfi de dimidia acra terre in Suth Lambheye.
    1. *versus* supplied from copy.
    (2) WAM 1808: paper copy made temp. Dean Gabriel Goodman (1561–1601).
    Endorsed: (a) A piece of evidence of the manor of Batteirsesby. (b) Land given to the abbey to pusche the water . . . in the Thame.
    Marginalia: (1) Memorandum de cursu aque de Winterborne prope Southlambeth. (2) Extracta et concordata cum libro vocato Domesdaie boke folio 171. (3) Gabrielle Goodman. (4) Per me Robertum Allatt Registrar decano et capitulo Westmonasterii.
Note: Text is entered in WAD on a folio headed Battersea. This transaction was prob. designed to facilitate the water-transport of produce from the abbey's manors in Surrey.

487. Notification by Peter Fitz Herbert to the barons of the Exchequer and justices of the Bench that he has received £100 from the abbot and convent of Westminster, and that they treated him favourably in all other matters, according to a concord made between them in the king's court over the manor of Parham (Sussex). He requests the barons that according to the form of the concord, they should make a cirograph in the king's court. Since he cannot be present in person, on account of the king's business, he assigns Mr Jocelin the king's marshal to take delivery of that cirograph on his behalf, and he will ratify anything negotiated between Jocelin and them. He also appoints Jocelin to take delivery of the charter which the abbot should make him, according to the concord, and to render them his (Peter's) charter. [1214]

Omnibus baronibus de Scaccario et justiciis domini regis de Banco, et omnibus has litteras visuris et audituris, Petrus filius Herberti, salutem. Noverit universitas vestra me recepisse centum libras de abbate et conventu de Westmonasterio et quod ipsi fecerunt gratum meum de omnibus aliis, secundum concordiam factam inter nos coram vobis in curia domini regis pro manerio de Pereham. Inde est quod vos precor diligenter, quatinus secundum formam concordie inter nos facte, cirographum in curia domini regis faciatis, et quare ad presens pro negocio domini regis in propria persona interesse non possum,

Magistrum Jocelinum marescallum domini regis ad cirographum illud recipiendum loco mei assigno gratum et ratum habiturus quicquid vos et ipse inde feceritis, et preterea eundem Jocelinum in loco meo assigno ad recipiendam cartam predicti abbatis et conventus quam michi facere debent, secundum formam dicte concordie, et ad faciendam eisdem cartam meam secundum formam eandem. Valete.

MS: WAD, f. 571v–572.
    Rubric: Littera Petri filii Herberti super manerio de Pereham.
Date: Peter Fitz Herbert's dispute with the abbey over Parham ran between 1211 and 1214 (*Curia Regis Rolls* VI, 119, 133, 176–7, 215, 287, 296, 393; VII, 239. See also R. V. Turner, *The King and his Courts* (Ithaca, N.Y., 1968), 256.
Note: Peter Fitz Herbert was a prominent *curialis* (Turner, ibid.).

488. Memorandum of a restoration by Robert Dispenser, for his soul, of the land and manor of Comberton (Worcs.), part of the abbey's demesne, which he bought from Gilbert Fitz Turold from the estate of the abbey. He also restored to the abbey the land called Wick which he held at farm from Abbot Gilbert in that manor, and which was a member of the manor of Pershore (Worcs.). In the presence of Bp. Walchelin of Winchester and other named witnesses, Robert's wife and his brother Urse [d'Abetot] placed on the [high] altar of St Peter this restoration [symbolised] by two silver candelabra; a thurible, altar cloth and a tapestry. [1095–96 × *ante* 1098]

Robertus Dispensator reddidit in vita sua Sancto Petro Westmonasterii, pro anima sua, terram et manerium Cumbrinton, quod de beneficio eiusdem ecclesie emerat a Gisleberto filio Toraldi. Et insuper reddidit eidem ecclesie terram quam de abbate Gisleberto eiusdem monasterii ad firmam tenebat in manerio ipsius ecclesie quod dicitur Wich, et est membrum manerii de Persore. Testes huius redditionis sunt: Episcopus Walchelinus; Urso frater eiusdem Roberti; Herbertus camerarius, Reg[inaldus] de Winton', Ivo Taillebosc et homines ipsius Roberti, Godardus, Robertus de Echinton, Hugo de Holavessael; de aliis baronibus regis: Hugo de Belcampo; Willelmus Bainardus; Petrus de Valunnis; Willelmus camerarius; Hugo de Bochelanda; Otto Aurifex, et multi alii, clerici et laici; homines ipsius abbatis: Otbert de Surreia, Willemus clericus, Girardus frater eius, Hugo de Coleham, Richerius. Hanc redditionem, presente episcopo Walchelino et predictis testibus, posuerunt super altare Sancti Petri uxor ipsius Roberti et Urso frater eiusdem Roberti, per duo candelabra argentea, unum turribulum, unum pallium, unum tapete.

MSS: (1) WAD, f. 292v.
    Rubric: Teligraphus Roberti Dispensatoris de terra et manerio de Cumbertona.
    Marginalia: Cumbertona.
    (2) CAY, f. lxix *verso*: *telligraphus* (memorandum).
Pd: *Gilbert Crispin*, 146, no. 27.

Cal: Bentley, 33, no. 254, from CAY.
Date: Bishop Walchelin d. 3 Jan. 1098 (*Fasti* II, 85). Robert's latest
attestation is 1095 × 1096 (*Regesta* I, no. 388, cf. no. 479).
Note: Cf. **66**; *Gilbert Crispin*, 146–7; Harvey, *WA*, 361, 364. In 1086,
Gilbert Fitz Turold was the tenant of the abbey in Comberton, and
Robert Dispenser was not recorded as having any interest in this estate
(*DB* I, f. 175). The makeshift nature of restoration, by proxy, suggests
that Robert, a well-known *curialis* (*Beauchamp Cartulary*, xx–xxj), was
gravely ill.

489. Mandate of Waleran, count of Meulan, to his bailiffs and officers in
Worcs. and reeves and officers in Wick that the church of St Peter and the
monks of Westminster are to have their tithe from his rents in Wick as in
the time of H I. [Dec. 1135 × summer, 1141]

G[ualeranus] comes de Mellent omnibus ballivis et ministris suis de
Wirecestreschira et omnibus prepositis et ministris de Wych, salutem.
Precipio quod ecclesia Sancti Petri et monachi de Westmonasterio ita
bene et in pace et honorifice et iuste habeant decimam suam in redditibus
meis de Wych, sicut melius aut quietius aut honorificencius habuerunt
tempore Regis Henrici. Et super hoc nullus disturbet inde homines vel
servientes eorum etcetera. T[estibus].

MS: F, ff. 279v–280.
Rubric: Item littera de decima de Wich Capitulum xciiij.
Date: Possibly issued before Waleran was created earl of Worcester, late
in 1138, since he already had territorial interests there (David Crouch,
The Beaumont Twins (1986), 39). He finally left England in the summer
of 1141 (ibid. 51–2).

490. Notification by Geoffrey de St Leger that he has become the man of
Abbot Walter for two knights' fees in Strensham (Worcs.), for which his
father Reginald was the man of the previous abbots, saving the use of the
tenement for his mother while she lives. He will pay to the abbot the full
relief of £10 if his mother dies or becomes a religious or otherwise gives up
the land; when he pays the relief the abbot or his successors is to give him
a charter. [1175 × 1190]

Sciant presentes et futuri quicumque has litteras viderint vel audierint
quod ego Galfridus de Sancto Ligerio deveni homo Walterii abbatis
Westmonasterii de feodo duorum militum in Strengesham de quo
Reginaldus de Sancto Ligerio, pater meus, fuit homo antecessorum
suorum, salvo eo tenemento ad opus matris mee quamdiu ipsa vixerit et
terram tenere voluerit, videlicet: quod non inquietabo nec aliquid
dominium vel magisterium propter hoc homagium super illam faciam in
predicto tenemento. Et sciendum preterea quod ego debeo prenominato
abbati plenum relevium meum, decem videlicet libras reddendas, si
mater mea decesserit, vel habitum religionis susceperit, vel michi terram
meam sponte reddiderit vel quocumque alio modo illam dimiserit. Et
sciendum quia quum reddam ei relevium suum ipse vel successores sui

faciant michi rationabilem cartam meam. Hiis testibus: Alexandro monacho; Radulfo monacho; Martino monacho; Alexandro fratre abbatis; Galfrido Picot; Magistro Nicholao; Petro de Wicha; Willelmo Picot; Randulfo, serviente abbatis; Bartholomeo de Assewell; Nicholao filio Roberti; Radulfo de Kuden'; Bartholomeo de Hannia; Willelmo de Kuden; Jordano filio Nicholai filii Roberti, et multis aliis.

MSS: (1) WAD, f. 293.
Rubric: Scriptum Galfridi de Sancto Ligerio de homagio feodi duorum militum et de relevio decem librarum.
(2) CAY, f. lxix *verso* (memorandum).
Cal: Bentley, 33, no. 254, from CAY.
Date: Term of office of Abbot Walter.
Note: Neither Geoffrey nor his father is readily identifiable in the *carta* returned by Abbot Laurence in 1166 (*Liber Niger Scaccarii*, 51; *RBE*, I, 188).

APPENDIX

There survive some genuine pre-Conquest charters for Westminster Abbey, but the majority purporting to date from before the reign of W I have subsequently been amended to a greater or lesser extent, even when they are not complete forgeries. These texts include one charter of Offa of Mercia; two of Edgar; one of Ethelred Unraed; two of St Dunstan and thirty-three of King Edward. From the commentaries listed by Sawyer, it will be apparent that there is often disagreement on the authenticity of the texts. Some may represent genuine grants, copied in the decades after the Norman Conquest; others have clearly been amended and expanded, while some are outright forgeries, reflecting the activities of Osbert de Clare and the scribes who were influenced by him.

WRITS AND CHARTERS ALLEGEDLY DATING FROM BEFORE THE NORMAN CONQUEST, BUT CONTAINING INDICATIONS OF POST-CONQUEST HANDIWORK:

GRANTOR	HARMER	SAWYER	HARVEY, WA
Offa of Mercia	501	no. 124	345
Edgar	338–9	no. 774	341–2; 344–6; 349, 351, 354, 358
Edgar	—	no. 1450	21, 352
Ethelred Unraed	287	no. 894	350, 352–4
St Dunstan	—	no. 1293	21, 23, 37, 350, 352–4, 359
St Dunstan	—	no. 1295	352
Edward (First Charter)	288–9	no. 1043	
Edward (Second Charter)	59n.1	no. 1011	
Edward (Third Charter)	290	no. 1041	
Edward (Telligraphus)	290	no. 1039	
Edward	no. 100	no. 1144	344, 363
Edward	no. 84	no. 1128	343
Edward	no. 80	no. 1124	
Edward	291	no. 1040	
Edward	no. 93	no. 1137	358
Edward	no. 101	no. 1145	344, 363
Edward	no. 89	no. 1133	351
Edward	no. 103	no. 1147	356 and n.
Edward	no. 92	no. 1136	359 and n.
Edward	no. 81	no. 1125	

GRANTOR	HARMER	SAWYER	HARVEY, *WA*
Edward	no. 104	no. 1148	356 and n.
Edward	no. 98	no. 1142	354
Edward	no. 97	no. 1141	338, 354
Edward	no. 85	no. 1129	345
Edward	no. 76	no. 1120	
Edward	no. 78	no. 1122	345
Edward	no. 91	no. 1135	72, 74
Edward	no. 90	no. 1134	
Edward	no. 79	no. 1123	346
Edward	no. 74	no. 1118	342
Edward	no. 73	no. 1117	344
Edward	no. 86	no. 1130	354
Edward	no. 77	no. 1121	349
Edward	no. 94	no. 1138	47
Edward	no. 102	no. 1146	344, 363
Edward	no. 82	no. 1126	
Edward	no. 105	no. 1149	
Edward	no. 75	no. 1119	
Edward	no. 106	no. 1150	

INDEX

Persons are indexed by Christian name, with cross-references from other names; names of places are indexed under their modern forms as far as possible. Witnesses to the charters calendared as **1–233** are not indexed. References in the form p1, etc., are to pages in the introduction; all other references are to the **bold** numbers of the charters.

Amalric, brother of Abbot Gervase, 258, 263, 269
Amand, clerk, 255
Amauric, 486
Amauric of Box (Hall), 472
Anagni, Italy, 167–70, 173–4
Andrew, 352
Andrew Albus (white), and his son Henry, 381
Andrew, brother of Robert son of Brictric, 352
Andrew Buccuinte (justiciar of London), 112
Andrew Bucherel, 342–3, 352
Andrew de Hwath, 270
Andrew, ironmonger (*ferunarius*), 376
Andrew le Blund, 369
Andrew of the Exchequer, 311–12, 321, 336, 409, 424–5, 446, 457; and his son William, 480
Andrew Revel, 474
Andrew, son of Ralph son of Adam, and his brothers Adam and Nicholas, 290
Andrew, son of Terric son of Albric, 293
Anjou, count of, 123; seneschal of, 386
Ankerwyke (Berks), nuns, 356
Ansegod, 394
Ansegod de Barra, 397
Ansell, 290
Anselm (of Aosta), abbot of Bec, p14; 26, 50
Anselm, son of Hakon of London, 363
Ansgod, cordwainer (*corveser*), 309
Ansgod, monk of Westminster, 258, 271
Ansgot (Angot) Duredent, 453–5
Apethorpe (Northants, Apetorp), priest, 270
Aqua, *see* John
Arbor, *see* Henry
Archbold, 288
Arden (Darden), *see* Geoffrey
Ardre, *see* Robert
Argentan, *see* Reginald
Arnald (Arnold) of Hurley, 289, 297, 319, 409
Arnold, brother of Constantine son of Alulf, 381
Arnulf of Greenford, 462
Arnulf Postard, brother of Abbot William, 321
Arras (Flanders), *see* Wibert
Arundel, *see* Ralph, abbot of Westminster; Ralph
Aschetill de Sartrin, and his son, William, 404
Asculf, *see* Hasculf
Ashwell (Herts, Assewell), chapels, 176; church, 176, 179
Ashwell, *see also* Bartholomew
Asketin, 374; William his son, 406

Ate, draper, 458
Aubigny, *see* Nigel; William
Aubrey de Vere, 246–7, 331; earl of Oxford, 464; grandfather of William de Mandeville, 464; his chamberlain, 246; sheriff of Essex, 91, 94; sheriff of London, 79
Aubrey de Vere III, earl of Oxford, and his parents, 456
Aucus, *see* Robert, gooseherd
Augustine Fitz Ailwin, 389, 391
Augustine, hosier (*calicerius*), 358–60, 389
Augustine Malet, 454–5
Aumary, *see* Robert
Aurea Valle, *see* Hugh
Avallon, *see* Hugh
Aveley (Essex), soke, 35
Avenay, *see* William
Avice of Longditch, 446–8
Aylwin, sheriff of Sussex, 272
Ayot St Laurence (Herts), manor, 37
Azo, son of Alfred, and his maternal aunt Alice, 256

Baalun, *see* Alan
Bailliol, *see* Jocelin
Bacheler, *see* Nicholas
Bagnor, *see* Robert
Baldric de Sigillo, archdeacon of Leicester, 452
Baldwin, 31, 380
Baldwin, abp of Canterbury, 138
Baldwin Crisp, 275–6
Baldwin of Parham, 325
Baldwin, son of Baldwin, 404
Baldwin, son of Ingelric, 258
Balham (Surr), 21
Balie, *see* Richard
Balta, *see* Richard
Banastre, *see* Gilbert
Baratrus, 462
Bardolf, Bardulf, *see* Hugh
Barentin, *see* Alexander; Richard; Thomas
Barill, *see* Reinald
Barking (Essex, Berchengis, Berching, Berking, Berkinge, Braking), abbess, 365; clerk, 461; nunnery, 6
Barking, *see also* Lucy; Peter; Richard; Stephen; William
Barra, *see* Ansegod; Edith; Geoffrey; William
Barre, *see* Richard
Bartholomew (Berth), butler (*pincerna*), 333, 476; usher (*hostiarius*), 402, 466–7
Bartholomew de Vendome, abp of Tours, formerly parson of Ockendon, 463
Bartholomew of Ashwell, 490
Bartholomew of Hanney, 490
Bartholomew, son of Godwin (le fiz Godwine), 309

Bartholomew, son of Hugh, 335
Bartholomew, son of John Fitz Herlicun, 381
Basset, *see* Isabel; Ralph; Richard; William
Bassingbourn, *see* Robert
Bat, *see* Simon; William
Bastard, *see* William
Battersea (Surr, Patricheseye), 6, 82–3, 314, 330; aqueduct, 330; church, 19, 169, 177, 231–2; manor, 17–18, 120–1, 197; vicar, 231–2; wood, 19, 330
Bauderic, clerk, later canon of St Mary Overy (Southwark), 357
Bayeux (Baioc'), bp, 17, 19–20, 48, 76
Baynard (Bainard), *see* Ralph; William
Beatrice, daughter of Iseult (Ysoude), daughter of Gilbert of Stevenage, 471
Beauchamp, *see* Hugh
Beaumont, *see* Henry; Ralph; Robert
Bec (Normandy), abbot, pp14–15; 26, 50, 361; monks, 361
Becche, *see* Osbert
Becham (? Beckenham, Kent), clerk, 298; park, 298, 330; priest, 298
Becket, *see* Agnes; Mary; John; Thomas
Bedford, *see* Geoffrey; Robert
Beggi (Begi), *see* John
Belet, *see* Henry; Michael
Bella Aqua, *see* Hugh
Bellus, *see* Hugh
Belmeis family, 105; *see also* Richard de Belmeis I and II
Belton (Lincs), church, 46
Benchesham, *see* Godfrey
Benedict, abbot of Stratford Langthorne, papal judge-delegate, 225
Benedict, capeler, 396–7
Benedict, linen-draper (*lingedraper*), 378
Benedict, Mr, 486
Benedict of Sawston, canon of St Paul's, London, 219
Benedict, tenant (*sentarius*), 294–5
Benfleet, South, (Essex, Bainflete, Bemflet, Benflet, Bienflet), p18; 339; church, 214, 299–300, 317, 344; manor, 299, 317, 332, 345; manorial court, 300; men, free and unfree, 332; parson, 214–15; vicar, 215
Benfleet, *see also* Robert; William
Berdena (? Bardney, Lincs), tithes, 462
Berengar (Bereng'), *see* Ralph
Berengier, *see* William
Berkshire (Barrocscire), 462
Berkswell, *see* Peter
Bermondsey (Surr, Bermundesseye), priory of St Saviour, p15; monks, 220, 287, 368; prior, 287; prior, as papal judge-delegate, 194, 220, 368
Bernard, bp of St Davids, 242

Bernard, brother of St James's hospital, Westminster, 288
Bernard, cook, 386
Bernard, sacrist of St Paul's cathedral, 255
Berners, *see* Ralph
Berniville, *see* Osbert
Bertherol, *see* Robert
Bertram, 380; clerk, son of Leodbert, 255
Bertram, prior of St Saviour, Bermondsey, 287
Beslun, *see* Robert
Bidun, *see* Walter
Bifort, *see* Hugh
Bigod, *see* Hugh; Roger
Bishop (Bissope), *see* Ernis
Bisley (Surr), 65
Bisset, *see* Manasser
Black, *see* Osbert Niger; Robert Niger
Blancfront (Blancfrunt), *see* Roland; Walter
Blessed Virgin Mary, cult, p17; heir of land donated to Westminster, 346
Bloet, *see* Robert
Blois (France), archdeacon, 202; count and countess, 105
Blois, *see also* Peter
Bloxham (Oxon, Bloccesham, Blockesham, Blokesham), 286; church, p12, p15; 225, 253, 286, 323, 481; parson, 286
Blund (Blunt, le Blund), *see* Andrew; David; Edward; Geoffrey; Henry; John; Matthew; Norman; Ralph; Richard; Robert; Roger; Simon; Stephen
Bohun, *see* Henry
Bonehaie, *see* Henry
Bordwadestone (Boston House in Brentford, Mddx), St Laurence's hospital, church and cemetery, 206
Bordewate, *see* Wulfric
Borel, *see* Norman; William
Bosworth, *see* Simon
Boulogne (Bolonia), *see* Ralph; Ralph Fitz Stephen; Stephen
Boulogne, count, 6, 13, 21, 61, 475
Boveney, *see* William
Box Hall, *see* Amauric
Bradmere, *see* William
Brampton (Hunts), 73
Branc', *see* Roger
Brand, Brant, *see* Hamo; Henry; Ralph
Bray, *see* Nicholas
Breton (Bretun), *see* Ralph
Brichtmar of Haverhill, 355; and Denise his wife, 388
Bricklehampton (Worcs, Brythelmeton), vill, 305
Bridport, *see* John

335

344

345

347

350

353

Index

355

LONDON RECORD SOCIETY

The London Record Society was founded in December 1964 to publish transcripts, abstracts and lists of the primary sources for the history of London, and generally to stimulate interest in archives relating to London. Membership is open to any individual or institution; the annual subscription is £7 ($15) for individuals and £10 ($23) for institutions, which entitles a member to receive one copy of each volume published during the year and to attend and vote at meetings of the Society. From 1 January 1989 membership subscriptions will be £12 ($22) for individuals and £18 ($35) for institutions. Prospective members should apply to the Hon. Secretary, Miss Heather Creaton, c/o Institute of Historical Research, Senate House, London, WC1E 7HU.

The following volumes have already been published:
1. *London Possessory Assizes: a calendar*, edited by Helena M. Chew (1965)
2. *London Inhabitants within the Walls, 1695*, with an introduction by D. V. Glass (1966)
3. *London Consistory Court Wills, 1492–1547*, edited by Ida Darlington (1967)
4. *Scriveners' Company Common Paper, 1357–1628, with a continuation to 1678*, edited by Francis W. Steer (1968)
5. *London Radicalism, 1830–1843: a selection from the papers of Francis Place*, edited by D. J. Rowe (1970)
6. *The London Eyre of 1244*, edited by Helena M. Chew and Martin Weinbaum (1970)
7. *The Cartulary of Holy Trinity Aldgate*, edited by Gerald A. J. Hodgett (1971)
8. *The Port and Trade of Early Elizabethan London: documents*, edited by Brian Dietz (1972)
9. *The Spanish Company*, by Pauline Croft (1973)
10. *London Assize of Nuisance, 1301–1431: a calendar*, edited by Helena M. Chew and William Kellaway (1973)
11. *Two Calvinistic Methodist Chapels, 1743–1811: the London Tabernacle and Spa Fields Chapel*, edited by Edwin Welch (1975)
12. *The London Eyre of 1276*, edited by Martin Weinbaum (1976)
13. *The Church in London, 1375–1392*, edited by A. K. McHardy (1977)
14. *Committees for Repeal of the Test and Corporation Acts: Minutes, 1786–90 and 1827–8*, edited by Thomas W. Davis (1978)
15. *Joshua Johnson's Letterbook, 1771–4: letters from a merchant in London to his partners in Maryland*, edited by Jacob M. Price (1979)
16. *London and Middlesex Chantry Certificate, 1548*, edited by C. J. Kitching (1980)

edited by H. Horwitz; *London Pollbooks, 1713*, edited by W. A. Speck and W. A. Gray (1981)

18. *Parish Fraternity Register: fraternity of the Holy Trinity and SS. Fabian and Sebastian in the parish of St Botolph without Aldersgate*, edited by Patricia Basing (1982)
19. *Trinity House of Deptford: Transactions, 1609–35*, edited by G. G. Harris (1983)
20. *Chamber Accounts of the sixteenth century*, edited by Betty R. Masters (1984)
21. *The Letters of John Paige, London merchant, 1648–58*, edited by George F. Steckley (1984)
22. *A Survey of Documentary Sources for Property Holding in London before the Great Fire*, by Derek Keene and Vanessa Harding (1985)
23. *The Commissions for Building Fifty New Churches*, edited by M. H. Port (1986)
24. *Richard Hutton's Complaints Book*, edited by Timothy V. Hitchcock (1987)
25. *Westminster Abbey Charters, 1066–c. 1214*, edited by Emma Mason (1988)

All volumes are still in print; apply to Hon. Secretary. Price to individual members £7 ($15) each; to institutional members £10 ($23) each; and to non-members £12 ($28) each.